Using
Liferay Portal

A Complete Guide

THE LIFERAY DOCUMENTATION TEAM
Rich Sezov, Jr.
Jim Hinkey
Stephen Kostas
Jesse Rao
Cody Hoag

Liferay Press

CONTENTS

PREFACE

Welcome to the world of Liferay Portal! This book was written for anyone who has any part in setting up, using, or maintaining a web site built on Liferay Portal. For the end user, it contains everything you need to know about using the applications included with Liferay. For the administrator, you'll learn all you need to know about setting up your site with users, sites, organizations, and user groups, as well as how to manage your site's security with roles. For server admins, it guides you step-by-step through the installation, configuration, and optimization of Liferay Portal, including setting it up in a clustered, enterprise-ready environment. Use this book as a handbook for everything you need to do to get your Liferay Portal installation running smoothly, and then keep it by your side as you configure and maintain your Liferay-powered web site.

What's New in the First Edition

First edition?!? Well, we've renamed the book (it used to be the *Administrator's Guide*), so we figured we'd start the numbering over. There's so much new in this edition that it just about encompasses the whole book. Of course, everything from the old book has been updated to reflect the release of Liferay Portal 6.1. We also have complete coverage of Liferay's new features, such as dynamic data lists—and the form designer that goes with them—, the rules engine, the audit framework, a revamped chapter on enterprise configuration, and more.

There is, of course, coverage of Liferay Marketplace as well as the Plugin Security Manager. The Document Library and Image Gallery have been combined into a robust, powerful Documents and Media portlet, and you'll find full documentation of it here. You'll learn about Liferay's OpenSocial integration, the new faceted search feature, and how to use the related assets feature.

The new release is feature-packed, and so the documentation must be also: we have over 650 pages of goodness awaiting you in these pages.

Conventions

The information contained herein has been organized in a way that makes it easy to locate information. We start at the beginning: put a list of stuff that's at the beginning here.

Sections are broken up into multiple levels of headings, and these are designed to make it easy to find information.

Source code and configuration file directives are presented monospaced, as below.

```
If source code goes multi-line, the lines will be \

separated by a backslash character like this.
```

Italics are used to represent links or buttons to be clicked on in a user interface.

`Monospaced type` is used to denote Java classes, code, or properties within the text.

Bold is used to describe field labels and portlets.

Page headers denote the chapters, and footers denote the particular section within the chapter.

Publisher Notes

It is our hope that this book is valuable to you, and that it becomes an indispensable resource as you work with Liferay Portal. If you need any assistance beyond what is covered in this book, Liferay offers training, consulting, and support services to fill any need that you might have. Please see http://www.liferay.com/services for further information about the services we can provide.

It is entirely possible that some errors or mistakes made it into the final version of this book. Any issues that we find or that are reported to us by the community are documented on the Official Liferay Wiki. You can view them or contribute information that you've found about any issues at our Documentation Errata page.[1]

As always, we welcome any feedback. If there is any way you think we could make this book better, please feel free to mention it on our forums. You can also use any of the email addresses on our Contact Us page.[2] We are here to serve you, our users and customers, and to help make your experience using Liferay Portal the best it can be.

---

[1] http://www.liferay.com/community/wiki/-/wiki/Main/Documentation+Errata
[2] http://www.liferay.com/contact-us

CHAPTER 1

WHAT IS LIFERAY?

If you're reading this, we're going to make a wild guess and say that you're probably looking for some software to help you run your web site. Creating a dynamic web site that's more than brochureware is complicated these days. You have to think about all kinds of things like user registration, security, community-building, collaboration, and of course your own, unique functionality and the design of your site.

To create all this, you can pursue several different strategies. You can decide to build the whole thing yourself from scratch. The reason usually given for pursuing this strategy is that you have the most freedom, since you can write whatever you want. A closer inspection, however, reveals that instead of freedom, you become a slave, writing all kinds of code that's not core to your web site. You have to write code for user registration, login, security, and session management; code for standards support, such as Facebook login, OpenID, OpenSocial, or RSS feeds; and code for general features, such as comments, tags, and ratings. You also take the most risk: you and/or your development team are responsible for every bug, glitch, user interface issue, or security hole–and the consequences for these–that can be found in your site. This strategy also requires the most *time* to implement, because you're building everything from scratch. When considering this option, therefore, you really need to think hard about whether you and your development team have the time and the expertise to handle building everything from the ground up.

Another option is to scrounge the web for software that has some of the features you want, and then "glue" it together into one integrated site. For example, every site has some kind of content, so you might pick a content management system. But you want users to interact in some way, so you also grab forum software. Prominent users might get a blog, so you'll need software to handle that. And, of course, don't forget that you have to write your own application(s). You're attempting to build a super app out of a collection of disparate, but best-of-breed individual applications. You've collected the applications, and now your job is to integrate all of these together so that users only have to log in once, the forum software can power comments on your content, and blogs are published in a nice, customizable feed on the home page. As you work on this, you find that gluing all these applications together isn't as easy as you thought. You might get all of it working, but then you have a different problem down the road: a maintenance nightmare. All of these software packages will be updated by their development teams separately, on different schedules, to fix bugs, add features, and plug security holes. Now that you've customized them all, every upgrade of every software package you've chosen becomes an exercise in re-implementing your "glue" code to make it all work.

You could also try using something like a blog that has a lot of functionality that can kind of be used as a content management system. But then, of course, things don't work exactly as you'd like them to, and features you need are missing. You either have to build those features and integrate them in, or do without them.

One final option, if you have a budget, is to buy something that mostly fits what you want to do, with the intention of customizing it to fit your needs. The goal here is to get something up and running as quickly as possible, by taking advantage of someone's product and support. The devil here, though, is in the details: it's the customization–particularly with products that are not open source–that can be most difficult. License agreements need to be negotiated to get you access to non-documented, internal APIs, and many products are simply not designed to be customized to the extent that you might want to have them customized. It can take more time to customize than you though, and you usually run into some limitation that keeps you from building exactly what you need. Alternatively, you may wind up having to pay expensive consultants to get the result that you want, and after that, you've paid more than you initially thought you would, and you have a complicated situation when it comes to upgrading your system.

As you can see, all of these options have pros and cons to them. There are times when building from scratch makes sense, and there are times when integration or purchasing a solution make sense. But what if you could have all of these strategies combined? What if there was a product that gave you the freedom to create whatever you want, had tons of reusable functionality, was designed for customization, and was a single, unified product with a clear upgrade path?

There is. This solution gives you all the freedom of creating your site from the ground up, all the benefits of existing, integrated, robust applications, and a development framework that makes your application a first class citizen. It's called Liferay Portal.

1.1 What makes Liferay Portal unique

Liferay Portal is a web experience platform that contains all of the common applications you'd use as building blocks for your web site. Because of this, using Liferay completely changes the way you'd approach building your site, because Liferay includes all the functionality mentioned above and more. In fact, depending on what you're building, it's possible to build some sites without writing any code at all! If you've got a great application in mind, then Liferay is also a fantastic web application development platform that you can use to your advantage to release your application faster. Why? Because you can focus on your application, and use the user management, security, standards support, and general features provided by Liferay Portal without having to write them yourself.

Of course, there are more features than just those. You can take advantage of functionality enabling users to connect with each other in social networks, to collaborate on whatever interests them, to create content, and so much more. In fact, it'll take this whole book to describe fully what Liferay can do, but we'll summarize it as best we can in the rest of this chapter.

In short, Liferay Portal is more than a development platform, more than a content management system, more than a social network, and more than a set of collaboration tools. It's the best way to build a web site.

1.2 Using Liferay Portal as a content management system

One of the most common uses of Liferay Portal is as a content management system. In fact, many use Liferay Portal just for content management, whether it be web content management or management of file-based content (documents, media files, and the like). They do this because Liferay Portal's content management system is so powerful and feature-rich that it could be offered as a totally separate, standalone system of its own. Of course, the fact that it's integrated with the rest of the applications in Liferay Portal makes it all the more attractive.

So what can it do? We'll answer that question, but take it in two parts. First, we'll look at Liferay Portal's role as a web content management system, and then we'll see how Liferay Portal excels at file-based content management.

Effectively building a site with Liferay WCM

The first thing you'll want to understand about Liferay WCM is that it scales to work for the tiniest of sites all the way up to the largest of sites. For example, on the small end of things you can fire up Liferay Portal, drop the Web Content Display application onto a page, and immediately start typing content into a WYSIWYG editor, in place. On the large scale of things, you can set up Liferay Portal to host many different web sites for many different purposes, all with their own domain names. Each site can take advantage of a separate staging server, where content and pages are created by teams of people using structures and templates, and updates to the production server are published on a schedule, only after having gone through a multi-step approval process.

That's powerful.

By default, Liferay Portal starts with a single site that has a single page. You can build any web site you wish out of this, complete with multi-nested page hierarchies, as the figure below shows.

These pages can have any layout you like: Liferay Portal ships with several built-in, and you can create your own custom layouts and deploy them easily. Pages can be added, removed, or reordered any time, and you have the full flexibility of all the HTML page attributes, such as meta tags and robot file declarations, that you need.

Pages are also integrated with Liferay's powerful permissions system, so it's easy to restrict access to certain portions of your site. You can give individual users sites of their own, with public pages that have their content and blog, and private pages that contain their calendar and email.

If you're running a large web site where you'll be creating and managing lots of different sub-sites for individuals and groups, you can take advantage of page templates and site templates. The former enables you to set up templates of pages with predefined layouts and applications already on them, and the latter enables you to create a whole site made up of multiple, predefined pages.

Figure 1.1: Liferay's page hierarchies are easy to create, using a tree structure that's familiar to anyone who has used a file manager.

There's even more. If you have a very large site, you might need multiple people to work on it. And you certainly don't want the live site changing before your users' eyes. For that reason, Liferay Portal provides a feature called *staging*, that lets you place your changes in a holding area while they're being worked on. You can have a local staging server, where the staged site resides on the same server as the live site, or you can have a remote staging server, where all web content work happens on a separate server from your live site. In either case, when you're ready, site changes can be pushed to the live site, either manually or on a schedule.

Figure 1.2: Staging supports publishing manually or on a schedule.

Liferay Portal's web content creation tools are easy and intuitive to use at all levels. If you need only basic content management capabilities for your site, you can jump right in. From the Dockbar, you can add the Web Content Display application anywhere in your page layout and enter content in place. It's easy to go from this basic level of content management to more sophisticated levels of functionality.

For example, suppose you wanted to build an online news-oriented site. Most of the content you'll publish is an article of some kind. Liferay's web content management system lets you create a *structure* for this, so that you can capture all the information from your writers that you'd need in an article. The figure below shows what this structure might look like to a journalist who'd be entering his or her article into the system.

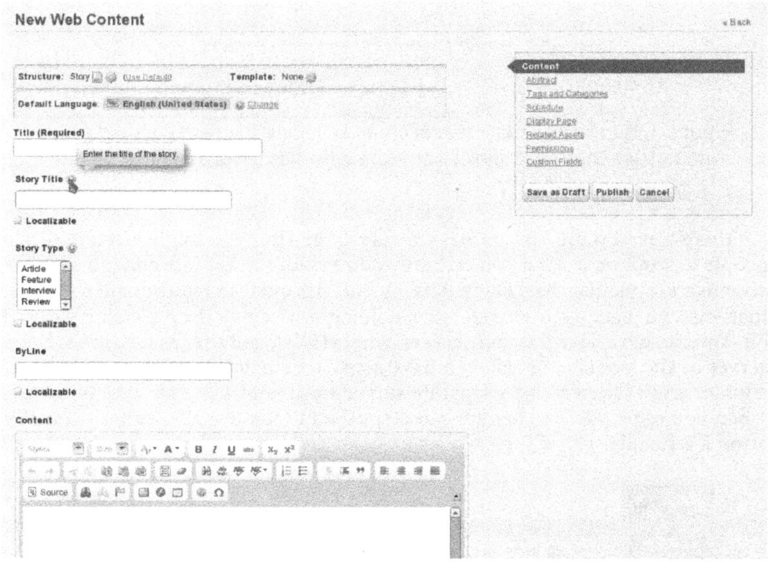

Figure 1.3: Structures allow you to specify exactly the type of data that makes up your content. You can also include tooltips to help your users understand what each field is for.

As you can see, you can use structures to make sure writers provide the title of the story, what type of story it will be, and the byline (i.e., the writer's name). You've made sure that all the relevant information for the story is captured in the system.

Web content is one example of what in Liferay is called an *asset*. Assets can have meta-data attached to them, and that metadata can be used to aggregate similar assets together in searches or as published content. One way to do this in the example above is that writers can tag and categorize their stories so they can be found more easily by users.

This is just one example, of course. But the concept is applicable to any kind of site you'd want to build. For example, if you were building a site for a zoo, you could use web content structures to help users enter data about animals in the zoo, such as their common names, their scientific names, their species, their locations in the wild, and more.

When it comes time to publish content, structures are combined with *templates*. Templates are instructions for how to display structures, written most of the time in Velocity or Freemarker–both of which are well-known templating languages used for mixing HTML with programmatic elements. Because of this, they're very easy to write, and can help you ensure that your site has a consistent look and feel.

There is much more to web content. You can create abstracts, schedule when content is published and when it should be taken down (or reviewed), define related assets, and more.

This is just the web content portion of Liferay's content management system. Liferay Portal is also great at managing file-based content.

Keeping track of documents, images, video, and more

It's rare to find in an open source project a full-featured content management system. Most of the time, you'll find web content management systems and file-based content management systems as separate projects. Liferay Portal, however, provides you with both. As shown above, the web content management system is as robust as any other you'll find, and its file-based content management system is the same.

Liferay Portal keeps the UI of its file-based content management system in an application called *Documents and Media Library*. This application resides in the control panel or can be added to any page, and, as shown below, looks very much like the file manager that you're already familiar with from your operating system.

Like a file manager, you can browse files and folders in nested hierarchies. You can also mount other repositories that you might have in your environment, such as Documentum (EE only) or any system that implements Content Management Interoperability Services (CMIS). It provides previews of just about every document type you can think of. And, like a file manager, you can copy and move files between folders by dragging and dropping them. Of course, if you still want to use your operating system's file manager, you can, because

Figure 1.4: Liferay Portal's Documents and Media library was purposefully designed to be familiar to anyone who uses a computer.

Liferay's Documents and Media library supports WebDAV, using the same credentials you use to log in to Liferay.

Liferay Portal's Documents and Media library, however, is much more robust than a file manager is, because it's a full content management system. You can define ways of classifying files that may be of different types, but are meant for the same, overarching purpose.

For example, you can define *metadata sets,* which are groups of fields describing attributes of a file. One of these that ships with the product is called *meeting metadata,* and it contains fields such as Meeting Name, Date, Time, Location, Description, and Participants. This is a generic set of fields that go together and that you'd want to use as a group. You can create as many of these as you want.

For files, you can define *document types.* They provide a more natural way of working with files. For example, you might create a document type called Meeting Minutes, because this is how we as humans conceptualize our documents. It doesn't really matter whether it's a Microsoft Word document, an HTML file, or a text file–the document contains meeting minutes. Once you've created the document type, you can attach the Meeting Metadata set that contains many of the fields you'd want, and you can also add extra fields, such as a field for action items. When users want to add a file containing their notes for meeting minutes, they can also add all the relevant metadata about the meeting (such as the time, location, and action items). This captures the context information that goes with the document, and it provides a much more natural way of working with documents than just dumping them into a shared file system.

Of course, the system goes much further than this. Folders can be set so that only certain document types can be added to them. Workflow rules can also be added to folders to run files through an approval process that you define. In short, Liferay's file-based content management system gives you all the features you need to manage and share files in a group.

Many Liferay Portal users see it as a robust content management system, and they use it primarily for that purpose. Now, hopefully, you can see why. We'll cover the system in-depth in the body of this book, but for now we need to look at some of the other ways you can use Liferay Portal, starting with its fantastic collaborative tools.

1.3 Using Liferay Portal as a collaborative platform

Many sites have grown organically. You may have grown your community by using separate tools: first a forums application, and then a wiki for collaborative documentation, and maybe even a chat application. It can be hard (and error-prone) to integrate all of these applications so your users can use them seamlessly. Thankfully, Liferay includes a suite of collaborative applications you can use, and they're all integrated together.

Liferay Portal offers every standard collaborative application that's available. These applications range from personal productivity applications like a calendar and email, to community-building applications like message boards, polls, and wikis.

Figure 1.5: Liferay Portal's message boards are as fully featured as any standalone forum application, with the added benefit that they're integrated with the rest of the system.

This is a suite of integrated applications with all the features of similar, standalone applications. For example, Liferay Portal's message boards include categories and subcategories, message threads, captcha, RSS feeds, email notification, posting via email, and much more. But more than this, the applications are integrated with the rest of Liferay Portal's framework. Users log in, and their profiles are used automatically by the message boards and all the other collaborative applications. And as we'll see later, functionality from the built in applications can be added to your own to provide features like comments in your own software, and you don't have to write any code to do it.

Liferay Portal's wiki is another example of a full-featured collaborative application. It has support for authoring pages in a WYSWYG editor, or more advanced users can use the easy-to-learn standard Wiki Creole syntax. Users can comment on wiki articles, and it keeps a full history of every change that's been made, allowing users to revert back to any change. It also supports RSS feeds (just about every Liferay application does) so you can subscribe to see new articles as they are posted. Each site can have one or more wikis, and each wiki can have one or more top-level nodes.

Figure 1.6: Liferay Portal's wiki enables users to collaboratively create complex articles. Clicking the *Details* link shows the full history of the article, including the author of each change.

We could go through all of Liferay Portal's collaborative applications in a similar fashion, but let's save that for the body of the book. Liferay Portal's suite of collaborative applications includes a blog (complete with blog aggregation features so you can publish multiple users' blog entries in one place), a chat application for users who are online at the same time, message boards, a wiki, a knowledge base that you can use to publish a library of technical articles, a polling system you can use to have users vote on certain questions, and personal productivity applications like a calendar and email.

Liferay Portal includes every application you'll need to enable users to collaborate. Next, we'll see how you can use Lifeay Portal as a social platform.

1.4 Using Liferay as a social platform

Whether you plan to build a social network or enable social applications as part of your overall user experience, Liferay Portal has the tools to make those features work for you. Starting with a suite of applications–including a profile summary, activities feeds, social requests, a wall, and more–and rounding things out with an API to handle relationships between users as well as publish their activities to each other, Liferay Portal helps you implement common features of social networks to enhance your existing site.

Figure 1.7: Liferay Portal provides feeds of social activities. These feeds can contain entries from any of Liferay's built-in applications or applications that you write.

Social relationships within Liferay Portal are ideally suited for many different kinds of implementations, whether you're building a public social network or want to enable social features in your corporate Intranet. Users can create relationships within the system, allowing them to see updates from those whose activity they need to track. That's far more powerful than having them subscribe to multiple individual RSS feeds or visit multiple profiles, because the system keeps track of the updates from those with whom you have a relationship, automatically.

More than this, however, Liferay is a great integration platform for social applications. It fully supports the OpenSocial framework. You can use Liferay Portal's built-in OpenSocial gadget editor to create and serve your own OpenSocial gadgets.

Figure 1.8: Liferay Portal's OpenSocial gadget editor lets you rapidly create social applications that can be served across the web to any other OpenSocial container.

Liferay Portal also supports the creation of Facebook applications; in fact, no additional coding is necessary to publish your Liferay applications on Facebook (you would, of course, need to use Facebook's API to use Facebook-specific features–such as posting on users' timelines). The only thing you need to do is get an API key and canvas page URL from Facebook.

Figure 1.9: Any Liferay application can be published to multiple social networks with a few clicks.

As you can see, Liferay Portal is built for social applications: adding social features to your web site, creating a social network of your own, creating social applications to be published on other web sites, or building a social application for Facebook.

As with social applications, Liferay Portal is also an easy to use, robust platform for any web application you're considering writing. In addition to this, Liferay Portal is easily configured to be used as a shared hosting platform for multiple web sites. Let's look at the benefits you can reap by using Liferay Portal in these ways.

1.5 Using Liferay as a web platform

We can't even begin to imagine what you're thinking of building, but whatever it is, you're going to put your heart and soul into it. Building it on Liferay's web platform can give you a leg up, by providing to you everything you need to support your application, so you can concentrate solely on what *you're* building, and not the rest of the features your users expect will come along with it.

Liferay as an application development platform

Imagine your application for a moment. Does it require users to register with your site? Will they be able to comment on content contained within your application? Is there some asset that users can tag or categorize? If you think about the layout of the application, would it benefit from modularization? Could

you make use of a rich JavaScript framework with many components built into
it? How about security–will you need to make information available to some
users, but not to all users? Liferay Portal has all of this and more available to
the developer, so you don't have to write it yourself.

Liferay Portal's development framework is a great help when you're building
a web application. While the framework itself is covered in other resources such
as the *Liferay Developer's Guide* or *Liferay in Action*, the strengths of Liferay as
a platform are also apparent once you've finished writing your application.

For example, bug fixes to your applications are easy to apply, because Liferay
applications are hot deployed to the running server. Liferay's Marketplace gives
you a ready-made shopping center for your applications. And Liferay's web
services and JSON architecture make it easy for you to share data from your
applications to other systems running on different platforms.

You get all this–not to mention the automatic Facebook and OpenSocial integration mentioned above–simply by using Liferay's development platform. It's
a very powerful platform, and certainly worth your investigation.

A great integration platform

If you're building an enterprise system, portals were designed in the first place
to be a single point of entry to your users' applications and content. Since Liferay Portal integrates well with user directories such as LDAP and Active Directory, and single sign-on systems such as SAML and OpenSSO, it fits well into
your enterprise systems. This allows you to use it as an integration platform for
existing applications.

Liferay Portal, since it adheres to the JSR standard for portlets, was designed
from the ground up for application integration. You can mix and match any
application installed in the system on any page within the portal. You can make
use of any APIs provided by other systems to integrate their data into an application window in Liferay. And applications you create with Liferay's Service
Builder API are web service-enabled from the start.

Hosting multiple sites on Liferay Portal

Liferay Portal excels as a multi-site hosting platform. You can use it to host
multiple sites under the same overall architecture (like Facebook, MySpace, or
Pinterest offer to their users), or you could host several completely different web
sites based solely on Liferay's ability to serve multiple instances of itself from
the same physical installation.

In the first scenario, Liferay Portal's Sites architecture lets you create multiple, different web sites that have public and/or private sets of pages and as many pages within those sets as you'd like. Users join the web site, and once they're members, they can join and leave open sites with one click. Some sites can be defined as restricted or private, and users can't access those unless they're added by site administrators. All of these sites can have canonical domain names such as baseballcards.liferay.com or progrock.liferay.com.

Using this construct, you can build anything from Facebook, to Yahoo Groups, to SourceForge, to the now-defunct-but-once-loved Geocities. There is no limit to the number of sites you can have: some Liferay installations have only one or two, but others have many thousands.

In the second scenario, Liferay Portal lets you create completely separate instances of itself from the same installation. Users, groups, organizations, sites, and roles from each instance are kept completely separate. If a user registers for a user id on one instance, he or she would have to register as a new user on another instance as well.

This lets you host many different, separate web sites from one Liferay Portal installation. Users of each instance have access to the same powerful content management, collaboration, social, and web development platform that they'd have if they were operating from a single, standalone installation.

1.6 Extending and customizing Liferay for your own needs

Beyond using Liferay as a development platform for new applications, Liferay Portal has also been designed to be extended and modified. As an open source project, its source code is available, but Liferay Portal's developers have designed the product to make it easy to build whatever you want out of it.

Special software components called *hook* and *ext* plugins enable developers to change any aspect of Liferay's interface and behavior–without having to modify any of Liferay Portal's source code. This provides you all the benefits of the "build from scratch" strategy we mentioned earlier, but without all the effort to build from scratch. If you want to make a change to the user registration screens, add support for a proprietary single sign-on mechanism that you've written, revise the user interface for the message boards application, or anything else, you can make those customizations. And if you're a developer, we're sure you know that it's a whole lot easier to customize something that *almost* does things exactly the way you want than it is to write that feature from scratch. With Liferay Portal, you *can* have your cake and eat it too.

1.7   Summary

So what is Liferay? As you can see, it's hard to describe, because it does so much. What we've essentially done is say it's a totally awesome content and document managing, user collaborating, socially enabling, application developing, corporate integrating, completely customizable platform for building the Internet. If we'd said that up front, you'd probably have doubted us. Hopefully now, you can see that it's true.

If you're interested in using Liferay Portal for *your* product, continue reading. We'll go through all of these features (and more that we couldn't mention) throughout the rest of the book.

CHAPTER 2

WEB CONTENT MANAGEMENT

Web Content Management is a system which allows non-technical users to publish content to the web without having advanced knowledge of web technology or programming of any sort. Liferay WCM empowers you to publish your content with a simple point and click interface and it helps you to keep your site fresh. You'll find yourself easily creating, editing and publishing content within just a few minutes of being exposed to its features. But Liferay WCM doesn't sacrifice power for simplicity. If need be, you can use your developer skills to create complex presentation layer templates that make your content "pop" with dynamic elements. Once these templates have been deployed into the portal, your non-technical users can manage content using these templates as easily as they would manage static content. All of this makes Liferay WCM an appropriate choice for sites with only a few pages or sites with gigabytes of content.

In this chapter, we'll cover the following topics:

- Features of Liferay WCM
- Creating sites and managing pages
- Authoring content
- Publishing content

- Workflow

- Site memberships and permissions

As you'll see, Liferay's WCM is a full-featured solution for managing your web site. We'll start with an overview of what it has to offer and then we'll dive down into its features. Note that web content is just one kind of asset on Liferay. Other types of content (blog posts, wiki articles, message board posts, etc.) are also considered assets. Liferay provides a general framework for handling assets that includes tags, categories, comments, ratings, and more. Please see chapter 5 for more information on Liferay's asset framework.

2.1   How Can Liferay's WCM Help You?

With Liferay's WCM you have the ability to create, edit, stage, publish and approve content with easy to learn yet powerful tools. Liferay's WCM streamlines the content creation process for end users. It's much faster to use Liferay's WCM than it would be to create all the content for your site in HTML. Some ways Liferay WCM makes this possible include:

- Once set up, non-technical users can manage the site.

- Liferay's fine-grained permissions system ensures your content gets to the right users.

- To manage the site, no programming is required.

- Content can be staged.

- Content can be passed through a workflow.

- Content can be published on a schedule.

- WCM is integrated with Liferay's services so advanced template developers can use them to query for data stored elsewhere in Liferay.

Once you get familiar with Liferay WCM you'll wonder how you ever got along without it.

What Features Does Liferay WCM Have?

Liferay's WCM has a host of features the makes managing the content of your site easier.

- **WYSIWYG Editor**: A complete HTML editor that allow you to modify fonts, add color, insert images and much more.

- **Structure Editor**: Easily add and remove fields you want available to content creators and then dynamically move them around. This editor includes an entire suite of form controls you can drag and drop onto your structure.

- **Template Editor**: Import template script files that inform the system how to display the content within the fields determined by the structure.

- **Web Content Display**: A portlet that allows you place web content on a page in your portal.

- **Asset Publisher**: A portlet which can aggregate different types of content together in one view.

- **Scheduler**: Lets you schedule when content is reviewed, displayed and removed.

- **Workflow Integration**: Run your content through an approval or review process.

- **Staging**: Use a separate staging server or stage your content locally so you can keep your changes separate from the live site.

Liferay's Web Content Management is a powerful and robust tool for creating and organizing content on your web site. Let's begin by examining some basic concepts involving sites and pages.

2.2 Creating sites and managing pages

With most products, you would learn what the software can do in terms of setting up your users and security model and then start building your system. You'd design your infrastructure and get your server environment up and running while your developers write the applications that live on your web site. With Liferay Portal, however, you start farther ahead. Liferay Portal is more than just a *container* for applications with a robust security model. It already includes many of the applications you'll need, out of the box, ready to go and integrated with all the user management and security features you've already learned about.

Nearly all Liferay users use Liferay's Web Content Management system (WCM). After all, all every web site has content that needs to be managed. Liferay's WCM empowers you to manage all the content on your site quickly and easily within your browser. Beyond managing existing content, Liferay WCM lets users easily create and manage everything from a simple article containing text and images to fully functional web sites. Web publishing works alongside Liferay Portal's larger collection of applications, which means you can add shopping cart functionality, visitor polls, web forms, site collaboration tools and more. Everything is done with our collection of easy-to-use tools with familiar rich-text editors and an intuitive interface.

In this section we'll cover some basic aspects of Liferay WCM, including:

- Page types

- Layouts

- Page and content permissions

- Importing and exporting content

- Content creation and editing

- Content publishing

- WCM Workflow

By the time we're done, you should be able to apply all these concepts to your own content. To demonstrate Liferay's Content Management features, we'll create and manage content on the portal for *Nose-ster*, a new social network where people are connected based on what their noses look like.

First, a little housekeeping. If we're going to be *Nose-ster*, our portal should also be called Nose-ster. To set general information about your portal like the name and mail domain, go to the Control Panel and select *Portal Settings* under the Portal heading. You could set up the configuration for Nose-ster as follows.

You can also customize the logo in the top left corner of every page by selecting *Display Settings* under the *Miscellaneous* tab on the panel to the right. Once you've made the changes, we can begin creating pages.

Figure 2.1: Changing Portal Settings

Creating and managing pages

You have a few options for accessing the page creation interface. To simplify this, we'll cover the Dockbar's *Manage* menu slightly out of order. There are two interfaces to be aware of: *Site Pages* and *Page*. You can get to these from multiple places. Depending on what you're editing and where you are on the portal, you'll use either the *Manage* menu or the Control Panel to work with your pages. From the Control Panel, make sure you have the correct site selected in the context menu selector and click the *Site Pages* link in the content section. If you've already navigated to the site you wish to manage, click *Manage* from the Dockbar and select *Site Pages*. This is the exact same interface you see in the Control Panel. To manage the specific page of the site you've navigated to, click *Manage* and select *Page*.

For convenience, you can also navigate to the Sites page under the Portal section of the Control Panel and click *Actions* → *Manage Pages*. To quickly add a single page while to the site you're browsing, click *Add* from the Dockbar and select *Page*. Just enter a name for the page and it's added immediately. Click

Figure 2.2: Managing Individual Pages

the name of the page in the navigation menu to visit it and start working on it.

Site Pages is an interface to view existing pages, create new pages, view pages and export or import pages using Liferay Archive (LAR) files. Note that you can switch between managing a set of pages and managing a single page using the left-hand side navigation menu. Click on *Public Pages* or *Private Pages* to manage the group or click on an individual page to manage just that one. Switching views like this changes the list of available tabs to the right. By default, liferay.com, which we renamed to nosester.com, contains a single public page called *Welcome*.

Liferay's page groups are always associated with sites. Even users' personal pages are part of their personal sites. All pages belong to one of two types of page sets: public pages and private pages. By default, public pages are accessible to anyone, even non-logged in users (guests). Private pages are accessible only to users who are members of the site which owns the pages. This means the private pages of an organization's site would be viewable only by members of the organization.

Regardless of whether the pages are public or private, Liferay uses the same interface to manage them. Let's look at this interface more closely.

More page management tools

From the Manage Site Pages dialog box, you can add a page to the site by clicking the *Add Page* button. Because *Public Pages* is selected on the left, clicking *Add Page* here adds a top level page next to the Welcome page. You can, however,

Site Pages ☝

Figure 2.3: Managing Site Pages

nest pages as deeply as you like. To create a sub-page under the Welcome page, select the *Welcome* page first and then create your page. If you later decide you don't like the order of your pages, you can drag and drop them in the list to put them in whatever order you want. Let's go ahead and add another top level page and name it *Community*. We'll use this page for the Recent Bloggers and Wiki portlets.

Figure 2.4: Adding Pages

When you create a new page, you can create either a blank page or a page prepopulated with portlets from a page template. When you're entering the name of the page, you can select from a list of page templates that are currently available. To view the pages once you add them, click the *View Pages* button. This is how you'd populate your pages with content and applications. This is covered in succeeding chapters.

If you're using the Manage Pages interface to create a new page, you'll have some additional options to create different types of pages. There are **Portlet Pages**, **Panel Pages**, **Embedded Pages**, **URL Pages** and **Link to Page**. By default, all pages are created as portlet pages but in some situations you might want to use one of the other options.

Portlet Pages are the pages we're usually talking about. They have a layout which you can drag and drop portlets into. Most of the pages you create will be portlet pages.

Panel Pages can have any number of portlets on them, as selected by an administrator, but only one will be displayed at a time. Users select which portlet they want to use from a menu on the left side of the page and the selected portlet takes up the entire page.

Figure 2.5: A panel page

Embedded Pages display content from another website inside of your portal. An administrator can set a URL from in the page management interface and that page will appear in the context and within the navigation of your Liferay portal.

URL Pages are just redirects to any URL specified by an administrator. You can use URL pages to create links to pages belonging to other sites of your portal or to pages of an external site. Use URL pages cautiously since blind redirects create a poor user experience.

Link to Page creates a portal page which functions as an immediate redirect to another page within the same site. You can select which page to link to from a dropdown in the page management interface. You could use a *Link to Page* to place a deeply nested page in the primary navigation menu of your site, for example.

Once you've created pages and populated them with content, Liferay provides a way for you to back them up to separate files. Let's see how that works.

Backing up and Restoring Pages Next to the *Add Page* button in the Manage Site Pages screen are two buttons labeled *Export* and *Import*. The Export button exports the pages you create into a single file, called a LAR (Liferay Archive). You can then import this file into any server running Liferay to re-create the pages. If you have a LAR you would like to import, use the *Import* button. Exporting and Importing LARs is a great way to take content from one environment (say, a development or QA environment) and move it all in one shot to your production server. Note that you should not make this a regular occurrence. If you want to regularly move pages from one server to another, you should use Liferay's staging environment, which is covered in chapter 3.

LARs are also a good way to back up your site's content. You can export them to a specific location on your server which is backed up, and if you ever have to restore your site, all you need to do is import the latest LAR file. One limitation on LAR files, however, is that they are version dependent, so you can't use an export from an old version of Liferay and import it into a newer version.

Let's be good administrators and export a LAR file for backup purposes. Click on the *Export* button and then name the file `nosesterv1.lar`. Use the check boxes to determine what you'd like to export. For this initial export, select everything. Note that if you select the *More Options* link, the list expands to include data from many of Liferay's applications, including the Documents and Media Library, Message Boards and Web Content. You can also export the theme you're using.

Once you click *Export*, your browser prompts you to save the file. Once you have the file, you can copy it to a backup location for safekeeping or import it into another installation of Liferay Portal. If you must rebuild or wish to revert back to this version of your site, you can import this file by clicking the *Import* button from the Manage Site Pages dialog box, browsing to it and selecting it.

Next, we'll look at the options on the right side menu, starting with Look and Feel.

Customizing the Look and Feel When you open the Manage Site Pages dialog box it defaults to the Look and Feel tab. On this tab, you're presented with an interface that allows you to choose a theme for the current site. Themes can transform the entire look of the portal. They are created by developers and are easily installed using the Liferay Marketplace. Since we don't have any themes beyond the default one installed yet, we'll use the default theme for our pages.

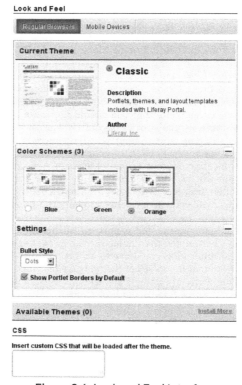

Figure 2.6: Look and Feel Interface

Many themes include more than one color scheme. This allows you to keep the existing look and feel while giving your site a different flavor. Change the color scheme from blue to green by selecting *Green* under *Color Schemes.* If you now go back to the site (by clicking *Back to nosester.com* in the top left corner of the Control Panel), you'll see some parts of the page are now tinged in a greenish hue.

If you apply a color scheme to a set of public or private pages it is, by default, applied to each page in the set. If, however, you open the Manage Pages dialog box for a particular page, you can select *Define a specific look and feel for this page* to make the color scheme apply to this page only. You can use this feature to choose a different color scheme for a particular page than the one defined for the set of public or private pages to which it belongs.

There are a few more configurable settings for your theme. You can switch the bullet style between dots and arrows and you can choose whether or not to show portlet borders by default.

Also notice themes can apply to regular browsers or mobile devices. You could create another site for mobile users attached to the http://m.nosester.com address and serve up a page designed for the smaller screens on phones.

The *CSS* section allows you to enter custom CSS that will also be served up by your theme. In this way, you can tweak a theme in real time by adding new styles or overriding existing ones.

The next option configures the logo that appears for your site.

Using a custom logo   If you want to use your own logo for a specific site, use the Logo tab. Adding a custom logo is easy: select the Logo tab and browse to the location of your logo. Make sure your logo fits the space in the top left corner of the theme you're using for your web site. If you don't, you could wind up with a site that's difficult to navigate, as other page elements are pushed aside to make way for the logo.

In the logo tab, you can also choose whether or not to display the site name on the site. If you check the box labeled *Show Site Name* the site name will appear in the the top right corner of the page. This option is enabled by default and cannot be disabled if the *Allow Site Administrators to set their own logo* option is disabled in *Portal Settings*. It is also not available for the default site – only newly created sites and user pages have the option to have the name display.

Changing options for individual pages

When you select a single page, some different options appear. Let's look at what these do.

Details: lets you name the page for any localizations you need. You can also set the HTML title that appears in the browser window for the page. Plus you can set an easy to remember, friendly URL for the page.

SEO: provides several means of optimizing the data the page provides to an indexer that's crawling the page. You can set the various meta tags for description, keywords and robots. There's also a separate Robots section that lets you tell indexing robots how frequently the page is updated and how it should be prioritized. If the page is localized, you can select a box to make Liferay generate canonical links by language. If you want to set some of these settings for the entire site, you can specify them from the Sitemaps and Robots tabs of the Manage Site Settings dialog box (see below).

> In previous versions of Liferay, it was possible that a single page could be indexed multiple times. In Liferay 6.1, all URLs that direct to the same page will only create one entry in the index. Previously, the simple URL *http://www.nosester.com/web/guest/blog/-/blogs/thenose* and different versions of the URL which provided additional information about the referring page had different entries in the index. As of Liferay 6.1, each asset (web content article, blog entry, etc.) has a unique URL. From the search engine's point of view, this will make your pages rank higher since any references to variations of a specific URL will all be considered references to the same page.

Look and Feel: lets you set a page-specific theme.

Layout: lets you specify how portlets are arranged on a page. Choose from the available installed templates to modify the layout. It's very easy for developers to define custom layouts and add them to the list. This is covered more thoroughly in both the *Liferay Developer's Guide* and in *Liferay in Action*.

JavaScript: gives you the ability to paste custom JavaScript code to be executed on this page.

Custom fields: If custom fields have been defined for pages (which can be done from the *Custom Fields* page of the Control Panel), they appear here. These are metadata about the page and can be anything you like, such as author or creation date.

Advanced: contains several optional features. You can set a query string to provide parameters to the page. This can become useful to web content templates, which you'll see in the next chapter. You can set a target for the page so that it either pops up in a particularly named window or appears in a frameset. And you can set an icon for the page that appears in the navigation menu.

Mobile Rule Groups: allows you to apply rules for how this page should be rendered for various mobile devices. You can set these up in the *Mobile Device Rules* section of the Control Panel.

Customization Settings: lets you mark specific sections of the page you want users to be able to customize.

Note that the *Manage* → *Page Layout* menu directs you to the same Layout tab that's in *Manage* → *Page*.

Modifying Page Layouts

Page layouts allow you to arrange your pages so the content appears the way you want it to. Liferay comes with many layouts already defined. Developers can create more and they can be deployed to your portal for your use.

To prepare for the portlets we'll soon be adding, let's change the layout of the Collaboration page. To access layouts, select *Manage* → *Page Layout* from the Dockbar.

Now, select the *2 Columns (70/30)* layout and click *Save*. Once saved, you'll return to the page and it'll seem as though nothing has happened. Once we start adding portlets, however, you'll notice the page is now equally divided into two columns. You can stack portlets on top of each other in these columns. There are, of course, more complicated layouts available and you can play around with them to get the layout you want.

Sometimes a particular layout is *almost* what you want but not quite. In this case use the Nested Portlets portlet to embed a layout inside another layout. This portlet is a container for other portlets. It lets you select from any of the layouts installed in Liferay, just like the layouts for a page. This gives you virtually unlimited options for laying out your pages.

The next option in the *Manage* menu is page customizations.

Page Customizations

Page Customizations are a new feature in Liferay 6.1. With page customizations, any user with the appropriate permissions can create personalized versions of any public page. Before users can create personalized versions of pages, customizations must first be enabled by an administrator. Administrators can activate or deactivate customizations for any row or column on any page. When users customize a page, they have the option to use either their version or the default version of a page. Users can't see alternate versions of pages other than their own.

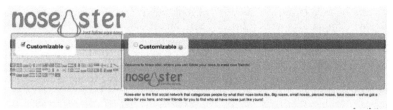

Figure 2.7: Setting Customizable Columns

When an administrator activates page customizations for a page, any portlets that are in a *Customizable* row or column can be moved around the page or removed from the page. Users can add new portlets of their own choosing to these columns of the page and can also customize portlet configurations. If at any time users determine they don't like their customizations, they can click *Reset My Customizations* to revert their pages back to the default. For more information about page customizations, please refer to the Page Customizations section of chapter 6.

Now that you know how to enable page customizations, let's look at the settings for the site as a whole.

Configuring Site Settings

As with Site Pages, you can access Site Settings through the Control Panel or directly from the site using the Dockbar (*Manage* → *Site Settings*).

You'll find options to specify details and metadata about your site, set up friendly URLs and virtual hosts, configure search engine optimization settings, turn staging on or off and specify a Google Analytics ID. Let's take a closer look.

Details: allows an administrator to change the description and membership type of a site and also to specify tags and categories for the site. The membership type can be set as open, restricted or private based on the privacy needs of the site. Users can join and leave an open site at will. To join a restricted site, a user has to be added by the site administrator. A user can also request to be added through the Sites section of the Control Panel. A private site is like a restricted site but doesn't appear in the Sites section of the Control Panel for users who aren't members.

Pages: From Site Settings, click on *Pages* to manage some basic features of the pages on a site. If no pages have been defined yet, you can set site templates

Figure 2.8: Site Settings

for the public or private pages. If pages already exist, links are provided to view them. You can also change the site's application adapter, which is a special type of hook plugin that customizes out of the box functionality for specific sites.

Site URL: Set a friendly URL and/or a virtual host for your site here. The *Friendly URL* option lets you manage the path to your site in the portal's URL. Friendly URLs are used for both public and private pages. For public pages, the friendly URL is appended to http://localhost:8080/web. For private pages, the friendly URL is appended to http://localhost:8080/group. Each friendly URL needs to be a unique name, of course. Having a human-readable friendly URL assists indexing bots and is critical to good search engine optimization.

For example, suppose you were creating a portal for a bank called the Best Bank. If you set the friendly URL of your portal's default site to /best-bank, the URL of your default site's public home page would change to

http://localhost:8080/web/best-bank/home

If your portal's default site had private pages, the URL of the default private home page would change to

http://localhost:8080/group/best-bank/home

Note that if you're adding a friendly URL for your portal's home page, you should update your portal's Home URL field so that page requests to your domain name redirect properly. To do this, navigate to the Portal Settings page of the Control Panel and find the Home URL field in the Navigation section. For our bank example, we would enter */web/best-bank/home* into the Home URL field. Once you've entered this setting, page requests to localhost:8080 will redirect to the friendly URL of your portal's new homepage: http://localhost:8080/web/bestbank/home.

Virtual Hosts make web navigation much easier for your users by connecting a domain name to a site. This tab allows you to define a domain name (i.e., www.mycompany.com) for your site. This can be a full domain or a subdomain. This enables you to host a number of web sites as separate sites on one Liferay server.

For instance, if we set this up for Nose-ster's Development Network, users in that site could use developers.nosester.com to get to their site, provided Nose-ster's network administrators created the domain name and pointed it to the Liferay server.

To set this up, the DNS name *developers.nosester.com* should point to your portal's IP address first. Then enter *http://developers.noseter.com* in the Virtual Host tab for the Developers site. This helps users quickly access their site without having to recall an extended URL.

Site Template: If you've created the site from a site template, this section displays information about the link between the site template and the site. Specifically, you can see which site template was used and whether or not it allows modifications to the pages inherited from it by site administrators. If you're not using site templates for this site, you can safely ignore this section.

Sitemap: lets you send a sitemap to some search engines so they can crawl your site. It uses the sitemap protocol, which is an industry standard. You can publish your site to Yahoo or Google and their web crawlers will use the sitemap to index your site. Liferay Portal makes this very simple for administrators by generating the sitemap XML for all public web sites.

By selecting one of the search engine links, the sitemap will be sent to them. It's only necessary to do this once per site. The search engine crawler will periodically crawl the sitemap once you've made the initial request.

If you're interested in seeing what is being sent to the search engines, select the *Preview* link to see the generated XML.

Robots: If you're using virtual hosting for this site, you can configure `robots.txt` rules for the domain. The Robots page gives you the option to configure your `robots.txt` for both public and private pages on a site. If you don't have Virtual Hosting set up, this tab is rather boring.

Staging: enables you to edit and revise a page behind the scenes, then publish changes to your site once they have been completed and reviewed. For a full explanation of Staging, see chapter 3: Advanced web content management.

Analytics: allows you to integrate your pages with Google Analytics. Liferay provides seamless integration with Google Analytics, allowing you to place your ID in one place, then it will get inserted on every page. This enables you to focus your efforts on building the page, rather than remembering to put the code everywhere. Google Analytics is a free service which lets you do all kinds of traffic analysis on your site so you can see who visits, where visitors are from and what pages they most often visit. This helps you tweak your site so you can provide the most relevant content to your users.

Now that you know how to configure sites, let's look at page templates and site templates.

Page Templates and Site Templates

Page Templates and *Site Templates* are invaluable tools for building similar pages on larger portals. As you continue to add pages to sites in your portal, you'll notice repeatable patterns in the designs of those pages. Page templates enable you to preconfigure a single page and then apply it to any new page you create. Site Templates allow you to do the same thing but on the scale of a site–if you have multiple sites that use a similar structure of pages, you can create a single site template and use it to create as many sites as desired. For a full explanation of Page Templates and Site Templates, see chapter 3.

Site Content

Liferay 6.1 makes it easier to access Web Content management without using the Control Panel. You can now click *Manage* and then *Site Content* to access the same Web Content controls featured in the Control Panel right from your portal page.

You can manage the following kinds of content:

- Recent Content
- Web Content
- Documents and Media
- Bookmarks
- Calendar
- Message Boards
- Blogs
- Wiki

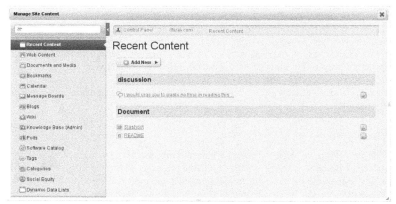

Figure 2.9: Site Content

- Polls
- Software Catalog
- Tags
- Categories
- Social Equity
- Dynamic Data Lists

For details about Liferay's social collaboration suite, see chapter 10.

Creating the Nose-ster pages

There are a lot of other things you can do beyond placing portlets on a page. So let's start working on the Nose-ster site. You can do this by going up to the Dockbar and clicking *Go to → Nose-ster*.

We'll use the *Community* page you created earlier in the chapter. Navigate to the *Community* page and select *Manage → Page* from the Dockbar.

This screen should now be familiar to you but let's recap.

The Page tab allows you to:

- Change the name of the page

- Enter HTML code for the title

- Choose the page type

- Hide the page from the theme navigation

- Define a friendly URL to the page

- Choose an icon to be displayed

- Choose a frame target for the page

- Copy an existing page

You can also enter custom meta tags or JavaScript to the page if you're a web developer. Additionally, if you click the *Permissions* button, you can define which users, groups, roles or organizations can view or edit the page.

The Children tab lets you create child pages underneath the page you've selected. You can nest pages as deep as you like but for every page below the top level hierarchy you must provide navigation to it via a Navigation or Breadcrumb portlet, at least with most themes (including the default). Developers can create themes which have cascading menu bars which show the full hierarchy. Some examples of that are in Liferay's plugin repositories.

For now, click *Return to full page*. You should be able to define and manage pages in Liferay at this point so let's look at what you'd put on a page.

Portlets

As we discussed earlier, Liferay Portal pages are composed of portlets. All of your site's functionality, from blogs to shopping, is composed of portlets.

Adding portlets to a page is simple. Let's add some to our Collaboration page.

1. In the Dockbar, select *Add → More*.

2. In the menu that appears, expand the *Collaboration* category.

3. Drag the *Blogs Aggregator* portlet off the Add Application window onto the right column of our page.

4. Next, drag the *Wiki* portlet to the *left column.*

See how easy it is to add applications to your pages? We've gone one step further: we've got the Wiki portlet, the Blogs Aggregator portlet and then a nested portlet with a different layout and the Alerts, Search and Dictionary portlets in the figure below.

Figure 2.10: Yeah, we're showoffs. But as you can see, your page layout options are virtually limitless.

You'll find it's easy to make your pages look exactly the way you want them to. If the layout options provided aren't enough, you can even develop your own. More information about that can be found in Liferay's official guide to development, *Liferay in Action*.

Page Permissions

By default, public pages are just that: public. They can be viewed by anybody, logged in or not logged in. And private pages are really only private from non-members of the site. If someone has joined your site or is a member of your organization, that person can see all the private pages. You can, however, modify the permissions on individual pages in either page group so only certain users can view them.

Let's say we wanted to create a page only for administrators to see. We can do this with the following procedure:

1. Go to the Dockbar and select *Manage* → *Control Panel*.

2. Ensure you've selected the default site in the context selector.

3. Click the *Site Pages* link.

4. Click the *Private Pages* tab to switch to the Private Pages. Remember, these pages by default are viewable only by members of the site.

5. Create a page called *Admin Tips*.

6. Click on the page in the tree on the left and then click *Permissions*.

7. Uncheck the *View* and *Add Discussion* permissions next to the Site Member role.

8. Click the *Save* button.

Figure 2.11: Permissions for Admin Tips

Congratulations! You've just changed the permissions for this page so only site administrators can view it. Any users you add to this role can now see the page. Other users, even members of this site, won't have permission to see it.

Pages in Liferay are as flexible as pages you'd create manually without a portal. Using a point and click interface, you can define your site any way you want. You can create and remove pages, export and import them, set their layouts, define how they are indexed by search engines and more. You've also been introduced to Liferay's concept of sites. Again, using a point and click interface, you can create multiple web sites and define how users can access them, whether they are linked to a domain name and create all of their pages.

You now understand how to manage pages in Liferay Portal. It's time to move on to adding content to those pages. Liferay's Web Content Management (WCM) is a highly powerful, yet flexible, set of tools that enables you to successfully manage your web site.

You'll soon discover that Liferay's WCM is easy to learn and highly configurable. If you already have experience with WCM, you'll see some new features and improvements to old ones. If you're new to Liferay's WCM, then you'll be surprised at how fast you will be adding, editing and scheduling content on your site. Once you're familiar with portlets such as Web Content Display and Asset Publisher, your ability to manage an immense site with a large amount of content will simply amaze you.

We'll be using Liferay's WCM to publish simple pieces of content, develop templates to define how content is to be displayed, set up a workflow for content to be approved, schedule when content is to be published and much, much more.

2.3   Authoring (basic) content

You've been assigned the task to build a web site for an innovative new social networking site called Nose-ster. You've decided to take advantage of Liferay Portal and its rapid deployment features as well as its ability to get a fully functional, content-rich web site with integrated social features up and running in little time. Together, we can get you started.

We'll walk through the creation of Nose-ster's web site, starting by creating and publishing some simple content using Liferay's built-in WYSIWYG editor. We'll then take advantage of Liferay's robust structure editor. We'll use templates to display the content and then explore some of the advanced publishing features such as the built-in workflow and Asset Publisher.

Creating content the simple way

As we've stated above, content is the reason web sites exist. Liferay Portal has made it easier than ever to get content published to your site. Because Liferay

Portal is so flexible, you can use basic authoring tools right away or take advantage of the more advanced features. It's adaptable to your needs.

We'll begin by creating simple content using Liferay's WYSIWYG Editor and then we'll publish it to the home page of Nose-ster's web site. This is a fast and straightforward process that demonstrates how easy it is to create and publish content on your Liferay Portal instance. Let's learn about the Web Content section of the control panel so we can create and publish our first pieces of content.

Figure 2.12: Choosing a Site in the Content Section

When you manage web content from the Control Panel you can select the location where the content resides. For instance, you can add content that's available to a specific site or globally across the portal. The Content section of the Control Panel displays as its heading the name of the site you're currently working on. This heading is called the *context menu selector*: you can change the scope of where you'd like to view, edit or create content by using the drop-down selector attached to the heading.

Rich, WYSIWYG Editing

Once you have the Nose-ster site selected, click on the *Web Content* link in the Control Panel. Next, click the *Add* button under the *Web Content* tab. This is a highly customizable form that by default has two fields: a title and a powerful WYSIWYG editor. We could customize this form to contain whatever fields our content needs but let's keep things simple for now. We'll cover more advanced features such as structures, templates and content scheduling later in this chapter.

For now, type the words *Welcome to Nose-ster* in the *Name* field. Notice that content can be localized in whatever language you want. If you click on the *localize* checkbox, two select boxes appear which allow you to pick the language you're working in and the default language. You can enter translations of your content for any language in the list. The screenshot below shows this interface but for now, we won't be using it, so you can leave it unchecked. In the content field, add a short sentence announcing the web site is up and running.

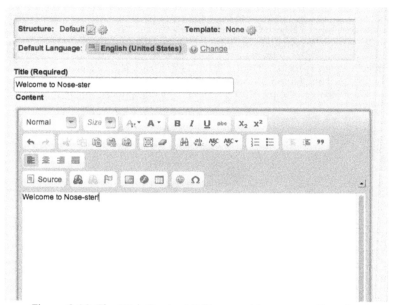

Figure 2.13: The Web Content Editor provides many options for
customization.

Getting a new web site up and running is an exciting step for anyone, whether
it is a large corporation or a small non-profit charity. To celebrate this momen-
tous achievement at Nose-ster, let's give our announcement some of the pomp
and circumstance we think it deserves!

Using the editor, select all the text and then change the style to *Heading 1*
and the color to *Dark Green*.

You could insert an image here or even more text with a different style, as
demonstrated in the screenshot below. You can also add bullets, numbering,
links to another site or custom images. You can even add an emoticon. Let's
add a smiley face at the end of our announcement.

The WYSIWYG editor is a flexible tool that gives you the ability to add text,
images, tables, links and more. Additionally, you can modify the display to
match the purpose of the content. Plus it's integrated with the rest of Liferay

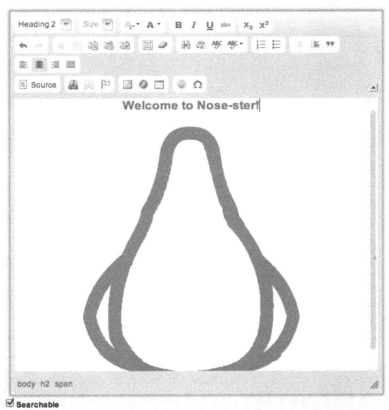

Figure 2.14: View your content changes directly in the editor.

Portal: for example, when you upload an image to be added to a page, that image can be viewed and manipulated in the Documents and Media portlet.

If you're HTML savvy, Liferay WCM doesn't leave you out in the cold. You can click the *Source* button and write your own HTML if you wish.

On the right of the New Web Content form are options that allow you to customize your web content.

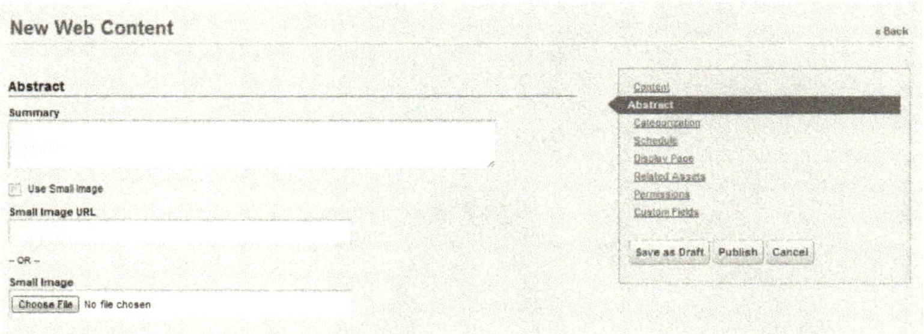

Figure 2.15: New web content can be customized in various ways using the menu on the right.

Abstract: lets you to create a brief summary of the web content. You can also pair the text with a small image.

Categorization: specifies the content type from a list of options. They are *Announcements, Blogs, General, News, Press Release*, and *Test*. You can also create tags to make the content easier to find in a search. Note that these categories are defined by a property in the properties file; see the `journal.article.types` property in chapter 20 for further information.

Schedule: customizes the date and time your content publishes and/or expires.

Display Page: lets you determine where the web contents are displayed when linked from other pages. The concept of the Canonical URL is new to Liferay 6.1. The Canonical URL is unique for articles that redirect the visitor to the article's default display page.

Imagine you have a newspaper with a sports section and a technology section. You add a Sports page and a Tech page to your site, each one with a specific banner and look and feel. You want the articles to appear in the appropriate pages, but you know in Liferay articles are not related to pages. You can add an article as often as you like in different web content display portlets or in configured Asset Publishers. But if you have a *View in context* link, where will you show your article? This is where you'd use a default display page. Articles that have a default display page defined are shown with other related articles in the same display page.

Imagine you have 100 sports articles and 100 tech articles. In previous versions of Liferay you'd need to create a page for each article to show it. Now with only one sports page and one tech page, you can show all articles in one place in a consistent fashion.

Creating a display page There are two ways of creating a display page. You can use a *Content Display Page* template, which automatically creates everything you need, or you can create one manually. The Content Display Page template is found under *Page Templates* in the Portal section of the Control Panel.

To create a display page manually, add an Asset Publisher to a page. Then make it the Default Asset Publisher for the page. This defines this Asset Publisher as the one that displays the content if several Asset Publishers are on the same page. Set this up by clicking *Configuration* on your Asset Publisher. Under the *Setup* tab, navigate to *Display Settings* and check the checkbox labeled *Set as the Default Asset Publisher for This Page.*

Once you've given an article its default display page, links to the article redirect the user to its default display page. To see how this works, add an Asset Publisher to another page, like the Home page of the newspaper, and configure it to *View in a Specific Portlet.* This setting is found in the *Asset Link Behavior* menu under Display Settings. If you click on the link, you'll be redirected to the Default Display Page of the article.

You now see that the link looks something like this:

www.nosester.com/nose-article

This is an example of a canonical URL, and it's a nice enhancement for Search Engine Optimization (SEO) because the article's URL becomes the page URL. To a search engine that's crawling your site, this means that the location of your article never changes. And if you decide to use the content on another page in the future, the article is still available at this URL. This feature is used in search results, in related assets and in Asset Publishers. For more information on Liferay's Display Pages, see chapter 5.

Related Assets: enables you to connect any number of assets within a site or across the portal, even if they don't share any tags and aren't in the same category. You can connect your content to a Blogs Entry, Message Boards Message, Web Content, Calendar Event, Bookmarks Entry, Documents and Media Document, and a Wiki Page.

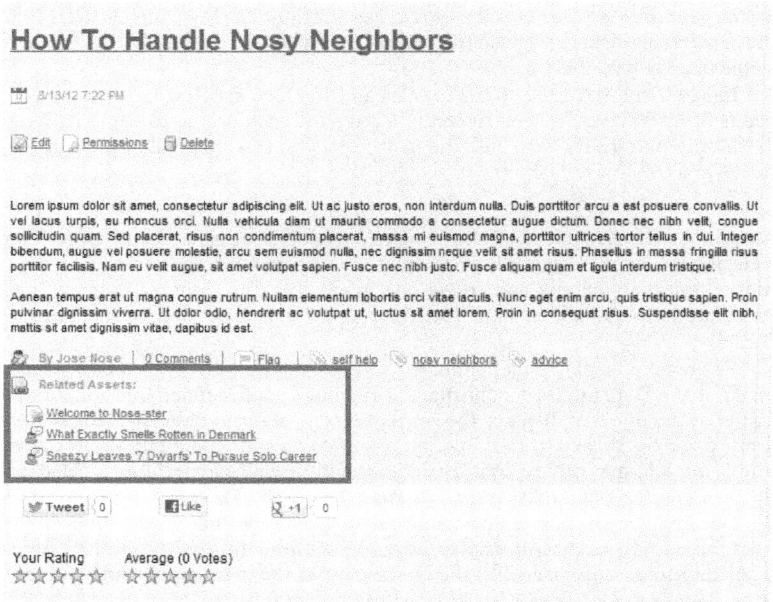

Figure 2.16: This blog entry has links to three Related Assets: one web content display and two blog entries.

You'll learn how to publish links to related assets using the Related Assets portlet in the *Defining content relationships* section of chapter 5.

Permissions: customize who has access to the content. By default, content is viewable by Anyone (Guest Role). You can limit viewable permissions by selecting any Role from the drop-down or in the list. Additionally, Liferay Portal provides the ability to customize permissions in more detail. Select the *More Options* link next to the drop down button and you'll find the different activities you can grant or deny to your web content.

Custom fields: customize metadata about the web content. The fields can represent anything you like, such as the web content's author or creation date. If custom fields have been defined for web content (which can be done from the *Custom Fields* page of the Control Panel), they appear here.

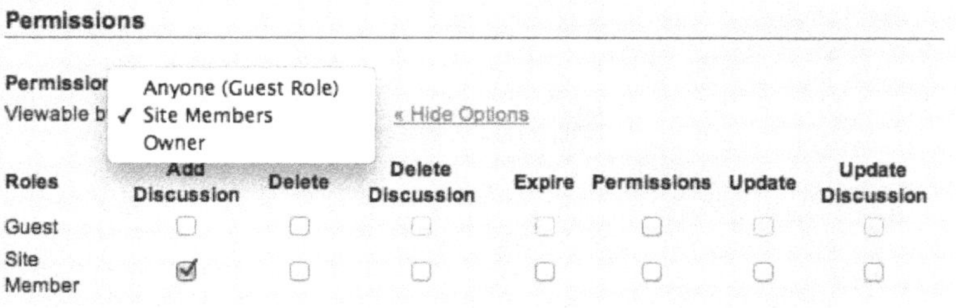

Permissions

Permission	Anyone (Guest Role)						
Viewable b	✓ Site Members		« Hide Options				
	Owner						

Roles	Add Discussion	Delete	Delete Discussion	Expire	Permissions	Update	Update Discussion
Guest	☐	☐	☐	☐	☐	☐	☐
Site Member	☑	☐	☐	☐	☐	☐	☐

Figure 2.17: Permissions for Web Content allow you to fine-tune how your content is accessed.

For more information on Custom Fields see the Custom Fields section in chapter 16.

For this piece of web content, we don't need to change anything. After you're finished with permissions, click *Save as Draft*. This saves the content in draft form. Once you're satisfied with your changes, select *Publish*. This makes the content available for display, but we still have some work to do to enable users to see it. In Liferay WCM, all content resides in a container, which is one of two portlets: Web Content Display or Web Content List. By far the most frequently used is the *Web Content Display* portlet. Let's look at how it works.

2.4 Publishing (basic) content

Now that we've created and published our first piece of web content for Nose-ster, it's time to display it. First, add the *Web Content Display* portlet to our Welcome page by selecting *Add → Web Content Display* from the Dockbar.

Once the portlet appears, drag it to the position on the page where you want your content to appear. You can have as many Web Content Display portlets on a page as you need, which gives you the power to lay out your content exactly the way you want it.

To add existing web content, select the *gear* icon on the lower left of the portlet. You will see the message *Please select a web content from the list below.* You have several options here.

Naturally, if your content appears in the list, you can simply select it. If there is lots of published content available, you could search for the content by name, ID, type, version, content and site (click the *Advanced* link to see all the

Figure 2.18: Adding the Web Content Display Portlet

options). You can also show the available locales for your content. If you're working on the page for a particular language, you can select the translation of your content that goes with your locale.

If you have enabled OpenOffice.org integration with your portal, you can also enable document conversion for your content. This gives your users the ability to download your content in their format of choice. This is especially handy if you are running a research or academically oriented site; users can very quickly download PDFs of your content for their research projects.

Note that you also have other options, such as enabling a Print button, enabling ratings so users can rate the content, enabling comments and enabling ratings on comments.

The Print button pops the content up in a separate browser window that contains just the content, without any of the web site navigation. This is handy for printing the content. Enabling ratings shows one of two ratings interfaces Liferay has: five stars or thumbs up and thumbs down. This can be set globally in the `portal-ext.properties` file. See chapter 12 for further information about this.

Enabling comments creates a discussion forum attached to your content which users can use to discuss your content. Enabling ratings on comments gives your users the ability to rate the comments. You may decide you want one, some or none of these features, which is why they're all implemented as simple check boxes to be enabled or disabled at need.

If you click the *Supported Clients* tab, you'll see you can choose the type of client to which you want to expose content. This lets you target the large screens of users' computers for expansive graphics and lots of special effects or target the small screens of mobile devices with pertinent information and a

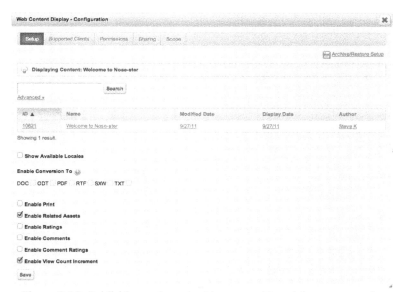

Figure 2.19: Publishing web content is a snap. At a minimum, you only have to select the content you wish to publish. You can also enable lots of optional features to let your users interact with your content.

lightweight page. For now, leave both checked and click the *Save* button. You can now close the configuration window.

To publish new content, select the *page and green plus icon* on the lower left of the portlet. This launches the same full-featured editor you've already seen in the Control Panel, which lets you add and edit content in place as you are working on your page.

This is another example of the flexibility that Liferay Portal offers. At times, you may want to add content directly into the Web Content Display portlet of the page you're managing, especially if you are in the process of building the page. At other times, you may want to use the Control Panel to create content, because at that moment you're more concerned with the creation of the content and not where the content will later be displayed. Liferay WCM supports both processes.

Editing content that's already been published is just as easy as creating new content is. You'll use the same exact tools.

Editing Content   Once the content is displayed–whether you've selected content or created it in the Web Content Display portlet–you can edit the content directly from the Web Content Display portlet or from the Control Panel. To edit it from the Web Content Display portlet, select the *pencil* icon to the lower left of the portlet. This launches the WYSIWYG editor and from there you can make any necessary changes.

Figure 2.20: Edit, Select and Add Icons of Web Content Display Portlet

When you publish your content this way, it becomes available immediately (unless, of course, you have a workflow enabled, which we'll see below). This happens whether you edit it in place or in the Control Panel.

Note: if you want to view your page the way your users will see it (i.e., without all those portlet controls and icons), go up to the Dockbar and select *Toggle Edit Controls*. This makes all those extra controls you see as a portal administrator disappear. If you need to use those controls again, just select *Toggle Edit Controls* again.

That's pretty much all there is to simple content creation. Whole sites have been created this way. But if you want to take advantage of the full power of Liferay's WCM, you'll want to use structures and templates found in chapter 3. Next, let's see how you can manage your content with an approval process called workflow.

2.5   Using Liferay's workflow with WCM

Workflow is essentially a predetermined sequence of connected steps. In Liferay WCM, workflow is designed to manage the creation, modification and publication of web content. You can set up a workflow so content can't be published without going through an approval process you design. In this way, content is published to the site only after it has been reviewed and approved.

Liferay's workflow engine is called Kaleo workflow and it ships with Liferay CE. If you have uninstalled it or are using EE, it needs to be installed and configured separately. This is covered in chapter 6. Since we have somewhat of a "What came first–the chicken or the egg?" problem, for now, we'll assume it's installed and look at how you can take advantage of workflow in getting your content through any approval steps between creation and publication.

You may have noticed something appears to be missing from the staging process discussed above. In particular, you might be asking the question, "How do I reject changes?" Starting with Liferay 6.1, Staging is integrated with Liferay's Workflow engine. To have a review process for staged pages, you need to make sure you have a workflow engine configured and you have staging set up in the workflow. To do this, select the workflow definition desired for page revisions in the Workflow Configuration.

When using a workflow, clicking *Submit for Publication* submits the staged pages into the workflow. Once all necessary approvals have been completed, the page status is marked as ready for publication. The *Publish to Live Now* and *Schedule for Publication* options publish the last version of the selected pages marked as ready for publication.

To enable workflow for Web Content, navigate to the Control Panel and select *Workflow Configuration*. From there, select a workflow that has been deployed to Liferay.

Figure 2.21: Enabling Workflow for Content Management

As you'll discover in chapter 10, you can design workflows to suit your organization's approval process. For Nose-ster's implementation we'll use the *Single Approver* workflow which ships with the product.

Defining Workflows for Web Content

Let's set up Liferay's Workflow for the Nose-ster web site. You must have the
Kaleo workflow plugin installed in order for the workflow categories to appear
in the Control Panel. Liferay's Kaleo workflow engine ships with CE versions
of Liferay. For installation instructions for Liferay EE, please see chapter 10.

1. Go to the Control Panel and select *Workflow Configuration* from the left
   panel.

2. From the select box, choose *Single Approver* for Web Content. Click *Save*.
   Note that you can add workflow to many of Liferay's portlets.

That's all it takes to set up workflow for web content. Now that workflow is
enabled, publishing content works a little bit differently. Let's go through the
process of publishing details for new class offerings at Nose-ster. Return to the
home page and click the *Add Web Content* icon on the Web Content Display
portlet. Call the new content *Course Offerings* and enter some content. Notice
that the Publish button is now gone. In its place is a *Submit for Publication*
button. Go ahead and click it.

Next, go to the *Workflow Tasks* in Control Panel and then select *My Workflow
Tasks*. You will see the option to Review Content for Sales Goals. It shows because you are logged in as an Administrator. There is also a Content Approvers
role which is defined by this workflow and anyone in this role can approve content as well.

To approve the content, you must first take ownership of it. Click on the
task. You should see the screen below.

Taking ownership of, reviewing and approving content is very easy:

1. Click the *Assign to Me* button. Alternatively, you could assign it to someone else in the Content Approvers role or create / update a due date for the
   content's approval.

2. Once you've assigned it to yourself, buttons allowing you to approve or reject
   the content appear. Click *Approve*.

3. You're asked to submit a comment. You'd have to do this for either *Approve*
   or *Reject*. Add a comment and click *Save*.

4. The content is now approved.

In a real world situation, you obviously wouldn't want the person who created the content to be the one who approves it. Instead, you would have one or more roles designed for users who will be creating content and you would have specific users assigned to one or more roles for approving content. Our example was of a very straightforward workflow, as it has only a single approver. Kaleo workflow allows you to design workflows that go through as many steps as you need to conform to your business processes. We look at Kaleo workflow in more detail in chapter 6.

2.6 Summary

This chapter has provided an introduction to Liferay Web Content Management. We've seen how to create and manage pages within a site in Liferay. We've also seen how easy it is to create and edit web content using Liferay's rich WYSIWYG editor. This powerful tool enables users who don't have much experience with HTML and CSS to easily create and style web content of any type that you'd like to publish on the web.

Liferay WCM also includes a powerful workflow engine, allowing you to set up custom publishing rules to fit your organization. You can set up custom approval processes for different sites as well as for different kinds of content within a site. We'll examine sites in more detail in chapter 3. We'll also cover some more advanced web content management tools such as web content structures and templates, page templates and site templates, staging, and mobile device rules.

ADVANCED WEB CONTENT MANAGEMENT

In the previous chapter we looked at some basic ways you can use Liferay to handle your web content. In this chapter we'll delve deeper into slightly more complex web content management techniques. But don't be alarmed, it's not too intense. We'll cover the following topics:

- Web content structures and templates
- Leveraging Liferay's multi-site capabilities
- Using page templates and site templates
- Allowing users to customize site pages
- Staging
- Creating teams to allow for flexible management of site permissions
- Mobile device rules

We'll examine how web content structures and templates provide additional power and flexibility to the web content management system we saw in chapter 2. You'll also learn how easy it is to set up and administer multiple sites in Liferay. Next, we'll learn how you can empower your users to create personal customizations of site pages. We'll also examine how you can use staging to manage the publication of pages and content on your site. Well conclude with sections on creating teams and rules for presenting site pages to mobile devices. Once finished with this chapter, you'll be the envy of your peers as they'll think you really know what you're doing.

3.1 Advanced content with structures and templates

If you've ever launched a web site, you know that as it grows, you can experience growing pains. This is the case especially if you've given lots of people access to the site to make whatever changes they need to make. Without preset limitations, users can display content in any order and in any manner they desire (think huge, flashing letters in a font nobody can read). Content can get stale, especially if those responsible for it don't maintain it like they should. And sometimes, content is published that should never have seen the light of day.

Thankfully, Liferay WCM helps you handle all of those situations. You can use *Structures* to define which fields are available to users when they create content. These can be coupled with *Templates* that define how to display that content. Content won't get stale, because you can take advantage of the *Scheduling* feature to determine when content is displayed and when it's removed. Additionally, you can configure Liferay's built-in *Workflow* system to set up a review and publishing process so only what you want winds up on the live site. Liferay Portal gives you the management tools you need to run everything from a simple, one-page web site to an enormous, content-rich site.

All of this starts with structures.

Using structures

Structures are the foundation for web content. They determine which fields are available to users as they create new items for display. Structures not only improve manageability for the administrator, they also make it much easier for users to quickly add content.

For example, say you're managing an online news magazine. All your articles need to contain the same types of information: a title, a subtitle, an author and one or more pages of text and images that comprise the body of the article. If Liferay only supported simple content as has been described above, you'd have no way to make sure your users entered a title, subtitle, and author. You might also get articles that don't match the look and feel of your site. If titles are supposed to be navy blue but they come in from your writers manually set to light blue, you need to spend time reformatting them before they are published.

Structures give you the ability to provide a format for your content so your users know what needs to be entered to have a complete article. Using structures, you can provide a form for your users which spells out exactly what is required and can be formatted automatically using a template.

You create a structure by adding form controls such as text fields, text boxes, text areas (HTML), check boxes, select boxes and multi-selection lists. Also you can add specialized, Liferay-specific application fields such as Image Uploader and Documents and Media right onto the structure. Furthermore, you can move the elements around by dragging them where you want them. This makes it easy for you to prototype different orders for your input fields. Additionally, elements can be grouped together into blocks which can then be repeatable. Template writers can then write a template which loops through these blocks and presents your content in innovative ways, such as in sliding navigation bars, content which scrolls with the user and more.

Let's look at how we can create and edit structures through the Manage Structures interface.

Editing a Structure

Go back to the Control Panel and select *Web Content* from the content section. The first way to access the Manage Structures interface is simply by clicking *Manage → Structures*. This opens a popup showing all the web content structures that exist in your currently selected scope. Here, you can add new web content structures, edit existing ones, manage the templates associated with a structure, edit the permissions of a structure, and copy or delete structures. Copying web content structures can be useful if you'd like to create a new web content structure that's similar to an existing one, but you don't want to start from scratch. Liferay generates a unique portal ID for the copied structure, but every other attribute of the copied structure, including the name, is the same as that of the original. Once you've copied a web content structure, you should enter a new name for it to avoid confusing it with the original. When you copy a web content structure, you'll be prompted to choose whether to copy any detail templates or list templates associated with the structure. For information on detail templates and list templates, please refer to chapter 9 on Dynamic Data Lists.

The second way to access the Manage Structures interface is directly from the web content article WYSIWYG editor. Click *Add → Basic Web Content* from the Web Content page to add another piece of content to your portal. Instead of

Figure 3.1: You can access the Manage Structures interface by clicking *manage* → *Structures* from the Web Content page of the Control Panel.

going right for the content, this time we'll first create a structure. To access the Manage Structures interface, simply click on *Select* next to the *Structure* heading near the top of the page. To create a new structure in your chosen scope, simply click on the *Add* button in the Manage Structures popup.

It's very easy to create and edit structures: all you have to do is drag elements into the structure and then give them names. For instance, select the *Checkbox* element under the *Form Controls* tab and drag it onto the structure. You can do the same with any of the elements. To remove it from the structure, simply select the *Delete* icon (black circle with X) in the upper right corner of the element. Take a moment to add, delete and rearrange different elements.

Liferay supports the following elements in structures:

FORM FIELDS

Text Field: Used for items such a titles and headings.

Text Box: Used for the body of your content or long descriptions.

Text Area (HTML): An area that uses a WYSIWYG editor to enhance the content.

Checkbox: Allows you to add a checkbox onto your structure. Template developers can use this as a display rule.

Selection List: Allows you to add a select box onto your structure.

Multi-selection List: Allows you to add a multi-selection list onto your structure.

APPLICATION FIELDS

Image Uploader: Allows you to add the upload image application into your structure.

Documents and Media: Allows you to add the Documents and Media folder hierarchy to your structure.

MISCELLANEOUS

Link to Page: Inserts a link to another page in the same site.

Selection Break: Inserts a break in the content.

These form elements provide all you need to model any information type you would want to use as web content. Liferay customers have used structures to model everything from articles, to video metadata, to databases of wildlife. You're limited only by your imagination. To fire that imagination, let's look more closely at the form elements.

Editing form elements

When creating a new structure, it is essential that you set variable names. Template writers can use these variables to refer to elements on your form. If you don't set variable names, Liferay generates random variable names, and these can be difficult for a template writer to follow. For example, consider a field called *Author*. You might create this field in your form but the underlying variable name in the structure might look something like `TextField4882`. The template writer needs to create markup for your structure and place the Author field in a certain spot in the markup. How will he or she know which field is Author when they're all named randomly?

To solve this problem, all you need to do is set a variable name for each field as you add it to your structure. Let's do this now. In your structure, add an element *Text Area (HTML)* which has the Field Label *Instructions*. If we wanted to give it the variable name `Steps`, we can do it very easily: at the bottom of every form element is a **Variable Name** field. Replace the generated name with the name you want to use. Now your template writer has a variable by which he or she can refer to this field.

Below each field is a button labeled *Edit Options*. This contains several other ways to configure your fields:

Field Type: changes the field type, in case you dragged the wrong field type to this location in the form.

Field Label: changes the displayed label for the field.

Index Type: Choose how you want Liferay to index your field for search. You can have it indexed by keyword, which filters out common words such as *and, but, the,* and so on, or you can have it index the full text of the field. By default, indexing is turned off.

Predefined Value: Specifying predefined values for structure forms is a way to specify defaults. When a user creates a new web content article based on a structure that has predefined values for various fields, the predefined values appear in the form as defaults for those fields.

Instructions for the User: Check this box and type a description of what the field is for to display it as a tooltip for the user.

Repeatable: If you want this field to be a repeatable element, check this box. Your users can then add as many copies of this field as they like. For example, if you're creating a structure for articles, you might want a repeatable Author field in case you have multiple authors for a particular article.

Required: Check the box to mark the field required. If a field is required, users must enter a value for it in order to submit content using this structure.

For the Nose-ster structure, type something in the *Instructions for the User* field that helps users know what to put into the Body element (example: *this is an HTML Text area for the body of your content*). Also enable the *Display as Tooltip* box. Now, when users hover over the Help icon near your title, your instructions are displayed.

Structure Default Values

Structure Default Values allow you to create one structure that uses common data from multiple articles.

Returning to our newspaper scenario again, let's say you want all sports articles to have the same display page (sports page), the same categories, or the same set of tags. Instead of adding them for each article or wondering if your users are adding them to every web content, you can add these characteristics once for every sports article by creating default values for the structure. There are two ways to edit structure default values: creating a new structure or editing an existing structure.

For a new structure, you must first create the structure before editing its default values. Navigate to *Web Content* in the Control Panel and click the *Structures* tab, then select the *Add Structure* button. Under the *XML Schema Definition* section of the new structure form, use the *Add Row* button to create different types of fields for the structure. Or you can use the editor to create the structure manually: the Launch Editor button allows you to edit the XML for the structure if you wish to do it via code. When you are done, click *Save and Continue* to go to the Structure Default Values form.

To edit an existing structure, go to *Web Content* in the Control Panel and click the *Structures* tab to see the structures list. Find the *Actions* button for the desired structure and select *Edit Default Values* from the menu to view a window like the one below. This form allows you to manage the structure settings.

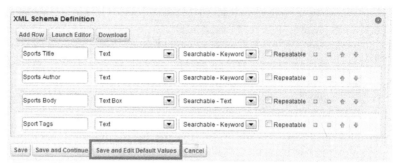

Figure 3.2: You can create fields for structure default values via the XML Schema Definition section of the new structure form.

Every new web content you create with this structure is preloaded with the data you inserted.

As with everything else in Liferay, you can set permissions on structures. Let's see how you'd do that.

Assigning Permissions

Setting permissions on structures is done using the same procedure as permissions everywhere else in Liferay. Most users should not have the ability to edit structures. Structures are coupled with templates, which require some web development knowledge to create. This is why only trusted developers should be able to create structures and templates. Users, of course, should be able to view structures. The View permission enables them to make use of the structures to create content.

You can grant or deny permissions based on Roles and this is the recommended way to handle permissions for structures.

Now that you understand what structures are used for, you need to understand the other half of Liferay's web content management system: templates.

Using templates

Developers create templates to display the elements of the structure in the markup they want. Content can then be styled properly using CSS, because markup is

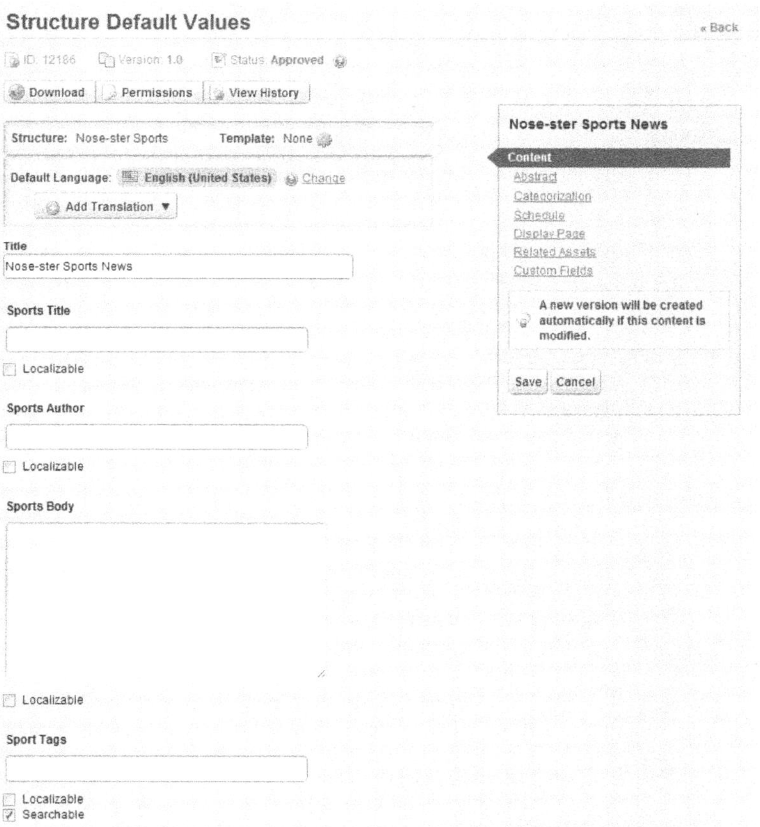

Structure Default Values

« Back

ID: 12186   Version: 1.0   Status: Approved

Download   Permissions   View History

Structure: Nose-ster Sports   Template: None

Default Language: English (United States) Change

Add Translation ▼

Title

Nose-ster Sports News

Sports Title

☐ Localizable

Sports Author

☐ Localizable

Sports Body

☐ Localizable

Sport Tags

☐ Localizable
☑ Searchable

Nose-ster Sports News

Content
Abstract
Categorization
Schedule
Display Page
Related Assets
Custom Fields

A new version will be created automatically if this content is modified.

Save   Cancel

Figure 3.3: You can edit default values via the Actions button of the structure form.

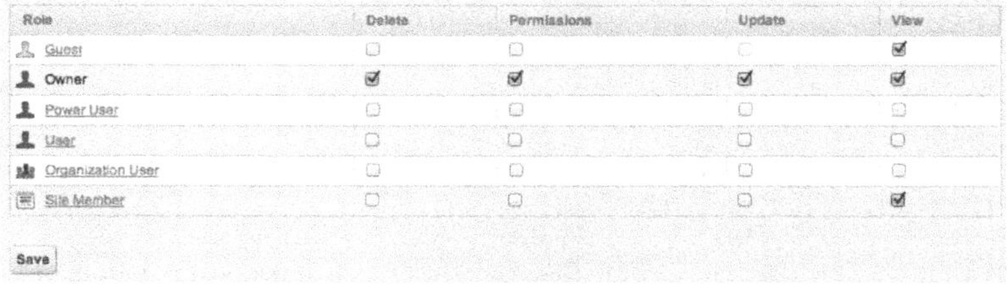

Role	Delete	Permissions	Update	View
Guest	☐	☐		☑
Owner	☑	☑	☑	☑
Power User	☐	☐	☐	☐
User	☐	☐	☐	☐
Organization User	☐	☐	☐	☐
Site Member	☐	☐	☐	☑

Save

Figure 3.4: View Permission for a Structure

generated consistently by the template when structured content is displayed. In essence, templates are scripts that tell Liferay how to display content in the structure. Any changes to the structure require corresponding changes to the template, because new or deleted fields produce errors on the page. If users enter content into a structure, it *must* have a matching template. Without a template, the portal has no idea how to display content which has been created using a custom structure.

Let's look more closely at the types of templates Liferay supports.

Template Types (VM, XSL, FTL and CSS)

Liferay supports templates written in four different templating languages, to support the skill sets of the largest number of developers. This increases the chances you can jump right in and use whichever one you've already used before. If you haven't yet been exposed to any of them, your best bet is Velocity or Freemarker, as they are less "chatty" than XSL and extremely simple to understand.

VM (Velocity Macro): Velocity is a scripting language that lets you mix logic with HTML. This is similar to other scripting languages, such as PHP, though Velocity is much simpler. Because it's been in the product the longest, it is probably the most widely used language for templates in Liferay WCM. If you haven't used any of the template languages before, we recommend using Velocity: you'll get up to speed the fastest.

XSL (Extensible Style Sheet Language): XSL is used in Liferay templates to transform the underlying XML of a structure into markup suitable for the browser. While it may not be as clean and compact as Velocity or FTL, it's widely used for transforming XML into other formats and it's very likely your developers have already been exposed to it.

FTL (FreeMarker Template Language): Freemarker is a templating language which could be considered a successor to Velocity, though it is not yet as popular. It has some advantages over Velocity for which it sacrifices some simplicity, yet it is still easy to use.

CSS (Cascading Style Sheets): You can use CSS if your structure is very straightforward and modifications are simple (colors, fonts, layouts, etc.). If your structure is more complex, however, you'll need to use one of the other options.

Adding a Template

Liferay WCM makes it easy to create structures, templates and content from the same interface. Let's go through the entire flow of how you'd create a structure, link it to a template and then create content using them both. We'll use Velocity for our template and we'll lay out the structure fields systematically to go along with the format we've defined for our content.

1. Go back to the Web Content section of the Control Panel and click *Add* under *Web Content.*

2. Click *Select* next to the Structures heading to access the Manage Structures interface.

3. Add the following fields:

Field Type	Variable Name
Text	*title*
Text Box	*abstract*
Image	*image*
Text Area	*body*

4. Name the structure *News Article* and click *Save.*

5. Back on the Manage Structures interface, click *Actions → Manage Templates* next to the News Article structure that you created.

6. Click *add.*

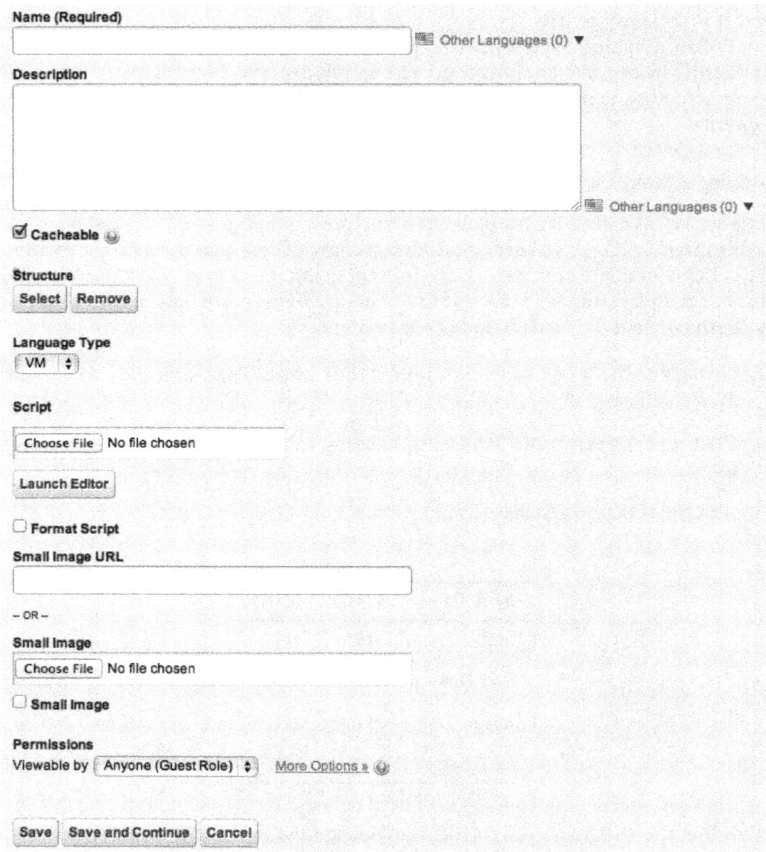

Name (Required)

[   ] 🔲 Other Languages (0) ▼

Description

[   ]
[   ]
[   ]
[   ]
[   ] 🔲 Other Languages (0) ▼

☑ **Cacheable** ⊚

Structure

[Select] [Remove]

Language Type

[VM ▾]

Script

[Choose File] No file chosen

[Launch Editor]

☐ **Format Script**

Small Image URL

[   ]

– OR –

Small Image

[Choose File] No file chosen

☐ **Small Image**

Permissions

Viewable by [Anyone (Guest Role) ▾]   More Options » ⊚

[Save] [Save and Continue] [Cancel]

Figure 3.5: Adding Template Interface

7. Enter the name *News Article* and add a description.

8. Make sure Velocity is selected as the script language (it's the default).

9. If you've written the script beforehand, you can select *Browse* to upload it from your machine. Otherwise, you can click *Launch Editor* to type the script directly into the small editor window that appears.

10. Click *Save.*

11. Click *Back.*

12. Select the News Article structure.

13. On the New Web Content form, you'll see the Title, Abstract, Image, and Body fields that you defined for the News Article structure. The News Article template should also be selected.

14. Populate the fields and click *Publish* to publish your News Article.

   Below is the template script for this structure. It is written in Velocity:

```
#set ($renderUrlMax = $request.get("render-url-maximized"))
#set ($namespace = $request.get("portlet-namespace"))
#set($readmore = $request.get("parameters").get("read_more"))
<h1>$title.getData()</h1>
#if ($readmore)
<p>$abstract.getData()</p>
<p>$body.getData()</p>
#else
<p>
<img src="${image.getData()}" border="0" align="right">
$abstract.getData()</p>
<a href="${renderUrlMax}&${namespace}read_more=true">Read More</a>
#end
```

   This template is pretty small but it actually does quite a bit. First, a portlet URL which maximizes the portlet is created. Once this is done, the template gets the namespace of the portlet. This is important to avoid URL collisions with other URLs that might be on the page.

   After this, the template attempts to get a request parameter called `read_more`. Whether or not this was successful is the key to the rest of the script:

- If the template got the `read_more` parameter, it displays the abstract and the body below the title (which is always displayed).

- If the template didn't get the `read_more` parameter, it displays the image, the abstract and the link created above, which sets the `read_more` parameter.

When this template is rendered, it looks like this:

Learn More About Nose-ster

New to our website? Why don't you take a couple minutes to learn the ins and outs of how to make new friends.

Read More

Figure 3.6: Initial View

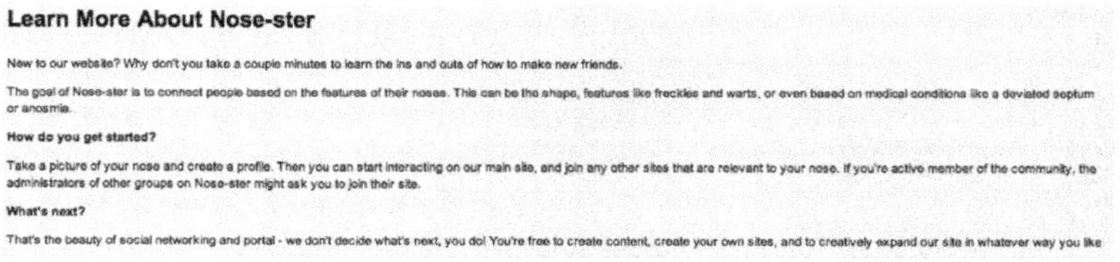

Learn More About Nose-ster

New to our website? Why don't you take a couple minutes to learn the ins and outs of how to make new friends.

The goal of Nose-ster is to connect people based on the features of their noses. This can be the shape, features like freckles and warts, or even based on medical conditions like a deviated septum or anosmia.

How do you get started?

Take a picture of your nose and create a profile. Then you can start interacting on our main site, and join any other sites that are relevant to your nose. If you're active member of the community, the administrators of other groups on Nose-ster might ask you to join their site.

What's next?

That's the beauty of social networking and portal - we don't decide what's next, you do! You're free to create content, create your own sites, and to creatively expand our site in whatever way you like

Figure 3.7: After Clicking "Read More"

Now that you've created a handsome template, it's time to decide who the lucky people are that get to use it.

Assigning template permissions

Permissions for templates are similar to permissions for structures. As with structures, you only want specific developers editing and creating templates. You may, however, want to make the templates viewable to some content creators who understand the template scripting language but are not directly writing the scripts. You can determine who views the template by selecting from the *Viewable By* select box beneath the *Permissions* tab. By default the *Anyone (Guest Role)* is selected.

You'll also want to determine how users can interact with the template. You can do this by selecting the *More* link.

From the *More* link, you can grant or deny permissions based on Roles. For instance, you may create a role with the ability to update the template and create a second role that can both update and delete. Liferay Portal makes it possible to assign permissions based on the roles and responsibilities within your organization.

Now that you understand the role structures and templates play in creating web content, let's look at how you can use Liferay to manage multiple sites.

3.2   Leveraging Liferay's multi-site capabilities

As stated in chapter 1, a site is a set of pages that can be used to publish content or applications. Sites can be independent or they can be associated with an organization and serve as the website for that organization. With Liferay, you can create as many different sites as you like within the context of a single portal.

You can use sites in Liferay to build many different kinds of web sites. Whether you're builing a large corporate website, a company intranet, or a small site designed to facilitate collaboration among team members, Liferay's framework provides all the tools you need. To support different kinds of collaboration and social scenarios, Liferay's sites provide three membership types:

- Open: Users can become members of the site at any time. Users can join sites from the *My Sites* portlet.

- Restricted: Users can request site membership but site administrators must approve requests in order for users to become members. Requests can be made from the *My Sites* portlet.

- Private: Users are not allowed to join the site or request site membership. Private sites don't appear in the *My Sites* portlet. Site administrators can still manually select users and assign them as site members.

In addition to these memberships, when a site is associated with an organization, all the users of that organization are automatically considered members of the site.

Members of a site can be given additional privileges within the site by using Liferay's permission settings. It is also possible to assign different roles within the site to different members. This can be done through *site roles* which are defined equally for all sites or *teams* which are unique for each site.

Liferay's sites have two categories of pages called page sets. There are two kinds of page sets: public pages and private pages. A site can have only public pages, only private pages or both. Private pages can only be accessed by site members. Public pages can be accessed by anyone, including users who haven't logged in. It's possible to restrict access to pages at the page set level or at the level of individual pages through the permission system. Public pages and private pages have different URLs and can have different content, applications, themes, and layouts.

Building a corporate Intranet provides a typical use case for Liferay sites. A corporate Intranet could have sites for all the organizations in the company: Sales, Marketing, Information Technology, Human Resources and so on. But what about the corporate health and fitness center? That's something everybody in the company, regardless of organization, may want to join. This makes it a good candidate for an open and independent site. Similarly, the home page for a corporate intranet should probably be placed in an open independent site so any member of the portal can access it.

For other kinds of web sites, you may want to use independent sites to bring people together who share a common interest. If you were building a photo sharing web site, you might have independent sites based on the types of photos people want to share. For example, those who enjoy taking pictures of landscapes could join a Landscapes site and those who enjoy taking pictures of sunsets could join a Sunsets site.

Liferay always provides one default site, which is also known as the main site of the portal. This site does not have its own name but rather takes the name of the portal. By default the portal name is *liferay.com* but this value can be changed through the simple configuration of the setup wizard. The portal name can also be changed at any time through the Control Panel within *Portal Settings*.

Tip: Prior to Liferay 6.1, there were two ways of creating sites: organizations and communities. This has been simplified to provide more ease of use and allow for more flexibility. The main role of organizations is still to organize the users of the portal in a hierarchy, but they can also have associated sites. Communities can still be created through independent sites, but the new name reflects the fact that sites can be used for many different purposes besides communities.

Sites can be created through the Control Panel by a portal administrator. To add a site, click on *Sites* under the Portal section of the Control Panel and then click *Add*. If there is at least one site template available, a dropdown menu appears. Site templates provide a preconfigured set of pages, portlet applications, and content that can be used as the basis of a site's public or private page set. To create a site from scratch, select *Blank Site*. Otherwise, select the name of the site template you'd like to use. If you opt to create a site from a site template, you have to choose whether to copy the site template's pages as your new site's public or private page set. If other site templates are created, they will appear in the Add menu as they become available. The following figure shows the form that needs to be filled when creating a *Blank Site*.

The following figure shows the form that needs to be filled when creating a *Blank Site*.

Figure 3.8: Adding a Site

Name: is the name of the site you wish to create.

Description: describes the site's intended function.

Membership Type: can be open, restricted or private. An open site appears in the My Sites portlet and users can join and leave the site whenever they want. A restricted site is the same except users must request membership. A site administrator must then explicitly grant or deny users' requests to join. A private site does not appear in the My Sites portlet and users must be added to it manually by a site administrator.

Active: determines whether a site is active or inactive. Inactive sites are inaccessible but can be activated whenever a site administrator wishes.

Once you've created a site, it appears in the Sites page of the Control Panel. Once the site has been created you can specify more details about the site using three categories: Basic Information, Search Engine Optimization and Advanced.

Figure 3.9: Editing a Site

Details: lets you edit the information you entered when you created the site and allows you to choose a site template for the public or private pages of your site. If you select a site template, leave the *Enable propagation of changes from the site template* box checked to automatically update your site if the associated site template changes. The update will only be done to pages which have not been changed within the specific site. If you uncheck this box but recheck it later, the template pages are then reapplied to your site, overwriting any changes that may have been made. Only users who have the permission "Unlink Site Template" will be able to disable the propagation of changes. When the propagation is enabled, the site template might prevent modification of some or all pages to ensure the propagation occurs.

Categorization: allows you to apply categories and tags to the site.

Site URL: lets you set friendly URLs and virtual hosts for your web site.

Site Template: provides additional information about the site template associated to the pages of the site (if any).

Sitemap: lets you use the sitemap protocol to notify search engines your web site is available for crawling.

Robots: lets you use a `robots.txt` file to specify certain pages and links you don't want to be indexed by search engines. You need to set a virtual host before you set a `robots.txt` file.

Staging: lets you turn on either Local Live staging or Remote Live staging. To enable staging, the *Enable propagation of changes from the site template* box on the Details tab must be unchecked. With staging enabled, changes to the site template are automatically propagated to the staged site, not to the live site. The changes still must be approved before the site is published to live.

Analytics: lets you set a Google Analytics ID that is used for your site.

When creating a site from a site template, the initial form provides a new option that lets you decide if you want to copy the pages from the template as public pages or as private pages. By default, the site is linked to the site template and changes to the site template propagate to any site based on it. A checkbox appears that allows users to unlink the site template if the user has permission to do so.

Site templates are very powerful for managing many similiar sites. Let's examine how they work.

3.3 Using site templates

Site Templates can be administered from the Control Panel. They allow portal administrators to create multiple sites with the same default set of pages and content. Site templates can contain multiple pages, each with its own theme,

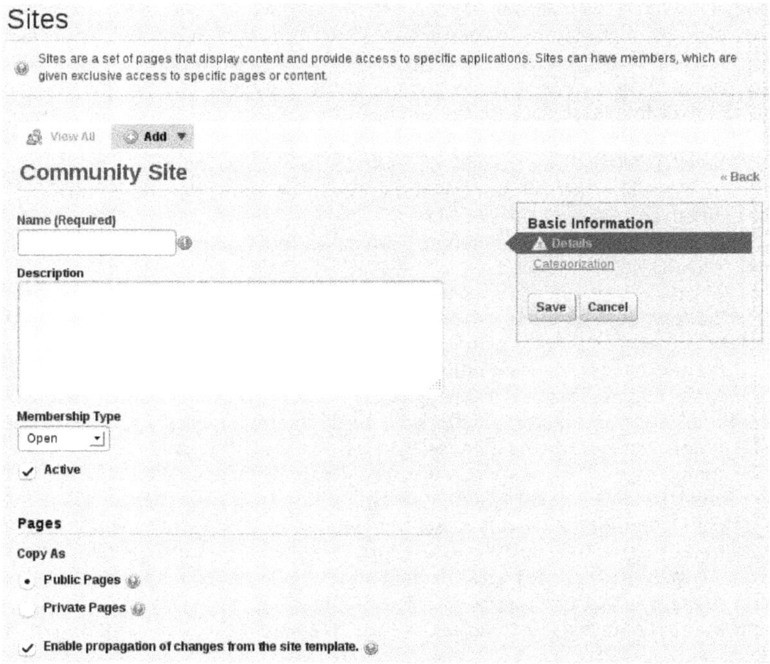

Figure 3.10: When creating a site from a site template, you need to choose whether the site template should be copied into the site's public pages or private pages.

layout template, portlets, and portlet configurations. Site templates can also contain content just like actual sites. This allows administrators to use site templates to create new sites that are each created with the same default pages, portlets, and content. After they've been created, these sites and their pages can be modified by site administrators. Using site templates can save site administrators a lot of work even if each site that was created from a given site template ends up being very different.

To get started, click on *Site Templates* in the Portal section of the Control Panel. Here, you can add, manage, or delete site templates. You can also configure the permissions of site templates. As long as a site is linked to the site template it was created from, changes to the site template's pages, portlets, and portlet configurations are propagated to the site. Changes to a site template's content, however, are not propagated to existing sites that are linked to the site template. We discuss the propagation of changes between site templates and sites in more detail in the section on site templates use cases below.

To manage the pages of a site template, click on *Site Templates* in the Control Panel and then click *Actions* → *Manage Pages*. From here, you can add or remove pages from a site template or select themes and layout templates to apply to the site template. Click on a specific page if you'd like to select a different theme or layout template for that page. To edit the pages themselves, click *Actions* → *View Pages*. You can add specific portlets to each page of a site template and configure the preferences of each portlet. Each page can have any theme, any layout template, and any number of portlet applications, just like a page of a regular site. As with site pages, you can organize the pages of a site template into hierarchies. When you create a site using a site template, the configuration of pages and portlets is copied from the template to the site. By default, all changes made to the site template are automatically copied to sites based on that template.

Tip: If you want to publish a piece of web content to many sites and ensure modifications are applied to all, don't use site template content for that purpose. Instead, place the content in the global scope and then reference it from a *Web Content Display* application in each site.

By default, the following site templates are provided:

- **Community Site:** Provides a preconfigured site for building online communities. The home of a *community site* provides message boards, search, a display of a poll, and statistics of the activity of community members. The site is also created with a page for a community calendar and a page for a wiki.

- **Intranet Site:** Provides a preconfigured site for an intranet. The Home page displays the activities of the members of the site, search, a language chooser and a list of the recent content created in the intranet. It also provides 3 additional pages for *Documents and Media, Calendar* and external *News* obtained through public feeds.

Figure 3.11 displays the form shown when editing the *Community Site* template:

To view and manage the pages of a site template, click the *Open site template* link. This opens the template in a new browser window (or tab) and it can be navigated or managed like a regular site.

Site Templates Example

Suppose we need to create the following three sites for Nose-ster's internal use: Engineering, Marketing, and Legal. These should be private sites that are only accessible to members of these respective departments. We could design each site separately but can save ourselves some work if we create a site template to use instead.

To create a site template, navigate to the Control Panel and click *Site Templates*. Then click *Add* and enter a name for your template: we'll use *Department* for our example. Leave the *Active* and *Allow Site Administrators to Modify the Pages Associated with This Site Template* boxes checked. The *Active* box must be checked for your template to be usable. If your template is still a work in progress, you can uncheck it to ensure that no one uses it until it's ready. Checking *Allow Site Administrators to Modify the Pages Associated with This Site Template* allows site administrators to modify or remove the pages and portlets that the template introduces to their sites—if you want the templates to be completely static, you should uncheck this.

From the list of site templates, click on the *Department* site template that you created. Then click on the *Open site template* link to begin adding pages and portlets and configuring the layouts. When you click this link, the site template opens in a new browser tab or window. For our example, we would like our site template to include four pages. First, we'd like a Home page with the Activities,

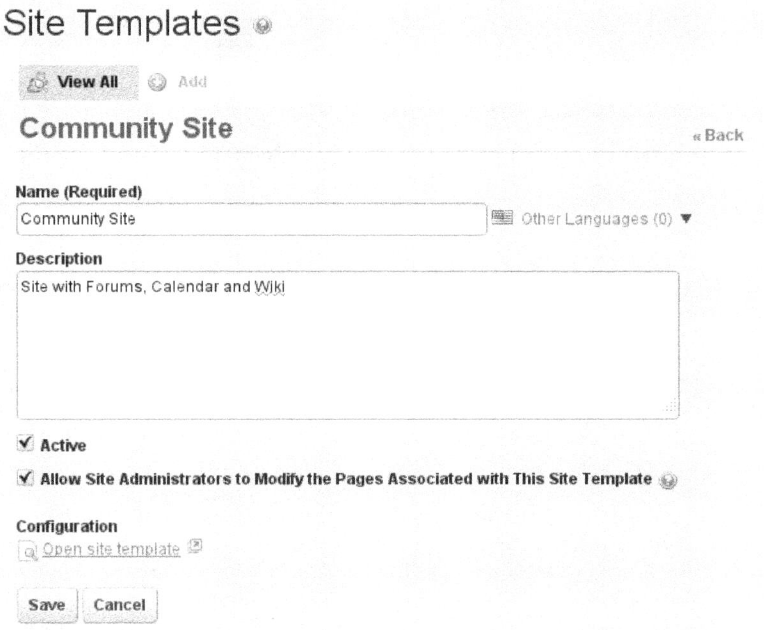

Site Templates ◎

View All   Add

Community Site

«Back

Name (Required)

Community Site   Other Languages (0) ▼

Description

Site with Forums, Calendar and Wiki

☑ **Active**

☑ **Allow Site Administrators to Modify the Pages Associated with This Site Template** ◎

Configuration

Open site template

Save   Cancel

Figure 3.11: Site Templates

Announcements, and Calendar portlets. Next, we'd like a Documents and Media page with the Documents and Media portlet. Finally, we should create a Wiki page with the Wiki and Tag Cloud portlets and a Message Boards page with the Message Boards and Tag Cloud portlets. When you're done creating and configuring the pages of your site template, just close the browser tab or window that opened when you clicked *Open site template*. Changes to site templates are automatically saved as you make them, so you don't need to return to the Site Templates page of the Control Panel and select *Save*.

Next, let's use our site template to create our Engineering, Marketing and Legal sites. Go to the Control Panel and click on *Sites*. Then click *Add → Department*. Enter *Engineering* for the site name and set the Membership Type

Figure 3.12: You can see the name of the site template you're currently editing

to *Private*. Recall that private sites don't appear in the My Sites portlet so that regular portal users won't even know that the Engineering site exists. Also, the only way users can be added to a private site is via an invitation from a site administrator. Leave the *Active* box checked so that your site can be used immediately. Select the *Copy as Private Pages* option since our Engineering site is intended for internal use only. Leave the *Enable propagation of changes from the site template* box checked so that the Engineering site receives updates if the Department site template is modified. Finally, click *Save* to create your the Engineering site.

Repeat these steps to create the Marketing and Legal sites. The new sites have all the pages and portlets you created in the site template. To view the pages of the new sites, click on *Sites* in the Control Panel and then click on *Actions → Go to Private Pages* next to one of your new sites. Using site templates streamlines the site creation process for administrators, making it easy to create sites quickly. Now each Nose-ster department has its own calendar, documents and media library, wiki, and message boards application. Although the pages and portlets of each department's site are the same, each site will quickly be filled with department-specific information as users add and share content within the sites. Also, site administrators can add new pages, portlets, and content to their sites, further differentiating each department's site from the others.

Propagating changes from site templates to sites

It's possible for site template administrators to add, update, or delete site template pages. Changes made to a site template can be propagated to sites whose pages sets are linked to the site template. Such a link is created when you create a site based on a site template and leave the *Enable propagation of changes from the site template* box checked. To disable or re-enable this link for a site, select the site in the Control Panel's context menu selector. Then click on *Site Settings* and uncheck or recheck the *Enable propagation of changes from the site template* checkbox. You can can also access the Site Settings interface via the Dockbar by clicking *Manage → Site Settings*. In this section, we explain the propagation of changes from site templates to sites and discuss the options available to site administrators and site template administrators.

If a site's page set has been created from a site template and the propagation of changes from the site template is enabled, site administrators can add new pages but cannot remove or reorder the pages imported from the site template. If a site has both pages imported from a site template and custom site pages, the site template pages always appear first; custom pages added by site administrators appear after the site template pages. Only site template administrators can remove, reorder, or add site template pages. Site administrators can add or remove custom site pages. They can also reorder custom site pages as long as they're all positioned after the site template pages. Site template administrators cannot add, remove, or reorder custom site pages.

If a site administrator changes a page that was imported from a site template and refreshes the page, the following message appears:

This page has been changed since the last update from the site template. No further updates from the site template will be applied. Click *Reset* to overwrite the changes and receive updates from the site template.

If the site administrator clicks the *Reset* button, changes are propagated from the site template to all the pages of the site that were imported from the site template. Clicking the *Reset* button makes two kinds of updates. First, changes made by site administrators to pages that were imported from the site template are undone. Second, changes made by site template administrators to site template pages are applied to the site pages.

Site template administrators can set preferences for portlets on site template pages. When a portal administrator creates a site from a site template, the portlet preferences are copied from the site template's portlets, overriding any default portlet preferences. When merging site template and site changes, e.g., when resetting, portlet preferences are copied from site template portlets to site portlets. Only global portlet preferences or local portlet preferences which don't refer to IDs are overwritten.

Site administrators can also add data to site template portlets. For example, site template administrators can add the Wiki portlet to a site template page and use the Wiki to create lots of articles. When a portal administrator creates a site from a site template, data is copied from the site template's portlets to the site's portlets. The preferences of the site's portlets are updated with the IDs of the copied data. For example, if a site is created from a site template that has a Wiki portlet with lots of wiki articles, the wiki articles are copied from the site template's scope to the site's scope and site's Wiki portlet is updated with the IDs of the copied wiki articles. Portlet data is only copied from a site template to a site when the site is first created; data is not copied copied during a site reset.

Now that we've learned how site templates work, let's discuss how to use page templates.

3.4   Using page templates

Click on *Page Templates* in the Control Panel to see a list of page templates. Page templates function similarly to site templates but at the page level. Each page template provides a pre-configured page to reuse. Within a page template, it's possible to select a theme, a layout template, to add portlets to the page and to configure portlet preferences. Both sites and site templates can utilize page templates for creating new pages.

You can edit or delete existing page templates, configure their permissions, or add new page templates. By default three sample page templates are provided:

- **Blog**: provides a page with three applications related to blogging. It has two columns: the main left column contains the blogs portlet and the small right column provides two side portlets, Tag Cloud and Recent Bloggers. The tag cloud application shows the tags used within the site and allows navigating through the blog entries shown in the main blogs portlet.

- **Content Display Page**: provides a page preconfigured to display content. It has three auxiliary applications (Tags Navigation, Categories Navigation, and Search) and an Asset Publisher. The most significant aspect of this page is that the Asset Publisher is preconfigured to be display any web content associated with this page. This means that you can select any page created from this page template as a *Display Page* for a web content article. You can choose a display page for a web content article when creating a new web content article or when editing an existing one. When you create a new web content article, a unique (canonical) URL for the web content pointing to this page will be assigned to it.

- **Wiki**: provides a page with three applications related to authoring a wiki. It also has two columns, the main left column with the wiki application

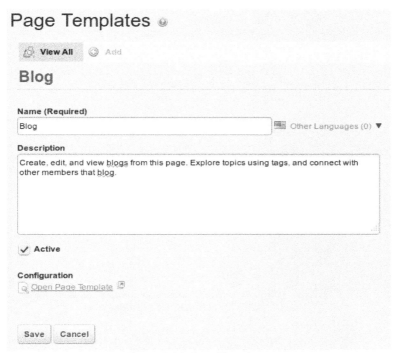

Figure 3.13: Page Templates

and two right side portlets to allow navigating through pages by tags and categories.

To add a new page template, click the *Add* button. Then enter a name and description for your template. Leave the *Active* button checked. Click *Save* and then identify your page template in the list. Click its name or use the Actions button to edit the page template. The *Open Page Template* link opens a new browser window which you can use to configure your new page. Any changes you make are automatically saved so you can close the new browser window once you're done.

Note that after a new page template has been created the default permissions are to only allow the creator to use the page template. To give other users access to it, use the actions menu in the list of templates and choose *Permissions*. Once you see the matrix of roles and permissions, check the *View* permission for the role or roles needed to see the page template in the list of available page templates when creating a new page. If you want any user who can create a page to be able to use the page template, just check the *View* permission for the *User* role.

Figure 3.14: Selecting a Page Template

To use your template to create a new page, just navigate to a page over which you have site administrator privileges and select *Add → Page* from the Dockbar. You'll be able to select a page template and type a name for the new page. Alternatively, you can use the Control Panel. First, in the context selector menu, select the site to which you'd like to add a page and then click on the *Site Pages* link. Then click the *Add Page* button, type a name, select your template from the drop down menu and click *Add Page* to finish.

Note that by default, when a site administrator creates pages based on a page template, any future changes to the template are automatically propagated to those pages. Site administrators can disable this behavior by unchecking the *Automatically apply changes done to the page template* box.

If staging has been enabled, changes to the page template are automatically propagated to the staged page. These changes still need to be approved before the page is published to live. For this reason, the automatic propagation of page template changes to the staged page cannot be turned off and the *Automatically*

Figure 3.15: Choosing whether or not to automatically apply page template changes to live pages

apply changes done to the page template checkbox does not appear.

We'll discuss staging in more detail later in this chapter. For now let's look at importing and exporting templates.

Exporting and Importing Site Templates and Page Templates

If you want to export a site that uses site or page Templates to a different environment (trough a LAR file or remote publication), the Templates must be exported and imported manually in advance or the import will fail.

To export a Site using a Site Template, use the following process: 1. Go to Control Panel → Site Templates and click Actions → Manage Pages for the Site Template your site is using. 2. Click *Export* to obtain a LAR file with the content of the Site Template. Be sure to choose the applications and data you want exported. 3. In your target environment, go to Control Panel → Site Templates and create a new Site Template. 4. Click Actions → Manage Pages for that Site Template and then click *Import*. 5. Upload the LAR file containing your site template's content.

Now the site can be exported and imported normally to this new environment.

For page templates, the process very similar: 1. Go to Control Panel → Page Templates. 2. Next to the page template you would like to export, click Actions → Export. This produces a LAR file you can import later. 3. On the target environment, go to Control Panel → Page Templates and create a new Page Template. 4. Next to the new template, click Actions → Import. 5. Upload the LAR file containing the exported page template from step 3.

The page template can now be imported normally to this new environment.

Next, let's examine the tools Liferay provides for handling translations.

Localization

Previous versions of Liferay had the ability to create and manage different translations of your web content but with Liferay 6.1 we've added several improvements.

When you create a new piece of Web Content, you have the ability to choose a default language. If you click *Change*, you can select your default language from a large number of languages Liferay supports. Before you can create a translation, you must finish creating the content in your default language and save it. Once you've done that, editing the content provides you with the option to *Add Translation*.

After you click *Add Translation*, you can select a language by scrolling through the list or by entering the language you want to use in the search box. When you select a language, a lightbox opens within your browser window enabling you to easily compare the original with the new translation. Once you are done with the translation, click *Save* and the translation is added to the list of *Available Translations*.

The ability to completely delete a translation in one step has also been added. Instead of simply disabling a translation or having to go through a multistep process to remove it, you can now simply open the translation you don't want and click *Remove Translation*.

When you create a new web content structure, each field you create has a *Localizable* checkbox displayed next to it. This enables you to control what can and can't be changed in the translation process. For example, if you don't want images or content titles to be changed when the content is translated, you can make sure those fields aren't listed as localizable. When you follow the steps above to localize content, only fields within the structure that had the *Localizable* box checked appear within the translation window.Next, we'll discuss how to let users customize their site pages.

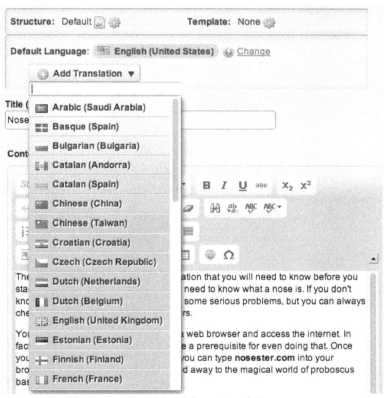

Figure 3.16: Adding a translation

Figure 3.17: Adding a translation

3.5   Allowing users to customize site pages

As we discussed before, as your site becomes larger and more complex, management of the content becomes more challenging. We've gone over Liferay management tools that help you create content quickly and in an orderly fashion. You created a simple announcement with Liferay's structure editor that allows you to quickly design a structure and prepare it for the template designers. Then you applied a template to the structure. You know how to display content using the Web Content Display portlet. Now, you're ready to take advantage of Liferay's advanced publishing options.

If a web site isn't properly managed, it can quickly become stale and that drives viewers away. If people are finding your site because of search engines, you don't want them presented with outdated (and possibly inaccurate) web content.

You also want your content to be found easily by your users. This is done through tags and categories.

Additionally, you may want to create content and send it through an approval and review process weeks before you want it displayed on the web site. Liferay gives you this flexibility with the *Schedule* and *Workflow* features.

Scheduling Web Content

Liferay's WCM lets you define when your content goes live. You can determine when the content is displayed, expired and/or reviewed. This is an excellent way to keep your site current and free from outdated (and perhaps incorrect) information. The scheduler is built right into the form your users access to add web content, in the same column as the structure and template selectors.

Display Date: Sets (within a minute) when content will be displayed.

Expiration Date: Sets a date to expire the content. The default is one year.

Never Auto Expire: Sets your content to never expire.

Review Date: Sets a content review date.

Never Review: Sets the content to never be reviewed.

As you can see, the scheduling feature in Liferay Portal gives you great control in managing when, and for how long, your web content is displayed on your web site. Additionally, you have the ability to determine when your content should be reviewed for accuracy and/or relevance. This makes it possible to manage your growing inventory of content.

Similar to scheduling, Liferay's staging feature also allows you to manipulate time, in a manner of speaking.

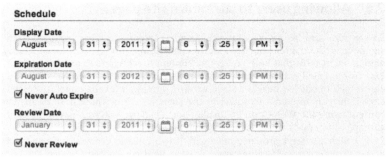

Figure 3.18: Schedule for Publishing Content

3.6   Staging page publication

Staging is an important feature of Liferay WCM. The concept of staging is a simple one: you can modify your site behind the scenes and then publish all your updates in one shot. You don't want users seeing your web site change before their eyes as you're modifying it, do you? Liferay's staging environment allows you to make changes to your site in a specialized *staging area*. When you're finished, you can publish all your site changes at once.

Liferay provides site administrators with two different ways to set up staging: Local Live and Remote Live. With Local Live staging, both your staging environment and your live environment are hosted on the same server. When Local Live staging is enabled for a site, a clone of the site is created containing copies of all of the site's existing pages. Portlet data is also copied, depending on which portlets are selected when staging is enabled. The cloned site becomes the staging environment and the original site becomes the live environment.

When Remote Live staging is enabled for a site, a connection is established between the current site and another site on a remote Liferay server. The remote site becomes the live environment and the current site becomes the staging environment—an instance of Liferay Portal used solely for staging. Content creators can use the staging server to make their changes while the live server handles the incoming user traffic. When changes to the site are ready to be published, they are pushed over the network to the live server. Whether you enable Local Live or Remote Live staging, the interface for managing and publishing staged pages is the same.

So when should you use Local Live staging and when should you use Remote Live Staging? Local Live staging allows you to publish site changes very quickly, since the staged and live environments are on the same server. It's also easier to switch between the staged and live environments using Local Live staging. However, since the staged content is stored in the same database as the production content, the content isn't as well protected or backed up as with Remote Live staging. Also, you can't install new versions of portlets for testing purposes in a Local Live staging environment since only one version of a portlet can be installed at any given time on a single Liferay server.

With Remote Live staging, your staging and live environments are hosted on separate servers. This allows you to deploy new versions of portlets and content to your staging environment without worrying about interfering with your live environment. With Remote Live staging, you can also use one Liferay instance as the staging server for multiple production servers. However, publishing is slower with Remote Live than with Local Live since data needs to be transferred over a network. And, of course, you need more hardware to run a separate staging server.

Liferay 6.1 added a feature to staging called Page Versioning. This feature works with both Local Live and Remote Live staging and allows site administrators to create multiple variations of staged pages. This allows to several different versions of sites and pages to be developed at the same time. Variations can be created, merged, and published using a Git-like versioning system. Let's jump in to see how to use staging.

Enabling Local Live staging

Site administrators can enable Staging for a site via the Site Settings UI. To reach this interface via the Control Panel, select a site in the context menu selector, click on *Site Settings* in the Control Panel menu, then click on *Staging* at the left. Under Staging Type, select either *Local Live* or *Remote Live* and additional options appear. Staging allows changes to be made in a staging environment so that work can be reviewed, possibly using a workflow, before it's published to a live site. Enabling Local Live staging is easy. Just select *Local Live* and decide whether you'd like to enable page versioning. You can enable page versioning on a site's public pages, private pages, both, or neither. Page versioning allows you to work in parallel on different versions of pages and maintains a history of all page modifications. We discuss page versioning in more detail below.

Enabling Remote Live staging

When you enable Remote Live staging, the remote site becomes the live environment and the current site becomes the staging environment. The remote (live) Liferay server and the local (staging) Liferay server should be completely separate systems. They should not, for example, share the same the database. When Remote Live staging is enabled, all the necessary information is transferred over the network connecting the two servers. Before a site administrator can enable Remote Live staging for a site, the remote Liferay server must first be added to the current Liferay server's list of allowed servers. The current Liferay server must also be added to the remote Liferay server's list of allowed servers. You can make these configurations in your Liferay servers' `portal-ext.properties` files. Your first step should be to add the following lines to your current Liferay server's `portal-ext.properties` file:

```
tunnel.servlet.hosts.allowed=127.0.0.1,SERVER_IP,[Remote server IP address]
axis.servlet.hosts.allowed=127.0.0.1,SERVER_IP,192.168.0.16,[Remote server IP address]
```

Then add the following lines to your remote Liferay server's `portal-ext.properties` file:

```
tunnel.servlet.hosts.allowed=127.0.0.1,SERVER_IP,[Local server IP address]
axis.servlet.hosts.allowed=127.0.0.1,SERVER_IP,192.168.0.16,[Local server IP address]
```

Remember to restart both Liferay servers after making these portal properties updates. After restarting, log back in to your local Liferay portal instance as a site administrator. Then navigate to the Control Panel and choose a site in the context menu selector. Then click on *Site Settings* in the Control Panel menu and then on *Staging* in the menu at the left. Select *Remote Live* under Staging Type and additional options appear.

First, enter your remote Liferay server's IP address into the Remote Host/IP field. If the remote Liferay server is a cluster, you can set the Remote Host/IP to the load balanced IP address of the cluster in order to increase the availability of the publishing process. Next, enter the port on which the remote Liferay instance is running into the Remote Port field. You only need to enter a Remote Path Context if a non-root portal servlet context is being used on the remote Liferay server. Finally, enter the site ID of the site on the remote Liferay server that will be used for the Live environment. If a site hasn't already been prepared for you on the remote Liferay server, you can log in to the remote Liferay server and create a new blank site. After the site has been created, note the site ID so you can enter it into the Remote Site ID field on your local Liferay server. You can find any site's ID by selecting *Actions → Edit* next to the site's name on the Sites page of the Control Panel. Finally, check the *Use a Secure Network Connection* field to secure the publication of pages from your local (staging) Liferay server to your remote (live) Liferay server.

That's all you need to do to enable Remote Live Staging! However, when a user attempts to publish changes from the local (staging) server to the remote (live) server, Liferay passes the user's credentials to the remote server to perform a permission check. In order for a publishing operation to succeed, the operation must be performed by a user that has identical credentials and permissions on both the local (staging) and the remote (live) server. This is true regardless of whether the user attempts to publish the changes immediately or attempts to schedule the publication for later. If only a few users should have permission to publish changes from staging to production, it's easy enough to create a few user accounts on the remote server that match a selected few on the local server. However, the more user accounts that you have to create, the more tedious this job becomes and the more likely you are to make a mistake. And you not only have to create identical user accounts, you also have to ensure that these users have identical permissions. For this reason, we recommend that you use LDAP to copy selected user accounts from your local (staging) Liferay server to your remote (live) Liferay server. Liferay's Virtual LDAP Server application (EE-only), available on Liferay Marketplace, makes this easy.

Example: Enabling Local Live staging

Let's create a Local Live staging environment for Nose-ster's home page. Before we begin, let's add a new page. Click *Add → Page* from the toolbar in the default site and name the new page *News and Events*. Next, click the *View Pages* button to navigate to the pages. Then add the Alerts and Announcements portlets to the News and Events page.

When you activate Local Live staging, Liferay creates a clone of your site. This clone became the staging environment. Because of this, we recommend only activating staging on new, clean sites. Having a few pages and some portlets (like those of the example site we've created) is no big deal. However, if you have already created a large amount of content you might not be able to enable staging on that site. Also, if you intend to use page versioning to track the history of updates to your site, we recommend that you enable it as early as possible, *before* your site has many pages and lots of content. Your site's update history won't be saved until you enable page versioning. Page versioning requires staging (either Local Live or Remote Live) to be enabled.

Now we're ready to activate staging for this site. Go to the Control Panel then to *Site Settings* and select *Staging* from under the *Advanced* heading. We'll assume we don't have a separate staging server so we'll select the *Local Live* staging type. If you do have a separate server to use for staging, follow the instructions in the previous section for configuring it and your local server for remote staging. Either way, once you make a selection (either *Local Live* or *Remote Live*), more options become available for page versioning and staged portlets.

Enabling Page Versioning and Staged Portlets

Enabling page versioning for a site allows site administrators to work in parallel on multiple versions of the site's pages. Page versioning also maintains a history of all updates to the site from the time page versioning was enabled. Site administrators can revert to a previous version of the site at any time. This flexibility is very important in cases where a mistake is found and it's important to quickly publish a fix. If you're following the Nose-ster example, check *Enabled On Public Pages* to enable page versioning for the Nose-ster site and then click *Save*.

Before you activate staging, you can choose which portlets' data should be copied to staging. We'll cover many of the collaboration portlets listed under the Staged Portlets heading when we come to chapter 8. For now, you just need to be aware that you can enable or disable staging for any of these portlets. Why might you want to enable staging for some portlet types but not others? In the case of collaborative portlets, you probably *don't* want to enable staging since such portlets are designed for user interaction. If their content were staged, you'd have to manually publish your site whenever somebody posted a message on the message boards to make that message appear on the live site. Generally, you'll want web content to be staged because end users aren't creating that kind of content—web content is the stuff you publish to your site. But portlets like the Message Boards or the Wiki would likely benefit from *not* being staged. Notice which portlets are marked for staging by default: if you enable staging and accept the defaults, staging is *not* enabled for the collaborative portlets.

Using the staging environment

After enabling staging (either Local Live or Remote Live) for a site, you'll notice a colored bar with some new menus just below the Dockbar when you navigate to the site. These new menus help us manage staged pages. You'll also notice that most of your page management options have been removed, because now you can't directly edit live pages. You now must use the staging environment to make changes. Click on *Staging* to view the staged area. Your management

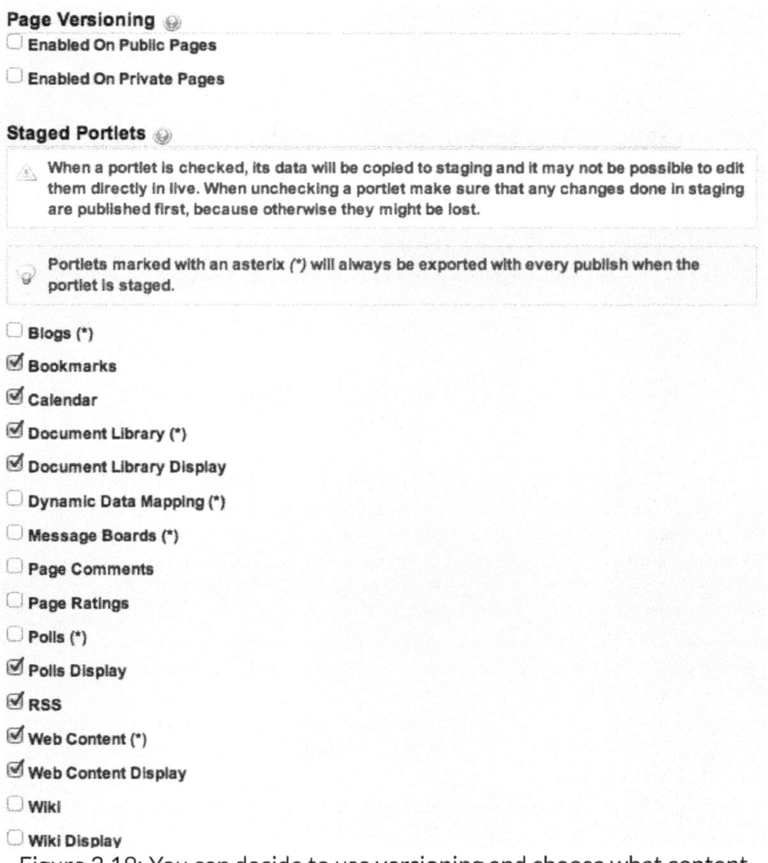

Page Versioning ⊙

☐ Enabled On Public Pages

☐ Enabled On Private Pages

Staged Portlets ⊙

⚠ When a portlet is checked, its data will be copied to staging and it may not be possible to edit them directly in live. When unchecking a portlet make sure that any changes done in staging are published first, because otherwise they might be lost.

💡 Portlets marked with an asterix *(*)* will always be exported with every publish when the portlet is staged.

☐ Blogs (*)

☑ Bookmarks

☑ Calendar

☑ Document Library (*)

☑ Document Library Display

☐ Dynamic Data Mapping (*)

☐ Message Boards (*)

☐ Page Comments

☐ Page Ratings

☐ Polls (*)

☑ Polls Display

☑ RSS

☑ Web Content (*)

☑ Web Content Display

☐ Wiki

☐ Wiki Display

Figure 3.19: You can decide to use versioning and choose what content should be staged.

options are restored and you can access some new options related to staging. If you're following along with the Nose-ster example, navigate back to the News and Events page and click on *Staging* to get your page editing capabilities back.

Figure 3.20: You can see the new bar staging adds to the top of your screen.

Add the Calendar portlet and then click on *Live* from the Dockbar. Notice that the Calendar portlet isn't there. That's because you've staged a change to the page but haven't published that change yet to the live site. Go back to the staged page and look at the options you have available. From here you can *Undo* changes, view a *History* of changes, *Mark as Ready for Publication* and *Manage Page Variations*.

Undo/Redo: allows you to step back/forward through recent changes to a page, which can save you the time of manually adding or removing portlets if you make a mistake.

History: shows you the list of revisions of the page, based on publication dates. You can go to any change in the revision history and see how the pages looked at that point.

Manage Page Variations: allows you to work in parallel on multiple versions of a staged page. We will explain this later.

After you're done making changes to the staged page, click the *Mark as Ready for Publication* button. The status of the page changes from *Draft* to *Ready for Publication* and any changes you've made can be published to the Live Site. When you publish a page to live, only the version which was *Marked as Ready for Publication* is published.

The dropdown next to the Staging link at the top gives you the option to *Publish to Live Now* or *Schedule Publication to Live*.

Publish to Live Now: immediatiately pushes any changes to the Live Site.

Schedule Publication to Live: lets you set a specific date to publish or to setup recurring publishing. You could use this, for example, to publish all changes made during the week every Monday morning without any further intervention.

Click on *Mark as Ready for Publication* and then *Publish to Live Now* to publish your Calendar portlet to the live site.

Content publication can be also controlled using staging. Calendar events are staged by default (this can be changed in Staging Configuration). If you create an event in the staged site, it isn't visible in the live site until you publish it to the live site following the same steps you just performed (you can select which types of content are published when you publish to the live site). If workflow is enabled for Calendar Events, the event needs to go through the workflow process before it can be published to the live site.

Figure 3.21: Ready to publish to the live site.

One of the most powerful features of staging is page variations. Let's see how to use them to create multiple different variations of your site's pages for different purposes.

Site Pages Variations

Let's say you're working on a product-oriented site where you'll have several major changes to a page or a set of pages over a short period of time. Also you need to be working on multiple versions of the site at the same time to ensure everything has been properly reviewed before it goes live. With staging in Liferay 6.1 you can do this using **Page Variations**.

For example, you can create several page variations, enabling the marketing team to give your site a completely different look and feel for Christmas. At the same time, the product management team can work on a different version that will be published the day after Christmas for the launching of a new product. Additionally, the product management team is considering two different ideas for the home page of the site, so they can create several page variations of the home page inside their product launch site.

Variations only affect pages and not the content, which means all the existing content in your staging site is shared by all your variations. In different site page variations you can have different logos, different look and feel for your pages, different applications on these pages, different configuration of these applications and even different pages. One page can exist in just one site page variation or in several of them.

By default, we only have one site page variation which is called **Main Variation**. To create a new one, use the dropdown next to the *Staging* link and click on *Manage Site Pages Variations*. This brings you to a list of the existing site page variations for your site. Click *Add Site Pages Variation* to create a new one. From the *Add Site Pages Variation* screen, you can set a Name, Description and also set your new variation to copy the content from an existing variation. There are several options to choose in this selector.

Any existing Site Pages Variation: creates a new site page variation that contains only the last version of all the pages that exist in this variation. The current variation must be marked as ready for publication.

All Site Pages Variation: creates a new variation that contains the last version marked as ready for publication from any single page existing in any other variation.

None: creates a new, empty variation.

You are also able to rename any variation. For example, edit the Main Variation and change its name to something that makes more sense in your site, such as *Basic, Master, Regular* and create a variation for Christmas.

You can switch between different variations by clicking on them from the staging menu bar. It's also possible to set permissions on each variation, so certain users have access to manage some, but not all variations.

You can now go to the home page of your Christmas variation and change the logo, apply a new theme, move portlets around, change the order of the pages and configure different portlets. The other variations won't be affected. You can even delete existing pages or add new ones (remember to *Mark as Ready for Publication* when you are finished with your changes).

When you delete a page, it is deleted only in the current variation. The same happens when you add a new page. If you try to access a page which was deleted in the current variation, Liferay informs you this page is not *enabled* in this variation and you must enable it. To enable it, navigate to the *Manage →Site Pages* screen. Here all the existing pages for all the variations are shown in a tree. Pages not enabled for the current variation are shown in a lighter color.

To publish a variation to the live site, click on *Publish to Live now* in the dropdown next to the variation name. Publications can also be scheduled independently for different variations. For example, you could have a variation called *Mondays* which is published to the live site every Monday and another one called *Day 1* which is published to the live site every first day of each month.

You can also have variations for a single page inside a site page variation, which allows you to work in parallel in different versions of a page. For example, you might work on two different proposals for the design of the home page for the Christmas variation. These page variations only exist inside a site Page variation.

To create a new page variation, click *Manage Page Variations* on the staging toolbar. This brings you to a list of existing page variations for the current page (by default, there is only one called *Main Variation*). You can create more or rename the existing one. You can switch between different page variations using the toolbar containing the page variations below the site pages variations toolbar. When you decide which page variation should be published, mark it as *Ready for Publication.* Only one page variation can be marked as ready for publication and that is the one that gets published to the live site.

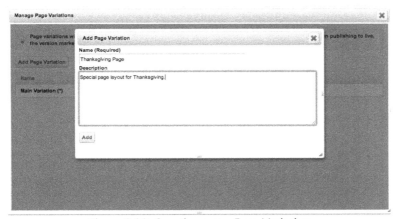

Figure 3.22: Creating a new Page Variation

For example, we could create a page variation called Thanksgiving for the News and Events page inside of the Christmas variation and another one called

Christmas Day to display different content on those particular days.

Figure 3.23: The Thanksgiving Page Variation.

Another powerful feature is the possibility of *merging* Site Pages Variations. To merge two Site Pages Variations, you need to go to the Manage Site Variations screen. From there, click on *Merge* on the Site Pages Variation you want to use as the base. You will be asked to choose the Site Pages Variation to merge on top of it. Merging works in the following way:

- New pages that don't exist in the base Variation, will be added.

- If a page exists in both Site Pages variations, and at least one version of the page was marked as ready for publication, then the latest version marked as ready will be added as a new Page Variation in the target page of the base Variation. (Note that older versions or page variations not marked as ready for publication won't be copied. However, merge can be executed as many times as needed and will create the needed pages variations in the appropriate page of the base Site Pages Variation).

- Merging does not affect content nor will overwrite anything in the base Variation, it will just add more versions, pages and page variations as needed.

Let's finish our discussion of staging by outlining a few more features.

Wrapping up staging

You can enable staging on an individual site basis, depending on your needs. This makes it easy to put strict controls in place for your public web site, while opening things up for individual sites that don't need such strict controls. Liferay's staging environment is extremely easy to use and makes maintaining a content-rich web site a snap.

Liferay 6.0 introduced a new feature to the permissions system called teams. Let's examine them next.

3.7   Creating teams for advanced site membership management

Teams don't appear as a link in the Control Panel because they exist *within* sites. Teams allow site administrators a greater degree of flexibility than was possible using just user groups and roles. They allow site administrators to create various sets of users and permissions for site-specific functions. Teams are the preferred method for collecting permissions within a single site.

If you create a team for one site, the permissions defined for it are not available to any other sites. In contrast, if you assigned a custom role to a user group, the role would be available portal-wide even though the specific permissions defined by it would only apply within the scope of a designated site. Furthermore, team members, unlike user group members, are guaranteed to be members of the desired site.

To create a team within a site, first naviagte to the *Control Panel* → *Sites* page then and then select *Actions* → *Manage Memberships* for the site within which you want to create a team. Finally, click *View* → *Teams* and click the Add Team button.

After you've clicked the *Add Team* button and entered a name and a description, click *Save*. Your new team will appear in the list. To add members, simply click on *Actions* → *Assign Members*.

Permission management for teams is handled at the individual portlet level, using the *Options* → *Configuration* → *Permissions* tab of the portlet itself. Remember the portlet options link is the wrench symbol at the top of a portlet. This enables users who wouldn't have access to all of the necessary options in the Control Panel to manage permissions through teams.

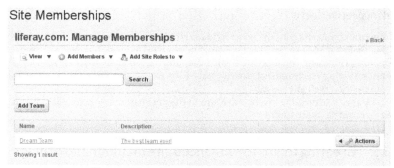

Figure 3.24: Creating a Team within a Site

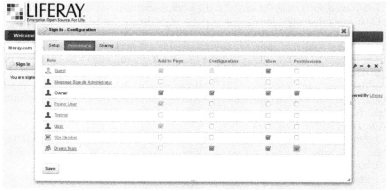

Figure 3.25: Assigning Portlet Permissions to a Team

To give a team access to a particular portlet function, access the *Permissions* tab of a portlet residing on a page, check the boxes corresponding to permissions you want to assign to the teams, then click *Save*. That's it! Now your team is ready to perform their functions. Next, let's look at how to configure Liferay for mobile devices.

3.8 Displaying site pages to mobile devices

Mobile device rules allow you to configure sets of rules to alter the behavior of the portal based on the device being used to access Liferay. The proportion of mobile device users browsing the web has been steadily increasing, so it's important to be able to handle different kinds of devices appropriately. For instance, you can configure the look and feel of Liferay pages accessed by smartphone or tablet users differently from those accessed by PC users.

Both sites and individual pages can be configured with any number of rule groups. A rule group is designed to describe a group of devices; think of a rule group as a mobile device family. It can contain one or more rules that describe a category of devices, such as all Android devices or all iOS tablets. You can define as many rules in a rule group as you need to classify all the devices for which you'd like to define actions. Rule groups can be prioritized to determine which one applies to a given page request.

In order to configure mobile device rules, you need a way to find out the characteristics of the device. While some of the characteristics are provided by the device, most are not. For this reason, there are databases that contain information about thousands of devices. These databases make it possible to learn every detail about a device from the device type, which is included in each request sent to the portal. Liferay's Mobile Device Rules can connect to device databases so that you can use their device characteristics in your rules.

Among the plugins available on Liferay Marketplace, you can find the Device Recognition Provider plugin. This plugin provides out of the box integration with WURFL, an open source database licensed with the AGPLv3 license. Commercial licenses are also available. It's also possible to develop plugins that integrate with other device databases. Even if you don't have a device database, you can still set up mobile device rules. They won't, however, be effective until a database is deployed, because the portal won't have enough information about the devices being used to make page requests.

To configure mobile device rules, you must install the Device Recognition Provider plugin. This plugin uses the WURFL database to enable Liferay to detect which mobile device or operating system is being used for any given request. To install the plugin, navigate to the Store section of the Control Panel, located under the Marketplace heading. Click on the *Utility* section and then on *See All*. Search for the appropriate Device Recognition Provider plugin (CE or EE) and click on it. Finally, click on *Free* to acquire the plugin. Once you've acquired the plugin, you need to download and install it. To do so, navigate to the Purchased section of the Control Panel, find your Device Recognition Provider plugin, and click on *Download* and then *Install.*

Installation Note: If your server doesn't have access to the outside Internet, an error appears in your log:

```
SLF4J: Failed to load class "org.slf4j.impl.StaticLoggerBinder
```

This occurs because WURFL by default downloads device information from the web. You can provide the same information to WURFL manually. Download the SLF4J distribution from http://www.slf4j.org/download.html, unzip the resulting file, copy `slf4j-log4j12.jar` to `[WEB_APP_HOME]/wurfl-web/WEB-INF/lib` folder, and restart your Liferay instance. On some application servers, you'll need to add this .jar file to the `wurfl-web.war` file first (in the directory noted above) before deploying the file to your server.

You can access the Mobile Device Rules administrative page from the Content section of the Control Panel. Select the appropriate scope using the context menu selector so your rule groups are available where you expect them to be. The Mobile Device Rules administrative page displays a list of defined rule groups and lets you add more. To add rules to a rule group, select *Actions* → *Manage Rules*, or click on a rule group to edit it, and then click the *Manage Rules* link.

The rules defined for a rule group, along with the priorities of the rule groups selected for a particular site or page, determine which rule group's actions are applied to a given request. From the Manage Rules page for a specific rule set, you can add a rule by specifying a rule type. Remember that you can add as many rules to a rule group as you need in order to classify the devices on which you'd like to take actions. Note that, by default, only the Simple Rule type is available. The rules are designed, however, to be extensible, and additional rule types can be added by your developers. Once added, you can edit the rule to specify a device type and operating system.

Once you've created some mobile device rule groups and added some rules to them, you'll be ready to set up some actions. The actions defined for a rule group determine what happens to a particular request when the device is detected and the rule group has been found to apply.

You can add actions to a rule group from the Site Pages page of the Control Panel. Select either the public or private pages and then look for the *Mobile Rule*

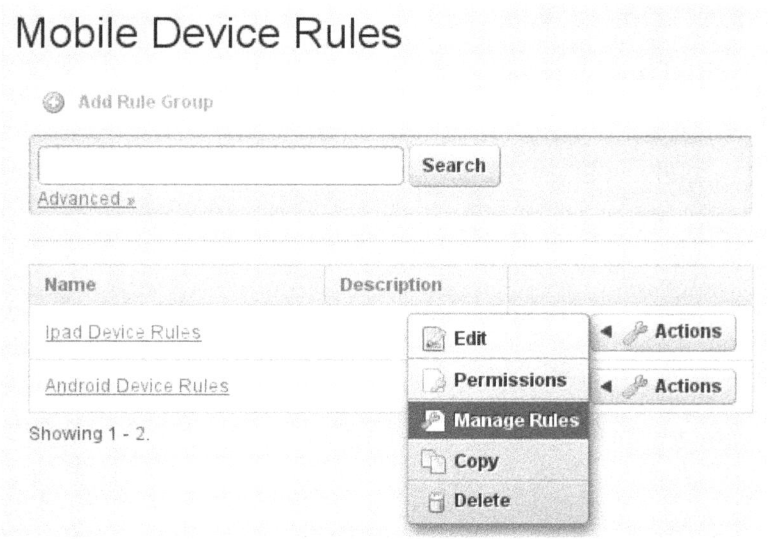

Figure 3.26: You can manage device rules from the Mobile Device Rules administrative page.

Groups link in the right-hand menu. Use the *Select Rule Group* button to select rule groups to be applied either to a site or to a single page. If you select the page group itself from the left-hand menu, the selected rule group applies to all the pages of the site by default. If, however, you select an individual page and then click the *Select Rule Group* button, the rule groups apply only to that page. You can select multiple rule groups for a particular site or page and order them by priority. The rule groups are checked in decreasing order of priority: the actions defined by the first rule group that applies are executed.

To add actions to a selected rule group, use the *Actions* → *Manage Actions* button and then click *Add Action*. By default, there are four kinds of actions that can be configured for mobile rule groups: layout template modifications, theme modifications, simple redirects, and site redirects. Layout template modifications let you change the way portlets are arranged on pages delivered to mobile devices, and themes modifications let you select a specific look and feel.

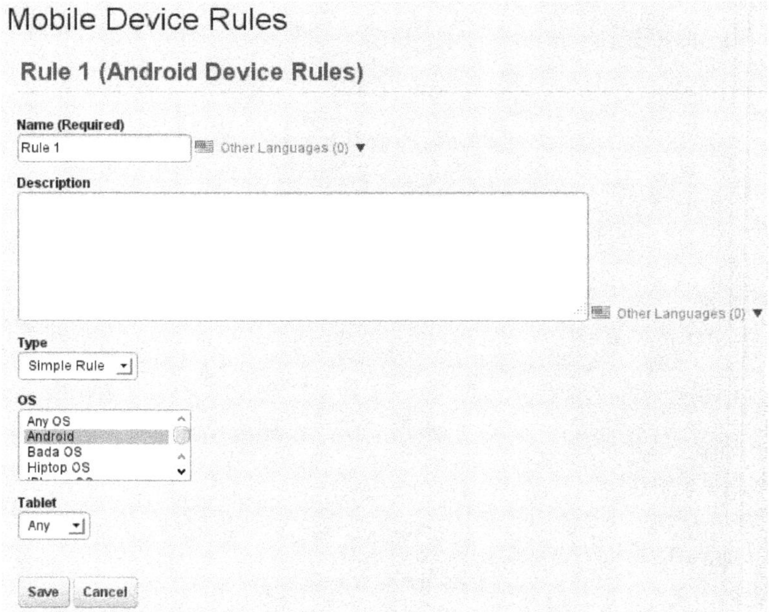

Figure 3.27: You need to install the Device Recognition Provider plugin to populate the OS list.

If it makes more sense for you to create separate mobile versions of certain sites or pages, you can use a redirect to make sure mobile device users get to the right page. To define a simple redirect, you need to specify a URL. To define a site redirect, you need only specify the site name and page name of the page to which you're redirecting. Like mobile device rules, mobile device actions are designed to be extensible. Your developers can define custom actions in addition to the four actions provided by default.

To review, if you'd like to configure an action or actions that take place when mobile device requests are received, take the following steps:

1. Create a mobile device rule group to represent the family of devices for which to define an action or actions.

Figure 3.28: You can select a mobile device rule group to apply for a site or page from the Site Pages section of the Control Panel.

2. Define one or more rules for your rule group that describe the family of devices represented by your rule group.

3. Apply your rule group to an entire page set of a site (all the public pages of a site or all the private pages) or to a single page.

4. Define one or more actions for your rule group that describe how requests should be handled.

To see how this might work in practice, let's discuss a few examples of how you can use mobile device rules. First, suppose you have a separate version of a site on your portal that's specifically designed for mobile phones running Android or Bada. For our example, we'll make a site called Android/Bada Liferay and we'll configure the default Liferay site to redirect incoming requests from Android or Bada mobile phones to the Android/Bada Liferay site. Our first step is to create the Android/Bada Liferay site: go to the Sites page of the Control Panel and click *Add → Blank Site*. Enter the name *Android/Bada Liferay* and click *Save*. Then, with Android/Bada selected in the context menu selector, click on *Site Pages*. By default, the newly created site doesn't have any pages, so click on *Add Page*, enter the name *Welcome*, and click the *Add Page* button. Now our Android/Bada Liferay site has a public Welcome page just like our default Liferay site.

Next, select *Liferay* in the context menu selector and go to the Mobile Device Rules page of the Control Panel. Click on *Add Rule Group*, enter the name
Android and Bada Mobile Phones, and click *Save*. You'll see the message, *No rules
are configured for this rule group*.

Mobile Device Rules

Android and Bada Mobile Phones

Name (Required)

| Android and Bada Mobile P | 🖾 Other Languages (0) ▼ |

Description

💡 **No rules are configured for this rule group.**

🔧 Manage Rules

| Save | Cancel |

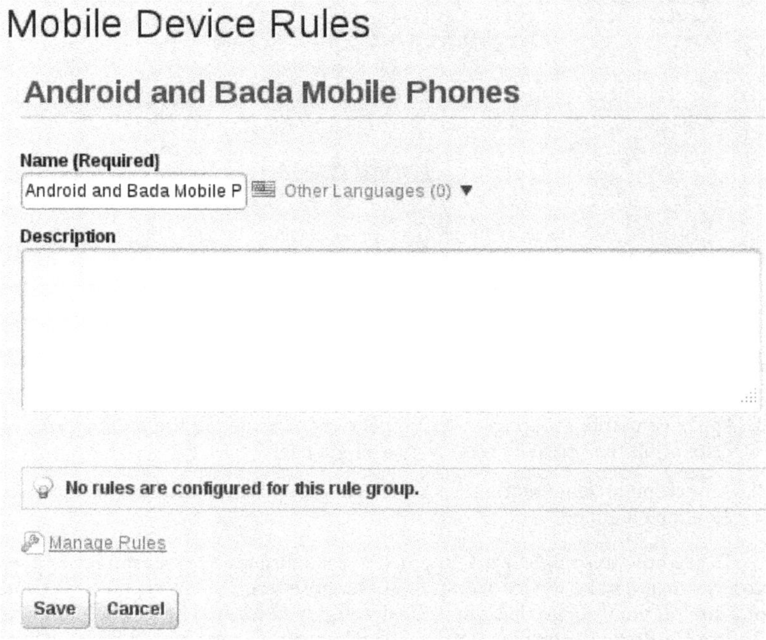

Figure 3.29: After adding a new rule, you'll see a message indicating that
no rules have been configured for the rule group.

Click the *Manage Rules* link and we'll configure our rule group to apply only
to mobile phones running Android or Bada. Click *Add Rule*, enter *Rule 1* for
the name and select *Simple Rule* for the type, then click *Save*. Then click on the
rule to edit it or click *Actions* → *Edit*. Under OS, select *Android* and *Bada OS*
(hold down Control to make multiple selections), select *False* under Tablet since
we want our rule group to apply only to mobile phones, and click *Save*. Now

we just need to define the redirect action for our rule group. Make sure Liferay is still selected in the context menu selector and click on *Site Pages*. Click on *Mobile Rule Groups* in the navigation menu to the right.

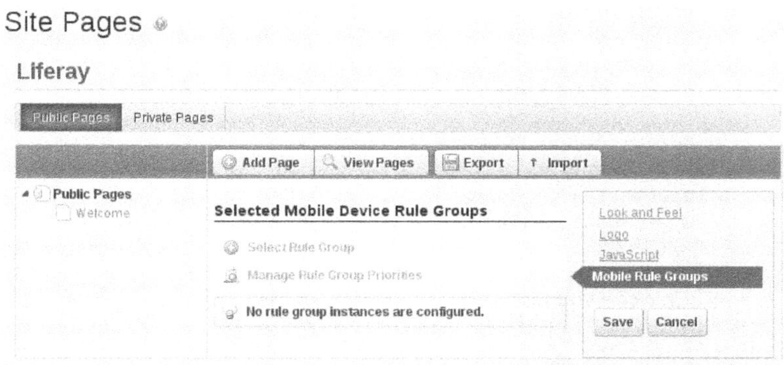

Figure 3.30: To apply a mobile device rule group to a page set of a site, select the site in the context menu selector, click on *Mobile Rule Groups*, click *Select Rule Group*, and select the desired rule group.

Click *Select Rule Group* and then click the *Android and Bada Mobile Phones* rule group that you configured. Once you've selected your rule group, click *Mobile Rule Groups* again and click either on your rule group or *Actions* → *Manage Actions* next to it. Then click *Add Action*, enter the name *Android/Bada Liferay Redirect*, and select *Site Redirect* under Type. Under the Site dropdown menu that appears, select *Android/Bada Liferay* and under the Page dropdown menu that appears, select the *Welcome* page that you created earlier. Lastly, click *Save*. That's it! Now Android and Bada mobile phone users are redirected to the Android/Bada Liferay site from the Liferay site.

Let's look at one more example of using mobile device rules before we move on. Suppose you'd like to create another rule so that when a site is accessed by an Android or iOS tablet, a different layout is used. To set this up, we need to follow the same four steps described above. First, make sure that the Liferay site is selected in the Control Panel's context menu selector and navigate to the Mobile Device Rules page of the Control Panel. Add a new rule group called *Android and iOS Tablets*. Add a simple rule called *Rule 1* to this rule group. As with the previous example, we only need one rule to describe our device family.

Edit *Rule 1* and select *Android and iPhone OS* under the OS heading and *True* under the Tablet heading, then click *Save*.

Next, click on *Site Pages* in the Control Panel, select *Mobile Rule Groups*, and select the *Android and iOS Tablets* rule group. Notice that you've now selected two rule groups for the Liferay site's public pages and they've been assigned priorities. If a device making a request belongs to both of the device families represented by the rule groups, the priority of the rule groups determines which rule group's actions are executed. Note that in our example, the first rule group contains only mobile phones and the second rule group contains only tablets, so no devices can belong to both rule groups. Now we just need to define an action for our Android and iOS Tablets rule group to use a different layout: On the Site Pages page of the Control Panel, click on *Mobile Rule Groups*, and then on *Actions → Manage Actions* next to Android and iOS Tablets. Click on *Add Action*, enter the name Layout Template Modification*, and select the *Layout Template Modification* action type. Lastly, select the *1 Column* layout template (or whichever one you like) and click *Save*. Good job! Now the Liferay site's pages are presented to Android and iOS tablet users with the 1 Column layout template.

3.9 Summary

This chapter has been your guide to Liferay site management and advanced Web Content Management. We've seen how you can use Liferay to manage both simple content and advanced content with structures and templates. We've learned how you can use Liferay to create multiple sites with different membership types. We've also learned how to use page and site templates to simplify the site creation process.

Liferay WCM also includes a powerful staging environment, allowing you to stage content locally on the same server or remotely to another server. You can publish your site when you want it, on the schedule you choose. You can even create different variations of your site that can be worked on simultaneously.

You saw how to allow users to create personal customizations of site pages. We discussed how site administrators can create teams as a flexible means of delegating site permissions. We also saw how to configure mobile device rules so that site pages are presented differently depending on the device making a page request.

Whether your site is small and static or large and dynamic, Liferay's WCM enables you to plan and manage it. With tools such as the WYSIWYG editor, structures and templates, you can quickly add and edit content. With the Web

Content Display and Asset Publisher, you can rapidly select and configure what content to display and how to display it. By using Liferay's integrated workflow, you can set up custom publishing rules to fit your organization. And by using Liferay's staging and scheduling mechanisms, you can manage various branches of pages and content and control when they are published to your live portal instance. You will find that managing your site becomes far easier when using Liferay's Web Content Management system.

CHAPTER 4

DOCUMENT MANAGEMENT

Liferay's Documents and Media library provides a mechanism for storing files online using the same type of structure that you use to store files locally. You can use it to store files of any kind; it serves as a virtual shared drive. The Documents and Media portlet takes its name from the fact that it represents a redesign of two portlets from previous versions: the Document Library and the Image Gallery. First, the Documents and Media library serves as a repository for all types of files; there's no need to store image files in a separate Image Gallery anymore. Second, the Media Gallery portlet introduced in Liferay 6.1 does not serve as a repository but just displays selected content from the Documents and Media library. It can display image, audio and video files. Other new features include customizable document types and metadata sets, automatic document preview generation, and support for mounting multiple external repositories. The new document types and metadata sets are an addition to, not a replacement for, the portal's system of tags and categories. Let's start exploring how to use the Documents and Media portlet.

4.1 Getting Started with Documents and Media

The Documents and Media portlet is non-instanceable. This means that each page on your portal can host at most one such portlet. Furthermore, if you add multiple Documents and Media portlets to pages in the same site, these portlets will share the same data sets since they are scoped by site by default. However, you can add multiple Documents and Media *Display* portlets to a page. Then you can choose content from actual Documents and Media repositories to display. Remember that users, by default, have their own personal sites with public and private pages. They can use their personal sites to host Documents and Media portlets for storing or sharing their own files.

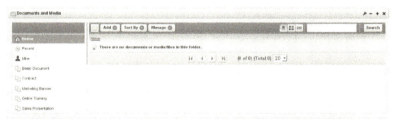

Figure 4.1: Initial View of the Documents and Media Portlet

The default view of the Documents and Media portlet displays the contents of the *Home* folder. The links on the left side of the portlet windows are filters. You can use these filters to choose what you want the main window of the portlet to display. *Recent Documents* displays documents users have recently uploaded, edited or downloaded. *My Documents* shows *your* documents; in other words, the documents you have uploaded. *Basic Document* and the document types listed below it are also filters. If you click on one of these filters, the main portlet window shows only documents that belong to the selected document type. When you add custom document types, which we discuss below, they are added to the filter list. Next, let's look at how to navigate around Documents and Media.

Navigating the Documents and Media Portlet

In the main window of the Documents and Media portlet, you can click on a document to view details about it. Its version number, version history, status, as well as its uploader and the user who last edited it. Depending on the document, some automatically extracted metadata may also be displayed, such as the document creator, author, title, content type, creation date and last modification date. In the case of audio or video files, the duration would also be displayed. You can perform several actions on the document here:

Download: lets you download the document.

Get URL: displays the URL of the document on the server.

Get WebDAV URL: displays the WebDAV URL of the document on the server. See the WebDAV access section below for more information.

Edit: lets you change contents of a document, point it to a different file, change its title, description or document type, or add tags, categories or related assets.

Move: lets you choose a new location in the Documents and Media repository to store the document.

Checkout/Checkin: prevents others from modifying the document while you are working. Other users can still view the current version of the document if they have permission. You can check the document back in when you're done working.

Permissions: allows you to configure file-specific permissions for the document.

Delete: lets you remove the document from the Documents and Media library.

If comments are enabled, you can also view comments, add comments or subscribe to comments about documents. Comments are enabled by default.

The menu at the top of the Documents and Media portlet contains Actions, Add, Sort By and Manage buttons. There are also buttons for switching between icon view, descriptive view and list view. If there are lots of documents in the Documents and Media library, the search field can help you find the documents you're looking for. If your portlet contains more documents than it can display at once, you can use the navigation tool at the bottom of the portlet window to either switch your view to another page or configure the page to display more documents per page.

Actions

The Actions menu will only be displayed if you have selected one or more documents with the check boxes.

Cancel Checkout: lets you check in a document that you had checked out but did not make any changes to. Using this option will prevent the Documents and

Figure 4.2: Viewing a Document

Media portlet from incrementing the document's version number and saving an identical version of the document.

Checkin: lets you check in a document that you have edited. Its version number will increment and the previous version will be saved.

Checkout: lets you check out a document that you would like to edit. This option prevents anyone else from modifying it while you are working.

Move: allows you to choose a new location for a document or folder within the portlet's file system. You can move multiple documents and folders at the same time. Moving documents and folders is also possible via drag & drop.

Delete: allows you to remove a document or folder from the portlet. You can delete multiple documents and folders at the same time.

Add

From the Add button, you can add documents, folders and shortcuts just like on your local file system.

Folder: lets you create a new location in your portlet's file system.

Shortcut: allows you to create a shortcut to any document that you have read access for. You can set permissions on the shortcut to specify who can access the original document through the shortcut.

Repository: is a new feature of Liferay 6.1. This option allows you to add an entirely new repository to your Documents and Media portlet. To do this you need to specify the repository type and choose an ID. If you are using the AtomPub protocol you'll also have to specify the AtomPub URL.

Multiple Documents: allows you to upload several documents at once.

Basic Document: allows you upload a single file that you would like the default document type, "Basic Document," to apply to. By default, basic documents are not described by any metadata sets.

The remaining items in the Add menu are default document types that are each described by a unique metadata set. When you add a document belonging to a specific document type, you're presented with a form to not only specify the file to upload but also to fill out the fields defined by the document type's metadata set. We describe the "Contract" document type by way of example.

Contract: lets you upload a file that you would like the "Contract" document type to apply to. This document type is intended to be used to describe legal contracts. By default, contracts are described by effective date, expiration date, contract type, status, legal reviewer, signing authority and deal name fields. Document types are discussed below.

Any custom documents types that have been defined also appear in the Add menu. If a document type has been created that matches the document you would like to upload, you can select that document type from the Add menu. This will associate the metadata fields associated with the document type to your document and you will be asked to fill out the fields.

Sort

You can sort the items displayed in the main window of the Documents and Media portlet using the Sort By menu. You can sort by title, create date, modified date, downloads or size.

Title: lets you alphabetically sort documents by title.

Create Date: lets you sort documents by the time they were created.

Modified Date: lets you sort documents by the last time they were modified.

Downloads: lets you sort documents by the number of times they were downloaded.

Size: lets you sort documents by how much disk space they use.

Manage

The Manage menu allows you to view the names of document types and metadata sets, as well as the last times they were edited.

Document Types: shows you a list of defined document types.

Metadata Sets: shows you a list of defined metadata sets as well as their portal IDs.

4.2 Document Types and Metadata Sets

Customizable document types and metadata sets are new features in Liferay 6.1. When a user assigns a document type to a document, the user is required to fill out the fields defined by the metadata set of the document type. This encourages users not to forget to enter important information about their documents. For example, you could create a "copyrighted" document type and require users to enter a license for all "copyrighted" documents. More importantly, document types and metadata sets can improve document searchability. The values that users enter into the fields determined by their document type's metadata set become searchable entities within the portal. You can use Liferay's search portlet to search for these terms. Document types and metadata sets are accessible from the Manage Button at the top of the Documents and Media portlet window.

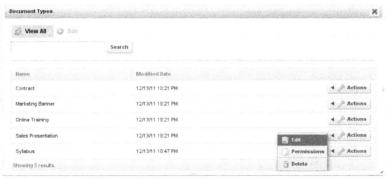

Figure 4.3: Document Types Dialog Box

You can add a new document type using the Add button at the top of the dialog box. To do so, you need to define one or more metadata sets to associate with your document type. When creating a new document type, you can define "Main Metadata Fields" or select "Additional Metadata Fields". Main metadata fields are directly tied to their document type and cannot be made available to other document types. Additional metadata fields, by contrast, can be defined independently and can be used in many different document types. You can differentiate the document types that implement the same additional metadata set by defining different main metadata fields for them. However, Additional metadata fields need to be defined and saved before creating a document type that will implement them.

Figure 4.4: Adding a New Document Type

As an example, we could create a document type called "Syllabus" and define a metadata set. What metadata should we associate with syllabi? Let's choose for our syllabi to have course title, professor, semester, course description and course requirements fields. All syllabi in our portal should maintain entries for these fields. This ensures that a syllabus will show up in a portal search if its course title, professor or semester is searched for. Since we don't want to use our metadata set for any document type other than "Syllabus," let's create our metadata set under the Main Metadata Fields area. Alternatively, we could create our metadata set independently using *Manage → Metadata Sets → Add* and then select it as an Additional Metadata Field.

Figure 4.5: Selecting Additional Metadata Sets

You can view, edit or add metadata sets from the *Manage → Metadata* window. A metadata set consists of a group of fields. If you click the Add button,

you can use same UI for defining a metadata set that you used in the Add Document Type window.

Figure 4.6: Adding a New Metadata Set

Make sure the Fields tab is selected on the left. Then, to define a metadata set,
just choose fields to use from the area on the left and drag and drop them into
the area on the right. The drag and drop interface allows for nested fields so you
need to be careful about where you drop the fields. Default values, mouse-over
tips, widths and other settings can be configured for most fields. To configure
these settings, just double-click on a field from the area on the right. This au-

tomatically selects the Settings tab on the left. Then double-click on a value to edit. Liferay supports the following kinds of fields for metadata sets:

Boolean: is a checkbox.

Date: lets you enter a date. A valid date format is required for the date field, but you don't have to enter a date manually. When you select the date field a mini-calendar pops up which you can use to select a date.

Decimal: lets you enter a decimal number. The value will be persisted as a double.

Documents and Media: lets you select a file from one of the portal's Documents and Media libraries.

File Upload: lets you select file to upload from your local system.

Integer: lets you enter an integer. The value will be persisted as an int.

Number: lets you enter a decimal number or an integer. The value will be persisted either as a double or an int, depending on the type of input.

Radio: displays several clickable options. The default number is three but this is customizable. Only one option can be selected at a time.

Select: is just like the radio field except that the options are hidden and have to be accessed from a drop-down menu.

Text: lets you enter a single line of text.

Text Box: is just like the text field except you can enter multiple lines of text or separate paragraphs.

Remember that metadata sets created independently are reusable. Once they have been created they can be included in any number of document types as additional metadata sets. Next, let's take a look at tags. Tags can be attached to most forms of web content that can be created in Liferay, including documents.

4.3 Alternative File Repository Options

By default, Liferay stores documents and media files on the file system of the server where it's running. You can choose a specific location for the document library store's root directory by adding the following property to your 'portal-ext.properties' file and replacing the default path with your custom path:

```
dl.store.file.system.root.dir=${liferay.home}/data/document_library
```

You can also use an entirely different method for storing documents and media files. The following documents and media library stores are available:

- Advanced File System Store

- CMIS Store (Content Management Interoperability Services)

- DBStore (Database Storage)

- File System Store

- JCRStore (Java Content Repository)

- S3Store (Amazon Simple Storage)

For example, you can store documents and media files in your Liferay instance's database using DBStore. To enable DBStore, add the following line to your `portal-ext.properties` file:

```
dl.store.impl=com.liferay.portlet.documentlibrary.store.DBStore
```

Remember to restart your Liferay server after updating your `portal-ext.properties` file in order for your customizations to take effect. Please refer to the Document Library Portlet section of your `portal.properties` file for a complete list of supported customizations. You can customize features such as the maximum allowed size of documents and media files, the list of allowed file extensions, which types of files should be indexed, and more.

Next, let's look at mounting external repositories.

4.4   Using External Repositories

Adding repositories in Documents and Media is a new feature in Liferay 6.1. Content Management Interoperability Services (CMIS) is a specification for improving interoperability between Enterprise Content Management systems. Documents and Media allows users to connect to multiple third-party repositories that support CMIS 1.0 with AtomPub and Web Services protocols.

Some of the features supported with third-party repositories include:

- Reading/writing documents and folders

- Document check-in, check-out, and undo check-out

- Downloading documents

- Moving folders and documents within the repository

- Getting revision history

- Reverting to revision

There are some subtle differences in setting up the different kinds of third-party repositories for use in Documents and Media. But there are plenty of similarities too.

Common Liferay configuration steps:

- Adjust the portal properties.

- Add any user accounts required by the repository.

- Add the repository.

Lastly, keep in mind your third-party repository may require installation and deployment of an appropriate Liferay plugin. Plugins for SharePoint and Documentum are available through Liferay's Marketplace.

Let's go through those steps, starting with setting our portal properties.

Adjusting portal properties The admin must ensure that the same credentials and authentication are being used in Liferay and in the external repository. This is normally synchronized using a mechanism like LDAP. If you don't have LDAP, you need to ensure manually that the credentials and authentication are the same. In order to authenticate with the third-party repository, you need to store passwords for the user sessions. Set the following portal property in your `portal-ext.properties`:

```
session.store.password=true
```

Next, we need to make sure the login and password for Liferay are the same as the external repository. This is easily accomplished by using identical screen names, so in `portal-ext.properties` add the following:

```
company.security.auth.type=screenName
```

Alternatively, configure these properties in the Control Panel under *Portal Settings → Authentication.*

Adding required repository users   Once these properties are set, you must create a user in Liferay with a screen name and password matching the administrative user of your external repository. Be sure to assign appropriate roles (e.g. Administrator) to that user. Sign out of Liferay and sign in again as that new user. See sections of the *Management* chapter on adding and managing users.

Adding the repository   You can add new repositories from the UI by clicking the *Add* button from the Home folder. Repositories can only be mounted in the Home folder.

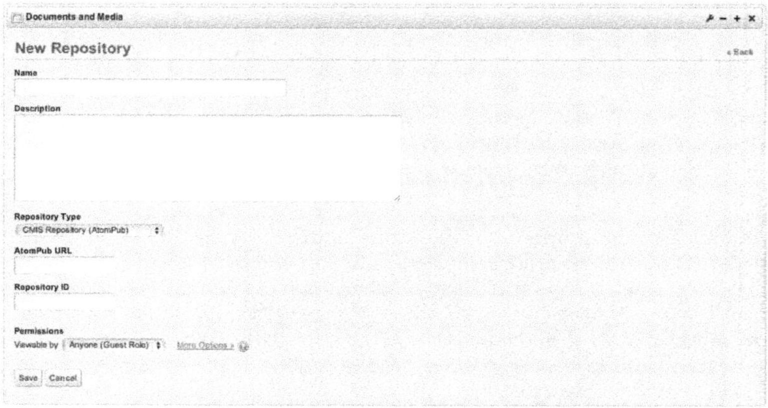

Figure 4.7: Adding a new repository

All fields in this form are required, except for *Repository ID*. Leave this field blank, and a repository ID is automatically generated by the system.

When finished, the repository is displayed in the left side of the window in the Home folder.

Using this information, we can now add an example repository. As noted previously, there are several repositories that work well with Liferay using CMIS. One that is familiar to many users is SharePoint. In the exercise below, we'll set up SharePoint as a Documents and Media repository.

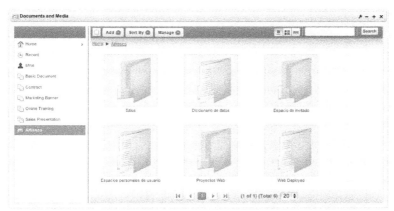

Figure 4.8: Viewing a repository

Example Repository Setup: SharePoint

With Liferay Portal you can connect to an external SharePoint server and add it as a Documents and Media repository. This lets users collaborate and share documents more easily between both environments. We will mount a SharePoint repository via CMIS AtomPub and SharePoint SOAP web services.

Liferay uses a combination of SOAP and Representational State Transfer (REST), based on the Atom convention, to connect to the SharePoint repository. SharePoint provides various SOAP services for modifying and querying data from its document library. Liferay uses Axis2 to generate SOAP calls to the SharePoint server.

To use SharePoint as a Liferay Documents and Media repository, we'll do the following:

- Configure the CMIS Connector on SharePoint.

- Activate a SharePoint site as a CMIS Producer.

- Acquire your SharePoint document library's repository ID.

- Enable Basic Authentication on the SharePoint host.

- Add SharePoint as a Liferay Documents and Media repository.

Note that this section is geared towards portal system administrators and SharePoint system administrators.

Before you can use SharePoint as an external repository with Liferay portal, you must verify that SharePoint is properly configured. Several services must be set up on the SharePoint server before synchronizing with Liferay.

Configuring the CMIS Connector on SharePoint

SharePoint utilizes a CMIS Connector and a CMIS Producer to interface with Liferay Portal. The Connector is installed with the SharePoint Administrator Toolkit using a solution package called a Windows SharePoint file (.wsp). If you don't have it already, install the SharePoint Administrator Toolkit for its CMIS Connector. Install and deploy the CMIS Connector as a Farm Solution on SharePoint.

The folder `Content Management Interoperability Services (CMIS) Connectors` contains the `spscmis.wsp` file. Choose the appropriate deployment settings and deploy that file. When deployment completes, Solution Properties shows the solution is successfully deployed to all target sites. Now it's time to configure the CMIS Producer.

Activating a SharePoint site as a CMIS Producer

The Producer makes SharePoint repositories available through the CMIS Connector. Choose the SharePoint site containing the document libraries to be used as document repositories. Every document library in this site is made available as a repository through the CMIS connector.

Go to *Site Actions* → *Site Settings* → *Manage Site Features*. Enable the *Content Management Interoperability Services (CMIS) Producer* by clicking *Activate*.

Now any document library created under this site is CMIS enabled. Before we leave our SharePoint console, let's take note of our SharePoint document library's repository ID.

Acquiring the SharePoint document library's repository ID

Acquiring your SharePoint document library's repository ID, or list ID, is important as it must be specified in the AtomPub URL Liferay uses to connect with the external repository. Finding it, however, can be a little confusing. The easiest way to find the repository ID is by accessing the SharePoint repository using a browser such as Mozilla Firefox.

Follow these steps to get the repository ID:

1. In SharePoint, open the desired library.

2. Under Library Tools select *Library*.

3. Click on *Library Settings*, located to the far right.

4. The browser window refreshes displaying the repository ID between curly braces '{' and '}' in the browser's address bar.

Figure 4.9: The repository ID can be found by displaying the repository's URL in a Firefox browser.

The repository ID is highlighted in the figure above. For this example, the repository ID is 6DFDA9-B547-4D1D-BF85-976863CDF533. Therefore, the AtomPub URL you'd use when adding this repository in Documents and Media would resemble this:

```
http://liferay/CMIS/_vti_bin/cmis/rest/6DFDA9-B547-4D1D-BF85-976863CDF533?getRepositoryInfo
```

Be sure to copy down this URL so you can use it to configure SharePoint as a repository in Documents and Media. Next, let's enable Basic Authentication on the SharePoint host.

Enabling Basic Authentication on the SharePoint host

For the CMIS connector and producer to work, Basic Authentication on IIS must be enabled. This lets Liferay's SharePoint hook authenticate against the SharePoint web services. Enable Basic Authentication on your SharePoint host.

You are now prepared to mount SharePoint as an external repository.

Adding SharePoint as a Liferay Documents and Media repository

With the SharePoint server configured, we now turn our attention to Liferay. As mentioned in the common steps for adding an external repository, be sure to adjust the portal properties and add any user accounts required by the repository.

Here are the steps specific to configuring Liferay to use SharePoint:

1. Download and install the SharePoint hook from Marketplace. See the *Downloading and Installing Apps* section of the *Leveraging the Liferay Marketplace* chapter of this document for more information.

2. Add the Documents and Media portlet to a page, if you haven't done so already.

3. In the Documents and Media portlet click *Add Repository* and enter the following information:

   Name: Enter an arbitrary name for the repository.

   Description: Describe the repository.

   Repository Type: Select *SharePoint (AtomPub)*.

   AtomPub URL: Enter the applicable URL using the format below, substituting the SharePoint server's host name for *[host]* and the SharePoint document library's repository ID for *[repository ID]*:

   ```
   http://[host]/CMIS/_vti_bin/cmis/rest/[repository ID]?getRepositoryInfo
   ```

   Repository ID: Leave this field empty. Liferay searches for the first repository using the given parameters and sets this value to that repository's ID.

   Site Path: Enter data using the format below, the SharePoint server's host information for *[host]* and the SharePoint document library's repository name for *[repository path]*:

   ```
   http://[host]/[repository path]
   ```

4. Click *Save*.

The left navigation panel of your Documents and Media portlet now lists your new repository.

In the site path example below, notice how the repository path has a folder *Shared Documents* consisting of two words.

```
http://[host]/CMIS/Shared Documents/Forms/AllItems.aspx
```

The space between the words in the repository name must be accounted for when setting the site path in Liferay. Replace the empty space with the string *%20* so the site path value now looks like this:

```
http://liferay-20jf4ic/CMIS/Shared%20Documents/Forms/AllItems.aspx
```

This should be done for any multi-word repository name.

Remember that connecting to an external SharePoint server and adding it as a Documents and Media repository is a great way to give users flexibility for sharing and collaborating on Microsoft Office documents.

To further enhance your use of Microsoft Office documents with Documents and Media, Liferay provides integration directly with Microsoft Office. Let's look at that next.

4.5 Microsoft Office integration

Liferay lets you open Microsoft Office files that reside in Documents and Media. You can open the files from Microsoft Internet Explorer or open them directly from your Microsoft Office applications. Let's open a file from your browser first.

Liferay lets you launch Microsoft Office right from folders in Documents and Media. First, find the Microsoft Office file that you want to edit. Then click the drop-down icon in the upper-left corner of the document's thumbnail and click the *Open in MS Office* link. Liferay launches Microsoft Office and prompts you to log in using your Portal credentials. Once logged in, the file opens in your Microsoft Office application.

When you save the file, it is stored automatically in the Documents and Media folder from which you opened it.

This feature currently limits you to opening Documents and Media files whose titles end in their file's extension (e.g., `.doc`, `.docx`, `.xls`, `.xlsx`, `.ppt`, or `.pptx`). See the related issue[1] for more information.

---

[1]http://issues.liferay.com/browse/LPS-31223

Note that 64-bit Microsoft Internet Explorer and 64-bit Microsoft Office versions do not currently support this feature. It is only supported on 32-bit Microsoft Internet Explorer versions with 32-bit versions of Microsoft Office. See the related issue[2] for more information.

Next we'll show you how to navigate your Documents and Media folders and open a file from the Microsoft Office application.

Liferay lets you access Microsoft Office files in Documents and Media directly from your Microsoft Office applications. Liferay implements the MS-DWSS SharePoint protocol to allow saving and retrieving documents from Liferay Portal as if it were a SharePoint server. You can conveniently update your Microsoft Office (Office) files without having to exit your Office program.

For example, if you are working in Microsoft Word locally on your machine, you can open a file from Documents and Media to view or edit it. Simply select *File→ Open* in Word and enter `http://localhost:8080/sharepoint/` in the file name field. Click *Open* and log in using your Portal credentials.

Figure 4.10: Enter the URL of your `sharepoint` location on Liferay to access Documents and Media.

In the list of folders displayed, navigate to *guest → document_library* and select *All Files* to see your Documents and Media files. Open the desired Word file to make changes. Click *Save* when you are finished and close the file.

Now anyone with appropriate permission can see the latest version of the file with these updates. Liferay takes care of version control as well as file check out and check in. Users can add comments, ratings, and tags.

Liferay's integration with Microsoft Office lets users leverage Documents and Media in managing their Office files. Collaboration is simplified as users share their most up-to-date versions of Office files.

Now let's look at configuring the Documents and Media portlet.

---

[2]http://issues.liferay.com/browse/LPS-28718

4.6 Configuring the Documents and Media portlet

To configure the Documents and Media portlet, click on the wrench icon at the top of the portlet window and select *Configuration*. The portlet-specific customizations appear on the Setup tab. To change your Documents and Media portlet's top-level folder, click *Select* next to *Root Folder*, browse to the folder you'd like to be your new top-level folder, and click *Save*. The root folder is the highest-level folder that's accessible from the Documents and Media portlet. For example, suppose you created a folder called *My Documents* in the Documents and Media portlet's default Home folder. If you set the My Documents folder to be your portlet's new root folder, the original Home folder would no longer be accessible.

By default, the Documents and Media portlet contains a search bar to help users quickly find relevant files. If you'd like the search bar not to appear, uncheck the *Show Search* box. The *Maximum Entries to Display* dropdown menu lets you set a limit on how many folders and files can be displayed in the portlet window at once. By default, the Documents and Media portlet contains three display style views: icon, list, and descriptive. Icons for each appear in the portlet window, allowing users to select the display style with which they're most comfortable. Under the Display Style Views heading, you can select which display styles users are able to choose and you can arrange the order of the selected display styles. The topmost display style in the list becomes the portlet's default display style.

Related assets are enabled by default for Documents and Media files. Related assets allow users to link assets together even if the assets don't share any tags or categories. To disable related assets for files in your Documents and Media portlet, uncheck the *Related Assets* box. For more information on related assets, see the section on defining content relationships in chapter 6.

Under the Show Columns heading, you can customize which columns appear when your Documents and Media portlet uses the list display style. By default, file names, sizes, downloads, and actions are displayed. You can also configure the portlet to display files' create dates and modified dates. To add or remove columns from being displayed, move them to the Current box or to the Available box. You can arrange the columns in the Current box to control the order in which the columns appear in the portlet: the topmost column in the box appears as the leftmost column in the portlet.

Comment ratings are also enabled by default for Documents and Media files. If users decide that a certain comment about a file is useful or informative, they can rate it as good by clicking on the thumbs up icon next to the rating. If they

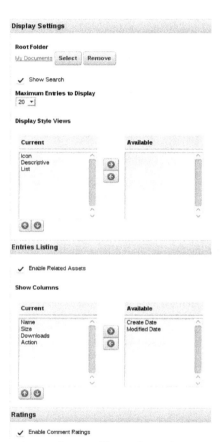

Figure 4.11: To make portlet-specific configurations for Documents and Media, click on the wrench icon at the top of the portlet window and select *Configuration*.

think the comment is unhelpful or misleading, they can click on the thumbs down icon. If you'd like to disable comment ratings for files within your portlet, uncheck the *Enable Comment Ratings* box.

4.7 Automatic Previews and metadata

Whenever possible, Liferay 6.1 generates previews of documents added to the Documents and Media library. Out of the box, Liferay only ships with Java-based APIs to generate previews for documents. The only tool available that is 100% Java and has a compatible license to be distributed with Liferay is PDF-Box. From a vanilla installation of Liferay 6.1, if you upload a PDF file to the Documents and Media portlet, Liferay will process the PDF in a separate thread to generate a preview. This process may last only a few seconds for a small file. The larger the file is, the longer it takes.

The first time you run a conversion like this, look for a console message that indicates something like the following:

```
Liferay is not configured to use ImageMagick for generating Document Library
previews and will default to PDFBox. For better quality previews, install
ImageMagick and enable it in portal-ext.properties.
```

While a default implementation of image generation for document previews and thumbnails is provided via PDFBox, you'll need to install and configure some additional tools to harness the full power of Liferay's Documents and Media library. These tools include *OpenOffice* or *LibreOffice*, *ImageMagick*, which requires *Ghostscript*, and *Xuggler*. With these tools installed and configured, Documents and Media content is displayed using a customized viewer depending on the type of content. Configuring Liferay to use OpenOffice or LibreOffice in server mode allows you to generate thumbnails and previews for supported file types (.pdf, .docx, .odt, .ppt, .odp, etc.), lets you view documents in your browser and lets you convert documents. ImageMagick allows for faster and higher-quality previews and conversions. Xuggler allows for audio and video previews, lets you play audio and video files in your browser and extracts thumbnails from video files. Please see the *External Services* section of chapter 16 for instructions on how to configure Liferay to use these tools.

With the above tools installed and enabled, the Documents and Media library looks like this:

You can view a document with a customized viewer that allows you to navigate through the different pages of the document and read its content.

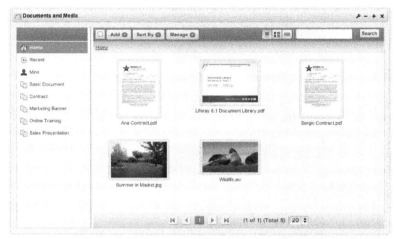

Figure 4.12: Previews in Documents and Media

You can view a multimedia document (audio or video) and play it online. If the browser supports HTML5, it uses the native player of the browser. Otherwise it falls back to a Flash player.

Document previews are powerful and help users browse media more successfully to find what they're looking for.

Automatic extraction of RAW Metadata

When adding new documents or viewing existing documents, a process is triggered automatically that extracts the file's metadata. The library used by this process is TIKA and it's already included in Liferay out of the box.

You can see the metadata when viewing the document, in the right side of the window.

Document type restrictions and workflow per folder

You can force users to add only certain document types to a folder. By default, child folders inherit the restrictions of their parent folder. You can change this behavior by editing the folder and selecting the allowed document types.

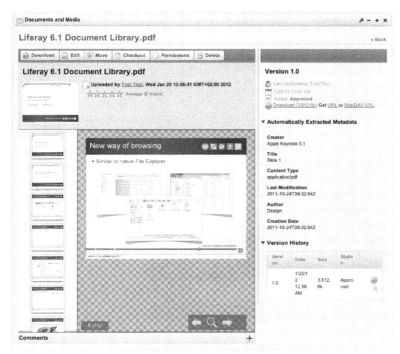

Figure 4.13: Viewing an office document

If workflow is enabled, you can specify different workflow definitions per folder. Furthermore, you can specify different workflow definitions per document type and per folder. You can set this by editing the folder. Then the UI will look like this:

Document types are a powerful way to enforce rules for documents uploaded by users. Next, we'll see a way to make it incredibly easy for users to access documents stored in Liferay's Documents and Media repositories.

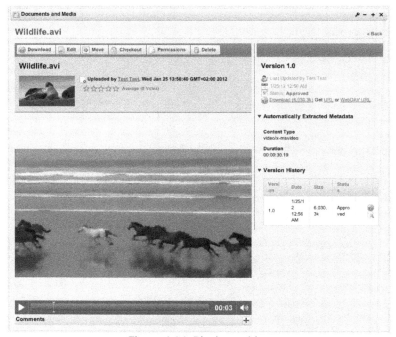

Figure 4.14: Playing a video

WebDAV access

Wouldn't it be great if you could access documents and folders belonging to
Liferay's Documents and Media library from your own machine's file manager?
You can, thanks to the Documents and Media library's WebDAV integration.
WebDAV stands for Web-based Distributed Authoring and Versioning. It's a
set of methods based on HTTP that allows users to create, edit, move or delete
files stored on web servers. WebDAV is supported by most major operating
systems and desktop environments, including Linux (both KDE and GNOME),
Mac OS and Windows.

Suppose you've created an *Image Gallery* folder using a Documents and Me-

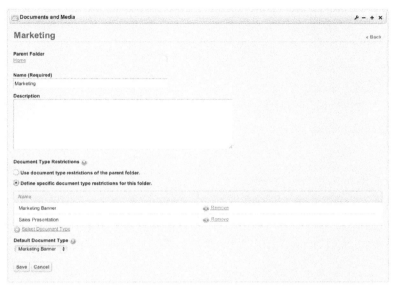

Figure 4.15: Restrict Marketing folder to use specific document types

dia portlet and uploaded some images to it. Portal users with the appropriate permissions can access this folder, and the image files it contains, using a
browser and Liferay's web interface. WebDAV provides an alternative way to
do this using a file manager instead of a web browser. To access a folder stored
in a Documents and Media portlet on a remote server, you'll need log in credentials for the portal and the WebDAV URL of the folder you'd like to access.

Next, navigate to the Documents and Media portlet hosting the folder you'd
like to access. Mouse over the folder (*Image Gallery* for our example) and select
Access from Desktop.

Copy the WebDAV URL. On Windows, right-click on My Computer and select *Map Network Drive*. Select an unused drive, paste the WebDAV URL, and
click *Finish*. You're prompted to enter your Liferay credentials and then, provided you have the required permissions, the *Image Gallery* folder appears. You
can now add, edit, move or delete files in this directory.

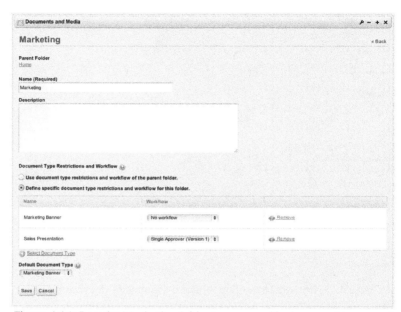

Figure 4.16: Restrict Marketing folder to use specific document types and workflow

Figure 4.17: Select *Access from Desktop* to get the WebDAV URL of a folder.

On Mac OS X, select *Go* → *Connect to Server* in Finder. Then enter the Web-DAV URL of the folder you'd like to access in the Server Address field, click *Connect* and you should be prompted for your Liferay credentials.

On Linux, you must slightly modify the WebDAV URL of your folder in your file manager. For KDE's Dolphin, change the URL's protocol so that it says `webdav://` instead of `http://`. For GNOME's Nautilus, change the URL's protocol so that it says `dav://` instead of `http://`. Then press *Enter* and you're prompted for your Liferay credentials.

Note that Liferay increments the version numbers of files edited and uploaded via WebDAV so you don't have to worry that using your file manager will bypass the functionality of Liferay's web interface. The Documents and Media application is a powerful way to manage any types of files your users need to use. Next, let's look at how you can leverage Liferay Portal's Asset framework.

Now you know just how easy it is to store your files using Liferay's Documents and Media portlet. In the next section we'll review some ways to organize and manage your assets so you're getting the most out of your content.

4.8   Liferay Sync

Liferay Sync, released in September 2012, is an add-on product for Liferay 6.1 CE and EE that synchronizes files between your Liferay server and users' desktop and mobile environments. With Liferay Sync, your users can publish and access shared documents and files from their native environments without using a browser. Windows and Mac OS desktops and Android and iOS-based mobile platforms are currently supported. As users add and collaborate on documents and files, Liferay Sync automatically synchronizes them across all configured Sync clients. Liferay Sync is fully integrated into the Liferay Platform so that features such as authentication, versioning, workflow, and social collaboration function in the supported environments. Liferay Sync stores files locally so that they're always available, even when you're offline. It automatically synchronizes your files upon reconnection.

How does it work?

Liferay Sync manages documents and site information through Liferay 6.1's built-in web services. Clients securely communicate to Liferay using user-supplied credentials such that each user can only access those documents and sites for which they have permission. Changes made through Liferay Sync are immediately available to the rest of the Liferay Platform, including users accessing Liferay through traditional web-based interfaces.

For desktop environments, a new folder structure is created and used for synchronizing files. Files found therein can be treated as any ordinary file. Credentials, sync frequency, and other folder options can be configured in-client. Native desktop notification events keep you abreast of what Sync is doing, and native menu and taskbar integration keep Sync controls within easy reach.

Mobile environments are naturally dependent on the way in which documents are handled. For Android and iOS, documents are maintained in a file list, and can be viewed by clicking on the files themselves. External files accessible from other apps can be "opened" using Liferay Sync, thereby dropping them into your Sync folder and synchronizing them across other Sync clients. In iOS devices, "pulling down" on the Sync file list forces a refresh. In Android, click on the *Refresh* icon within the menu.

Liferay Sync is designed to work with both Liferay 6.1 Community Edition and Enterprise Edition. Using Sync with Liferay CE limits users to syncing one site. Using Sync with Liferay EE enables users to synchronize documents and files across all the sites which they can access.

Liferay Sync is also designed to work with Liferay Social Office. You can sync one site from Social Office CE as well as one site from Liferay Portal CE. If you've installed Social Office CE on Liferay Portal EE, then you can sync any site from Portal, but only one from Social Office. If you've installed Social Office EE on Liferay Portal EE, then you can sync any and all sites.

Installing Liferay Sync

For Windows or Mac OS, visit the Liferay Sync product page Liferay Sync Product Page, and click *Get it Now* (on the right-side navigation menu) to download the client application for your desktop environment. For Windows, the client application installer should be named `liferay-sync-<version>-<date>.exe`. For Mac OS, it should be `liferay-sync-<version>-<date>.dmg`. Follow the on-screen instructions of the installer wizard to configure your client to connect to an existing Liferay 6.1 deployment using your Liferay credentials.

Windows

Upon launching the Windows application installer, you'll be prompted to choose an installation location for Liferay Sync. Browse to an appropriate location on your machine and click *Next*.

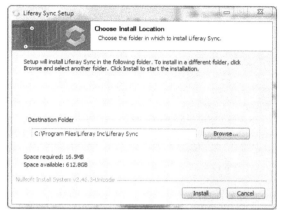

Figure 4.18: Use the Liferay Sync Installation wizard to choose an installation location.

Leave the *Run Liferay Sync* button checked to automatically start Liferay Sync after you click *Finish*.

The first time you run Liferay Sync, you'll have to enter some account information. Sync needs to know where you'd like to locally store the files it's supposed to sync with your Liferay server. And, of course, it needs to know your server's URL and the account credentials with which it should authenticate.

The options for the Mac OS application installer are similar.

Mac OS

Liferay Sync for Mac is packaged in a DMG file. Double-clicking on a DMG mounts it as a disk image, and opens a window showing the contents of the image. To install Sync, drag the Liferay Sync icon to the Applications folder. Once it's installed, go to your Applications folder to run it.

When you launch Liferay Sync, the first thing you need to do is provide it with the URL for the Liferay server that you'll be using Sync with, along with your Liferay credentials. After that, you'll need to run through the brief setup process that was described above for Windows.

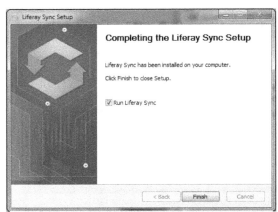

Figure 4.19: You'll see the following screen once Liferay Sync has been
installed. Click *Finish* to exit the installation wizard.

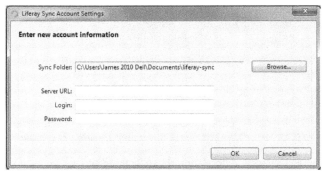

Figure 4.20: The first time you run Liferay Sync, you'll have to tell it how to
communicate with your Liferay server.

Figure 4.21: Drag the Liferay Sync icon to the Applications folder.

Once you've finished your configuration and have clicked *OK*, Liferay Sync starts running in the background, and an icon appears in your top menu bar. If you wish to change any of your settings, click the icon to open the Liferay Sync menu and click on *Preferences*. Note that on Windows, the Sync menu says *Properties*, not *Preferences*.

Mobile

For iOS, visit the App Store, search for Liferay, and install the Liferay Sync App.

For Android, go to Google Play, search for Liferay, and install the Liferay Sync App.

Once the mobile apps are installed, follow the on-screen instructions as below.

Using Liferay Sync on the Desktop

Once installed, you'll see a Liferay Sync icon in your taskbar whenever it's running. A green checkmark means Liferay Sync has a working connection to your Liferay server and is updating the files in your Sync folder according to the interval you specified in the wizard. Click the Liferay Sync icon in your taskbar to bring up the menu.

Open Sync Folder opens your Liferay Sync folder in your native file manager.

Open Website provides links to the pages containing the Documents and Media portlets which you have permission to access. By default, you can find links

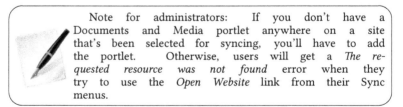

Figure 4.22: You can provide the same information requested by the Windows application installer.

to your personal Documents and Media repository as well as links to the Documents and Media repositories of all the other sites you belong to.

> Note for administrators: If you don't have a Documents and Media portlet anywhere on a site that's been selected for syncing, you'll have to add the portlet. Otherwise, users will get a *The requested resource was not found* error when they try to use the *Open Website* link from their Sync menus.

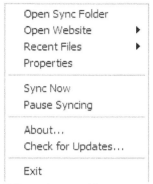

Figure 4.23: Open the Liferay Sync taskbar menu to access the following options.

Recent Files shows a list of recently created or modified files from all the repositories you can access.

Properties (*Preferences*, on Mac OS) lets you change properties like starting on login, desktop notifications, and sync frequency. It also allows you to edit the account information you provided when you started Sync for the first time. For example, you can enter a new URL for your Liferay server and enter a different set of Liferay credentials.

There are three items listed in the *General Settings* section. *Start Liferay Sync on Login* is checked by default. If you don't want Sync to start automatically, uncheck this. *Show Desktop Notifications* is also checked by default. Unless you uncheck this, when a file that you have synced is changed, a small notification will appear in the corner of your screen. The *Check Server For Updates Every:* field enables you to set how frequently it will check to see if anything has changed. This can be set anywhere between 5 seconds and 30 minutes.

Click the *Edit Settings* button in the *Account Settings* section to specify your server's URL and enter your Liferay credentials. Use the *Test Connection* button to make sure Liferay Sync can communicate with the server. Editing your settings also allows you to specify your Sync folder, the folder where Sync will store files on your machine. By default, files are stored in the *liferay-sync* sub-

Figure 4.24: Open the Liferay Sync menu and select *Properties* (*Preferences*, on Mac OS) to edit the settings you configured during setup.

folder of your personal Documents folder.

Finally, the *Site Settings* section allows you to choose which sites you wish to sync media from. By default, it will list all of the sites that you are a member of, but you can uncheck any of those sites if you don't want to sync those files.

Sync Now instructs Liferay Sync to check the Liferay server for updates immediately.

Pause Syncing instructs Liferay Sync to suspend syncing until further notice. If someone added a very large file to one of your shared folders that's taking a very long time to sync, you might want to use this option and resume syncing at a later time.

About displays Liferay Sync version information, copyright information, and a link to Liferay's home page.

Check for Updates checks to see if a new version of Liferay Sync is available from liferay.com and allows you to set whether or not Liferay Sync should automatically check for updates.

Using your Sync folder

Once Liferay Sync has been configured and is running, any files you add to or modify in your Sync folder are automatically detected and uploaded to your Liferay server. Also, changes from other users are downloaded to your Sync folder.

Liferay Sync handles deletions via a special `liferay-sync.deletions` file. This mechanism prevents users from accidentally deleting shared files. When you delete files from your Sync folder, a `.liferay-sync.deletions` file is created there with the names of the files you deleted. This lets Liferay Sync know that you don't want these files in your Sync folder, so it won't download them the next time it syncs. Note that the files listed in your `.liferay-sync.deletions` file are only local deletions. You can remove entries from your `.liferay-sync.deletions` file to have Liferay Sync download them the next time it syncs. Of course, you can use Sync for more than just local deletions. If you have the required permissions, you can delete files from the server.

You can run through the following exercise to familiarize yourself with how to create, edit, download, and upload files with Liferay Sync. First, open your Liferay Sync folder in your file manager (use the *Open Sync Folder* option of the Liferay Sync menu from the taskbar), and create a new file called `README.txt`. Edit this file and enter the word *test*. Then use the *Sync now* option of the Liferay Sync menu to make sure that your `README.txt` file gets uploaded to your Liferay server. Next, check that you can access this file from your Liferay site. Open your browser, navigate to your Liferay site, and sign in with your Liferay account credentials. Then, navigate to the control panel. Make sure the site you chose to sync with is selected in the context menu selector and click on *Documents and Media*. You should see your `README.txt` file listed there.

Download the file (click the small triangle icon at the top right corner of the *README.txt* icon and select *Download*) to a convenient location on your machine and check that it still says *test*. Now open the `README.txt` file in your Sync folder and edit it so that it says *second test*. Choose *Sync now* again, and then go back to your browser and refresh your Documents and Media page. Click on the *README.txt* icon, look at the information displayed to the right, and you'll see that its version number has incremented.

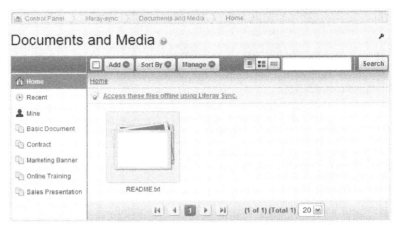

Figure 4.25: You can access the same files from Liferay Sync that you can from Liferay's web interface.

Download the file again, and you'll see that it now says *second test*–your edit was uploaded to the server. You can be confident that this edit was also downloaded by all other Liferay Sync clients connected to your site.

Demonstrating Liferay Sync Permissions

Liferay Sync uses the default Liferay permissions to determine which files and folders are synced to the user's machine. This means that whatever files a user can access from a certain site are the ones that will be pulled down by Liferay Sync if that site is selected in the Sync client. You can test the functionality of Liferay Sync permissions by performing the following steps. First, create a new file on your desktop called *secret.txt*. Enter the text *classified information* into this file. Then use your browser to log into Liferay and create a new user called *secretagent* with the email address *secretagent@liferay.com* and the password *test*. Also, create a new private site called *Secret Site*. Then assign the *secretagent* user to the *Secret Site* and grant the *Site Administrator* role to this user. There will be no other members of this site unless they are assigned by an administrator. Log in as the *secretagent* and use *Go to* → *Control Panel*, select *Secret Site* in the context menu selector, and click on *Documents and Media*. Then upload the

Figure 4.26: Updating a file through Liferay Sync increments the file's version number. You can view a file's version number through the web interface.

secret.txt document.

Next, we'll configure our Liferay Sync client to log in with the *secretagent* user's credentials and access the *Secret Site*. Open the Liferay Sync menu from the taskbar and select *Properties*. Click on the *Edit Settings* button, choose a new Sync folder, enter your server's URL, and enter the secret agent's credentials: *secretagent@liferay.com* and *test*. Lastly, uncheck all Liferay sites except the *Secret Site*, and click *OK*. Confirm that the *secret.txt* file that you uploaded to the *Secret Site*, is downloaded to your new Sync folder. Open it and check that it says *classified information*. If you reconfigure your Sync client connect to your Liferay instance using the credentials of another user who doesn't belong to the *Secret Site*, the *secret.txt* will not be downloaded. Congratulations! You've successfully set up a Liferay Sync folder that can only be accessed by the *secretagent* user and your administrators.

Using Liferay Sync Mobile

Once you've installed Liferay Sync on your Android or iOS mobile environment, you'll be able to access the same functionality that's available when using Sync on a desktop environment. However, the interface differs from that of the Sync desktop clients.

Android

After installing Liferay Sync for Android, an empty screen appears asking you to set up the app. This screen appears whenever preferences are missing.

Figure 4.27: First screen

Touch the screen and it displays the *Settings* view. You can always go back to *Settings* by clicking on the wrench icon at the top right corner of the screen.

Enter your Liferay server credentials by filling in your *Login*, *Password*, and *Server* information. Your *Login* is either your user account's email address or screen name. Use the same credentials you use to log in to the portal in a browser. In the *Server* field, enter your portal's URL. In this example, the server URL is *http://www.liferay.com*. Click the key icon on the top right to test your connection and check if everything is correct.

Note for Gingerbread users: If you can't see some of the features described here, click on the menu button to view a list of all possible actions. This includes options to refresh, open the settings menu, upload files, take photos, test your connection, etc.

After you have successfully tested your connection, hit the *back* button and you'll see a list of Liferay sites you have access to.

Figure 4.28: Android settings

Figure 4.29: Gingerbread

Figure 4.30: Sites

You can browse the files of a site by tapping on any of them. This opens a list of the folders and files belonging to the site that you have permission to view.

Figure 4.31: Folder and files

From here, you can click on a folder and browse deeper into the folder hierarchy or click the *Back* button to navigate back to parent folders up to the initial *Sites* list.

Single-tap on a file to open it. If the file has never been downloaded before, Sync will download it and open after it has finished downloading. You can only view the file's contents if your device has an app installed that can open the file type. For example, in order to open a PDF, you must have at least one PDF viewer app installed. Otherwise, you will see a message informing you that no viewer is available and you need to install an app that can open the file.

Long-press on any folder or file to find a list of actions you can take on it: *Add to Favorites, View Details, Download, Rename* or *Delete.* This actions menu varies depending on which entry type is selected: file or folder.

On Gingerbread, the actions menu looks like this:

On Ice Cream Sandwich and above, you can find the action icons and menu at the top right:

Clicking on *Add to Favorites* (Gingerbread) or the gray star (Ice Cream Sandwich) adds the selected file to the *Favorites* list. *Favorites* are special files that can be accessed and viewed even when you are offline (more details below). If a file is already marked as a favorite, you'll see a *Remove from Favorites* or blue star instead. Clicking on it removes the selected file from the *Favorites* list.

Clicking on *View Details* (Gingerbread) or the round icon with the letter "i" (Ice Cream Sandwich) opens the details view, which displays the entry's metadata such as creation date, author, version, description, etc.:

Figure 4.32: Gingerbread menu

Figure 4.33: ICS menu

Figure 4.34: View details

If you click on *Download* (floppy disk icon on Ice Cream Sandwich), it down-loads and overwrites the local file copy.

You can rename a folder or file by clicking on the *Rename* option. This re-names the entry in the portal.

Clicking on *Delete* deletes the file/folder from the remote portal, and other users won't be able to view or download it. On Ice Cream Sandwich and above, you can select multiple entries for deletion:

Figure 4.35: Actions

Some actions are not related to a specific folder or file. You can find these actions in the menu on the top action bar when no entry is selected (Gingerbread users need to click on the device menu button). Depending on the device screen width, some icons may overflow to the three dots button on the right. Click on this button to see all of the available actions.

The *Refresh* button fetches and updates the list of folders and files that have been changed in the portal.

The *Camera* button allows you to quickly take a picture and upload the image to the current folder. The image file name is automatically generated with a time stamp.

The *New Folder* button asks you for the name of the folder you want to create in the portal.

The *Upload* button displays the types of local files you can upload to the portal. Choosing *Image*, for example, shows all images that are stored locally on your device. Once you choose the files and confirm, these files are uploaded to the portal and are placed in the current folder. By default, you can upload images, videos, and audio files. If you have installed an app on your device that

Figure 4.36: More options

can open and browse any type of file, you will also see an option called *Other files*.

Figure 4.37: Upload local files

The *Favorites* menu option opens the favorites list. All files that have been marked as favorites show up in this list. You should mark your most important files as favorites because, as mentioned earlier, the *Favorites* feature gives you quick offline access to them. You can view the contents of items in the *Favorites* list, view their metadata and, of course, remove them from the list.

Next, let's look at the iOS Sync app.

Figure 4.38: Favorites

iOS

After installing Liferay Sync for iOS, an empty screen appears asking you to set up the app. This screen appears whenever preferences are missing.

Figure 4.39: iOS Settings

Click on *Settings* in the toolbar and enter your Liferay server credentials by filling in your *Login, Password,* and *Server* information. Your *Login* is either your user account's email address or screen name, whichever you use to log in to the portal in a browser. In the *Server* field, enter your portal's URL. In this example, the server URL is *http://www.liferay.com.* Click on *Test Connection* to check if your configuration is correct.

After you have successfully tested your connection, tap on the *Documents* toolbar section and you'll see a list of Liferay sites you have access to.

You can browse the files of a site by tapping on its name or icon. This opens a list of the folders and files belonging to the site that you have permission to

Figure 4.40: iOS Settings

Figure 4.41: Sites

view.

From here, you can click on a folder to browse deeper into the folder hier-archy. You can also click on the *Back* button to navigate back to parent folders up to the initial *Sites* list.

You can refresh the list by pushing it down. This updates all the files and folders that have been changed in the portal.

When you click on a file, this file is downloaded from the remote portal and if a previewer for this file type is available, you can view the contents of the file. The next time you open a file, it won't download it again; instead, it opens the local copy.

There are three icons at the bottom of the screen when you open a file. Click-ing on the leftmost round icon with the letter "i" opens the details view, which displays the entry's metadata such as creation date, author, version, description, etc.:

Clicking on the star icon at the center adds the selected file to the *Favorites*

Figure 4.42: Folder and files

Figure 4.43: Refreshing

Figure 4.44: Opening a file

Figure 4.45: View details

list. *Favorites* are special files that can be accessed and viewed even when you are offline (more details below). If a file has already been marked as a favorite, clicking on the star icon removes the file from the *Favorites* list.

Clicking on the rightmost icon displays sharing options. You can, for example, send the file as an email attachment, print the file, or copy it to your clipboard. Some external apps may also appear in this list. For example, you can share your file with social apps and messengers if they are available.

Figure 4.46: Share options

In the file list, there's an Edit button. Clicking on it switches the app to the edit mode as shown below:

Selecting one or more files or folders and clicking on the *Delete* button deletes the selected files or folders from the remote portal. Once you delete files or folders from the remote portal, other users won't be able to view or download them.

Figure 4.47: Edit mode

Selecting only one file or folder enables the *Rename* button. Click on it to change the entry's name locally and remotely.

To quickly delete a file or folder from the portal, you can also swipe right and click on the *Delete* button in the file list view:

Figure 4.48: Deleting a file

If you want to upload an image or video to the portal, click the *Plus* button at the top right corner. You should see three options:

Take a photo or video opens your camera app and lets you take a photo or record a video and upload it.

Choose Existing allows you to upload multiple photos or videos stored on your device.

Create New Folder lets you type the name of the folder and creates it in the portal.

The *Favorites* toolbar section opens the favorites list. All files that have been marked as favorites show up in this list. You should mark your most important

Figure 4.49: Upload photos and videos

files as favorites because, as mentioned earlier, the *Favorites* feature gives you quick offline access to them. You can view the contents of items in the *Favorites* list, view their metadata and, of course, remove them from the list.

Figure 4.50: Favorites

All downloaded files are stored on your device indefinitely.

If you want to delete downloaded files locally but don't want to remove them from the portal, go to *Settings* and click on the *Clear Cache* button.

4.9 Summary

In this chapter, we examined Liferay's Documents and Media Library, a powerful and customizable virtual shared drive. Liferay 6.1 introduced the ability to mount multiple external repositories to the Documents and Media library. The Documents and Media library can be used to store files of any kind. The

Figure 4.51: Deleting local copies

Documents and Media Display portlet is meant to be configured to show chosen hierarchies of folders and files from the Documents and Media library. The Media Gallery is meant for presenting media files such as images or videos.

Document types and metadata sets provide a flexible way to distinguish between different types of files and to define custom metadata fields for them. Document previews are automatically generated by default, but Liferay supports integration with external tools that offer greater speed, higher quality, and additional functionality. Finally, we discussed Liferay Sync, an add-on product for Liferay 6.1 that allows your Liferay server to directly synchronize files on users' desktop and mobile environments.

CHAPTER 5

LEVERAGING THE ASSET FRAMEWORK

Any type of content in Liferay is considered an asset. In chapters 2 and 3, we already examined Liferay's most common type of asset: web content. Other types of assets include blog posts, wiki articles, message board posts, bookmarks, and documents. It's possible for developers to define custom asset types that utilize Liferay's asset framework. Originally, the asset framework was created to provide a mechanism for adding tags to blog entries, wiki articles, and web content without reimplementing the same functionality multiple times. The asset framework has been greatly extended since then and it now supports tags, categories, vocabularies, comments, ratings, and asset relationships.

This chapter covers the following topics:

- Tagging and categorizing content

- Using targeted, single value, and multi-value vocabularies

- Using Faceted Search

- Using the Asset Publisher

- Setting up display pages

- Adding relationships between assets

The Asset Publisher portlet is designed to display multiple assets. It has quite a few configuration options which we'll cover in this chapter. By default, abstracts (previews) of recently published assets are displayed by the Asset Publisher portlet and links to their full views are provided. You can configure the Asset Publisher portlet to display a table of assets, a list of asset titles, or the full content of assets. You can also configure the Asset Publisher to display only certain kinds of assets and you choose how many items to display in a list. The Asset Publisher portlet is very useful for displaying chosen types of content, for displaying recent content, and for allowing users to browse content by tags and categories. The Asset Publisher is designed to integrate with the Tags Navigation and Categories Navigation portlets to allow this.

5.1   Tagging and Categorizing Content

Tags and categories are two important tools you can use to help organize information on your portal and make it easier for your users to find the content they're looking for through search or navigation. Tagging and categorizing web content is easy. You can do it at the bottom of the same form you use to add content. If you open the *Categorization* section of the form, you'll be presented with an interface for adding tags and categories.

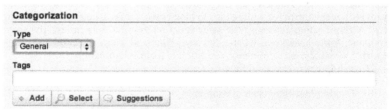

Figure 5.1: Tagging and categorizing content can be done at the same time you create it.

The Control Panel contains an interface for managing tags and categories for each site in the portal. This interface can be used to manage all your tags and categories in one place. It is important that you both tag and categorize your content when you enter it. Let's take a closer look at tags and categories.

Tags

Tags are an important tool that you can use to help organize information on your portal and make it easier for your users to find content that they're looking for. Tags are words or phrases that you can attach to any content on the website. Tagging content will make your search results more accurate, and enable you to use tools like the Asset Publisher to display content in an organized fashion on a web page. There are two ways to create tags: you can do it through the administrative console in the Control Panel, or on the fly as content is created.

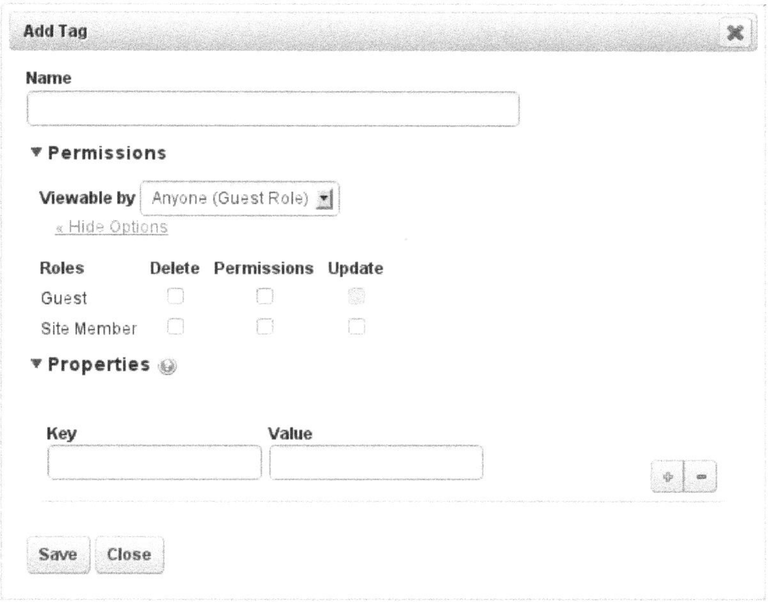

Figure 5.2: The Add Tag Dialog

To create tags in the Control Panel, select the site that you want to create tags for, and select *Tags*. From this screen, you will be able to view any existing tags and make new ones. To create a new tag, simply click *Add Tag*. You'll then be asked for the name of the tag, and you'll have the ability to set permissions for viewing or managing the tag. You can also add properties to a tag. Properties basically act like tags for your tags. Structurally, properties are key-value pairs associated with specific tags that provide information about your tags. You can edit existing tags from the *Tags* window of on the Control Panel. You can change the tag name, change the tag's permissions, delete the tag, or add properties.

Tags are not the only portal-wide mechanism for describing content: you can also use categories.

Categories

Categories are similar in concept to tags, but are designed for use by administrators, not regular users. Hierarchies of categories can be created, and categories can be grouped together in *vocabularies*. While tags represent an ad hoc method for users to group content together, categories exist to allow administrators to organize content in a more official, hierarchical structure. You can think of tags like the index of a book and categories like its table of contents. Both serve the same purpose: to help users find the information they seek.

Adding vocabularies and categories is similar to adding tags. Once you've selected the site you want to work on, select *Categories* from the content section of the Control Panel, and you will be presented with the categories administration page.

Figure 5.3: Categories Administration Page

Clicking on a vocabulary on the left displays any categories that have been created under that vocabulary. You can create new vocabularies simply by clicking *Add Vocabulary* and providing a name for it. You can create categories in a similar fashion by choosing a vocabulary on the left, and then selecting *Add Category*. Like tags, you can also provide properties for categories. Once you have created some vocabularies and categories, you can take advantage of the full capabilities of categories by creating a nested hierarchy of categories. To nest categories, select what you want to be the parent category, then drag any category that you want to become a child category onto it. You will see a plus sign appear next to the name of the category you are dragging if you can add it to the selected parent category; if you see a red *x* that means that you cannot add that category as a subcategory of parent category that you have selected.

Once you have created a hierarchy of categories, your content creators will have them available to apply to content that they create. Navigate to the Web Content page of the Control Panel and click *Add Content*. Click the Categorization link from the right-side menu and click *Select* on the vocabulary you would like to use. A dialog box will appear with your categories. Select any relevant categories by checking the box next to them, and they will be applied to the content.

There are a several new enhancements to vocabularies and categories in Liferay 6.1. The three main features are targeted vocabularies, single/multi-valued vocabularies, and separated widgets for every vocabulary.

5.2   Targeted Vocabularies

Targeted Vocabularies allow you to decide which vocabularies can be applied to an asset type and which vocabularies are required for an asset type. To configure these settings, go to the categories administration page and mouse over the vocabulary in the list until you see the edit icon to the right. Select the icon to reveal a dialog box like the one below.

The default value for *Associated Asset Types* is *All Asset Types*. You can fine tune your choices by using the + and - buttons, which narrows the scope of the vocabulary to specific assets. In the screenshot above, notice how the vocabulary Famous Noses is configured to be available for Blogs and Web Content, but it is not required. It is mandatory, however, for Documents and Media Documents.

Single and Multi-valued Vocabularies

You can now decide if the user can choose one or more categories from the same vocabulary to categorize an asset. If a vocabulary is single-valued you can only choose one, and if it allows more, you can choose several categories.

Setting vocabulary values is done through the categories administration page. Edit a vocabulary and deselect the *Allow Multiple Categories* checkbox to set sin-

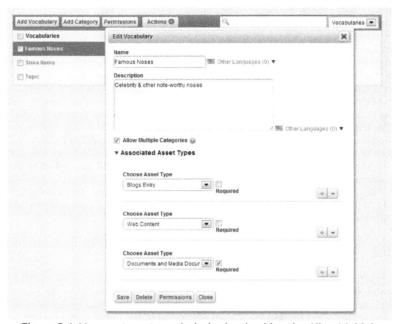

Figure 5.4: You can target vocabularies by checking the *Allow Multiple Categories* checkbox and then selecting the Asset Types.

Figure 5.5: Single-valued vocabularies, on the left, use radio buttons while multi-valued vocabularies use checkboxes.

gle value vocabularies or use the default option to set multi-value vocabularies.

Separated Widgets

The third important improvement is every vocabulary has its own separated widget. These widgets appear in the Categorization section of every asset and they allow users to easily select appropriate categories for that asset.

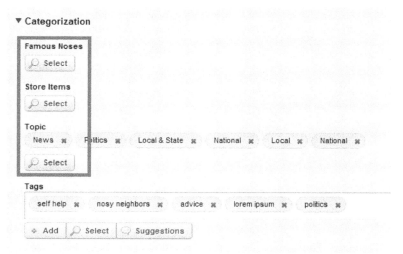

Figure 5.6: Now that vocabularies have their own widgets, it's easy to select available categories.

It's important to use tags and categories with all your content, so that content is easier for users to find. Let's look at one of the ways users will make use of tags and categories: searching for content.

5.3   Using Faceted Search

To stay organized, I (RS) used to use a paper-based planner. It had various sections for various areas of my life. Its initial incarnation came from a commercial company, but over the years I tweaked it into something that worked for me. This final version (before I went digital) had different tabs for different areas of my life that I wanted to keep track of: daily items like tasks, notes, a spiritual section, and agenda pages that kept track of things I needed to go over with specific people. A Planning section had tabs for projects, family, future items, and reference.

Of course, since this was paper-based, it had its limitations. It was kind of hard to find stuff. Did I put the note I'd written about that new toy my daughter wanted in the Notes section or in the Family section? Or maybe it was on my *While Out* list, so I would remember to buy it before her birthday?

Liferay content can be like this. That important information you remember seeing–was it in a wiki article, a message boards post, or web content? Did you remember to tag it? If you don't have this kind of information, browsing to the content you're looking for could be difficult. Thankfully, Liferay includes a powerful, faceted search function, which means you can drill down through the different types of content, tags, and categories to refine your search and find what you want. Let's see how to use it.

Searching for Portal Content

To get started, drop the Search portlet on a page and search for something. You'll see a page with results on the right and a collection of *facets* on the left.

Figure 5.7: The first set of facets is content types. You can drill down to specific types of content that contain the search terms you entered.

A facet is a combination of the information about a specific indexed field, its terms, and their frequency. Facets are typically named by the field in question. The default facets are asset types (pictured above), asset tags, asset categories, and modified time range.

The frequency in which the term was found for each facet is listed in parentheses after the facet. It may jog your memory to see that the term you searched for appears in a blog entry, and that may be all you need to find what you were looking for. If, however, your memory is more foggy than that, or you're searching for something you're not sure is actually there, then the asset tags or asset categories facets may be more helpful to you.

Figure 5.8: Asset tag facets provide you with more information list, and the results to the right are refined by the facet you selected.

Figure 5.9: Drilling down creates a list of what you selected at the top of the screen.

Here we can see that we've selected one of the tags, *liferay*, to further refine the search. The tag appears in a list at the top, and there's a red X next to it that lets us remove it from our filter as we work to increase the relevancy of our search. But maybe selecting only the tag isn't enough to filter our search into something small enough to sort through. In this case, we can further refine the search by selecting another facet, as below.

Figure 5.10: Selecting another facet further refines the search.

Now we've selected web content, which is one particular content type within Liferay, and the list of potential hits on our search terms has been dramatically reduced. In this way, you can interactively tweak the search results to narrow them down, making it easier to find that proverbial needle within the haystack.

Asset Types

Searching can only be done on assets. As has already been described in this chapter, just about any entity in the portal is an asset and can be indexed and searched. Under the hood, this means that these entities use Liferay's Asset API and have an Indexer defined.

Developers can create custom searchable assets within the portal. This is described in the Developer's Guide. For this reason, you may have additional asset types defined in your portal beyond the ones that Liferay ships with by default. If this is the case, you may wish to tweak the `frequency threshold` and the `max terms` settings to increase the number of asset types displayed past the default of 10. This is covered in the section below on search options.

Asset Tags

If tags have been applied to any asset that appears in the result set, it may be displayed in the Asset Tag facet. Tags are handled in a similar way to how asset types are handled: not all tags may appear. There may be many more than the 10 tags listed, but the default configuration for this facet is to show the top 10 most frequent terms. As with asset types, this can be modified by setting max terms property.

Asset Categories

If categories have been applied to any asset that appears in the result set, they may be displayed in the Asset Categories facet. Yadda, yadda, yadda, same thing as the two sections above. That last sentence was written to check if you're still reading.

Let's move on to advanced searching.

Advanced Searching

The Search portlet's search box is deceptively simple. Though you have only a single field for search, there's a search syntax inherited from Lucene that lets you create very powerful search queries. Let's look at some ways you can use search queries.

Searching for specific fields: By default, searches are performed against a long list of fields. Sometimes you want results for a term within a particular field. This can be achieved using the field search syntax [field] : [term]. For example, to search in the *Title* field for *Liferay*, use the following syntax:

```
title:liferay
```

If you search for a phrase within a field, surround the term with double quotation marks:

```
title:"Liferay Portal"
```

Wildcards: You can use wildcards in exactly the way you use them with your operating system: for a single character wildcard, use ?; for the multiple character wildcard, use *.

Boolean operators: You can use logic operators, such as AND, OR, NOT, +, and – in your searches. The AND operator matches assets in which the terms between the AND operator exist. For example, to search for both Liferay and Kaleo Workflow, use this query:

```
"liferay" AND "kaleo workflow"
```

The OR operator is the default; if there's no operator between two terms, the OR operator takes effect. OR finds matches if any term exists in an asset.

The + operator requires that the term exists somewhere in some field in the asset. If you wanted to search for something that *must* contain *liferay* and *may* contain *portal*, use this query:

```
+liferay portal
```

The NOT operator excludes assets that contain the term after the NOT operator. It requires that at least two terms be present:

```
"Liferay Portal" NOT "Liferay Social Office"
```

The − operator is similar: it excludes assets that contain the term after the − symbol:

```
"Liferay Portal" - "Liferay Social Office"
```

Grouping: You can use parentheses within your queries to form sub-queries, in a similar fashion to an SQL statement. For example, to search for *liferay* or *social office* and *website*, use this query:

```
(liferay OR "social office") AND website
```

As you can see, the search syntax is very powerful. There's more you can do with it than what is listed here; to view the full syntax, visit the Lucene URL above.

Next, we'll look at how the Search portlet can be configured.

Setting Search Options

As with Liferay's other portlets, you can configure the Search portlet via the configuration screen, which looks like the below illustration.

Display Asset Type Facet: Toggles whether the Asset Type facet appears.

Display Asset Tags Facet: Toggles whether the Asset Tags facet appears.

Display Asset Categories Facet: Toggles whether the Asset Categories facet appears.

Display Modified Range Facet: Toggles whether the date modified range facet appears.

Display Results in Document Form: Never use this in production. Developers use this feature to view search responses in their generic, Document-based

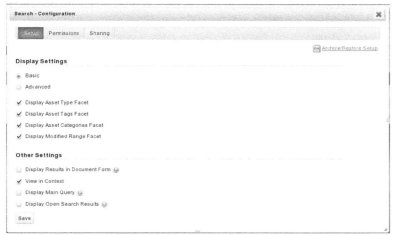

Figure 5.11: Basic search configuration is pretty straightforward.

format. Part of a developer's job when writing search indexers is to convert Documents (the objects that get indexed) to the actual object and back again. This option allows developers to see how their objects are being indexed.

View in Context: When an asset is clicked, show it in the portlet to which it belongs.

Display Main Query: Show the exact search query that the portlet generated to the search engine. Again, never use this in production; this is for development purposes only.

Display Open Search Results: Shows results from third party Open Search plugins, if they are installed. This is for backward compatibility only: developers are encouraged to re-design their search code as described in *Liferay in Action*, and then custom assets are aggregated with native portal assets seamlessly.

These are the basic options, but surely you didn't miss the fact that there are also advanced options.

Configuring advanced search requires a bit more technical acumen than you might expect, because there are so many properties to tweak. Thankfully, in most instances, you shouldn't need to change a thing. If you do, however, the configuration is done through a JSON object.

If you don't know what a JSON object is, don't worry: it's not a difficult concept. JSON stands for JavaScript Object Notation. An Object is a software development term for anything that can be represented in code. Objects have *attributes*, or sometimes these are called *fields*, and they are very similar to fields you'd find on a form that you're filling out. Software developers use the word *object* to refer generically to anything like this that they can describe in the software; for all intents and purposes, objects could just as easily have been called Things. For example, one type of object used in Liferay is a User. A User can be represented in code, and it has many *fields*, such as a name, an email address, and more. JSON is one way of describing objects like this.

The object we're concerned with is called `facets`. Here's what it looks like, in all its glory, in JSON. Explanation of the settings follows the object below.

```
{"facets": [
    {
    "displayStyle": "asset_entries",
    "weight": 1.5,
    "static": false,
    "order": "OrderHitsDesc",
    "data": {
        "values": [
        "com.liferay.portlet.bookmarks.model.BookmarksEntry",
        "com.liferay.portlet.blogs.model.BlogsEntry",
        "com.liferay.portlet.calendar.model.CalEvent",
        "com.liferay.portlet.documentlibrary.model.DLFileEntry",
        "com.liferay.portlet.journal.model.JournalArticle",
        "com.liferay.portlet.messageboards.model.MBMessage",
        "com.liferay.portlet.wiki.model.WikiPage",
        "com.liferay.portal.model.User"
        ],
        "frequencyThreshold": 1
    },
    "label": "asset-type",
    "className": "com.liferay.portal.kernel.search.facet.AssetEntriesFacet",
    "fieldName": "entryClassName"
    },
    {
    "displayStyle": "asset_tags",
    "weight": 1.4,
    "static": false,
    "order": "OrderHitsDesc",
    "data": {
        "maxTerms": 10,
        "displayStyle": "list",
        "frequencyThreshold": 1,
        "showAssetCount": true
    },
    "label": "tag",
    "className": "com.liferay.portal.kernel.search.facet.MultiValueFacet",
    "fieldName": "assetTagNames"
    },
    {
```

```
"displayStyle": "asset_tags",
"weight": 1.3,
"static": false,
"order": "OrderHitsDesc",
"data": {
    "maxTerms": 10,
    "displayStyle": "list",
    "frequencyThreshold": 1,
    "showAssetCount": true
},
"label": "category",
"className": "com.liferay.portal.kernel.search.facet.MultiValueFacet",
"fieldName": "assetCategoryTitles"
},
{
"displayStyle": "modified",
"weight": 1.1,
"static": false,
"order": "OrderHitsDesc",
"data": {
    "ranges": [
    {
        "range": "[past-hour TO *]",
        "label": "past-hour"
    },
    {
        "range": "[past-24-hours TO *]",
        "label": "past-24-hours"
    },
    {
        "range": "[past-week TO *]",
        "label": "past-week"
    },
    {
        "range": "[past-month TO *]",
        "label": "past-month"
    },
    {
        "range": "[past-year TO *]",
        "label": "past-year"
    }
    ],
    "frequencyThreshold": 0
},
"label": "modified",
"className": "com.liferay.portal.kernel.search.facet.ModifiedFacet",
"fieldName": "modified"
    }
]}
```

Now that you've seen the object, don't be daunted by it. Here are all the settings within the object that you can tweak.

"**className**": This field must contain a string value which is the FQCN (fully qualified class name) of a java implementation class implementing the Facet interface. Liferay provides the following implementations by default:

```
com.liferay.portal.kernel.search.facet.AssetEntriesFacet
com.liferay.portal.kernel.search.facet.ModifiedFacet
com.liferay.portal.kernel.search.facet.MultiValueFacet
com.liferay.portal.kernel.search.facet.RangeFacet
com.liferay.portal.kernel.search.facet.ScopeFacet
com.liferay.portal.kernel.search.facet.SimpleFacet
```

"**data**": This field takes an arbitrary JSON object (a.k.a. {}) for use by a specific facet implementation. As such, there is no fixed definition of the data field. Each implementation is free to structure it as needed. The value defined here matches the implementation that's selected in the `className` attribute above.

"**displayStyle**": This field takes a string value and represents a particular template implementation which is used to render the facet. These templates are normally JSP pages (but can also be implemented as Velocity or Freemarker templates provided by a theme if the portal property `theme.jsp.override.enabled` is set to `true`). The method of matching the string to a JSP is simply done by prefixing the string with /html/portlet/search/facets/ and appending the .jsp extension.

For example, `"displayStyle": "asset_tags"` maps to the JSP

```
/html/portlet/search/facets/asset_tags.jsp
```

Armed with this knowledge a crafty developer could create custom display styles by deploying custom (new or overriding) JSPs using a JSP hook. See the *Developer's Guide* or *Liferay in Action* for more information on hook plugins.

"**fieldName**": This field takes a string value and defines the indexed field on which the facet operates.

For example, `"fieldName": "entryClassName"` indicates that the specified facet implementation operates on the `entryClassName` indexed field.

Note: You can identify available indexed fields by enabling the Search portlet's *Display Results in Document Form* configuration setting and then expanding individual results by clicking the [+] to the left of their titles.

"**label**": This field takes a string value and represents the language key that is used for localizing the title of the facet when it's rendered.

"**order**": This field takes a string value. There are two possible values:

`OrderValueAsc`: This tells the facet to sort it's results by the term values, in ascending order.

`OrderHitsDesc`: This tells the facet to sort it's results by the term frequency, in descending order.

"**static**": This field takes a boolean value (`true` or `false`). The default value is false. A value of `true` means that the facet should not actually be rendered in the UI. It also means that it should use pre-set values (stored in its `data` field) rather than inputs dynamically applied by the end user. This allows for the creation of pre-configured search results.

Imagine you would like to create a pre-configured search that returns only images (i.e. the asset type is `DLFileEntry` and the indexed field extension should contain the values bmp, gif, jpeg, jpg, odg, png, or svg). We would need two static facets, one with "fieldName": "entryClassName" and another with "field-Name": "extension". This could be represented using the following facet configuration:

```
{
    "displayStyle": "asset_entries",
    "static": true,
    "weight": 1.5,
    "order": "OrderHitsDesc",
    "data": {
    "values": [
        "com.liferay.portlet.documentlibrary.model.DLFileEntry"
    ],
    "frequencyThreshold": 0
    },
    "className": "com.liferay.portal.kernel.search.facet.AssetEntriesFacet",
    "label": "asset-type",
    "fieldName": "entryClassName"
},
{
    "displayStyle": "asset_entries",
    "static": true,
    "weight": 1.5,
    "order": "OrderHitsDesc",
    "data": {
    "values": ["bmp", "gif", "jpeg", "jpg", "odg", "png", "svg"],
    "frequencyThreshold": 0
    },
    "className": "com.liferay.portal.kernel.search.facet.MultiValueFacet",
    "label": "images",
    "fieldName": "extension"
}
```

"weight": This field takes a floating point (or double) value and is used to determine the ordering of the facets in the facet column of the search portlet. Facets are positioned with the largest values at the top. (yes, the current implementation is counter-intuitive and perhaps could be reversed in future versions).

Configuring search using a JSON object is a bit unusual, but as you can see, it's not as hard as it looks initially.

Summary

Search is a powerful component of Liferay Portal's asset framework. The proclivity of assets means that there is an extensible, robust, and configurable search mechanism throughout the portal that allows administrators to optimize the search experience of their users. Users also get an easy to use search interface that makes use of the tags and categories that they themselves apply to various pieces of content, regardless of the type of content. This makes Liferay's search truly "for the people."

Power users can learn an extended search syntax that lets them craft very specific searches. These searches can be used on large installations with lots of data to find the proverbial needle in the proverbial haystack. Administrators can tune the configuration of search portlets so that they are optimized for the contents of their communities.

Next, we'll look at how the Asset Publisher portlet makes even more extensive use of Liferay's asset framework to bring relevant content to users.

5.4 Using the Asset Publisher

As we create web content, it's important to keep in mind that to Liferay, the pieces of content are assets, just like message board entries and blog posts. This allows you to publish your web content using Liferay's Asset Publisher.

You can use the Asset Publisher to publish a mixed group of various kinds of assets such as images, documents, blogs, and of course, web content. This helps in creating a more dynamic web site: you can place user-created wiki entries, blog posts or message board messages in context with your content. Let's look at some of its features.

Querying for Content

The Asset Publisher portlet is a highly configurable application that lets you query for mixed types of content on the fly. By giving you the ability to control what and how content is displayed from one location, the Asset Publisher helps you to "bubble up" the most relevant content to your users.

To get to all the portlet's options, click the *Configuration* link in the portlet's menu (the wrench icon).

The ability to configure how content is displayed and selected by your users further demonstrates the flexibility of the Asset Publisher. You get to choose how content is displayed. You can select it manually for display in a similar

way to the Web Content Display portlet or you can set up predefined queries
and filters and let the portal select the content for you, based on its type or its
tags and categories.

Let's first look at how we might select content manually. You'll see that it's
very similar to the Web Content Display portlet.

Selecting assets manually   By selecting *Manual* from the select box beneath
Asset Selection, you tell the Asset Publisher that you want to select content manually. You can select what you want to be published within the portlet, or you
can create new content from within the Asset Publisher.

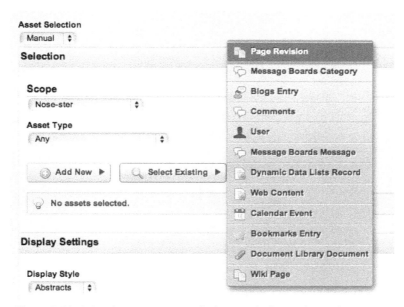

Figure 5.12: Selecting assets manually is very similar to the Web Content
Display portlet, except you have many other content types to choose from.

Clicking *Add New* gives you a menu of options, enabling you to create the
content right where you are. You can create blogs, bookmarks, calendar entries,

documents, images, and of course, web content. Anything you create here is added to the list below of assets that are displayed by the portlet.

Clicking *Select Existing* gives you a similar menu, except this time you can pick from existing content in the portal that either you or your users have created. Has someone written an excellent wiki page that you want to highlight? Select it here, and it will be displayed.

The Asset Publisher enables you to mix and match different content types in the same interface. Once you have your content selected, you can move on to the display types to configure how the content appears.

Most of the time, however, you'll likely be using the Asset Publisher to select content dynamically.

Selecting assets dynamically   The Asset Publisher's default behavior is to select assets dynamically according to rules that you give it. These rules can be stacked on top of each other so that they compliment each other to create a nice, refined query for your content. You have the following options for creating these rules:

Scope: Choose the sites or organizations from which the content should be selected.

Asset Type: Choose whether you'll display any asset or only assets of a specific type, such as only web content, only wiki entries, or any combinations of multiple types.

Filter Rules: Add as many filters on tags or categories as you like. You can choose whether the content contains or does not contain any or all categories or tags that you enter.

Once you've set up your filter rules for dynamically selecting your content, you can then decide how the content will be displayed.

The Display Settings section gives you precise control over the display of your assets. There are a multitude of options available to configure how you want your content to appear. You can configure the style, length of abstracts, behavior of the asset link, maximum items to display, pagination type and file conversions. Additionally, you can enable printing, flags, ratings, comments and comment ratings, and these work the same way they do in the Web Content Display portlet.

You can display the content returned by the filters above in order by title, create date, modified date, view count and more in ascending or descending order. For instance, you may have a series of "How To" articles that you want displayed in descending order based on whether the article was tagged with the *hammer* tag. Or, you may want a series of video captures to display in ascending

Figure 5.13: You can filter by tags and categories, and you can set up as many filter rules as you need.

order based on a category called *birds*. You can also group by *Asset, Type* or *Vocabularies*. Vocabularies are groups of categories defined by administrators in the *Categories* section of the Control Panel.

In the *Ordering and Grouping* section of the Asset Publisher, you have great control over how content is ordered and grouped in the list, but this is only one aspect of how your content will be displayed. You can refine the display through many other display settings.

5.5   Setting up Display Pages

The Display Settings section gives you precise control over the display of your assets. There are a multitude of options available to configure how you want your content to appear. You can configure the style, length of abstracts, behavior of the asset link, maximum items to display, pagination type and file conversions. Additionally, you can enable printing, flags, ratings, comments and comment ratings, and these work the same way they do in the Web Content Display portlet.

Display Style   Abstracts: Shows the first 200-500 characters of the content, defined by the **Abstract Length** field.

Table: Displays the content in an HTML table which can be styled by a theme developer.

Title List: The content's title as defined by the user who entered it.

Full Content: The entire content of the entry.

Other Settings   Asset Link Behavior: The default value is *Show Full Content*. With this value selected, when the link to an asset is clicked, the full asset is displayed in the current Asset Publisher. If the value *View in a Specific Portlet* is selected, clicking on an asset causes that asset to be displayed in the portlet to which the asset belongs. For example, a blog entry would be displayed in the Blogs portlet where it was created. Likewise, a forum post would be displayed in the Message Boards porlet where it was created. Similarly, a generic Web Content article would be displayed in the Asset Publisher of its configured Display Page. See the secton below on Display Pages for more information.

Maximum Items to Display: You can display 1-100 items.

Pagination Type: Select Simple or Regular. Simple shows previous and next navigation; regular includes a way of selecting the page to which you'd like to navigate.

Exclude Assets with 0 Views: If an asset has not been viewed, exclude it from the list.

Show Available Locales: Since content can be localized, you can have different versions of it based on locale. This will show the locales available, enabling the user to view the content in the language of his or her choice.

Enable Conversion To: If you have enabled Liferay Portal's OpenOffice.org integration, you can allow your users to convert the content to one of several formats, including PDF.

Below these options are the same ones in the Web Content Display portlet: enable print, enable comments, enable ratings, etc.

Show Metadata: Allows you to select from the available metadata types (see below).

Enable RSS Subscription: This lets users subscribe to the content via RSS Feeds.

The Display Settings section of the Asset Publisher has numerous options to help you configure how your content selections are displayed to your users. Even though there are many choices, it's easy to go through the options and quickly adjust the ones that apply to you. You'll want to use the Asset Publisher

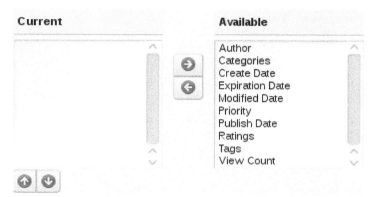

Figure 5.14: Available metadata types

to query for mixed assets in the portal that have relevant information for your users.

Next, we'll look at Display Pages, an addition to the asset framework introduced by Liferay 6.1.

Display Page

If you've been using Liferay for a while, or you've just spent a little bit of time with this guide, you might have noticed something about how Liferay handles web content–content is never tied directly to a page. While this can be useful (because it means that you don't have to recreate content if you want to display the same thing on multiple pages), it also means that you don't have a static URL for any web content, which is bad for search engine optimization.

As an improvement, Liferay has introduced the concept of Display Pages and Canonical URLs. Each web content entry on the portal has a canonical URL, which is the official location of the content that is referenced any time the content is displayed. A Display Page can be any page with an asset publisher configured to display any content associated with the page. When adding or editing web content articles, you can select a Display Page, but only pages with a configured asset publisher are available for selection.

To create a Display Page, you can create a page yourself, add an Asset Publisher portlet and configure it yourself. Alternatively, you can use the *Content*

Display Page page template included with Liferay. If you're creating a Display Page manually, once you've added an Asset Publisher portlet to the page, open its configuration window. Then check the *Set as the Default Asset Publisher for This Page* box.

You may now be thinking, "Wait, you just told me that each Web Content item has its own URL, and that this is somehow related to pages where we display a whole bunch of content on the same page?" Yes. That's exactly what I said. Just watch–create a display page called *My Web Content Display Page* somewhere on your portal, using the *Content Display Page* template. Now, on a different page, add a Web Content Display portlet. Click the *Add Web Content* button, enter a title and some content, click on *Display Page* at the right, and select the Display Page you just created. Then click *Publish*.

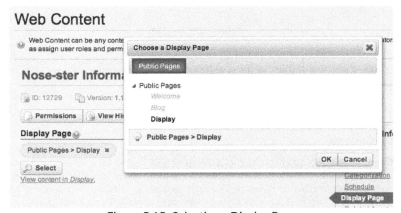

Figure 5.15: Selecting a Display Page

In the Asset Publisher of the *My Web Content Display Page*, you can now click the *Read More* link to display the content. Notice that the canonical URL for content appears in your browser's address bar. If you create your own custom display page, any additional portlets that you place on the page are displayed along with the content when you access it via the canonical URL. If you used the *Content Display Page* page template for your Display page, it not only features a configured Asset Publisher portlet but also a Tags Navigation, a Categories Navigation, and a Search portlet. These tools help users to quickly identify relevant content.

Figure 5.16: The Canonical URL

Let's move on to another new featured introduced by Liferay 6.1.

5.6 Defining content relationships

Related Assets is a new feature in Liferay 6.1 that enables you to connect any number of assets within a site or across the portal, even if they don't share any tags and aren't in the same category. We've already seen that you can show related assets within the display for a specific asset, and with the Related Assets portlet you can show links to any assets which are related to content displayed on that page.

The Related Assets portlet is based on the Asset Publisher and possseses essentially the same interface with one key difference. The Asset publisher displays any content that meets the criteria selected in the portlet configuration. The Related Assets portlet only displays content that meets the criteria, and also is listed as a related asset for a piece of content that is currently published on the page where it is placed. Let's take a look at the the Related Assets portlet.

As a prerequisite for the Related Assets portlet to display related assets, you configure it to show the content you want displayed. To do this, go to the Asset Publisher portlet and select the *wrench* icon in the upper right corner of the portlet. Under the *Setup* tab, set type of asset(s) to display using the *Asset Type* menu. The default value is set to *Any*. You can narrow the scope of the portlet to display any single category of asset type or select multiple assets from the menu.

Filter options let you set minimum requirements for displaying assets by their categories, tags, and custom fields. Ordering and Grouping allows you to organize assets using the same criteria. Display settings allow you to customize how asssets are shown in the portlet. They can be listed by title, in a table, by abstract or full content. You can convert assets to different document types like ODT, PDF, and RTF. You can choose to show various metadata fields such as author, modification date, tags, and view count. You can even enable RSS subscriptions and customize their display settings.

When you are finished setting the Source and Filter options, click *Save*. But hold on a minute. You saw the message that says, You have successfully updated the setup, but there still aren't any assets displayed in the related assets portlet. Why? You cannot see any related assets until you select an asset in the Asset Publisher.

Figure 5.17: Select an asset in the Asset Publisher to see its related assets displayed in the Related Assets portlet.

Once you select an asset, its related assets will display in the Related Assets portlet, similar to the image above.

5.7   Summary

In this chapter, we explored Liferay's asset framework. Any type of content in Liferay is considered an asset and can utilize the features provided by the asset framework: tags, categories, comments, ratings, and relationships. We examined the Asset Publisher portlet and looked at the many configuration options for choosing what kinds of assets to display and how to display them. We saw that the Asset Publisher portlet is designed to integrate with the Tags Navigation and Categories navigation portlets to allow users to browse content more easily. We also learned about the Display Page attribute of web content, the Content Display Page page template, and canonical URLs for assets. Assets can have display page associated with them so that the full view of the asset is displayed on the display page. The display page of an asset is used in the asset's canonical URL.

CHAPTER 6

PERSONALIZATION AND CUSTOMIZATION

In this chapter, we discuss several ways Liferay users can customize pages, applications, and the way they use your portal. We'll cover the following topics:

- Personal Sites

- Customizable Pages and Applications

- Using a Rules Engine

Personal sites allow each portal user to manage and customize a set of public and/or private pages and any associated content or applications. Public pages provide a means of making content publicly available while private pages provide a means of hiding information from other users. Liferay 6.1 introduced customizable pages and applications. Administrators can designate certain pages or applications as "customizable," which allows each user to make and save their own customizations. Liferay Enterprise Edition provides a rules engine which allows administrators to create custom portal rules and simplify complex blocks of code containing lots of `if-else` statements. Let's start by discussing personal sites.

6.1   User Personal Sites

By default, newly created users in Liferay are each granted a personal site. Each user functions as the site administrator of his or her personal site. Personal sites are fully customizable but cannot have more than one member. The public pages of personal sites provide a space for users to publish content that they'd like to make accessible to anyone, including guests. User blogs are often placed on public personal site pages. Content and applications that users would like to reserve for personal use are often placed on the private pages of personal sites. For example, each user can add a Documents and Media portlet to his or her private pages and use it as an online private file repository.

If you'd like to disable personal sites for your portal, just add the following properties to your `portal-ext.properties` file:

```
layout.user.public.layouts.enabled=false
layout.user.private.layouts.enabled=false
```

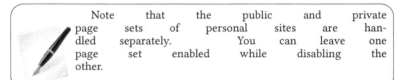

Note that the public and private page sets of personal sites are handled separately. You can leave one page set enabled while disabling the other.

What if you initially had user personal sites enabled for your portal but then disabled them? Each existing user's personal site remains on your portal until the next time they log in, at which point it's removed.

You can allow users to create personal sites but not have them automatically created for new users. To do this, first make sure that `layout.user.public.layouts.enabled` and `layout.user.private.layouts.enabled` are not set to `false`. You don't need to explicitly set them to `true`—`true` is the default. Then add the following properties to your `portal-ext.properties` file:

```
layout.user.public.layouts.auto.create=false
layout.user.private.layouts.auto.create=false
```

If all of these properties are set to `true`, which is the default, then users will have personal sites and public and private pages will be automatically created for new users. There are number of portal properties you can use to customize the automatically created pages. You can customize the names of the default pages, the portlets that appear on the pages, the themes and layout templates of the default pages, and more. Please refer to the Default User Public Layouts and Default User Private Layouts sections of chapter 20 for details.

Prior to Liferay 6.1, administrators could disallow users from being able to modify the pages and portlets of their personal sites by setting the following properties:

```
layout.user.public.layouts.modifiable=true
layout.user.private.layouts.modifiable=true
```

As of Liferay 6.1, this property is obsolete. However, you can customize the modifiable portions of personal sites through Liferay's permissions system by removing permissions from roles. To disallow all portal users from modifying something, remove the permission from the User role.

Historically (prior to Liferay 5.1), only power users received personal sites. Back then, they were called personal communities. If you'd like only power users to receive personal sites, add the following properties to your **portal-ext.-properties** file:

```
layout.user.public.layouts.power.user.required=true
layout.user.private.layouts.power.user.required=true
```

Personal sites are a dynamic feature of Liferay Portal. They allow users to manage and customize their own pages and content on your portal. Next, let's look at how users can customize applicatons.

6.2 Page Customizations

Liferay 6.1 introduced the concept of page customizations. Administrators can designate public pages or sections of public pages to be customizable. When a user visits such a page, a notification will appear stating that the user can customize the page. Users can make customizations only in the sections of pages designated by administrators. Customizations are based on the rows and columns of a page layout. Page customizations are only visible to the user who made the customizations. By default, site members can make page customizations but non-site members and guests can't.

To enable page customizations as an administrator, first navigate to the page you'd like to let site members modify. Then select *Manage → Page Customizations* from the Dockbar.

Figure 6.1: To enable page customizations, select *Manage → Page Customizations* from the Dockbar.

Once you've selected *Manage → Page Customizations*, you'll see one or more red regions, depending on the layout template of your page. Check one or more of the *Customizable* boxes to allow site members to customize certain sections of the page. Regions that you've designated as customizable are colored green.

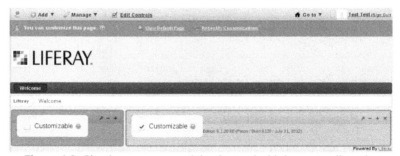

Figure 6.2: Check one or more of the *Customizable* boxes to allow site members to customize certain sections of the page.

When site members visit your customizable page, they'll see a notification saying, "You can customize this page." Site members can toggle between viewing their customized page and viewing the default page by clicking the *View Default Page* or *View My Customized Page* links just below the Dockbar. There's also a *Reset My Customizations* link that restores a user's customized page to the match the default page. This allows users to discard one set of customizations and start a new set without having to manually undo each customization that they'd previously made.

Note that non-administrator site members can access the Add menu from the Dockbar when viewing their customizable page even if they don't ordinarily have permission to view this menu. This allows them to add portlets to the sections of the page that they're allowed to customize. If they click *View Default Page*, the Add menu will disappear from the Dockbar since they're not allowed to modify the default page.

Figure 6.3: Non-administrator site members can customize their own versions of customizble pages but can't modify the default page.

Administrators of customizable pages have the same two views as site members: the *default page* view and the *customized page*. Changes made to the *default page* affect all users, whereas changes made to the *customized page* affect only the administrator who made the changes. Changes made by administrators to non-customizable sections in the *default view* are immediately applied for all users. However, changes made by administrators to customizable sections do *not* overwrite users' customizations.

Users can make two kinds of customizations to customizable regions. First, they can configure any portlet applications within the customizable regions. Second, they can add portlets to or remove portlets from the customizable regions. As a simple example, suppose that you, as an administrator, selected the right column of the default portal homepage to be customizable. A member of the default site could take the following steps to make a personal customization of the portal homepage:

1. Navigate to the portal homepage by clicking *Go To* → *Liferay* from the Dockbar. (The portal homepage belongs to an automatically created site called *Liferay*, by default.)

2. Remove the Hello World portlet remove from the right column of the page.

3. Add the Language portlet to the right column by clicking *Add* → *More* in the Dockbar, expanding the *Tools* category, and clicking *Add* next to *Language*.

4. Configure the Language portlet by clicking on the wrench icon and selecting *Configuration* and then opening the *Display Style* dropdown menu and
   choosing *Select Box*.

The Language portlet is useful to have on your portal homepage if you expect
users who speak different languages to access your portal. Users can select their
language in the Language portlet to view a translation of the portal into their
native language. After closing the Configuration dialog box of the Language
portlet, the customized portal homepage looks like this:

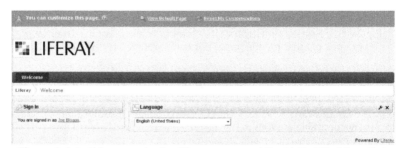

Figure 6.4: In this example, Joe Bloggs removed the Hello World portlet,
added the Language portlet, and changed the display style from icons to a
select box.

To allow users to customize a page, administrators must grant users permission to *Customize* pages under the Site section. This can be achieved by
assigning permission to a role, then assigning this role to the appropriate users.
For example, if we want any logged user to be able to customize our customizable pages, we could assign the *Customize* permission to the role *User*. If we
want site members to be able to customize the customizable pages of their sites,
we would accept the default setting. By default, the *Customize* permission is
assigned to the role *Site Member*.

In addition to granting the ability to customize portlet configurations, the
Customize permission allows users to customize the look and feel of portlets
and to import or export portlet settings. Next, let's look at how to use Liferay's
rules engine.

 EE Only Feature

6.3 Using Liferay's rules engine

Liferay Portal Enterprise Edition provides an implementation of a JSR-94 compliant rules engine. This rules engine is provided as a Web Plugin and is based on the popular open source Drools project.

Why use a rules engine?

If you are not familiar with rules engines, you may be wondering why you would want to use one. In most applications, complex rule processing often takes the form of nested `if-else` blocks of code which can be very difficult to decipher and to maintain. If rules change, a developer must work with a business user to define the new rules. The developer must then read through the existing logic to understand what is happening and make the necessary modifications. The changes must then be recompiled, tested, and redeployed. A rules engine provides a means to separate the rules or logic of an application from the remaining code. Separating these rules provides several distinct advantages.

- A rule engine allows for a more declarative style of programming where the rules define what is happening, without describing how it is happening. This makes it much easier to read than nested 'if-else' blocks of code. It's also easier to make changes without introducing bugs in your code.

- The rules are written in a language that is easier for non-developers to understand. This makes it easier for business users to validate and even modify the rules without having to involve developers.

- A rule engine allows for changes to be made to the rules without requiring that you recompile your application. If your code must pass through a strict deployment workflow, this can be a huge time saver and can also save a significant amount of money.

After all this, you may be interested in using Liferay's rules engine, so let's get started with it.

Installation

The Drools Web Plugin is available to Liferay Enterprise Edition customers through Liferay Marketplace. Its name is `Drools EE`, and you'll find it categorized as a Utility app.

The Drools Web Plugin provides a rules engine implementation, but by itself it doesn't provide any observable changes to the portal user interface or any additional functionality. To see the rules engine in action, you can download and install a Sample Drools Portlet that contains two rule definitions that illustrate how to leverage the rules engine in your custom code. The Sample Drools Portlet is available through the Customer Portal.

Let's examine the sample portlet to see how it works.

Configuring the sample Drools portlet

Begin by downloading and installing the Sample Drools Portlet. The Sample Drools Portlet is available to Liferay Enterprise Edition customers through the customer portal. The name is `sample-drools-portlet`, and you'll find it in the list of web plugins.

After installation is complete, add the portlet to a page. Initially, the portlet indicates the name of the currently logged in user and a message that says there are no results. To see results in the portlet we'll need to create and tag assets in the site to which you added the portlet.

Log in as an administrative user and navigate to the Control Panel. Once in the Control Panel, add a new Web Content entry to your site. Before publishing the Web Content entry, tag the article with *west coast symposium*. While still in the control panel, navigate to *My Account* and select the Address link on the right side of the screen. Enter a Canadian, Mexican, or US based address and save the record. Now, navigate back to the liferay.com site and the Web Content should be displayed in the Sample Drools Portlet.

The default rule that's being evaluated displays a list of assets based on the current user's address. For example, if the current user's country is set to Canada, Mexico, or the United States, the Sample Drools Portlet displays a list of assets that have been tagged with the *west coast symposium* tag.

The Sample Drools Portlet plugin also contains a second rule that returns personalized content based on the user's net worth set in the My Account → Custom Fields section of the Control Panel. To see this rule in action, add a second instance of the Sample Drools Portlet to a page. Once added to the page, select the *Options* icon (*the wrench*) and then select *Configuration*. You need to replace the rules defined in the *Rules* section of the Configuration screen with contents of the *rules_user_custom_attribute_content.drl* file. The rule file can be found in the deployed portlet at

```
sample-drools-portlet/WEB-INF/src/com/liferay/sampledrools/dependencies/rules/_user/ \
    _custom/_attribute/_content.drl
```

In the same Configuration screen, add `networth` to the user-custom-attribute-names field. Save your changes and close the pop-up window. Navigate to the Control Panel and add a Custom Field on the User object with the Key `networth`. Navigate to *My Account* and select the Custom Fields link on the right side of the screen. Enter a net worth of 150000 and save the record. While still in the Control Panel, add a new Web Content entry to the default liferay.com site. Before publishing the Web Content entry, tag the article with *high net worth* and then save the entry. Now, navigate back to the liferay.com site and the Web Content should be displayed in the second Sample Drools Portlet added to the page.

Now that you can see how it works in practice, let's look closer at the rules themselves.

Rules Definitions

Rule definitions can be written using Drools' declarative language. Rule files are text files that often have a .drl extension. A rule file can contain multiple rules. In addition to the standard Drools' declarative language, a domain specific language (DSL) can be created for your specific problem domain. Creating a DSL can make your rules even easier for business users to create and maintain your applications rules but does require some additional work up front. For additional information on creating a DSL for your problem domain please refer to the Domain Specific Languages section of the official Drools Documentation at docs.jboss.org.

To see examples of a rules definition file, access the following directory in the Sample Drools Portlet:

```
sample-drools-portlet/WEB-INF/src/com/liferay/sampledrools/dependencies
```

To see how rules work in action we'll look at the rule defined in `rules/_user/_address/_content.drl`.

At first glance, this .drl file looks a lot like a Java class file. This example starts with a comment describing the rule. Single line comments can begin with either a # or // and multi-line comments begin with /* and end with */.

```
## ## Rules ## ## This sample program will return personalized content
```

based on the user's ## addresses set in the My Account section of the Control Panel. ## ## For example, suppose the current user has an address in the United States and ## is a member of the Liferay site. All assets within the Liferay site ## that are tagged with "West Coast Symposium" will be returned. ##

Following the comments is a `package` declaration. The package declaration is optional in a Drools, but if it appears, it must be at the beginning of the file. The package denotes a collection of rules. Unlike Java, the package name does not represent a folder structure; it's only a unique namespace. The ; at the end of the package declaration and all other statements is optional.

```
package com.liferay.sampledrools.dependencies;
```

After the package declaration are a series of `import` statements. Import statements in the rule file are used the same as the import statements in Java classes. Classes that are imported can be used in the rules.

```
import com.liferay.portal.kernel.util.KeyValuePair; import
com.liferay.portal.kernel.util.StringUtil; import
com.liferay.portal.model.Address; import com.liferay.portal.model.Contact;
import com.liferay.portal.model.User; import
com.liferay.portal.service.AddressLocalServiceUtil; import
com.liferay.portlet.asset.model.AssetEntry; import
com.liferay.portlet.asset.service.persistence.AssetEntryQuery; import
com.liferay.portlet.asset.service.AssetEntryLocalServiceUtil; import
com.liferay.portlet.asset.service.AssetTagLocalServiceUtil;

import java.util.ArrayList; import java.util.List;
```

The next line declares the `dialect` for the package. In this case, we will be using Java for any of the code expressions that we'll encounter. The other possible value for dialect is `MVEL`. If necessary, the dialect can also be specified at the rule level to override the package level dialect.

```
dialect "java"
```

In this rule file, we have only a single function, which is listed next. Functions allow you to insert Java code that can be evaluated at run time into your rule file. Functions are commonly used as a as part of the consequence clause of the rule statement. Functions are similar to Java methods, but to define a function you use the *function* keyword. The function's parameters and the return type are declared as they would be in a Java method. In this example, the `getAssetEntries` function returns a `java.util.List` object that contains `AssetEntry` objects based on the `groupIds`, `classNameIds`, and `names` provided in the function call.

```
function List getAssetEntries( long[] groupIds, long[] classNameIds,
String[] names) {

    long[] assetTagIds =
AssetTagLocalServiceUtil.getTagIds(groupIds, names);

    List<AssetEntry> assetEntries = new ArrayList<AssetEntry>();

    if (assetTagIds.length > 0) { AssetEntryQuery assetEntryQuery =
new AssetEntryQuery();

        assetEntryQuery.setAnyTagIds(assetTagIds);
assetEntryQuery.setClassNameIds(classNameIds);
assetEntryQuery.setGroupIds(groupIds); assetEntryQuery.setVisible(true);

        assetEntries.addAll(AssetEntryLocalServiceUtil.getEntries(assetEntryQuery));
}

    return assetEntries; }
```

Alternatively, this function could've been written in a helper class and then imported using a *function import*. So if we had created a helper class called **AddressContentHelper** the import would look like this:

```
import function

com.liferay.sampledrools.dependencies.AddressContentHelper.getAssetEntries;
```

The last section of the rules file contains the actual rules. The syntax of a rule is very straightforward.

```
rule "name" attribute when condition then consequence end
```

The rule name is required and it must be unique within the package as declared above. Names with spaces must be enclosed in double quotes. It is considered a best practice to always enclose your rule names in double quotes.

```
rule "Initialize Rules"
```

The attributes section is optional. In our first rule, we have a single attribute called **salience**. The salience attribute is an integer value that acts as a priority weighting. The number can be positive or negative and defaults to the value of 0. Rules with a higher salience value are given a higher priority. It is considered a best practice to write attributes one to a line. In our example, the first rule is one that should be evaluated before any other so it is given a high salience value of 1000. None of our other rules have a salience attribute set, so they all default to a value of 0.

```
salience 1000
```

The **when** keyword marks the conditional section of the rule. It is also referred to as the Left Hand Side (LHS). The **when** keyword is followed by zero or more condition elements that must be met before the consequence will be called. If there are no condition elements, then the condition is always evaluated as true.

The most common type of conditional element is a *pattern*. Patterns match against *facts*. Facts are statements that are known to be true. Facts can be inserted by the Java code that invokes the rules engine or they can be declared in the rule file itself.

In the first rule of our rule file (**Initialize Rules**), the only condition is that the rule must operate on a User object.

```
when user : User();
```

In more complex rules, the pattern may include constraints or may evaluate the properties of Java objects. For example, the second rule of this rule file is called *Get European Symposium Content*. This rule includes the following pattern which ensures that a user's address contains the country name France, Germany, or Spain.

```
userAddress : Address(country.name in ("France", "Germany", "Spain"));
```

The consequence section of the rule follows the conditional section. It's also known as the Right Hand Side (RHS) or action part of the rule. The consequence section begins with the keyword **then** and it is intended to modify the working memory data. Drools provides some convenience methods that make it easier to modify the working memory. In this rule, we use the **insertLogical** method which places a new object into the working memory and retracts it when there are no more facts supporting the truth of the current rule. After the consequence section of the rule, the rule is terminated with the keyword **end**.

```
then List<Address> userAddresses = AddressLocalServiceUtil.getAddresses(
user.getCompanyId(), Contact.class.getName(), user.getContactId());

    for (Address userAddress : userAddresses) {
insertLogical(userAddress); } end
```

Following the initial rule in our example, there are three additional rules that will be evaluated. Each of these rules evaluates the **userAddress** that was inserted into the working memory to determine what type of content should be displayed to the end user.

For additional documentation on the Drools rules language, please see the official Drools documentation.[1]

6.4 Summary

In this chapter, we discussed personal sites for portal users. We showed how to enable or disable them, how to set whether or not pages should be automatically created, and how to customize automatically created pages. We also examined general customizable pages that don't belong to personal sites. Administrators can designate certain pages or portions of pages to be customizable and site members can configure these portions of the pages, add or remove portlet applications, and save their configurations.

We also discussed how you can use Liferay's rules engine with Liferay EE. As you can see from the Sample Rules Portlet, using a rules engine can be a powerful way to decouple the rules of your application from the front-end and back-end code. These rules are written in a declarative language that business users can read and verify. Additionally, rule definitions can be modified without modifying the underlying Java code, re-compiling, or redeploying your applications.

---

[1]http://docs.jboss.org/drools/release/5.2.0.Final/drools-expert-docs/html/

CHAPTER 7

COLLABORATION SUITE

Liferay Portal ships with a robust suite of collaboration applications which you can use to build communities of users for your site. These applications provide all the features that you would expect of standalone versions outside of a portal setting. The difference with Liferay's collaboration suite, however, is that all of the applications share a common look and feel, security model and architecture. They inherit the strengths of being part of Liferay's development platform so you can use them in combination with Liferay's user management and content management features to build a well-integrated, feature-rich web site.

This chapter focuses on how to use Liferay's collaboration suite. We explain how to set up and administer:

- Blogs

- Calendars

- Message Boards

- Wikis

- Polls

- Chat

- Mail

We'll discuss how these features work together to facilitate information flow within your portal and provide an enhanced experience for your users.

7.1 Understanding Liferay's common configuration options

Just like siblings have common features inherited from their parents, applications that ship with Liferay also share common features. These include look and feel, communication, scoping, sharing, permissions, archive configurations, and exporting/importing portlet data. So before we get into the nitty gritty of the applications themselves, it's best to cover these common features first, starting with the look and feel configuration options.

Look and Feel

An administrator can access the look and feel configuration menu of any Liferay portlet by clicking on the wrench icon at the top right corner of the portlet and selecting *Look and Feel*. The location of the wrench icon and other portlet icons (minimixe, maximize, and remove) may vary, depending on your theme. Liferay portlets' look and feel dialog boxes contain seven tabs:

- Portlet Configuration
- Text Styles
- Background Styles
- Border Styles
- Margin and Padding
- Advanced Styling
- WAP Styling

After making customizations on any tab, remember to click the *Save* button to apply your changes. To see the effect of your changes, you may have to refresh the page. If you don't like the effect of your changes, click the *Reset* button to discard them.

On the Portlet Configuration tab, you can check the *Use Custom Title* box to rename your portlet's title. The value you enter in the Portlet Title box will be displayed at the top of the portlet window on the page. You can also select a language from the Portlet Title dropdown menu. If you've provided a language key translation for the language you select, the your portlet's title will be displayed in the selected language.

Figure 7.1: The Portlet Configuration tab of the Look and Feel Box allows you to define a custom portlet title, link porlet URLs to a specific page, and select whether or not portlet borders should be displayed.

If you select a page in the *Link Portlet URLs to Page* dropdown menu, all portlet URLs will point to the page you selected. The current page is the default. Note that you can use the Asset Publisher's View in a Specific Portlet feature and web content articles' Display Page attribute to achieve a more elegant solution for displaying the full view of web content articles on specific pages. Please see the Display Page section of chapter 5 for details.

You can also choose whether or not to display borders around your portlet. By default, borders are displayed. Be careful about turning portlet borders off; some themes assume that portlet borders are turned on and may not display correctly with them turned off.

The Text Styles tab allows you to configure format of the text that appears in the portlet. The fonts you can choose from include Arial, Georgia, Times New Roman, Tahoma, Trebuchet MS, and Verdana. Arial is the default. You can set the text to bold, italics, or both. You can set the font size anywhere from 0.1 em to 12 em, with 0.1 em increments. 1 em is the default. You can set the text color to any six digit hex color code. If you'd like help choosing a color, click on the pencil icon to open the color palette. You can set the text alignment to left, center, right, or justified. (Justified text is both left and right aligned.) You can set an underline, overline, or strikethrough as the text decoration. The default text decoration is none.

Figure 7.2: The Text Styles tab lets you configure the format of the text that appears in the portlet.

You can set the word spacing anywhere from -1 em to 0.95 em, with 0.5 em increments. 0 em is the default. You can set the line height anywhere from 0 em to 12 em, with 0.1 em increments. 0 em is the default. Finally, you can set the letter spacing anywhere from -10 px to 50 px, with 1 px increments. 0 px is the default.

The Background Styles tab allows you to specify the portlet's background color. You can enter any six digit hex color code or you click on the pencil icon to use the color palette.

On the Border Styles tab, you can configure your portlet's border width, border style, and border color. For each of these attributes, leave the *Same for All* box checked to apply the same settings to top, right, bottom, and left borders.

For border width, you can specify any % value, em value, or px value. For border style, you can select dashed, double, dotted, groove, hidden, inset, outset,

Figure 7.3: The Background Styles tab lets you specify the portlet's background color.

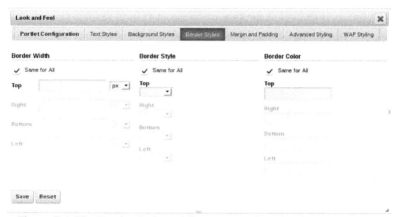

Figure 7.4: The Border Styles tab lets you specify a border width, style, and color for each side of the portlet.

ridge, or solid. For border color, you can enter any six digit hex color code, just like for the text color and background color. You can also use the color palette.

The Margin and Padding tab allows you to specify margin and padding lengths for the edges of your portlet. Just like for border styles, leave the *Same for All* box checked to apply the same settings to each side (top, right, bottom, and left) of the portlet.

Figure 7.5: The Margin and Padding tab allows you to specify margin and paddings lengths for the sides of your portlet.

For both padding and margin, you can specify any % value, em value, or px value.

The Advanced Styling tab displays current information about your portlet, including your portlet's Liferay ID and CSS classes.

On this tab, you can also enter custom CSS class names for your portlet and custom CSS code. Clicking the *Add a CSS rule for just this portlet* or *Add a CSS rule for all portlets like this one* links adds the CSS code shells into your custom CSS text box. If you check the *Update my styles as I type* box, your CSS code will be dynamically applied to your portlet so you can see the effects of your edits.

The WAP Styling tab allows you to specify a custom portlet title that will be displayed when mobile devices using the Wireless Application Protocol make page requests. You can also set the initial window state to normal or minimized. Normal is the default.

Next, let's discuss exporting and importing portlet data.

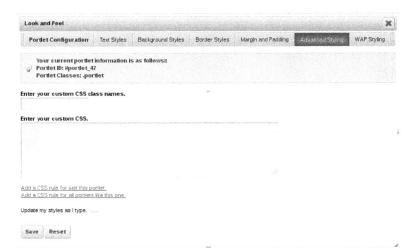

Figure 7.6: The Advanced Styling tab displays your portlet's Liferay ID and allows you to enter CSS code to customize the look and feel of your portlet.

Figure 7.7: The WAP Styling tab lets you enter a custom portlet title to be displayed to devices making page requests via WAP; it also allows you to specify an initial window state.

Export/Import

Some Liferay portlets allow you to export or import portlet data. These include many of Liferay's collaborative applications, such as the Blogs, Wiki, and Message Boards portlets. To export or import portlet data, right-click on the wrench icon of your portlet and select *Export/Import*. Exporting portlet data produces a `.lar` file that you can save and import into another portlet applicaton of the same type. To import portlet data, you must select a `.lar` file. Be careful not to confuse portlet-specific `.lar` files with site-specific `.lar` files. See the Backing up and Restoring Pages section of chapter 2 for a discussion of exporting and importing data across an entire site.

Figure 7.8: When exporting portlet data, you can choose which categories of information to include.

Each portlet has different configuration options. Checking the *Setup* box selects the portlet's saved configuration for export. Checking the *User Preferences* box selects saved portlet configurations of specific users. The *Data* box is the most important one–check this to select your portlet's data (like blog entries, message board posts, or wiki articles, for example) for export. When you check the *Data* box, more options appear, allowing you to choose specific kinds of metadata to include and to select a data range. Check the *Permissions* box if you'd like to export your the permissions defined for your portlet. When you check this box, a subbox called *Permissions Assigned to Roles* appears. If you wish, you can export your portlet's permissions but not the permissions assigned to roles. Finally, you can check the *Categories* box to include cate-

gories for export. When selected, all categories referenced by portlet data will
be exported or imported, keeping their hierarchy.

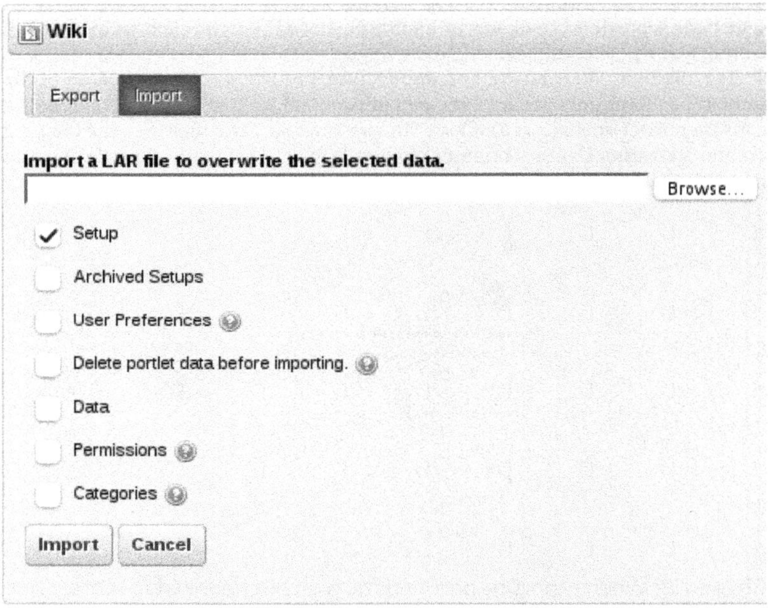

Figure 7.9: When importing portlet data, you can choose which categories
of information to use.

When you import portlet data, only the data types you select will be overwritten. If you'd like to import portlet data, you have to select a `.lar` file. You
can import any items that were included when your `.lar` file was created. Note
that user preferences can only be successfully imported when the user UUIDs
match. Additionally, you can import any archived setups into your portlet, if
any. Archived setups provide a means to save multiple portlet configurations
and to switch between them. We discuss archived setups below. If you check
the *Delete portlet data before importing* box, *all* data created by the portlets will
be deleted just before the import process. Be careful, some portlets on others
pages may be referencing this data.

Next, let's discuss the concept of a portlet's scope.

Scope

As we learned earlier, roles can be scoped by the portal, by a site, or by an organization. A role only takes effect within its scope. For example, a Message Boards Administrator role with complete access to the Message Boards portlet has different permissions based on the role's scope. If it's a portal role, members have permission to administer message boards across the entire portal. If it's a site role, members only have permission to administer message boards within the site where they've been assigned the role. For organizations with sites, site roles are automatically assigned to organization members based on the organization roles they have. So for an organization-scoped Message Boards administrator role, members only have permission to administer message boards within the site of the organization that assigned the role to them.

We also use the word *scope* to refer to the data set of a portlet. By default, when a portlet is added to a page in a site, it is *scoped* for that site. This means that its data belongs to that site. If the portlet is added to a page in a different site, it employs a completely different data set. This enables you to place a Message Boards portlet in one site with one set of categories and threads, and place another Message Boards portlet in different site with a different set of categories and threads.

Scoping by site means that you can only have one Message Boards portlet per site. If you add one Message Boards portlet to a page in a site and add another Message Boards portlet to a different page in the same site, the second Message Boards portlet contains exactly the same data as the first. This is because, by default, the Message Boards portlet is scoped by site. Most of Liferay's other portlets also default to being scoped by site.

To avoid this limitation, many Liferay portlets can be scoped by page. In this case, the data sets of page-scoped portlets serve a single page, not an entire site. If you set the scope of a portlet to *page* instead of *site*, you can add any number of these portlets to different pages, and then they have different sets of data. This allows you to have more than one message board per site if you wish. Most portlets, however, default to the "native" configuration, and have their scopes set to the site where they are placed.

Unless otherwise noted, all the portlets in this chapter support scoping by portal (global), site (default), or page (select layout $\rightarrow$ current page). This grants you some flexibility in how you want to set up your portal. You can configure the scope of a portlet with just a few simple steps.

1. Click the *Menu* icon in the portlet window (the wrench).

2. Select *Configuration*.

3. Select the *Scope* tab.

4. Use the drop-down menu to set the scope.

5. Click *Save*.

Figure 7.10: Changing the scope of a portlet

That's all it takes to change the scope for a particular portlet instance. By setting the scope to *Current Page*, you can add as many of these portlets to a site as you want, provided they are all added to separate pages.

Another useful feature of Liferay's portlets is Archived Setups.

Archived Setups

Once you've configured a portlet, Archived Setups enables you to save those settings in an "archive". If someone goes in and changes the settings of a particular portlet, it then becomes easy to revert those changes back to the original, archived configuration.

To create an archived setup, click the *Configuration* option from the menu in the portlet's title bar. If the current settings of the portlet you're configuring are the ones you want to archive, click the *Archive/Restore Setup* link. If not, change and save the settings until you have the portlet configured the way you want it, and then click the *Archive/Restore Setup* link.

There is only one field to fill out. Enter a name for your archive and click *Save*. You should now see your archive in the list. If you ever need to revert the portlet to these archived settings, you can click *Actions → Restore* next to the archived setup you want to restore.

Unless otherwise noted, all of the portlets in this chapter support this feature. This is particularly useful for portlets that have a lot of configuration options, such as the Message Boards portlet.

Next, we'll see how permissions apply to Liferay portlets in general.

Permissions

All of Liferay's portlets support Liferay's robust, fine-grained permissions system. Some higher level permissions can be configured in the permissions tab of the portlet configuration dialog box. You can grant roles permission to add the portlet to a page, configure the portlet, or view the portlet. To set these permissions, go to the *Configuration* menu and click on *Permissions*. This shows you a table of roles defined in the portal. Use the check boxes to grant certain permissions to different roles. Click *Submit* after you have made your selections.

Beyond this, specific permissions are generally defined for specific applications. For example, the message boards portlet contains a *Ban User* permission. This makes no sense in the context of another portlet, say, the blogs portlet. We'll go over permissions for specific applications in the sections for those applications. For now, let's move on to sharing applications.

Communication

Liferay implements several communication mechanisms across portlets including those specified by the JSR-286 standard: public render parameters and events. Public render parameters are easy to use and can be quite powerful. Some Liferay portlets provide a configuration UI to help you get the most out of this communication mechanism. To access this UI, open your portlet's configuration window by clicking on the wrench icon and selecting *Configuration*. Then click on the *Communication* tab.

The screenshot above is for the Wiki portlet, which has six public render parameters: categoryId, nodeId, nodeName, resetCur, tag, title. For each of these parameters, you can configure the portlet to ignore the values coming from other portlets to read the value from another parameter.

Why might it be useful to ignore the values for certain parameters that come from other portlets? Consider a common use case for the Wiki portlet. The Wiki portlet is often used along with the Tags Navigation portlet so that when a user clicks on a tag of the latter, the Wiki portlet shows a list of pages with that tag. In some cases, an administrator may want the Wiki portlet to always show the front page independently of any tag navigation done through other portlets.

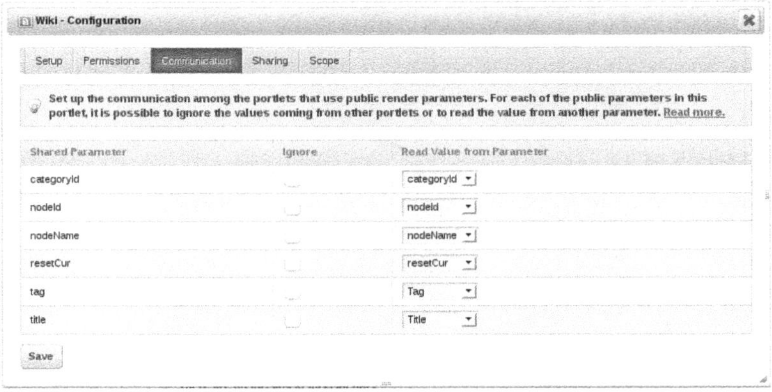

Figure 7.11: You can configure portlets to communicate with each other using public render parameters.

This can be achieved by checking the *Ignore* checkbox so that the values of the parameter coming from those other portlets are ignored.

Reading the value of a parameter from another portlet is an advanced but very powerful option that allows portlets to communicate with each other even if their developers didn't intend them to. For example, imagine that the Wiki portlet is being used to publish information about certain countries. Imagine further that there's another portlet that allows browsing countries for adminis- trative reasons. The second portlet has a public render parameter called *country* with the name of the country. We'd like the Wiki to show the information from the country that's selected in the administration portlet. This can be achieved by setting the value of the title parameter of the Wiki portlet to be read from the country parameter of the administration portlet. Cool, isn't it?

Sharing

The web was once thought of as a number of islands of applications in a vast universe of "cyberspace." Many web sites attempted to make their island the biggest. Some succeeded to a large extent and some failed. More recently, the concept of the web as an application itself has taken hold, and so widgets have become very popular nowadays. This concept is part of the "Web 2.0" concept and is very much enabled by widgets. What is a widget? A widget is a small piece of code which provides a piece of functionality, can be included on any web site, but does not necessarily have to be hosted by that web site. If you have ever embedded a YouTube video on your own web site so that users could watch a video without actually having to visit http://youtube.com, then you've already used a widget.

Liferay supports serving its portlets as widgets. You can embed a particular instance of a portlet running on your site into another site, such as Facebook. This opens up a whole new avenue of exposure to your web site that you would not have had otherwise. In fact, this is how all those Facebook games work.

Figure 7.12: Sharing Tab of the Portlet Configuration Dialog Box

To share one of your portlets as a widget, open the *Configuration* dialog box from the portlet's title bar and select the *Sharing* tab. There are five subtabs under sharing: Any Web Site, Facebook, Google Gadget, Netvibes, and Friends.

Any Web Site

Copy and paste the provided snippet of JavaScript code into the web site to which you want to add the portlet as a widget. That's all you need to do. When a user loads the page on the other web site, the code will pull the relevant portlet from your site and display it.

Facebook

You can add any Liferay portlet as an application on Facebook. To do this, you must first get a developer key. A link for doing this is provided to you in the Facebook tab. You'll have to create the application on Facebook and get the key and canvas page URL from Facebook. Once you've done this, you can copy and paste their values into the Facebook tab. Your portlet will now be available on Facebook as a Facebook application.

Figure 7.13: Liferay's Forums on Facebook

Incidentally, this makes Liferay a fantastic platform upon which to build applications for Facebook. See the *Liferay Developer's Guide* or *Liferay in Action* for more details.

OpenSocial Gadget

OpenSocial comprises a container and a set of APIs for social networking and other web applications. iGoogle is a service provided by Google that lets users create a customizable page and add *Gadgets* to that page. Liferay can serve up portlets to be used as Open Social Gadgets on iGoogle or other OpenSocial-compatible pages.

To serve a Liferay portlet on iGoogle, check the box labeled *Allow users to add [portlet-name] to iGoogle.* Then copy and paste the URL provided into Google's *Add a feed or gadget* feature on the iGoogle configuration page. Your Liferay portal instance will serve that portlet directly onto your iGoogle page. The URL provided is unique to the specific instance of the portlet, so you could serve multiple instances of the same portlet as different Google Gadgets.

You could use this feature to allow users to view what's happening on your portal at a glance, using asset publishers or custom RSS feeds. You could also use Liferay's API to build your own portlet and provide the URL for users to place on their iGoogle pages.

Netvibes

Netvibes offers a similar service to iGoogle–users can log in, create their own personal portal, called a *dashboard,* and add customizable widgets to the dashboard that they create. To set up Netvibes support for a particular portlet, check the *Allow users to add [portlet-name] to Netvibes pages* box. You can then use the provided URL to create a custom Netvibes widget based on the instance of the portlet that you're using.

Friends

The final sub-tab of the *Sharing* tab is called *Friends.* This tab has a single check box that allows you to give your friends permission to add the application as a widget to another web site. This could be particularly useful for your blog or calendar if you wish to share them.

Now that we've seen all the common options available in Liferay's portlet applications, we can move on to specific applications, starting with blogs.

7.2 Expressing yourself using Blogs

The word *Blog* is an apostrophe-less contraction of the two words *web* and *log.* Blogs were first popularized by web sites such as Slashdot (http://slashdot.org)

which have the format of a running list of entries to which users could at-tach comments. Over time, more and more sites such as Digg, del.icio.us, and Newsvine adopted the format, empowering users to share their opinions and generating lively discussions.

Over the course of time, blogging sites and applications began to appear, such as blogger.com, blogspot.com. TypePad, WordPress, and Web Roller. These applications allow *individuals* to run their own web sites in the same format: a running list of short articles to which readers who are registered with the site can attach threaded comments. People who run a blog are called *bloggers*, and sometimes they build a whole community of readers who are interested in their blog posts. Anyone can have a blog, in fact, there are several famous people who run their own blogs. It gives people an outlet for self-expression that they would not otherwise have, and the ubiquity and wide reach of the Internet ensures that if you have something important and interesting to say, somebody will read it.

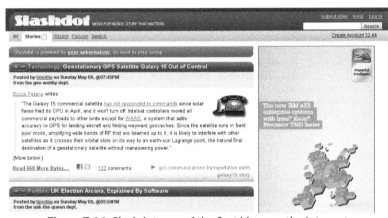

Figure 7.14: Slashdot, one of the first blogs on the Internet

Liferay Portal has a Blogs portlet which allows you to provide a blogging service to users of your web site. In fact, Liferay extensively uses the Blogs portlet on http://www.liferay.com to provide employees with blogs of their own. In addition to the Blogs portlet, there's also a Blogs Aggregator portlet which can take entries from multiple users' blogs and put them all in one larger list. We will go over how to use both of these portlets to create a blogging site for your users.

The Blogs Portlet

The Blogs portlet is available from the *Collaboration* section of the *Add* → *More* menu. Notice that it is an instanceable portlet, meaning that it supports scopes. This allows you to use the Blogs portlet to create a shared blog to build a site like Slashdot or to create multiple personal blogs to build a site like http://blogger.com. What's the difference? Adding the Blogs portlet to a site page creates a shared blog for members of the site that the page belongs to. Adding the Blogs portlet to a user's personal site creates a blog just for that user. The Blogs portlet works the same way in both cases. And of course, you can change the Blog portlet's scope to have different blogs on different pages in the same site.

Figure 7.15: Initial View of the Blogs Portlet

By default, the Blogs portlet displays the latest entry in its entirety. When you first add the portlet to a page, it has no entries, so the portlet is empty. There are several display options to let you configure it to look the way you want it to look. Before we start adding entries, let's configure the portlet so that it displays entries the way you want them.

Configuring the Blogs Portlet

The Blogs portlet is easy to configure. Click on the *Menu* icon in the portlet's title bar and select *Configuration*. Beneath the Setup tab, there is another row of options.

Email From: defines the *From* field in the email messages that users receive from the Blogs portlet.

Entry Added Email: defines a subject and body for the emails sent out when a new Blog entry has been added.

Entry Updated Email: defines a subject and body for the emails sent out when a new Blog entry has been updated.

Display Settings: changes various display options for the Blogs portlet. To choose the right settings, you should think about the best way to display your entries as well as how you want users to interact with bloggers.

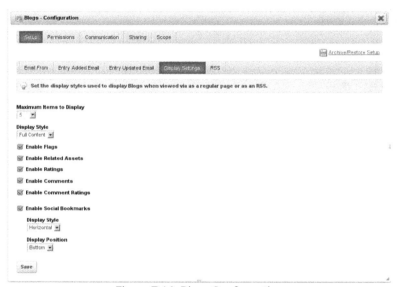

Figure 7.16: Blogs Configuration

Maximum Items to Display: choose the total number of blog entries to display on the initial page. You can select up to one hundred to be displayed.

Display Style: choose between full Content, abstract, or just the title. Setting this to Abstract shows the abstract, or if there isn't one, only the first 30 words of your blog entries, with a Read More link at the bottom of each that expands to the whole entry.

Enable Flags: flag content as inappropriate and send an email to the administrators.

Enable Related Assets: select related content from other portlets to pull into their blog entry for readers to view.

Enable Ratings: lets readers rate your blog entries from one to five stars.

Enable Comments: lets readers comment on your blog entries.

Figure 7.17: Related Assets

Enable Comment Ratings: lets readers rate the comments which are posted to your blog entries.

Enable Social Bookmarks: lets users tweet, Facebook like, or +1 (Google Plus) about blog posts.

Maximum Items to Display: determine how many blog entries will be displayed at once. The default is set to twenty.

Display Style: select a simple, vertical, or horizontal display style for your blog posts.

Display Position: choose a top or a bottom position for your blog posts.

RSS: choose how blogs are displayed to RSS readers. Here, you can choose how you want your blog entries to be published as feeds to readers and outside web sites.

Maximum Items to Display: choose the total number of RSS feeds to display on the initial page. You can choose up to one hundred to be displayed.

Display Style: choose between full content, abstract, and title. These options work just like the ones above for blog entries.

Format: choose which format you want to deliver your blogs: RSS 1.0, RSS 2.0, or Atom 1.0.

Now that you have the Blogs portlet looking the way you want it, you'll want to review permissions for it–especially if you're working on a shared blog.

Permissions

If you have a personal blog, the default permissions should work well for you. If you have a shared blog, you may want to modify the permissions on the blog. The default settings make it so only the owner of the site to which the portlet has been added is able to add entries. This, of course, is great if the Blogs portlet has been added to a user's personal pages, but doesn't work so well for a shared blog. But don't worry: it's easy to share a blog with multiple users.

First, create a role for your bloggers and add them to the role (roles are covered in chapter 12 of Part 2). Next, click the *Permissions* button on the Blogs portlet. A list of both portal and site roles is displayed, and currently only the owner is checked. Check off any other role or team that should have the ability to add blog entries, and then click *Save*. Once this is done, users in the roles or teams that you selected are able to post to the shared blog.

Now that everyone's able to post, let's look at how posts work.

Adding Blog Entries

Now you're ready to begin adding blog entries. Click the *Add Blog Entry* button. The following data entry screen appears:

There isn't much difference between this screen and any other data entry screen within Liferay Portal. You get a title, a way of scheduling when the entry is to appear, and a rich editor that allows you to format your entry the way you want, complete with embedded images, videos, and the like. Note also that as you type, the entry is automatically saved as a draft at periodic intervals. This gives you peace of mind in using the portlet from within your browser, since you won't lose your entry in the event of a browser crash or network interruption. You can also tag your entries using the same tagging mechanism found everywhere else in the portal.

The Blogs portlet also supports trackbacks and pingbacks. Trackbacks are special links that let you notify another site that you linked to them. For example, if you wanted to write an entry in your blog and reference some other site's entry, you might put the URL to the other entry in the *Trackbacks to Send* field. If you have multiple URLs you want to send trackbacks to, separate them with spaces.

If you want others who link to your blog to let you know about the link via trackbacks, leave the *Allow Trackbacks* box checked. This generates a URL that is displayed with your blog entry. Others who want to link to your entry can use this URL for the link, to send trackbacks to your blog.

Note that trackbacks only work when the protocol is supported by both the linker and the linkee. A newer way to support similar link notification functionality is *pingbacks*. Pingbacks are XML-RPC requests that are similar to trackbacks except they're automatically sent when you link to another site. They're easier to use because you don't have to do anything extra: if you link to another site in your blog entry, Liferay sends a pingback to the other site to notify that

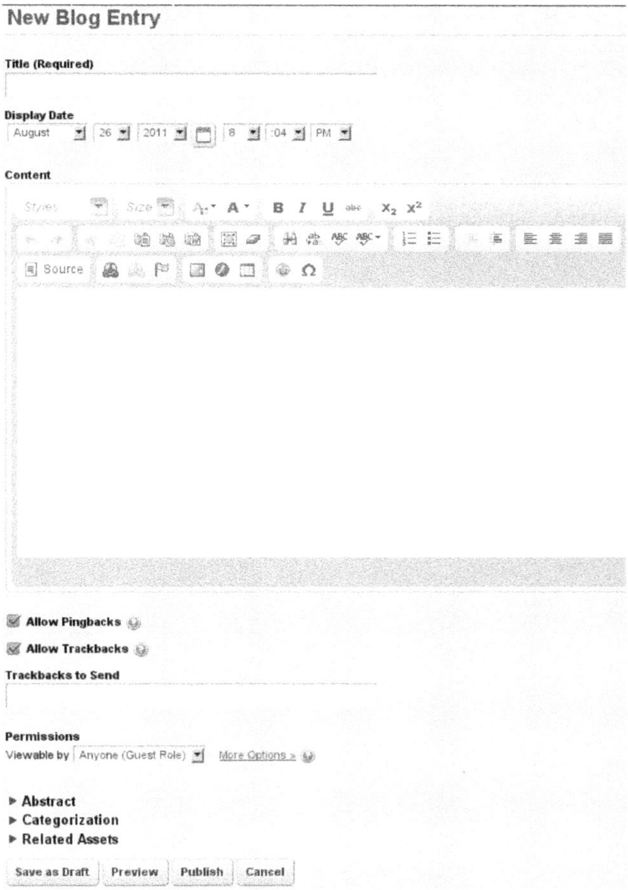

Figure 7.18: Adding a Blog Entry

site that you linked to it. Similarly, if someone links to your blog entry, Liferay can receive a pingback from that person's site and record the link.

You can enter a description of your post beneath the Abstract heading, and this can be used by the Abstract display style. Below this is the Categorization heading, where you can attach tags and/or categories to your blog entry. You should definitely consider doing this: it improves search results for blog entries, and it gives you more navigation options that you can pass on to your users. For example, you can add the Tags Navigation portlet to another column on your blogs page, allowing users to browse blog entries by tag.

Below this is the Related Assets heading. If there's some other content in the portal that's related to your blog, you can choose it here. For example, you might want to write a blog entry talking about a particular discussion that happened on the forums. To link those two assets together, select the forum thread under Related Assets.

Once you've finished your blog entry, click *Publish*. You'll go back to the list of entries, and now your entry is displayed. Here is what it looks like when the display style is set to *Full Content* and the number of entries is set to ten:

Figure 7.19: First Blog Entry Added

You can see that in the summary view, you don't see the trackback/pingback link, and you only see the number of comments that have been added. If you were to click the *Read More* link, you would see the entirety of the article, all the comments in a threaded view, and the trackback/pingback link which others can use to link back to your blog entry.

The full view of the blog entry also contains links to share blog entries on so-cial networks, such as Twitter, Facebook, and Google Plus. This gives your read-ers an easy way to share blog entries with friends, potentially driving further traffic to your site. As you can see, the Blogs portlet is a full-featured blogging application that gives you and your users the ability to enter the blogosphere with an application that supports anything a blogger needs.

Of course, Liferay is a portal, and as a portal, it excels at aggregating infor-mation from multiple places. For that reason, it also includes the Blogs Aggre-gator portlet so that you can "bubble up" blog entries from multiple users and highlight them on your site. Let's look next at how that works.

Aggregating Blog Entries

You can set up a whole web site devoted just to blogging if you wish. The Blogs Aggregator portlet allows you to publish entries from multiple bloggers on one page, giving further visibility to blog entries. This portlet is also very straight-forward to set up. You can add it to a page from the Collaboration category in the Dockbar's *Add* → *More* menu.

If you click *Configuration* from the menu button in the title bar of the port-let, the Blogs Aggregator's configuration page appears. From here, you can set several configuration options.

Figure 7.20: Blogs Aggregator Configuration

Selection Method: select Users or Scope here. If you select Users, the Blogs Aggregator aggregates the entries of every blogger on your system. If you want to refine the aggregation, you can select an organization by which to filter the users. If you select Scope, the Blogs Aggregator contains only entries of users who are in the current scope. This limits the entries to members of the site where the Blogs Aggregator portlet resides.

Organization: select which organization's blogs you want to aggregate.

Display Style: select from several different styles for displaying blog entries: title, abstract, body, image, or quote.

Maximum Items to Display: select maximum number of entries the portlet displays.

Enable RSS Subscription: creates an RSS feed out of the aggregated entries. This lets users subscribe to an aggregate feed of all your bloggers.

Show Tags: for each entry, displays all the tags associated with the blogs.

When you've finished setting the options in the portlet, click *Save*. Then close the dialog box. You'll notice the Blogs Aggregator looks very much like the Blogs portlet, except that the entries come from more than one author. This makes it nice and familiar for your users to navigate.

The Blogs Admininistrator Portlet

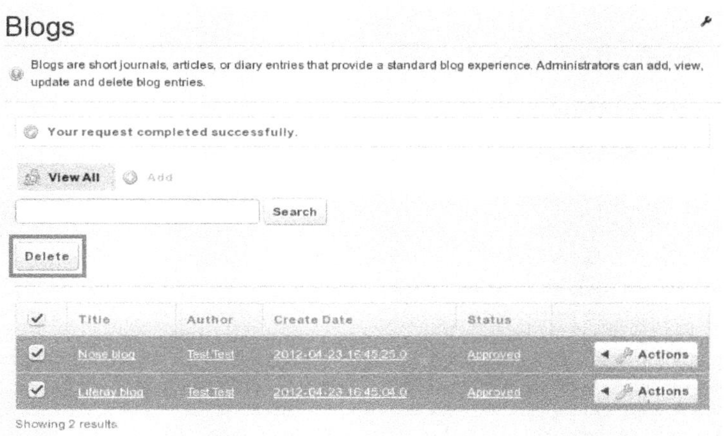

Figure 7.21: The Blogs Administrator portlet lets you delete large sets of blog entries.

In the Control Panel there's a portlet for managing your site's blog entries. Most of the time, the Blogs portlet is the only tool you'll need to manage your blog entries. If, however, you need to massively delete blog entries, the blogs administrator portlet is the perfect tool for you.

Note that it's only for batch processing of blog entries; for the full set of tools for managing blog entries, your best bet is to use the Blogs portlet.

We've already talked a little bit about connecting content across the portal by using Related Assets; now let's take a look at the Related Assets portlet.

7.3 Organizing and sharing events with the Calendar

Liferay's Calendar portlet is a complete calendaring solution. You can schedule any number of events of different types, receive alarms via email or text message, import and export your calendar, and much more. Additionally, you can import and export the calendar to and from the popular iCalendar format for use in other applications.

In a similar way to the Blogs portlet, you can use the Calendar portlet as a shared calendar on a web site or as a personal calendar – or both. Let's look at how to configure it.

Configuring the Calendar Portlet

Open the *Configuration* dialog box from the menu in the portlet's title bar. The Setup tab allows you to configure three different options in subtabs: *Email From*, *Event Reminder Email*, and *Display Settings*.

Email From: set the *Name* and *Email Address* system generated emails come from. The address that you enter in the Email Address field must be properly formatted, but it doesn't need to be an address that actually exists.

Event Reminder Email: customize the email message the Calendar sends for event reminders. It contains the same rich text editor that you see everywhere else in Liferay, and this allows you to HTML format the message for easy recognition. As with other Liferay email notifications, there are several variables which allow you to insert runtime values into the message, and these are listed underneath the text editor so that you can use them in the appropriate place in your template. For example, you might want the event start date and time and the event title included in the email reminder that you receive. Use the variables to insert that information in the appropriate place.

Display Settings: customize how the portlet shows itself to the user. There are several settings here:

- *Default Tab*: select which tab of the calendar portlet is displayed to the user by default.

- *Summary Tab*: select whether it has a horizontal or vertical layout. You can also use checkboxes to choose whether or not the calendar portlet shows a mini month, shows today's events, or enables related assets, comments, or ratings.

Now that you've successfully set up your calendar, let's look at how to use it.

Using the Calendar Portlet

The Calendar portlet inherits its interface from the rest of Liferay's portlet library, so you should find shared features in the same place that you find them in other Liferay portlets.

Figure 7.22: The Liferay Calendar Portlet

To get started, you may want to click the *Permissions* button. Here you'll find an interface that should be becoming familiar: a list of roles with check boxes. For the Calendar, these denote whether the role has the *Add Event* or the *Export All Events* permission. By default, only the owner has permission to do these things, which means that the Calendar portlet is set up for personal use. The reason for this is that out of the box, Liferay puts a Calendar portlet on all users' private pages. If you want to use the Calendar as a shared calendar, you'll need to make an additional configuration.

First, create a portal or site role. Then add the users responsible for maintaining the calendar to this role. This process is described in chapter 12. You can add multiple roles if you like. Once you have the role or roles set up, come back to the Calendar portlet and click the *Permissions* button. Check the boxes next to the roles that should have access to one or both of the functions *Add Event* and *Export All Events*. Then click *Submit*.

Now you are ready to begin using your calendar. Click the *Add Event* button. A form appears that allows you to fill out all the information for your event.

Start Date/Time: enter a date and time for the event.

Duration: specify how long the event will last.

All Day Event: disassociate time from the event and make it last all day.

Time Zone Sensitive: make sure that the portal keeps track of the event regardless of time zone.

Title: provide a title for the event.

Description: describe your event.

Location: specify the physical location of the event.

Type: select a pre-configured event type. You can change these in the `por-tal-ext.properties` file.

Permissions: manage who can view and edit the event.

Categorizations: tag and categorize the event.

Related Assets: attach a piece of content from another portlet to the event.

Repeat: select the schedule (daily, weekly, monthly. etc.) for repeatable events.

End Date: enter the end date for events that repeat on a schedule but have a specified last meeting.

Reminders: select whether to send a reminder, how long before the event to send it, and through what medium (email, SMS text message, or instant message) to send it. Note that this feature is integrated with users' profiles on the portal, so users need their information filled out and current in order to receive notifications.

When you have finished adding your event, click *Save*. You can view calendar events by day, week, month, year, or in a simple list.

As you can see, the Calendar portlet is easy to use and convenient for users of the portal. Next, let's look at one of the most widely used applications provided by Liferay: its message boards.

7.4   Discuss, ask and answer using the Message Boards

Liferay's Message Boards portlet is a state of the art forum application similar to many forums in which you may have participated. The difference, of course, is that Liferay's message boards can inherit the abilities of the Liferay development platform to provide an integrated experience that others cannot match.

There are countless web sites out there where it is clearly evident that there is no link whatsoever between the main site and the message boards. In some cases, users are even required to register twice: once for the main site and once for the message boards. Sometimes it is three times: for the site, for the message boards, and for the shopping cart. By providing a message boards portlet along with all of the other applications, Liferay provides a unique, integrated approach to building web sites. You can concentrate on building your site while Liferay does the integration work for you.

The Message Boards portlet has a lot of configuration options, but they are straightforward to use and are the reason why this portlet is a full-featured forum application for your web site. To get started, add a Message Boards portlet to your site. Once it is added, click the *Menu* icon in the portlet's title bar and click *Configuration*. There are two rows of tabs. The first tab in the top row is titled *Setup*. This is where you can configure the application the way you want it to behave on your site.

General

The first tab beneath *Setup* is labeled *General*. Here, you can enable anonymous posting, subscribe by default, flags, ratings, and thread as question by default. You can also choose whether you want the message format to be BBcode or HTML. Anonymous posting, subscribe by default, flags, and ratings are selected by default and the default message format is BBcode.

Enabling *Allow Anonymous Posting* allows users without an account on the system to post messages to your message boards. Whether or not you you'll want to do this depends on the type of community you are building. Allowing anonymous posting opens your site to anyone who might want to spam your forums with unwanted or off topic advertising messages. For this reason, most of those who implement message boards turn anonymous posting off by unchecking this box.

Enabling the *Subscribe by Default* option automatically subscribes users to threads they participate in. Whenever a message in a thread is added or updated, Liferay sends a notification email to each user who is subscribed to the thread.

You can set the *Message Format* to either BBCode or HTML. This determines the markup language of users' actual message board posts. Different WYSIWYG editors are presented to users depending on which option is enabled. Both editors have a *Source* button which allows users to view the underlying BBCode or HTML of a message. Users can compose messages using either the WYSIWYG or Source view and can switch between views during message composition by clicking on the *Source* button.

Enabling *Enable Flags* allows your users to flag content which they consider to be objectionable. If you are allowing anonymous posting, you might use flags in combination with it if you have someone administering your message boards on a day-to-day basis. That way, any unwanted messages can be flagged by your community, and you can review those flagged messages and take whatever action is necessary. Using flags is also a good practice even if you're not allowing anonymous posting.

Enabling *Enable Ratings* enables your users to give certain posts a score. This score is used by Liferay Portal's social activity system to rank your site members by how helpful their contributions are. You can read more about social activity later in this chapter and in chapter 9.

Enabling the *Thread as Question by Default* option automatically checks the mark as question box in the new thread window. Threads marked as questions display the flag "waiting for an answer." Subsequent replies to the original message can be marked as an answer.

Email From

This tab allows you to configure the name and email address from which message board email notifications are sent. The default name and email address are those of the default administrator account: the name is `Test Test` and the email address is `test@liferay.com`. Make sure to update this email address to a valid one that can be dedicated to notifications.

Message Added Email

This tab allows you to customize the email message that users receive when a message is added to a topic to which they are subscribed.

Enabled: allows you to turn on the automatic emails to subscribed users. Uncheck the box to disable the message added emails.

Subject Prefix: lets you choose a prefix to be prepended to the subject line of the email. This is usually done so that users can set up message filters to filter the notifications to a specific folder in their email clients.

Body: allows you to write some content that should appear in the body of the email.

Signature: lets you add some content to appear as the signature of the email.

Below the fields is a section called *Definition of Terms* which defines certain variables which you can use in the fields above to customize the email message. Some of these variables are for the message board category name, the site name, and more.

Message Updated Email

The Message Updated Email tab is identical to the Message Added Email tab, except it defines the email message that users receive whenever a topic is updated.

Thread Priorities

You can define custom priorities for message threads on this tab. These allow administrators to tag certain threads with certain priorities in order to highlight them for users. By default, three priorities are defined: Urgent, Sticky, and Announcement. To define a thread priority, enter its name, a URL to the image icon that represents it, and a priority number which denotes the order in which that priority should appear.

There is also a field on this form that allows you to select a localized language for your priorities. If you need to do this, you can select the language from the selection box.

User Ranks

On this tab, users can be ranked according to the number of messages they have posted. You can set up custom ranks here. Defaults have been provided for you, going from zero messages all the way up to one thousand.

In addition to ranks, you can also choose labels for certain users to have displayed in their profiles as shown by the Message Boards application. These labels correspond to memberships these users have in your portal. Below are examples of using the label *Moderator*. The Moderator label in this configuration is applied for anyone who is a part of any of the Message Boards Administrator groups: the site role, the organization, the organization role, the regular role, or the user group. Of course, you probably wouldn't want to create a role, organization, organization role, site role, and user group all with the same name in your portal, but you get the idea.

```
Moderator=site-role:Message Boards Administrator

Moderator=organization:Message Boards Administrator

Moderator=organization-role:Message Boards Administrator

Moderator=regular-role:Message Boards Administrator

Moderator=user-group:Message Boards Administrator
```

As you can see, all you need to do is set the rank, the collection type, and the name of the type. In the example above, anyone who has a site role, an organization role, a regular role, or is in a user group called *Message Boards Administrator*, or anyone who is the organization owner gets the moderator rank.

As with thread priorities, on this tab you can define whether your ranks are localized in a particular language.

RSS

Message board threads can be published as RSS feeds. This tab allows you to define how the feeds are generated.

Maximum Items to Display: lets you select the number of items to display in the feed.

Display Style: lets you select the style. You can publish the full content, an abstract, or just the title of a thread.

Format: allows you to choose the format: RSS 1.0, RSS 2.0, or Atom 1.0.

Permissions

The default page that the Message Boards portlet displays has three buttons on it. Click the one labeled *Permissions*. This allows you to define which roles have the ability to add a category of threads or to ban abusive users from the message boards. Select the roles and permissions you want to configure and then click *Submit*.

Adding Categories

You are now ready to add categories to your message boards. Click the *Add Category* button. You may merge with a Parent Category by enabling the *Merge with Parent Category* check box and clicking the *Select* button. Enter a name for the category and a description of the category.

Starting with Liferay 6.1, categories can have different display styles. The available categories must be set in portal property `message.boards.category.display.styles` and the default category in `message.boards.category.display.styles.default`. When creating a new category, you can select the display style you like for that category. By default, Liferay provides two predefined display styles, although many more can be easily added:

Default: classic display style for general purpose and discussions.

Question: designed for discussions in a format of questions and answers.

You can add as many categories to your message boards as you wish. As we saw above, categories can have subcategories. You can add any number of top-level categories to a message board. You can also edit any category and add subcategories to an unlimited level. For usability reasons, you don't want to nest your categories too deep, or your users will have trouble finding them. You can always add more categories as your message boards grow. Finally, each category can have any number of threads.

At the bottom of the form for creating or editing a message board category is a check box for enabling the mailing list function. If don't want to add a mailing list to the category you're creating, click *Save* now. You can always edit an existing category to add, edit, or remove a mailing list.

Figure 7.23: Editing a Message Boards Category

Liferay's Message Boards portlet supports two different mechanisms for sending email notifications: user subscriptions and mailing lists. Let's discuss user subscriptions first and then mailing lists.

User Subscriptions and Mailing Lists

The first mechanism Liferay uses for sending email notifications is user subscriptions. Users can subscribe to particular categories and threads. Liferay uses the message board's configured *Email From* address to send email notifications to subscribed users whenever a new post is created or an existing post is updated. Liferay can import email replies to message board notifications directly into the message board. This is a very useful features since it allows users to interact on the message board via email without needing to log in to the portal and view the message board page directly. However, this feature is not enabled by default. To enable this feature, add the following line to your `portal-ext.properties` file:

```
pop.server.notifications.enabled=true
```

As this property suggests, Liferay's message boards user subscription mechanism uses the POP mail protocol. When an email reply to a message board notification is read by Liferay, the reply is posted to the message board and then deleted from the mail server. Deleting the message from the mail server is the POP protocol's default behavior and Liferay assumes that your POP mail server behaves this way. Most POP clients offer an option to leave mail on the mail server after it's been downloaded but you shouldn't exercise this option. If you configure mail to be left on the mail server, Liferay will repeatedly send copies of each retained message along with each new email notification that's sent to subscribed users.

When enabling message boards to import replies to email notifications, you should decide whether or not you want to you a mail server subdomain to handle notifications. By default the following line is set in your portal properties:

```
pop.server.subdomain=events
```

This property creates a special MX (mail exchange) subdomain to receive all portal-related email (e.g., events.liferay.com). If you don't want to use the subdomain approach, you can unset this value to tell Liferay to use the *Email From* address specified in the portlet preferences to receive message board notification email replies. For example, the *Email From* address could be set to *replies@liferay.com*.

If you don't want to use a mail server subdomain, add the following line to your `portal-ext.properties` file:

```
pop.server.subdomain=
```

If you're not using a mail subdomain, Liferay parses the message headers of emails from the *Email From* address to determine the message board category and message ID. If you keep the `pop.server.subdomain=events` default, the email notification address takes the following form:

```
mb.[category_id][message_id]@events.liferay.com
```

In this case, Liferay parses the email address to find the category and message ID. Parsing the email address is safer than parsing message headers since different email clients treat message headers differently. This is why the `events` subdomain is enabled by default.

Additionally, you can configure the interval on which the `POPNotifica-tionListener` runs. The value is set in one minute increments. The default setting is to check for new mail every minute, but you can set it to whatever you like:

```
pop.server.notifications.interval=1
```

The second mechanism Liferay uses for sending email notifications is mailing lists. Any category in a Liferay message board can have its own mailing list. Liferay's mailing list mechanism, unlike its user subscription mechanism, supports both the POP and the IMAP protocols. POP is the default protocol but each message board's mailing list is configured independently. If you choose the IMAP protocol for a category's mailing list, make sure to configure the IMAP inbox to delete messages as they are pulled by the email client that sends messages to the users on the mailing list. Otherwise, each email message that's retained on the server is sent to the mailing list each time there's a new post or an update in the category.

When a mailing list is enabled for a message board category, Liferay listens to the specific email inbox that's configured for the mailing list. Enabling the mailing list function allows users on the mailing list to simply reply to the notification messages in their email clients. Liferay pulls the messages from the email inbox it's configured to listen to and automatically copies those replies to the appropriate message board thread.

With both user subscriptions and mailing lists, users can reply to message board notification emails and Liferay imports their replies to the message board. However, with mailing lists, users reply to the mailing list and Liferay listens to the specific inbox configured for the mailing list and copies messages to the appropriate message board category. With user subscriptions, by default, email replies to message board notifications are not imported to the message boards. This feature has to be enabled in your `portal-ext.properties` file. Once this feature has been enabled, users can reply to a specific address and have their replies copied to the message board.

Note: Since any number of sites can use a globally scoped message board, globally scoped message boards do not support user subscriptions or mailing lists. Make sure to use a site-scoped or page-scoped message board if you need user subscriptions or a mailing list with your message board.

To enable the mailing list functionality for a category, you need a dedicated email address for the category. Once you click the *Active* check box, a number of other options appear. When a mailing list is activated, Liferay imports messages it receives from the mailing list to the message board. Liferay looks for a Liferay user with the sender's email address. If the sender isn't a Liferay user and the *Allow Anonymous Emails* box is unchecked, the message is thrown away and not posted to the message board. If the *Allow Anonymous Emails* box is checked, anyone can send email to the message board category's dedicated email account and Liferay copies the messages to the message board.

Email Address: lets you enter the email address of the account that will receive the messages.

Next, there are two sections: *Incoming* and *Outgoing*. These define the mail settings for receiving mail and for sending mail. The Incoming tab has the following options:

Protocol: lets you select POP or IMAP.

Server Name: lets you enter the host name of the mail server you are using.

Server Port: allows you to specify the port on which your mail service is running.

Use a Secure Network Connection: lets you use an encrypted connection if your server supports it.

User Name: lets you enter the login name on the mail server.

Password: lets you enter the password for the account on the server.

Read Interval (Minutes): allows you to specify how often Liferay will poll the server looking for new messages to post to the message board.

The Outgoing section has the following options:

Email Address: lets you enter the email address that messages from this category should come from. If you want your users to be able to reply to the categories using email, this should be the same address configured on the *Incoming* tab.

Use Custom Outgoing Server: allows you to use a different mail server than the one that is configured for the portal. If you check this box, more options appear.

Server Name: lets you enter the host name of the SMTP mail server you are using.

Server Port: allows you to specify the port on which your mail service is running.

Use a Secure Network Connection: allows you to use an encrypted connection if your server supports it.

User Name: lets you enter the login name on the mail server.

Password: lets you enter the password for the account on the mail server.

When you're finished configuring the mailing list for your category, click *Save*.

Using the Message Boards

Upon seeing Liferay's Message Boards portlet, your users will immediately recognize that the interface is similar to many other implementations they've seen before. Message boards are nothing new to the Internet, and many people have been using them for quite a long time. For that reason, Liferay's message boards will seem very familiar to your users.

Threads can be viewed in many ways. At the top of the portlet is a set of tabs: *Recent posts*, *My Posts*, *My Subscriptions*, and for administrative users, *Statistics* and *Banned Users*. The Recent Posts tab shows all posts from all categories by date, so you can keep up on all the most recent discussions in the message boards. The My Posts tab shows all of the posts for the user that is currently logged in. This is a convenient way to get back to a previous conversation in order to retrieve some pertinent information. The My Subscriptions tab allows a user to manage thread subscriptions. If you lose interest in a particular topic, you may want to visit this tab and unsubscribe from a thread.

For administrators, the Statistics tab shows the number of categories, the number of posts, and the number of participants in your message boards. It also has a list of who the top posters to your message boards are. The Banned Users tab shows all of the users who have been banned from posting on the message boards.

Posting New Threads

To post a new thread simply select the *Post New Thread* button. You will see a message editing form. The body field on this form is different from that of the other portlets in Liferay. The reason for this is to support *BBCode*, which is a standard form of markup used in many message board products. Before BBCode was invented, many message board products would allow users to enter HTML to format their messages. This, however, enabled attackers to insert malicious code into the message board. BBCode was invented to provide users a way of formatting their messages without allowing them to enter HTML. Similarly, Liferay supports BBCode in the message boards portlet because the other editor–which is used for the Content Management System, the Blogs portlet, and other portlets–produces HTML. This is appropriate for those other portlets, as they are only used by privileged users, but it is not appropriate for the message boards. Besides this, many users of message boards are familiar with BBCode and are used to it, and the editor that is provided for Liferay's Message Boards portlet makes it very easy to use.

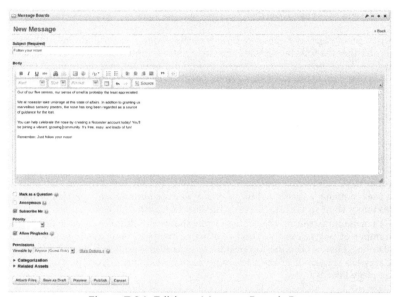

Figure 7.24: Editing a Message Boards Post

The message boards editor is quite rich. It supports bold, italicized, under-lined, and crossed-out text, links, images, colors, lists, tables, alignments, quo-tation blocks, code blocks, different fonts and font sizes, and more. There are even a bunch of smiley faces that you can use.

Users who have Moderator access to the board can modify the priority of messages. You can also use the editor to quote from messages that you are replying to, to insert emoticons, to add preformatted text, and more. Messages that are posted to the message boards are shown by default in a threaded view so that replies are attached to the proper parent message. This makes it easy to follow along with conversations.

When viewing a message board thread, users are given several options. At the top right of the thread are three icons, allowing users to view threads in a flat view, in a tree view, or in a combination view. A flat view shows all of the messages in the order in which they are posted. A tree view shows all of the

Figure 7.25: Emoticons Available in the Editor

messages in a threaded view, so that replies are next to the messages they are replying to. A combination view shows the threads at the top as subjects only, with the flat view underneath.

When viewing a thread, users can click links allowing them to post a new thread, subscribe to the thread they are viewing, or if they have administrative access, lock a thread or move a thread to another category. Subscribing to a thread causes Liferay to send the user an email whenever a new message is posted to the thread. If you have enabled the mailing list feature for the category in which the thread resides, users can simply reply to these messages in order to post back to the thread, without having to visit your site.

The Message Boards portlet is also highly integrated with Liferay's user management features. Posts on the message board show users' pictures if they have uploaded one for themselves, as well as the dates that users created an ID on your site.

Message Board Administrative Functions

The Message Boards portlet provides for the day to day administration of the message threads. You may wish to separate this function out by a role, and then delegate that role to one or more of your users. That would free you up to concentrate on other areas of your web site. To do this, you can create a role called Message Board Administrators. This role can be scoped by the portal, an organization, or a site. If you have a portal scoped role, members of this role will be able to administer any Message Boards portlet in the portal. If it is an organization or site scoped role, members of this role will be able to administer a Message Boards portlet in only the organization or site which assigned the role to them.

Go to the Control Panel and create this role. Once it is created, click *Actions → Define Permissions*. Click the *Add Permissions* dropdown list. Browse the list until you find the Message Boards portlet under the Site Content section and then click on it. You will then see a screen which allows you to configure the various permissions on the portlet.

Select the permissions you would like message board administrators to have and then click *Save*. You can add users to this role and they will inherit the permissions. Message Board administrators can perform all of the functions we have already presented, including creating and deleting categories and posting threads. In addition to these, a number of other functions are available.

Moving Threads

Many times a user will post a thread in the wrong category. Administrators may in this case want to move a thread to the proper category. This is very easy to do. You can select the *Actions* menu to the right of the thread and choose *Move Thread*. Or, if you are already viewing the thread and you have administrative access, there is a link at the top of the thread labeled *Move Thread*. Click this link. You will be presented with a simple form which allows you to select a category to which to move the thread and a check box which allows you to post a message explaining why the thread was moved. This message will be posted as a reply to the thread you are moving. When finished, click the *Move Thread* button and the thread will be moved.

Deleting Threads

Users with administrative access to the message boards can delete threads. Sometimes users begin discussing topics that are inappropriate or that reveal confidential information. In this case, you can simply delete the thread from the message boards. This is easy to do. First, view the list of threads. Next to every thread is an *Actions* button. Click *Actions → Delete* to delete the thread. This

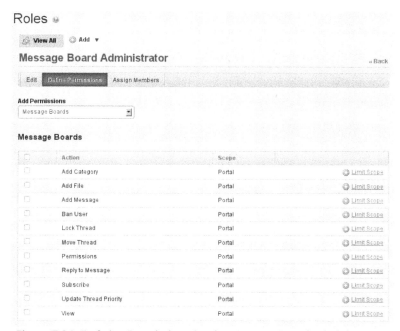

Figure 7.26: Defining Permissions for the Message Board Administrators Role

does not prevent users from re-posting the information, so you may need to be vigilant in deleting threads or consider the next option.

Banning Users

Unfortunately, sometimes certain users become abusive. If you wind up with a user like this, you can certainly make attempts to warn him or her that the behavior he or she is displaying is unacceptable. If this does not work, you can ban the user from posting on the message boards.

Again, this is very easy to do. Find any post which was written by the abusive user. Underneath the user's name/profile picture is a link called *Ban this User.*

Click this link to ban the user from the message boards.

If after taking this action the user apologizes and agrees to stop his or her abusive behavior, you can choose to reinstate the user. To do this, click the *Banned Users* tab at the top of the Message Boards portlet. This will show a list of all banned users. Find the user in the list and select *Unban this User*.

Splitting Threads

Sometimes a thread will go on for a while and the discussion completely changes into something else. In this case, you can split the thread where the discussion diverges and create a whole new thread for the new topic. Administrative users will see a *Split Thread* link on each post. To split the thread, click the link. You will be brought to a form which allows you to add an explanation post to the split thread. Click *Ok* to split the thread.

Editing Posts

Administrative users can edit anyone's posts, not just their own. Sometimes users will post links to copyrighted material or unsuitable pictures. You can edit these posts, which allows you to redact information that should not be posted or to censor profanity that is not allowed on your message boards.

Permissions

Permissions can be set not only on threads, but also on individual posts. You can choose to limit a particular conversation or a post to only a select group of people. To do this, click the *Permissions* link on the post and then select among the *Delete, Permissions, Subscribe, Update, and View* permissions for the particular role to which you want to grant particular access. This function can be used, for example, to allow some privileged users to post on a certain thread, while others are only allowed to view it. Other combinations of the above permissions are also possible. Next, let's discuss Liferay's Wiki portlet.

7.5   Working together with the Wiki

Liferay's Wiki portlet, like the Message Boards portlet, is a full-featured wiki application which has all of the features you would expect in a state of the art wiki. Again, though, it has the benefit of being able to take advantage of all of the features of the Liferay platform. As such, it is completely integrated with Liferay's user management, tagging, and security features.

So, what is a wiki? Basically, a wiki is an application which allows users to collaboratively build a repository of information. There are, of course, many implementations of this idea, the most famous of which is Wikipedia. Wikipedia is a full online encyclopedia developed collaboratively by users from all over the world, using a wiki. Another example would be Liferay's wiki, which is used for collaborative documentation of the Community Edition of Liferay Portal.

A wiki application allows users to create and edit documents and link them to each other. To accomplish this, a special form of markup is used which is sometimes called wikitext. Unfortunately, the proliferation of many different wiki applications resulted in slightly different syntax for wikitext in the various products, as each new wiki tried to focus on new features that other wikis did not have. For that reason, a project called WikiCreole was started. This project resulted in the release of WikiCreole 1.0 in 2007, which is an attempt to define a standard wiki markup that all wikis can support.

Rather than define another wikitext syntax, Liferay's Wiki portlet supports WikiCreole as its syntax. This syntax is a best-of-breed wiki syntax and should be familiar to users of other wikis. The portlet provides a handy cheat sheet for the syntax on the page editing form, with a link to the full documentation if you wish to use some of WikiCreole's advanced features.

Getting Started with the Liferay Wiki

The Wiki portlet works just like the other portlets developed by Liferay. Add the portlet to a page using the *Add* → *More* menu and then click *Configuration* in the portlet menu in the Wiki portlet's title bar. You'll see some options are likely to be familiar to you by now such as sharing the application with websites, Facebook, Google Gadgets, etc. You will also notice that the communication tab has some additional options not seen in the other portlets.

The communication tab of the configuration window allows you to configure communication across portlets, using predefined public render parameters. From here you can modify six public render parameters: categoryId, nodeId, nodeName, resetCur, tag, and title. For each parameter you can:

- Ignore the values for this parameter that come from other portlets. For example, the wiki portlet can be used along with the tags navigation portlet. When a user clicks on a tag in the tags navigation portlet, the wiki shows a list of pages with that tag. In some cases an administrator may want the wiki portlet to always show the front page independently of

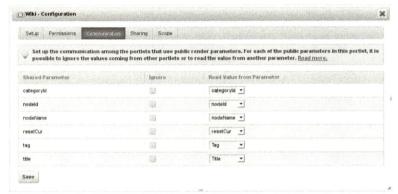

Figure 7.27: Communication Tab of the Wiki Portlet

any tag navigation done through other portlets. This can be achieved by checking the Ignore check box so that the values of the parameter coming from those other portlets are ignored.

- Read the value of a parameter from another portlet. This is an advanced but very powerful option that allows portlets to communicate without configuring it beforehand. For example, imagine that the wiki portlet is used to publish information about certain countries. Imagine further that a custom portlet that allows browsing countries for administrative reasons was written and placed on the same page. We could associate to this second portlet a public render parameter called *country* to designate the name of the country. Using this procedure, we can cause the wiki to show the information from the country being browsed through in the other portlet. You can do this here for the wiki by setting the value for the title parameter to be read from the country parameter of the other portlet.

Once you have set the options the way you want them, click *Save*.

Managing Wikis

The Wiki portlet can contain many wikis. By default, it contains only one, called *Main*. To manage Wikis, navigate to the *Control Panel* and select *Wiki*. This page allows you to add, modify, and delete wikis. The Main wiki has already been added for you.

At the top of this screen is a *Permissions* button. Clicking this allows you to define which roles have access to create wikis. If you have created a specific role for creating wikis, you can click the box in the *Add Node* column and then click *Submit*, and that role will have access to create new wikis in this portlet.

Clicking the *Add Wiki* button prompts you to enter a name and description for the new wiki. You can also set up some default permissions. When you create a new wiki, it appears in a list at the top of the main page of the Wiki portlet.

Next to each wiki in the list of wiki nodes is an *Actions* button. This button contains several options:

Edit: lets you edit the name and description of the wiki.

Permissions: lets you define what roles can add attachments to wiki pages, add pages to the wiki, delete pages, import pages to the wiki, set permissions on the wiki, subscribe to the wiki, update existing pages, and view the wiki.

Import Pages: allows you to import data from other wikis. This lets you migrate off of another wiki which you may be using and use the Liferay wiki instead. You might wish to do this if you are migrating your site from a set of disparate applications (i.e. a separate forum, a separate wiki, a separate content management system) to Liferay, which provides all of these features. Currently, MediaWiki is the only wiki that is supported, but others are likely to be supported in the future.

RSS: opens a new page where you can subscribe to an RSS feed using Live Bookmarks, Google, or Yahoo.

Subscribe: allows you to subscribe to a wiki node, and any time a page is added or updated Liferay will send you an email informing you what happened.

Delete: deletes the wiki node.

To go back to your wiki, click on its name in the list of wikis. Note that there is also a wrench icon leading to a configuration menu on this portlet in the Control Panel. This contains several other options which you may have seen on other portlets.

The *Email From*, *Page Added Email*, and *Page Updated Email* tabs are similar to the ones for notification email settings for other portlets, allowing you to customize who wiki emails come from and the format and text of the email that is sent when a page is added or updated.

The *Display Settings* tab gives you several options for how the wiki should be displayed. *Enable Related Assets*, *Enable Page Ratings*, *Enable Comments*, and *Enable Comment Ratings* are similar to the same options in other portlets. They give you the ability to set how you want users to interact with wiki documents:

a little, a lot, or not at all. Below this, you can set which wikis are visible in the Wiki portlet by default and which are hidden. You might host two wikis on a given site, exposing one to the public and keeping the other private for site members.

Finally, the Wiki portlet also supports RSS feeds as the other collaboration portlets do, and you can configure its options in the *RSS* tab.

Adding and Editing Wiki Pages

By default, there is one page added to your wiki, called *FrontPage*. To get started adding data to your wiki, click the *Edit* link at the top right of the portlet. You will be brought to a blank editing page.

Figure 7.28: Editing the Default Page in the Wiki Portlet

You can now begin to add content to the page. Notice that there is a very convenient "cheat sheet"? which can help with the wiki syntax. You can use this syntax to format your wiki pages. Consider, for example, the following wiki document:

```
== Welcome to Our Wiki! ==
\index{Wiki}

This is our new wiki, which should allow us to collaborate on
documentation. Feel free to add pages showing people how to do stuff.
Below are links to some sections that have already been added.

{[}{[}Introduction{]}{]}

{[}{[}Getting Started{]}{]}

{[}{[}Configuration{]}{]}

{[}{[}Development{]}{]}

{[}{[}Support{]}{]}

{[}{[}Community{]}{]}
```

This would produce the following wiki page:

This adds a simple heading, a paragraph of text, and several links to the page. Since the pages behind these links have not been created yet, clicking one of those links takes you to an editing screen to create the page. This editing screen looks just like the one you used previously when you wrote the front page. Liferay displays a notice at the top of the page stating that the page does not exist yet, and that you are creating it right now. As you can see, it is very easy to create wiki pages. All you have to do is create a link from an existing page. Note that at the top of the screen you can select from the Creole wiki format and the HTML editor that comes with Liferay. We recommend that you stick with the Creole format, as it allows for a much cleaner separation of content and code. If you want all of your users to use the Creole format, you can disable the HTML format using the `portal-ext.properties` file. See chapter 14 for details about how to configure this.

At the bottom of the page editing screen, you can select *Categories* for the article. Categories are hierarchical lists of headings under which you can create wiki pages. This allows you to organize your content in a more formal fashion. You can create categories using the Control Panel, in the *Categories* section.

Page Details

When viewing a page, you can view its details by clicking the *Details* link which appears in the top right of the page. This allows you to view many properties of the page. There are several tabs which organize all of the details into convenient categories.

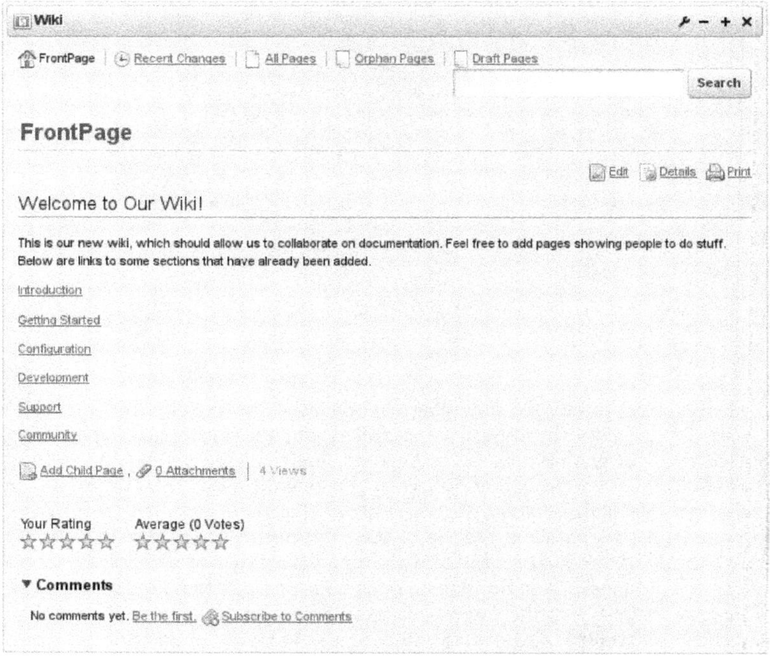

Figure 7.29: Wiki Text Added to Front Page

Details

The Details tab shows various statistics about the page, and also allows you to perform some actions on the page.

Title: displays the title of the page.

Format: displays the format for the page – either Creole or HTML.

Latest Version: displays the latest version of the page. The wiki portlet automatically keeps track of page versions whenever a page has been edited.

Created By: displays the user who created the page.

Last Changed By: displays the user who last modified the page.

Attachments: displays the number of attachments to the page.

RSS Subscription: displays links which allow you to subscribe to the page as an RSS feed in three formats: RSS 1.0, RSS 2.0, and Atom 1.0.

Email Subscription: contains links allowing you to subscribe to the entire wiki or just to this page.

Advanced Actions: contains links allowing you to modify the permissions on the page, make a copy of the page, move (rename) the page, or delete the page.

History

This tab shows a list of all of the versions of the wiki page since it was created. You can revert a page back to a previous state and you can also compare the differences between versions by selecting the versions and then clicking the *Compare Versions* button.

Incoming/Outgoing Links

The next two tabs are for incoming and outgoing links. These are wiki links to and from the page. You can use this tab to examine how this page links to other pages and how other pages link back to this page.

Attachments

The last tab is for attachments. You can attach any file to the wiki. This is mostly used to attach images to wiki articles which can then be referenced in the text. Referencing them using the proper WikiCreole syntax renders the image inline, which is a nice way to include illustrations in your wiki documents.

Navigating in the Wiki Portlet

At the top of the portlet is a list of links which allow you to navigate around the wiki. Next to the *Manage Wikis* button is a list of wikis that are currently created in the portlet. Simply click on the wiki's name to begin browsing that wiki. After this is a set of navigation links:

Recent Changes: takes you to a page which shows all of the recently updated pages.

All Pages: takes you to a flat, alphabetical list of all pages currently stored in the wiki.

Orphan Pages: takes you to a list of pages that have no links to them. This can happen if you take a link out of a wiki page in an edit without realizing it's the only link to a certain page. This area allows you to review wiki pages that are orphaned in this way so that you can re-link to them or delete them from the wiki if they are no longer relevant.

Draft Pages: takes you to a list of pages which have not yet been published. Users can edit pages and save their changes as drafts. They can come back later to finish their page changes and publish them once they have been approved.

Search: allows you to a term here and click the *Search* button to search for items in the wiki. If the search term is not found, a link will be displayed which allows you to create a new wiki page on the topic for which you searched.

The Wiki portlet is another full-featured Liferay application with all of the features you expect from a state of the art wiki. Next, we'll look at how Liferay handles live chat.

7.6   Find out what others think or do using Polls

How well do you know your users? Do you ever wonder what they're thinking? Is using your site easy for them? How do they feel about the hot-button issues of the day? Do they prefer dogs over cats? What about the new policy that management wants to implement? What's their favorite ice cream flavor? When you use Liferay's Polls feature you can find out the answer to these and other questions that should help you better understand your users.

There are two portlets involved in making and displaying a poll: the Polls portlet, which is accessed through the Control Panel, and the Polls Display portlet, which can be added to any page in the portal.

The Polls portlet helps you set up the poll question and the possible answers users can select. The Polls Display portlet is an instanceable portlet that lets you select which poll to display, and is the portlet you put on the page so users can vote.

The Polls portlet allows users and administrators to create multiple choice polls that keep track of the votes and display results on the page. Many separate polls can be managed; a separate portlet called Polls Display can be configured to display a specific poll's questions and results.

The Polls Display Portlet allows users to vote for a specific poll's questions and see the results. Questions must be created from the Polls portlet in the Control Panel. You can display one question at a time or you can combine several questions inside a nested portlet to create a survey.

We'll begin by creating a poll in the Control Panel.

Creating a Poll

In the Control Panel, navigate to the *Polls* link under Content. Click the *Add Question* button. A form appears that allows you to fill out all the information for your poll.

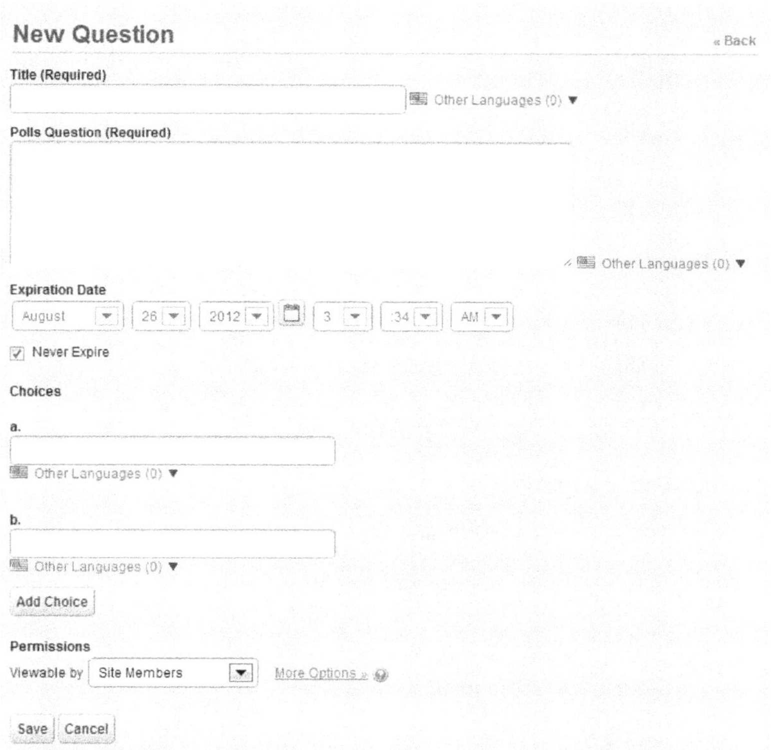

Figure 7.30: Besides the Title and the Polls Question, you must enter data for each of the Choices fields when creating a new poll.

Title: Enter the name of the poll question.

Polls Question: Enter the text of the poll question.

Expiration Date: Enter the date and time you want the poll to expire.

Choices: Enter at least two answer options for the poll question.

Add Choice: Enter additional answer options for the poll question.

Permissions: Manage who can view and edit the poll.

When you have finished creating your poll, click *Save*, and it is added to the Polls portlet.

As more polls are created in the Control Panel, they become accessible through the Polls Display portlet until they are either deleted or they expire. You can set an expiration date for a poll by selecting the day and time in the Add Poll form or in the New Question form. The default is set to *Never Expire*.

When a poll expires, users can't enter votes any more, but if a Polls Display portlet is still publishing it, the poll results are displayed on the page. To remove an expired poll from a page, remove the Poll Display portlet or configure it to show another poll question. See the section below for more details about the Polls Display portlet.

Permissions can be set on individual polls as they are set elsewhere in Liferay Portal. Permissions can be used, for example, to allow some privileged users to vote on a certain poll question, while others can only view it. For further information about permissions, please see chapters 15 and 16.

As you can see, creating a poll is fairly straightforward. Next, let's complete the two-step process and put your poll on a page.

Adding a Poll to a Page

Now that you have created your poll question, it's time to present it to your users. Navigate to your portal and add the Polls Display portlet to a page. It is available from the *Content Management* section of the *Add → More* menu.

The Polls Display portlet may look strange when it first appears on your page. That's because it's not configured. Before visitors to your site can use the poll, they must be able to access it. Click on the link labelled *Please configure this portlet to make it visible to all users*, and a dialog box like the one below appears.

Under the Setup tab is a menu option labeled *Question*. Selecting this option displays the name of the poll you created. Choose it, click *Save*, and it is displayed on the page. That, in a nutshell, is how you create a poll, but there is another way to add a question to the Polls Display portlet.

Start by navigating to your portal and placing the Polls Display portlet on a page. Using the icons in the lower left of the portlet, choose the *Add Question*

Polls Display - Configuration
Setup
Permissions
Sharing
Archive/Restore Setup
Question
Save

Figure 7.31: In the initial configuration of the Polls Display portlet, the Question field will remain blank until you select the appropriate poll question.

button. A new form appears that lets you create another question. When you are done filling out the form, click *Save* and you new poll appears on the page.

Once the poll question has been successfully placed on the page, you can perform other tasks by using the icons in the lower left corner of the portlet. Besides adding questions, you can also edit the currently selected question or select existing questions.

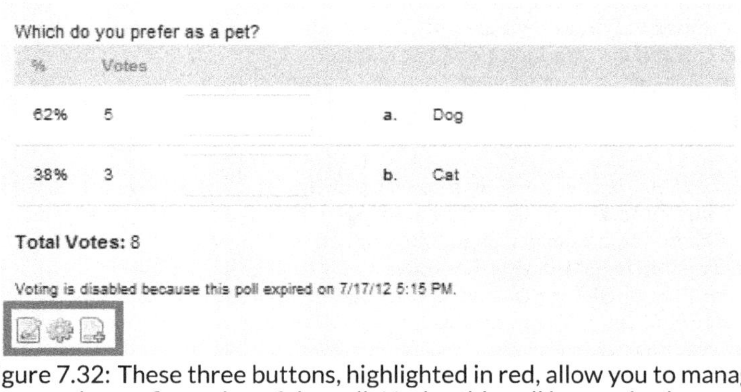
Which do you prefer as a pet?
% Votes
62% 5 a. Dog
38% 3 b. Cat
Total Votes: 8
Voting is disabled because this poll expired on 7/17/12 5:15 PM.

Figure 7.32: These three buttons, highlighted in red, allow you to manage the configuration of the poll. Notice this poll has expired.

Edit Question: Displays a similar dialog box to the one used to create the poll.

Select Question: Displays the same dialog box as Configuration, allowing you to choose different questions from the dropdown menu.

Add Question: Allows you to create a new question.

You can also manage the Polls Display portlet by clicking the wrench symbol in the upper right corner of the portlet's title bar. Now let's see the poll results.

Viewing the Poll Results

When you create a poll question, it appears in a list in the Control Panel. After users vote in the poll, the data is collected here. If you select it, the name and the question, as well as a breakdown of the poll results appears, including percentages and total number of votes per answer and the total number of votes cast.

Below this is an item called *Charts*. This option shows the poll results represented in various graphs. The graphs are *Area*, *Horizontal Bar*, *Line*, *Pie* and *Vertical Bar*.

There is also a listing of the users who voted in your poll, how they voted, and a time/date stamp of when their votes were cast. Registered users are represented by their screen name while Guest users are represented by a number.

With Liferay Polls you can do many things. You can ask users very specific questions or you can use Polls to create a little fun for your community. As with most things in Liferay, you are only limited by your imagination. Now let's see what you can do with Liferay's Chat feature.

7.7   Staying in touch with the Chat

Liferay's Chat portlet provides a convenient way of allowing users to send each other instant messages when they are logged into your web site. It appears as a bar at the bottom of every page, showing who is logged on, their statuses, and any chats the logged-in user has open.

The Chat portlet is distributed with the Liferay bundles, but is not included as part of the `.war` distribution, as it is a separate plugin. If you installed the Liferay `.war` manually on your application server, you can install the Chat portlet by going to the Control Panel, clicking *Plugins Installation*, and then clicking the *Install More Portlets* button. Find the Chat portlet in the list, click on it, and then click *Install*.

The Chat portlet is very simple to use. To change the settings, click *Settings* (found near the lower right corner next to *Online Friends*). Here you can set your status, choose whether or not to show that you are online, and whether or not to play a sound if someone sends you a message while you have the window

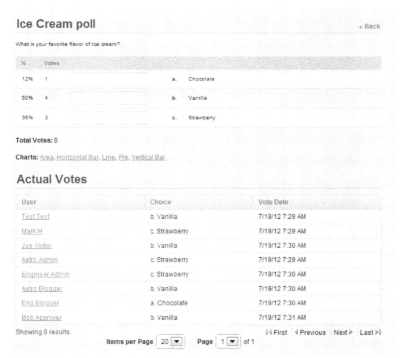

Figure 7.33: Selecting a poll in the Polls portlet allows you to see all the information related to the poll results.

Vote Results

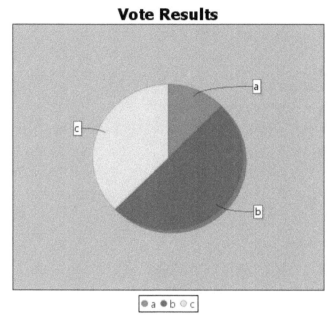

Figure 7.34: This is what the pie chart for the Ice Cream poll results looks like.

or tab in the background. The Chat portlet displays the number of your friends who are online. Click the *Online Friends* link and then click on a friend's name to open a chat window. You can have multiple chats open at a time, and can have one or more of them minimized.

Jabber Server Integration

Liferay 6.1 introduced Jabber server integration to Liferay's Chat portlet. Jabber is the original name of the XMPP (Extensible Messaging and Presence Protocol) protocol, an open-standard communications protocol based on XML. Using a chat server helps Liferay's chat scale to very large installations and allows for

Figure 7.35: Liferay's Chat Portlet

communication between different chat clients. For example, Jabber server integration allows users using the chat portlet in their browser windows to chat with other users using desktop clients like Empathy, Pidgin, or Kopete.

Jabber server integration is not enabled by default since it requires a running Jabber server. Once you have installed and started a Jabber server, you can enable Jabber server integration by creating a `portlet-ext.properties` file to override some properties of your Chat portlet's `portlet.properties` file. You could modify your Chat portlet's `portlet.properties` file directly, but it's a best practice to override it instead.

Installation Steps

You can use any chat server that supports Jabber. The Chat portlet's Jabber server integration feature was tested with versions 3.7.0 and 3.7.1 of Openfire, a real time collaboration server distributed under the Open Source Apache License. You can download Openfire from the web site[1]. To enable Jabber chat integration, follow these steps:

---

[1]http://www.igniterealtime.org/projects/openfire/

1. Start your chat server. If you are using Openfire on a Linux/Mac system, you can start/stop the chat server by executing the openfire shell script in the `openfire/bin` directory. Usage: `./openfire start` or `./openfire stop`

2. Override the `portlet.properties` file in your /chat-portlet/WEB-INF/src/ directory with a `portlet-ext.properties` file in the same directory. When you deploy the portlet, the properties files should be copied to your /chat-portlet/WEB-INF/classes/ directory. If you have already deployed the Chat portlet, create the `portlet-ext.properties` file in your /chat-portlet/WEB-INF/classes/ directory. The contents of your `portlet-ext.properties` file should like this:

```
jabber.enabled=true
jabber.import.user.enabled=true
jabber.host=localhost
jabber.port=5222
jabber.service.name=<Host Name>
jabber.resource=Liferay
jabber.sock5.proxy.enabled=false
jabber.sock5.proxy.port=-1
```

Note that you must change `jabber.service.name` to the "Host Name". If you are using Openfire, you can find the Host Name by using the Openfire administration web tool. If you did not set up administrative credentials when you started Openfire, the default credentials are username: admin, password: admin.

Additionally, make sure that you set `jabber.enabled` to `true` and have added the correct values to `jabber.host` and `jabber.port`. If you installed your chat server on a remote machine or chose to not use the default port, change `jabber.host` and `jabber.port` accordingly.

3. Deploy your Chat portlet. Remember that this portlet must be of version 6.1 or higher.

Single Sign On

If the property `jabber.import.user.enabled` is set to `true`, the Chat portlet will import the user automatically to Jabber after he logs in to the portal. Once the user is imported, he can use any Jabber client using the same screen name and password he uses to log in to the portal. His buddies will be also imported as they become online in the Chat portlet.

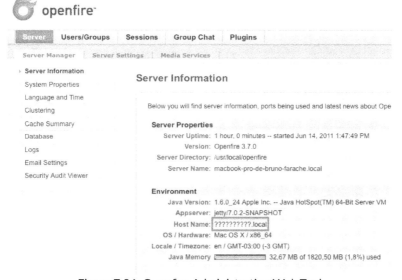

Figure 7.36: Openfire Administration Web Tool

Note that it's a "lazy import". Users are imported only after they log in to the portal and their buddies will be added to his list only if they see each other within the Chat portlet. They won't be able to use other Jabber chat clients until they log in to the portal.

If `jabber.import.user.enabled` is set to `false`, users need to create their Jabber account and add buddies manually. They have to create their accounts using the same screen name and password they use in the portal. If they don't, the Chat portlet won't be able to connect to their Jabber account.

Alternatively, since Openfire integrates with LDAP, if you are using Openfire and your portal is also using LDAP for authentication, you can disable the `jabber.import.user.enabled` property.

Next, let's look at how you can integrate your email addresses with Liferay's Mail portlet.

7.8   Integrating your email with Liferay Mail

Liferay's Mail portlet enables your users to interact with their email using an easy to use, ubiquitous web interface. If your mail system supports the IMAP protocol, you can use the Mail portlet to integrate your users' mail with the rest of your web site. You can also connect the Mail portlet to a mail account provided by Google.

The Mail portlet is distributed with the Liferay bundles, but is not included as part of the .war distribution, as it is a separate plugin. If you installed the Liferay .war manually on your application server, you can install the Mail portlet by going to the Control Panel, clicking *Plugins Installation*, and then clicking the *Install More Portlets* button. Find the *Mail* portlet in the list, click on it, and then click *Install.*

Figure 7.37: Liferay's Mail Portlet

To connect the Mail portlet with an email account, click the *Add a New Email Account* link. From there, you are given a choice between a Custom email Account or a Gmail Account. Choose the option that you wish, and fill out the form that appears.

For a Gmail account, all you need to do is provide your email address and your password, and the portlet will take care of the rest.

For a Custom Mail Account, the following fields are necessary:

Address: lets you enter the email address which receives mail for this account.

Login: lets you choose a user name for logging into the account.

Password: lets you choose a password for logging into the account.

Incoming Settings: allows you to specify the host name for your IMAP (Internet Mail Access Protocol) or POP server.

Incoming Port: allows you to specify the port upon which the IMAP or POP service is running.

Use Secure Incoming Connection: allows you to use an encrypted connection to the server provided that your server supports it.

Outgoing SMTP Server: lets you enter the host name of your SMTP (Simple Mail Transfer Protocol) server.

Outgoing Port: allows you to specify the port upon which the SMTP service is running.

Use Secure Outgoing Connection: allows you to use an encrypted connection to the server provided that your server supports it.

When finished, click *Save*. Your new email account now appears as a tab at the top of the page along with the button for adding a mail account. In this way, you can add as many mail accounts as you want in order to view them in the portlet.

Click the tab for the mail account you just configured to be brought to an interface which allows you to read your mail and compose new messages. To read a message, click on it. To compose a new message, click the *Compose Email* link on the left side of the portlet. A form appears which allows you to compose an email message using the same rich text editor that appears everywhere else in Liferay. You can read, reply, and create messages, as well as manage all of your folders in Liferay's Mail portlet.

The Mail portlet is a great way to integrate a familiar service with other the collaboration features that Liferay provides.

7.9 Summary

We have explored many of the portlets in Liferay's collaboration suite. You have seen how you can configure all of the portlets in a similar fashion using a unified user interface. After this, we went over all of the portlets in succession.

The Blogs and Blogs Aggregation portlets can be used to manage shared blogs or blogs belonging to a group of people at once. These portlets have all the features you would want in a blog, including rich text editing, links to news aggregators, tags, RSS feeds, and more.

The Calendar portlet likewise can be used to manage a shared calendar or a group calendar. It includes features for events, event notification, repeatable events, and import and export to and from the standard iCalendar format.

Discussion becomes easy with Liferay's Message Boards portlet. This portlet can be used to manage heavily trafficked discussion forums with ease. It inherits all of the security features of the Liferay platform and includes administrative functions for thread priorities, moving threads, nested discussion categories, banning users, and more.

Liferay's Wiki portlet is a state of the art wiki application that users can make use of to collaborate on web pages. Again, it inherits the strengths of the Liferay platform in the form of security, interface, and search. You can use the wiki portlet to manage several wiki nodes or use many wiki portlets to manage one node each.

The Polls portlet is a fun way to interact with users of your site to get an understanding of what they're thinking at any given time. It allows you to create multiple choice polls that keep track of the votes and display results on the page. You can view these results in a number of ways, including charts.

Liferay provides a chat solution for your portal that's very easy to use. It allows logged-in users to see who else is logged in to the portal and view their status. Users can go invisible if they don't want others to know that they're online. Users can chat with each other via instant messages. You can also set up a Jabber chat server and configure Liferay to use it; this allows users who have logged in to your portal via their browsers to chat with users using traditional desktop clients.

Integrating mail with your portal is easy with the Mail portlet. You can add as many custom or Gmail mail accounts as you wish, and this portlet can keep them all organized in one place, together with the rest of the things Liferay is aggregating for you.

Liferay's collaboration platform is a full suite of integrated applications that empower users to work together. You can use them to great effect to enhance your portal and to build a vibrant, active community.

CHAPTER 8

SOCIAL NETWORKING

Since the first social networks rose to popularity, concepts such as *Friend* and later *Like*—previously reserved for direct human interaction—have taken on new meaning in an always-online, information driven culture. It could be argued that social networks have transformed the way people interact with their friends, relatives and colleagues. Friends, connections, followers, circles and lists have enabled people to connect and stay connected in ways they'd never been able to before. Initially, these concepts proved to be highly successful for casual web sites but they didn't take to the business world as quickly. But many organizations are now realizing the importance of leveraging social interactions for more than just recreation. Liferay's robust social features make it a great platform for business web sites, casual web sites and everything in between.

Social applications have many differences when compared to Standard applications that are vital to a social networking site. Standard applications have general and user specific data, whereas social applications can share data within a defined network. This variation is a huge advantage when trying to communicate important information to a large group of people. This difference in communication settings is illustrated below:

Liferay has a constantly improving set of social features which enable you to encourage social interactions on your own portal and to leverage the power and popularity of other social networks. In this chapter, we'll discuss:

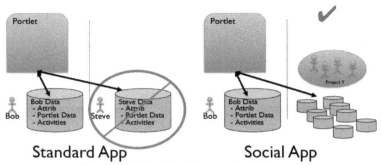

Standard App   Social App

Figure 8.1: Standard Apps vs. Social Apps

- General use social portlets
- Social portlets for personal pages
- Configuring personal pages for social networking
- How to connect users using Liferay social relations
- Social equity
- Integrating Liferay with other social sites

When we're finished, you'll be well equipped to use Liferay to power your social network.

8.1 Leveraging Social Portlets, Activities Tracking and User Connections

Liferay has many portlets available for social interaction and collaboration. Some of these portlets are designed to help you work together as a team, while others are designed to foster social interactions between team members at your organization.

Some of the social portlets should be used on the public pages of your portal, while others should be used as part of a user's personal site. As you might guess, the portlets for personal page use are more focused on simple social interactions, while the ones which can be placed on any site help improve productivity.

Unless otherwise noted, these portlets are all provided with minimal configuration options. Most of them have two configuration options–the option to change permissions for the portlet view and sharing options for connecting the portlet to other web sites. They do not have any way to change options like feed length or display styles. Some styling changes, however, can be made through custom CSS.

Installing the social portlets

The social portlets are all included with the Liferay Community Edition distribution, but need to be installed separately for Enterprise Edition. If you're using Liferay Enterprise Edition, or had previously removed the social portlets from Community Edition, you can use Liferay's plugin installer to easily add social features to your portal.

If you're logged in as an administrator, go to the control panel and click on *Plugins Installation* in the *Server* section. From here, click on *Install More Portlets* and search for *Social Networking*. Once the results come up, select the latest version of the Social Networking Portlet and click *Install*. Once the install process finishes, you can start using the social networking portlets.

Using social networking on public pages

There are several social portlets that are designed for use on public portal pages. The goal of these is to use social connections to help a group work together more closely. These include the **Members**, **Meetups**, **Summary**, and **Activities** portlets.

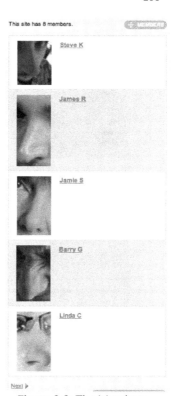

Figure 8.2: The Members Portlet

The Members portlet is a simple list of all the current site's members. The only configuration options you have are permissions, which are the

Figure 8.3: The Meetups Portlet

Figure 8.4: The Activities
Portlet

same for every portlet. For example, you might change the permissions so only members of the current site can view the portlet.

The Meetups portlet is a tool for creating casual meetings for users of your portal. Anyone can create a "meetup" and give it a title, description, date/time, maximum number of attendees, price and provide an image. Any meetups that are created are displayed in the portlet for anyone to view. Users can register for the meetup, which lets the organizer keep track of who's coming.

The options for creating a meetup are essentially the same as those for creating a calendar event and the Meetups portlet shares some functionality with the Calendar. For more information on the Calendar portlet and configuring events, see chapter 7.

The Activities portlet comes in two varieties: the standard Activities portlet and the Members' Activities portlet. The basic function of the portlets are the same–they both display a feed of what users are doing on the portal. The difference is that Activities displays what's going on across the entire portal, while Members' Activities displays only what members of the current site have been doing. There's also a Friend's Actvities portlet that's intended for use on users' personal pages. In the Configuration dialog box of any variety of the Activities portlet, you can use the *Maximum Activities to Display* dropdown menu to set a limit on how many activities can be displayed at once in the portlet window.

The Map portlet allows you to view the locations of site members, both locally and internationally. Only members of the site to which the Map portlet has been added are displayed. In order to configure the Map portlet, you need to install the IP Geocoder portlet (available from Liferay Marketplace) and configure it to access MaxMind GeoIP or GeoLite on your server. For more information on configuring geolocation services, visit the MaxMind support page[1]. Once you've installed the Geocoder portlet and configured it to access MaxMind GeoIP or GeoLite, you'll need a key from Google to access Google's Maps API so your Map portlet will work. Visit the Google Maps web site[2] to learn how to obtain a valid Google API key. To configure the Map portlet using the GeoLite City database, use the following steps:

Figure 8.5: The Map Portlet

1. Install the Social Networking plugin, if you haven't already done so.

2. Install the IP Geocoder portlet. (Both the Social Networking and IP Geocoder apps can be installed from Martketplace.)

3. Shut down your application server.

4. Download the Geo Lite City database.[3].

5. Unzip the `.dat` file to your desired storage location on your server.

6. Create a `portlet-ext.properties` file in the `/{ROOT}/webapps/ip-geo-coder-portlet/WEBINF/classes/` directory of your Liferay installation.

7. Add the property `maxmind.database.file={GeoIP Lite City database .dat file path}` to this file.

---

[1]http://www.maxmind.com/app/installation?city=1
[2] http://code.google.com/apis/maps/documentation/javascript/v2/introduction.html#Obtaining_Key
[3]http://www.maxmind.com/download/geoip/database/GeoLiteCity.dat.gz

8. Create a `portlet-ext.properties` file in the `/{ROOT}/webapps/social-networking-portlet/WEB-INF/classes/` directory of your Liferay installation.

9. Add the property `map.google.maps.api.key={Your API Key}` to this file. If you haven't done so already, you'll need to generate a Google Maps API Key.

10. Restart your application server.

11. Enjoy the Maps portlet!

Next, let's look at the social networking portlets designed for use on personal pages.

Using social networking on personal pages

In addition to the portlets available for general use, there are a handful that can only be used on personal pages. These include the Summary, Wall, Friends, and Friends' Activities portlets. These portlets can be used to create profile pages similar to Facebook's or Google+'s.

The Summary portlet provides a quick overview of a user's profile. When posted in a user's personal site, it displays the user's name, profile picture and job title. Users can add additional personal information by clicking on *Edit* in the portlet and filling in information in the *About Me* section. This portlet is essential to any social implementation on Liferay, because it has the *Friend Request* button. This enables users to initiate social relationships. Note that this portlet simplifies a much more powerful underlying social networking API that defines many different kinds of relationships, including friends. Your developers can take advantage of this API to create powerful social applications. For more information on this, see *Liferay in Action* (Manning Publications) or the *Liferay Developer's Guide.*

The Wall portlet provides a place for users to leave messages on other users' profiles. The messages can only be plain text as no formatting or HTML is supported. Once a post is added to their wall, users have the ability delete it or respond to it with a quick link to post on the original poster's wall.

The Friends portlet shows a list of all the user's friends with links to their profiles. The Friends' Activities portlet displays information about a user's friends' activities on the portal.

Now that we've discussed the functions of the suite of social networking portlets that ships with Liferay, let's put them all together and make a social web site.

Figure 8.6: Social Networking Portlets in a Facebook-like Layout

Liferay's social tools in action

To get started with Liferay's social features, let's set up the public pages of our users' personal sites to include social apps. Because of Liferay's flexible page layout options, we have a large number of options for how to set the pages up. For simplicity's sake, we'll make something that's fairly similar to the original Facebook layout.

Setting up users' personal pages

Before we start adding portlets to pages, we should configure Liferay so that everyone (or some subset of everyone) has the same social features. We have two ways to do this with advantages and disadvantages to each.

User Groups: Placing users into a group enables you to create a user group site for them. The pages and portlets defined by the user group site are copied to members' personal sites. With the user group site, you can control whether users can modify pages and you can push changes out to users in the future. Once the site template is assigned to a user group, you can set the *Default User Associations* to have all users be the member of a particular group in *Portal Settings* in the control panel. The advantage of this is that it can be managed entirely through the GUI and it's easy to configure. If you base your user group's site on a template, you can use the *Enable propagation of changes from the site template* option to manage all user pages simply by changing the template. This is the recommended way to manage personal pages across the portal. For more information on user group sites, see chapter 15.

Portal Properties Configuration: The legacy way to do this is with the configuration file. You can specify a default layout and portlets for personal pages in your `portal-ext.properties` file. Note that this method applies changes to all users' personal sites. However, it does not provide as much maintainability or as many customization options as does using user group sites. User group sites allow you to choose what's modifiable by the user. For more information on the `portal-ext.properties` method, see *Default User Private Layouts* and *Default User Public Layouts* in chapter 20.

Because it's the recommended method, we'll use the user group method to create the layouts. As an administrator, go to the control panel and select *Site Templates* from under the *Portal* section. Click *Add* and fill out the form. We'll call our new site template *Social Layout*. Click *Save*.

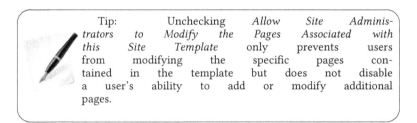

Figure 8.7: Creating the Site Template

> Tip: Unchecking *Allow Site Administrators to Modify the Pages Associated with this Site Template* only prevents users from modifying the specific pages contained in the template but does not disable a user's ability to add or modify additional pages.

Once you've created the template, choose *Actions → Manage Pages* for *Social Layout* from the Site Templates page, then click *View Pages*. Let's change the name of the page from the default to *My Profile* and add some portlets to the page. In the screenshot below, we removed the borders to make the page look more integrated, and also used Nested Portlets to make the layout more interesting.

Back in the control panel, select *Users and Organizations* from the *Portal* section. Once there click *Add → User Group*. Name the group *Social Users*.

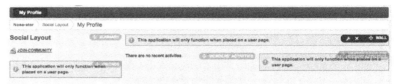

Figure 8.8: Social Profile Site Template

When creating a user group, you have the option to set a user group site; use this option and select the Social Layout template for your Public Pages.

Now go to *Portal Settings* and select *Users* from the submenu. From the Users page, go to the *Default User Associations* tab and enter *Social Users* in the User Groups section. Now all users on the portal get a Social Profile page. Now the question is, how do we encourage users to visit each others fancy new profile pages?

Connecting users through collaboration

There are many ways that social networks connect users. These generally involve some kind of mutual interest or experience. On a site like Facebook, you can connect with people from school, from work or from other personal connections. On a music based networking site like Last.fm, you can connect with people who have similar tastes to yours. With Liferay's social networking collaboration is the key to connection.

Using our example site of nosester.com, we can take a closer look at ways users can be connected through hierarchies and ways they can connect to each other. We'll look at a handful of portlets, both those designed specifically for connecting users and those that can create connections as a side-effect of just getting work done.

The Directory portlet can provide a simple way for users to connect. If we have a site dedicated to people with big noses, we can place a directory portlet on that site, listing all the users that have joined that site. Users can connect by sending requests to other users on that list. This isn't the worst way to get users connected but it probably won't be very effective. Why not? Well, other than sharing some very basic common interests, we haven't really had any interactions.

The Activities portlet provides a similar but more effective means of connection. Because it shows a list of what other users are doing, this portlet helps users discover who is among the most active across the site or the portal, and thus who might be a good connection.

Probably the most effective way users can connect is by interacting with other users. Every portlet in the Collaboration category provides information on who is contributing, regardless of how. You can see who is creating a thread in a message board, editing a wiki article, blogging or creating a calendar event. Users can use these to connect based on content–if I find your blog interesting, or if you answer my question on the message board, we can use that as a point to connect as friends to further our interactions. This way, instead of our connection being forced or arbitrary, we've connected based on the fact that we've directly interacted and share a common interest–just like people did before they had the internet.

"Friend" is only the default social relationship as implemented by Liferay's social portlets. You can design things so that users are automatically connected through Site and Organization membership. And there are many other relationship types beyond Friend: your developers can take advantage of these by using Liferay's social API. This is covered in *Liferay in Action* and the *Liferay Developer's Guide.* Now that you've got all these social applications running on your system, you might wonder: how can I measure social interaction? How do I make identify the best contributors to my site? Liferay has an answer: social activity measurements.

8.2   Measuring social activity

When you have a lot of user interaction on your web site, it can be helpful to try to separate the signal from the noise. Liferay contains a lot of applications which end users can use to communicate with each other and provide information. Some of this information is good and helpful and some of it can be rather unhelpful. Using Liferay's Social Activity feature will help show which users are making real, valuable contributions.

To activate Social Activity, you'll first need to determine which collaboration applications you want to use Social Activity. There are currently three types of content you can use with Social Activity - Blogs Entries, Message Board Messages, and Wiki Pages. Activation is a la carte - so you can use it on one, two, or all three applications. Social Activity tracks three metrics from within each of these applications two are for the user - *Participation* and *Contribution* - and the other, *Popularity*, is for the asset involved.

Let's activate Social Activity for Blogs Entries. Check the box next to *Blog Entry.* You now have options to set point values and limits on several different

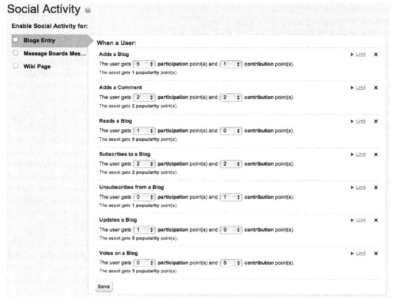

Figure 8.9: The Social Activity Page of the Control Panel

actions for blogs. You'll notice each item on the list has dropdowns you can use to set the number of participation and contribution points; popularity points are tied directly to contribution points. In addition to that, you can expand the box by clicking *Limits* in the top right of each list item. You can use this to set a limit on how many times a use can perform this activity with a specific asset and receive the requisite points. For some activities, you can set limits on both participation and contribution points but on new content creation you can only set limits on participation points.

It might not be immediately obvious, but for all actions that do not involve the creation of a new asset, all of the contribution points always go to the original asset creator and all popularity points go to the original asset. That means if *Votes on a Blog* is set to have 1 *Participation* point and 5 *Contribution* points (and therefore 5 *Popularity* points), the user who votes on the asset will receive

1 participation point, the user who created the asset will receive 5 contribution points, and the asset will receive 5 popularity points.

Figure 8.10: Setting limits in Social Activity

It's easy to assign points–you can arbitrarily assign points for just about anything–the challenge is making the points significant in some way. As mentioned before, the primary purpose of social activity tracking is to make sure that users who regularly contribute to the portal and participate in discussions are recognized as such. So the central piece of the social equity display is the *User Statistics* portlet.

The User Statistics portlet displays a list of users ranked by an amalgamation of their participation and contribution scores. By clicking on the Configuration icon for the portlet, you can change some of the specifics of the rankings. There are four check boxes that you can enable or disable:

Rank by Contribution: If this is checked, a user's contribution score will be used as a factor in calculating their rank.

Rank by Participation: If this is checked, a user's participation score will be used as a factor in calculating their rank.

Show Header Text: Determines whether the title shows or only the rankings.

Show Totals: Toggles the display of the users activity score next to their name.

Display Additional Activity Counters: You can toggle the display of any number of other pieces of information next to the users name in the statistics, ranging from the number of comments on assets a user has created to the number of wiki articles that the user has created. If you want to display multiple data points, you can click the *plus* button to add one and the *minus* button to remove one. You can have as many data points displayed as you want, but displaying too many might make your portlet a little unwieldy.

The **Group Statistics** portlet provides some more advanced data analytics. If you add it to a page, and click on the configuration icon, you see that by default, it will display one metric *Activities on Assets*. You can click the *plus* button to add additional slots, and choose from the dozen or so metrics available for each

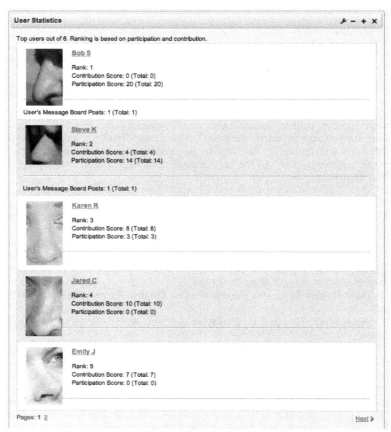

Figure 8.11: The User Statistics portlet

slot, covering virtually any action that a user can perform on content on the portal. If you decide that you're displaying too many metrics, you can click the *minus* button for a particular slot on the configuration view to remove it.

There are a wide-ranging number of actions that you can provide social credit for. Users can receive credit for everything from subscribing to a blog to writing wiki articles. You can easily tweak the numbers in the control panel if it becomes clear that certain activities are weighted too high or too low.

Social Activity can be an invaluable tool for portals that are heavily driven by community-created content. It allows you to easily recognize users who are major contributors and it indicates to new users whose advice will be most trustworthy. Social Activity is easy to set up and can be configured differently for each site, increasing the flexibility of your portal.

Beyond Liferay's social API, there is also support for the OpenSocial standard.

8.3 Exporting portal applications as widgets and OpenSocial gadgets

OpenSocial is a framework designed for the creation of socially themed application programming interfaces (APIs). OpenSocial applications, called *gadgets*, can be used in any web-based application that supports them. They are characterized as simple, widely available, and easy to deploy. Gadgets are especially popular on social networking sites. They can, however, be used in many different ways throughout your site.

Liferay allows any OpenSocial gadget to be used on a page. An OpenSocial gadget is specified in an XML document and consists of embedded HTML and JavaScript. Liferay allows gadgets to communicate with each other and with portlets. This allows your gadgets to run seamlessly without your having to constantly check or update their content. They automatically update based on their connections with other applications. OpenSocial gadgets support numerous open web technologies such as *OAuth*, which we'll discuss in more detail later in the chapter.

Gadgets are socially aware and can share data across a community of users. You can define your own groups and create gadgets to communicate information based on pages (community/team pages), applications (gadgets/widgets/portlets), data, users, roles and authorization, and policies. In short, you can develop gadgets to allow individuals to access and share data within their social networks.

Adding OpenSocial gadgets

The OpenSocial plugin can be installed through Liferay Marketplace for both Liferay CE and EE. Installing the OpenSocial plugin enables you to add OpenSocial gadgets to pages, just like you'd add portlets. There are two types of gadgets:

- "Adhoc" gadgets that users can add to a page via URL

- Gadgets published by the Control Panel that are available portal-wide

First, we'll go through steps to add an Adhoc gadget to a page.

Adding Adhoc gadgets

This method is a quick way to add a gadget to a single page. To do this, go to the *Add → More* menu and add *OpenSocial Gadget* to the page. The portlet displays a link to pick a gadget for display:

Figure 8.12: Configure a gadget to display in your portlet.

Click the configure link and a configuration window opens. Next, you need to insert a URL to an OpenSocial gadget. We'll insert the URL for a colorful calculator which is:

```
http://www.labpixies.com/campaigns/calc/calc.xml
```

Figure 8.13: Configuring an adhoc gadget with your portlet is as easy as pasting the gadget's URL.

After pasting the URL into the text field, click *Save* and your new gadget is visible on your page.

Figure 8.14: The calculator gadget displays seamlessly on your page.

This particular gadget allows you to change its "skins" to fit your needs. Likewise, there are many other user-friendly interactive gadgets that give you flexibility to fit them into your themed sites. As you find gadgets that would work nicely throughout your portal, you can publish them for portal-wide use. You'll learn that next.

Adding gadgets for portal-wide use

You can easily make gadgets available for adding to pages as you would any other application. We'll demonstrate this by adding a *To-Do List* gadget for portal-wide use.

1. Go to the Control Panel and select *OpenSocial Gadget Publisher* under the *Portal* heading

2. Click *Publish Gadget*

3. Insert the URL for the *To-Do List* gadget:

   ```
   http://www.labpixies.com/campaigns/todo/todo.xml
   ```

4. Select an appropriate category for your gadget

5. Click *Save*

Figure 8.15: Configure new gadgets with ease.

Figure 8.16: Publish gadgets for portal-wide use via the OpenSocial
Gadget Publisher.

Your *OpenSocial Gadget Publisher* should now look like the next figure.

Clicking *Actions* next to the gadget enables you to edit, refresh, change permissions on, or delete the gadget. Here is a brief listing of what these four buttons do:

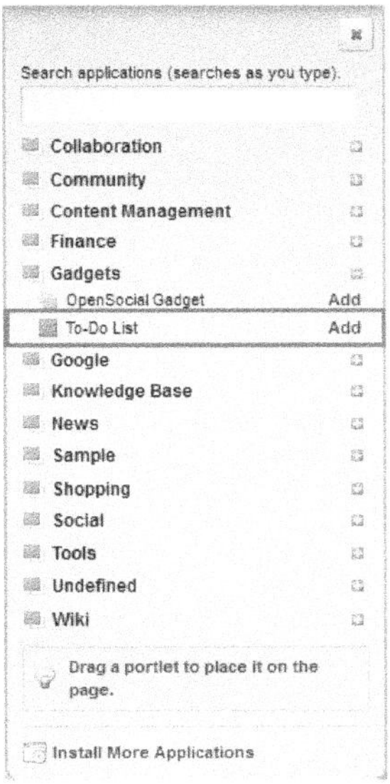

Edit: allows you to change the URL or category.

Refresh: manually refreshes the gadget cache to reflect changes that have been made to the gadget that may not currently be displayed in the portlet.

Permissions: gives you the basic *View, Update, Delete,* and *Permissions* options for each role on your site.

Delete: removes the listing for the gadget.

If you navigate to *Add → More → Gadgets,* you should see the *To-Do List* gadget.

In the next section, we will demonstrate how to share OpenSocial gadgets with other sites.

Sharing OpenSocial Gadgets

OpenSocial consists of a set of APIs for social networking. Liferay implements the OpenSocial standard, so you can be assured that your gadgets run on Liferay. That also means gadgets hosted by a Liferay Portal instance can be deployed and run in any standard OpenSocial container. It may be beneficial for you to share gadgets from your Liferay server with other sites, such as iGoogle. Google's iGoogle lets users customize their own page and add gadgets to their page. Your Liferay Portal users can share their portlets and other OpenSocial gadgets on iGoogle or any other OpenSocial-compatible site.

Figure 8.17: You can conveniently list your gadgets within the *Gadgets* category.

Let's try this now.

For our example, we'll share Liferay's *Loan Calculator* on iGoogle.

1. Add the *Loan Calculator* portlet onto your Liferay page

2. Click the wrench icon in the upper right corner of the portlet and select *Configuration*

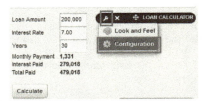

Figure 8.18: Select the *Configuration* button.

3. Select the *Sharing* tab and the *OpenSocial Gadget* sub-tab

4. Check the box labeled *Allow users to add Loan Calculator to iGoogle*. Enter the name of your public domain and port.

5. Click Save

6. Close out the window and navigate back to the wrench icon in the upper right corner of your portlet. There is a new option named *Add to iGoogle* available. Click on this button to add your portlet to your iGoogle page.

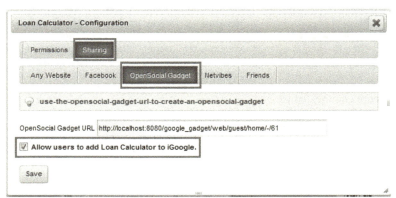

Figure 8.19: Allow users to add your portlet as an OpenSocial Gadget in iGoogle.

Your portlet is now available on your iGoogle page!

By going through this process, Liferay shared the URL of your portlet to iGoogle. The URL you provided is unique to your specific instance of the portlet. This allows you to share multiple instances of the same portlet as different Google Gadgets.

Figure 8.20: Users simply click the *Add to iGoogle* button to add your portlet to their iGoogle page.

You could use this sharing capability to let users view what's happening on your portal at a glance. As you can imagine, you can share all kinds of information from your portal gadgets and portlets with your various circles of friends, colleagues, and fellow community members.

Gadget Personalization

Liferay allows gadgets on your site to be personalized with data from third-party applications. Some of the third-party sites that authorize users to access application data include Evernote, Facebook, Google, Netflix, Photobucket, and Yahoo. Of course, many users feel uncomfortable giving away their private credentials to access these applications. Fortunately, Liferay allows you to use *OAuth* to protect your credentials while you access resources on these sites.

Keep these concepts in mind when going through the OAuth sections:

Service Provider: a web application that uses OAuth for access

Protected Resources: data controlled by the service provider, which can be accessed by the gadget through authentication

Consumer Key: a value used by the gadget to identify itself to the service provider

Consumer Secret: a secret the gadget uses to establish ownership of the consumer key

Request Token: a value the gadget uses to obtain user authorization, which is exchanged for an access token

Access Token: a value the gadget uses to gain access to the protected resources on behalf of the user, instead of using the user's service provider credentials

OAuth is an open standard that authorizes third-party applications to interact with a user's resources. Users can share their private resources from one
site with another site without supplying typical credentials, such as their user
name and password. OAuth uses request and access tokens as well as a token
secret to authenticate the users of your gadget.

A popular characterization for the OAuth client is the "valet key for your
web services." Let's say you're hosting Liferay Portal and have users and customers coming to your web site. You want them to have access to a third party
resource, like Twitter, and be able to access their accounts from your site. In
the past, they would have to provide their Twitter user names and passwords,
but not if you use OAuth. OAuth is a "handshake mechanism" where, instead of
requiring personal information, Liferay redirects users to Twitter, where they
can tell Twitter to allow Liferay limited access to their accounts. This example is similar to our earlier "valet key" characterization. You wouldn't want a
valet driver opening your glove box, storage spaces, hood, and other personal
compartments within your vehicle. You would only want him or her to access
things he or she needs to park your car. OAuth is based on this same idea: it
allows a site just enough information to do what it needs and nothing more.
This assures the user that his personal information is safe but gives him freedom to take advantage of valuable resources he typically uses from the service
provider's site.

OAuth Admin Configuration

OpenSocial defines a specification that allows gadgets to incorporate OAuth to
access protected resources from service providers. A brief example is provided
to demonstrate how easy it is to leverage OAuth within gadgets on your site.

For this example, we'll set up a demo Twitter account gadget using OAuth.
First we must configure your gadget. Follow the steps below to acquire the
consumer key and secret given by the service provider.

1. Similar to previous examples, add the Twitter Demo gadget to your page.
   Go to the Control Panel and click on *OpenSocial Gadget Publisher* under the
   Portal heading. Click *Publish Gadget* and insert the Twitter Demo URL:

   ```
   http://opensocialdeju.googlecode.com/svn-history/r15/Twitter/TwitterDemo.xml
   ```

2. Click *Save*

3. For OAuth-enabled gadgets, you can select the *Manage OAuth* button from
   the *Actions* tab. Select *Manage OAuth* for your Twitter gadget. As shown

below, you have several options under "twitter" that you must fill in to configure your gadget. You must also register your gadget with Twitter to access
the Consumer Key and Consumer Secret.

Figure 8.21: Twitter allows you to manage OAuth for your Twitter gadget.

4. Go to https://www.twitter.com and, before logging in, scroll to the bottom of
the page and select *Developers*. Then click *Create an app* to begin registering
your gadget.

Figure 8.22: Select the *Developers* tab on Twitter.

5. Fill in the *Name*, *Description*, and *Website* fields with what you prefer.

   a. For the *Callback URL* field, enter Liferay's default callback URL:

   ```
   http://myLiferayServer/opensocial-portlet/gadgets/oauthcallback
   ```

   Replace "myLiferayServer" with an appropriate value – for this demonstration, we'll use 127.0.0.1:8080.

   b. Finally, select the *Create your Twitter application* tab at the bottom of the
   page.

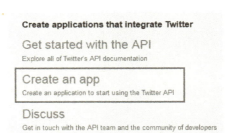

Figure 8.23: Select *Create an app* from within the *Developers* page.

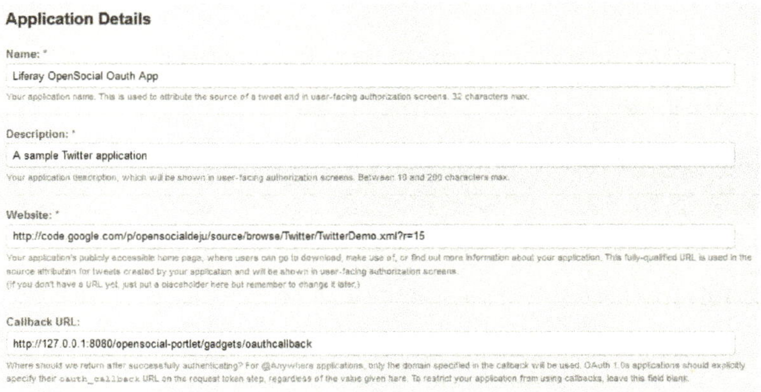

Application Details

Name: *

Liferay OpenSocial Oauth App

Your application name. This is used to attribute the source of a tweet and in user-facing authorization screens. 32 characters max.

Description: *

A sample Twitter application

Your application description, which will be shown in user-facing authorization screens. Between 10 and 200 characters max.

Website: *

http://code.google.com/p/opensocialdeju/source/browse/Twitter/TwitterDemo.xml?r=15

Your application's publicly accessible home page, where users can go to download, make use of, or find out more information about your application. This fully-qualified URL is used in the source attribution for tweets created by your application and will be shown in user-facing authorization screens.
(If you don't have a URL yet, just put a placeholder here but remember to change it later.)

Callback URL:

http://127.0.0.1:8080/opensocial-portlet/gadgets/oauthcallback

Where should we return after successfully authenticating? For @Anywhere applications, only the domain specified in the callback will be used. OAuth 1.0a applications should explicitly specify their oauth_callback URL on the request token step, regardless of the value given here. To restrict your application from using callbacks, leave this field blank.

Figure 8.24: Fill in *Application Details* to setup connectivity between your Twitter gadget and your portal.

6. You are given the OAuth setting that you need to configure your gadget on
   Liferay. Copy the Consumer Key and Consumer Secret to your clipboard.

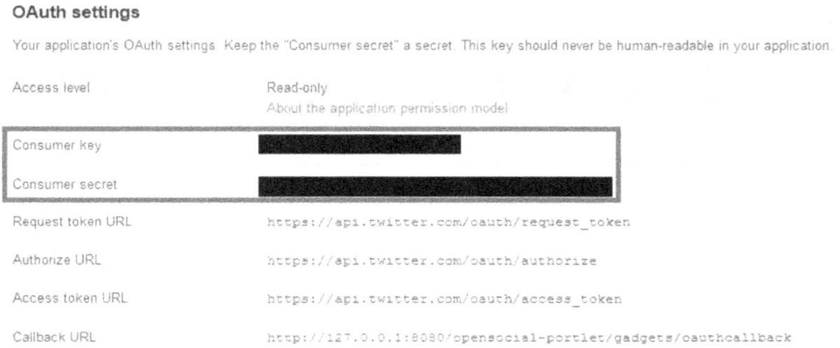

OAuth settings

Your application's OAuth settings. Keep the "Consumer secret" a secret. This key should never be human-readable in your application.

Access level	Read-only
	About the application permission model
Consumer key	██████████████████
Consumer secret	███████████████████████
Request token URL	https://api.twitter.com/oauth/request_token
Authorize URL	https://api.twitter.com/oauth/authorize
Access token URL	https://api.twitter.com/oauth/access_token
Callback URL	http://127.0.0.1:8080/opensocial-portlet/gadgets/oauthcallback

Figure 8.25: Here are the *Consumer Key* and *Consumer Secret* (values are
blacked out for security).

7. Enter your Consumer Key and Consumer Secret under the *Manage OAuth*
   that you navigated to earlier. Also, select HMAC_SYMMETRIC for the *Key Type*
   and then click *Save*.

   Note: Liferay offers PLAINTEXT and RSA_PRIVATE as alternative key types.
   HMAC symmetric and RSA private are commonly used production key types,
   whereas plain text should never be used in real-world settings.

8. Navigate to the *Settings* tab

9. Under *Application Type*, select *Read and Write*. Then click *Update this Twitter
   application's settings* at the bottom of the page.

   Congratulations! Your Twitter gadget is now configured with OAuth.
   Next, we'll configure the gadget within Liferay Portal.

Incorporating OAuth within your site

Now that your gadget is registered with Twitter and is configured with OAuth,
you can add it to your Liferay Portal. The OAuth client you configured in the

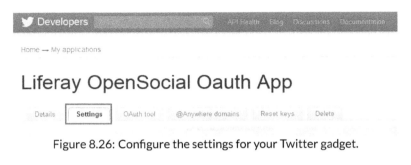

Figure 8.26: Configure the settings for your Twitter gadget.

Application Type

Access:

○ Read only

◉ Read and Write

○ Read, Write and Access direct messages

What type of access does your application need? Note: @Anywhere applications require read & write access. Find out more about our Application Permission Model.

Figure 8.27: Select the *Read and Write* option to enable two way communication.

previous section allows users to protect their credentials while accessing resources on your site. For this section, we'll demonstrate how to add the OAuth-configured gadget to your page.

1. Navigate to *My Private Pages* and click *Add → More... → Twitter Gadget*. If your gadget is configured correctly, it should appear like this:

2. Click on *Personalize this gadget* to be redirected to the service provider.

3. Fill in your Twitter user name and password and select *Authorize app*

4. Your Twitter Gadget should now show your last 20 tweets from your timeline. Your gadget should look similar to the snapshot below:

Twitter Gadget
Personalize this gadget

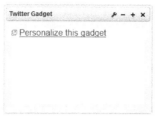

Figure 8.28: Your OAuth configured Twitter gadget awaits personalization with your Twitter account.

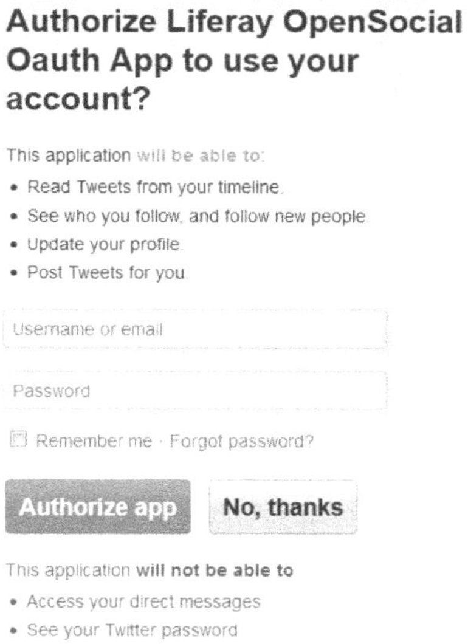
Authorize Liferay OpenSocial Oauth App to use your account?
This application will be able to:
Read Tweets from your timeline.
See who you follow, and follow new people.
Update your profile.
Post Tweets for you.
Username or email
Password
Remember me · Forgot password?
Authorize app
No, thanks
This application will not be able to
Access your direct messages
See your Twitter password

Figure 8.29: Authorizing your OpenSocial application to use your account is straightforward.

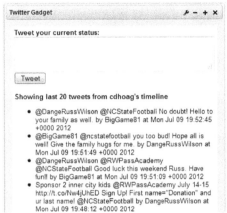

Figure 8.30: Check out your Twitter gadget timeline!

5. Using this gadget, you can tweet your current status and have it display on your Liferay site and Twitter page. To change the amount of tweets displayed, click on the wrench icon in the upper right corner and select *Configuration*. Under the *Setup* tab, you can type the number of tweets to display.

Figure 8.31: Configure the number of Tweets to display.

6. Lastly, you can tweet and view your Twitter timeline. The snapshot below displays what the Twitter Gadget looks like when tweeting.

Figure 8.32: Here is your Twitter gadget just the way you like it!

As you can see, OAuth is easy to configure and offers users the freedom to securely add valuable data from third-party sites.

Creating and editing OpenSocial gadgets

OpenSocial gadgets are XML documents, so as part of Liferay's OpenSocial integration, a gadget editor is included. The gadget editor is a complete development environment for gadgets providing syntax highlighting, a preview function, undo/redo options, and built in tabs for working on multiple gadgets at once. You can also organize and manage gadgets through a simple file manager embedded into the portlet. To access the gadget editor, go to the control panel and click on *OpenSocial Gadget Editor* in the *Content* section.

Once you have created and saved a gadget using the editor, click on the wrench next to the file to rename, delete, publish or get the URL for your gadget. If you want to display your gadget somewhere, click *Publish* to choose a category and display your gadget in the application menu or click *Show URL* to get a URL to display your gadget on any site that supports OpenSocial.

In addition to the social interactions that you can create on your portal, Liferay can integrate with some other popular social networks. This enables you to leverage their power and popularity for your portal's content.

8.4   Integrating with Facebook

Facebook is currently the number one social network in the world with somewhere in the neighborhood of 750 million active users. If you're trying to build a community on your portal, you don't want to neglect a bridge to nearly a billion possible users. With that in mind, Liferay provides a few easy ways for you to integrate your portal with Facebook.

Facebook sign on

Like many web sites you may visit, any portal running on Liferay can be set up to use Facebook for sign in. This makes it easier for users to sign in to your site, since they won't need to remember another user name and password, For more information on setting up Facebook sign on, see chapter 15.

Using your portlets as Facebook applications

You can add any Liferay portlet as an application on Facebook. To do this, you must first get a developer key. A link for doing this is provided to you in the Facebook tab in any portlet's Configuration screen. You will have to create the application on Facebook and get the key and canvas page URL from Facebook. Once you've done this you can copy and paste their values into the Facebook tab. Your portlet is now available on Facebook.

This integration enables you to make things like Message Boards, Calendars, Wikis and other content on your portal available to a much larger audience (unless you already have a billion users on your site, in which case, kudos to you).

8.5   Summary

Websites like Facebook and Twitter have attracted hundreds of millions of users by simply giving users a way to connect and communicate with each other. With Liferay, you have the power to either build a portal around social features or enhance a portal built around content and collaboration by providing users with the tools to connect and interact.

To get started, you can use a selection of portlets designed to make users' personal public pages a place where they can interact with each other by learning about other users and communicate using a simple messaging system. Using the now ubiquitous concept of "friends," users can also form a long term connection with other users they frequently work with or with whom they share similar interests.

Outside of users' personal pages, you have a variety of portlets, like the activity portlets, which are designed to help users identify other users that might be working on similar projects, and keep track of what's going on around the portal. You can even use the Social Activity feature to give credit where credit is due and recognize the users who contribute the most.

Reaching even further out, Liferay provides integration with other sites and services that enable you to connect with users outside of your portal, either by pulling content from other websites using OpenSocial integration, or by pushing content on your portal out to a broader audience using Facebook integration. We've outlined the tools you have available, now it's up to you to leverage Liferay's Social Networking features in the way that best fits your portal.

CHAPTER 9

USING WEB FORMS AND DYNAMIC DATA LISTS

As needs change in business and organizations, the technology used to fulfill those needs must adapt as well. People use electronic means to do things that years ago were done using manual processes. For example, you may want your team to sign up on your web site for a holiday party. Or maybe every fall, you need to put up a job posting board, only allowing administrators to create new job posts. Maybe you want to allow users to manage a notebook or To-Do list on their private pages. In all of these cases, you want to enter in custom sets of data, allow your users to add their information and be able to access the set of data.

In the past, you'd need to be a developer to accomplish any of this. Today, you can do it without writing a single line of code. Enter Liferay's *Dynamic Data Lists*. This is an easy way to create, aggregate and display new data types. Data Lists are flexible enough to handle all types of data, and you don't have to write any code. Simply put, Liferay gives you the power to:

- Define your own data definitions

- Create new lists from those definitions

290

- Customize the input forms for ease of use

- Customize the output format

- Integrate lists into Workflow

All of this capability is easily distilled into two concepts: data defining and data displaying. These data lists are dynamic for a reason: they are flexible and powerful. Whether you want to collect simple input from the user or develop an entire data entry system for real estate listings, Dynamic Data Lists have your use case covered. Combined with the flexibility provided through templates and the power of languages like Velocity, entire applications can be built in a short time.

9.1 Building a list platform in Liferay

To expand and extend the social capabilities of our site, we want to build a new, radical platform on Liferay: custom-built lists that users can share and collaborate on with their friends (or enemies, depending on their Social Relation type). Marketing has come up with a great name for our new service: `list.it`. Our beautiful `list.it` dashboard will give users the power to generate their own lists, see the lists of their friends and tally the results of certain types of lists (surveys, anyone?). Liferay makes this as simple as throwing some Dynamic Data List Display and Form portlets on a user's private and public user pages.

9.2 Defining data types

When new users log in to `list.it`, they are going to want to build a few lists for themselves. Chances are, many of the lists they would want to create–to do lists, shopping lists and memos come to mind–are already defined in the portal. All the user has to do is create a new list, choose that pre-defined data type, and have at it! A number of data definitions ship with the portal to help you get started: *To Do, Issues, Meeting Minutes* and *Contacts*. Use these on their own to generate new data lists or tweak them to fit your use case.

If none of the built-in data definitions suits your needs, you can define your own. Perhaps we want to allow our `list.it` users (who would probably call themselves "list-ers" or "list-ies") to create their own data types for lists they create. In this case, they would need to have unfettered access to the content of their private user site where they can create a new data type.

Using data lists to outline a new data model is as simple as point and click. You now have a `list.it` account and have been dying to bug your friends and family to sign up for "volunteer" work: helping you move into a new apartment. Using an intuitive visual editor, you can quickly draw up the skeleton for that volunteer list in minutes. Since data lists exemplify a unique type of content for your site, you can find them in the content section of the control panel, selecting *Go To → Control Panel → Content → Dynamic Data Lists* or *Manage → Site Content → Dynamic Data Lists*. Within the dynamic data lists section, you can either create a new data type (*Manage Data Definitions*) or a new list from an existing data type.

Figure 9.1: Data Lists in
the control panel.

If you have a new data type, you need to create a definition for it first. Click *Manage Data Definitions* and click the *Add* button. The first thing you should enter is a name for the definition and a description. Call it *Volunteer Sign-Up*. When creating a new data definition, you have a palette of fields to lay out, as well as a blank canvas to construct the definition. The interface looks similar to creating and editing web content structures covered previously. Let's explore the different data types at our disposal:

Boolean: presents a checkbox to the user and stores either a `true` (checked) or `false` (unchecked) based on state.

Date: a preformatted text field that displays a convenient date picker to assist in selecting the desired date. The format for the date is governed by the current locale.

Number: a text box that only accepts numbers as inputs, but puts no constraints on the kind of number entered.

Integer: similar to `Number`, except that it constrains user input to non-fractional numbers.

Decimal: similar to `Number`, except that it requires a decimal point (`.`) be present.

Documents and Media: select an existing uploaded document to attach to the data record.

File Upload: upload a document to attach to the data record. Uploads are stored in Documents and Media, in an existing folder or in the user's default upload location.

Radio: presents the user with a list of options to choose from using radio button inputs. Values are stored as `Strings`. Similar to `Select`.

Select: a selection of options for the user to choose from using a combo box. Can be configured to allow multiple selections, unlike `Radio`.

Text: a simple text field for any `String` input.

Text Box: a large text box for long text input.

Figure 9.2: Data definition fields.

Using that reference as a nice cheat-sheet, you can now create the data type you need for "Volunteer Work Sign-Up." Use a `Text` type for the name. For all the tasks your friends and family can volunteer to do for you, use `Select` (obviously set to allow multiple options). Finally, you don't want to forget a `File Upload` so they can upload images of themselves. After all, how much more official-feeling and fun is it if you can print out some nifty badges? To add these fields, drag them from the palette on the left to the work area on the right

When creating data definitions, you can also customize the appearance of the input fields and provide helpful tips and hints for those entering data. Some data types have specific configuration options but all have some in common. The following properties can be edited in three ways: 1) by double-clicking on any field, 2) by clicking the gear icon in the upper-right corner of the field or 3) by clicking the *Settings* tab when the field is selected. Let's take a look at the properties you can edit for each of these field types:

Type: Lists the type of field placed in the definition. This is not editable but is available to reference from a list template.

Field Label: Sets the text that can be displayed with the field. This is the human-readable text that the user sees.

Show Label: When set to `Yes`, the label is shown with the form field.

Required: When set to `Yes`, this field must have data in it for a new entry to be submitted.

Name: The name of the field internally, automatically generated. Since this is the variable name that you can read the data from in a list template, you should give a more memorable name here.

Predefined value: If you would like example data or a default value for the user to start with, enter it here. The field's value defaults to this when adding a new entry.

Tip: Each field can have a small help icon, with a tooltip attached that displays helpful information. If you would like to provide text for the tooltip you may enter it here.

Multiple (Select): When set to `Yes`, allows the user to select more than one option. This defaults to no.

Allowed File Extensions (File Upload): By default, form validation accepts any file type to be submitted. Set this value to a comma-delimited list of extensions, including the character ., and Liferay checks the extension before the file can be uploaded.

Folder (File Upload): Set the location the document is uploaded to in Documents and Media. You can choose from an existing folder, create one or default to Documents and Media's home location.

Width (Text, Text Box, Decimal, Integer, Number): Sets the visual width of the form on the page. It does not affect the values that are stored. Possible values are `Small`, `Medium` and `Large`.

In addition to dragging the fields around to create your desired forms, you can stack inputs within inputs by dragging a field within another field. You can organize your data into unlimited levels of hierarchy, creating the clearest, most logical data model. There is also a duplicate button on each field (the middle button), allowing you to easily clone any field as many times as you need.

That really covers the basic tools that users of `list.it` need to get rolling with an unlimited array of custom types. Plus, you can always come back and change your form. If you find you needed to add some more information, simply come back to the data definition and fix it. All your data lists that use it are then instantly updated with the new or changed fields.

All that's left to do is build a new data list and let your users play with it.

Figure 9.3: Data field properties.

9.3   Creating data lists

Building out new lists really isn't all that different from creating new pieces of web content. Just as you can create new Web Content Structures to control the input of a particular type of web content, you can use Data List Definitions to control the input of new list types. Similarly, just as you create a new piece of web content, selecting the Structure you would like to use with it, `list.it` users (we'll call them *Listies*) choose the Definition they want to use when creating a new list. Now that a data definition is in place, all that remains is to create a new data list to capture the information we're going after. This is the easiest step in creating the list, with only a few clicks between a data definition and robust data entry and delivery.

To create a new volunteer list with the "Volunteer Sign-Up" definition:

1. From the *Content* section of the Control Panel, select Dynamic Data Lists.

2. Click on *Add* to create a new list based on a data definition, which in our case is the volunteer sign-up.

3. Give the data list a name, like *Spring Move-In* and a description to assist administrative users in the future.

4. Last and most importantly, click *Select* under the *Data Defition* section–this is where you set the data model that drives this list.

5. Choose the *Volunteer Sign-Up* data definition you created, then click *Save*.

Now that you've created your brand new volunteer list, you can pester everyone you know to sign up. But what would it look like for them to add an entry to this list? The data definition you've previously created (or selected) defines the layout as well, which means the form looks just the way you laid it out.

But how will this data appear? How will my awesome, new Volunteer Sign-Up sheet or that boring Jobs Listing look? The answers to these pressing, burning questions bring us to the mecca that is the display side of this equation.

Using data list forms

A nice way to enable people to use your forms is the Dynamic Data List Forms portlet. This portlet is tailored to entering new records. When you deploy that data list for your users to sign up for a retreat, or your family members to volunteer to help you move, using the data list form allows you to simplify the sign-up process and hide the contents of the list.

Using the Dynamic Data List Form is exactly the same as using the Web Content Display portlet: just set it up, point it to a list (either existing or new) and let it go. This is very easy to do.

To display a list inside the portlet, add the Dynamic Data List Form portlet to a page from the Dockbar: *Add → More → Dynamic Data List Form*. With the portlet on the page, click on the small gear icon in the lower left corner. This takes you to the configuration page, where you can select a list to use for the form entries. Each time a user visits your page with the volunteer sign-up, they are presented with a form to fill out. If they have already filled out an entry, a message is displayed instead.

Unlike the Web Content Display portlet, however, the Dynamic Data List Forms portlet may not be installed already in your portal. If not, just head over to Liferay Marketplace, grab it and install it.

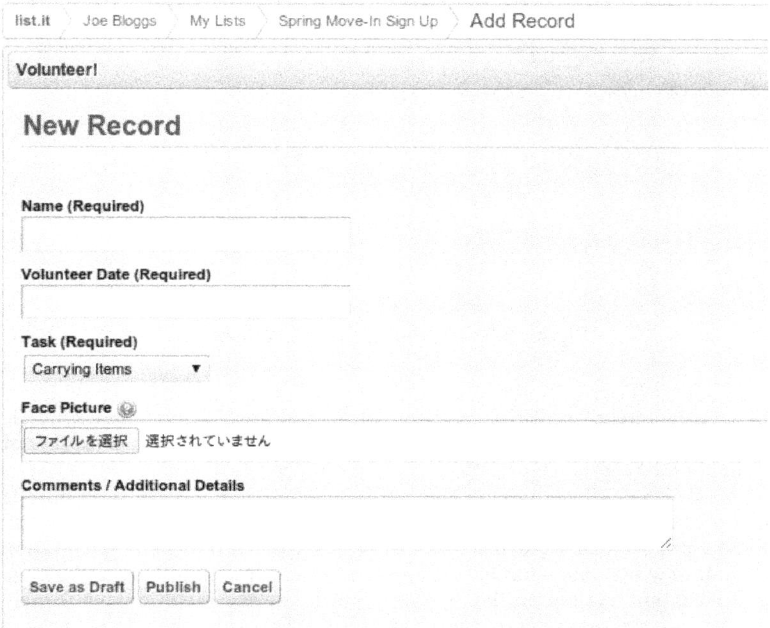

Figure 9.4: Entering a new data record.

You can publish your lists anywhere in your portal too. Read on to find out more about that.

Using default displays

Lists are published in the portal through the Dynamic Data List Display portlet. If Listies don't customize the display, their lists look something like this:

This isn't all that exciting, but it allows users to see the list's contents, and if they have permission, to add and/or edit list items. Within a site like `list.it`, this type of interaction is used for display-only lists that the user chooses to expose to others, or for the user's own private lists. But you can improve the display. You can show the data in a spreadsheet, so you can view the responses

Figure 9.5: The default data list display.

to your Volunteer Sign-Up in a comfortable, easy-to-read format. The Dynamic Data List Display portlet provides an easy way for a user (such as a member of a site) to interact with whatever list is active and available.

While it's possible to ask everyone to contribute to the data list within the control panel, it's much better to give them a simple way to access the list. Liferay provides the Dynamic Data List Display portlet to ease the integration of your new list onto your site. With your list in hand, head over to the page you want and add the portlet. It works much like the Web Content Display portlet: use the gear icon to select a list for display or use the pen/paper icon to add a new list. The default display spills out the contents of the list, but can be configured to use a different display template, which is explored later in this chapter. The two important configuration options to consider are:

Editable: allows users that have permission to add new entries to the list. By default, this is disabled and when enabled, administrators are the only ones with add permission. To easily grant access to other users, edit the permissions on the list you'd like to grant access to, and grant the `Add Record` permission.

Spreadsheet View: displays the list in a dynamic spreadsheet view. This allows users with permission to interact with the list in the same way as in a standard spreadsheet program.

Now, as useful as this default display is, and it's certainly useful for my to do list and my memo notes, it can be an awkward way to ask my volunteers to sign up. In fact, any time I want other Listies to interact with my lists and contribute responses, I really just want a simple form to show them. They don't need to see the full range of responses. And in some cases, it can be hazardous to your

Dynamic Data Lists

Spring Move-In Sign Up

Name (Required)	Volunteer Date (Required)	Task (Required)	Face Picture	Comments / Additional Details
Awesome Mother	2012-01-19	Organising Boxes		I'm the best!
Reluctant Brother	2012-01-19	Carrying Heavy Items		Uh...yeah....

Add 1 ▾ more rows at bottom.

Figure 9.6: The spreadsheet view

health for everyone to see the responses. Then you don't have to explain why your sister-in-law won't work with your brother on the same task because of his B.O. problem. For reasons like that, you'll need to customize the data entry form or the display of the list. Liferay lets you do exactly that using a custom *detail template* or *list template*.

9.4   Make it pretty: creating custom displays

When creating custom lists and data definitions, you can control not only how
the input form appears to your users but also how the list itself displays. Eventually you may realize you need to create another sign-up sheet but you don't
need the asme level of detail provided by the Volunteer Sign-Up data definition
you created. Liferay empowers you to customize both the input and output
of your lists to unlimited levels. Dynamic data lists provide two areas to customize: detail templates and list templates. This covers the forms of lists (*detail
templates*), as well as the display of the list contents (*list templates*).

Detail templates

The default data entry form is the entire data model you created in a data definition, including required and optional fields. Listies who create new lists using
a data definition will see every item in that definition on the input form. What
if, however, you want a quick sign-up form to find out who's coming to dinner
tonight? Using a detail template you can customize the form's display any way
you want. You can limit the fields displayed for entry or change the order of
elements. To access and create new templates, go to *Control Panel* → *Content*
→ *Dynamic Data Lists* → *Manage Data Definitions*, choose the data model you
want to modify, click the *Actions* button and choose *Manage Templates*. When
you click on *Add Detail Template*, you're presented with the same kind of graphical, drag-and-drop interface used for creating the data definition. Move items
around, delete unwanted fields from view and save when ready.

Note that data definitions can have multiple templates. You can choose the
template you want to use for display in either a dynamic data list display or a
dynamic data list form portlet (see below). You should create as many templates
as you might need, and you can prototype them in the portlets to see how each
feels.

Now your friends and enemies alike will be impressed with your `list.it`
skills. It may look to the untrained eye like you've singlehandedly created three
or four different data types for your lists but you know better. You used the
power that detail templates provide, using one data model that encompasses the
maximum information you might need (like preferred activity, favorite color
and ideal schedule). Then you quickly churned out four different detail templates with a few mouse clicks. Now that you have such a vast amount of data
collection options, how will you display them? However you want, as you're
about to find out.

List templates

For every data definition, you have an unlimited number of displays you can create. If you created a special "Thanksgiving Dinner Sign-Up" list using your "Volunteer Sign-Up" definition, you wouldn't want to confuse fellow Listies by displaying data fields you never asked for. "Preferred task?" a friend might say, "I don't remember seeing *that* on the sign-up form!" To avoid such embarassing situations, you should create a custom display to match that list. Taking it even further, you could provide a fancy, JavaScript-driven image carousel preview of all the attendees of the party. This would complement your other displays and be another bragging right on `list.it`. List templates give you the power to do all this and more.

Just like detail templates, list templates are found in the Manage Templates section of a data definition. With list templates you can customize the display of a list in precisely the same way as you can customize web content. List templates can be written in Freemarker or Velocity, pulling data from the data definition in the same way that web content templates pull data from their structures. We'll look at a simple example, but for more information on using template scripts to pull data from a backing structure, see web content templates in chapter 3.

The first thing we need to do is create a new list template for our "Volunteer Sign-Up" data definition. Like other features in Liferay, there are several ways to do this, depending on your context.

From the Dynamic Data List Display portlet:

1. Navigate to where your DDL Display portlet is and make sure your list is selected.

2. Find the *Create List Template* icon on the bottom-left of the portlet window and click it to create a new template. If you don't see the icon, sign in as a user with rights to create templates.

From the Dockbar:

1. Go to *Manage → Site Content*.

2. When loaded, navigate to *Dynamic Data Lists → Manage Data Definitions*.

3. Find your data definition in the list, then click *Actions → Manage Templates*

4. Now you can click on *Add List Template* to create a new template.

From the control panel:

1. Navigate to *Dynamic Data Lists* → *Manage Data Definitions.*

2. Find your data definition in the list, then click *Actions* → *Manage Templates*

3. Now you can click on *Add List Template* to create a new template.

Fill out the form with a title and a description. Next, choose a templating language. Just like web content templates, you can choose between Freemarker or Velocity. There is no functional difference between the two. Once you choose the script language, you can upload a template file or choose *Launch Editor* to type in a script manually. Inside the editor you can also choose to use plain text editing or a rich editor that features line numbers and syntax highlighting.

We want to use our template to give us a summary of who is helping on the tasks in our move. To do that, we need to access the records for the list and pull out the name and task for each volunteer. Within the template, we have access to a few helper variables to find out what records we have access to:

```
reserved_ddm_structure_id

reserved_record_set_description

reserved_record_set_id

reserved_record_set_name
```

Inside a template, these variables give us the ID for the record set (that contains all of the volunteers in our list), as well as the name, description and data definition. We can easily retrieve all the records through a service call to DDLRecordLocalService. To gain access to this service, we need to use a helper utility called serviceLocator that retrieves an instance of the service for us. Once we have the service, we can retrieve the list of records (our list of volunteers). Accessing the service with the serviceLocator is a single line of code:

```
#set ($ddlRecordsUtil =
       $serviceLocator.findService(
       "com.liferay.portlet.dynamicdatalists.service.DDLRecordLocalService"))
```

We store a handle to our service in ddlRecordsUtil so we can then use the service to retrieve our list of volunteers:

```
#set ($records = ${ddlRecordsUtil.getRecords($recordSetId)})
```

Now that we have our records, we can iterate through the list and display the data from each record that we want to show. To access a field from a record entry (such as the volunteer's name), we call the `getField` method and pass in the field's name. Each field has a number of methods on it as well, but the one you will use most often is `getValue`, which returns the content of the field. Each field has the set of properties discussed above and can be accessed in the same way (`get + FieldName`):

```
#set ($name = $record.getField("name").getValue())
```

Now all we have to do is set the results in some appealing way. In this example, we've made it very simple by using an unordered list for the results (`<ul>`). Here is the complete source for the template:

```
<h1>Task Summary</h1>

Here are the tasks that people have signed up for on "$reserved_record_set_name.data".
#set ($ddlRecordsUtil = $serviceLocator.findService(
    "com.liferay.portlet.dynamicdatalists.service.DDLRecordLocalService"))

#set ($recordSetId = $getterUtil.getLong($reserved_record_set_id.data))
#set ($records = ${ddlRecordsUtil.getRecords($recordSetId)})

<ul>

#foreach ($record in $records)

    #set ($name = $record.getField("name").getValue())
    #set ($tasks = $record.getField("task").getValue())

    <li><em>${name}</em> will help with <strong>$tasks</strong> </li>
#end
</ul>
```

Once you've typed your source into the editor window, click *Update* and then save the list template. With the list template selected, your list display can now be a summary of tasks as shown below.

All the knowledge you have accrued through building out your award-winning content can be brought to bear in list templates. With the full power of Velocity templates at your fingertips, you have easy access to all the data in the list, as well as the full complement of helper methods and the Alloy UI Javascript library to make easy work of dynamic displays.

If you're not a Listie, and you happen to be deploying custom lists in an environment that requires approval from other users, then it's not enough to just create the list and display a form. What you need is a real integration with Workflow. Workflow integrates smoothly with Dynamic Data Lists.

Figure 9.7: A list template in action

Using workflow

Liferay integrates the powerful features of workflow and the data capabilities of dynamic data lists in *Kaleo Forms*. Workflow is not enabled in the dynamic data list portlets by default, so you can focus on the core task of building custom forms backed by a data list. After this is done, you can deploy custom workflows to the form and its data. Though Kaleo Forms is only available in Enterprise Edition, you can still apply a workflow to a list when creating it in the Community Edition.

If you don't have a workflow engine installed, install the Kaleo Web plugin by going to *Control Panel* → *Server* → *Plugins Installation* → *Install More Portlets* → *Web Plugins* and finding Kaleo Web in the list. You can also copy the Kaleo .war file to the deploy folder of you application server. Once workflow is installed, you have a new option when creating a list:

Figure 9.8: Enabling workflow on a list

Choose the workflow you would like to use, then every record has to go through the workflow process. Now if you need to preview or edit entries as they're coming in, it's easy to work in to your daily workflow.

Creating a Kaleo Form

 EE Only Feature

Kaleo Forms is a plugin that enables you to have greater control over the list creation and entry process. For lists to appeal to companies all over the world (and make your new site not just a resounding success but attract profitable businesses), business users must be able to control the workflow of list entry and review those entries when made. There should also be a cool dashboard you can use to make all of your changes.

Inside Kaleo Forms, users can create lists that follow a workflow, called a *process*, or create new *entries* in a process. Creating a new process is easy, straightforward, and effective.

Starting a new Process

Defining processes that must be followed in data collection and entry is a fundamental part of business. Historically, this hasn't been fun or easy but Kaleo forms makes it as easy as possible. A process is just another way to describe a workflow you want on a list. When you place a Kaleo Forms portlet on a page, you are presented with a dashboard with two tabs: *Summary* and *Processes*. The summary view shows entries you have added to established processes, while also allowing you to add new entries. The processes view allows you to manage process definitions you have created.

To build a list in Kaleo Forms with a workflow:

1. Within the Kaleo Forms portlet click on the *Processes* tab.

2. Click on *Add Process* and a form appears.

3. Enter a name and description, helping your users understand the purpose of this process.

4. Select the appropriate list, workflow and forms you want to use in this process.

5. Click *Save* to save your process.

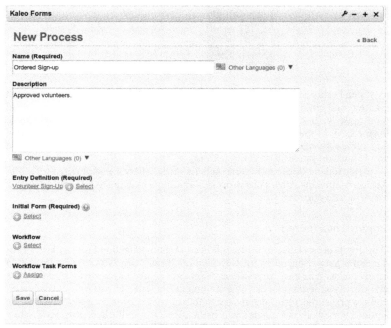

Figure 9.9: New Kaleo Forms process

While the form looks complicated, it can be straightforward. There are a few pieces that make up a process and clicking on each one takes you to the relevant list of options to insert.

Selecting an Entry Definition   The first part of a new Kaleo process is also the simplest: the entry definition. This is just another way to refer to a data definition. All of the avaliable data definitions can be chosen, including our awesome "Volunteer Sign-Up List." Just like with normal data lists, you can always create a new entry definition from the list view by clicking on *Add new definition*.

Selecting an Initial Form   One of the great advantages to using Kaleo forms to present your list as a process is having total control over the detail template. You can always use a default template, which displays all the fields from your entry definition. Greater flexibility comes, however, from creating multiple detail templates for use in different stages of the process. When you create a detail template you have the option of what *mode* to put it in:

Create: *Create* mode gives a display for creating the initial entry. The first stage of any workflow requires you to create a new entry, so this should be the mode chosen for the initial form. All fields marked `required` must be included on create mode forms.

Edit: *Edit* mode is used for any stage of the workflow process. For instance you may want to separate information that shouldn't be saved from information that should. Other stages in the workflow may be a great place to store that additional information. No required fields have to be present on an edit mode form.

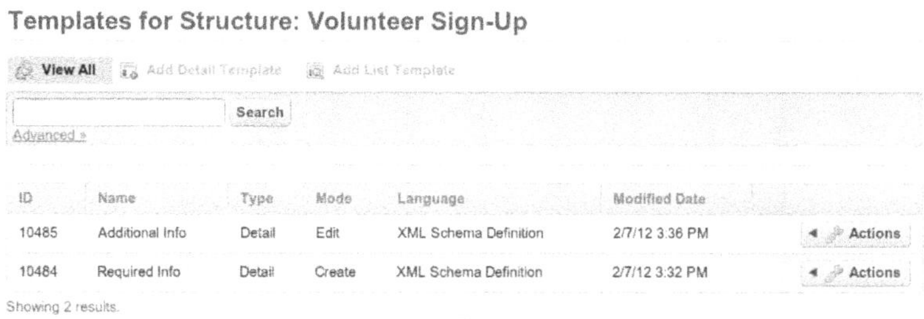

Templates for Structure: Volunteer Sign-Up

Figure 9.10: Selecting a detail template as the initial form

Once you have chosen the initial display you want, all that's left to do is configure the workflow for your process.

Selecting a Workflow   You can now select a workflow to apply to your new list-defined process. All the avaliable workflows can be chosen and you can create new ones from the selection screen. Simply choose *Add Workflow* and a

Workflow Designer screen appears allowing you to define a new workflow by dragging elements in a flow chart.

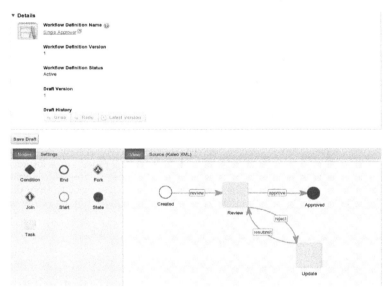

Figure 9.11: Creating a new workflow with Kaleo Designer

We'll keep ours simple and just choose "Single Approver Definition." This gives us a starting point (entry creation) and a 'review' task, which we can use to add additional information in a secondary form.

Assigning Workflow Task Forms   Many workflows offer you the option of having multiple editorial and review stages. During these stages, you might want to offer different forms that allow the user to add more information to the entry. Kaleo forms offers you the opportunity to fine-tune the stages of workflow to use different forms.

When inside the view to assign forms to tasks:

1. Choose the workflow task by clicking on it. This selects the task in the chart.

2. In the details pane on the left-hand side there is a property called `Forms`. Double click to edit the *value*.

3. Start typing the name of a detail template and it appears.

4. Click *Save* to save the form assignment.

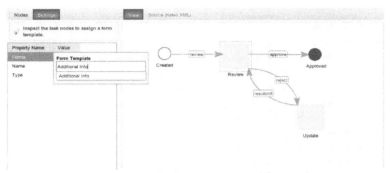

Figure 9.12: Assigning forms to workflow tasks

You can assign forms to as many tasks as you need until you're satisfied with the workflow. After this stage, save the process and it's ready to be used in Kaleo Forms.

Using a Kaleo Form

 EE Only Feature

Once you have a new Kaleo Form process, you can add new entries through the Summary tab in Kaleo Forms. Once the form is filled out and submitted, it enters the workflow you selected for the process.

After you have created an entry, the next task in the workflow may have an additional form to complete. If so, there is also an option to enter it:

Figure 9.13: Adding a new entry to a process

1. Next to the entry in progress click the *Actions* button.

2. Click *Complete form*.

Figure 9.14: Completing a form in the next workflow task

After the new entry has worked its way through the entire workflow, it is added to the data set collected. The owner of that data set (who created the Kaleo process) can view and edit the entries collected.

If you are a Listie, or a `list.it` developer, you're now prepared to show your lists to the world. That is, in fact, the reason you created `list.it` in the first place, right?

9.5 Summary

Our `list.it` experience is now much more enjoyable than when we first signed up. As new Listies, we had no idea how to define our own data types for our lists, let alone how to create a list. You can now be the envy of your co-workers as you breeze through list setup and data definitions. Once you have your new lists set up, you can work through building new, custom input forms for the data. Your friends on `list.it` will thank you and wonder how you were able to accomplish it all. That's nothing next to the masterpiece of design that you can show off in your custom displays through list templates. Once the lists have the precise look and feel you envisioned, then living among the Listies will not only be easy, but fun and exciting.

With the ability to create dynamic sets of data and customize both the data display as well as the entry, the possible combinations are limitless. Dynamic Data Lists can be viewed as a way to deliver small-scale applications that display desired information quickly. Whether you're building a site like `list.it` or a real estate listing service, you'll find the limitless power of dynamic data lists enticing, easy to use, and above all, empowering.

CHAPTER 10

USING WORKFLOW

Liferay Portal includes a workflow engine called Kaleo. In Greek, this word means "called ones," which is appropriate for a workflow engine that calls users to participate in a process designed for them. Kaleo workflow allows a user to define any number of simple to complex business processes/workflows, deploy them, and manage them through a portal interface. The processes have knowledge of users, groups and roles. You don't have to write a single line of code to accomplish this: all you have to do is create a single XML document. And if you're a Liferay EE customer, you get a graphical workflow designer which gives you a point and click interface to create workflows.

To explain how to use Kaleo Workflow, this chapter covers:

- Installation

- Creating workflow definitions

- Configuring assets to use workflow

- How users interact with workflow

We introduced Kaleo workflow in chapter 2, where we discussed how to set up an approval process for basic web content. Once we're done with this chapter, you should be familiar with how to use Liferay's Kaleo workflow to set up approval process for any kind of content before it is published to your portal.

10.1 Enabling workflow

Liferay's Kaleo workflow engine ships with CE versions of Liferay. If you have EE or if you uninstalled it, the plugin can be installed through the Liferay marketplace. The name is `kaleo-web` and you'll find it in the list of web plugins. Installing the plugin adds a number of new options to the control panel:

- My Workflow Tasks

- Workflow Configuration

- My Submissions

- Workflow

There is one workflow that comes bundled with the `kaleo-web` plugin: Single Approver Workflow. This workflow requires one approval before an asset can be published. One of the conveniences of using Liferay's workflow engine is that any roles specified in the workflow definition are created automatically when the definition is deployed. This provides a level of integration with the portal that third party engines cannot match. The Single Approver Workflow contains three roles each with different scopes. The scope of each role can be deduced by their names: Site Content Reviewer, Organization Content Reviewer and Portal Content Reviewer.

Let's jump right in and create a workflow process definition.

10.2 Creating new workflow definitions

A Kaleo workflow, called a *process definition*, is defined in an XML file and is executed by users on the portal. You can create as many different workflow definitions as needed to manage the work done on your portal. You can define new user roles in the workflow to manage the approval process or use roles that already exist in your portal.

The XML file has several parts which define the workflow. To get an idea of how this works, we'll examine the default `single-approver-definition.xml` file which is included in the the Liferay Kaleo plugin.

The key parts of the workflow definition are the asset that's running through the workflow, the nodes of the workflow and the transitions between nodes. The asset is any kind of asset registered in Liferay: web content, wiki articles, message board threads and more. Developers can create their own assets as well to be used with workflow (see *Liferay in Action* or *Liferay Developer's Guide* for more information). Nodes represent stages of the workflow and there are several types. Transitions occur between nodes and indicate what the next node should be.

Think of workflow as a state machine made up of nodes. A node can be a state, a task, a condition, a fork, a join or a timer. Transitions are used to move from one node to another. Each type of node has different properties. For example, states execute actions automatically and require no user input. Tasks block until user input completes a transition to another state. The transition then moves the workflow to the next task or state. This cycle continues until the end Approved state is reached. For example, you could create a workflow which goes through two approvers. Initiating the workflow puts it in the In Review state and then transitions to a task which requires user input. Users approve or reject the asset as part of the task. When the first user approves the workflow, a condition checks to see if there are two approvals. Since there is only one, workflow transitions back to the task. When the second user approves the workflow, the condition finds there are two approvers and it triggers a different transition to the Approved state.

Let's look in detail at how you'd create a workflow using a single approver.

Starting a workflow definition

Below is a diagram of a single approver workflow definition. It has only two tasks and two states.

First you define the schema. For Liferay workflows using Kaleo, `liferay-workflow-definition-6_1_0.xsd` should be your schema. You can find this schema in the `definitions` folder of the Liferay source or a good XML editor can cache it from Liferay's web site.

```
<workflow-definition
xmlns="urn:liferay.com:liferay-workflow_6.1.0"
xmlns:xsi="http://www.w3.org/2001/XMLSchema-instance"
xsi:schemaLocation="urn:liferay.com:liferay-workflow_6.1.0
http://www.liferay.com/dtd/liferay-workflow-definition_6_1_0.xsd"
>
```

Next you define a name and description for the workflow. This appears in the control panel when users choose and configure workflows.

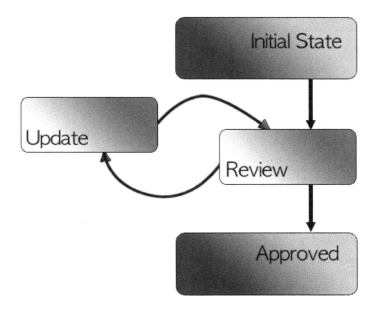

Figure 10.1: The default single approver workflow. Arrows represent transitions and boxes represent states and tasks.

```
<name>Single Approver</name>
<description>A single approver can approve a workflow
content.</description>
<version>1</version>
```

After that, you define your initial state.

Creating an initial state

In this case, the state is simply that the asset has been created. States can contain actions and transitions. Actions can contain scripts. You can specify the language of the script with the `<script-language>` tag. Scripts can be written in Groovy, JavaScript, Ruby or Python (see chapter 18 for more information on leveraging scipts in workflow). For a state, the action is triggered automatically and then executes a transition. Transitions move you to a new state or task.

```
<state>
    <name>created</name>
    <initial>true</initial>
```

From the initial state, you transition to a new task, where further processing is blocked so the asset can be reviewed.

```
    <transitions>
        <transition>
        <name>review</name>
        <target>review</target>
        <default>true</default>
        </transition>
    </transitions>
</state>
```

The next step is to create a task.

Creating tasks

The task has several parts and is the most complex part of the definition. Tasks are linked with roles in order to choose who should complete the task. Roles are notified that there's new content in need of review. If you define a role that doesn't exist, it is created automatically.

The first task listed in the `single-approver-definition.xml` workflow definition is the *update* task. Though it appears first in the file, it's actually not the first task in the workflow. The *update* task is the task that's assigned by the workflow if the asset is rejected by an approver. It's listed first because it's the default task: when this task is triggered, the workflow process is reset back to the beginning. In this task, the asset is assigned back to the content creator, who receives an email notification and is required to resubmit the asset. Once the task is resubmitted, it goes back to the review stage.

You can also see the task is assigned to `<user/>`. This tag always assigns the task back to the user who created the asset.

```
<task>
<name>update</name>
<actions>
    <notification>
    <name>Creator Modification Notification</name>
    <execution-type>onAssignment</execution-type>
    <template>Your submission was rejected by a reviewer, please modify and resubmit.</template>
```

```
    <template-language>text</template-language>
    <notification-type>email</notification-type>
    </notification>
</actions>
<assignments>
    <user />
</assignments>
<transitions>
    <transition>
    <name>resubmit</name>
    <target>review</target>
    <default>true</default>
    </transition>
</transitions>
</task>
```

The *review* task is the first task in the workflow. This is where portal users with the proper role review the content and decide to reject it (move it back to the beginning) or accept it (transition it to the next step).

Once the transition has been made to this task, a notification is sent to those who are assigned to the task. You can edit the name or content of the notification in the XML file.

```
<task>
<name>review</name>
<actions>
    <notification>
    <name>Review Notification</name>
    <execution-type>onAssignment</execution-type>
    <template>You have a new submission waiting for your review in the workflow.</template>
    <template-language>text</template-language>
    <notification-type>email</notification-type>
    </notification>
</actions>
```

You must also assign the task to a specific role or roles. This role doesn't have to be the role you notified. For example, you might want to notify all the content creators any time a new item is submitted. Regardless of who you're notifying, you definitely want to send a notification to anyone who is responsible for approving content.

Sending notifications

Notifications need an `execution-type` which can be `onAssignment`, `onEntry` or `onExit`.

- `onAssignment` generates and sends the notification when the user is assigned the task in the workflow. **Note:** `onAssignment` notification will not work if you wish to notify a user that is not part of the workflow.

- onEntry generates and sends the notification when entering the work-flow task or state.

- onExit generates and sends the notification when exiting the workflow task or state.

Notifications also need a notification-type which can be email, im or private-message. Note the private-message type is a placeholder for now; that functionality is in Liferay's Social Office product but has not yet been integrated into Liferay Portal. Your notification type and execution type should complement each other. You wouldn't want to use an onExit execution type with a private message, because the user won't receive that message until he or she logs back in. Generally speaking, email notifications work best with onExit or onAssignment, while IM or private message work better with onEntry.

Email and private message notifications can also be created as plain text or you can create formatted content using Freemarker or Velocity templating languages. When creating the notification, you need to specify the template-language as text, freemarker or velocity.

In this workflow, anyone who is capable of approving the content is notified onAssignment. This includes administrators and site and organization owners. The role-type tag helps the system sort out who should receive the notification based on the scope and can be set as *community, organization* or *portal.*

```
<assignments>
    <roles>
    <role>
        <role-type>community</role-type>
        <name>Community Administrator</name>
    </role>
    <role>
        <role-type>community</role-type>
        <name>Community Content Reviewer</name>
    </role>
    <role>
        <role-type>community</role-type>
        <name>Community Owner</name>
    </role>
    <role>
        <role-type>organization</role-type>
        <name>Organization Administrator</name>
    </role>
    <role>
        <role-type>organization</role-type>
        <name>Organization Content Reviewer</name>
    </role>
    <role>
        <role-type>organization</role-type>
```

```
        <name>Organization Owner</name>
    </role>
    <role>
        <role-type>regular</role-type>
        <name>Portal Content Reviewer</name>
    </role>
    <role>
        <role-type>regular</role-type>
        <name>Administrator</name>
    </role>
    </roles>
</assignments>
```

Once the content is approved you'll want to transition to a new state.

Using transitions

In this case, you only need a single approver, then the transition goes to the final approved state. In more complex workflows, you might transition to a second tier approver.

```
<transitions>
    <transition>
    <name>approve</name>
    <target>approved</target>
    <default>true</default>
    </transition>
    <transition>
    <name>reject</name>
    <target>update</target>
    <default>false</default>
    </transition>
</transitions>
</task>
```

Finally, we define our end state. Remember states automatically run all actions that are assigned to them, so a script executes and sets the state of the content to *approved*. Workflow scripts are completely contained within XML workflow definitions.

You could also write a customized script if there were actions outside the standard one that you need to perform on your asset. The script below, written in JavaScript, sets the status of the asset to *approved*. Of course, there's much more you can do with scripts. You don't even have to use JavaScript: if you want, you can change the `<script-language>` to another supported language (Ruby, Groovy or Python) and rewrite the action with additional details to meet your needs.

```
<state>
<name>approved</name>
<actions>
    <action>
    <name>approve</name>
    <execution-type>onEntry</execution-type>
    <script>
    <![CDATA[Packages.com.liferay.portal.kernel.workflow.WorkflowStatusManagerUtil.  \
        updateStatus(Packages.com.liferay.portal.kernel.workflow.WorkflowConstants.  \
            toStatus("approved"), workflowContext);]]>
    </script>
    <script-language>javascript</script-language>
    </action>
</actions>
</state>
```

To create longer workflows, you'd create additional states, tasks and transitions according to your requirements. For instance, if you wanted to have a second level of review before an item is approved, you'd create a new task in between the *review* task and the *approved* state. The task itself might have similar content to *review* but you would assign it to a different role. The *review* task would transition to your new task and the new task would transition to the *approved* state.

You can also use *forks* and *joins* to create more complex workflows.

Using forks and joins

Forks and joins are used for parallel processing. For example, say you have a new offer you'd like to put up on your site but it needs to go through both the sales manager and the marketing manager first. You can set up a workflow that notifies both managers at the same time so they can approve them individually. This way, you're not waiting for one manager's approval before you can send the notification to the other manager. The below illustration shows how a workflow with a fork and a join might be designed.

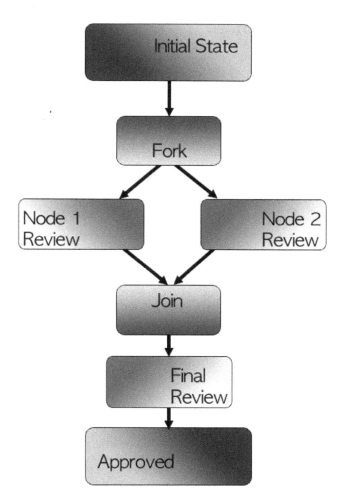

You can transition to a fork from a task or state. From the fork, you can transition to multiple tasks or states which occur in parallel. In the previous example, when we have multiple transitions from one task, they're mutually exclusive: you either trigger one or the other. The transitions are also serial, meaning one must occur before the next one can occur. With a parallel workflow, you can have different approvals going through different users at the same time. For example, you could use this to separate two different departments' approval chains on a single asset. A fork should be formatted like this:

```
<fork>
    <name>review_fork</name>
    <transitions>
        <transition>
            <name>node_1</name>
            <target>review_one</target>
        </transition>
        <transition>
            <name>node_2</name>
            <target>review_two</target>
        </transition>
    </transitions>
</fork>
```

To bring a fork back together, transition both nodes of the fork back to a single join. A join is formatted similarly to a fork, except that any transitions are serial, not parallel, as in the example below.

```
<join>
    <name>approved</name>
    <transitions>
        <transition>
            <name>result</name>
            <target>done</target>
            <default>true</default>
        </transition>
    </transitions>
</join>
```

Another important consideration when creating parallel approvals is each node needs its own "rejected" state for cases where content is approved in one node but rejected in another. Another feature you can use in custom workflows along with forks and joins is Timers. While using parallel workflow enables you to speed up your process by getting content in front more people at once, instead of making them wait in line, timers allow you to add some urgency to the process.

10.3 Timers

Timers are a new workflow feature in 6.1 that help make sure important tasks in a workflow aren't forgotten or left undone because of an oversight or the absence of someone on the critical path. The basic concept of the timer is that after a period of time specified, a specific action occurs. There are two main elements for a Timer, the **Task Timer** and the **Timer Action**.

Timers occur within a Task element and are formatted like:

```
<task>
    ...
    <task-timers>
        <task-timer>
            <name></name>
            <delay>
                <duration></duration>
                <scale></scale>
            </delay>
            <timer-actions>
                ...
            </timer-actions>
        </task-timer>
    </task-timers>
    ...
</task>
```

The outer element is because you can have multiple timers with multiple actions. The specific then contains the element which has a and . The duration can be any number, whole or fractional, and it's significance is defined by the scale. The scale tells you what unit of time the duration is talking about - seconds, minutes, hours, days, weeks, months or years. Once you've determined the time, you'll want to pick an action - either a notification, reassignment or a custom script.

Notifications are pretty simple—if a certain amount of time passes and an action isn't completed yet, the user assigned to the task will receive a fresh notification. With the timer, you have all of the standard notification types available and you can choose a different notification type than was used for the original notifcation. For example, you could create a definition such that when a new item is submitted to the workflow, all members of the *Content Reviewer* role receive a notification. You could then use a timer to say if the content hasn't been reviewed within two hours each member of the *Content Reviewer* role will receive a second notification via instant messenger.

A Notification would be formatted like this:

```
<timer-actions>
```

```
<timer-notification>
    <name></name>
    <template></template>
    <template-language>text</template-language>
    <notification-type>im</notification-type>
</timer-notification>
</timer-actions>
```

Reassignments are designed to keep the workflow moving, even if a key person is out of the office. With a timer set to reassign, after the specified amount of time has passed, the task can be assigned to a new role. Building off of our example above, if the Content Reviewers all received the IM notification after two hours, but the content still wasn't approved after four hours, the workflow could be set to automatically reassign to the task to the *Adminstrator* role.

A Reassignment would be formatted like this:

```
<timer-actions>
    <reassignments>
        <assignments>
            <roles>
                <role>
                    <role-type></role-type>
                    <name></name>
                </role>
                ...
            </roles>
        </assignments>
    </reassignments>
</timer-actions>
```

Obviously we can't think of eveything, so if you have an idea for using timers in your workflow that doesn't fit into our design, you could access Liferay's scripting engine to create a custom action to happen after a specified amount of time. For example, if you had means of sending electric shocks through employees chairs if they weren't doing their work, and had created a Liferay portlet to access the shock mechanism, you could use a custom script to zap any users who were at their desk that hadn't reviewed content assigned to them.

```
<timer-actions>
    <action>
        <name></name>
        <script>
            <![CDATA[
            ]]>
        </script>
        <script-language></script-language>
        <execution-type></execution-type>
    </action>
</timer-actions>
```

For more information on using scripting in Liferay, please refer to chapter 18.

Using workflows and approvals is necessary for virtually any organization and timers are an excellent way to help mitigate the potential headaches caused by having multiple bottlenecks through the process. Using timers in conjunction with other workflow features can help you create powerful workflows for your organization.

Putting it all together

The Kaleo workflow engine is deeply integrated with Liferay Portal. It can generate roles scoped for organizations, sites and for the whole portal based on workflow definitions. You can also customize workflow options for individual sites.

Users are the most important part of the workflow, since they're the ones who do all the work. To make a user a part of the workflow process, you assign them a role which you defined in your workflow . When you're creating your workflow definition, you can create new roles by defining them in the XML file or by using roles which you have already created in your portal. Roles created automatically are always portal scoped, so if you want to use site or organization scoped roles, create the roles before deploying your workflow to the portal.

A portal administrator can create a default workflow definition scheme for each application which applies for the entire portal and site and organization administrators can customize the settings for their sites and organizations. Now that we've seen how to create workflow definitions, let's discuss how to use them.

10.4 Configuring assets to use workflow process definitions

Most of your workflow configuration is done via the control panel. Everything you need to do in the portal can be done through simple GUI controls.

You can find the Workflow section under the Portal heading in the control panel. There are three options under Workflow: *Definitions, Default Configuration* and *Submissions.*

If you created a new workflow definition, you need to add it so it can be used in the portal. Click *Definitions.* By default, only the Single Approver workflow appears here. Clicking *Add* allows you to enter a title for a new workflow definition and upload the XML file. Once you add a file here, it's added to the portal and is immediately available for use.

Figure 10.3: Adding a
Workflow Definition

Under *Default Configuration*, you can set the workflow behavior (if any) for all workflow-enabled applications on the portal. You can choose to use no workflow, which is the default, or select any installed workflow definition. Setting the default configuration causes any newly created sites to default to that configuration. An administrator can then edit the definitions for each one individually through the *Workflow Configuration* page.

Clicking on *Submissions* will let you view any currently pending assets or any assets which were previously approved.

Configuring workflow

After you have uploaded workflow definitions and set the default workflow behavior you can go up to *Workflow Configuration* and tweak the definitions you're using for each site individually.

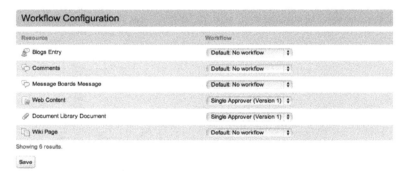

Figure 10.4: The Workflow Configuration Page

Using the context selector drop-down menu in the control canel, you can select any site in the portal. All the options under that heading, including Workflow Configuration, now apply to that particular site. Using workflow is just as easy.

My Workflow Tasks

My Workflow Tasks is a personalized version of the Workflow Tasks and it's found in your personal section of the control panel. Here are specific tasks which have been assigned to you or assigned to a role of which you are a member. You can also view your completed tasks.

Figure 10.5: My Workflow Tasks Page

It's here workflow users review and approve content. By clicking on the actions next to a piece of content, a user can view the content, then choose to approve or reject it and add comments.

My Submissions

My Submissions is found under your user's personal information in the control panel. From this screen you can view any assets you have submitted to review. Those currently under review are listed under the *Pending* tab and those that have been reviewed are listed under the *Completed* tab.

Besides viewing your work, you can also withdraw a submission from the review process by clicking on *Withdraw Submission* from the *Pending* tab.

Using Kaleo Workflow Processes in Liferay Portal

Before workflow can be used, you must define which types of assets on the portal are workflow-enabled. If you have created additional definitions, you

Figure 10.6: The My Submissions Page

must also choose the workflow definition to use for each asset that is workflow-enabled.

Figure 10.7: You can select which site to work on by using the drop-down menu in the Content section of the control panel.

To demonstrate how this works, we'll create a press release. Press releases should be posted in the *Newsroom* section of the web site, so before setting specific workflow configuration options or creating content, create the Newsroom site and switch to it in the control panel. In Workflow Configuration, set Web Content to use the Single Approver workflow.

Next, create two users, a Content Creator and a Content Reviewer. The Content Creator logs in and creates a new press release for Nose-ster and clicks *Submit for Publication*. This triggers the workflow process and notifies the Content Reviewer. When the Content Reviewer logs in, he or she can assign the workflow task to him- or herself and approve the content.

Figure 10.8: Before a Content Reviewer can approve content, he must assign it to himself or have an administrator assign it to him.

Once the content is approved, it can be posted on the Press Releases page in a web content display portlet.

There's more. EE customers get extra features that enable them to create workflows without having to deal with XML.

10.5 Using workflow with other applications

We saw an example of how to use workflow with Liferay web content in chapter 2. In this section, we'll discuss how to use workflow with other applications. First, we'll look at using workflow with Documents and Media. After that, we'll look at using workflow with Blogs, Wikis, and Message Boards.

Documents and media

You can enable workflow for most portal resources, including page revisions for staging, web content, and collaborative applications, from the Control Panel. However, workflow for Documents and Media can only be enabled within a Documents and Media portlet since it must be defined at the folder level. To see how this works, create a new page in the default site called *Documents and Media* and add the Documents and Media portlet to this page. Then click *Add → Folder*, enter the name *My Documents*, and click *Save*. Mouse over your new

My Documents folder, click on the gray icon that appears at the top right corner of the folder, and select *Edit*.

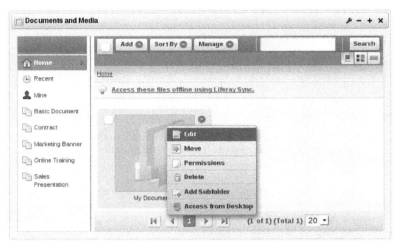

Figure 10.9: Workflow for Documents and Media must be enabled at the folder level. Edit a folder to select a workflow.

By default, the *Use document type restrictions and workflow of the parent folder* button is selected. To enable workflow for this folder, select the *Define specific document type restrictions and workflow for this folder* button. After you've selected this button, a *Default Workflow for all Document Types* dropdown menu appears. By default, you can select *No workflow* or *Single Approver*. Any custom workflows that you added also appear in this dropdown menu. You can add custom workflows through the Workflow page in the Portal section of the Control Panel.

After you've selected the *Single Approver* workflow and clicked *Save*, workflow takes effect for the My Documents folder. Try adding a new document to your My Documents folder—notice that the *Publish* button now says *Submit for Publication* since workflow is enabled. Any users assigned to the (Portal, Organization, or Site) Content Reviewer roles can see that your document has been submitted for publication by navigating to the Control Panel and clicking on *My Workflow Tasks*. Ordinarily, the same user who submitted a document for

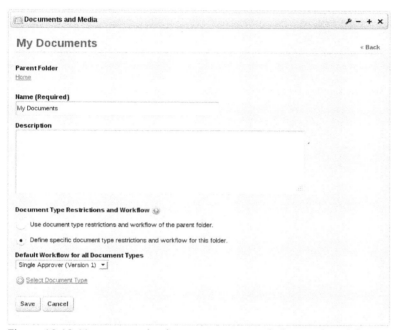

Figure 10.10: You can use the document type restrictions and workflow of the parent folder or you can define specific document type restrictions and workflow for this folder.

publication wouldn't also approve it but we'll do this to demonstrate how the process works.

Navigate to the Control Panel and click on *My Workflow Tasks*. The document that you submitted for publication appears under *Assigned to My Roles* since you're an administrator. Click *Actions → Assign to Me* next to your document. Then click *Actions → Approve* next to the document when it appears in the *Assigned to Me* category. That's it–your document has passed through the workflow!

Collaboration

To enable workflow for collaborative applications, first navigate to the Control Panel and select a scope in the context menu selector. You can enable workflow globally, or for a specific site. Once you've chosen a scope, click on *Workflow Configuration* in the content section of the Control Panel. This page lists the portal resources for which you can select a workflow.

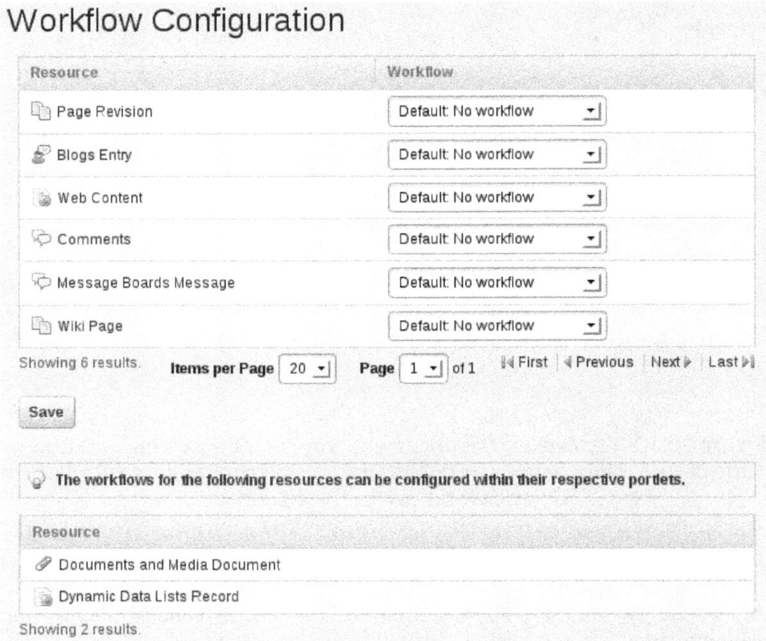

Workflow Configuration

Resource	Workflow
🗋 Page Revision	Default: No workflow ▾
📑 Blogs Entry	Default: No workflow ▾
🌐 Web Content	Default: No workflow ▾
💬 Comments	Default: No workflow ▾
💬 Message Boards Message	Default: No workflow ▾
🗋 Wiki Page	Default: No workflow ▾

Showing 6 results.   **Items per Page** 20 ▾   **Page** 1 ▾ of 1   ◄◄ First   ◄ Previous   Next ►   Last ►◄

Save

💬 The workflows for the following resources can be configured within their respective portlets.

Resource
📎 Documents and Media Document
🌐 Dynamic Data Lists Record

Showing 2 results.

Figure 10.11: The Workflow Configuration page of the Control Panel lists the resources for which can select a workflow for your chosen scope.

To select a workflow, click on the Workflow dropdown menu and choose a workflow. By default, you can only select *No workflow* or *Single Approver*. Custom workflows that you added also appear in this dropdown menu. You can add custom workflows through the Workflow page in the Portal section of the

Control Panel. To enable workflow for the collaborative applications, select the *Single Approver* for the Blogs Entry, Message Boards Message and Wiki Page resources, then click *Save*.

To test the workflow for collaborative applications, add a page called *Collaboration* to the site whose scope you selected when you enabled workflow. Then add the Blogs, Message Boards, and Wiki portlets to this page. Using each portlet, add a blog entry, post a new message board thread, and write some content for the Wiki frontpage. For each application, notice that the *Publish* button is replaced by a *Submit for Publication* button since workflow is enabled.

The workflow process for collaborative applications works the same way as in the examples you've already seen. Any users assigned to the (Portal, Organization, or Site) Content Reviewer roles can see that your blog post, message board thread, and wiki article have been submitted for publication by navigating to the Control Panel and clicking on *My Workflow Tasks*. Of course, since you submitted these items for publication, it wouldn't make sense in a real-world use case for you to approve them. However, to see how the workflow process works, go ahead and approve these items yourself; you can do this since you're an administrator.

Navigate to the Control Panel and click on *My Workflow Tasks*. The items you've submitted for publication appear under *Assigned to My Roles*. Click *Actions → Assign to Me* next to the items you've submitted. Then click *Actions → Approve* next to each item when it appears in the *Assigned to Me* category. That's it–your blog post, message board thread, and wiki article have passed through the workflow!

10.6 Summary

In this chapter, we explained how to install the Kaleo workflow plugin for Liferay EE. Liferay's Kaleo workflow engine is included with Liferay CE. We discussed how to create new workflow definitions and examined the XML schema for them. We looked at how to choose different workflow processes for different asset types. We also explained how end-users can interact with the approval process. Finally, we discussed how to use workflow with different types of applications such as Documents and Media and Blogs, Wikis, and Message Boards. In the next chapter, we'll look at Kaleo forms and the Kaleo workflow designer.

CHAPTER 11

KALEO FORMS: DEFINING BUSINESS PROCESSES

EE Only Feature

In the last chapter, we looked at the elements that comprise a workflow definition and discussed how to create a workflow definition. In this chapter, we introduce the Kaleo Workflow Designer for Liferay EE which allows you to create workflow definitions using an intuitive UI. Using the workflow designer saves you the time and trouble of having to deal directly with the XML.

Developers who are used to working with XML are generally able to create workflow definitions. Other users may not be so comfortable with it. In fact, even skilled developers can make mistakes that break a definition and require time to troubleshoot. To help streamline the creation of workflow definitions and empower more users to create custom workflows, Liferay provides the Kaleo Workflow Designer in Liferay 6.1 EE.

There are two pieces to the workflow designer: *Kaleo Forms* and *Kaleo Designer*. Kaleo Forms is an extension of the Dynamic Data Lists feature (covered in chapter 9). This enables you to create web forms and basic applications, then apply a workflow to govern the processing of those forms. Kaleo Designer is a drag and drop interface for creating new workflow definitions. It can be used in conjunction with Kaleo Forms or standalone to create workflow definitions without having to write XML.

Let's look at Kaleo Forms first.

11.1 Kaleo Forms

Add the Kaleo Forms portlet to a page. In the portlet's initial state, the *Summary* tab displays similar information to what you might see in the *My Workflow Tasks* portion of the Control Panel. Because the Kaleo Forms portlet is scoped to Kaleo Processes, tasks related to other assets cannot be managed from Kaleo Forms. Any forms available for processing through the workflow can be initiated through the *Submit New* button, as the below image indicates.

Figure 11.1: Kaleo Forms give you a convenient way to manage all available workflows in the portal.

Click on *Processes* to view any existing workflow processes or to create new ones. All available processes are listed here. If you're coming here for the first time, however, there won't be any, so let's create one. Click *Add*. You'll see the screen below.

Set a name and a description. Next, you'll define an *Entry Definition* and an *Initial Form*, choose or create a *workflow* and *Workflow Task Forms*.

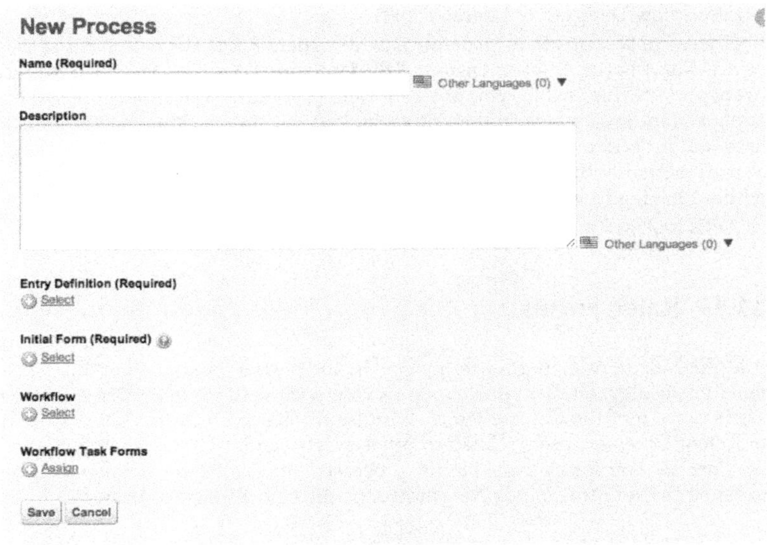

Figure 11.2: The Workflow Process Creation Page

Entry Definition: This is a Dynamic Data List Definition, you can use an existing definition here or create a custom one through the UI.

Initial Form: You can customize the display of the Entry Definition with the Initial Form. This can include things like adding Pagination or altering some other display feature.

Workflow: You can choose any existing workflow definition here or define a new one.

Workflow Task Forms: This is where you can define how the workflow definition interacts with form definitions. You can trigger a workflow action to occur along with a form action, such as a notification, or have a multi-step process where part of the form is completed but needs to be approved before the user can complete another part of the form.

You probably noticed when choosing a workflow, you also have the option to create a new one. This is where the Kaleo Workflow Designer can help you build a workflow without having to write any XML. Let's see how this works.

11.2 Kaleo Designer

Kaleo Designer provides a drag and drop interface for users to create custom workflows. It's an incredibly powerful tool for managing workflow definitions. The Workflow Designer can only be accessed through the Kaleo Forms portlet but definitions created can be used for other processes as well.

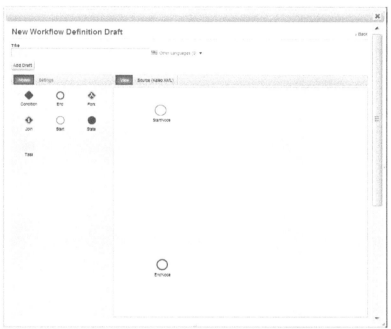

Figure 11.3: Define business processes using Kaleo Workflow Designer.

There are seven types of nodes you can add to a definition. The node types are **Condition**, **End**, **Fork**, **Join**, **Start**, **State** and **Task**. If you've read the entire chapter, you'll notice Start and End aren't node types we've previously discussed; that's because they're actually just State nodes, with certain fields prefilled to help streamline the creation process. Since every workflow has a start and end state, you'd have to do this anyway.

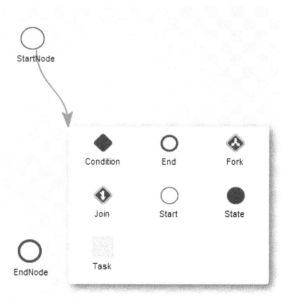

Figure 11.4: The Node Configuration Menu shows options to edit or delete your node.

Each node you add has a pop-up menu letting you edit or delete the node. As you hover your mouse over the edges of a node, notice your mouse pointer changes to a cross. The cross indicates you can connect the current node to another node. Hold down your mouse button and drag the mouse to start drawing your transition to another node. If you stop before reaching the edge of the next node, a pop-up displays node types you can create and connect to on-the-fly. To connect with an existing node, continue dragging the connector to that node.

Figure 11.5: Create transitions to existing or new nodes. The connector pop-up let's you create and connect to new nodes on-the-fly.

To get a feel for how the designer works, let's use the workflow designer to duplicate the default workflow definition. When we choose the option to *Add Definition* from the Kaleo Forms portlet, it creates a blank workflow definition with start and end nodes. To make this work, we'll add two tasks, fill in the relevant information, assign the tasks properly and create the transitions.

First add two tasks, then use the edit icon to name them *Review* and *Update*.

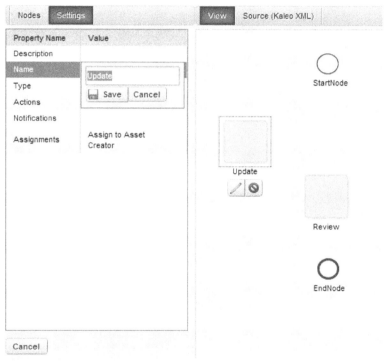

Figure 11.6: Edit a node by clicking on its edit icon and modifying its settings.

Next, connect the nodes so Review has four nodes, as follows: one receiving the transition from **StartNode**, one sending a transition to **Update**, one receiving a transition from **Update**, and one sending a transition to **EndNode**.

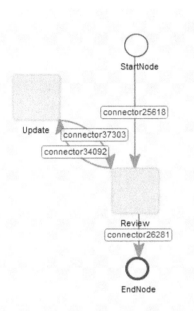

Figure 11.7: Your workflow should look like this.

Next, we want to add the correct assignments and notifications. Click on *Review*. The box on the left shows all the properties of the Review node. In the *assignments* category, assign the task to the *Portal Content Reviewer* role. Click on *Notifications* and create a notification with the type *On Assignment*. Now move to the Update node and assign it to the *Content Creator* with its own notification.

Next, let's go through all the transitions and make sure they're named correctly. What are the transitions? Workflow transitions connect one node to another. On exiting the first node, processing continues to the node pointed to by the transition. Every time you created an arrow from one node to another it created a transition. By default, these transitions get system generated names so we'll rename them all to something more human readable. First, click on the arrow going from the Start node to the Review node and set the name as *Submit* and set *Default* to true–we'll leave all the others as false. Set the name of the transition from Review to Update to *Reject* and the one from Update to Review to *Resubmit*. Lastly, set the name of the transition from Review to the EndNode to *Approve*.

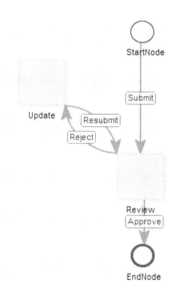

Figure 11.8: Your completed workflow should look like this.

Now let's take a look at the generated XML. It should look a lot like our default workflow, only a tiny bit messier, as the nodes display in the order they were created, not in the logical order that happens when a human writes the code. Save your definition and it's ready to use.

11.3 Summary

As you can see, Liferay Portal and the Kaleo Workflow engine combine to create a very robust environment for web content management. The Kaleo Forms portlet allows you to manage all available workflows in the portal. You can create your portal's workflows by using the Kaleo Designer's unique drag and drop interface. Simple workflows can be managed using the default configuration and GUI tools, while more complex workflows can be created to meet the workflow management needs of almost any portal. Through this chapter and the previous one, we've taken a look at the various elements of a workflow and shown how to use those elements to create your own custom workflows. We've also seen how to properly use the various elements of a workflow like Assignments and Notifications, as well as newer and more advanced features like Parallel Workflows, Timers, and Custom Scripts.

It's not enough to understand each individual step of the workflow process; one of the keys to using Kaleo workflow is to understand how each step interacts with the other elements. If you understand these relationships, you can figure out which features will to work best for your organization. We hope you'll use the information we've covered on workflow to craft suitable processes for you portal.

CHAPTER 12

LIFERAY UTILITY APPLICATIONS

In this chapter we'll look at some Liferay utility applications that might be useful for you. The Software Catalog is currently packaged with Liferay but will soon be replaced by Liferay Marketplace. Please see chapter 13 for information about Liferay Marketplace and managing Liferay plugins. The Knowledge Base application is an EE-only plugin. In this chapter we'll discuss several of these applications:

- Bookmarks

- Software catalog

- Shopping

- Knowledge Base

Liferay's Bookmarks application is a simple way for users to keep track of URLs in the portal that can also be used by an administrator to publish relevant links to groups of users. The Software Catalog allows you to define a set of software items to display to visitors. The Knowledge Base application allows you to create articles and organize them into full books or guides that be published on your portal.

12.1   Capturing Web Sites with the Bookmarks Portlet

Many of us enjoy collecting things we value. They may be stamps, comic books, sea shells, or fabulous shoes. The list goes on and on. But have you considered URLs collectible? Having a thorough collection of links can be a great way to add value to your portal's usability.

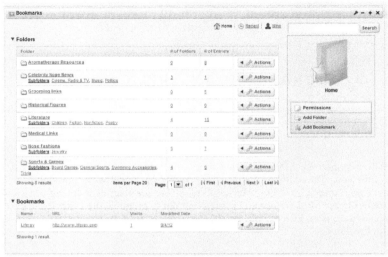

Figure 12.1: Individual bookmarks, not associated with a folder, are listed separately.

With Liferay's Bookmarks application, users collect and manage URLs in the portal. They can add, edit, delete, export and import bookmarks. Users can use links to access regularly visited web sites. Administrators can publish links tailored to specific groups of users. Both internal pages as well as external sites can be bookmarked.

Organizing Bookmarks by Folder

You can store all your important links in one place and you can manage this data easily using folders. You can create, edit, and delete bookmark folders. You get to decide how many bookmarks or folders are displayed on a page. Bookmark folders can have any number of subfolders.

Here's an example of what one bookmarks portlet might look like. Bookmark Folders are displayed above individual bookmarks.

In this example, there are eight bookmark folders, four of which have subfolders. The columns showing the number of folders and the number of entries show the subfolders and the entries contained within each top level folder. Note that total number of bookmarks includes those in the subfolders.

Using the Actions button on the right, you can edit the folder, manage folder permissions, delete the folder, add a subfolder, or add a bookmark to the folder.

As your collection of links grows, you may need to add more subfolders to keep things in order. Should you decide a link needs to move from one folder to another, you can manage this using the Edit option for that link.

Moving a Link

Just for fun, let's move a link from the main bookmarks folder into a subfolder one level down. We'll move the Liferay link into the Nonfiction subfolder in the Literature folder. The Nonfiction subfolder is a child of the Literature folder. We need to move the link to the Literature folder first before moving it into the Nonfiction subfolder.

To achieve this, we select *Edit* from the Actions button for the link. In the Edit view, find the section called *Folder*. When applicable, this section contains breadcrumb links to allow you to navigate freely among the other folder levels. Currently, there are two buttons here labeled Select and Remove. Click the *Select* button and a new window appears, like the one below. Clicking the *Remove* button here doesn't affect the link. It is used

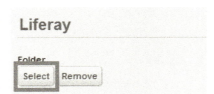

Figure 12.2: You can move a link one level at a time by selecting the Select button.

solely for moving links out of folders and subfolders back into the main Bookmarks view.

Now choose the *Literature* folder. When you do this, notice how the link's Folder section changes to reflect the new location of the link.

Home

Add Folder   Choose This Folder

Folder	# of Folders	# of Entries	
Aromatherapy Resources	0	8	Choose
Celebrity Nose News	3	1	Choose
Grooming links	0	5	Choose
Historical Figures	0	0	Choose
Literature	4	5	Choose
Medical Links	0	0	Choose
Nose Fashions	5	7	Choose
Sports & Games	4	0	Choose

Showing 8 results.   Items per Page 20 ▼   Page 1 ▼ of 1   ◄ First   ◄ Previous   Next ►   Last ►|

Figure 12.3: Select the Choose button next to the desired folder.

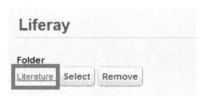

Figure 12.4: When you choose a folder, the folder navigation changes to reflect the new location of the link.

When you choose *Save*, you return to the Bookmarks portlet. Notice that the Liferay link is no longer under the Bookmarks section. Select *Literature* to reveal its contents. In the example below, you can see the Liferay link is now in the bookmarks section of the Literature folder.

Select *Edit* from the Actions button next to the Liferay link, then click *Select*. Choose the *Nonfiction* subfolder and again notice the change in the folder-level breadcrumbs. Click *Save* and the Literature folder view appears. Select *Nonfiction* to see your link in the subfolder's bookmarks list. Piece of cake, right?

To move a link out of a subfolder and into a higher-level folder, Edit the link in the subfolder and choose *Select*.

Figure 12.5: When you move a link to a folder, it remains in the bookmarks section until it's moved into a subfolder.

Figure 12.6: To move a link up to a higher-level folder, choose the appropriate folder from the breadcrumbs in the Select view.

In the resulting window, select the appropriate folder from the breadcrumbs at the top. In this example, we selected *Literature* for consistency. This opens a new window, like the one below, showing the other folder options.

You can choose one of the other subfolders from the list, or you can choose *Home* from the breadcrumbs at the top. When you verify that the desired folder is the one currently displayed in the breadcrumbs, click *Choose This Folder*. Then click *Save* and you're done. If you don't like any of the subfolders listed, you can place the link into a new subfolder by using the *Add Subfolder* button.

If you choose *Remove* instead of Select in the above example, you take the link out of both subfolders and return it to the main bookmarks view.

Now that you have an understanding of how bookmark folders are used, let's

Home

Home ▶ Literature

Add Subfolder   Choose This Folder

Folder	# of Folders	# of Entries	
Children	0	6	Choose
Fiction	0	2	Choose
Nonfiction	0	3	Choose
Poetry	0	5	Choose

Showing 4 results.

Figure 12.7: In this view, you can move the link into several different locations.

create some new bookmarks.

Adding and Using Bookmarks

Navigate to your portal and add the Bookmarks application to your page by selecting *Add → More*. The portlet looks like this by default:

Across the top of the portlet are links labeled Home, Recent, and Mine. There is also a Search field and button.

Home: returns you to the top level of the portlet.

Recent: displays a list of the latest bookmarks that have been added.

Mine: displays a list of the bookmarks you added to the portlet.

Search: lets you search for bookmarks by name, category, or tags.

When you select the *Permissions* button on the right, a list of Roles and their associated permissions appears. The options are Add Entry, Add Folder, Permissions, and View. When you are finished selecting the permissions click *Save*.

Clicking the *Add Folder* button in the Bookmarks application reveals this form:

Here you can choose the folder's name, a description of its contents, and who can view it. Under More Options, you can set portlet permissions for various Roles to the folder. Click *Save* when you are finished.

Figure 12.8: Initially, no bookmarks are listed in this form until they're created.

Figure 12.9: It's not necessary to enter a description for a Bookmarks folder.

To create a bookmark, click the *Add Bookmark* button. This form is similar to the New Folder form but has a few more options.

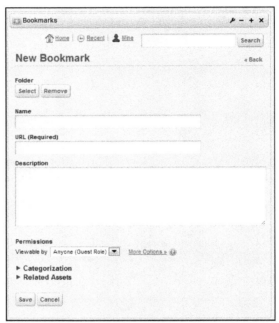

Figure 12.10: When you use the Add Bookmark form, you must enter a valid URL in the required field.

Click *Select* to choose the folder for the new bookmark. Click *Remove* to delete a bookmark from the selected folder. As stated above, a removed link goes into the list of general bookmarks that aren't associated with a folder. These are listed in the bookmarks section, below the folders, in the portlet.

Below the Permissions there are additional options for Categorization and Related Assets, just like in other Liferay applications. Please see chapter 5 on the Asset Framework for further information about this.

Once you have added a new bookmark, it appears in the portlet. From here, you can manage your bookmark using familiar Liferay editing features. Collecting and organizing your links is a snap when you use Liferay's Bookmarks application.

12.2 Creating Your Own Plugin Repository

As your enterprise builds its own library of portlets for internal use, you can create your own plugin repository to make it easy to install and upgrade portlets. This will allow different departments who may be running different instances of Liferay to share portlets and install them as needed. If you are a software development house, you may wish to create a plugin repository for your own products. Liferay makes it easy for you to create your own plugin repository and make it available to others.

You can create your plugin repository in two ways:

1. Use the Software Catalog in the Control Panel to create the repository by using its graphical interface and an HTTP server.

2. Create an XML file using the Liferay Plugin Repository DTD and an HTTP server.

Both methods have their benefits. The first method allows users to upload their plugins to an HTTP server to which they have access. They can then register their plugins with the repository by adding a link to it via the Control Panel's graphical user interface. Liferay will then generate the XML necessary to connect the repository to a Control Panel running on another instance of Liferay. This XML file can then be placed on an HTTP server and its URL can be added to the Plugin Installer, making the portlets in this repository available to the server running Liferay.

The second method does not require an instance of Liferay to be running. You can upload plugins to an HTTP server of your choice, then create an XML file called `liferay-plugin-repository.xml` manually. If you make this file available on an HTTP server (it can be the same one which is storing the plugins or a different one), you can connect the repository to a Plugin Installer in the Control Panel running on an instance of Liferay.

We will first look at creating a plugin repository using the Software Catalog in the Control Panel.

Software Catalog

You will want to use the Software Catalog if you will have multiple users submitting portlets into the repository and if you don't want to worry about creating the liferay-plugin-repository.xml file yourself.

Figure 12.11: The Software Catalog with Nothing Installed

Each site in your portal can have an instance of the Software Catalog. The Control Panel presents you with the software catalog for whichever site you are working on. This means different sites can have different software repositories, so you can host several software repositories on the same instance of Liferay if you wish, they just have to be in different sites. Choose the site that will host the plugin repository and go to the Control Panel. You will see at the top of the screen a message that says "Content for [Site]," where [Site] is the site you were on when you selected the Control Panel from the dockbar. If you want to administer the software catalog for a different site, you can select it from the selection box.

The Software Catalog has several tabs. The first tab is labeled Products. The default view of the portlet, when populated with software, displays what plugins are available for install or download. This can be seen in the version on Liferay's home page.

We will use an example site in order to better illustrate how to use the Software Catalog portlet. Assume you, as the portal administrator, have created a site called *Old Computers*. This site will be for users to collaborate on setting up and using old computers with obsolete hardware and operating systems. Users who participate in the site will eventually get upgraded to a more privileged status and get their own blog page. To implement this, you have created a My Summary portlet which displays the user's name, picture and description from his or her user profile. Because this portlet is generic enough that it could be

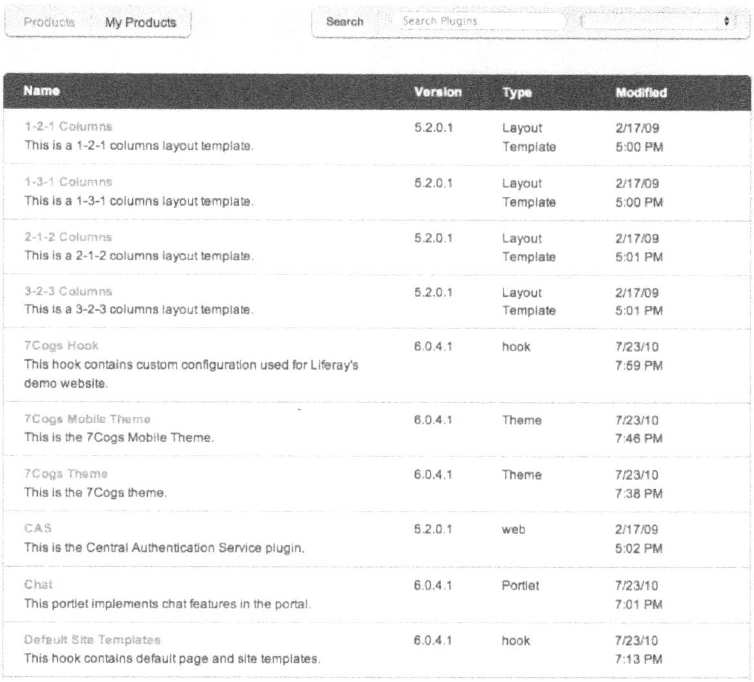

Products	My Products		Search	Search Plugins	

Name	Version	Type	Modified
1-2-1 Columns This is a 1-2-1 columns layout template.	5.2.0.1	Layout Template	2/17/09 5:00 PM
1-3-1 Columns This is a 1-3-1 columns layout template.	5.2.0.1	Layout Template	2/17/09 5:00 PM
2-1-2 Columns This is a 2-1-2 columns layout template.	5.2.0.1	Layout Template	2/17/09 5:01 PM
3-2-3 Columns This is a 3-2-3 columns layout template.	5.2.0.1	Layout Template	2/17/09 5:01 PM
7Cogs Hook This hook contains custom configuration used for Liferay's demo website.	6.0.4.1	hook	7/23/10 7:59 PM
7Cogs Mobile Theme This is the 7Cogs Mobile Theme.	6.0.4.1	Theme	7/23/10 7:46 PM
7Cogs Theme This is the 7Cogs theme.	6.0.4.1	Theme	7/23/10 7:38 PM
CAS This is the Central Authentication Service plugin.	5.2.0.1	web	2/17/09 5:02 PM
Chat This portlet implements chat features in the portal.	6.0.4.1	Portlet	7/23/10 7:01 PM
Default Site Templates This hook contains default page and site templates.	6.0.4.1	hook	7/23/10 7:13 PM

Figure 12.12: Populated Software Catalog from liferay.com

useful to anyone using Liferay, you have decided to make it available in your own software catalog.

The first step in adding a plugin to your software repository is to add a license for your product. A license communicates to users the terms upon which you are allowing them to download and use your software. Click the *Licenses* tab and then click the *Add License* button that appears. You will then see a form which allows you to enter the title of your license, a URL pointing to the actual license document and check boxes denoting whether the license is open source, active or recommended.

When you have finished filling out the form, click the *Save* button. Your license will be saved. Once you have at least one license in the system, you can begin adding software products to your software catalog. Click the *Products* tab, then click the *Add Product* button.

Your next step will be to create the product record in the software catalog. This will register the product in the software catalog and allow you to start adding versions of your software for users to download and/or install directly from their instances of Liferay. You will first need to put the .war file containing your software on a web server that is accessible without authentication to the users who will be installing your software. In the example above, the *Old Computers* site is on the Internet so you would place the file on a web server that is accessible to anyone on the Internet. If you are creating a software catalog for an internal Intranet, you would place the file on a web server that is available to anyone inside of your organization's firewall.

To create the product record in the Software Catalog portlet, click the *Products* tab, then click the *Add Product* button. Fill out the form with information about your product.

Name: The name of your software product.

Type: Select whether this is a portlet, theme, layout template, hook or web plugin.

Licenses: Select the license(s) under which you are releasing this software.

Author: Enter the name of the author of the software.

Page URL: If the software has a home page, enter its URL here.

Tags: Enter any tags you would like added to this software.

Short Description: Enter a short description. This will be displayed in the summary table of your software catalog.

Long Description: Enter a longer description. This will be displayed on the details page for this software product.

Permissions: Click the *Configure* link to set permissions for this software product.

Group ID: Enter a group ID. A group ID is a name space which usually identifies the company or organization that made the software. For our example, we will use *old-computers*.

Artifact ID: Enter an Artifact ID. The artifact ID is a unique name within the name space for your product. For our example, we will use *my-summary-portlet*.

Screenshot: Click the *Add Screenshot* button to add a screen shot of your product for users to view.

When you have finished filling out the form, click the *Save* button. You will be brought back to the product summary page and you will see your product has been added to the repository.

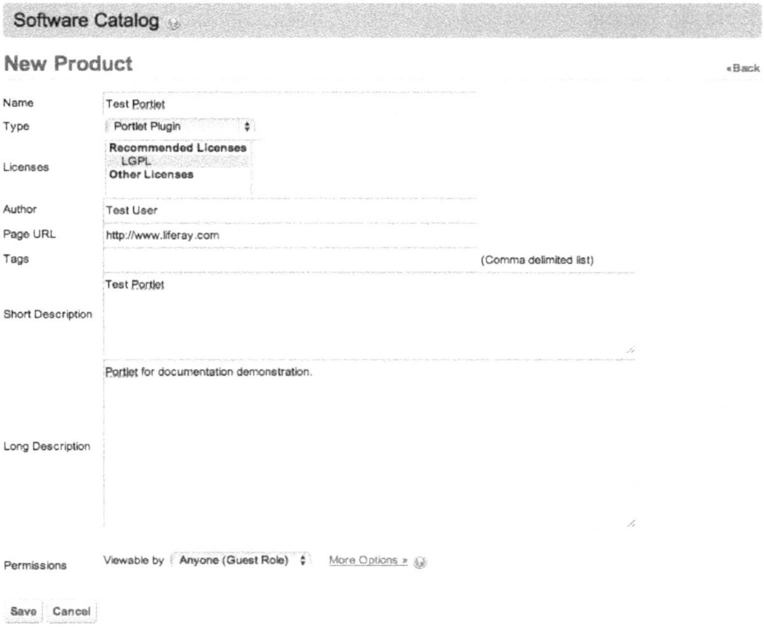

Figure 12.13: Adding a Product to the Software Catalog

Notice in the version column, *N/A* is being displayed. This is because there are not yet any released *versions* of your product. To make your product downloadable, you need to create a version of your product and point it to the file you uploaded to your HTTP server earlier.

Before you do that, however, you need to add a *Framework Version* to your software catalog. A Framework version denotes what version of Liferay your plugin is designed for and works on. You cannot add a version of your product without linking it to a version of the framework for which it is designed.

Why is this so important? Because as Liferay gains more and more features, you may wish to take advantage of those features in future versions of your product, while still keeping older versions of your product available for those who are using older versions of Liferay. This is perfectly illustrated in the example My Summary portlet we are using. Liferay had a My Summary portlet of its own, which does exactly what we have described here. This portlet was added to the suite of portlets which Liferay provides in the Social Networking plugin. This plugin makes use of the many social networking features which have been added to Liferay. So rather than just displaying a summary of your information, the Social Networking portlet adds features such as status updates, a "wall" for each user in his or her profile that other users can *write* on, the ability to become *friends* with other users—thereby granting them access to their profiles—and more.

None of this would work in older versions of Liferay, because the core engine that enables developers to create features like this is not there. So in this case, you would want to keep the older My Summary portlet available for users who have not yet upgraded and make the newer social portlets available to those using latest version of Liferay. This is what *Framework Versions* does for you. If you connect to Liferay's software repositories with an old version of Liferay Portal, you will see the My Summary portlet. If you connect to Liferay's software repositories with new version of Liferay, you will see the social portlets.

So click the *Framework Versions* tab and then click the *Add Framework Version* button.

Give the framework a name, a URL and leave the *Active* check box checked. For our example, we have entered 6.0.3 for the name, because our portlet should work on that version and higher, and http://www.liferay.com for the URL. Click *Save.*

Now go back to the *Products* tab and click on your product. You will notice a message is displayed stating the product does not have any released versions. Click the *Add Product Version* button.

Version Name: Enter the version of your product.

Change Log: Enter some comments regarding what changed between this version and any previous versions.

Supported Framework Versions: Select the framework version for which your software product is intended. Enter a + at the end of the version number if you want to specify a version plus any future versions.

Download Page URL: If your product has a descriptive web page, enter its URL here.

Direct Download URL (Recommended): Enter a direct download link to your software product here. The Plugin Installer portlet will follow this link in order to download your software product.

Include Artifact in Repository: To enable others to use the Plugin Installer portlet to connect to your repository and download your plugin, select *yes* here.

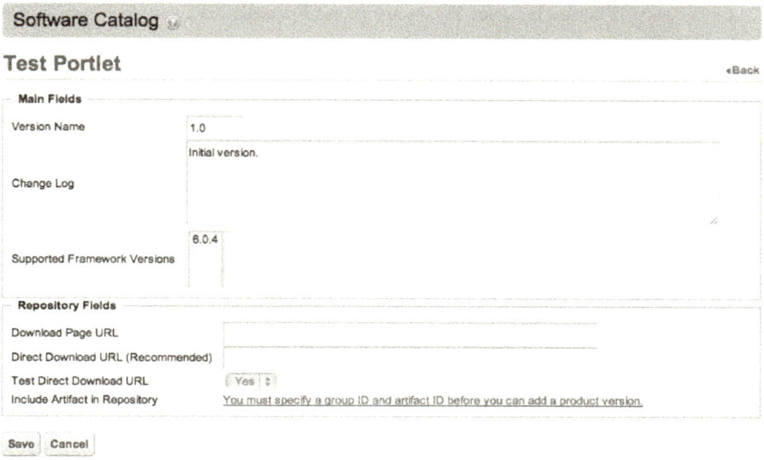

Figure 12.14: Adding a Product Version to the Software Catalog

When you are finished filling out the form, click the *Save* button. Your product version will be saved and your product will now be available in the software repository.

Generating The Software Catalog

The Software Catalog works by generating an XML document which the Plugin Installer reads. Using the data from this XML document, the Plugin Installer knows where it can download the plugins from, what version of Liferay the plugins are designed for and all other data about the plugins that have been entered into the Software Catalog portlet.

In order to get your Software Catalog to generate this XML data, you will need to access a particular URL. If you have created a friendly URL for your site (for example, the default site, which is called *guest*, has a friendly URL of /guest already configured for it), you can use the friendly URL. If not, you will first need to know the Group ID of the site in which your Software Catalog portlet resides. You can do this by accessing the Manage Pages interface and looking at the URLs for any of the pages. The URL will look something like this: http://localhost:8080/web/10148/1.

Obviously, it is much easier if you are using Friendly URLs, which we highly recommend.

Next, go to your browser and go to the following URL:

http://:/software_catalog?

For example, if you are on the same machine as your Liferay instance, and that instance is running on port 8080, and your group ID from the database is 10148, you would use the following URL:

http://localhost:8080/software_catalog?10148

If you have also created a friendly URL called *old-computers* for this site, you would use the following URL:

http://localhost:8080/software_catalog?old-computers

If you have configured everything properly, an XML document should be returned:

```
<?xml version="1.0" encoding="UTF-8"?>

<plugin-repository>

    <settings/>

    <plugin-package>

        <name>My Summary</name>

        <module-id>old-computers/my-summary-portlet/1.0/war</module-id>

        <modified-date>Thu, 23 Apr 2009 20:40:16 +0000</modified-date>

        <types>

            <type>portlet</type>

        </types>

        <tags>

            <tag>social</tag>

            <tag>profile</tag>

        </tags>

        <short-description>My Summary</short-description>

        <long-description>My Summary</long-description>

        <change-log>Initial Version</change-log>

        <download-url>
        http://www.liferay.com/portlets/my-summary-portlet-6.0.4.war
```

```
        </download-url>

            <author>Rich Sezov</author>

            <screenshots/>

            <licenses>

                <license osi-approved="true">MIT License</license>

            </licenses>

            <liferay-versions/>

        </plugin-package>

</plugin-repository>
```

You can now give the URL to your software repository out on your web site and other administrators of Liferay can enter it into the Plugins Installation module of their Liferay Control Panels to connect to your repository.

If you want to serve your repository off of a static web server, you can save this document to a file called `liferay-plugin-package.xml` and put this file on your HTTP server. You can then give out the URL to the directory which holds this file on your web site and anyone with an instance of Liferay will be able to point their Plugin Installer portlets to it.

Benefits of the Software Catalog

As you can see, the Software Catalog makes it easy for you to create a repository of your software. Users of Liferay can configure their Plugin Installers to attach to your repository and the proper versions of your software will be automatically made available to them by a single click. This is by far the easiest way for you to keep track of your software and for your users to obtain your software.

Another benefit of the Software Catalog is that you can make available to your users a standard interface for manually downloading your software. For those who prefer to manually download plugins, your Software Catalog gives them an interface to go in, find your software either by browsing or by searching, preview screen shots and download your software—and you don't have to build any of those pages yourself. Simply configure your software in the portlet and all of that is done for you.

How can you do this? The Software Catalog is also available as a portlet. You can add it to any page on your web site through the *Add Application* menu. You can find the portlet in the *Tools* category.

Manually Creating A Software Catalog

If you do not wish to use the Control Panel to create your software catalog, you can create it manually by manually typing out the XML file that the Software Catalog section of the Control Panel would normally generate. Note that if you do this, you will not be able to use the Software Catalog portlet as a graphical user interface to your software that end users can use to download your software manually: you will have to build this yourself. Keep in mind many instances of Liferay Portal sit behind a firewall without access to the Internet. Because of this, if you are making your software available to Internet users, some of them will have to download it manually anyway, because their installations are firewalled. In this case, the Software Catalog portlet is the easiest way to provide a user interface for downloading your software.

If you still wish to use a text editor to create your software catalog, you can. To manually create a software catalog, obtain the DTD for the XML file from Liferay's source code. You will find this DTD in the *definitions* folder in the Liferay source or on the Liferay web site[1] It is a file called `liferay-plugin-package_-6_1_0.dtd`. Use this DTD with a validating XML editor (a good, free choice is jEdit with all the XML plugins) to create your software catalog manually.

Connecting to a Software Catalog

If there is a software catalog of plugins you would like to point your instance of Liferay to, all you need is the URL to the catalog. Once you have the URL, go to the Plugin Installer in your Control Panel and click the *Configuration* tab. You will see there are two fields in which you can enter URLs to plugin repositories: *Trusted Plugin Repositories* and *Untrusted Plugin Repositories*. Currently, the only difference between the two is to provide a visual cue for administrators as to which repositories are trusted and untrusted.

Enter the URL to the repository to which you wish to connect in one of the fields and click *Save*. The portlet will connect to the repository and items from this repository will be shown in the list.

If all this talk of catalogs has put you in the mood to do some shopping, then it's probably a good time to get acquainted with Liferay's Shopping application. Let's go down that aisle next.

---

[1]`http://www.liferay.com/dtd/liferay-plugin-repository_6_1_0.dtd`

12.3 Shopping

Would your organization like to make some money selling promotional items? Are you an artist looking to share your work with the world? Perhaps your company produces a publication that customers want to purchase? If you have something of value the visitors of your site want or need, then Lifeary's Shopping application can help you get these items to your customers with a secure transaction.

The Shopping portlet uses PayPal and allows you to choose the credit cards your store accepts. You can organize your inventory with categories and subcategories. A search function helps users find items quickly. Users place items in a shopping cart, allowing them to purchase multiple items at once. There is also an email notification system to alert customers when their transactions are processed.

Before we start printing money, let's first create an online store.

Setting up shop

Figure 12.15: Start setting up the store by entering items and categories in the shopping portlet.

To begin setting up a store, place the Shopping application on a page in your site. Like the Message Boards portlet, the Shopping portlet takes up a lot of space. It's best, therefore, to dedicate an entire page to the application. The

Shopping portlet is available from the *Add* → *More* menu in the Dockbar under Shopping.

The shopping portlet has four tabs across the top:

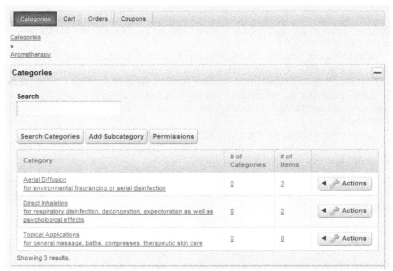

Figure 12.16: In this figure there are three subcategories for the Aromatherapy category. The first subcategory has three items, the second has two, and the third is empty.

Categories: shows the categories of items in your store. For example, if you're selling music, you might have categories for various genres, such as pop, rock, metal, hip hop, and the like. The portlet defaults to this view.

Cart: shows the items the user has selected to purchase from your store. It displays the order subtotal, the shipping cost, and a field for entering a coupon code. There are buttons for updating the cart, emptying the cart, and checking out.

Orders: displays a list of all previous orders placed, containing options to search for orders by the order number, status, first name, last name and/or email address.

Coupons: lets you define coupon codes to offer discounts to your customers. You can enter the coupon code, discount type, and whether it is active or not. Search looks for a particular coupon offer while Add Coupon opens a new form to key in the coupon data. Delete removes a coupon.

Below the tabs are breadcrumbs for navigating between the categories and subcategories you create. In fact, this would be a good time to start creating some categories.

Creating Categories

It's not difficult to create categories. Simply click the *Add Category* button to display the Category form. In this form enter the *Name*, *Description*, and set the *Permissions* for the category. That's all there is to it.

When you click *Save*, your new category is listed in the portlet, along with the number of subcategories and the number of items that are in the category. You can edit the category, set permissions for it or delete it using the *Actions* button.

Each category can have unlimited subcategories and you can add subcategories to any category. Notice as you add categories and subcategories, navigational breadcrumbs appear in the portlet. Use these to move through the store inventory.

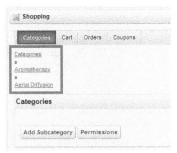

Creating Items

When you select a category, you'll see its items appear. You create items the same way you create categories. Use the *Add Item* button to open the new item form. Enter data for the SKU number, name, description, and item properties. You can select checkboxes to specify whether the item requires shipping and whether it is a featured item. Enter the stock quantity to

Figure 12.17: Breadcrumbs are an important navigational tool in the shopping portlet.

record how many items are available and set the appropriate permissions.

The Fields area is where you add additional fields to set specific characteristics for the item. These can include things like sizes and colors. The additional fields appear in the item form as pull-down menus, as in the figure below.

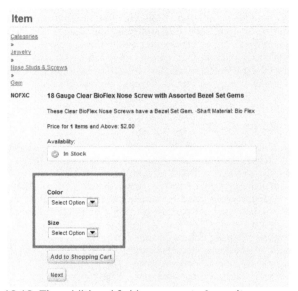

Figure 12.18: The additional fields you create for an item appear in the item description form as menu options.

The Prices area is for all data pertaining to the item's cost, minimum and maximum quantities, quantity discounts, taxes, and shipping costs.

The Images area lets you add photos to the item form. You can add a link to the photo or upload the file locally. Choose from three sizes of images. You must select the appropriate check box for the image you want to display. When you're finished creating a new item, click *Save*.

As products are added, they are listed in the Items section of the portlet. If the item you just created needs to go into one of your new categories or subcategories, you can assign it to the category by editing the item. Choose the *Select* button (next to the *Remove* button), and this displays a dialog box listing all the shop categories.

Choose the desired category from the list to relocate the item to its new location. Notice how the breadcrumbs reflect this change in the item form.

Figure 12.19: The image in this figure is the medium sized option.

Categories

Category	# of Categories	# of Items	
Aromatherapy	3	5	Choose
Grooming	0	4	Choose
Jewelry	12	14	Choose
Swimming Accessories	0	4	Choose

Showing 4 results.

Figure 12.20: To put an item in a category, edit the item and choose *Select* to see the available categories.

Figure 12.21: When an item moves into a category, the breadcrumb navigation updates accordingly.

You can make changes to any item through *Actions* → *Edit*. Finding an item is easy, using the *Search* function.

That's how you create an item for the store. Now let's examine some of the shopping portlet's configuration options.

Configuration

By selecting the *wrench* icon in the top right of the portlet, you can manage the configuration options of the shopping application. In the Setup view, there are tabs for Payment Settings, Shipping Calculation, Insurance Calculation, and Emails.

Payment Settings

The payment settings section is where you configure all the functions related to transactions for your store.

PayPal Email Address: is the address of your store's PayPal account which is used for payment processing.

Note that PayPal can be disabled by entering a blank PayPal address in the field. Credit cards can likewise be disabled. Payments to the store are not required when these settings are disabled. The credit card function does not process payments; it instead stores the card information with the order so you can process the transaction separately.

Credit Cards: sets the type of credit cards your store accepts.

The Current column holds the cards your store takes. The Available column holds cards not accepted by your shop. These can be moved easily from one column to another by selecting a card and clicking one of the arrow buttons. The arrows below the Current window allow you to choose the order credit cards are displayed on the form.

Currency: sets the appropriate currency your shop accepts.

Tax State: sets the applicable state where your business is responsible for paying taxes.

Tax Rate: sets the percentage of taxes your store is responsible for paying. This rate is added as a sales tax charge to orders.

Minimum Order: sets the minimum amount required for a sale.

Shipping and Insurance Calculation

Both the Shipping and Insurance forms have identical options.

Formula: sets the equation for determining shipping and insurance costs. They're calculated on either a flat rate based on the total purchase amount or on a percentage of the total amount spent.

Values: sets the shipping and insurance fees based on a range of figures that the total order amount falls under.

Emails

This form sets the addresses for customer email notifications. Use the list of term definitions below to customize the correspondence with your customers.

Emails From: sets the email address from which order and shipping notifications are sent.

Confirmation Email: Use this form to customize the email message customers receive when an order is received.

Shipping Email: Use this form to customize the email message customers receive when an order has been shipped.

So far we have added the shopping portlet to your site, created categories and items for your store, set up payment options, and configured customer communication options. These are the basics required to get your store up and running. Now let's review the buying process.

Using the shopping cart

Logged in users are given a shopping cart to store the items they wish to buy. Customers can manage items and their quantities directly from the cart, allowing them to purchase a single product or multiple products at once. Customers can also key in coupon codes to take advantage of any discounts your store has to offer. Products can be placed in the cart from any category or subcategory. The cart's appearance can be customized to reflect the overall design of your store.

When buyers select an item, they see the item's description displaying all of its relevant information. The figure below is typical of what an item's description might look like.

Below the product description is the Availability field indicating whether the item is in stock. There are also two buttons for managing the shopping experience:

Add to Shopping Cart: places the item in your cart for checkout.

Figure 12.22: Shopping emails can be configured in a myriad of ways to suit your needs.

Figure 12.23: You can include images of each item in your store. (Medium sized images display on the item's description form).

Next: lets you to scroll through all the items in the category, giving you the option to add to the cart as you go.

After adding an item to the cart, click << *Back* to return to the product description and continue shopping by navigating the category breadcrumbs at the top of the form. You can also continue shopping by scrolling through a category, item by item, using the *Previous* and *Next* buttons at the bottom of the product description.

Each time you add an item to the cart, a running tally of the cart's contents is kept. Quantities for each item are controlled using drop-down menus. The order subtotal and shipping costs appear above a field where coupon codes can

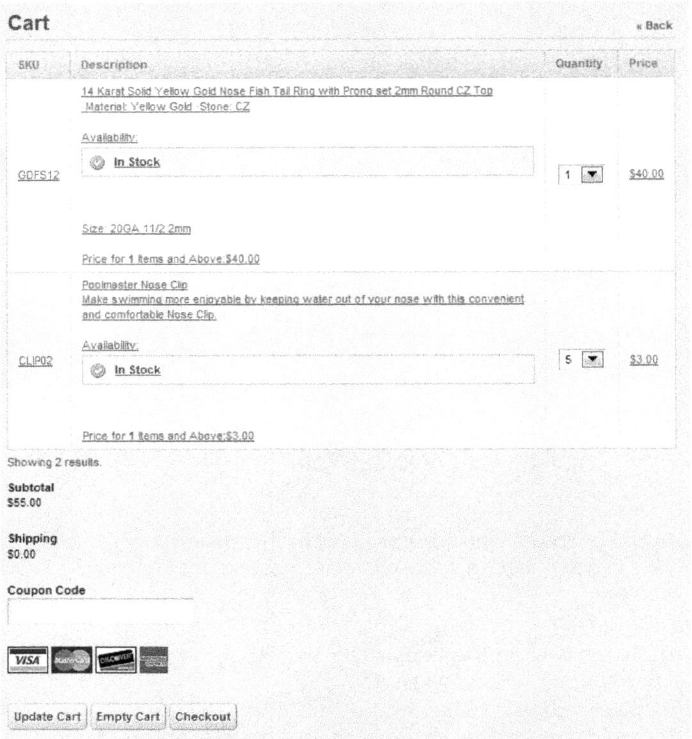

Figure 12.24: This shopping cart has two items in it so far.

be entered. When you have finished adding products to the cart, you have three options:

Update Cart: lets you change the quantity of an item being purchased. If a minimum number of items has been set in the item description, the field under the Quantity column shows that number by default. You can adjust the exact number of items you want with the drop-down menus in the cart.

Empty Cart: lets you clear the contents of the cart to either start shopping again or to stop shopping.

Checkout: sends you to a new form to verify the billing address, shipping address, and the credit card information. You can also add comments about the order if necessary.

When all the data has been entered correctly, click *Continue* to see the order summary. After reviewing the summary, click *Finished* and you are given confirmation the order has been placed, along with the order number. Use this number to search for the order history and keep track of its status.

Customizing the shopping cart with a hook

If you think the shopping cart looks a little basic for your purposes, you can customize it by using a hook. To learn more about changing the appearance of the shopping cart, consult the *Liferay Developer's Guide* or see section 8.3 in *Liferay in Action*.

Now your online store is set up, you have inventory, you have a payment system, and you have sales rolling in. All is good. Some day there will be customers with questions about their orders. Let's go over the orders next.

Managing Orders

Under the Orders tab there are fields for finding specific orders. Search for orders using the order number, order status, first or last name on the order or by the email address associated with the account. For more information on searching in Liferay Portal, see the Faceted Search section in chapter 5.

Below the search fields is the orders list. Orders can be deleted or edited using the *Actions* button. When you select an order from the Orders tab, cr if you edit an order, you see a summary of the order details along with some options across the bottom.

Invoice: creates a printer-friendly copy of the order that can be sent to a customer.

Resend Confirmation Email: lets you notify the customer that the order has been received and is being processed.

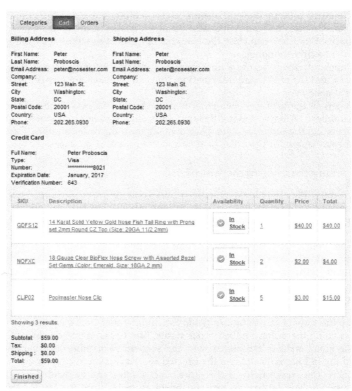

Figure 12.25: All the information pertaining an order can be seen in the order summary view.

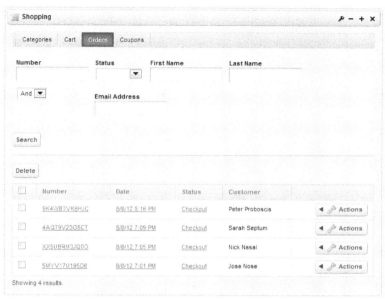

Figure 12.26: Search for orders in the Orders view or select one from the list.

Send Shipping Email: notifies the customer that the order is *en route*. You can also include a tracking number with this email to allow the customer to follow the delivery process.

Delete: removes the order from the system.

Cancel: closes the Edit view and returns the user to the main orders view.

You can also add comments about the order and subscribe to the comments to get any updates on the order.

Managing Coupons

The Coupons view of the Shopping application lets you provide coupon codes for special sale events or other discounts. You can determine the type of dis-

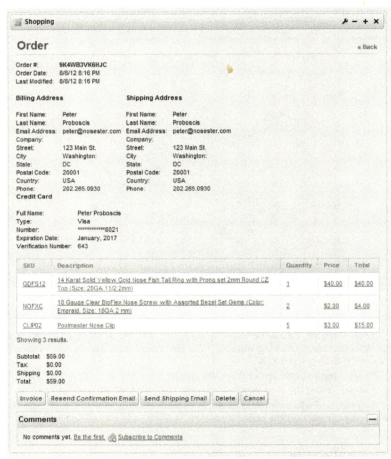

Figure 12.27: Review order specifics in the Edit view.

count to apply and whether it is currently active. You can search for coupons and create new coupons from this form.

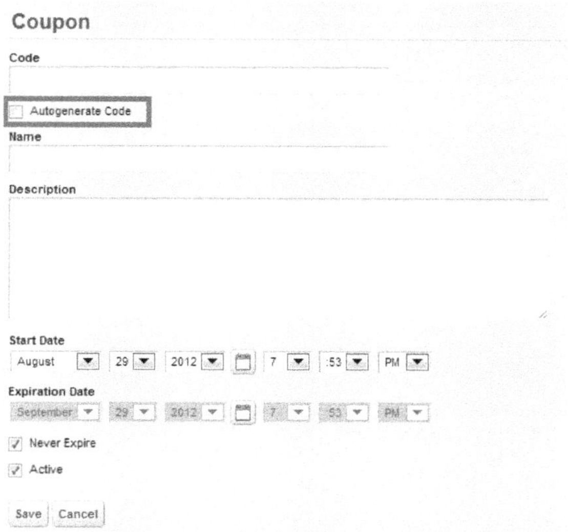

Coupon

Code

☐ Autogenerate Code

Name

Description

Start Date

August ▼ 29 ▼ 2012 ▼ 📅 7 ▼ :53 ▼ PM ▼

Expiration Date

September ▼ 29 ▼ 2012 ▼ 📅 7 ▼ :53 ▼ PM ▼

☑ Never Expire

☑ Active

Save Cancel

Figure 12.28: Create a coupon code automatically when you select the Autogenerate Code box.

To add a coupon, enter the coupon code in the Code field. If no code is specified, you can create one automatically by selecting the *Autogenerate Code* checkbox. After entering the coupon's name and description, you can set the coupon's start and expiration dates. Additional options let you activate the coupon and set it to never expire.

Under the Discount section, you can set the minimum order amount required for the discount, the discount amount, and the discount type. Types can be based on a percentage, a fixed amount, free shipping, or a tax free sale. The Limits section lets you set coupon restrictions based on a list of categories and/or SKU numbers.

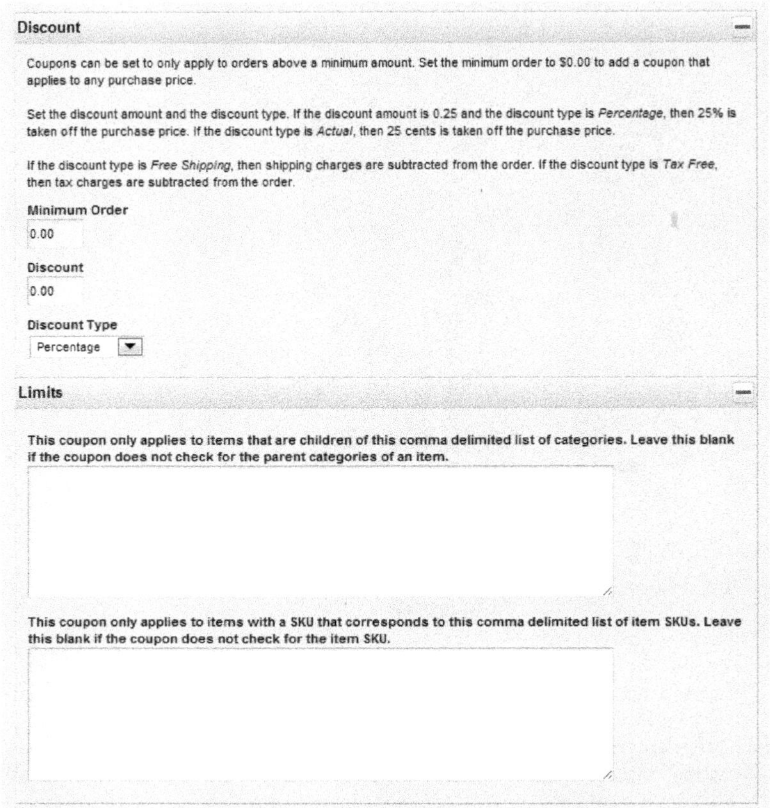

Discount   —

Coupons can be set to only apply to orders above a minimum amount. Set the minimum order to $0.00 to add a coupon that applies to any purchase price.

Set the discount amount and the discount type. If the discount amount is 0.25 and the discount type is *Percentage*, then 25% is taken off the purchase price. If the discount type is *Actual*, then 25 cents is taken off the purchase price.

If the discount type is *Free Shipping*, then shipping charges are subtracted from the order. If the discount type is *Tax Free*, then tax charges are subtracted from the order.

Minimum Order

0.00

Discount

0.00

Discount Type

Percentage ▼

Limits   —

This coupon only applies to items that are children of this comma delimited list of categories. Leave this blank if the coupon does not check for the parent categories of an item.

This coupon only applies to items with a SKU that corresponds to this comma delimited list of item SKUs. Leave this blank if the coupon does not check for the item SKU.

Figure 12.29: Customize your coupon parameters under Discounts and Limits.

Integrating the Amazon Rankings portlet

If your store sells books, you can use Liferay's Amazon Rankings application to display them alongside the main shopping portlet. Both of these are found in the Shopping category under *Add → More* in the Control Panel. The Amazon Rankings application lets you highlight the books in your store's inventory outside of the typical category structure. Books are arranged in ascending order according to Amazon's Best Sellers Rank. Book cover images displayed in the portlet come from the images in the product's description.

Setting up your Amazon Web Services account To use Amazon rankings, you must first setup an Amazon Associates Program account. This gives you the *associate ID tag* you need to enter in your `portal-ext.properties` file. Then you need to join the Amazon Product Advertising API group. This yields the *access key id* and the *secret access key* that also must go into your `portal-ext.properties` file.

Amazon License Keys are available at their web site[2].

Add the following lines to your `portal-ext.properties` file and populate the values for the associate ID tag, access-key id, and secret access key. Ensure there are no spaces between the = sign and the property values.

```
amazon.access.key.id=
amazon.associate.tag=
amazon.secret.access.key=
```

Note that these keys are provided by Amazon for personal use only. Please consult Amazon at http://www.amazon.com for more information.

If your Amazon Web Services key is set improperly, you can't add books to your Shopping portlet.

Setting up the Amazon Rankings portlet After setting up your Amazon Web Services account, choose the books to display in your store. Select *Configuration* from the Amazon Rankings portlet in the upper right corner. Go to the *Setup* tab and enter the International Standard Book Numbers (ISBNs) in the textbox, separated by spaces. The portlet accepts 10-digit ISBNs rejecting ISBNs that letters.

When you are finished setting up the rankings, books appear in the portlet similar to the example below. Clicking on the book's cover image opens the book's Amazon page.

---

[2]https://aws-portal.amazon.com/gp/aws/developer/registration/index.html/

Figure 12.30: Separate ISBNs with single spaces.

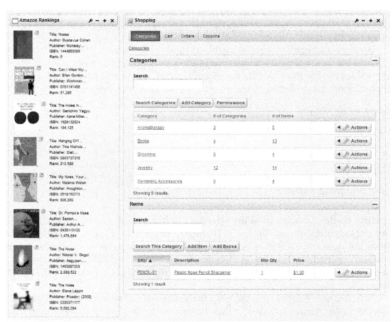

Figure 12.31: Using the Amazon Rankings application can be a nice
addition to your store.

Now that you have a good grasp on Liferay's Shopping and Amazon Rankings applications, let's see what the Knowledge Base application has to offer.

12.4 Knowledge Base

Liferay's Knowledge Base portlet provides a means for creating and organizing articles within a site. The knowledge base is perfect for creating and organizing information more formally than in a wiki. For example, it can be used to organize and display professional product documentation. It's easy to set up the knowledge base with a workflow that requires articles to be approved before they are published. Additionally, it allows administrators to create article templates. Templates can be used to insure certain kinds of articles possess a common structure and include certain kinds of information. Knowledge base articles can be categorized to make them easy to find. They can also be organized hierarchically to form complete books or guides. The Knowledge Base portlet is available as an app from Liferay Marketplace. Please see chapter 2 for installation instructions.

Knowledge Base Display Portlet

The Knowledge Base app actually consists of four portlets that can be placed on site pages as well as one that adds a page to the Control Panel. The four portlets that can be placed on a page are Knowledge Base (Display), Knowledge Base Search, Knowledge Base Article and Knowledge Base Section. When placed on a page, the Knowledge Base display portlet presents many of the same options to an administrator that are available from the Knowledge Base page of the control panel.

You can use the four links at the top of the Knowledge Base display portlet to control what it displays.

Knowledge Base Home: shows you a list of all top level articles.

Recent Articles: shows you a list of articles in order from most recent activity to least recent activity.

Administrator: shows you a list of all articles, regardless of which ones are parents or children of the others.

My Subscriptions: shows you a list of articles you are subscribed to.

The *Add Article* button is available from the Knowledge Base Home or Administrator view of the Knowledge Base display portlet or from the Articles tab of the Knowledge Base page of the Control Panel. Use this button to create an

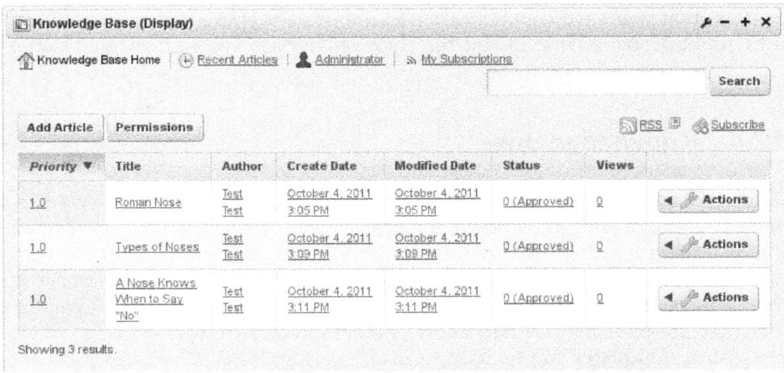

Figure 12.32: Knowledge Base Display Portlet

article for the knowledge base. When creating an article, you can use the same WYSIWYG editor you used to create wiki pages. Articles, however, are not the same as wiki pages: they must be created in HTML, not MediaWiki or Creole. Click the *Source* button in the editor to view the HTML source of what you've written or write some HTML yourself.

In addition to entering a title and creating content for your article, you can use the editor to add attachments, add tags and set permissions. By default, view permission is granted to the guest role, meaning anyone can view your article. After you're done using the editor, you can save it as draft and continue working on it later or you can submit it for publication. Your article may need to be approved before being published, depending on the workflow defined for your portal.

You can find the *Permissions* button next to the Add Article button in the Knowledge Base display portlet or on the Knowledge Base page of the control panel. Click this button to define permissions that apply to the Knowledge Base display portlet generally, not to particular articles. Here, you can define which roles can add articles and templates, which are granted knowledge base administrator privileges, which can change permissions on articles, which can subscribe to articles and which can view templates.

Users may need to be granted access to the knowledge base page of the control panel in order to exercise some of the above permissions. For example, suppose the user role has been granted the Add Article and the View Templates

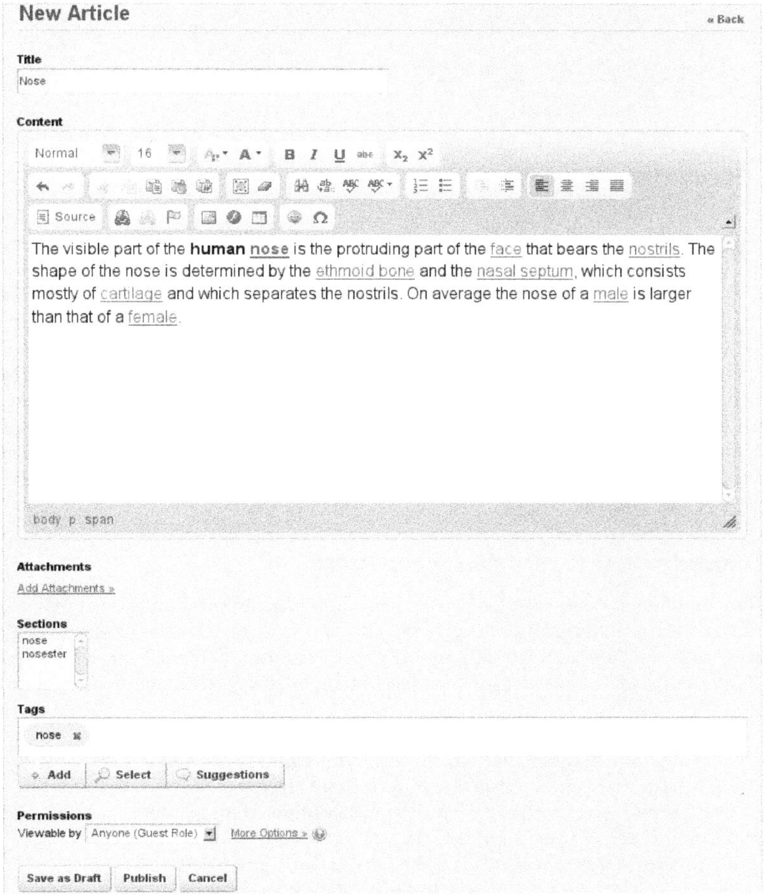

Figure 12.33: New Knowledge Base Article

Figure 12.34: Knowledge Base Permissions

permissions. A user will be able to add articles from the knowledge base display portlet but will need access to the knowledge base page of the Control Panel in order to view templates. Note that the Knowledge Base (Display) permissions are distinct from the Knowledge Base (Admin) portlet. The display permissions define what a user can do with the Knowledge Base display portlet on a page while the admin permissions define what a user can do on the Knowledge Base page of the Control Panel.

Knowledge Base Page of the Control Panel

The Knowledge Base page of the Control Panel has two tabs: one for articles and one for templates. The articles tab shows all the articles in the knowledge base and lets you perform actions on them. The templates tab shows all the templates defined in the knowledge base and lets you perform actions on them.

Administrators can perform the following actions on an article:

View: displays an article. From here, you can add a child article, edit the article, change its permissions, move it or delete it.

Edit: allows you to change the title and content of an article as well as add attachments, select topics and add tags.

Permissions: lets you configure the permissions on a specific article.

Subscribe: lets you to choose to be notified of any updates to a particular article.

Move: lets you change an article's position in the hierarchy by choosing a new parent article for it.

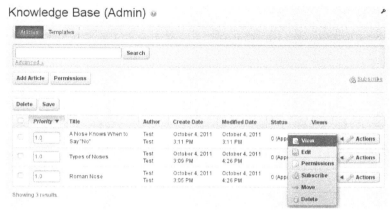

Figure 12.35: Knowledge Base Control Panel Page

Delete: lets you remove an article from the knowledge base.

These actions are similar to the ones that can be performed from the Administrator view of the Knowledge Base display portlet. However, the Knowledge Base display portlet is intended to be placed on a page for the end user so an additional action is available: *RSS* is a link to an RSS feed of an article. Also, the *View* action is only available from the Control Panel since the Knowledge Base Article portlet can be used to display an article on a page.

The templates tab of the Knowledge Base page of the Control Panel allows administrators to create templates to facilitate the creation of articles. A template basically functions like a starting point for the creation of certain types of articles. Click the *Add Template* button on the Templates tab of the Knowledge Base page of the Control Panel to create a new template.

Navigate back to the templates tab of the Knowledge Base page of the control panel. You can perform the following actions on a template:

View: displays a template. From here, you can use the template to create an article, edit the template, modify the permissions on the template or delete it.

Edit: allows you to change the title and content of a template.

Permissions: allows you to configure the permissions on a template. You can choose roles to have permission to update, view, delete or change the permissions on templates.

Delete: lets you remove a template from the knowledge base.

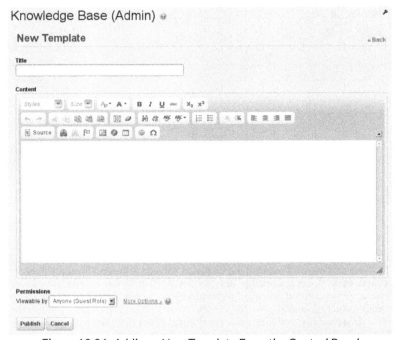

Figure 12.36: Adding a New Template From the Control Panel

To use a template to create a new article, you have to view the template and then click *Use this Template*. This brings you to the New Article editor with the contents of the template copied for you.

Knowledge Base Article Portlet

The Knowledge Base Article portlet can be placed on a page to display an entire article. When you first place this portlet on a page it displays the message *Please configure this portlet to make it visible to all users*. This message is a link to the configuration dialog box for the portlet. Click *Select Article* to choose an article to display. Pick an article and then click *Save*. When your page refreshes it will

Figure 12.37: Knowledge Base Section Portlets

display the article in the portlet.

Figure 12.38: Knowledge Base Article Portlet

The Knowledge Base Article portlet allows users to rate and comment on the article it displays. There are also links at the top of the portlet users can use to subscribe to an RSS feed of the knowledge base, subscribe to the article, view the history of the article or print the article.

Knowledge Base Section Portlet

The Knowledge Base Section portlet allows administrators to selectively show articles associated with a specific section. For example, a news site might have a *World* section, a *Politics* section, a *Business* section and an *Entertainment* section. In order to use sections, you need to set the `admin.kb.article.sections` property in your knowledge base portlet's `portlet.properties` file and re-deploy the portlet. You can find the `portlet.properties` file in the knowledge base portlet's source directory. Updating the one in your server's directory won't work. Use comma delimited section names to set the property, for example:

```
admin.kb.article.sections=World,Politics,Business,Entertainment
```

Figure 12.39: Knowledge Base Section Portlets

Once you have defined some sections in your knowledge base's `portlet.properties` file, your users will see a multi-select box in the Add Article and Edit Article screens that allows them to select which section an article belongs to.

You can add any number of Knowledge Base section portlets to a page and you can configure each portlet to display articles from any number of sections.

The Knowledge Base section portlet has some additional configurations that allow an administrator to select a display style (title or abstract), an article window state (maximized or normal), how to order the articles, how many articles to display per page and whether or not to show pagination.

Knowledge Base Navigation

Wikis often have deeply nested articles that can be hard to find by browsing. Liferay's knowledge base's ability to selectively display articles makes it easier to browse than a Wiki. The knowledge base also features some other aids to navigation. The Knowledge Base Search portlet allows you to search for articles in the knowledge base. This portlet presents the search results to you in order from most relevant to least relevant.

Figure 12.40: Knowledge Base Search Portlet

You can also use the Categories Navigation portlet in conjunction with the Knowledge Base display portlet. When both of these portlets are placed on a page you can select a topic in the Categories Navigation portlet and the Knowledge Base display portlet will show all of the articles that match the topic. You can create topics from the Categories page of the Control Panel.

You can select topics for articles when you are creating or editing them.

Figure 12.41: Knowledge Base Category Navigation Portlet

12.5   Summary

In this chapter, we examined two Liferay utility applications: the Software Catalog and the Knowledge Base. The Software Catalog allows you to define a set of software items to make available to visitors to your portal. Remember that the Software Catalog will be replaced by Liferay Marketplace and will soon be deprecated. The Knowledge Base application is an EE-only application that allows you to create articles and organize them into full books or guides that be published on your portal. Next, let's take a tour of the Liferay Marketplace and learn how to manage Liferay plugins.

CHAPTER 13

LEVERAGING THE LIFERAY MARKETPLACE

Liferay Marketplace is an exciting new hub for sharing, browsing and downloading Liferay-compatible applications. As enterprises look for ways to build and enhance their existing platforms, developers and software vendors are searching for new avenues to reach this market. Marketplace leverages the entire Liferay ecosystem to release and share apps in a user-friendly, one-stop site.

This chapter covers the following topics:

- Users, Companies, and Apps

- Accessing Liferay Marketplace

- Finding, Downloading, and Installing Apps

- Managing Apps

- Plugins and Plugin Management

- Portlets, Themes, Layout Templates, Hooks, and Web Plugins

- Installing Plugins from Repositories

- Installing Plugins Manually

- Plugin Troubleshooting and Configuration Issues

In a nutshell, the Liferay Marketplace is a repository for applications built on the Liferay Platform. You can find and download applications directly from the Marketplace on the web or use an existing Liferay installation to access and install applications onto the running Liferay web site. Once installed, you can manage the applications through Liferay's control panel.

13.1 Marketplace Concepts: Users, Companies, and Apps

Anyone can browse the apps available on Liferay Marketplace,[1] but a `liferay.com` user account is required for purchasing and downloading apps, whether from the Marketplace website or from an existing Liferay installation. Many official Liferay apps, as well as some third party apps, are available free of charge. Other apps require you to pay a fee in order to access them. When you purchase an app, you can do so on your own behalf or on behalf of a company. Apps purchased on your own behalf are associated with your personal `liferay.com` user account. Apps purchased on behalf of a company are associated with the company's account and can be accessed by any users who belong to the company. Once you've purchased an app, you're free to download and install any available version of the app whenever you like. We'll explain how to set up a company account, manage company apps and join companies after we discuss how to access Liferay Marketplace.

13.2 Accessing the Liferay Marketplace

There are two ways to access the Marketplace.

1. Via the website–Using your favorite browser, you can navigate to the marketplace at http://liferay.com/marketplace.

2. Via Liferay–If you have a site up and running based on Liferay, you can use the Marketplace section of the control panel to access Marketplace content.

---

[1]http://liferay.com/marketplace

The Basics

No matter which method you choose, you will see the same content and apps.

If you are new to the Marketplace, the easiest way to access it is by using your browser to navigate to http://liferay.com/marketplace. You will be presented with the Marketplace home page.

Figure 13.1: Marketplace Home Page

In the center of the page, you will see a number of icons. Each icon represents an individual app and they are grouped into a couple of different areas:

- New To Marketplace: The latest apps added to the marketplace

- Featured Products: Liferay features a different set of apps each month

- Most Viewed: The top 10 most viewed apps

If you click on the title of an app, you can access details about the app, including a description, the author's name, screenshots, price, latest version, number of users, number of weekly installs, a link to the developer's `liferay.com` profile page, a link to the developer's own website, a link to report abuse and a Purchase button. You'll also be able to view version history, read reviews left by other users or write your own review.

Figure 13.2: Marketplace App Details

If you click on the Purchase button, you'll be prompted to choose a purchase type. You can purchase an app for your personal account or for your company. If your company has already been registered, select it in the drop-down list.

If your company hasn't been registered, click the *Register Your Company* link to register your company with Liferay Marketplace. Please see the *Creating a Company* section below for details.

The left side of each page in the http://liferay.com/marketplace site contains a Marketplace navigation menu. This menu contains links to various categories of apps and themes available from Marketplace. Clicking on the individual categories will allow you to browse apps in that category. To view all apps or themes at once, click the *Apps* or *Themes* link and then the *See All* link in the Apps or Themes portlet.

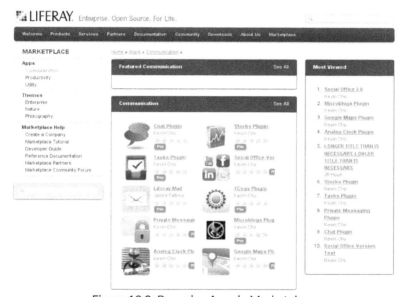

Figure 13.3: Browsing Apps in Marketplace

Below the navigation menu is the search bar. This allows you to search for apps with specific titles. Type in search terms and click *Search* to perform the search.

Logging In

You do not need a `liferay.com` account in order to browse the Marketplace. However, if you wish to purchase and download an app (or if you are a developer and wish to create and upload new apps), you will need to establish a `liferay.com` account and agree to the Marketplace Terms of Use. To get a new `liferay.com` account, visit http://www.liferay.com, click *Sign In*, then *Create Account*, and sign up! Once you are signed in, you will be able to fully utilize the Marketplace to find and use Marketplace apps.

Marketplace Profile

On your existing `liferay.com` Home page, you'll notice a new link entitled *App Manager*. The App Manager allows you to access information about the apps you've purchased and apps you've uploaded to Marketplace. It also provides a mechanism for uploading new apps to Marketplace. Once you submit your app, it will be reviewed before appearing on the `liferay.com` Marketplace.

Your `liferay.com` Home page is a private page. It's distinct from your public `liferay.com` Profile page.

Managing Apps

The App Manager shows you relevant information related to your usage of Marketplace. You'll find three tabs to help you manage your Marketplace apps: *Purchased*, *Apps* and *Add an App*.

The Purchased tab lists the apps you have purchased. From this screen, you can find information about the authors of the apps you have purchased. You can also download or re-download the app (for example, if you lost your copy or have re-installed Liferay and wish to re-deploy the app). This option is also useful for downloading apps and deploying them to offline instances of Liferay that do not have direct access to `liferay.com`.

If possible, it's best to log into your portal instance and install purchased applications through the My Marketplace link in the control panel. This will provide your portal instance with automatic update notices should they become available. If you download applications this way, they can be hot-deployed.

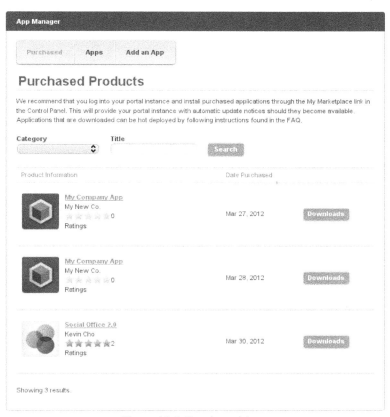

Figure 13.4: Purchased Apps

The Apps tab lists apps you have authored and uploaded, showing you details such as the number of downloads, the current price and other relevant information. From here you can manage the apps you have created (please see the Marketplace chapter of the Developer Guide for details on this topic).

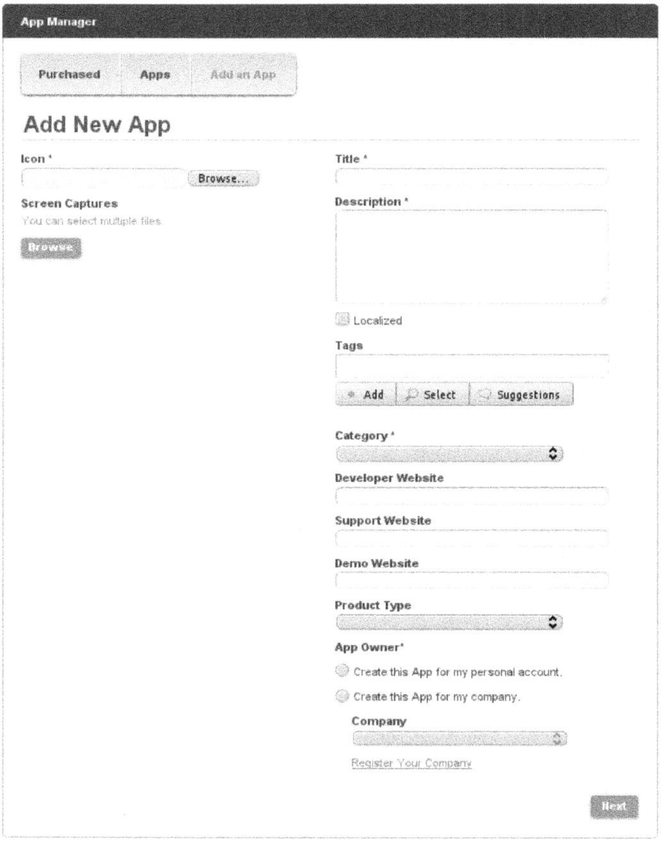

Figure 13.5: Upload an App

Clicking on *Add an App* allows you to upload a new app and make it available in the marketplace. Please see the Marketplace Developer Guide for more detail on authoring your own app.

Creating a Company

To create and register a company with Liferay Marketplace, click the *Create a Company* link in the left-hand navigation menu. Your first step is to see if your company already exists on Liferay Marketplace. Enter your company name into the search box and check if it's already been registered. If someone else from your company has already created a company account on Liferay Marketplace, you can click the *Request to Join this Company* button. This will send an email notification to your company's Marketplace admin (the one who created your company's Marketplace account). Your company's Marketplace admin will then be able to add you to the company. If the company name you'd like to use is available, click the *Register Your Company* button to move on to the next step.

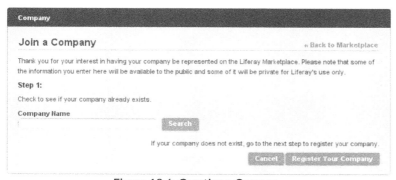

Figure 13.6: Creating a Company

Your second step is to fill out your company's information. The public information you must provide includes a company logo, the company name, a company description, a company email address and a homepage URL. The private information you must provide includes a company address, your company's country, region, city, postal code and phone number. Additonal private information required for validation includes a company email address and a legal tax document. Once your company's Marketplace registration has been approved, you will be your company's Marketplace admin! This means you'll be responsible for handling Marketplace users' requests to join your company. Don't worry, you don't have to be stuck with this responsibility. Once you've added other users to your company, you can promote some of them to be company Marketplace admins too.

13.3   Finding Apps

Figure 13.7: Browsing Categories

There are several ways to search for and find apps you are interested in.

1. Browsing Categories. Click on a category (for example, *Communication* or *Productivity*) to see a list of interesting apps in that category. Upon clicking a category, you are presented with a list of featured apps for that category,

as well as a canonical listing of all apps. Also, on the right, are lists of the Most Viewed apps within that category.

2. Searching. To search for an app, type in search criteria in the search box under the navigation menu on the left and click *Search*. Apps matching the specified search criteria are displayed.

Versions

Apps are often updated to include new features or fix bugs. Each time an app is updated, its version number is changed. The version number is specified by the app developer and often follows established norms, such as 1.0 → 1.1 → 2.0 or 1.0.1 → 1.0.2 → 1.2.0 and so on. Generally, the higher the numbers, the younger the version.

When viewing an app's details, click on the *Version History* tab to see a list of versions of the app. In some cases, not all historical versions of apps are available, depending on the app. Usually, you will want to download and install the latest available app for the version of Liferay you are using (See Compatibility below).

MARKETPLACE

Apps
  Communication
  Productivity
  Utility

Themes
  Enterprise
  Nature
  Photography

Marketplace Help
  Create a Company
  Marketplace Tutorial
  Developer Guide
  Reference Documentation
  Marketplace Partners
  Marketplace Community Forum

Figure 13.8:
Marketplace Search
Box

Compatibility

Some apps are written to work across a wide range of Liferay Platform releases. Others are dependent on a specific Liferay Platform release (or a handful of such releases). When viewing individual apps, each version of the app that is available also describes the range of Liferay Platform versions the app is compatible with. Make sure to choose a version of the app that is compatible with your Liferay Platform release.

To check if an app is compatible with your version of Liferay, click on the App and then click on the *Version History* tab. The Version History tab displays not only the list of versions of the app but also the app's supported framework versions and the dates of each version of the app. The supported framework version of the app tells you whether or not the app is compatible with your version of Liferay.

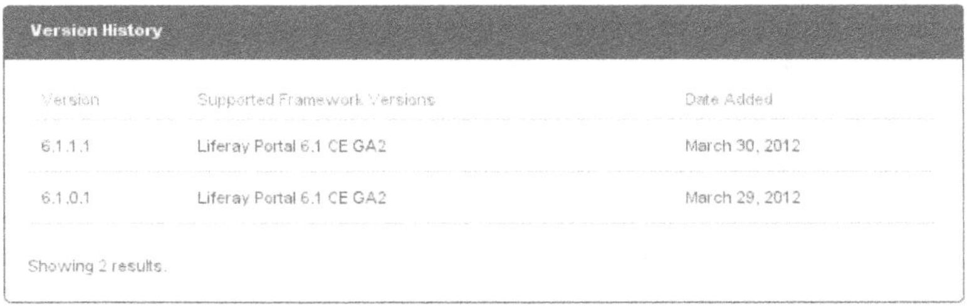

Version History		
Version	Supported Framework Versions	Date Added
6.1.1.1	Liferay Portal 6.1 CE GA2	March 30, 2012
6.1.0.1	Liferay Portal 6.1 CE GA2	March 29, 2012
Showing 2 results.		

Figure 13.9: Marketplace App Version History

13.4 Downloading and Installing Apps

Once you've found an app you wish to download and use, click on the name of the app to display its detailed information screen.

Figure 13.10: Detailed App Information

On this screen, there are a number of items to assist in learning more about the app. You can find the primary information about the app on the left side of the screen. In the center display, you see a set of screenshots along with a description of the app. On the left, below the icon for the app, is some basic information about the app.

- Author: The creator of the app

- Rating: The average rating of the app on a scale from zero to five stars. The number of ratings is also shown.

- Latest Version: The latest released version of this app

- Supported By: Who to contact if you need support for this app

- Users: The total number of users of the app

- Weekly Installs: The average number of installations per week

- Developer Profile: A link to the app developer's `liferay.com` profile page

- Developer Website: A link to the developer's own website

- Purchase: The button to click on to purchase the app. You must purchase an app before you can download it.

In the lower section, you will find Reviews and Version History tabs for this app. Check here to find out what other people are saying about this app. In addition, on a separate tab, you will find the history of versions for this app, where you can download other versions (for example, if you are using an older version of the Liferay Platform, you may need to download a specific version of this app that is compatible with the version of the Liferay Platform you are using).

Downloading and Installing

You've chosen an app, read the reviews and want to download and use the app! There are two ways to install the app. Ultimately, both methods result in the same outcome: the app you've chosen is installed onto your local running Liferay instance.

Figure 13.11: Detailed App Information

Liferay Hot Deploy

Apps on the Liferay Marketplace consist of individual Liferay Plugins (for example: a portlet, a hook, or a collection of multiple plugins). Ultimately these apps must be installed on a running Liferay instance before they can be used. Deploying an app to a running Liferay instance is automatically done through the process of *hot deploy*. When using *Control Panel* to install apps from the Marketplace, when you click *Purchase* or *Install* to download and use a given app, it will be downloaded and hot deployed to your local running Liferay instance.

For some Liferay installations, the hot deploy mechanism is disabled, in order for the site administrator to manage (or prevent) the deployment of plugins. In this case, the app will still be downloaded and stored in the hot deploy directory (with a .lpkg extension in its filename), but must be manually deployed using the custom process used for deploying other plugins.

Please see the later section *Installing Plugins Manually* To learn more about hot deploy, its behavior on various app servers, and how to manually deploy Marketplace apps in situations where hot deploy cannot be used.

Installing through the Control Panel

The easiest way to install an app is to do so from your Liferay control panel. This requires that you have already installed Liferay on your local machine and that you can log in as an administrator. Once you are logged in as an administrator, click the *Go to* menu on the Dockbar and choose *Control Panel*.

Click on either the *Store* or the *Purchased* link in the Marketplace category at the upper-left. Before you can access Marketplace via the control panel, you need to associate your `liferay.com` login credentials with your local administrator account. Enter your `liferay.com` email address and password so your Liferay installation can connect to the `liferay.com` Marketplace.

Figure 13.12:
Marketplace from the
Control Panel

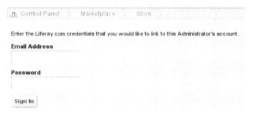

Figure 13.13: Marketplace Login Screen

Once you've successfully linked the accounts, you will be presented with the same Marketplace screens as you would have if you were directly accessing the Marketplace. You will be able to browse, search, and install directly from the Marketplace. Click on the *Store* link under the Marketplace heading in the control panel to browse the apps available from the `liferay.com` Marketplace. Browse to the app you wish to install, click the *Purchase* button, and then the *Buy* button on the next screen. The app will be downloaded and deployed to your local Liferay installation.

Any local user with administrative privileges can use the Marketplace to browse and install apps from the Marketplace, by entering their `liferay.com` credentials in the above login screen. This allows multiple administrators to manage the apps installed on the local Liferay instance. Once a link is established between a local administrator account and a `liferay.com` account, there is no way to undo this, short of re-installing Liferay.

All apps that you've bought are listed on the *Purchased* page of the Marketplace control panel. Clicking on the *Purchased* link will show you a list of those apps which you have downloaded in the past, including apps you may have purchased/downloaded while using other Liferay installations.

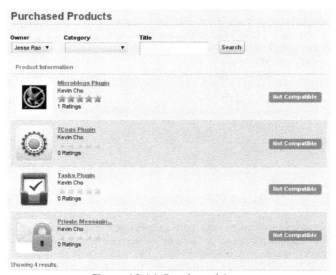

Figure 13.14: Purchased Apps

The apps which you downloaded and installed on the currently running instance of Liferay are listed as Installed. Apps which you have previously downloaded or purchased on other Liferay instances that are incompatible with the current one are listed as Not Compatible. You need to re-download/re-install the appropriate version of these apps if you wish to use them on your running instance of Liferay.

Downloading through liferay.com

The second way to install an app is to download it first, then in a separate step, deploy it to your running Liferay instance. This is especially useful in situations where you do not wish to deploy the app directly to your production environment, or in cases where the target Liferay instance that is to receive the app is behind a corporate firewall or otherwise does not have direct access to the Marketplace.

In this case, using your browser, you will find the app on Liferay Marketplace.[2] Once found, click on the *Purchase* button when viewing the individual app. This will cause the app to be placed in your *Purchased* list on your personal Home page. Navigate to your Home page, click on *App Manager* and visit the *Purchased* tab. Each app is listed. Find the app you just purchased and click *Downloads*. You'll find a list of app versions and Liferay versions. Choose the version of the app you want, making sure the Liferay version corresponds to the version of the Liferay installation into which you'd like to install the app. Click *Download App* and the app is downloaded to your local machine in the same way any other file would be downloaded. This file can then be hot-deployed to Liferay by copying it to Liferay's hot deploy directory.

13.5   Creating and Uploading Apps

Creating apps for the Liferay Marketplace is very easy and intuitive. To find out more information about creating your own Liferay apps, visit the Liferay Marketplace Developer Guide and get started creating apps today!

Next, we'll discuss general Liferay plugin management. We'll explain the differences between the various types of Liferay plugins and show how to manually deploy plugins to Liferay.

13.6   Plugin Management

One of the primary ways of extending the functionality of Liferay Portal is by the use of plugins. *Plugin* is an umbrella term for installable portlet, theme, layout template, hook, Ext and web module Java EE `.war` files. Though Liferay comes bundled with a number of functional portlets, themes, layout templates, hooks and web modules, plugins provide a means of extending Liferay to be able to do almost anything.

Portlets

Portlets are small web applications that run in a portion of a web page. The heart of any portal implementation is its portlets, because all of the functionality of a

---

[2]`liferay.com/marketplace`

portal resides in its portlets. Liferay's core is a portlet container. The container's job is to manage the portal's pages and to aggregate the set of portlets that are to appear on any particular page. This means the core doesn't contain application code. Instead, all of the features and functionality of your portal application must reside in its portlets.

 Tip: Liferay 4.4.2 and below support the Portlet 1.0 standard: JSR-168. Liferay 5.0 and above support the Portlet 2.0 standard: JSR-286. You cannot run Portlet 2.0 portlets in Liferay 4.4.2, but because the Portlet 2.0 standard is backwards-compatible, portlets written to the 1.0 standard will run in Liferay 5.x and above.

Portlet applications, like servlet applications, have become a Java standard which various portal server vendors have implemented. The JSR-168 standard defines the portlet 1.0 specification and the JSR-286 standard defines the portlet 2.0 specification. A Java standard portlet should be deployable on any portlet container which supports the standard. Portlets are placed on the page in a certain order by the end user and are served up dynamically by the portal server. This means certain *givens* that apply to servlet-based projects, such as control over URLs or access to the `HttpServletRequest` object, don't apply in portlet projects, because the portal server generates these objects dynamically.

Portal applications come generally in two flavors: 1) portlets can be written to provide small amounts of functionality and then aggregated by the portal server into a larger application or 2) whole applications can be written to reside in only one or a few portlet windows. The choice is up to those designing the application. The developer only has to worry about what happens inside of the portlet itself; the portal server handles building out the page as it is presented to the user.

Most developers nowadays like to use certain frameworks to develop their applications, because those frameworks provide both functionality and structure to a project. For example, Struts enforces the Model-View-Controller design pattern and provides lots of functionality, such as custom tags and form validation, that make it easier for a developer to implement certain standard features. With Liferay, developers are free to use all of the leading frameworks in the Java EE space, including Struts, Spring MVC and Java Server Faces. This allows developers familiar with those frameworks to more easily implement portlets and also facilitates the quick porting of an application using those frameworks over to a portlet implementation.

Additionally, Liferay allows for the consuming of PHP and Ruby applications as portlets so you do not need to be a Java developer in order to take advantage of Liferay's built-in features (such as user management, sites, organizations, page building and content management). You can also use scripting languages such as Groovy if you wish. You can use the Plugins SDK to deploy your PHP or Ruby application as a portlet and it will run seamlessly inside of Liferay. We have plenty of examples of this; to see them, check out the Plugins SDK from Liferay's public code repository.

Does your organization make use of any Enterprise Planning (ERP) software that exposes its data via web services? You could write a portlet plugin for Liferay that can consume that data and display it as part of a dashboard page for your users. Do you subscribe to a stock service? You could pull stock quotes from that service and display them on your page, instead of using Liferay's built-in Stocks portlet. Do you have a need to combine the functionality of two or more servlet-based applications on one page? You could make them into portlet plugins and have Liferay display them in whatever layout you want. Do you have existing Struts, Spring MVC or JSF applications you want to integrate with your portal? It is a straightforward task to migrate these applications into Liferay, then they can take advantage of the layout, security and administration infrastructure that Liferay provides.

Themes

Figure 13.15: Envision Theme from Liferay's Theme Repository

Themes are hot deployable plugins which can completely transform the look and feel of the portal. Most organizations have their own look and feel standards which go across all of the web sites and web applications in the infrastructure. Liferay makes it possible for a site designer to create a theme plugin which can be installed, allowing for the complete transformation of the portal to whatever look and feel is needed. There are lots of available theme plugins on Liferay's web site and more are being added every day. This makes it easier for those who wish to develop themes for Liferay, as you can now choose a theme which most closely resembles what you want to do and then customize it. This is much easier than starting a theme from scratch. You can learn more about theme development in *Liferay in Action*.

Figure 13.16: Murali Theme from Liferay's Theme Repository

Layout Templates

Layout Templates are ways of choosing how your portlets will be arranged on a page. They make up the body of your page, the large area into which you can drag and drop portlets. Liferay Portal comes with several built-in layout templates. If you have a complex page layout (especially for your home page), you may wish to create a custom layout template of your own. This is covered in *Liferay in Action*.

Hook Plugins

Hook plugins were introduced with Liferay 5.2. As the name implies, they allow "hooking" into Liferay's core functionality. This means they enable developers to override or replace functionality that is in the core of the system. You can hook into the eventing system, model listeners and portal properties. You can also override Liferay's core JSPs with your own. Hooks are very powerful and have been designed to replace most of the reasons for using the extension environment with something that is easier to use and hot deployable.

Web Plugins

Web plugins are regular Java EE web modules designed to work with Liferay. Liferay supports integration with various Enterprise Service Bus (ESB) implementations, as well as Single Sign-On implementations, workflow engines and so on. These are implemented as web modules used by Liferay portlets to provide functionality.

Installing Plugins from Repositories

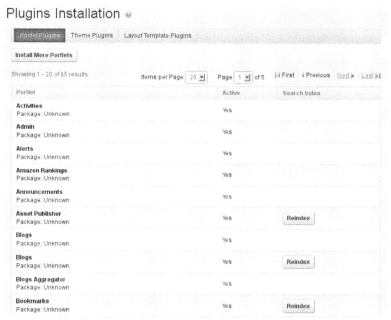

Figure 13.17: Plugins Installation Portlet Tab Default View

Liferay Portal has a section of the control panel called Plugins Installation, which you can find under the Server heading. This section not only allows you to see what plugins are installed in your portal, but also it enables you to run the search indexer on those portlets that support it and install new portlets.

Use the dockbar's *Go to* menu to select *Control Panel*. Under the Server heading, select *Plugins Installation*. You should now see the page which allows you to configure and install portlets.

The default view of the Plugins Installation page shows which plugins are already installed on the system and whether or not they are active. The Portlet Plugins tab allows you reindex certain portlets to improve their searchability.

The Theme and Layout Template Plugins tabs display which portal roles can access them.

Figure 13.18: Plugins Installation Theme Tab Default View

If you would like to see what plugins are available, you can do so by clicking the *Install More* button, where changes based on which tab you are viewing. Please note the machine running Liferay must have access to the Internet to read the Official and Community repositories. If the machine does not have Internet access, you will need to download the plugins from the site and install them manually. We will discuss how to do this later in this chapter.

It's easy to navigate from the initial page of the Plugin Installer to different pages since the plugins are listed alphabetically. You can also change the number of items per page and navigate to a specific page if you know where a particular plugin appears in the list. This is a standard feature of Liferay and you will see it in most of Liferay's portlets.

After you click the *Install More* button, a new view appears. This view has

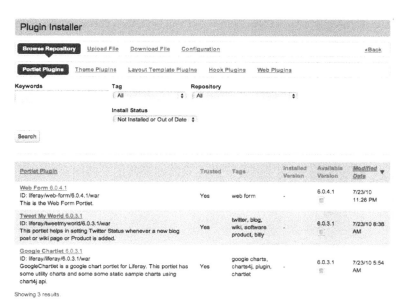

Figure 13.19: Installing Plugins

multiple tabs, and by default, displays the *Portlet Plugins* tab. Note the list displayed is a list of all of the plugins available across all of the repositories to which the server is subscribed. Above this is a search mechanism which allows you to search for plugins by their name, by whether or not they are installed, by tag or by which repository they belong to. To install a plugin, choose the plugin by clicking on its name. For example, if you want to use online web forms on your web site, you might want to install the Web Form portlet. This portlet provides a handy interface which allows you to create forms for users to fill out. You can specify an address to which the results will be emailed.

Find the Web Form Portlet in the list by searching for it or browsing to it. Once you have found it, click on its name. Another page will be displayed which describes the portlet plugin in more detail. Below the description is an *Install* button. Click this button to install your plugin.

Once you click *Install*, your chosen plugin will automatically download and be installed on your instance of Liferay. If you have the Liferay console open, you can view the deployment as it happens. When it is finished, you should be able to go back to the Add Application window and add your new plugin to a page in your portal.

The same procedure is used for installing new Liferay themes, layout templates, hooks and web modules. Instead of the *Portlet Plugins* tab, you would use the appropriate tab for the type of plugin you wish to install to view the list of plugins of that type. For themes, convenient thumbnails (plus a larger version when you click on the details of a particular theme) are shown in the list.

Figure 13.20: Installing the Web Form Portlet

After clicking on the *Install* button for a theme, the theme becomes available on the *Look and Feel* tab of any page.

Installing Plugins Manually

Installing plugins manually is almost as easy as installing plugins via the Plugin Installer. There are several scenarios in which you would need to install plugins manually rather than from Liferay's repositories:

- Your server is firewalled without access to the Internet. This makes it impossible for your instance of Liferay to connect to the plugin repositories.

- You are installing portlets which you have either purchased from a vendor, downloaded separately or developed yourself.

- For security reasons, you do not want to allow portal administrators to install plugins from the Internet before they are evaluated.

You can still use the control panel to install plugins that are not available from the online repositories. This is by far the easiest way to install plugins.

If your server is firewalled, you will not see any plugins displayed in the Portlet Plugins or Theme Plugins tabs. Instead, you will need to click the *Upload File* tab. This gives you a simple interface for uploading a .war file containing a plugin to your Liferay Portal.

Click the *Browse* button and navigate your file system to find the portlet or theme .war you have downloaded. The other field on the page is optional: you can specify your own context for deployment. If you leave this field blank, the default context defined in the plugin (or the .war file name itself) will be used.

That's all the information the Plugin Installer needs in order to deploy your portlet, theme, layout template, hook or web module. Click the *Install* button and your plugin will be uploaded to the server and deployed. If it is a portlet, you should see it in the *Add Content* window. If it is a theme, it will be available on the *Look and Feel* tab in the page definition.

Figure 13.21: Installing a Plugin Manually

If you do not wish to use the Update Manager or Plugin Installer to deploy plugins, you can also deploy them at the operating system level. The first time Liferay starts, it creates a *hot deploy* folder which is, by default, created inside the Liferay Home folder. This folder generally resides one directory up from where your application server is installed, though it may be elsewhere depending on which application server you are running. To find out where the Liferay Home folder is for your application server, please see the section on your server in chapter 1. The first time Liferay is launched, it will create a folder structure in Liferay Home to house various configuration and administrative data. One of the folders it creates is called *deploy*. If you copy a portlet or theme plugin into this folder, Liferay will deploy it and make it available for use just as though you'd installed it via the Plugin Installer in the control panel. In fact, this is what the Plugin Installer is doing behind the scenes.

You can change the defaults for this directory structure so it is stored anywhere you like by modifying the appropriate properties in your `portal-ext-.properties` file. Please see the above section on the `portal-ext.properties` file for more information.

To have Liferay hot deploy a portlet or theme plugin, copy the plugin into your hot deploy folder, which by default is in `[Liferay Home]/deploy`. If you are watching the Liferay console, you should see messages like the following:

```
16:11:47,616 INFO [PortletAutoDeployListener:71] Copying portlets for
/liferay-portal-6.0.4/deploy/weather-portlet-6.0.4.1.war

Expanding:
/liferay-portal-6.0.4/deploy/weather-portlet-6.0.4.1.war
into
/liferay-portal-6.0.4/tomcat-6.0.26/temp/20100729161147694

Copying 1 file to
/liferay-portal-6.0.4/tomcat-6.0.26/temp/20100729161147694/WEB-INF

Copying 1 file to
/liferay-portal-6.0.4/tomcat-6.0.26/temp/20100729161147694/WEB-INF/classes

Copying 1 file to
/liferay-portal-6.0.4/tomcat-6.0.26/temp/20100729161147694/WEB-INF/classes

Copying 1 file to
/liferay-portal-6.0.4/tomcat-6.0.26/temp/20100729161147694/META-INF

Copying 37 files to
/liferay-portal-6.0.4/tomcat-6.0.26/webapps/weather-portlet

Copying 1 file to
/liferay-portal-6.0.4/tomcat-6.0.26/webapps/weather-portlet

Deleting directory
/liferay-portal-6.0.4/tomcat-6.0.26/temp/20100729161147694

16:11:48,072 INFO [PortletAutoDeployListener:81] Portlets for
/liferay-portal-6.0.4/deploy/weather-portlet-6.0.4.1.war
copied successfully. Deployment will start in a few seconds.

Jul 29, 2010 4:11:50 PM org.apache.catalina.startup.HostConfig
deployDirectory

INFO: Deploying web application directory weather-portlet
```

```
16:11:50,585 INFO [PortletHotDeployListener:222] Registering portlets
for weather-portlet
\index{portlet}

16:11:50,784 INFO [PortletHotDeployListener:371] 1 portlet for
weather-portlet is available for use
```

The *available for use* message means your plugin was installed correctly and is available for use in the portal.

Plugin Troubleshooting

Sometimes plugins fail to install. There can be different reasons for installation failure based on several factors, including

- Liferay configuration

- The container upon which Liferay is running

- Changing the configuration options in multiple places

- How Liferay is being launched

You can often tell whether or not you have a plugin deployment problem by looking at the Liferay server console. If the hot deploy listener recognizes the plugin, you'll see a *plugin copied successfully* message. If this message is not followed up by an *available for use* message then you have an issue with your plugin deployment configuration, probably due to one of the factors listed above.

Let's take a look at each of these factors.

Liferay Configuration Issues

> **Tip:** This applies to Liferay versions prior to version 4.3.5. Liferay versions above 4.3.5 are able to auto detect the type of server it is running on, which makes things a lot easier. If you are running a newer version of Liferay, you can skip this section. If you are upgrading from one of these versions, continue reading.

Liferay by default comes as a bundle or as a .war file. Though every effort has been made to make the .war file as generic as possible, sometimes the default settings are inappropriate for the container upon which Liferay is running. Most of these problems were resolved in Liferay 4.3.5 with the addition of code that allows Liferay to determine which application server it is running on and adjust the way it deploys plugins as a result. If you have upgraded from one of these older versions, you may still have settings in your portal.ext.properties file that are no longer needed. One of these settings is the manual override of the default value of auto.deploy.dest.dir.

In versions of Liferay prior to 4.3.5, there is a property called auto.deploy.dest.dir that defines the folder where plugins are deployed after the hot deploy utilities have finished preparing them. This folder maps to a folder the container defines as an auto-deploy or a hot deploy folder. By default in older versions of Liferay, this property is set to ../webapps. This default value works for Tomcat containers (if Tomcat has been launched from its bin folder) but will not work for other containers that define their hot deploy folders in a different place. In newer versions of Liferay, this value is automatically set to the default for the application server upon which Liferay is running.

For example, Glassfish defines the hot deploy folder as a folder called auto-deploy inside of the domain folder in which your server is running. By default, this is in <Glassfish Home>/domains/domain1/autodeploy. JBoss defines the hot deploy folder as a root folder inside the particular server configuration you are using. By default, this is in <JBoss Home>/server/default/deploy. WebLogic defines this folder inside of the domain directory. By default, this is in <Bea Home>/user_projects/domains/<domain name>/autodeploy.

The best thing to do when upgrading to newer versions of Liferay Portal is to remove this property altogether. It is not needed, as the autodetection of the container handles the hot deploy location. If, for whatever reason, you need to customize the location of the hot deploy folder, follow the instructions below.

You will first need to determine where the hot deploy folder is for the container you are running. Consult your product documentation for this. Once you have this value, there are two places in which you can set it: in the portal-ext.properties file and in the Plugin Installer portlet.

To change this setting in the portal-ext.properties file, browse to where Liferay was deployed in your application server. Inside of this folder should be a WEB-INF/classes folder. Here you will find the portal-ext.properties file. Open this file in a text editor and look for the property auto.deploy.-dest.dir. If it does not appear in the file, you can add it. The safest way to set this property, as we will see later, is to define the property using an absolute path from the root of your file system to your application server's hot deploy folder. For example, if you are using Glassfish, and you have the server installed in /java/glassfish, your auto.deploy.dest.dir property would look like the following:

```
auto.deploy.dest.dir=/java/glassfish/domains/domain1/autodeploy
```

Remember, if you are on a Windows system, use forward slashes instead of back slashes, like so:

```
auto.deploy.dest.dir=C:/java/glassfish/domains/domain1/autodeploy
```

Save the file and then restart your container. Now plugins should install correctly.

Instead of changing the hot deploy destination directory in your portal-ext.properties file, you can do it via the Plugin Installer. To change the setting this way, navigate to the Plugins Installation page of the control panel, click the *Install More* button. This will bring you to the Plugin Installer page. Next, click on the *Configuration* tab of the Plugin Installer page. There are a number of settings you can change on this tab, including the default folders for hot deploy, where Liferay should look for plugin repositories and so on.

The setting to change is the field labeled *Destination Directory*. Change this to the full path to your container's auto deploy folder from the root of your file system. When you are finished, click the *Save* button at the bottom of the form. The setting will now take effect without your having to restart your container. Note the setting in the control panel overrides the setting in the properties file.

If you are having hot deploy trouble in Liferay versions 4.3.5 and greater, it is possible the administrator of your application server has changed the default folder for auto deploy in your application server. In this case, you would want to set auto.deploy.dest.dir to the customized folder location as you would with older versions of Liferay. In Liferay 4.3.5 and greater, this setting still exists but is blank. Add the property to your portal-ext.properties file and set its value to the fully qualified path to the auto deploy folder configured in your application server.

Deploy Issues for Specific Containers

Some containers, such as WebSphere®, don't have a hot deploy feature. Unfortunately, these containers do not work with Liferay's hot deploy system. But this does not mean you cannot install plugins on these containers. You can deploy plugins manually using the application server's deployment tools. Liferay is able to pick up the portlet plugins once they get deployed to the container

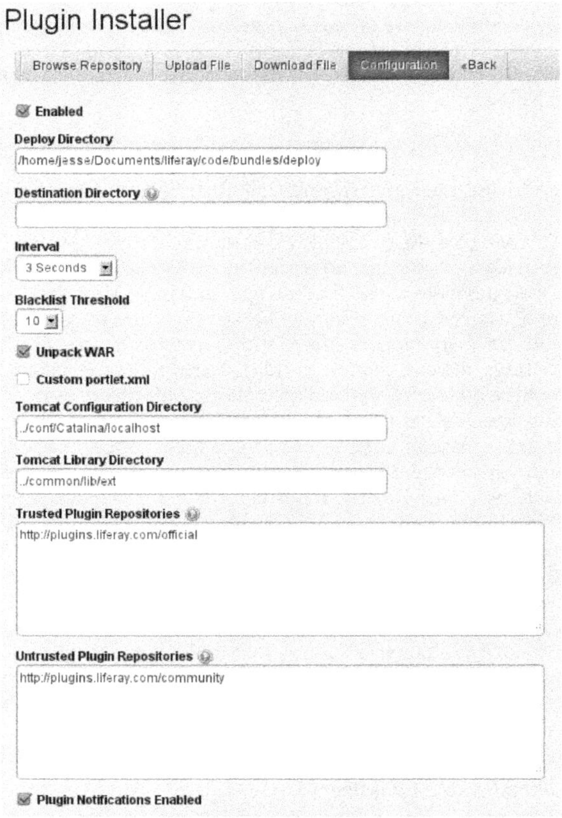

Figure 13.22: Changing the Hot Deploy Destination Directory

manually, especially if you add it to the same Enterprise Application project that was created for Liferay.

When Liferay hot deploys portlet and theme `.war` files, it sometimes makes modifications to those files right before deployment. In order to successfully deploy plugins using an application server vendor's tools, you will want to run your plugins through this process before you attempt to deploy them.

Navigate back to the *Configuration* tab of the Plugin Installer. Enter the location you would like plugin `.war` files to be copied to after they are processed by Liferay's plugin installer process into the *Destination Directory* field. You will use this as a staging directory for your plugins before you install them manually with your server's deployment tools. When you are finished, click *Save*.

Now you can deploy plugins using the Plugin Installer portlet or by dropping `.war` files into your auto deploy directory. Liferay will pick up the files, modify them and then copy the result into the destination directory you have configured. You may then deploy them from here to your application server.

Example: WebSphere ® Application Server

1. If you don't have one already, create a **portal-ext.properties** file in the Liferay Home folder of your Liferay installation. Add the following directive to it:

   auto.deploy.dest.dir=${liferay.home}/websphere-deploy

2. Create a folder called **websphere-deploy** inside your **$LIFERAY_HOME** folder. This is the folder where the Lucene index, Jackrabbit config and deploy folders are.

3. Make sure the **web.xml** file inside the plugin you want to install has the following context parameter in it:

   com.ibm.websphere.portletcontainer.PortletDeploymentEnabled

   false

   Liferay versions 5.2.2 and higher will automatically inject this into the **web.xml** file on WebSphere containers.

4. The WebSphere deploy occurs in two steps. You will first use Liferay's tools to "pre-deploy" the file and then use WebSphere's tools to do the actual deployment. This is because Liferay makes deployment-time modifications to the plugins right before they are actually deployed to the application server. For other application servers, this can usually be done in one step, because

Liferay can make the modifications and then copy the resulting .war file into an autodeploy folder to have it actually deployed. Because WebSphere does not have an autodeploy feature, we need to separate these two steps.

5. Deploy your .war file using Liferay's Plugin Installer or by copying it into `$LIFERAY_HOME/deploy`. Liferay will make its modifications, and because we changed the `auto.deploy.dest.dir` in the first step, it will copy the resulting .war file into `$LIFERAY_HOME/websphere-deploy`. You will see a *copied successfully* message in the log.

6. Use WebSphere's tools to deploy the .war file. Make the context root for the .war file equal to the file name (i.e., `/my-first-portlet`). Once the .war file is deployed, save it to the master configuration.

7. Go back to the *Applications* → *Enterprise Applications* screen in the WebSphere Admin Console. You will see your portlet is deployed but not yet started. Start it.

8. Liferay will immediately recognize the portlet has been deployed and register it. The portlet will be automatically started and registered upon subsequent restarts of WebSphere.

Experienced WebSphere system administrators can further automate this by writing a script which watches the `websphere-deploy` directory and uses `wsadmin` commands to then deploy plugins automatically.

Changing the Configuration Options in Multiple Places

Sometimes, especially during development when several people have administrative access to the server at the same time, the auto deploy folder location may inadvertently be customized in both the `portal-ext.properties` file and in the control panel. If this happens, the value in the control panel takes precedence over the value in the properties file. If you go into the control panel and change the value to the correct setting, plugin deployment will start working again.

13.7   Summary

In this chapter, we introduced Liferay Marketplace, your one-stop shop for browsing and downloading Liferay-compatible applications. We looked at how to browse, purchase, download, and install apps. You can do this either through liferay.com/marketplace or through Liferay Portal's control panel. When you purchase apps, you can do so via your personal account or on your company's behalf. For information about developing and uploading apps to Liferay Marketplace, please see the Marketplace chapter of the Liferay Developer guide at http://www.liferay.com/marketplace/developer-guide.

After discussing Liferay Marketplace, we discussed general plugin management. We covered Liferay portlet plugins as well as layout, theme, hook, Ext, and web plugins. Finally, we looked at how to manually deploy plugins to Liferay and discussed some configuration issues.

CHAPTER 14

INSTALLATION AND SETUP

Liferay Portal is one of the most flexible applications on the market today with regard to application server environments. You can install Liferay Portal on everything from a shared Tomcat installation to a multi-node cluster running a commercial application server and on everything in between. In fact, Liferay is used successfully in all of these scenarios every day.

You'll find that because Liferay is extremely flexible in its deployment options, it is easy to install as well. If you already have an application server, you can use the tools for deployment that came with your application server. If you don't have an application server, Liferay provides several application server bundles from which to choose. These are very easy to install and with a small amount of configuration can be made into production-ready systems.

14.1   Editions of Liferay

Liferay ships in two different editions: Liferay Portal Community Edition (CE) and Liferay Portal Enterprise Edition (EE). CE is the same Liferay Portal that has been available for years: frequently updated and bursting with the latest features, the Community Edition of Liferay Portal is offered for free under the Lesser GNU public license, an open source license. This license gives you the flexibility to link Liferay with your own code in your portlet, theme, hook, layout, Ext or web plugins, no matter what license you use for your code. If, however, you modify Liferay directly, those modifications need to be released as open source. This is really the best of both worlds: you have the freedom to do what you want with your code if you use plugins, but if you modify Liferay directly, the community receives the benefits of any enhancements that you've made.

Liferay Portal EE is a supported version of Liferay Portal for the enterprise. Hardened for security and designed to be rock solid stable, EE is offered with a subscription and support package, allowing organizations to build their portals on a stable version of the product that is offered over an extended period of time.

Because the release cycle for EE is longer than that for CE, each enterprise release is supported for four years. All bug fixes in Liferay Portal are backported to your version of Liferay for the duration of your subscription. This gives organizations the peace of mind that comes from knowing that their Liferay-powered web sites are stable and will run for years to come, enabling them to build their sites on a proven, stable platform. Additionally, Liferay offers training and consulting on the Enterprise Edition to ensure long-term support and stability for our clients.

Liferay's Versioning Schema

Liferay's release process follows a prescribed structure that is consistent from one release to the next. Each release has a specific number sequence attached to it signifying the type of release it is, whether it's a major, minor or maintenance release. Each release also has a term attached to it to indicate its intended level of quality.

EE subscribers have access to additional maintenance releases, along with specific *Fix Packs* and *Hot Fixes* that make applying updates to production environments safer and faster.

Let's start with an explanation of Liferay's version structure. Liferay versions are organized in a straightforward numerical system consisting of a three digit number. For example, 6.1.2. These numbers represent the type of the release: Major.Minor.Maintenance.

Major Release

A change in the first digit of the version (e.g., 6.x to 7.x) is a major release. This means that:

- There are major changes in functionality or new functionality based on high demand.

- There are architectural changes, changes to APIs (as part of the deprecation process), or changes to internal schema.

Minor Release

A change to the second digit of the version scheme (e.g., 6.0 to 6.1) is a minor release. This means that:

- There are new features and bug fixes from prior releases.

- Customizations may be affected when installing.

- Customers should leverage the upgrade tools and documentation.

Maintenance Release

A change in the third digit of the version scheme (e.g, 6.1.5 to 6.1.6) is a maintenance release. This means that:

- Each maintenance release provides an improved level of security and reliability.

- Customizations are generally safe, but we recommend doing a review.

- No new features are included.

These rules are relaxed when a minor or major release is still in beta quality. Now let's delve into the evolution of versions.

Release Process

Each version of Liferay has a surname that specifies the expected quality of that release. This is needed because pre-releases of Liferay look very much like maintenance releases when viewed solely through their version numbers. The surname in general replaces the third digit in the version, but is visible through the logs and administration UIs. Here is a description of each surname and what it means:

- **Milestone** and **Beta**: (6.2 M1, 6.2 B1, 6.2 B2, ...) There can be zero or more of these types within each minor or major release. These releases are meant for testing and to provide Liferay feedback through the beta testing category in the forums. There will likely be major changes in milestone releases, but beta releases are considered "feature complete" and should have only bug fixes.

- **Release Candidates**: (6.1 RC1, 6.1 RC2) There can be zero, one, or more of these right after the beta releases. These releases appear near the end of the release process and are candidates for release. As such, they should have minimal to no bugs, but because they are very new, some minor bugs may have slipped by.

- **General Availability**: (6.1 GA1, 6.1 GA2, ...) There can be one or more of these releases. A General Availability release is a re-label of the last release candidate, based on internal testing and feedback from beta testers. These releases are stable and are made available via Liferay's Downloads page for CE and on the Customer Portal for EE.

Comments and Recommendations

At this point you might be asking yourself questions like, which version should I use? What if I was using a previous version? Will the update to a new maintenance release cost a lot? Here are some comments and recommendations to address these questions.

- When starting a new project, always use the latest stable version available; that is, the latest available GA. At the time of writing, the most recent version is Liferay CE 6.1 GA2 (6.1.1) or Liferay EE 6.1 GA2 (6.1.20).

- Always update to the latest maintenance release available for the functional version (major or minor) that you are using. For example, if you started your project with Liferay 6.1.0 GA1, it is recommended that you switch to GA2 to take advantage of bug fixes and improvements. If you have a subscription, you can benefit from the fixes faster by requesting fix packs and hot fixes from the support team.

- You are always welcome to use any preview, beta or release candidate. In fact, that's why they exist–so as many people as possible start using it and provide us their feedback. Please note, we do not recommend using pre-releases (milestones, betas, or release candidates) in production. You

may not want to use these releases even during development if you have
tight deadlines, since you may find road blocks.

- Plugins that work in any GA or fix pack version will work in any later
  maintenance release. That is, a plugin developed for Liferay 6.1 GA1 will
  also work in Liferay 6 GA2 or a GA2 fix pack.

For more details on updating Liferay Portal, see Upgrading Liferay in chapter
17.

Liferay Portal is a very flexible application that runs well on several different
server environments. It's simple to install and comes in either a Community
Edition or an Enterprise Edition, depending on your needs. Liferay follows a
systematic versioning system that makes it easy to keep current with the latest
updates. The strength of the Liferay community helps detect potential issues
early that are then reported through the forums and are later fixed in a series of
maintenance releases.

Now let's learn about Liferay bundles.

14.2   Obtaining Liferay Portal

The CE version of Liferay is freely downloadable from our web site.[1]   Click
the *Downloads* link at the top of the page and you are presented with multiple
options for getting a copy of Liferay, including our convenient bundles or a .war
package for installation on your application server of choice.

The EE version of Liferay is provided to you as a result of your support subscription. Everything you need is provided in the Customer Portal, including
download links that allow you to obtain a copy of a Liferay bundle or a .war
package for installation on your application server of choice.

So what is a bundle anyway? A bundle is an open source application server
with Liferay preinstalled. This is the most convenient way to install Liferay.
Liferay is bundled with a number of open source application servers; all you
need to do is choose the one that best fits your needs. If you don't currently
have an application server, you may want to start with the Tomcat bundle, as
Tomcat is one of the smallest and most straightforward bundles to configure. If
you have an open source application server preference, choose the server you
prefer from the available Liferay Portal bundles. All of the bundles ship with a
Java Runtime Environment for Windows; if you are using a different operating

---

[1]http://www.liferay.com

system, you will need to have a JDK (Java Development Kit) installed prior to launching Liferay.

Please note that Liferay is not able to provide application server bundles for proprietary application servers such as WebLogic or WebSphere, because the licenses for these servers don't allow for redistribution. Liferay Portal, however, runs just as well on these application servers as it does on open source application servers. A .war file and dependency .jars are provided for proprietary application servers and you'll need to follow a procedure to install Liferay on them.

First we'll go over installing Liferay from a bundle and after this we'll provide instructions for installing Liferay manually on all the application servers it supports.

14.3   Installing a bundle

Liferay bundles contain the same directory structure regardless of application server. The top-level folder is named for the release of Liferay. This folder is called *Liferay Home* and we refer to it thoughout this documentation.

Inside this folder, there are folders for various purposes:

Data: This folder is used to store the embedded HSQL database which the bundles use, as well as the configuration and data for the Jackrabbit JSR-170 content repository and the Lucene search index.

Deploy: Plugins which you wish to deploy to Liferay can be copied into this folder. It is also used by Liferay Marketplace and Liferay's graphical plugin installer utility.

Figure 14.1: Bundle directory structure

[Application Server]: The name of this folder is different depending on which bundle you have downloaded. This folder contains the application server in which Liferay has been installed.

Installing a bundle is as easy as uncompressing the archive, copying a JDBC driver and then starting the application server. Let's use the Tomcat bundle as an example:

1. Unzip the bundle to a location of your choice.

2. If you're setting up Liferay to be an actual server, copy your database's JDBC driver .jar to [Tomcat]/lib/ext (see the setup wizard section below). If you're setting up Liferay for demo purposes, you can skip this step.

3. Start Tomcat in the same way as you would if you had downloaded it manually. Tomcat is launched by way of a script which is found in its `bin` folder. If
   you drop to a command prompt and go to this folder, you can launch Tomcat
   via the following command on Windows:

   startup

   or the following command on Linux/Mac/Unix:

   `./startup.sh`

The Liferay/Tomcat bundle then launches. If you are on Windows, another
command prompt window appears with Tomcat's console in it. If you are on
Linux, you can see the Tomcat console by issuing the following command:

`tail -f ../logs/catalina.out`

Once Tomcat has completed its start up, it automatically launches a web
browser that displays Liferay's setup wizard. If for some reason your browser
doesn't load the wizard, launch your browser and go to http://localhost:8080.

Liferay CE ships with a sample web site that showcases Liferay's features. It
contains many links describing the features of Liferay that we'll cover in detail
throughout this book.

If you're installing Liferay on your own machine to explore its features, you
likely want to leave the sample site there so you can examine it. If, however,
you're installing Liferay on your server to run your own site, it's best to start
with a clean system. Before running the setup wizard, you should remove the
sample data from your Liferay installation. You must do this before running
the setup wizard to get a clean database, and it's as simple as undeploying the
applications that install the sample data.

There are two applications included in the bundle that you need to remove:

- resources-importer-web

- welcome-theme

To remove them, all you have to do is undeploy them. The method for doing
this differs by application server and that, of course, depends on the bundle you
have chosen. For example, on Tomcat you delete the application folders from
the `[Tomcat Home]/webapps` folder. On Glassfish, you use the administrative
console to undeploy them.

If you forget to undeploy the sample applications before you run through
the setup wizard and connect Liferay to your real database, the sample data is

created in your database, and you won't have a clean installation. Make sure you get the sample data undeployed before setting up your server.

If you're using Liferay EE, you don't have the sample site so you don't need to worry about this. The next step is to run through the setup wizard, which we'll cover below.

As you can see, bundles are the easiest way to get started with Liferay. They come pre-configured with a running Liferay instance that can be used immediately to explore all of the things that Liferay can do. Bundles are the fastest way to create full production-ready Liferay installations. If you're using a bundle, skip to the section on the setup wizard below to continue your installation.

Of course, it's not always possible to use a bundle. You may already have an application server upon which you want to install Liferay. The bulk of this chapter describes how to install Liferay on all the application servers it supports, both open source and proprietary.

14.4 App servers

When it comes time to install Liferay Portal on your server, you'll find it's easiest to do this by starting with a bundle. But many enterprises can't do that. There may be an existing infrastructure into which you're installing Liferay or you may have standardized on a particular application server. You'll be happy to know that Liferay Portal has been designed to work well with all the leading application servers and that it's easy and straightforward to install. But before we get started, we need to go over a few concepts; namely, the Liferay Home folder, databases and Liferay's main configuration file. These were touched on in the section on bundles above but we'll look at them in more detail now.

Liferay Home

Liferay Portal uses a special folder defined as *Liferay Home*. This folder is one folder higher than the location of the application server itself. This is why the bundles place the application server one folder in from the bundle's root folder.

If Liferay is unable to create the resources it needs in this folder or if it finds itself running on certain application servers, it creates a folder called `liferay` in the home folder of the user ID that is running Liferay and that becomes Liferay Home.

As described above in the *Bundles* section, the home folder is very important to the operation of Liferay. The aforementioned folders (*data* and *deploy*) are created there and you can also put a special configuration file called `portal-ext.properties` there. This file is fully documented in chapter 20, a reference for Liferay properties.

> **Note:** To use database properties from a `portal-ext.properties` file you must disable the Setup Wizard by specifying `setup.wizard.enabled=false` in that `portal-ext.properties`. Also, note that property values in `portal-setup-wizard.properties` (the file created in Liferay Home by the Setup Wizard) override property values in `portal-ext.properties`.

Let's move on to examining the database.

Liferay's database

As stated above, if you create your database and grant a user ID full access to it, Liferay can use that user ID to create its indexes and tables automatically. This is the recommended way to set up Liferay, as it allows you to take advantage of Liferay's ability to automatically maintain its database during upgrades or through various plugin installs which may create tables of their own. It is by far the best way to set up your Liferay installation.

If you'll be setting up Liferay's database with the recommended permissions, you can skip to the next section.

> **Note:** This is not the recommended set up for Liferay installations but is documented here so enterprises with more restrictive standards can install Liferay with more strict – but suboptimal – database settings. If it's at all possible, Liferay recommends that you use the automatic method as documented above instead of the procedure outlined below.

Even though Liferay can create its database automatically, some enterprises prefer *not* to allow the user ID configured in an application server to have the permissions over the database necessary for Liferay and its plugins to maintain their tables. For these organizations, Select, Insert, Update and Delete are the only permissions allowed so we will go over how to set up the database manually. If your organization *is* willing to grant the Liferay user ID permissions to create and drop tables in the database – and this is the recommended configuration – by all means, use the recommended configuration.

Creating the database is simple: grant the ID Liferay uses to access the database full rights to do anything to the database. Then install Liferay and have it create the database. Once the database is created, remove the permissions for creating tables and dropping tables from the user ID.

There are some caveats to running Liferay like this. Many Liferay plugins create new tables when they're deployed. In addition to this, Liferay has an automatic database upgrade function which runs when the version of Liferay is upgraded to a new release. If the user ID that accesses the database doesn't have enough rights to create/modify/drop tables in the database, you must grant those rights to the ID before you deploy one of these plugins or start your upgraded Liferay for the first time. Once the tables are created or the upgrade is complete, you can remove those rights until the next deploy or upgrade. Additionally, your developers may create plugins that need to create their own tables. These are just like Liferay's plugins that do the same thing and they cannot be installed if Liferay can't create these tables automatically. If you wish to install these plugins, you will need to grant rights to create tables in the database before you attempt to install them.

Once you have your database ready, you can install Liferay on your server.

Liferay installation overview

Before we begin, it's important to go over the various facets of the installation. They are:

1. Create your database (see above).

2. Determine whether you want to use the Liferay managed data source or a data source managed by your application server. The Liferay managed data source is recommended.

3. Gather credentials for sending email notifications to users. Liferay supports a JNDI mail session as well as its built-in mail session.

4. Install Liferay according to the instructions for your application server (see below).

5. Create a `portal-ext.properties` file in the Liferay Home folder. This is a simple text properties file that you'll use to override Liferay's default properties (see below). This is where you'll place the mail session configuration credentials you collected in step 3.

The easiest way to install Liferay is to set up your database and then follow the instructions for your application server. This method uses the setup wizard to create a working configuration. We'll go through the steps in order, so first we'll look at the options for data sources.

Using data sources

Liferay comes bundled with its own built-in data source. It's configured by a number of properties which are set in a properties file. By default, the setup wizard asks you for the necessary values and creates a configuration file that uses the built-in data source to connect to the database.

Liferay always recommends that you use the built-in data source. Sometimes, however, organizations prefer to use the data source provided by their application server of choice. In this instance, a JNDI lookup provides a handle to the data source and the application server manages the connection pools. Liferay supports using your application server's data source if you wish to do that.

To do this, you'll need to create your own configuration file and skip the setup wizard. Since you'd be creating this file *after* the wizard anyway, this isn't such a big deal.

Since mail sessions are configured in a similar way to data sources, we'll look at them next.

Using mail sessions

Liferay's default configuration looks for a mail server on the same machine on which Liferay's running and it tries to send mail via SMTP to this server. If this is not your configuration, you'll need to modify Liferay's defaults. To do this, you'll use a `portal-ext.properties` file (see below).

In a similar fashion to databases, you have two ways to configure your mail server:

- Use your application server's mail session.

- Use the built-in mail session.

To use your application server's mail session, you must create it in your application server and it should point to your mail server. Once you've done that, you're ready to point Liferay to it. You can do this through the configuration file or through Liferay's control panel after it's been installed.

Let's look next at this configuration file and, if you're choosing not to use the setup wizard, show you how to get Liferay connected to your database and your mail server.

The portal-ext.properties file

Liferay's properties files differ from the configuration files of most other products in that changing the default configuration file is discouraged. In fact, the file that contains all the defaults is stored inside of a `.jar` file, making it more difficult to customize. Why is it set up this way? Because Liferay uses the concept of *overriding* the defaults in a separate file, rather than going in and customizing the default configuration file. You put only the settings you want to customize in your own configuration file and then you have a file that contains only the settings you need. This makes it far easier to determine whether a particular setting has been customized and it makes the settings more portable across different installations of Liferay.

The default configuration file is called `portal.properties` and it resides inside of the `portal-impl.jar` file. This `.jar` file is in Liferay Portal's WEB-INF/lib folder. The file used to override the configuration manually is `portal-ext.properties`.

Complicating matters, the setup wizard creates a file called `portal-setup-wizard.properties`. This file performs the same function as `portal-ext.properties`, and you can use it in place of that file if you wish. The `portal-ext.properties` file is read before the `portal-setup-wizard.properties file`, so if you have both files in your configuration, note that the settings in the setup wizard file override the ones in `portal-ext.properties`.

This file should be created in your Liferay Home folder. You'll use this file throughout this book to change many of Liferay's settings. An exhaustive list of the configurable properties is provided in chapter 20.

> **Warning:** The configuration you choose in the setup wizard is saved in a `portal-setup-wizard.properties` file in your Liferay Home directory. In the setup wizard, however, if you specify a different Liferay Home directory than the default, the `portal-setup-wizard.properties` file that's saved there will not be read upon restarting your server. To have Liferay read your `portal-setup-wizard.properties` file, create a `portal-ext.properties` file in your new Liferay Home directory and

add the following line to it, where `${liferay.home}` is the new Liferay
Home directory that you chose:

```
include-and-override=${liferay.home}/portal-setup-wizard.properties
```

Without this workaround, Liferay will not read the
`portal-setup-wizard.properties` file with your saved configuration when you restart your server and you'll see the setup wizard again.

You now have all the background information you need. Next you need
to make your decision: will you use Liferay's built-in data source, or the one
provided by your application server? If you're planning to use the one provided
by your server, you can't use Liferay's installation wizard, and you'll have to
follow the instructions in the section below titled Manual Configuration.

In either case, your next step is to install Liferay onto your application server.
Once this is done, if you're using the recommended built-in data source, you can
use the setup wizard, which we'll cover next.

14.5   Using Liferay's setup wizard

To make it easy to configure Liferay optimally for your use, the first thing you
see when browsing to your newly installed Liferay bundle is a setup wizard.
This gives you a convenient way to configure Liferay for your purposes.

The wizard is an extremely helpful tool, especially if you're
setting up Liferay for the first time or creating a completely fresh
portal instance. If you're a Liferay veteran and you already have
your database information and various properties set up, you can
skip the wizard by adding this line to your *portal-ext.properties*
file:

```
setup.wizard.enabled=false
```

There are three sections of the wizard: the portal, the adminstrator and the
database. For the portal, you need to supply the following information:

Portal Name: the name of the web site you're powering with Liferay. In this
book, we'll build a social network for your nose. This site is called Nosester so
we've supplied `Nosester` in the screenshot below.

Default Language: choose the default locale where your site resides.
For the adminstrator, you need to supply the following information:
First Name: the first name of the user that has the administrator account.
Last Name: the last name of the user that has the administrator account.
Email: the email address of the user that has the administrator account.

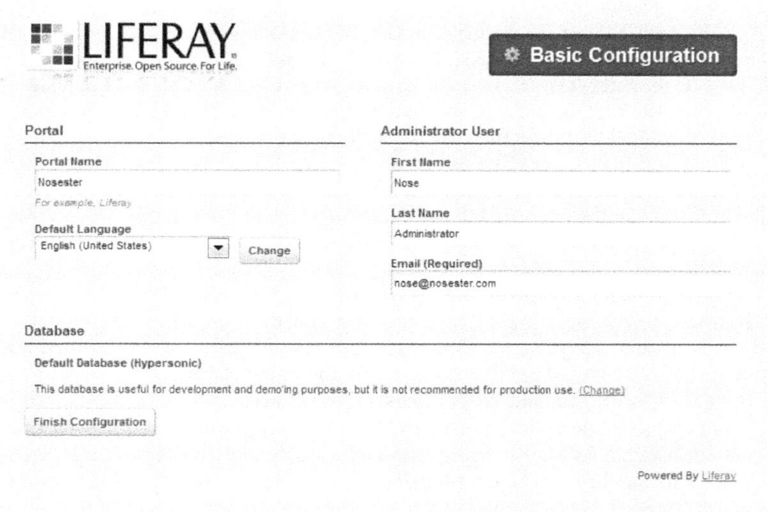

Figure 14.2: Supply the information for your site and your site's
administrative account in the setup wizard.

Liferay supports just about all the leading databases today:

- DB2
- Ingres
- MySQL
- Oracle
- PostgreSQL
- SQL Server

- Sybase

In addition to these, Liferay also supports a few embedded databases that are designed for development. We haven't listed these here because you're setting up a production Liferay server and you shouldn't use an embedded database with a production box.

Before you fill out the database section of Liferay's setup wizard, you should already have created a database for Liferay to use. This database must have UTF-8 as its character set, because Liferay is an internationalized application and needs the UTF-8 character set to display text in many different languages. Check the documentation for your database to see how to do this.

Once you have your database created, create a user that can do anything to the database, including create and drop tables. It's important that this user has complete rights over the Liferay database, because Liferay manages its own tables. Once you have your database and the credentials for this user, you can continue.

Open the Database section of the wizard. From the select box, choose your database. You'll see a form which lets you specify the URL to the database, the driver class and the user credentials (see below). Most of this is filled out already; all you should need to do is supply the name of your database and the server it's running on, as well as the user credentials.

Once you've filled out the form, click *Finish Configuration.* You'll see a message stating that Liferay is being installed as it creates the tables and data it needs in its database. When it's finished, it tells you the location of the configuration file (`portal-setup-wizard.properties`) where it saved all of your settings. From here, you can go to your home page.

In Liferay 6.1 GA2 (both 6.1.1 CE and 6.1.20 EE), the admin user test@liferay.com is created by the setup wizard even when a different user is specified. This means that two admin users are created: test@liferay.com and the specified user. Unless you're just installing Liferay for testing purposes, you should deactivate the test@liferay.com user after your database has been created.

Congratulations! You've just installed Liferay Portal! The next thing you need to do is set up your mail configuration, so Liferay can send email notifications to users. This is covered in the Manual Configuration section below.

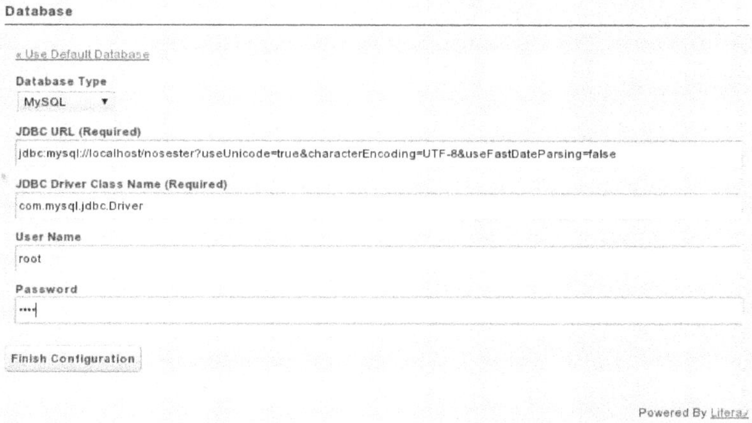

Database

x Use Default Database

Database Type

MySQL ▼

JDBC URL (Required)

jdbc:mysql://localhost/nosester?useUnicode=true&characterEncoding=UTF-8&useFastDateParsing=false

JDBC Driver Class Name (Required)

com.mysql.jdbc.Driver

User Name

root

Password

····|

Finish Configuration

Powered By Liferay

Figure 14.3: Fill out the information for your database. We've chosen MySQL in this example and have created a database called *nosester* to hold our Liferay data.

14.6   Manual Configuration

You don't have to use the setup wizard to configure Liferay. The setup wizard behind the scenes creates a configuration file that you can create manually. Create a text file called `portal-ext.properties` in your Liferay Home folder. This file overrides default properties that come with Liferay. The first setting you'll override is the default configuration that points Liferay to the embedded HSQL database.

As stated above, there are two ways to set up the connection:

- Use the built-in connection pool.

- Use your application server's connection pool.

Use the setup wizard if you're using the built-in connection pool. If you want to use your application server's pool, continue with this procedure.

If you want to use your application server's connection pool, you will have to create one in your application server that points to your database. It should be called `jdbc/LiferayPool`. To cause Liferay to use this connection pool, add the following directive to your `portal-ext.properties` file:

```
jdbc.default.jndi.name=jdbc/LiferayPool
```

Next, install Liferay according to the instructions for your application server. Once it's installed, you can set up the mail configuration.

For mail, you can use Liferay's control panel to create the configuration and this is the recommended way. Go to *Control Panel → Server Administration → Mail* and enter your settings for your mail session settings. If, however, you're setting up a lot of Liferay machines and they're all going to have similar mail configurations, it's easier to do the configuration once and then copy the configuration file to multiple machines. In this case, you'll want to use the `portal-ext.properties` file. To use the built-in mail session, use the following properties and customize their values for your environment:

```
mail.session.mail.pop3.host=localhost
mail.session.mail.pop3.password=
mail.session.mail.pop3.port=110
mail.session.mail.pop3.user=
mail.session.mail.smtp.auth=false
mail.session.mail.smtp.host=localhost
mail.session.mail.smtp.password=
mail.session.mail.smtp.port=25
mail.session.mail.smtp.user=
mail.session.mail.store.protocol=pop3
mail.session.mail.transport.protocol=smtp
```

To use your application server's mail session, create it first. Then specify it in the `portal-ext.properties` file:

```
mail.session.jndi.name=mail/MailSession
```

When you've finished, save the file.

Next, follow the instructions for installing Liferay on your particular application server in the section below.

14.7   Installing Liferay on an existing application server

This section contains detailed instructions for installing Liferay Portal using its .war file distribution. This allows system administrators to deploy Liferay in existing application server installations. It is recommended that you have a good understanding of how to deploy Java EE applications in your application server of choice.

Installing Liferay in five easy steps

There are five generic steps to installing Liferay on an existing application server:

1. Obtain the Liferay `.war` file and the dependencies archive.

2. Make sure you don't have an application listening at the root (/) of your server. If you do, move it to a different context or undeploy it.

3. Shut your application server down.

4. Extract the dependencies to a location on your server's global classpath. This allows both Liferay and plugins to access these dependencies.

5. Start your application server, deploy the Liferay `.war` file and start it.

The instructions below are specific for each application server that Liferay supports. Liferay supports a wide combination of application servers and databases. Because of this, this section assumes MySQL as the database, that the database has already been created and that you're using the setup wizard. If you're not using the setup wizard, see the sections above for information on how to set up Liferay manually.

We also assume your application server is already installed and running successfully. If you still need to install your application server, please follow your vendor's instructions first.

The following instructions assume an installation on a local machine. When installing to a remote server, substitute `localhost` with the host name or IP of the server.

Tip: Note that Liferay *requires* JDK 5 or greater. Do not attempt to install Liferay 6.x on an application server that runs under Java 1.4 or lower; it will not work. If you are running an application server that ships with a JDK and that JDK is 1.4 or lower, you'll need to upgrade your application server to run current versions of Liferay Portal.

Without further ado, let's get to the application servers. The first one we'll cover is Mule Tcat. If you don't have an application server preference, and you want support all the way down to the application server from Liferay, then Mule Tcat is your solution. After we cover Mule Tcat, we'll look at all the supported application servers in alphabetical order.

14.8   Installing Liferay on Mule Tcat

Liferay Portal Tcat Edition is a combination of Liferay Portal, the leading open source portal, and Tcat Server, an enterprise grade administration console for the Apache Tomcat application server.

Tcat Server provides several tools to make Tomcat more administrator friendly, especially in organizations used to leveraging administration consoles like those found in other more complex JEE application servers. You may use the console to:

- Monitor and control all Tomcat instances on multiple servers and across multiple environments

- Deploy and view applications across instances

- Troubleshoot problems across all instances, including view JMX parameters, viewing remote logs and more

- Provide granular entitlement controls for the above functions and more

This isn't a complete guide to Mule Tcat; it just covers Liferay installation. For full documentation, you'll find more detailed information at MuleSoft's web site.[2]

To obtain Liferay Portal Tcat Edition, you need access to the Liferay Customer Portal and the Mulesoft Tcat Server web site. If you are not a current Liferay customer and would like to try the product, please contact Liferay via email at sales@liferay.com.

For this section, we'll limit ourselves to the Windows and Linux 64-bit installation wizards. For more detailed installation instructions, please consult the Mulesoft Tcat Server installation documents located at:

http://www.mulesoft.org/documentation/display/TCAT/Home

- Installing Tcat Server on Linux

- Installing Tcat Server on Windows

- Installing Tcat Server on Solaris

- Installing Tcat Server on Mac OS X

- Adding Tcat Server Capabilities to an Existing Apache Tomcat Install

---

[2]http://www.mulesoft.org/documentation/display/TCAT/Home

First, download the Liferay Tcat bundle from the Liferay customer portal. You'll need two files:

- **Liferay Portal 6.1 EE Tcat Admin**: contains the Tcat administration console and Liferay Portal EE and all appropriate plugins.

- **Liferay Portal 6.1 EE Tcat Agent**: contains a vanilla Tomcat application server and the Tcat management agent.

Next, download the appropriate Tcat platform installation.[3] You may select installation wizards for Windows (32 and 64-bit), Mac, Unix, Solaris and Linux (32 and 64-bit) as well as a manual installation zip.

After obtaining the software bundles, you can proceed with installation and configuration of the Administration Console.

Installing the Administration Console on Windows

For Windows, Tcat comes with an installer to assist with installation and configuration. After downloading, execute the installer, accepting the appropriate license agreement.

Upon accepting the license agreement, the system presents you with two installation choices, a "standard" or "custom" installation.

Figure 14.4: Installation selection

---

[3]http://www.mulesoft.com/download-tcat

You should select the "Custom" installation option to provide better control of where Tcat Server is installed.

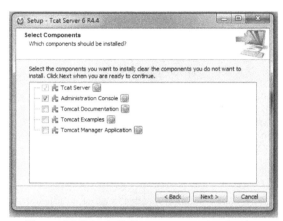

Figure 14.5: Installation component selection

After selecting the custom installation option, the Tcat installer prompts you to select the desired components.

- **Tcat Server**: a version of Apache Tomcat that includes the appropriate management agents used by Tcat.

- **Administration Console**: the administration console for monitoring and managing all available Tcat servers. This console contains tools used for application deployment, log access, server control and other administration tools.

- **Tomcat Documentation**: the documentation that comes normally with an Apache Tomcat distribution. You do not need to select this option.

- **Tomcat Examples**: the examples that comes normally with an Apache Tomcat distribution. You do not need to select this option.

- **Tomcat Manager Application**: the manager application that comes normally with an Apache Tomcat distribution. You do not need to select this option.

For this step in the installation process, select the Administration Console in addition to Tcat Server.

Figure 14.6: Installation location

After selecting Tcat Server and the Administration Console for installation, the installation wizard prompts you for an installation directory. Please select the desired installation directory for the Tcat Server.

After selecting the appropriate installation location, the installation wizard prompts you to specify the appropriate port numbers. If this is the first time installing Tcat and no other Apache Tomcat installations are present, then you may retain the above ports. However, if there are other installations, you will need to select new ports. For the purpose of this installation, we will assume the above ports are correct.

To ensure the operating system starts the Tcat Server and Administrator Console, you must configure the Tcat Server process as a Windows service. The next step in the installation wizard helps with this process.

In the Windows service installation screen, please select "Install Tcat Server as a Windows service." You may choose an appropriate service name other than *TcatServer*.

The final step in the installation wizard is to configure Start Menu shortcuts. You may choose to customize the shortcut location or accept the default.

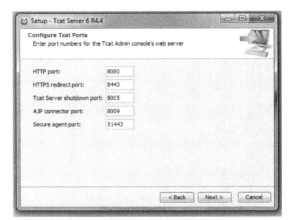

Figure 14.7: Port configurations

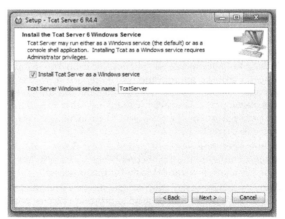

Figure 14.8: Windows service installation

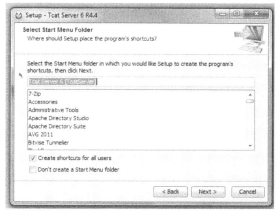

Figure 14.9: Start menu shortcuts

After configuring the shortcuts, the Tcat Server Windows installer performs the installation as previously configured.

Installing the Administraton Console on Linux (Ubuntu)

For Linux, Tcat comes with an installer to assist with installation and configuration. After downloading, execute the installer, accepting the appropriate license agreement. To execute the installer, make sure:

- you have added execution permissions to the installer file (`chmod a+x [file name]`)

- you execute it with root privileges (don't worry: the installed service is executed by a pre-defined system user with no root privileges)

Upon accepting the license agreement, the system presents you with two installation choices: a "standard" or "custom" installation.

You should select the "Custom" installation option to provide better control of where Tcat Server is installed.

After selecting the custom installation option, the Tcat installer prompts you to select the desired components.

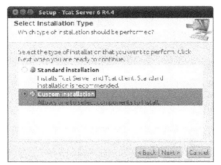

Figure 14.10: Installation type

Figure 14.11: Installation component selections

- **Tcat Server**: a version of Apache Tomcat that includes the appropriate management agents used by Tcat.

- **Administration Console**: the administration console for monitoring and managing all available Tcat servers. This console contains tools used for application deployment, log access, server control and other administration tools.

- **Tomcat Documentation**: the documentation that comes normally with an Apache Tomcat distribution. You do not need to select this option.

- **Tomcat Examples**: the examples that comes normally with an Apache Tomcat distribution. You do not need to select this option.

- **Tomcat Manager Application**: the manager application that comes normally with an Apache Tomcat distribution. You do not need to select this option.

For this step in the installation process, select the Administration Console in addition to Tcat Server, which is the default setting.

After selecting Tcat Server and the Administration Console for installation, the installation wizard prompts you for an installation directory.

Figure 14.12: Installation location

Please select the desired installation directory for the Tcat Server. The offered default directory is different if the installation process has been started as root.

After selecting the appropriate installation location, the installation wizard prompts you to specify the appropriate port numbers. If this is the first time installing Tcat and no other Apache Tomcat installations are present, then you may retain the above ports. However, if there are other installations, you will need to select new ports. For the purpose of this installation, we will assume the above ports are correct.

For security considerations, Tcat runs as a non-root system user. If the username specified at this step does not exist, it's created as a system daemon user.

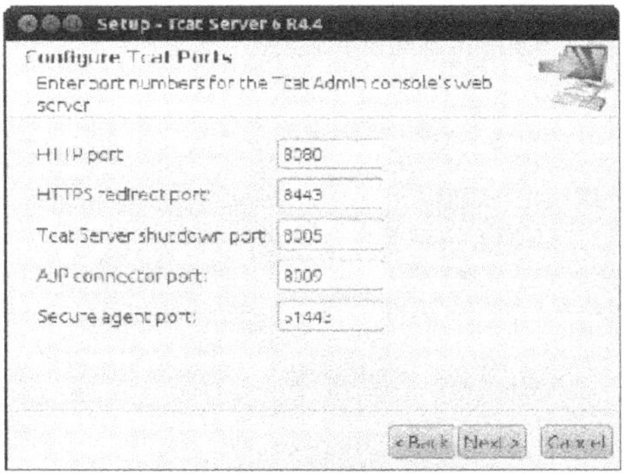

Figure 14.13: Port configuration

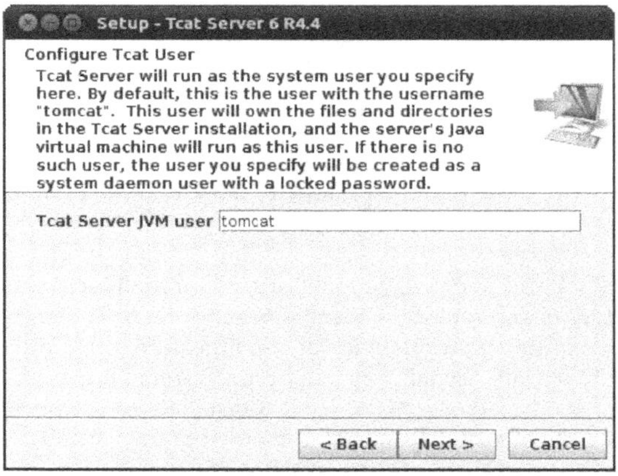

Figure 14.14: Configure Tcat system user

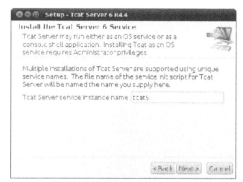

Figure 14.15: Install service

To ensure the operating system starts the Tcat Server and Administrator Console, you must create a service startup script in /etc/init.d. The next step in the installation wizard helps with this process.

In the service installation screen, you may enter an appropriate service name or use the default. If you have multiple installations of Tcat, you should select a more appropriate name than what is supplied by default.

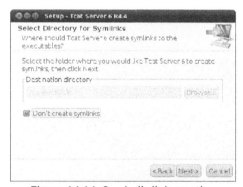

Figure 14.16: Symbolic link creation

The final configuration step before installation is the creation of a symbolic link so the Tcat executable can be accessed more easily. This step is optional and you may choose to not create the symbolic link.

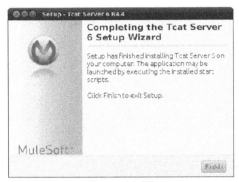

Figure 14.17:

Now that Tcat is installed, you can add Liferay to it.

Adding Liferay Portal packages

After completing the TcatServer Administration Console installation, you can configure the Liferay Portal packages for Tcat.

First, extract the previously downloaded Liferay Portal 6.1 EE Tcat Admin into a temporary directory. Once extracted, locate the file `tcat-init.groovy` and the directory `tcat\_init`.

The `tcat-init.groovy` file contains instructions for the TcatServer administration console to:

- Pre-load the Liferay Portal and Plugins WAR files into the application repository

- Load the appropriate Liferay application profile that should be applied to all other Tcat managed servers

- Load the Liferay specific deployment manager

Figure 14.18: Liferay Portal Tcat packages

The `tcat\_init` folder contains the managed server profiles, Liferay WAR files and administration scripts.

Copy the `tcat-init.groovy` file and `tcat\_init` folder to the previously configured installation location.

After successfully completing the installation on Windows, you should see a TcatServer entry in the Services console, similar to the screen shot below.

By default, the TcatServer service is inactive but is set to start automatically upon boot. Go ahead and choose to start the service.

If you're using Linux, you should see an entry for the Tcat service initialization script in `/etc/init.d`. The script name is the name you choose during the installation process.

To start the Tcat Server Administration Console, execute the service script in `/etc/init.d`.

Tcat Server Managed Server Installation

The steps to install the Tcat Server managed server are quite similar to those for installing the Tcat Server Administration Console.

First, launch the wizard. During the installation component configuration step, unselect "Administration Console" from the list of components.

The next step is to specify an installation location. If you have other installations of Tcat on this machine, you should choose another destination. For

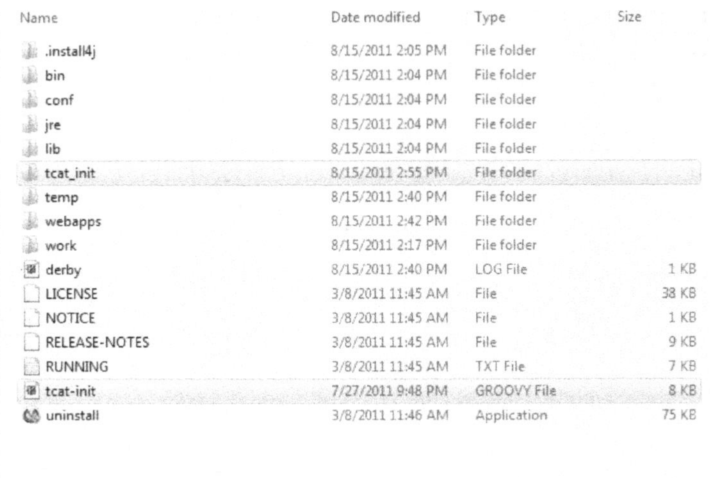

Name	Date modified	Type	Size
.install4j	8/15/2011 2:05 PM	File folder	
bin	8/15/2011 2:04 PM	File folder	
conf	8/15/2011 2:04 PM	File folder	
jre	8/15/2011 2:04 PM	File folder	
lib	8/15/2011 2:04 PM	File folder	
tcat_init	8/15/2011 2:55 PM	File folder	
temp	8/15/2011 2:40 PM	File folder	
webapps	8/15/2011 2:42 PM	File folder	
work	8/15/2011 2:17 PM	File folder	
derby	8/15/2011 2:40 PM	LOG File	1 KB
LICENSE	3/8/2011 11:45 AM	File	38 KB
NOTICE	3/8/2011 11:45 AM	File	1 KB
RELEASE-NOTES	3/8/2011 11:45 AM	File	9 KB
RUNNING	3/8/2011 11:45 AM	TXT File	7 KB
tcat-init	7/27/2011 9:48 PM	GROOVY File	8 KB
uninstall	3/8/2011 11:46 AM	Application	75 KB

Figure 14.19: The installation directory after copying the `tcat\_init` folder and `tcat-init.groovy` into the TcatServer installation directory.

example, if you have already installed the Tcat Server Administration Console to `C:\\TcatServer6`, you should perhaps install the managed server to `C:\\TcatServer6Managed`.

During the managed server installation, as with the administration console installation, you will be prompted to configure the appropriate port numbers. If you do not have another Tcat Server instance (e.g. administration console or another managed server), you may choose the default ports. Otherwise, you should select non-conflicting ports. For instance:

- HTTP port: 8180
- HTTPS redirect port: 81443
- Tcat Server shutdown port: 8105
- AJP connector port: 8109
- Secure Agent Port: 52443

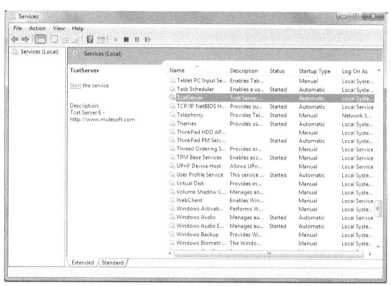

Figure 14.20: Windows services console

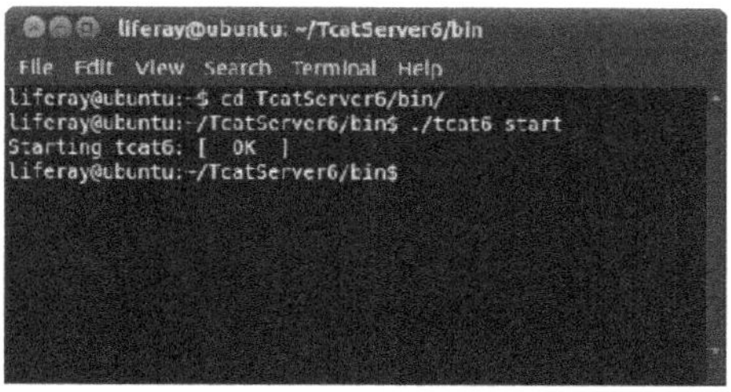

Figure 14.21: Tcat service startup on Linux

Figure 14.22: Installation location

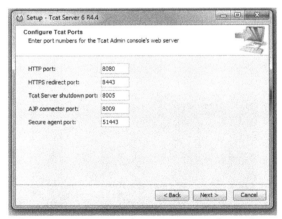

Figure 14.23: Managed server port configurations

To ensure the operating system starts the Tcat Server and Administrator Console, you must configure the Tcat process as a Windows service or Linux daemon. The next step in the installation wizard helps with this process.

The final step in the installation wizard is to configure Start Menu shortcuts. You may choose to customize the shortcut location or simply accept the default. Since this is for a managed server, you may wish to name it similar to the service name.

After configuring the shortcuts, the Tcat Server installer performs the installation as previously configured.

Once you have installed the managed server, there is one more step to perform on the managed server. You must modify the `catalina.properties` file located in the `conf` directory of your Tcat Server installation.

You will need to change the text:

```
common.loader=${catalina.base}/lib,${catalina.base}/lib/\*.jar,    \
  ${catalina.home}/lib,${catalina.home}/lib/\*.jar
```

To:

```
common.loader=${catalina.base}/lib,${catalina.base}/lib/\*.jar,    \
  ${catalina.home}/lib,${catalina.home}/lib/\*.jar,    \
  ${catalina.home}/lib/ext,${catalina.home}/lib/ext/\*.jar
```

By modifying the `common.loader` property, you instruct Tcat Server to load everything in the `lib/ext` folder as part of the classpath.

Registering the managed server

After completing the installation process and starting the appropriate TcatServer processes, open a browser to `[SERVER NAME]:[PORT]/console`. Using the previous installation example, you should point your browser to:

```
http://localhost:8080/console
```

The browser should render the TcatServer Administration Console shown below.

The default login is: admin/admin.

Once you have logged into the administration console, you will be presented with a global dashboard that you may customize once you have dismissed the "Tcat Server - Quick Start" panel.

First make sure that you have started the previously installed managed server. Clicking on the *Servers* tab in the console, you will see a server listed as *Unregistered*.

Figure 14.24: Tcat Admin Console log in

Unregistered servers are servers that have the Tcat management agent installed but are not added to the administration console. You may add the unregistered server by selecting either *Register* or *Register & Add To Group*.

If you choose to use *Register & Add To Group*, the server is added to the
desired server group (e.g. Development). For the purpose of this guide, we'll
register the server to the Development group.

After registering the server, you will have access to view its health status, log
files and more. Feel free to walk through the console to examine its capabilities,
like reviewing log files, current thread status and deployed web applications.

More information is available at MuleSoft's web site.

Managing and Monitoring Servers

- Using the Server Dashboard

- Working with Server Groups

- Monitoring Servers (View Apps, Threads, etc)

Figure 14.25: Customizable Tcat Admin Console

- Monitoring a JMX Agent

- Scripts to Save JMX Metrics to CSV Files

Managing Tcat Web Applications

- Monitoring Applications

- Deploying Applications

- Using the Repository

- Setting Security on Repository Artifacts

Figure 14.26: Monitoring a registered server

Deploying Liferay Portal

As part of the installation process, the current version of Liferay Portal and a number of Liferay Plugins have been provisioned into the Tcat repository. You can view them by clicking on the "Repository" tab.

There are two components in the Tcat Repository:

- **Profiles**: application profiles to be applied to the Tcat managed servers. Contains configuration, shared libraries and more.

- **Applications**: deployable WAR files for web applications and Liferay Plugins.

Figure 14.27: Tcat Repository profiles

To begin Liferay deployment, we must first create a Liferay license profile to be deployed to the managed server:

1. First create a new workspace under *Profiles*. Select *Profiles* in the left navigation and then click the *New Workspace* button.

2. Within the new workspace *Liferay Portal Trial License*, create another folder called deploy.

3. In the deploy folder, select *New Artifact* and upload a new license file.

After completing the above, you have successfully uploaded your Liferay Portal license file into the Tcat repository. The final step is to create a server profile from the *Administration* tab.

Figure 14.28: Tcat Repository: Applications

Server Profiles shows the list of available Server Profiles and the option to create a new profile.

When creating a server profile for the Liferay Portal Trial License, you will need to select the workspace folder created in the previous step. This ensures that when you apply the profile, Tcat uses the latest version of the license file.

Once you've created the server profile for your Liferay Portal EE license, you may begin deploying Liferay to the managed server.

The first step is to apply two server profiles, one for the license and the other for Liferay Portal. Applying the license profile does not require a restart of the server.

The second profile to be applied is the Liferay server profile. In the example shown we applied the profile for Liferay Portal EE 6.1.

The Liferay Portal server profile requires a server restart. If you have the managed server configured as a Windows or Linux service, you may restart the

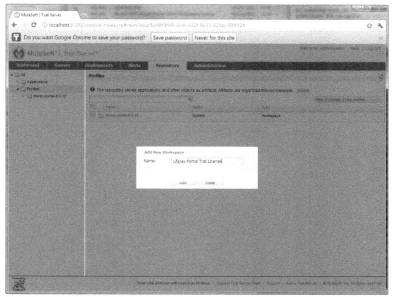

Figure 14.29: Creating a new workspace for Liferay license profile

server directly from the console by selecting the server and clicking "Restart".

With both profiles applied, we can now deploy the Liferay Portal WAR to the appropriate server.

The *Deployments* tab contains tools that assist in creating a deployment and targeting it to specific servers. Once you create a deployment, you may target it to any number of servers or deployment groups.

When creating a deployment, you may choose a WAR file already uploaded into the repository or you may choose to upload a new WAR file. We recommend using a WAR file from the repository for non-development deployments. This ensures you consistently deploy the correct version to your environments.

Since we are deploying Liferay Portal for the first time, we choose the ROOT.war file.

After selecting the appropriate web application, you may choose which Servers to deploy to. In this example, we deploy to the Tomcat instance labeled *Liferay*

Figure 14.30: Viewing server profiles

Portal Instance 1.

After choosing to deploy the application, the Tcat console informs you of the current deployment status (e.g. "Successful"). Assuming you followed the previous steps and the deployment successfully completes, you will be able to access Liferay Portal on the target Tomcat instance.

Deploying Liferay plugins on Mule Tcat

Liferay Portal Tcat Edition works with all the appropriate Liferay EE Plugins, including:

- Kaleo workflow engine

- Knowledge base

Figure 14.31: Apply Liferay Portal trial license

- Chat

- Private messaging

You may choose to deploy these plugins to the appropriate servers by following the same steps as for deploying Liferay Portal, specifying the appropriate plugin WAR file instead of the ROOT.war.

Other plugins that may be downloaded and added to this repository include:

- Audit

- Report engine and console

- Drools integration.

Figure 14.32: Apply Liferay profile

You may download these plugins from the Liferay Customer Portal and manually add them to the Tcat repository.

Mule Tcat provides an enterprise grade solution to managing Tomcat servers. If you need a complete stack, combining Liferay Portal with Mule Tcat gives you everything you need to run a fully supported and robust portal environment for your enterprise.

14.9   Installing Liferay on GlassFish 3

Liferay Home is three folders above your GlassFish domain folder.

For example, if your domain location is

```
/glassfish-3.1-web/glassfish3/glassfish/domains/domain1,
```

Liferay Home is

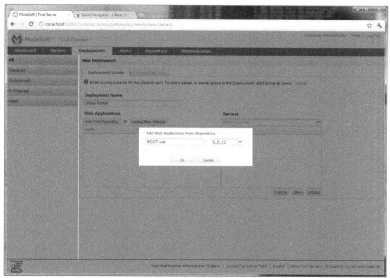

Figure 14.33: Choosing a web application for deployment

```
/glassfish-3.1-web/glassfish3/.
```

If you don't already have an existing GlassFish server, we recommend that you download a Liferay/GlassFish bundle.[4] If you have an existing GlassFish server or would like to install Liferay on GlassFish manually, please follow the steps below.

Before you begin, make sure you have downloaded the latest Liferay `.war` file and Liferay Portal dependencies.[5] The Liferay `.war` file should be called

```
liferay-portal-6.1.x-[date].war
```

and the dependencies file should be called

```
liferay-portal-dependencies-6.1.x-[date].zip
```

---

[4]http://www.liferay.com/downloads/liferay-portal/available-releases
[5]http://www.liferay.com/downloads/liferay-portal/additional-files

Figure 14.34: Completing Liferay Portal deployment

These instructions assume that you are running the latest supported version of Glassfish (currently 3.1.2.2), have already configured a domain and server, and that you have access to the GlassFish administrative console.

Let's start out by installing the JAR files you will need.

Dependency Jars

Liferay depends on jar files found in the Liferay Dependencies Archive. You should also have installed your database driver.

1. Navigate to the folder that corresponds to the domain in which you'll be installing Liferay. Inside this folder is a sub-folder named `lib`.

Unzip the Liferay dependencies archive so that its `.jar` files are extracted into this `lib` folder.

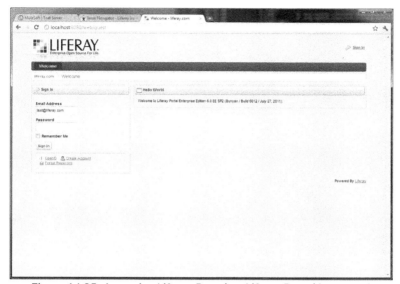

Figure 14.35: Accessing Liferay Portal on Liferay Portal Instance 1

2. Make sure the JDBC driver for your database is accessible to GlassFish as well. Obtain the JDBC driver for your version of the database server. In the case of MySQL, use `mysql-connector-java-{$version}-bin.jar`. You can download the latest MySQL JDBC driver.[6] Extract the JAR file and copy it to `lib`.

Terrific, you have your JAR files just where you'll need them. Next we'll configure your domain.

Domain Configuration   There are a couple of modifications you need to make in your domain to use Liferay Portal.

1. Before starting GlassFish, modify your domain's configuration to do the following:

---

[6]http://www.mysql.com/products/connector/

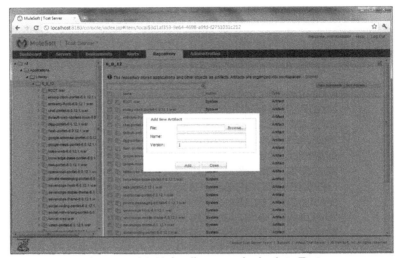

Figure 14.36: Uploading new plugins into Tcat

- Set the file encoding

- Set the user time-zone

- Set the preferred protocol stack

- Prevent the application server from setting static fields (final or non-final) to `null`

- Increase the default amount of memory available.
  Modify

```
/glassfish-3.1-web/glassfish3/glassfish/domains/domain1/config/domain.xml
```

merging in the following JVM options into the current list of JVM options within your `<java-config>` element:

```
<jvm-options>-Dfile.encoding=UTF8</jvm-options>
```

```
<jvm-options>-Djava.net.preferIPv4Stack=true</jvm-options>
<jvm-options>-Dorg.apache.catalina.loader.WebappClassLoader.    \
     ENABLE_CLEAR_REFERENCES=false</jvm-options>
<jvm-options>-Duser.timezone=GMT</jvm-options>
<jvm-options>-Xmx1024m</jvm-options>
<jvm-options>-XX:MaxPermSize=512m</jvm-options>
```

Be sure that any existing options with values such as

```
-Dfile.encoding
-Djava.net.preferIPv4Stack
-Dorg.apache.catalina.loader.WebappClassLoader.ENABLE_CLEAR_REFERENCES
-Duser.timezone
-XX:MaxPermSize
```

are replaced with the new values listed above.

For example, replace:

```
<jvm-options>-Xmx256m</jvm-options>
```

with this:

```
<jvm-options>-Xmx1024m</jvm-options>
```

2. Delete, rename or move the `domain1/docroot/index.html` file to another location to allow your Liferay Portal default page to be displayed.

Next, let's get your database configured.

Database Configuration

If you want to use GlassFish to manage your domain's data source, follow the instructions found in this section. If you want to use Liferay Portal to manage your data source, you can skip this section.

1. Start your domain's application server if it is not already running.

2. Go to the GlassFish console URL: http://localhost:4848.

3. Under *Common Tasks*, navigate to *Resources* → *JDBC* → *JDBC Connection Pools*

4. Click *New....*

Figure 14.37: Navigate to JDBC Connection Pools

Figure 14.38: Glassfish JDBC Connection Pool

5. In the first screen (Step 1 of 2), give your connection pool the name Liferay-Pool, the resource type of javax.sql.ConnectionPoolDataSource and select your database driver vendor (e.g. MySQL) as follows:

6. Click *Next* to advance to the next step in creating your JDBC connection pool.

7. On the this screen (Step 2 of 2), scroll down to the *Additional Properties* section.

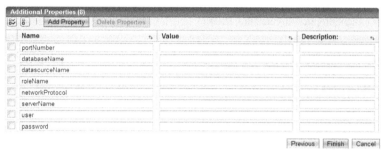

Figure 14.39: Glassfish JDBC Connection Pool Properties

8. Replace or add the following properties ...

   - **URL**: the URL of your connection pool.

   For example,

```
jdbc:mysql://localhost/lportal?useUnicode=true&amp;characterEncoding=UTF-8   \
   &amp;emulateLocators=true
```

Note, if you are using the above example, you should specify the name of your database in place of lportal. Likewise, if your database is not on the same host as GlassFish, specify your the database server's host name in place of localhost. Lastly, specify your database type in place of jdbc:mysql.

   - **user**: the name of your database user.

- **password**: your database user's password.

10. Click *Finish*.

    You should now see your `LiferayPool` connection pool listed under *Resources → JDBC → JDBC Connection Pools*

11. Test your connection by selecting your `LiferayPool` connection pool and clicking *Ping*.

    If you get a message stating *Ping Succeeded*, you've succeeded in setting up a connection pool of your data source!

13. Now, you'll setup a JDBC resource to refer to the `LiferayPool` connection pool you just created.

14. Navigate to *Resources → JDBC → JDBC Resources* to show the current JDBC resources listed by their JNDI names.

15. Click *New....*

16. Set the JNDI name to `jdbc/LiferayPool` and select `LiferayPool` as the pool name.

17. Click *OK*.

    Congratulations! You've now configured your domain's data source on Glass-Fish!

Mail Configuration

If you want to use GlassFish to manage your mail session, follow GlassFish's documentation on configuring a JavaMail session with a JNDI name of

```
mail/MailSession
```

If you want to use Liferay Portal to manage your mail session, you can skip this step.

Domain Configuration - Continued

Let's tie up some loose ends with regards to Liferay being able to access your database and mail session.

2. Shutdown your domain's application server if it is currently running.

3. Create a `portal-ext.properties` file in the *Liferay Home* folder mentioned at the beginning of this GlassFish installation section.

4. If you are using *Glassfish* to manage your data source, add the following to your `portal-ext.properties` file in your *Liferay Home* to refer to your data source:

    jdbc.default.jndi.name=jdbc/LiferayPool

Otherwise, if you are using *Liferay Portal* to manage your data source, follow the instructions in the *Deploy Liferay* section for using the setup wizard.

4. If want to use *Liferay Portal* to manage your mail session, you can configure the mail session within Liferay Portal. That is, after starting your portal as described in the *Deploy Liferay* section, go to *Control Panel → Server Administration → Mail* and enter the settings for your mail session.

If you are using *GlassFish* to manage your mail session, add the following to your `portal-ext.properties` file to reference that mail session:

```
mail.session.jndi.name=mail/MailSession
```

Liferay can now communicate with your database and mail session. So let's go ahead and deploy Liferay.

Deploy Liferay

Here are the steps you'll need to follow to deploy Liferay Portal to your domain's server. Before you deploy Liferay Portal, let's consider whether you want to also start the setup wizard.

  • **Start the setup wizard along with Liferay Portal** - Do this if you want to configure your portal, set up your site's administrative account and/or manage your database within Liferay.

If this is your first time starting Liferay Portal 6.1, the setup wizard is automatically invoked. If you want to re-run the wizard, specify `setup.wizard.enabled=true` in your properties file (e.g. `portal-setup-wizard.properties`).

```
setup.wizard.enabled=true
```

The setup wizard is then invoked during server startup.

- **Start Liferay Portal without invoking the setup wizard** - Do this if want to preserve your current portal settings.

To start the server without triggering the setup wizard, specify `setup.wizard.enabled=false` in your properties (e.g. `portal-setup-wizard.properties` or `portal-ext.properties` file).

```
setup.wizard.enabled=false
```

Once you run the setup wizard, the `portal-setup-wizard.properties` file it creates already has `setup.wizard.enabled=false` conveniently specified for you.

 Property values in `portal-setup-wizard.properties` override property values in `portal-ext.properties`.

1. Start your domain's application server.

2. Go to the GlassFish console URL: http://localhost:4848

3. Click *Applications* in the tree on the left.

4. Click *Deploy*.

5. Under *Packaged File to Be Uploaded to the Server*, click *Choose File* and browse to the location of the Liferay Portal `.war` file. Enter *Context Root:* /

6. Enter *Application Name:* `liferay-portal`

7. Click *OK*.

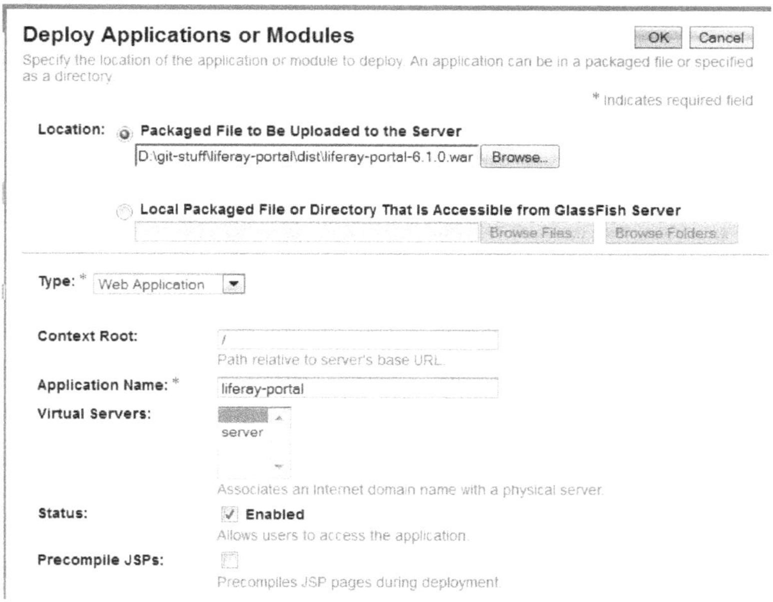

Figure 14.40: Deploying Liferay in GlassFish 3.1.x

- If you disabled the setup wizard, your site's home page opens in your browser at http://localhost:8080.

- Otherwise, the setup wizard opens in your browser.

See the section on the setup wizard above for how to use the setup wizard. Your installation of Liferay Portal on GlassFish is complete!

14.10   Installing Liferay on Jetty 7

Liferay Home is one folder above Jetty's install location.

For this section, we'll refer to Jetty server's installation location as

$JETTY_HOME

If you do not already have an existing Jetty server, we recommend you download a Liferay/Jetty bundle from Liferay's web site.[7] If you have an existing Jetty server or would like to install Liferay on Jetty manually, please follow the steps below.

Before you begin, make sure you have downloaded the latest Liferay `.war` file and Liferay Portal dependencies.[8] The Liferay `.war` file should be called `liferay-portal-6.1.x-<date>.war` and the dependencies file should be called `liferay-portal-dependencies-6.1.x-<date>.zip`.

Now that you have all of your installation files, you're ready to start installing and configuring Liferay on Jetty.

Dependency Jars

Let's work with the Liferay depenency jar files first.

1. Create folder `$JETTY_HOME/lib/ext/liferay`.

2. Unzip the jar files found in the Liferay Portal Dependencies zip file to your `$JETTY_HOME/lib/ext/liferay` folder. Take care to extract the zip file's `.jar` files directly into this folder.

3. Next, you need several `.jar` files which are included as part of the Liferay source distribution. Many application servers ship with these already on the class path but Jetty does not. The best way to get the appropriate versions of these files is to download the Liferay source code and get them from there. Once you have downloaded the Liferay source, unzip the source into a temporary folder. We'll refer to the location of the Liferay source as `$LIFERAY_SOURCE`.

   Copy the following jars from `$LIFERAY_SOURCE/lib/development` to your `$JETTY_HOME/lib/ext/liferay` folder:

   - `activation.jar`

   - `jta.jar`

   - `mail.jar`

   - `persistence.jar`

---

[7]http://www.liferay.com/downloads/liferay-portal/available-releases
[8]http://www.liferay.com/downloads/liferay-portal/additional-files

4. Make sure the JDBC driver for your database is accessible to Jetty. Obtain the JDBC driver for your version of the database server. In the case of MySQL, use `mysql-connector-java-{$version}-bin.jar`[9]. Extract the JAR file and copy it to `$JETTY_HOME/lib/ext/liferay`.

Now that your `.jar` files are in place, let's configure your domain.

Jetty Configuration

To get Jetty ready for running Liferay Portal, you must make a number of modifications that involve configuration files, initialization files and run scripts.

1. Create a `start.config` file to modify the behavior of Jetty's `start.jar`. It's best to base your `start.config` file on the default one found in `start.jar`.

2. Extract the default start config file `org/eclipse/jetty/start/start.config` from the `start.jar` into `$JETTY_HOME/etc`. The file `$JETTY_HOME/etc/start.config` should be in the `$JETTY_HOME/etc` folder.

3. Add the following property assignment to `$JETTY_HOME/etc/start.config` to specify where Jetty should write its logs:

   jetty.logs=$(jetty.home)/logs

4. Add the following directive to `$JETTY_HOME/etc/start.config` to load all of the `.jar` and `.zip` files found in your `$JETTY_HOME/lib/liferay` folder into your class path:

   $(jetty.home)/lib/liferay/*

Now that your class loading is specified, let's create initialization files and run scripts that invoke these configuration directives during Jetty's startup process.

2. Create initialization file: `$JETTY_HOME/bin/start.ini`

```
START=../etc/start.config
OPTIONS=Server,jsp,resources

../etc/jetty.xml
../etc/jetty-deploy.xml
../etc/jetty-webapps.xml
../etc/jetty-contexts.xml
../etc/jetty-testrealm.xml
```

---

[9]http://www.mysql.com/products/connector/

This initialization file does the following:

- Sets $JETTY_HOME/etc/start.config as your starting configuration file.

- Sets your server options.

- Specifies a sequence of deployment descriptor files to be processed.

3.Create a run script appropriate to your operating system:

- On Windows, create: $JETTY_HOME/bin/run.bat

```
@echo off

if "" == "%JAVA_HOME%" goto errorJavaHome

set "JAVA_OPTS=-Djetty.version=7.5.4 -Djetty.version.date=20111024    \
    -Dfile.encoding=UTF8 -Djava.io.tmpdir=../temp    \
    -Djava.net.preferIPv4Stack=true -Duser.timezone=GMT    \
    -Xmx1024m -XX:MaxPermSize=256m"

"%JAVA_HOME%/bin/java" %JAVA_OPTS% -jar ../start.jar

goto end

:errorJavaHome
    echo JAVA_HOME not defined.

    goto end

:end
```

- On Unix/Linux, create: $JETTY_HOME/bin/run.sh

```
#!/bin/sh

if [ ! $JAVA_HOME ]
then
    echo JAVA_HOME not defined.
    exit
fi

export JAVA_OPTS="-Djetty.version=7.5.4 -Djetty.version.date=20111024    \
    -Dfile.encoding=UTF8 -Djava.io.tmpdir=../temp    \
    -Djava.net.preferIPv4Stack=true -Duser.timezone=GMT    \
    -Xmx1024m -XX:MaxPermSize=256m"

$JAVA_HOME/bin/java $JAVA_OPTS -jar ../start.jar
```

3. Create a context file $JETTY_HOME/contexts/root.xml to specify the context, classpath and resource base of your web application:

```
<?xml version="1.0"?>
<!DOCTYPE Configure PUBLIC "-//Mort Bay Consulting//DTD Configure//EN"
    "http://jetty.mortbay.org/configure.dtd">
<Configure class="org.eclipse.jetty.webapp.WebAppContext">
    <Set name="contextPath"/></Set>
    <Set name="extraClasspath">
        <SystemProperty name="jetty.home" />/lib/jetty-server-
        <SystemProperty name="jetty.version" />.v
        <SystemProperty name="jetty.version.date" />.jar,
        <SystemProperty name="jetty.home" />/lib/jetty-util-
        <SystemProperty name="jetty.version" />.v
        <SystemProperty name="jetty.version.date" />.jar,
        <SystemProperty name="jetty.home" />/lib/jetty-webapp-
        <SystemProperty name="jetty.version" />.v
        <SystemProperty name="jetty.version.date" />.jar</Set>
    <Set name="resourceBase">
        <SystemProperty name="jetty.home" />/webapps/root</Set>
</Configure>
```

4. Lastly, create the following folders:

   - $JETTY_HOME/logs - for log files

   - $JETTY_HOME/temp - for temporary files. Note, this folder is specified to our JVM as a temporary folder in the run script you created previously.

Now that your general Jetty startup files are set in place, let's consider how you will manage your data source.

Database Configuration

If you want to manage your data source within Jetty, continue following the instructions in this section. If you want to use the built-in Liferay data source, you can skip this section.

1. Management of databases in Jetty is done via the file $JETTY_HOME/etc/jetty.xml. Edit jetty.xml and insert the following text within the root element <Configure> to specify the data pool for your data source. Be sure to pass in value jdbc/LiferayPool as the second argument.

```
<New id="LiferayPool" class="org.eclipse.jetty.plus.jndi.Resource">
    <Arg></Arg>
    <Arg>jdbc/LiferayPool</Arg>
```

```
<Arg>
    <New class="com.mysql.jdbc.jdbc2.optional.MysqlConnectionPoolDataSource">
        <Set name="Url">jdbc:mysql://localhost/lportal?
useUnicode=true&amp;characterEncoding=UTF-8</Set>
        <Set name="User">root</Set>
        <Set name="Password">root</Set>
    </New>
</Arg>
</New>
```

Be sure to replace the URL database value (i.e. `lportal`), user value and password value with values specific to your database.

2. Your data pool needs Jetty's JNDI and Jetty Plus libraries loaded to access those classes at runtime. Your `$JETTY_HOME/etc/start.config` file should have sections that load these libraries as long as `jndi` and `plus` *options* are specified at startup.

   To set these options, edit your `$JETTY_HOME/bin/start.ini` file and add `jndi` and `plus` as values for the `OPTIONS` variable:

```
OPTIONS=Server,jsp,resources,jndi,plus
```

Super! Now you have your database specified and ready for use with Liferay on Jetty. Let's consider your mail session next.

Mail Configuration

If you want to manage your mail session within Jetty, use the following instructions. If you want to use the built-in Liferay mail session, you can skip this section.

Management of mail sessions in Jetty is done via the configuration file `$JETTY_HOME/etc/jetty.xml`. Edit `jetty.xml` and insert the following text within the root element `<Configure>` to specify your mail session. Be sure to pass in value `mail/MailSession` as the first argument and to replace the mail session values with your own.

```
<New id="MailSession" class="org.eclipse.jetty.plus.jndi.Resource">
    <Arg>mail/MailSession</Arg>
    <Arg>
        <New class="org.eclipse.jetty.jndi.factories.MailSessionReference">
            <Set name="user"></Set>
            <Set name="password"></Set>
            <Set name="properties">
                <New class="java.util.Properties">
                    <Put name="mail.pop3.host">pop.gmail.com</Put>
```

```
                <Put name="mail.pop3.port">110</Put>
                <Put name="mail.smtp.host">smtp.gmail.com</Put>
                <Put name="mail.smtp.password">password</Put>
                <Put name="mail.smtp.user">user</Put>
                <Put name="mail.smtp.port">465</Put>
                <Put name="mail.transport.protocol">smtp</Put>
                <Put name="mail.smtp.auth">true</Put>
                <Put name="mail.smtp.starttls.enable">true</Put>
          <Put name="mail.smtp.socketFactory.class">javax.net.ssl.SSLSocketFactory</Put>
                <Put name="mail.imap.host">imap.gmail.com</Put>
                <Put name="mail.imap.port">993</Put>
                <Put name="mail.store.protocol">imap</Put>
            </New>
        </Set>
      </New>
    </Arg>
</New>
```

Great! Now you'll be able to use this mail session with Liferay.

Configuring data sources and mail sessions

Let's revisit your configuration to make sure we'll be able to access your data source and mail session from Liferay Portal.

1. First, navigate to the *Liferay Home* folder, which is one folder above Jetty's install location. Create a file named `portal-ext.properties`.

2. If you are using *Jetty* to manage your data source, add the following to your `portal-ext.properties` file in your *Liferay Home* to refer to your data source:

```
jdbc.default.jndi.name=jdbc/LiferayPool
```

Otherwise, if you are using *Liferay Portal* to manage your data source, follow the instructions in the *Deploy Liferay* section for using the setup wizard.

3. If want to use *Liferay Portal* to manage your mail session, you can configure the mail session within Liferay Portal. That is, after starting your portal as described in the *Deploy Liferay* section, go to *Control Panel → Server Administration → Mail* and enter the settings for your mail session.

Otherwise, if you are using *Jetty* to manage your mail session, add the following to your `portal-ext.properties` file to reference that mail session:

```
mail.session.jndi.name=mail/MailSession
```

Let's start your server and deploy Liferay Portal!

Deploy Liferay

Liferay can be deployed as an exploded web archive within $JETTY_HOME/web-
apps.

1. If you already have an application folder $JETTY_HOME/webapps/root, delete
   it or move it to a location outside of $JETTY_HOME/webapps.

2. Then extract the contents of the Liferay portal .war file into $JETTY_HOME/web-
   apps/root.

3. Before you start Liferay Portal, let's consider whether you want to also start
   the setup wizard.

   - **Start the setup wizard along with Liferay Portal** - Do this if you want
     to configure your portal, setup your site's administrative account and/or
     manage your database within Liferay.

If this is your first time starting Liferay Portal 6.1, the setup wizard is invoked
on server startup. If you want to re-run the wizard, specify `setup.wizard.en-
abled=true` in your properties file (e.g. `portal-setup-wizard.properties`).

```
setup.wizard.enabled=true
```

The setup wizard is invoked during server startup.

   - **Start Liferay Portal without invoking the setup wizard** - Do this if want
     to preserve your current portal settings.

To start the server without triggering the setup wizard, specify `setup.wiz-
ard.enabled=false` in your properties (e.g. `portal-setup-wizard.pro-
perties` or `portal-ext.properties` file).

```
setup.wizard.enabled=false
```

The `portal-setup-wizard.properties` file the setup wizard creates has
`setup.wizard.enabled=false` conveniently specified for you.

 Property values in `portal-setup-wizard.properties`
override property values in `portal-ext.properties`.

Now its time to launch Liferay Portal!

4. Start Liferay Portal by executing `run.bat` (Windows) or `run.sh` (Unix/Linux) script from `$JETTY_HOME/bin`.

   - If the setup wizard was disabled, your site's home page opens in your browser at http://localhost:8080.

   - Otherwise, the setup wizard opens in your browser.

   See the section on the setup wizard above for more information about the setup wizard.
   You've just installed and deployed Liferay Portal on Jetty - way to go!

14.11 Installing Liferay on JBoss 5.1

Liferay Home is one folder above JBoss's install location.

1. Download and install JBoss EAP 5.1.x into your preferred directory. This directory is referred to as `$JBOSS_HOME` throughout this section.

2. Download the latest version of the Liferay Portal `.war` file.

3. Download Liferay's Portal Dependencies.

   Now that you have all of your installation files, you are ready to start installing and configuring Liferay on JBoss.

Configuring Dependencies

First we'll take care of dependencies and potential conflicts.

1. Unzip Liferay's dependencies to `$JBOSS_HOME/server/default/lib`.

2. Download your database driver `.jar` file and put it into the folder as well. For demonstration purposes, we'll download the MySQL Connector/J driver from http://dev.mysql.com/downloads/connector/j/ and put its `.jar` file into the `$JBOSS_HOME/server/default/lib` folder.

3. Next we'll delete JBoss's Hibernate Validator and HSQL JARs to prevent conflicts with Liferay's JARs. Remove the following files from `$JBOSS_HOME/common/lib`:

```
hibernate-validator.jar
hsqldb.jar
hsqldb-plugin.jar
```

Next we need to clean up the entries for the JAR files that we deleted.

1. Open `$JBOSS_HOME/server/default/conf/login-config.xml` in a text editor.

2. Comment out the blocks with the name `HsqlDBRealm` and `JmsXARealm` around lines 41-64.

We'll also delete some other files that can cause conflicts with Liferay when it's deployed.

1. Remove the following files from `$JBOSS_HOME/../server/default/deploy`:

```
/messaging
ejb2-container-jboss-beans.xml
ejb2-timer-service.xml
ejb3-connections-jboss-beans.xml
ejb3-container-jboss-beans.xml
ejb3-interceptors-aop.xml
ejb3-timerservice-jboss-beans.xml
hsqldb-ds.xml
jms-ra.rar
mail-ra.rar
mail-service.xml
profile-service-secured.jar
uuid-key-generator.sar
```

2. Delete the following in `$JBOSS_HOME/../server/default/deployers`:

```
jboss-ejb3-endpoint-deployer.jar
messaging-definitions-jboss-beans.xml
```

Deploying Liferay

Now that we've added all of the necessary dependencies and removed unnecessary files, it's time to deploy Liferay.

1. Navigate to `$JBOSS_HOME/../server/default/deploy/ROOT.war` and delete all the content of the folder.

2. Extract the contents of the Liferay WAR file into this folder.

3. Create a file named `jboss-classloading.xml` in

```
$JBOSS_HOME/../server/default/ROOT.war/WEB-INF
```

and add the following contents to it:

```
<classloading xmlns="urn:jboss:classloading:1.0"
parent-first="false"
domain="LiferayDomain"
export-all="NON_EMPTY"
import-all="true">
</classloading>
```

This configuration file defines a domain that does not allow parent classes to load first. Instead, Liferay Portal's classes are exported. Since JBoss comes with its own Hibernate JARs, the above configuration is needed to tell Liferay to ignore these JARs and to use its own JARs instead. If you omit this configuration, you may encounter a Hibernate exception. It's also necessary to add a `jboss-classloading.xml` file to the `WEB-INF` folder of each Liferay plugin; see the *Deploying Plugins* section below.

4. Create a `portal.ext.properties` file in `$LIFERAY_HOME` (one level above `$JBOSS_HOME`) and add the following properties:

```
hibernate.validator.apply_to_ddl=false
hibernate.validator.autoregister_listeners=false
```

5. Delete the following files from the `$JBOSS_HOME/ROOT.war/WEB-INF/lib`:

```
jaxrpc.jar
stax.jar
xercesImpl.jar
xml-apis.jar
```

6. Add the following lines to your `portal.ext.properties` file:
   NOTE: The autodeploy folder must be set with the full name of the folder; you can't use any variables to define the location.

```
auto.deploy.jboss.dest.dir=${jboss.home.dir}/server/default/deploy
auto.deploy.deploy.dir=C:/JBoss-<version>/deploy
```

7. Start the JBoss Application Server.

   Liferay is now successfully installed on JBoss 5.1.

Deploying plugins

Add a `jboss-classloading.xml` to the `WEB-INF` folder of each plugin, with the following content:

```
<classloading xmlns="urn:jboss:classloading:1.0"
domain="PLUGINNAME-portlet"
parent-domain="LiferayDomain"
parent-first="false"
top-level-classloader="false"
export-all="NON_EMPTY"
import-all="false">
</classloading>
```

The `LiferayDomain` referenced in the above configuration is the domain we defined above during step 3 of the *Deploying Liferay* section. Configuring plugins to use the Liferay domain ensures that if JBoss and Liferay have different versions of a JAR file, the plugin uses Liferay's version. Without this configuration, Liferay plugins might end up using the wrong versions of JAR files. You can configure this before or after the plugin WAR is deployed, as long as JBoss is not running. Of course, it's best to make this configuration before deployment. Otherwise, if there's a JAR conflict, you'll have to shut down your server, configure the plugin to use the Liferay domain, and restart the server.

To set up a hot deploy folder and have plugins automatically copied to the right place, add the following lines to your `portal-ext.properties` file:

```
\index{plugin}
\index{hot deploy}
```

```
auto.deploy.jboss.dest.dir=${jboss.home.dir}/server/default/deploy
auto.deploy.deploy.dir=/opt/jboss-eap-5.1/deploy
```

The first line is the value for the default server; if you've installed Liferay in something other than the default, change it accordingly. The path in the second line should point to the `deploy` folder configured for JBoss.

Liferay also runs on JBoss 7. Let's see how we'd get it installed on that version of JBoss.

14.12   Installing Liferay on JBoss 7

Liferay Home is one folder above JBoss's install location.

1. Download and install JBoss AS 7.0.x into your preferred directory. This directory is referred to as `$JBOSS_HOME` throughout this section.

2. Download the latest version of the Liferay Portal `.war` file.

3. Download Liferay's Portal Dependencies.

Now that you have all of your installation files, you are ready to start installing and configuring Liferay on JBoss.

Dependency Jars

Let's work with the dependency jar files first.

1. Create folder `$JBOSS_HOME/modules/com/liferay/portal/main` and unzip the jar files found in the Liferay Portal Dependencies zip file to this folder. Make sure there are no subdirectories; the files should be in this folder directly.

2. Download your database driver `.jar` file and put it into the same folder as above. For demonstration purposes, we'll download the MySQL Connector/J driver from http://dev.mysql.com/downloads/connector/j/ and put its `.jar` file into the `$JBOSS_HOME/modules/com/liferay/portal/main` folder.

3. Create the file `module.xml` in the `$JBOSS_HOME/modules/com/liferay/portal/main` folder and insert the following contents.

```
<?xml version="1.0"?>

<module xmlns="urn:jboss:module:1.0" name="com.liferay.portal">
    <resources>
        <resource-root path="mysql-connector-java-5.1.18-bin.jar" />
        <resource-root path="portal-service.jar" />
        <resource-root path="portlet.jar" />
    </resources>
    <dependencies>
        <module name="javax.api" />
        <module name="javax.mail.api" />
        <module name="javax.servlet.api" />
        <module name="javax.servlet.jsp.api" />
        <module name="javax.transaction.api" />
    </dependencies>
</module>
```

If you're using a different database driver, replace the path of the MySQL resource root entry with that of your database driver.

Great! You have your `.jar` files ready for your domain.

Configuring JBoss

Let's make some adjustments in your configuration to support using Liferay.

You can specify the JBoss server instance's configuration in the XML file `$JBOSS_HOME/standalone/configuration/standalone.xml`. We'll refer to this file simply as `standalone.xml`. You must also make some modifications to your configuration and startup scripts found in the `$JBOSS_HOME/bin/` folder. But let's start with the changes to `standalone.xml`.

1. Make the following modifications to `standalone.xml`.

2. Disable the welcome root of the web subsystem's virtual server default host by specifying `enable-welcome-root="false"`.

```
<subsystem xmlns="urn:jboss:domain:web:1.0" default-virtual-server="default-host">
    <connector name="http" scheme="http" protocol="HTTP/1.1" socket-binding="http"/>
    <virtual-server name="default-host" enable-welcome-root="false">
        <alias name="localhost" />
        <alias name="example.com" />
    </virtual-server>
</subsystem>
```

3. Insert the following `<configuration>` element within the web subsystem element:

```
<subsystem xmlns="urn:jboss:domain:web:1.0" default-virtual-server="default-host">

    <configuration>
        <jsp-configuration development="true" />
    </configuration>
```

4. Add a timeout for the deployment scanner by setting `deployment-timeout="120"` as seen in the excerpt below.

```
<subsystem xmlns="urn:jboss:domain:deployment-scanner:1.0">
    <deployment-scanner name="default" path="deployments" scan-enabled="true"
scan-interval="5000" relative-to="jboss.server.base.dir" deployment-timeout="120"/>
</subsystem>
```

5. Add the following JAAS security domain to the security subsystem `<security-domain` defined in element `<subsystem xmlns="urn:jboss:domain:security:1.0">`.

```
<security-domain name="PortalRealm">
    <authentication>
    <login-module code="com.liferay.portal.security.jaas.PortalLoginModule" flag="required"/>
    </authentication>
</security-domain>
```

Now it's time for some changes to your configuration and startup scripts.

2. Make the following modifications to your standalone domain's configuration script file `standalone.conf` (`standalone.conf.bat` on Windows) found in your `$JBOSS_HOME/bin/` folder.

These modifications change the following options:

- Set the file encoding

- Set the user time-zone

- Set the preferred protocol stack

- Increase the default amount of memory available.

Make the following edits as applicable to your operating system:

- On Windows, comment out the initial `JAVA_OPTS` assignment as demonstrated in the following line:

  rem set "JAVA_OPTS=-Xms64M -Xmx512M -XX:MaxPermSize=256M

Then add the following `JAVA_OPTS` assignment one line above the : `JAVA_OPTS_SET` line found at end of the file:

```
set "JAVA_OPTS=%JAVA_OPTS% -Dfile.encoding=UTF-8 -Djava.net.preferIPv4Stack=true   \
   -Duser.timezone=GMT -Xmx1024m -XX:MaxPermSize=256m"
```

- On Unix, merge the following values into your settings for `JAVA_OPTS` replacing any matching attributes with the ones found in the assignment below:

```
JAVA_OPTS="$JAVA_OPTS -Dfile.encoding=UTF-8 -Djava.net.preferIPv4Stack=true   \
   -Duser.timezone=GMT -Xmx1024m -XX:MaxPermSize=256m
```

The prescribed script modifications are now complete for your Liferay installation on JBoss. Next we'll consider the database and mail configuration.

Database Configuration

If you want JBoss to manage your data source, follow the instructions in this section. If you want to use the built-in Liferay data source, you can skip this section.

Modify `standalone.xml` adding your data source and driver within the `<datasources>` element of your data sources subsystem.

1. First, add your data source within the `<datasources>` element.

```
<datasource jndi-name="java:/jdbc/LiferayPool"
            pool-name="LiferayPool"
enabled="true"
jta="true"
use-java-context="true"
use-ccm="true">

    <connection-url>
        jdbc:mysql://localhost/lportal
    </connection-url>
    <driver>
        mysql
    </driver>
    <security>
        <user-name>
            root
        </user-name>
        <password>
            root
        </password>
    </security>
</datasource>
```

Be sure to replace the URL database value (i.e. `lportal`), user value and password value with values specific to your database.

2. Then add your driver to the `<drivers>` element also found within the `<datasources>` element.

```
<drivers>
    <driver name="mysql" module="com.liferay.portal"/>
</drivers>
```

Your final data sources subsystem should look something like this:

```
<subsystem xmlns="urn:jboss:domain:datasources:1.0">
    <datasources>
        <datasource jndi-name="java:/jdbc/LiferayPool"
        pool-name="LiferayPool"
```

```
enabled="true"
jta="true"
use-java-context="true"
use-ccm="true">

                <connection-url>
                    jdbc:mysql://localhost/lportal
                </connection-url>
                <driver>
                    mysql
                </driver>
                <security>
                    <user-name>
                        root
                    </user-name>
                    <password>
                        root
                    </password>
                </security>
            </datasource>
            <drivers>
                <driver name="mysql" module="com.liferay.portal"/>
            </drivers>
        </datasources>
    </subsystem>
```

Now that you've configured your data source, let's go over how to configure your mail session within JBoss.

Mail Configuration

At the time this document was written, JavaMail was not yet supported in JBoss AS 7.0.1 - however, it was implemented in the JBoss AS 7.1 alpha (see https://issues.jboss.org/browse/AS7-1177. If you want JBoss to manage your mail session, use the following instructions which are based on the implementation found in JBoss AS 7.1 alpha. If you want to use the built-in Liferay mail session, you can skip this section.

Specify your mail subsystem in `standalone.xml` as in the following example:

```
<subsystem xmlns="urn:jboss:domain:mail:1.0">
    <mail-session jndi-name="java:/mail/MailSession" >
        <smtp-server address="smtp.gmail.com" port="465">
                <login name="username" password="password"/>
        </smtp-server>
        <pop3-server address="pop.gmail.com" port="110"/>
        <imap-server address="imap.gmail.com" port="993">
            <login name="username" password="password"/>
        </imap-server>
    </mail-session>
</subsystem>
```

You've got mail! Next, we'll make sure Liferay is configured to properly connect with your new mail session and database.

Configuring data sources and mail sessions

Now that your data source and mail session are set up, you need to ensure Liferay Portal can access them.

1. First, navigate to the Liferay Home folder, which is one folder above JBoss's install location (i.e. `$JBOSS/..`).

2. If you're using *JBoss* to manage your data source, add the following to your `portal-ext.properties` file in your *Liferay Home* to refer to your data source:

   ```
   jdbc.default.jndi.name=java:jdbc/LiferayPool
   ```

   If you're using *Liferay Portal* to manage your data source, follow the instructions in the *Deploy Liferay* section for using the setup wizard.

3. If you're using *Liferay Portal* to manage your mail session, this configuration is done within Liferay Portal. That is, after starting your portal as described in the *Deploy Liferay* section, go to *Control Panel* → *Server Administration* → *Mail* and enter the settings for your mail session.

   If you're using *JBoss* to manage your mail session, add the following to your `portal-ext.properties` file to reference that mail session:

   ```
   mail.session.jndi.name=java:mail/MailSession
   ```

   You've completed the steps necessary for your deployment of Liferay so Liferay Portal can now communicate with your data source and mail session—way to go! Now you're ready to deploy Liferay Portal.

Deploy Liferay

1. If the folder `$JBOSS_HOME/standalone/deployments/ROOT.war` already exists in your JBoss installation, delete all of its subfolders and files. Otherwise, create a new folder `$JBOSS_HOME/standalone/deployments/ROOT.war`.

2. Unzip the Liferay `.war` file into the `ROOT.war` folder.

3. To trigger deployment of `ROOT.war`, create an empty file named `ROOT.war.do-deploy` in your `$JBOSS_HOME/standalone/deployments/` folder. On startup, JBoss detects the presence of this file and deploys it as a web application.

4. Remove `eclipselink.jar` from `$JBOSS_HOME/standalone/deployments-/ROOT.war/WEB-INF/lib` to assure the Hibernate persistence provider is used instead of the one provided in the `eclipselink.jar`. Note, JBoss 7.0.2 has a known issue http://community.jboss.org/thread/169944 in determining which persistence provider to use.

5. Before you start Liferay Portal, let's consider whether you want to also start the setup wizard.

   • **Start the setup wizard along with Liferay Portal** - Do this if you want to configure your portal, set up your site's administrative account and/or manage your database within Liferay.

   If this is your first time starting Liferay Portal 6.1, the setup wizard is invoked on server startup. If you want to re-run the wizard, specify `setup.wizard.en-abled=true` in your properties file (e.g. `portal-setup-wizard.properties`).

   `setup.wizard.enabled=true`

   The setup wizard is invoked during server startup.

   • **Start Liferay Portal without invoking the setup wizard** - Do this if want to preserve your current portal settings.

   To start the server without triggering the setup wizard, specify `setup.wiz-ard.enabled=false` in your properties (e.g. `portal-setup-wizard.pro-perties` or `portal-ext.properties` file).

   `setup.wizard.enabled=false`

   The `portal-setup-wizard.properties` file the setup wizard creates has `setup.wizard.enabled=false` conveniently specified for you.

> Property values in `portal-setup-wizard.properties` override property values in `portal-ext.properties`.

Now it's time to start Liferay Portal on JBoss!

6. Start the JBoss application server.

  • If the setup wizard was disabled, your site's home page opens automati-
    cally in your browser at http://localhost:8080.

  • Otherwise, the setup wizard opens in your browser.

· See the section on the setup wizard above for how to use Liferay's setup
wizard.

Now you are truly *the boss* when it comes to deploying Liferay Portal on
JBoss!

14.13   Installing Liferay on JOnAS 5.2

JOnAS is somewhat unique among the open-source application servers for two
reasons: it is built entirely on an OSGi core, allowing for dynamic deployment
of simultaneous webapps and containers and allows the clean separation of the
configuration directory from the server itself. In fact, the separation of the configuration is recommended by the developers of JOnAS as a way to cleanly deploy so you can revert to default settings later.

If you don't have an existing JOnAS installation, it is recommeded to use the
available Liferay-JOnAS bundle.[10]

Given the unique nature of the server, there are a few steps to consider in
the configuration stage. Otherwise, installing on JOnAS follows much the same
pattern as other servers: configure, copy dependencies and deploy.

Configuring JOnAS for Liferay

A pristine JOnAS installation comes with a number of samples, tutorials and
template configuration files. A lot of this is unnecessary and irrelevant for installing Liferay. In addition, the server already contains an application deployed
to the root context, which you must remove prior to installing the Liferay .war
package (and which you'd want to remove anyway for a production configuration). JOnAS allows you to decide where to place all the server configuration
and deployment settings, also called $JONAS_BASE. The folder created by un-
zipping the JOnAS application (likely called jonas-full-5.2.2 or similar) is

---

[10]http://www.liferay.com/ja/downloads/liferay-portal/available-releases

referred to as $JONAS_ROOT. This allows a unique, clean separation between application and configuration.

The structure of $JONAS_BASE is:

```
/conf             - configuration files
/deploy           - main deployment directory (Liferay is deployed here)
/lib              - used for extending the main server classloaders
+----/ext         - extensions for unbundled applications
/logs             - logs for the running instance
/work             - the working directory, used by containers such as Tomcat
/repositories     - contains OSGi bundles for deployment; not used for Liferay installation
```

By default, the $JONAS_BASE directory is the same as $JONAS_ROOT. Creating a new $JONAS_BASE is a simple process, outlined in the JOnAS Configuration Guide.[11]

To remove sample files and unneeded configuration:

1. Navigate to the directory you unpackaged *JOnAS* into, $JONAS_BASE.

2. Find the following sample directories and remove them:

   - /examples

   - /tutorial

3. Navigate to $JONAS_BASE/conf and remove the following files:

   - db2.properties

   - FirebirdSQL.properties

   - HSQL1.properties

   - jetty*.xml

   - InstantDB1.properties

   - InterBase1.properties

   - MailMimePartDS1.properties

   - MailSession1.properties

   - McKoi1.properties

---

[11]http://jonas.ow2.org/JONAS_5_2_2/doc/doc-en/html/configuration_guide.html

- MySQL.properties
- Oracle1.properties
- PostgreSQL1.properties
- spy.properties
- Sybase1.properties

This disables the default settings for the databases available in JOnAS, as well as removing configuration for Jetty as a container to use for the webapp.

4. To remove the default application installed on the root context:

a. Go to the `$JONAS_BASE/deploy` directory and remove:

- ctxroot.xml
- doc.xml
- jdbc-ds.xml
- jonasAdmin.xml

b. Go to the `$JONAS_ROOT/repositories` directory to remove the application by removing:

- org/mortbay/
- org/ow2/jonas/documentation/
- org/ow2/jonas/jonas-admin/
- org/ow2/jonas/jonas-ctxroot/

This will fully remove the Maven deployment plan and artifact for the JOnAS default application, as well as the administration console from loading on the root context.

Now that JOnAS is prepared for configuring Liferay to run on the server as its root application, you can begin tuning the settings for Liferay. By default, JOnAS has its own deployment of Hypersonic it uses internally. This internal use of HSQL must be disabled, along with other JOnAS services, so they won't conflict with Liferay's.

To turn of HSQL and other JOnAS-level services:

1. Open the file `jonas.properties` in the directory `$JONAS_BASE/conf`.

2. Find the configuration section for the JOnAS database manager, starting around line 340:

```
#
##################### JOnAS DBM Database service configuration

...

jonas.service.dbm.datasources    hsql
```

3. Change the datasources definition around line 353 to read:

```
jonas.service.dbm.datasources
```

   Thereby preventing the HSQL database from being used internally.

4. Find the services configuration around line 82:

```
jonas.services    jtm,db,security,resource,ejb3,jaxws,web,ear,depmonitor
```

5. Modify the services being loaded to read:

```
jonas.services    jtm,resource,ejb3,jaxws,web,ear,validation,depmonitor
```

   This prevents the internal db and `security` services from interfering with Liferay.

6. To put JOnAS into production mode for proper deployment of Liferay, find the property around line 71:

```
jonas.development    true
```

   And change it to `false`:

```
jonas.development    false
```

   This allows JOnAS to startup appropriately with Liferay installed.

Configuring Containers in JOnAS

Now that the application server has all extraneous services and applications disabled, you can now tweak the configuration of the containers within JOnAS: Tomcat and OSGi. By default, the Tomcat container is set to listen on a different HTTP port and HTTPS port than Liferay uses by default.

To change the Tomcat ports for Liferay's use:

1. Open the file `tomcat6-server.xml` inside of `$JONAS_BASE/conf`.

2. Find the `Connector` definition around line 69:

```
<Connector port="9000" protocol="HTTP/1.1"
           connectionTimeout="20000"
           redirectPort="9043" />
```

   Change it to reflect the default ports:

```
<Connector port="8080" protocol="HTTP/1.1"
           connectionTimeout="20000"
           redirectPort="8443" />
```

3. If you are using any other settings in Tomcat's server settings, you can adjust the ports if needed (such as changing the AJP port from 9009 to 8009.

To modify the OSGI defaults to ensure required java packages are bootsrapped by the loader:

1. Open the file `defaults.properties` inside of `$JONAS_BASE/conf/osgi`.

2. Find the declaration for `javase-packages` around line 93:

```
javase-packages \${javase-\$\{javase.version\}\}
```

   And add the following packages to make it read:

```
javase-packages \${javase-\$\{javase.version\}\},
com.sun.jmx.mbeanserver, com.sun.crypto.provider,
org.apache.felix.framework
```

   To ensure the required packages are loaded.

Starting JOnAS

Once you have the required configuration in place, all that is left is to copy the portal dependencies and the Liferay .war file and start the server. JOnAS maintains libraries inside $JONAS_BASE/lib/ext and the application inside $JONAS_BASE/deploy.

To install liferay-portal-dependencies-6.1.x-<date>.zip:

1. Unzip the archive liferay-portal-dependencies-6.1.x-<date>.zip on your local filesystem.

2. Navigate to $JONAS_BASE/lib/ext.

3. Copy the .jar files from liferay-portal-dependencies-6.1.x-<date>/ to $JONAS_BASE/lib/ext.

4. Install any additional libraries needed, such as database connectors.

To deploy the liferay-portal-6.1.x-<date>.war file:

1. Copy the liferay-portal-6.1.x-<date>.war file from its current directory.

2. Navigate to $JONAS_BASE/deploy.

3. Paste the liferay-portal-6.1.x-<date>.war file into the deploy directory.

Once the necessary files have been installed, all that is needed is to start JOnAS:

1. Navigate to $JONAS_BASE/bin.

2. Run the command jonas.bat start on Windows and ./jonas start on UNIX-lixe systems.

JOnAS starts and Liferay opens a browser to http://localhost:8080.

14.14   Installing Liferay on Resin 4

Liferay Home is one folder above Resin's install location.

For this section, we will refer to your Resin server's installation location as $RESIN_HOME. If you do not already have an existing Resin server, we recommend you download a Liferay/Resin bundle.[12] If you have an existing Resin server or would like to install Liferay on Resin manually, please follow the steps below.

Before you begin, make sure you have downloaded the latest Liferay .war file and Liferay Portal dependencies.[13] The Liferay .war file should be called liferay-portal-6.1.x-<date>.war and the dependencies file should be called liferay-portal-dependencies-6.1.x-<date>.zip.

Now that you have all of your installation files, you are ready to start installing and configuring Liferay on Resin.

Dependency Jars

Let's work with the dependency jar files first.

1. Unzip the jar files found in the Liferay Portal Dependencies zip file to your $RESIN_HOME/ext-lib folder. Take care to extract the zip file's .jar files directly into this folder.

2. Next, you need several .jar files which are included as part of the Liferay source distribution. Many application servers ship with these already on the class path but Resin does not. The best way to get the appropriate versions of these files is to download the Liferay source code and get them from there. Once you have downloaded the Liferay source, unzip the source into a temporary folder. We'll refer to the location of the Liferay source as $LIFERAY_SOURCE.

3. Go to $LIFERAY_SOURCE/lib/development and copy saxpath.jar into $RESIN_HOME/lib.

4. Copy the following files from $LIFERAY_SOURCE/lib/portal to $RESIN_-HOME/lib.

---

[12]http://www.liferay.com/downloads/liferay-portal/available-releases
[13]http://www.liferay.com/downloads/liferay-portal/additional-files

```
log4j.jar
slf4j-api.jar
slf4j-log4j12.jar
```

If folder $RESIN_HOME/extlib doesn't exist, create it.

5. Make sure the JDBC driver for your database is accessible by Resin. Obtain the JDBC driver for the database you want to use. In the case of MySQL, use mysql-connector-java-{$version}-bin.jar. You can download the latest MySQL JDBC driver from http://www.mysql.com/products/connector/. Extract the JAR file and copy it to $RESIN_HOME/extlib.

Great! now you have your .jar files in place. Next, let's configure Resin for Liferay.

Configuring Resin

The primary file used in configuring your domain is $RESIN_HOME/conf/resin.xml. You need to make common modifications necessary to support Liferay Portal. You'll also create a run script and add a folder to hold Resin's logs. But let's start with the changes to resin.xml.

1. Make the following modifications to your resin.xml. These modifications to your application cluster make the following configuration changes:

   - Set the file encoding.

   - Set the preferred protocol stack.

   - Set the user time-zone.

   - Increase the default amount of memory available.

To accomplish this, insert the following <jvm-arg> elements as server defaults for your main application cluster. Please see the following example:

```
<cluster id="app-tier">
    ...
    <server-default>
        ...
        <jvm-arg>-Dfile.encoding=UTF-8</jvm-arg>
        <jvm-arg>-Djava.net.preferIPv4Stack=true</jvm-arg>
        <jvm-arg>-Duser.timezone=GMT</jvm-arg>
        <jvm-arg>-Xmx1024m</jvm-arg>
```

```
        <jvm-arg>-XX:MaxPermSize=256m</jvm-arg>
        ...
    </server-default>
</cluster>
```

2. Create an appropriate script in $RESIN_HOME/bin to help you start Resin.

    • If you're on Windows, create a batch script $RESIN_HOME/bin/run.bat
      and insert the following text in the script:

      ```
      ..\resin.exe console
      ```

    • If you're on Unix/Linux, create shell script $RESIN_HOME/bin/run.sh
      and insert the following text in the script:

      ```
      #!/bin/sh

      ./resin.sh $
      ```

3. Create the folder $RESIN_HOME/log if it doesn't already exist. As you run
   Resin, the server generates these log files here:

   ```
   access
   jvm-default
   watchdog-manager
   ```

Now that you've completed some important common configuration tasks to
support Liferay, let's consider database configuration.

Database Configuration

If you want to manage your data source within Resin, continue following the
instructions in this section. If you want to use the built-in Liferay data source,
you can skip this section.

Management of databases in Resin is done via the configuration file $RESIN_-
HOME/conf/resin.xml. Edit resin.xml and insert a <database> element for
your database. Be sure to give it the JNDI name jdbc/LiferayPool and add it
within the application tier cluster element as in the example below:

```
<cluster id="app-tier">
    ...
    <database>
        <jndi-name>jdbc/LiferayPool</jndi-name>
        <driver type="com.mysql.jdbc.Driver">
        <url>jdbc:mysql://localhost/lportal?useUnicode=true&amp;characterEncoding=UTF-8</url>
            <user>root</user>
            <password>root</password>
        </driver>
        <prepared-statement-cache-size>8</prepared-statement-cache-size>
        <max-connections>20</max-connections>
        <max-idle-time>30s</max-idle-time>
    </database>
    ...
</cluster>
```

Be sure to replace the URL database value (i.e. `lportal`), user value and password value with values specific to your database.

Resin is now managing your database connection. Let's consider next how to configure mail.

Mail Configuration

If you want to manage your mail session within Resin, use the following instructions. If you want to use the built-in Liferay mail session, you can skip this section.

Management of mail sessions in Resin is done via the configuration file `$RES-IN_HOME/conf/resin.xml`. Edit `resin.xml` and insert a `<mail>` element that specifies your mail session. Be sure to give it the JNDI name `mail/MailSession`. Add your mail element within the application tier cluster element. Use the example below, replacing its values with the values of your mail session.

```
<cluster id="app-tier">
    ...
    <mail jndi-name="mail/MailSession">
        <properties>
            mail.pop3.host=pop.gmail.com
            mail.pop3.port=110
            mail.pop3.user=
            mail.pop3.password=
            mail.smtp.host=smtp.gmail.com
            mail.smtp.password=password
            mail.smtp.user=user
            mail.smtp.port=465
            mail.transport.protocol=smtp
            mail.smtp.auth=true
            mail.smtp.starttls.enable=true
            mail.smtp.socketFactory.class=javax.net.ssl.SSLSocketFactory
            mail.imap.host=imap.gmail.com
            mail.imap.port=993
```

```
            mail.store.protocol=imap
          </properties>
      </mail>
        ...
  </cluster>
```

You can specify additional properties for your mail session as needed.

Now that your mail session is squared away, we'll make sure Liferay can access it.

Configuring data source and mail session

Let's make sure Liferay's connected to your data source and mail session.

1. First, navigate to the *Liferay Home* folder, which is one folder above Resin's install location (i.e. `$RESIN_HOME/..`).

2. If you're using *Resin* to manage your data source, add the following to your `portal-ext.properties` file in your *Liferay Home* to refer to your data source:

   jdbc.default.jndi.name=jdbc/LiferayPool

   If you're using *Liferay Portal* to manage your data source, follow the instructions in the *Deploy Liferay* section for using the setup wizard.

3. If want to use *Liferay Portal* to manage your mail session, configure the mail session within Liferay Portal. That is, after starting your portal as described in the *Deploy Liferay* section, go to *Control Panel* → *Server Administration* → *Mail* and enter the settings for your mail session.

   If you're using *Resin* to manage your mail session, add the following to your `portal-ext.properties` file to reference that mail session:

```
mail.session.jndi.name=mail/MailSession
```

Great! Now Liferay can access your database and your mail session. Now, let's deploy Liferay.

Deploy Liferay

Liferay can be deployed as an exploded web archive within $RESIN_HOME/webapps.

1. If you already have an application folder $RESIN_HOME/webapps/ROOT, delete it or move it to a location outside of $RESIN_HOME/webapps.

2. Extract the contents of the Liferay portal .war file into RESIN_HOME/webapps/ROOT. The following files should now exist in your RESIN_HOME/webapps/ROOT folder:

   - dtd (folder)

   - errors (folder)

   - html (folder)

   - layouttpl (folder)

   - META-INF (folder)

   - wap (folder)

   - WEB-INF (folder)

   - index.jsp

3. Before you start Liferay Portal, consider whether you want to also start the setup wizard.

   - **Start the setup wizard along with Liferay Portal** - Do this if you want to configure your portal, set up your site's administrative account and/or manage your database within Liferay.

   If this is your first time starting Liferay Portal 6.1, the setup wizard is invoked on server start up. If you want to re-run the wizard, specify setup.wizard.enabled=true in your properties file (e.g. portal-setup-wizard.properties).

   ```
   setup.wizard.enabled=true
   ```

   The setup wizard is invoked during server startup.

   - **Start Liferay Portal without invoking the setup wizard** - Do this if want to preserve your current portal settings.

To start the server without triggering the setup wizard, specify `setup.wiz-ard.enabled=false` in your properties (e.g. `portal-setup-wizard.properties` or `portal-ext.properties` file).

```
setup.wizard.enabled=false
```

The `portal-setup-wizard.properties` file the setup wizard creates has `setup.wizard.enabled=false` conveniently specified for you.

 Property values in `portal-setup-wizard.properties` override property values in `portal-ext.properties`.

4. Start Liferay Portal by executing your `run.bat` (Windows) or `run.sh` (Unix/Linux) script from `$RESIN_HOME/bin`.

   - If the setup wizard was disabled, your site's home page opens in your browser at http://localhost:8080.

   - Otherwise, the setup wizard opens in your browser.

Please see the section above describing how to use the setup wizard.
Congratulations! You've installed Liferay Portal on Resin and have it up and running.

14.15   Installing Liferay on Tomcat 7

Liferay Home is one folder above Tomcat's install location.
For this section, we will refer to your Tomcat server's installation location as `$TOMCAT_HOME`. If you do not already have an existing Tomcat server, we recommend you download a Liferay/Tomcat bundle.[14] If you have an existing Tomcat server or would like to install Liferay on Tomcat manually, please follow the steps below.
Before you begin, make sure you have downloaded the latest Liferay `.war` file and Liferay Portal dependencies.[15] The Liferay `.war` file should be called

---

[14]http://www.liferay.com/downloads/liferay-portal/available-releases
[15]http://www.liferay.com/downloads/liferay-portal/additional-files

liferay-portal-6.1.x-<date>.war and the dependencies file should be called
liferay-portal-dependencies-6.1.x-<date>.zip.
Next, let's get started by addressing Liferay's library dependencies.

Dependency Jars

Liferay Portal needs to have the Liferay Portal Dependency JARs, an appropriate
JDBC driver and a few other JARs installed.

1. Create folder $TOMCAT_HOME/lib/ext.

2. Extract the Liferay dependencies file to $TOMCAT_HOME/lib/ext. If the files
   do not extract to this directory, you can copy the dependencies archive to this
   directory, extract them and then delete the archive.

3. Next, you need several .jar files which are included as part of the Liferay
   source distribution. Many application servers ship with these already on
   the class path but Tomcat does not. The best way to get the appropriate
   versions of these files is to download the Liferay source code and get them
   from there. Once you have downloaded the Liferay source, unzip the source
   into a temporary folder. We'll refer to the location of the Liferay source as
   $LIFERAY_SOURCE.

4. Copy the following jars from $LIFERAY_SOURCE/lib/development to your
   $TOMCAT_HOME/lib/ext folder:

   • activation.jar

   • jms.jar

   • jta.jar

   • jutf7.jar

   • mail.jar

   • persistence.jar

2. Copy the following jar from $LIFERAY_SOURCE/lib/portal to your $TOMCAT_HOME/lib/ext
   folder:

   • ccpp.jar

Note: Tomcat 6 users should *not* copy the ccpp.jar file into their $TOM-CAT_HOME/lib/ext folder and should delete it from this folder if it already exists.

3. Copy the following jars from $LIFERAY_SOURCE/lib/development to your $TOMCAT_HOME/temp/liferay/com/liferay/portal/deploy/dependencies folder:

   - resin.jar

   - script-10.jar

4. Make sure the JDBC driver for your database is accessible by Tomcat. Obtain the JDBC driver for your version of the database server. In the case of MySQL, use mysql-connector-java-{$version}-bin.jar.[16] Extract the JAR file and copy it to $TOMCAT_HOME/lib/ext.

5. Liferay requires an additional .jar on Tomcat installations to manage transactions. This is included in the bundle but you need to add it if you're installing Liferay manually.[17] Place this file in Tomcat's lib/ext folder.

Now that you have the necessary libraries in place, we'll move on to configuring your domain.

Tomcat Configuration

The steps in this section focus on:

- Setting environment variables

- Creating a context for your web application

- Modifying the list of classes/JARs to be loaded

- Specifying URI encoding

Let's get started with our configuration tasks.

---

[16]You can download the latest MySQL JDBC driver from http://www.mysql.com/products/connector/

[17]You may find this .jar here: http://www.oracle.com/technetwork/java/javaee/jta/index.html

1. Create a `setenv.bat` (Windows) or `setenv.sh` file (Unix, Linux, Mac OS) in the $TOMCAT_HOME/bin directory. When you start Tomcat, Catalina calls `setenv.bat` or `setenv.sh`. Edit the file and populate it with following contents:

   setenv.bat:

   ```
   if exist "%CATALINA_HOME%/jre@java.version@/win" (
       if not "%JAVA_HOME%" == "" (
           set JAVA_HOME=
       )

       set "JRE_HOME=%CATALINA_HOME%/jre@java.version@/win"
   )

   set "JAVA_OPTS=%JAVA_OPTS% -Dfile.encoding=UTF8 -Djava.net.preferIPv4Stack=true    \
       -Dorg.apache.catalina.loader.WebappClassLoader.ENABLE_CLEAR_REFERENCES=false  \
       -Duser.timezone=GMT -Xmx1024m -XX:MaxPermSize=256m"
   ```

   setenv.sh:

   ```
   JAVA_OPTS="$JAVA_OPTS -Dfile.encoding=UTF8    \
       -Dorg.apache.catalina.loader.WebappClassLoader.ENABLE_CLEAR_REFERENCES=false    \
       -Duser.timezone=GMT -Xmx1024m -XX:MaxPermSize=256m"
   ```

   This sets the character encoding to UTF-8, sets the time zone to Greenwich Mean Time and allocates memory to the Java virtual machine.

2. Create the directory $TOMCAT_HOME/conf/Catalina/localhost and create a ROOT.xml file in it. Edit this file and populate it with the following contents to set up a portal web application:

   ```
   <!--<Realm
       className="org.apache.catalina.realm.JAASRealm"
       appName="PortalRealm"
       userClassNames="com.liferay.portal.kernel.security.jaas.PortalPrincipal"
       roleClassNames="com.liferay.portal.kernel.security.jaas.PortalRole"
   />-->

   <!--
   Uncomment the following to disable persistent sessions across reboots.
   -->

   <!--<Manager pathname="" />-->

   <!--
   Uncomment the following to not use sessions. See the property
   "session.disabled" in portal.properties.
   -->
   \index{portal.properties}

   <!--<Manager className="com.liferay.support.tomcat.session.SessionLessManagerBase" />-->
   ```

Setting `crossContext="true"` allows multiple web apps to use the same class loader. In the content above you will also find commented instructions and tags for configuring a JAAS realm, disabling persistent sessions and disabling sessions in general.

3. Open `$TOMCAT_HOME/conf/catalina.properties` and replace the line:

```
common.loader=${catalina.base}/lib,${catalina.base}/lib/*.jar,${catalina.home}/lib,    \
    ${catalina.home}/lib/*.jar
```

with:

```
common.loader=${catalina.base}/lib,${catalina.base}/lib/*.jar,${catalina.home}/lib,    \
    ${catalina.home}/lib/*.jar,${catalina.home}/lib/ext,${catalina.home}/lib/ext/*.jar
```

```
This allows Catalina to access the dependency jars you extracted to
`$TOMCAT_HOME/lib/ext`.
```

4. To ensure consistent use of UTF-8 URI Encoding, edit `server.xml` in the `$TOMCAT_HOME/conf` directory and add the attribute `URIEncoding="UTF-8"` to your connector on port 8080. Below is an example of specifying this encoding on the connector:

```
<Connector port="8080"
          protocol="HTTP/1.1"
          connectionTimeout="20000"
          redirectPort="8443"
          URIEncoding="UTF-8" />
```

5. Make sure there is no `support-catalina.jar` file in `$TOMCAT_HOME/webapps`. If you find one, remove it.

Excellent work! Now let's consider configuration of your database.

Database Configuration

If you want Tomcat to manage your data source, use the following procedure. If you want to use Liferay's built-in data source, you can skip this section.

1. Make sure your database server is installed and working. If it's installed on a different machine, make sure it's accessible from your Liferay machine.

2. Add your data source as a resource in the context of your web application specified in `$TOMCAT_HOME/conf/Catalina/localhost/ROOT.xml`.

Note the above resource definition assumes your database name is *lportal* and your MySQL username and password are both *root*. You'll have to update these values with your own database name and credentials.

Your Tomcat managed data source is now configured. Let's move on to your mail session.

Mail Configuration

If you want to manage your mail session within Tomcat, use the following in-structions. If you want to use the built-in Liferay mail session, you can skip this section.

Create a mail session bound to `mail/MailSession`. Edit `ROOT.xml` in the `$TOMCAT_ HOME/conf/Catalina/localhost` directory and configure a mail session. Be sure to replace the mail session values with your own.

```
<Context...>
    <Resource
        name="mail/MailSession"
        auth="Container"
        type="javax.mail.Session"
        mail.pop3.host="pop.gmail.com"
        mail.pop3.port="110"
        mail.smtp.host="smtp.gmail.com"
        mail.smtp.port="465"
        mail.smtp.user="user"
        mail.smtp.password="password"
        mail.smtp.auth="true"
        mail.smtp.starttls.enable="true"
        mail.smtp.socketFactory.class="javax.net.ssl.SSLSocketFactory"
        mail.imap.host="imap.gmail.com"
        mail.imap.port="993"
        mail.transport.protocol="smtp"
        mail.store.protocol="imap"
    />
</Context>
```

Super! Your mail session is configured. Next, we'll make sure Liferay will be able to access your mail session and database.

Configuring your database and mail session

In this section we'll specify appropriate properties for Liferay to use in connecting to your database and mail session.

1. If you are using *Tomcat* to manage your data source, add the following to your `portal-ext.properties` file in your *Liferay Home* to refer to your data source:

```
jdbc.default.jndi.name=jdbc/LiferayPool
```

Otherwise, if you are using *Liferay Portal* to manage your data source, follow the instructions in the *Deploy Liferay* section for using the setup wizard.

2. If want to use *Liferay Portal* to manage your mail session, you can configure the mail session within Liferay Portal. That is, after starting your portal as described in the *Deploy Liferay* section, go to *Control Panel → Server Administration → Mail* and enter the settings for your mail session.

Otherwise, if you are using *Tomcat* to manage your mail session, add the following to your **portal-ext.properties** file to reference that mail session:

```
mail.session.jndi.name=mail/MailSession
```

It's just that easy! Now it's time to deploy Liferay Portal on your Tomcat server.

Deploy Liferay

We'll deploy Liferay as an exploded web archive within your **$TOMCAT_HOME/webapps** folder.

1. If you are manually installing Liferay on a clean Tomcat server, delete the contents of the **$TOMCAT_HOME/webapps/ROOT** directory. This undeploys the default Tomcat home page. Then extract the Liferay **.war** file to

```
\$TOMCAT\_HOME/webapps/ROOT
```

2. Before you start Liferay Portal, consider whether you want to use the setup wizard.

   - **Start the setup wizard along with Liferay Portal** - Do this if you want to configure your portal, set up your site's administrative account and/or manage your database within Liferay.

If this is your first time starting Liferay Portal 6.1, the setup wizard is invoked on server startup. If you want to re-run the wizard, specify **setup.wizard.enabled=true** in your properties file (e.g. **portal-setup-wizard.properties**).

```
setup.wizard.enabled=true
```

The setup wizard is invoked during server startup.

- **Start Liferay Portal without invoking the setup wizard** - Do this if you
  want to preserve your current portal settings.

To start the server without triggering the setup wizard, specify `setup.wiz-ard.enabled=false` in your properties (e.g. `portal-setup-wizard.pro-perties` or `portal-ext.properties` file).

```
setup.wizard.enabled=false
```

The `portal-setup-wizard.properties` file the setup wizard creates should have `setup.wizard.enabled=false` conveniently specified for you.

 Property values in `portal-setup-wizard.properties` override property values in `portal-ext.properties`.

I bet you can't wait to start Liferay Portal—let's do it!

3. Start Tomcat by executing

```
$TOMCAT_HOME/bin/startup.bat
```

or

```
$TOMCAT_HOME/bin/startup.sh
```

- If the setup wizard was disabled, your site's home page opens in your browser at http://localhost:8080.
- Otherwise, the setup wizard opens in your browser.

To use the setup wizard, please see the section above.
Congratulations on successfully installing and deploying Liferay on Tomcat!

14.16   Installing Liferay on WebLogic 10

Liferay Home is one folder above the domain to which you will be installing Liferay. For example, if your domain location is

```
/Oracle/Middleware/user_projects/domains/base_domain
```

then your Liferay Home is

```
/Oracle/Middleware/user_projects/domains.
```

For this section, we will refer to your WebLogic server's installation location as `$WEBLOGIC_HOME`.

Before you begin, make sure you have downloaded the latest Liferay `.war` file and Liferay Portal dependencies.[18] The Liferay `.war` file should be called `liferay-portal-6.1.x-<date>.war` and the dependencies file should be called `liferay-portal-dependencies-6.1.x-<date>.zip`.

These instructions assume you have already configured a domain and server and that you have access to the WebLogic console.

 WebLogic 10.0 supports JDK 1.5 but does *not* support JDK 1.6.

Now that you have all of your installation files, you are ready to start installing and configuring Liferay on WebLogic.

Dependency Jars

Liferay requires several `.jar` files including the Liferay Dependency JARs and a JAR file for your database driver. The following steps describe how to install these `.jar` files properly.

1. Navigate to the folder which corresponds to the domain to which you will be installing Liferay. Inside this folder is a `lib` folder. Unzip the Liferay dependencies archive to this folder so the dependency `.jar` files are extracted into the `lib` folder.

---

[18]http://www.liferay.com/downloads/liferay-portal/additional-files

2. If WebLogic does not already have access to the JDBC driver for your database, copy the driver to your domain's lib folder as well.

3. You will also need the xercesImpl.jar copied to your domain's lib folder or you will get SAX parsing errors after you deploy Liferay. You may download this from http://xerces.apache.org.

4. Create a folder $WEBLOGIC-HOME/jrockit_150_15/jre/lib/endorsed. Then copy commons-lang.jar, liferay-rhino.jar, serializer.jar and xalan.jar to the endorsed folder you just created.

Now that you have your WebLogic installation is loaded up with JAR files for Liferay to use, let's consider how to configure your database.

Database Configuration

If you want WebLogic to manage your data source, use the following procedure. If you want to use Liferay's built-in data source, you can skip this section.

Figure 14.41: WebLogic Data Sources

1. Browse to your WebLogic Console. Click the *Lock & Edit* button above the Domain Structure tree on the left side of the page.

2. From the Domain Structure tree on the left, select *Data Sources*. Then click the *New* button on the right side of the screen.

3. Give the Data Source a name, such as `LiferayDataSource`.

4. Define the JNDI name as `jdbc/LiferayPool`.

5. Select your Database Type, the Driver class and then click the *Next* button.

6. Accept the defaults on the next screen by clicking *Next.*

7. On the next screen, put in your *Database Name, Host Name, Database User Name* and *Password.* If you have been following the defaults we have been using so far, you would use *lportal, localhost, root,* and no password as the values. Click *Next.*

8. The next screen allows you to test your database configuration. Click the *Test Configuration* button. If the test succeeds, you have configured your database correctly. Select the check box of the server to which you want to deploy this Data Source (`AdminServer` is the default). Click *Finish.*

9. Click the *Activate Changes* button on the left, above the Domain Structure tree.

Great work! Your data source can now be managed from within WebLogic. Next, let's consider the mail session for your domain.

Mail Configuration

If you want WebLogic to manage your mail sessions, use the following procedure. If you want to use Liferay's built-in mail sessions, you can skip this section.

1. In the Domain Structure tree, select *Mail Sessions.* Then click the *Lock & Edit* button again to enable modifying these settings.

2. Click the *New* button which is now enabled on the right side of the screen.

3. Give the Mail Session a name, such as `LiferayMail`.

4. Select your new LiferayMail session from the list by clicking on it.

5. On the screen that appears, define the JNDI name as `mail/MailSession` and set your JavaMail properties. Click the *Save* button.

6. Click the *Targets* tab. Select the check box of the server to which you want deploy this Data Source to (AdminServer is the default).

Figure 14.42: WebLogic: Mail Sessions

7. Click the *Activate Changes* button on the left side of the screen, above the Domain Structure tree.

Now you have your mail session specified and ready for Liferay to use.

Domain Configuration - Continued

Let's revisit domain configuration to make sure we'll be able to access your data source and mail session from Liferay Portal.

1. First, navigate to the *Liferay Home* folder.

2. Then, if you are using *WebLogic* to manage your data source, add the following to your `portal-ext.properties` file in your *Liferay Home* to refer to your data source:

   jdbc.default.jndi.name=jdbc/LiferayPool

   Otherwise, if you are using *Liferay Portal* to manage your data source, follow the instructions in the *Deploy Liferay* section for using the setup wizard.

3. If want to use *Liferay Portal* to manage your mail session, you can configure the mail session within Liferay Portal. That is, after starting your portal as described in the *Deploy Liferay* section, go to *Control Panel → Server Administration → Mail* and enter the settings for your mail session.

Otherwise, if you are using *WebLogic* to manage your mail session, add the following to your `portal-ext.properties` file to reference that mail session:

```
mail.session.jndi.name=mail/MailSession
```

Liferay can now communicate with your data source and mail session. It's now time to deploy Liferay!

Deploy Liferay

Follow the instructions in this section to deploy Liferay Portal to your domain.

Before you deploy Liferay Portal, consider whether you want to use the setup wizard.

- **Start the setup wizard along with Liferay Portal** - Do this if you want to configure your portal, set up your site's administrative account and/or manage your database within Liferay.

If this is your first time starting Liferay Portal 6.1, the setup wizard is invoked on server startup. If you want to re-run the wizard, specify `setup.wizard.enabled=true` in your properties file (e.g. `portal-setup-wizard.properties`).

```
setup.wizard.enabled=true
```

The setup wizard is invoked during server startup.

- **Start Liferay Portal without invoking the setup wizard** - Do this if you want to preserve your current portal settings.

To start the server without triggering the setup wizard, specify `setup.wizard.enabled=false` in your properties (e.g. `portal-setup-wizard.properties` or `portal-ext.properties` file).

```
setup.wizard.enabled=false
```

The `portal-setup-wizard.properties` file the setup wizard creates has `setup.wizard.enabled=false` conveniently specified for you.

> Property values in `portal-setup-wizard.properties`
> override property values in `portal-ext.properties`.

Now that you have enabled or disabled the setup wizard, let's move on to deployment of Liferay Portal.

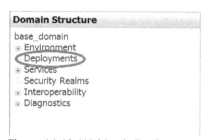

Figure 14.43: WebLogic Deployments

1. In the Domain Structure tree, select *Deployments*. Then click the *Lock & Edit* button above the Domain Structure tree.

2. Click the *Install* button on the right side of the screen.

3. Click the *Upload your file(s)* link.

4. Browse to where you have stored the Liferay `.war` file, select it and then click *Next*.

5. Select the Liferay `.war` file from the list and click *Next*.

6. Leave *Install this deployment as an application* selected and click *Next*.

7. Give the application a name (the default name is fine). Leave the other defaults selected and then click *Finish*.

8. WebLogic deploys Liferay. When it finishes, a summary screen is displayed. Click the *Activate Changes* link on the left above the Domain Structure tree.

9. In the Deployments screen, select the Liferay application and click the *Start* button. Select *Servicing All Requests* in the pop up.

10. Click *Yes* to continue on the next screen to launch Liferay Portal.

    - If the setup wizard was disabled, your site's home page opens in your browser at http://localhost:7001.

    - Otherwise, the setup wizard opens in your browser.

For more information on how to use the setup wizard, please see the section above.
Congratulations on your deployment of Liferay Portal on WebLogic 10!

14.17   Installing Liferay on Oracle WebLogic 10.3

Liferay Home is one folder above the domain to which you will be installing Liferay.
For example, if your domain location is

```
/Oracle/Middleware/user_projects/domains/base_domain
```

then your Liferay Home is

```
/Oracle/Middleware/user_projects/domains
```

For this section, we will use `$WEBLOGIC_HOME` to refer to your WebLogic server's installation `/Oracle/Middleware`.
Before you begin, make sure you have downloaded the latest Liferay `.war` file and Liferay Portal dependencies.[19] The Liferay `.war` file should be called `liferay-portal-6.1.x-<date>.war` and the dependencies file should be called `liferay-portal-dependencies-6.1.x-<date>.zip`.
These instructions assume you have already configured a domain and server and that you have access to the WebLogic console.
If you still have the `mainWebApp` module installed, remove it first.

 There is a known issue with the Sun and JRockit JVMs bundled with WebLogic 10.3.2.[20] To resolve, use Sun JVM 1.6.0_u24 or JRockit JVM 1.6.0_24.

Let's get started by installing the JAR files Liferay needs.

---

[19]http://www.liferay.com/downloads/liferay-portal/additional-files

Dependency Jars

Liferay needs the JAR files contained in the Liferay Dependencies Archive and the driver JAR file applicable for your database.

1. Navigate to the folder that corresponds to the domain to which you will be installing Liferay. Inside this folder is a `lib` folder. Unzip the Liferay Dependencies Archive to this folder so the dependency `.jar` files reside in the `lib` folder.

2. If WebLogic does not already have access to the JDBC driver for your database, copy the driver to your domain's `lib` folder as well.

So far so good. Your JAR files are in place and ready for Liferay.
Start Oracle WebLogic if you want to configure your database and/or mail session within Oracle WebLogic.

Database Configuration

If you want WebLogic to manage your data source, use the following procedure. If you want to use Liferay's built-in data source, you can skip this section.

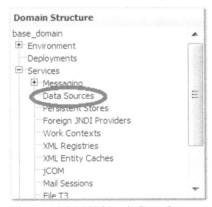

Figure 14.44: WebLogic Data Sources

1. Select *Services* → *Data Sources.* Click *New* → *Generic Data Source.*

2. Give your data source a name, such as *Liferay Data Source*. The JNDI name should be `jdbc/LiferayPool`.

3. Choose the type of database and click *Next*. From the screenshot, you can see we have chosen MySQL. The database driver class is selected automatically.

Figure 14.45: Creating a data source in WebLogic 10.3

4. Click *Next* three times. You should be on the *Connection Properties* screen. Enter the database name, the host name, the port, the database user name and the password. WebLogic uses this information to construct the appropriate JDBC URL to connect to your database. Click *Next*.

5. WebLogic next confirms the information you provided. For MySQL, some additional parameters must be added to the URL. Modify the JDBC URL so it has the proper parameters. Provide your database name, host name, user name and password as the values. Click *Next*.

6. Click *Test Configuration* to make sure WebLogic can connect to your database successfully. When it does, click *Finish*.

7. You will be back to the list of data sources. Notice your new data source has no value in the *Target* column. Click on your data source to edit it.

8. Click the *Targets* tab and check off the server instance(s) to which you wish to deploy your data source. Then click *Save*.

Next, let's configure a mail session in WebLogic.

Mail Configuration

If you want WebLogic to manage your mail sessions, use the following procedure. If you want to use Liferay's built-in mail sessions, you can skip this section.

Figure 14.46: WebLogic Mail Sessions

1. Select *Mail Sessions* and create a new mail session which points to your mail server.

2. Give it the name Liferay Mail and give it the JNDI name of `mail/MailSession` and click *Next.*

3. Choose your server and then click *Finish.*

Now let's make sure Liferay can access this mail session.

Domain Configuration - Continued

Let's revisit domain configuration to make sure we'll be able to access your data source and mail session from Liferay Portal.

1. Create a `portal-ext.properties` file in the Liferay Home folder, which is one folder up from your domain's home folder.

If you are using *WebLogic* to manage your data source, add the following to your `portal-ext.properties` file in *Liferay Home* to refer to your data source:

```
jdbc.default.jndi.name=jdbc/LiferayPool
```

If you are using *Liferay Portal* to manage your data source, follow the instructions in the *Deploy Liferay* section for using the setup wizard.

If want to use *Liferay Portal* to manage your mail session, you can configure the mail session in the Control Panel. After starting your portal as described in the *Deploy Liferay* section, go to *Control Panel → Server Administration → Mail* and enter the settings for your mail session.

If you are using *WebLogic* to manage your mail session, add the following to your `portal-ext.properties` file to reference that mail session:

```
mail.session.jndi.name=mail/MailSession
```

2. Lastly, you must provide WebLogic a reference to Java Server Faces (JSF) to use that library. Insert the following deployment descriptor within the `<weblogic-web-app>` element of `WEB-INF/weblogic.xml` found in your Liferay Portal `.war` :

```
<library-ref>
    <library-name>jsf</library-name>
    <specification-version>1.2</specification-version>
    <implementation-version>1.2</implementation-version>
    <exact-match>false</exact-match>
</library-ref>
```

Now its the moment you've been waiting for: Liferay deployment!

Deploy Liferay

Follow the instructions in this section to deploy Liferay Portal to your domain.

Before you deploy Liferay Portal, consider whether you want to use the setup wizard.

- **Start the setup wizard along with Liferay Portal** - Do this if you want to configure your portal, set up your site's administrative account and/or manage your database within Liferay.

If this is your first time starting Liferay Portal 6.1, the setup wizard is invoked on server startup. If you want to re-run the wizard, specify `setup.wizard.enabled=true` in your properties file (e.g. `portal-setup-wizard.properties`).

```
setup.wizard.enabled=true
```

The setup wizard is invoked during server startup.

- **Start Liferay Portal without invoking the setup wizard** - Do this if you want to preserve your current portal settings.

To start the server without triggering the setup wizard, specify `setup.wizard.enabled=false` in your properties (e.g. `portal-setup-wizard.properties` or `portal-ext.properties` file).

```
setup.wizard.enabled=false
```

The `portal-setup-wizard.properties` file the setup wizard creates has `setup.wizard.enabled=false` conveniently specified for you.

Property values in `portal-setup-wizard.properties` override property values in `portal-ext.properties`.

Now, let's deploy Liferay Portal.

1. Start WebLogic.

2. Select *Deployments* and click the *Install* button. Upload `jsf-1.2.war` from WebLogic's common files directory and select *Install this deployment as a library.*

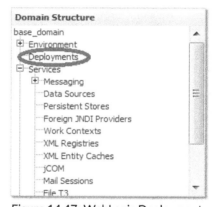

Figure 14.47: WebLogic Deployments

3. After installing the JSF libraries, go back to deployments and select the Liferay `.war` file from the file system or click the *Upload Your File(s)* link to upload it and then click *Next.*

4. Select *Install this deployment as an application* and click *Next.*

5. If the default name is appropriate for your installation, keep it. Otherwise, give it a name of your choosing and click *Next.*

6. Click *Finish*. After the deployment finishes, click *Save*.

Liferay launches in one of the following manners:

- If the setup wizard was disabled, your site's home page opens in your browser at http://localhost:7001.

- Otherwise, the setup wizard opens in your browser.

Please see the section above for how to use the setup wizard.

 Note: After Liferay is installed, you may see an error initializing the Web Proxy portlet. Because the XSL parser configured by default within WebLogic cannot compile a style sheet in this portlet, Liferay disables it by default. To re-enable this portlet, extract `xalan.jar` and `serializer.jar` from the Liferay `.war` archive and copy them to your JDK's endorsed folder for libraries. If you are using JRockit, this folder may be `[$WEBLOGIC_HOME]/jrockit_160_05/jre/lib/ext`; if you are using Sun JDK, this folder may be `[$WEBLOGIC_HOME]/jdk160_24/jre/lib/ext`.

Congratulations! You are now running Liferay on Oracle WebLogic.

14.18   Installing Liferay on WebSphere 8.0

Tip: Throughout this installation and configuration process WebSphere prompts you to Click Save to apply changes to Master Configuration. Do so intermittently to save your changes.

Liferay Home is in a folder called `liferay` in the home folder of the user ID that is running WebSphere.

Preparing WebSphere for Liferay

When the application server binaries have been installed, start the **Profile Management Tool** to create a profile appropriate for Liferay.

1. Click on *Create....* Choose *Application Server.* Click *Next.*

2. Click the Advanced profile creation option and then click *Next.* Why Advanced? You can specify your own values for settings such as the location of the profile and names of the profile, node and host. You can assign your own ports. You can optionally choose whether to deploy the administrative console and sample application and also add web-server definitions if you wish. Web server definitions are used with IBM HTTP Server. For more information about these options, please see the WebSphere documentation.

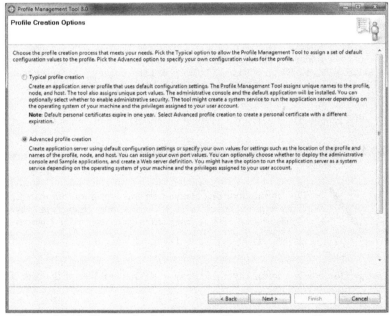

Figure 14.48: Choose the Advanced profile option to specify your own settings.

3. Check the box *Deploy administrative console*. This gives you a web-based UI for working with your application server. Skip the default applications. You'd only install these on a development machine. Click *Next*.

4. Set profile name and location. Ensure you specify a performance tuning setting other than *Development*, since you're installing a server for production use. Click *Next*.

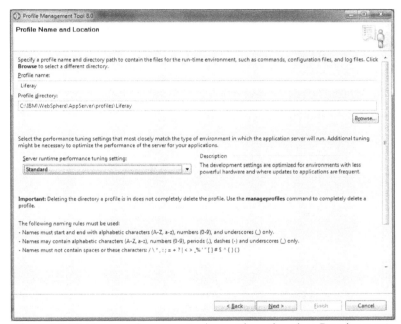

Figure 14.49: Use a performance tuning setting other than Development. We've selected Standard here. Please see the WebSphere documentation for further information about performance tuning settings.

5. Choose node and host names for your server. These will be specific to your environment. Click *Next*.

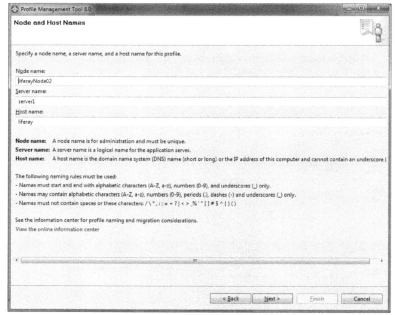

Figure 14.50: Choose node and host names appropriate to your environment.

6. Administrative security in WebSphere is a way to restrict who has access to the administrative tools. For simplicity, we've disabled it but you may want to have it enabled in your environment. Please see WebSphere's documentation for further information. Click *Next.*

7. Each profile needs a security certificate, which comes next in the wizard. If you don't have certificates already, choose the option to generate a personal certificate and a signing certficate and click *Next.*

8. Once the certificates are generated, set a password for your keystore. Click *Next.*

Figure 14.51: We've disabled administrative security but you may want to enable it.

9. Next, you can customize the ports this server profile uses. Be sure to choose ports that are open on your machine. When choosing ports, installation detects existing WebSphere installations and if it finds activity, it increments ports by one.

10. If you want WebSphere to start automatically when the machine is booted, you configure it next. This differs by operating system. When you're finished configuring this the way you want, click *Next*.

11. WebSphere ships with IBM HTTP Server, which is a rebranded version of Apache. If you want to front your WebSphere server with IBM HTTP Server

Figure 14.52: Set a password for your keystore.

you'd configure this next. Please see WebSphere's documentation for details on this. When finished, click *Next*.

12. WebSphere then creates your profile and finishes with a message telling you the profile was created successfully. You're now ready to install Liferay!

Copying portal dependencies

Liferay ships with dependency .jars it needs to have on the global classpath. These should be copied to WebSphere's global folder provided for this purpose:

```
[Install Location]/WebSphere/AppServer/lib/ext
```

Figure 14.53: WebSphere gives you a nice user interface for customizing the ports your server uses.

Once you've copied the .jars here, start the server profile you're planning to use for Liferay. Once it starts, you're ready to configure your database.

Database Configuration

If you want WebSphere to manage the database connections, follow the instructions below. Note this is not necessary if you're planning on using Liferay's standard database configuration; in that case, skip this section. You'll set your database information in Liferay's setup wizard after the install.

1. Start WebSphere.

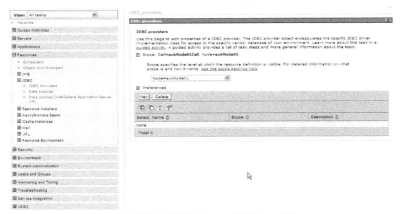

Figure 14.54: WebSphere JDBC providers

2. Open the Administrative Console and log in.

3. Click *Resources* → *JDBC Providers*.

4. Click *New*.

5. For name, enter the name of JDBC provider (e.g. *MySQL JDBC Provider*).

6. For Implementation class name, enter:

   com.mysql.jdbc.jdbc2.optional.MysqlConnectionPoolDataSource

7. Click *Next*.

8. Clear any text in classpath. You already copied the necessary `.jars` to a location on the server's class path.

9. Click *Next*.

10. Click *Finish*.

11. Click *Data Sources* under *Additional Properties*.

12. Click *New*.

13. Enter a name: *liferaydatabasesource*.

14. Enter JNDI: `jdbc/LiferayPool`.

15. Everything else should stay at the default values. Save the data source.

16. When finished, go back into the data source and click *Custom Properties* and then click the *Show Filter Function* button. This is the second from last of the small icons under the *New* and *Delete* buttons.

17. Type *user* into the search terms and click *Go*.

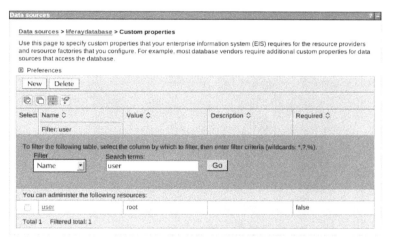

Figure 14.55: Modifying data source properties in WebSphere

18. Select the user property and give it the value of the user name to your database. Click *OK* and save to master configuration.

19. Do another filter search for the url property. Give it a value that points to your database. For example, the MySQL URL would be:

```
jdbc:mysql://localhost/lportal?useUnicode=true&characterEncoding=UTF-8   \
   &useFastDateParsing=false
```

Click *OK* and save to master configuration.

20. Do another filter search for the password property. Enter the password for the user ID you added earlier as the value for this property. Click *OK* and save to master configuration.

21. Go back to the data source page by clicking it in the breadcrumb trail. Click the *Test Connection* button. It should connect successfully.

Once you've set up your database, you can set up your mail session.

Mail Configuration

If you want WebSphere to manage your mail sessions, use the following procedure. If you want to use Liferay's built-in mail sessions, you can skip this section.

1. Click *Resources* → *Mail* → *Mail Providers*.

2. Click the Built-In Mail Provider for your node and server.

3. Click *Mail Sessions* and then click the *New* button.

4. Give it a name of *liferaymail* and a JNDI name of `mail/MailSession`. Click *OK* and save to master configuration.

5. Click *Security* → *Global Security* and deselect *Use Java 2 security to restrict application access to local resources* if it is selected. Click *Apply*.

Great! Now you're ready to deploy Liferay.

Deploy Liferay

1. Click *Applications* → *New Application* → *New Enterprise Application*.

2. Browse to the Liferay `.war` file and click *Next*.

3. Leave *Fast Path* selected and click *Next*, then click *Next* again.

4. Make sure your server is selected and click *Next*.

5. Keep the context root set to / and click *Next*.

6. Click *Finish*. When Liferay has installed, click *Save to Master Configuration*.

Start Liferay

1. If you plan to use Liferay's setup wizard, skip to the next step. If you wish to use WebSphere's data source and mail session, create a file called `por-tal-ext.properties` in your Liferay Home folder. Place the following text in the file:

```
jdbc.default.jndi.name=jdbc/LiferayPool
mail.session.jndi.name=mail/MailSession
setup.wizard.enabled=false
```

2. Select the Liferay application and click *Start.*

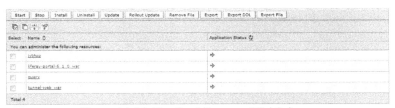

Figure 14.56: Starting Liferay on WebSphere.

3. In the setup wizard, select and configure your database type. Click *Finish* when you're done.

   Liferay then creates the tables it needs in the database.
   Congratulations! You've installed Liferay on WebSphere!

14.19 Making Liferay Coexist with Other Java EE Applications

Liferay Portal by default is configured to sit at the root (i.e., /) of your application server. Dedicating your application server to running only Liferay Portal is a good practice, allowing for separation between your portal environment and your web application environment. This is generally a best practice for portals, which by definition are application development platforms in and of themselves.

For that reason, your instance of Liferay is likely to be hosting many applications and even integrating several of them together on a single page. For this reason, you should design your system so your portal environment has all the resources it needs to do this. Configuring it so it is the sole consumer of any other `.war` files that get deployed to the application server helps to make sure your system performs optimally.

If, however, you want Liferay to share space on an application server with other applications, you can. In this instance, you may not want to make Liferay the default application in the root context of the server.

There are two steps to modifying this behavior:

1. Deploy Liferay in a context other than root (for example `/portal`).

2. Modify the `portal-ext.properties` file to tell Liferay the context to which it has been deployed.

To change the file, open it in a text editor. Place the `portal.ctx` property at the top of the file:

```
portal.ctx=/
```

This default setting defines Liferay Portal as the application that sits at the root context. If you change it to something else, say `/portal`, for example, you can then deploy Liferay in that context and it will live there instead of at the root context.

A full discussion of the `portal-ext.properties` file appears in Chapter 20.

Note for WebLogic Users: WebLogic also requires that you modify the `weblogic.xml` file which is included with Liferay. In this file are tags for the context root:

```
<context-root>/</context-root>
```

Change this so it matches the path you set in your `portal-ext.properties` file. You will have to modify the `weblogic.xml` file inside the Liferay `.war` before you deploy it. Extract the file from the `.war` file, modify it and then put it back in the `.war` file. Then deploy the modified Liferay `.war` file to the server in the proper context.

14.20 Summary

This chapter is a guide to everything about installing Liferay. Whether you choose a Liferay bundle or an existing application server, Liferay Portal integrates seamlessly with your enterprise Java environment. It is supported on more application servers than any other portal platform, allowing you to preserve your investment in your application server of choice or giving you the freedom to move to a different application server platform. Liferay is committed to providing you this freedom: we have 500 test servers certifying our builds with roughly 10,000 tests per version of Liferay Portal. Each of those tests are run on all of our different supported combinations of application servers, databases and operating systems. Because of this, you can be sure we are committed to supporting you on your environment of choice. You can feel safe knowing you have the freedom to use the software platform that is best for your organization and that Liferay Portal runs and performs well on it.

CHAPTER 15

MANAGEMENT

You know how all these retailers advertise themselves as a "one stop shop" for anything you want? The idea is they have so much stuff that chances are whatever you're looking for is there. Liferay's control panel is something like this. If you want to create users, sites, organizations, configure permissions and plugins and pretty much anything else, you'll do it with the control panel. The nice thing about the control panel is it makes all this very easy to do. This chapter takes all the concepts you learned about Liferay in chapter 1 (sites, organizations, and more) and makes them concrete. Here, you'll learn how to create and manage every aspect of Liferay's configuration.

This chapter explains how to use the Control Panel to manage the following items:

- Users

- Organizations

- User Groups

- Roles

- Password Policies

- Authentication Policies

- Global User Settings

Let's begin our examination of Liferay's control panel by looking at how to manage and organize users in Liferay Portal.

15.1   Managing Users

The Portal section of the control panel is used for most administrative tasks. You'll find there an interface for the creation and maintenance of

- Users, User Groups and Organizations

- Sites and Teams

- Site Templates

- Page Templates

- Roles

Additionally, you can configure many server settings, including:

- Password Policies

- Portal Settings

- Custom Fields

- Monitoring

- Plugins Configuration

15.2   The Portal Section of the Control Panel

The Portal section of the Control Panel is used for most administrative tasks. You'll find there an interface for the creation and maintenance of the following portal entities: users, organizations, user groups, sites, teams, site templates, page templates, and roles. Additionally, you can configure many settings, including the following ones: password policies, portal settings, custom fields, monitoring, and plugins configuration

Since we explained how to manage sites, teams, site templates, and page templates in chapters 2 and 3, we won't discuss them in detail here. In this chapter, we'll focus on using the Control Panel for user management. We'll finish our coverage of the Control Panel in the next chapter, discussing portal and server administration.

As a portal administrator, you'll use the Portal section of the Control Panel to create your portal structure, implement security, and administer your users. Configurable portal settings include mail host names, email notifications, and authentication options, including single sign-on and LDAP integration. Note that only users with the administrator role, which is a portal scoped role, have permission to view this section of the control panel. You can, of course, grant permissions to one or more sections to custom roles.

15.3   Adding users

Let's add a user account for yourself and configure this account so it has the same administrative access as the default administrator account. Go up to the Dockbar, mouse over *Go to* and click *Control Panel.* Then open the *Users and Organizations* page under the *Portal* category. Click the *Add* button and select *User.* Fill out the Add User form using your name and email address. When you are finished, click *Save.*

Figure 15.1: The Add User Screen

After you submit the form, the page reloads with a message saying the save was successful. An expanded form appears that allows you to fill out a lot more information about the user. You don't have to fill anything else out right now. Just note that when the user ID was created, a password was automatically generated and, if Liferay was correctly installed (see chapter 14), an email message with the password in it was sent to the user. This, of course, requires that Liferay can properly communicate with your SMTP mail server.

Figure 15.2: Liferay's User Account Editor

If you haven't yet set up your mail server, you'll need to use this page to change the default password for the user ID to something you can remember. You can do this by clicking on the *Password* link in the box on the right, entering the new password in the two fields and clicking *Save*. Next, you should give your user account the same administrative rights as the default administrator's account. This allows you to perform administrative tasks with your own ID instead of having to use the default ID. It also helps to make your portal more secure by deleting or disabling the default ID.

Click the *Roles* link. The control panel's Roles page shows the roles to which your ID is currently assigned. You should have one role: Power User. By default, all users are assigned the Power User role. You can give this role certain permissions if you wish or disable it altogether. You can also define the default roles a new user receives. We'll see how to do this later.

To make yourself an Administrator, click the *Select* link. A dialog box pops up with a list of all the roles in the system. Select the Administrator role from the list. The dialog box disappears and the role is added to the list of roles associated with your account. Next, click the *Save* button, which is at the bottom of the blue bar of links on the right. You are now an administrator of the portal. Log out of the portal and then log back in with your own user ID.

We'll next look at some aspects of user management.

15.4   User management

If you click the *Users* link on the left menu of the control panel, there are now two users in the list of users. If you want to change something about a particular user, you can click the *Actions* button next to that user.

Edit User: takes you back to the Edit User page where you can modify anything about the user.

Permissions: allows you to define which roles have permissions to edit the user.

Manage Pages: allows you to edit the personal pages of a user.

Impersonate User: opens another browser window which allows you to browse the site as if you were the user.

Deactivate: deactivates the user's account.

Note most users can't perform most of the above actions. In fact, most users won't even have access to this section of the control panel. You can perform all of the above functions because you have administrative access.

Let's look next at how to manage organizations.

Organizations

Organizations are used to represent hierarchical structures of users such as those of companies, businesses, non-profit organizations, churches, schools, and clubs. They are designed to allow distributed user administration. Organizations can be used, for example, to represent a sports league. The league itself could be modeled as a top-level organization and the various sports (soccer, baseball, basketball, etc.) could be modeled as suborganizations. The teams belonging to the various sports could be modeled as sub-organizations of the sports organizations. So, for example, you could have an organization hierarchy that looks like this:

- Atlantic Sports League

    – Atlantic Soccer Association

       * Midway Soccer Club
       * Fairview Soccer Club
       * Oak Grove Soccer Club
- Atlantic Baseball Association
       * Five Points Baseball Club
       * Riverside Baseball Club
       * Pleasant Hill Baseball Club
- Atlantic Basketball Association
       * Bethel Basketball Club
       * Centerville Basketball Club
       * New Hope Basketball Club

Whenever you have a collection of users that fit into a hierarchical structure, you can use organizations to model those users. In Liferay, organization administrators can manage all the users in their organization *and* in any suborganization. Referring to the hierarchy above, for example, an organization administrator of the Atlantic Sports League could manage any users belonging to the league itself, to any of the associations, or to any of the associations' clubs. An organization administrator of the Atlantic Soccer Association could manage any users belonging to the Atlantic Soccer Association itself, or to the Midway Soccer Club, Fairview Soccer Club, or Oak Grove Soccer Club. However, an administrator of the Atlantic Soccer Club would not be able to manage users belonging to the Atlantic Baseball Association or to the Bethel Basketball Club.

Organizations and suborganization hierarchies can be created to unlimited levels. Users can be members of one or many organizations. The rights of an organization administrator apply both to his/her organization and to any child organizations. By default, members of child organizations are implicit members of their parent organizations. This means, for example, that members of child organizations can access the private pages of their parent organizations. This behavior can be customized in your portal's 'portal-ext.properties' configuration file.

Since organizations are designed for distributed user administration, organization administrators have an entirely different set of privileges than site administrators. Site administrators are responsible for the pages, portlets, and content of their site. They are also responsible for managing the membership of their site. To this end, they can set the membership type to Open, Restricted, or Private. They can also add users to or remove users from their site but cannot manage the users themselves. Organization administrators, on the other hand, can edit users belonging to their organization or any suborganization. They cannot add existing users to their organization but they can create new users within their organization. Only portal administrators can add existing users to an organization.

Many simple portal designs don't use organizations at all; they only use sites (see chapters 2 and 3 for more information on sites). Remember that the main purpose of organizations is to allow for distributed user management. They allow portal administrators to delegate some of their user management responsibilities to organization administrators. If you don't anticipate needing to delegate user management responsibilities, your portal design need not include organizations. In order to decide whether or not your portal design should include organization, think about your portal's function. A simple photo-sharing web site, for example, could be powered by sites only. On the other hand, organizations are useful for corporations or educational institutions since their users can easily be placed into a hierarchical structure. In fact, organizations in Liferay are designed to model any group hierarchy, from those of government agencies all the way down to those of small clubs. Of course, users can belong both to organizations and to independent sites. For example, a corporation or educational institution could create a social networking site open to all portal users, even ones from separate organizations.

Additionally, organization administrators can assign organization-scoped roles to members of their organization. For example, consider an IT Security group in a corporate setting. You could have a suborganizaton of your IT organization that handles security for all of the applications company-wide. If you grant the IT Security organization the portal administrator role, all the members of the organization would have administrative access to the entire portal. Suppose further that a user in this organization was later hired by the Human Resources department. The simple act of removing the user from the IT Security organization also removes the user's administrative privileges, since the privilege came from the IT Security organization's role. By adding the user to the HR organization, any roles the HR organization has (such as access to a benefits system in the portal) are transferred to the user. In this manner, you can design your portal to correspond with your existing organization chart and users' permissions are granted according to their positions in the chart.

Of course, this is only one way to design it. If you have more complex requirements for permissions within an organization, you can create custom organization-scoped roles to assemble the permissions you wish to grant to particular users. Alternatively, you could consider attaching a site to your organization and using site teams to assemble the sets of permissions (see below).

We'll discuss roles and permissions in more detail later in this chapter.

Does your organization need to have its own site? Many organizations don't, but since some do, Liferay allows sites to be attached to organizations. If an organization has an attached site, the organization's administrators are treated as the site administrators of the attached site. This means that they can manage the pages, portlets, and content of the site as well as the users of the organization. Members of an organization with an attached site are treated as members of the organization's site. This means that they can access the private pages of the organization's site, along with any portlets or content there. The capability of attaching sites to organizations allows portal administrators to use organizations to facilitate distributed portal administration, not just distributed user administration. Next, let's learn how to create and manage organizations.

To add an organization, click the *Users and Organizations* link on the left side of the control panel. Then click the *Add* button and choose *Regular Organization*.

To attach a site when you create an organization, click the *Organization Site* tab at the right and check the *Create Site* box. If you don't know right now if your organization needs a web site, that's fine. You can always add one later if the need arises.

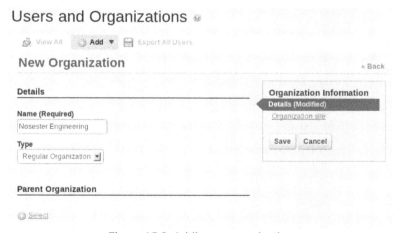

Figure 15.3: Adding an organization

Name: Enter a name for the organization.

Type: Choose whether this is a regular organization or a location. A location cannot have any suborganizations.

Parent Organization: Select an organization in the system to be the direct parent of the organization you are creating. Click the *Remove* button to remove the currently configured parent.

 Tip: Note that you're already a member of any organizations you create. By creating an organization, you become both a member and receive the Organization Owner role, which gives you full rights to the organization. You can, of course, add other users to this role to make them Organization Owners.

Fill out the information for your organization and click *Save*. As before with users, the form reappears and you can enter more information about the organization. Organizations can have multiple email addresses, postal addresses, web sites and phone numbers associated with them. The Services link can be used to indicate the operating hours of the organization, if any.

For now, click the *Back* button. This takes you back to the list of organizations.

Click the *Actions* button next to the new organization you created. This shows the actions you can take to manipulate this organization.

Edit: lets you specify details about the organization, including addresses, phone numbers, email addresses and websites.

Manage Site: lets you create and manage public and private pages for the organization's site.

Assign Organization Roles: lets you assign organization-scoped roles to users. By default, Organizations are created with three roles: Organization Administrator, Organization User and Organization Owner. You can assign one or more of these roles to users in the organization. All members of the organization automatically get the Organization User role so this role is hidden when you click Assign Organization Roles.

Assign Users: lets you search and select users in the portal to be assigned to this organization as members.

Add User: adds a new user in the portal and assigns the user as a member of this organization.

Add Regular Organization: lets you add a child organization to this organization. This is how you create hierarchies of organizations with parent-child relationships.

Add Location: lets you add a child Location, which is a special type of organization that cannot have any children added to it.

Delete: removes this organization from the portal. Make sure the organization has no users in it first.

If you click the *View* button at the top of the Users and Organizations page and select *View Hierarchy* you can view both a list of users who are members of this organization and a list of all the suborganizations of this organization.

Users can join or be assigned to sites when they share a common interest. Users can be assigned to organizations when they fit into a hierarchical structure. Users groups provide a more ad hoc way to group users than sites and organizations. Let's look at them next.

15.5 User Groups

User Groups are designed to allow portal administrators to create groups of users that traverse the organizations hierarchy. They can be used to create arbitrary groupings of users who don't necessarily share an obvious hierarchical attribute. Users can be assigned to multiple user groups. For example, consider a software company with many offices and departments within each office. The company's office/department structure could be modeled through organizations. In this situation, it might make sense to create user groups for developers, office managers, accountant, etc. User Groups are most often used to achieve one of the following goals:

- To simplify the assignment of several roles to a group of users. For example, in a University portal, a user group could be created to group all teachers independently of their organizations to make it easier to assign one or several roles at once to all the teachers.

- To simplify membership to one or more sites by specifying a group of users. Using the previous example, all teachers could be members of the sites *University Employees* and *Students and Teachers Collaboration Site* by adding the *Teachers* user group as a member.

- To provide predefined public or private pages to the users who belong to the user group. For example, the *Teachers* user group could be created to ensure the home page on all teachers' personal sites has the same layout and applications.

Creating a user group is easy. Navigate to the control panel, click the *Users Groups* link and then click the *Add* button. There are only two fields to fill out: Name and Description. Click *Save* and you will be redirected back to the *User Groups* page of the control panel.

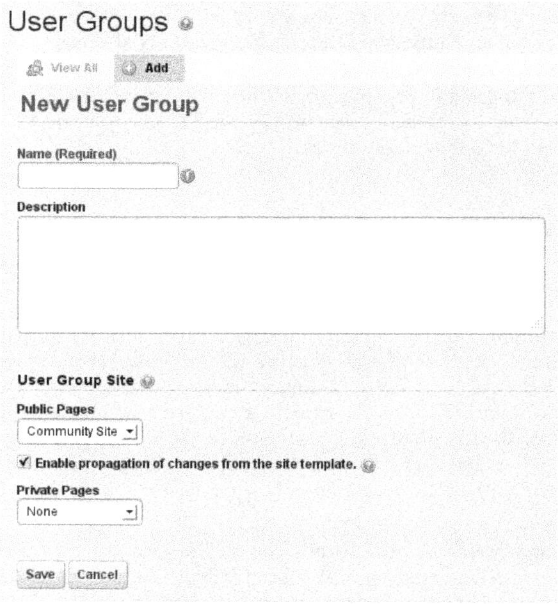

Figure 15.4: Creating a New User Group

Note in the figure above how each user group may have a site, with public and private pages. This is a special type of site that determines the base pages on all user group members' personal sites. The user group site works in a similar way to Site Templates, except in this case the User Group Site pages are not copied for each user but are rather shown dynamically along with any custom pages the user may have on his/her personal site. For this reason, users are not allowed to make any modifications to the pages that are *inherited* from the user group. Alternatively the administrators of the user group can define certain areas as customizable, just like they can for regular sites. This allows users to decide which applications they want to place in certain areas of each page, as well as change their configuration.

Figure 15.5: User Group Actions

As with the other resources in the portal, you can click the *Actions* button next to a user group to perform various operations on that group.

Edit: allows you to modify the name or description of the user group.

Permissions: lets you define which roles have permissions to view, edit, delete, assign members to the user group, etc.

Site Permissions: lets you define which roles have permissions to manage the user group site, to specify who can administer its pages, export and import pages and portlet content, manage archived setups and configure its applications.

Manage Site Pages: allows you to add pages to the user group site, import or export pages, organize the page hierarchy, modify the look and feel of the pages, add a logo or access other options from the Manage Site interface.

Assign Members: lets you search for and select users in the portal to be assigned to this user group as well as view the users currently belonging to the user group .

Delete: removes the user group.

If your user group has a site, two options named **Go to the Site's Public Pages** and **Go to the Site's Private Pages** also appear as links in your user group's Actions menu. Clicking one of these links opens the user group's site in a new browser window. Any changes you make to the site are saved automatically. You can safely close the browser window when you're done.

Creating and editing a User Group

A user group's site can be administered from the control panel. Select *User Groups* from the control panel to see a list of existing user groups. To edit a user group, click on its name or description. You can also click on the *Actions* button to see the full list of actions that can be performed on a user group. When editing a user group, you can view its site, if it exists, by clicking the *Open Pages* link under Public Pages or Private Pages (read below for details on user group sites).

As an example of how user group sites can be used, let's create a user group called *Bloggers* along with a simple template. We'll call the site template *Bloggers* too. It should contain a single *Blog* page with the Blogs and Recents Bloggers portlets on it. First, navigate to the User Groups page of the control panel. Then click *Add* and enter the name *Bloggers* for your user group, and optionally, a description. Click *Save* to create your user group.

Our next step is to assign an existing user to the *Bloggers* group.

Assigning Members to a User Group

Navigate to *Users and Organizations* and create a new user called *Joe Bloggs*. Then navigate to the User Groups page of the control panel and click *Actions* → *Assign Members* next to the Bloggers group. Click the *Available* tab to see a list of users that can be assigned to the group.

From that list, one or more users can be assigned as members of the user group.

For example, by default, newly created users are given *Welcome* pages on the public pages portion of their personal sites. This Welcome page contains the Language, Search and Blogs portlets. You can see the effect of the *Bloggers* site template on the public pages of Joe Bloggs's personal site in the figure above. When Joe Bloggs was added to the *Bloggers* group, he received a *Blogs* page with the *Blogs* and *Recent Bloggers* portlets.

After the user group has been created and several users have been added to it, you can add all those users at once as members of a site in one step from the *Site Memberships* UI of the site. You can also use the user group when assigning a role to users from the roles management UI.

The next section describes a more advanced usage of user groups: User Group Sites.

Figure 15.6: Assigning Members to a User Group

User Group Sites

Liferay allows users to each have a personal site consisting of public and private pages. Permissions can be granted to allow users to customize their personal sites at will. Originally, the default configuration of those pages could only be determined by the portal administrator through the `portal-ext.properties` file and, optionally, by providing the configuration in a LAR file. You can still configure it like this but it isn't very flexible or easy to use.

By using User Group Sites, portal administrators can add pages to the personal sites of all the users who belong to the site in an easy and centralized way. All the user group site's public pages are shown as part of the user's public personal site. All the user group site's private pages are shown as part of the user's private site. If a user belongs to several user groups, all of its pages are made part of his public and private site. In an educational institution's portal, for example, teachers, staff and students could get different default pages and applications on their personal sites.

The pages a user's personal site *inherits* from a User Group still belong to the User Group and thus cannot be changed in any way by the user. What the user group administrators can do is define certain areas of the pages as customizable to allow the users to choose which applications and what configuration should be shown in those areas. If a user has permission to add custom pages to his/her personal site, besides those *inherited* from a user group, the custom pages are always shown last.

Since the *inheritance* of pages is done dynamically, this new system introduced in Liferay 6.1 can scale to hundreds of thousands of users or even millions of them without an exponential impact in performance. Previous versions of Liferay used a different technique that required user group pages be copied to each user's personal site. For portals upgrading from previous versions of Liferay, you can keep the old behavior but it has been left disabled by default. You can enable it by adding the following line to your portal-ext.properties file:

```
user.groups.copy.layouts.to.user.personal.site=true
```

When this property is set to true, once the template pages have been copied to a user's personal site, the copies may be modified by the user. Changes done to the originals in the User Group will only affect new users added to the user group. Users with administrative privileges over their personal sites can modify the pages and their content if the *Allow Site Administrators to Modify the Pages Associated with This Site Template* box has been checked for the template. When a user is removed from a user group, the associated pages are removed from the user's personal site. Moreover, if a user is removed from a group and is subsequently added back, the group's template pages are copied to the user's site a second time. Note that if a user group's site is based on a site template and an administrator modifies the user group's site template after users have already been added to the group, those changes only take effect if the *Enable propagation of changes from the site template* box for the user group was checked.

 Tip: Previous to Liferay 6.1, pages from different user groups could be combined on users' personal sites by using a naming convention. Liferay 6.1 simplifies the way user groups' sites work by disallowing page combination. Set the property *user.groups.copy.layouts.to.user.personal.site* to true if you depend on that functionality.

You can create a user group's site manually or base it on a site template. To create a user group's site manually, use the *Actions* menu mentioned above and choose *Manage Site Pages*. You can add a new public or private page by selecting the appropriate tab and then clicking the *Add Page* button. Once the user group has at least one public or private page in place, you can go back to the *Actions* menu and click on the *Go to the Site's Public Pages* or *Go to the Site's Private*

Pages link to open the user group's site in a new browser window. In the new window, you can add more pages and portlets and configure site settings.

You can also base a user group's site on a template. When editing a user group, use the Public Pages and Private Pages drop down lists to select a site template. Leave the *Enable propagation of changes from the site template* box checked to automatically update users' personal sites if the associated site template changes. If you uncheck this box but recheck it later, the template pages are copied to the users' sites, overwriting any changes they may have made. You can allow users to make changes to the pages they receive from the user group by enabling the customization options on each page.

This flexibility lets you achieve almost any desired configuration for a user's personal site without having to modify it directly. When a user is assigned to a user group, the configured site pages are copied directly to the user's personal site.

Following with the example above, we will create a site for our sample user group. Edit the *Bloggers* group. Choose an existing Site Template from the drop down menu for the user group's public pages and click *Save*. After the page reloads you can click to see the pages and make any changes desired, add additional pages, etc.

Also, try visiting the public site of one of the users who belongs to the user group. You will see how all of the pages in the user group appear as part of the user site, including the ones copied from the site template and the ones added afterwards.

15.6 Roles and Permissions

Roles are used to collect permissions that define a particular function within the portal, according to a particular scope. Roles can be granted permissions to various functions within portlet applications. A roles is basically just a collection of permissions that defines a function, such as Message Board Administrator. A role with that name is likely to have permissions relevant to the specific Message Board portlets delegated to it. Users who are placed in this role will inherit these permissions.

The roles page of the control panel serves as a single interface which lets you create roles, assign permissions to them and assign users to the roles. Roles can be scoped by portal, site or organization. To create a role, click the *Roles* link and then click the *Add* button. You can choose a Regular, Site or Organization role. A regular role is a portal-scoped role. Make a selection and then type a name for your role, a title and a description. The name field is required but the

Figure 15.7: Selecting a Template for the User Group Site

title and description are optional. If you enter a name and a title, the title will be displayed in the list of roles on the Roles page of the control panel. If you do not enter a title, the name will be displayed. When you have finished, click *Save*.

In addition to regular roles, site roles, and organization roles, there are also teams. Teams can be created by site administrators within a specific site. The permissions granted to a team are defined and applied only within the team's site. The permissions defined by regular, site, and organization roles, by contrast, are defined at the portal level, although they are applied to different scopes. The differences between the four types of roles can be described as follows:

Regular role: Permissions are defined at the *portal* level and are applied at the *portal* level.

Site role: Permissions are defined at the *portal* level and are applied to one *specific site*.

Organization role: Permissions are defined at the *portal* level and are applied to one *specific organization*.

Team: Permissions are defined within a *specific site* and are assigned within that *specific site*.

For more information about teams, please refer to chapter 3.

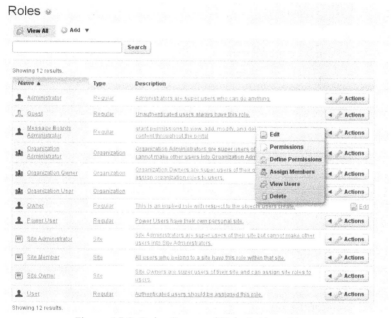

Figure 15.8: Roles Page and Role Actions Menu

After you save, Liferay redirects you to the list of roles. To see what functions you can perform on your new role, click the *Actions* button.

Edit: lets you change the name, title or description of the role.

Permissions: allows you to define which users, user groups or roles have permissions to edit the role.

Define Permissions: defines what permissions this role grants. This is outlined in the next section.

Assign Members: lets you search and select users in the portal to be assigned to this role. These users will inherit any permissions that have been assigned to this role.

View Users: allows you to view the users who have been assigned to this role.

Delete: permanently removes a role from the portal.

Next, let's examine how to configure the permissions granted by different roles.

Defining Permissions on a Role

Roles serve as repositories of permissions to be assigned to users who belong to them. So, to use a role, you need to assign members to it and define the permissions you want to grant to members of the role.

When you click the *Actions* button on portal-scoped role and select *Define Permissions*, you will be shown a list of all the permissions defined for that role. Click the *Add Permissions* drop-down menu to see a list of the permissions that can be defined. As of Liferay version 6.1, these permissions fall into seven categories: Portal, Site Content, Site Application, Control Panel: Personal, Control Panel: Site, Control Panel: Portal and Control Panel: Server. For non-portal scoped roles, you need to click on the *Options* link on individual portlets, then *Configuration*, then *Permissions* to assign permissions within the site or organization that owns the portlet.

Portal permissions cover portal-wide activities that comprise several categories, such as site, organization, location, password policy, etc. This allows you to create a role that, for example, can create new sites within the portal. This would allow you to grant users that particular permission without making them overall portal administrators.

Site Content permissions cover the content the installed portlets create. If you pick one of the portlets from this list, you'll get options for defining permissions on its content. For example, if you pick Message Boards, you'll see permissions for creating categories and threads or deleting and moving topics.

Site Application permissions affect the application as a whole. So, using our Message Boards example, an application permission might define who can add the Message Boards portlet to a page.

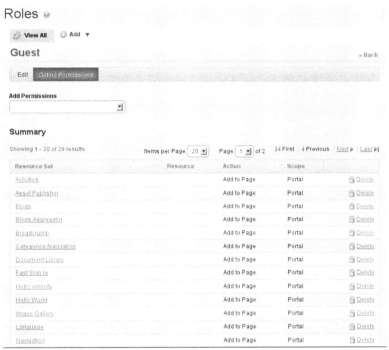

Figure 15.9: Defining Permissions on a Role

The control panel permissions affect how the portlet appears to the user in the control panel. Some control panel portlets have a Configuration button, so you can define who gets to see that, as well as who gets to see an application in the control panel.

Each possible action to which permissions can be granted is listed. To grant a permission, check the box next to it. If you want to limit the scope of the permission to a particular site, click the *Limit Scope* link and then choose the site. Once you have chosen the permissions granted to this role, click *Save*. For a portal-scoped Message Boards Administrator role, you might grant content permissions for every action listed. After you click *Save*, you will see a list of

Figure 15.10: Message Board Content Permissions

all permissions currently granted to this role. From here, you can add more permissions or go back by clicking a link in the breadcrumb list or the *Return to Full Page* link.

The list of permissions that you can define for a role may seem overwhelming. However, these permissions ensure that you can customize exactly which areas of your portal you'd like different collections of users to be able to access. Sometimes you might find that a certain permission grants more or less access than what you expected–always test the permissions yourself!

For example, suppose that you created a role called User Group Manager. You'd like to define the permissions for the User Group Manager role so that users assigned to this role can add users to or remove users from any user group. To do this, you might click on *Go To* → *Control Panel* and then *Roles* → *Add* → *Regular Role*. After naming your role, you'd click *Actions* → *Define Permissions*. Then you'd click on the *Add Permissions* dropdown menu and select *Users and Organizations* under the *Portal* heading. Since you'd like user group managers to be able to view user groups and assign members to them, you'd check the *Assign Members* and *View* permissions under the *User Group* heading. Then you'd go back to the *Add Permissions* dropdown menu and select *User Groups* under the *Control Panel: Portal* heading and check the *Access in Control Panel* and *View* permissions so that user group managers can manage user groups from the Control Panel.

You might expect that these permissions would be enough to allow users assigned to the User Group Manager role to add or remove any users to or from any user group. After all, we've granted user group managers permissions to view user groups and assign members and we've granted them access to User Groups in the Control Panel. However, we're forgetting an important permission. Can you guess what it is? That's right: we haven't granted the User Group Manager role permission to view users! Although user group managers can assign members to user groups, they don't have permission to view users at the portal level. This means that if they click *Assign Members* for a user group and click on the *Available* tab, they'll see an empty list.

To fix this, click *Go To* → *Control Panel*. Click on *Roles* and then *Actions* → *Define Permissions*. Then click on the *Add Permissions* dropdown list and select *Users and Organizations* under the *Portal* heading. On this page, check the *View* permission under the *User* heading. Once you've saved, users who've been assigned to the User Group Manager role will be able to browse the portal's entire list of users when assigning users to a user group.

Roles are very powerful and allow portal administrators to define various permissions in whatever combinations they like. This gives you as much flexibility as possible to build the site you have designed.

Figure 15.11: Make sure to test the permissions you grant to custom roles.

Figure 15.12: Users assigned to the User Group Manager role can't find any users to add!

Special Note about the Power Users Role

Prior to Liferay 6.0, the default configurations of many Liferay portlets allowed power users, but not regular users, to access them. Liferay 6.0 and subsequent versions grant the same default permissions to both power users and regular users. This way, portal administrators are not forced to use the power users role. However, Liferay encourages those who do to create their own custom permissions for the role.

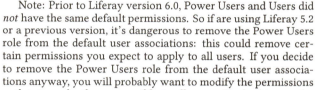

Note: Prior to Liferay version 6.0, Power Users and Users did *not* have the same default permissions. So if are using Liferay 5.2 or a previous version, it's dangerous to remove the Power Users role from the default user associations: this could remove certain permissions you expect to apply to all users. If you decide to remove the Power Users role from the default user associations anyway, you will probably want to modify the permissions on certain portlets to make them accessible to all users. To do this, see the section on Plugins Configuration below.

Now that we've seen how to use organizations and user groups to manage users and how to use roles to define permissions, let's examine the general portal settings you can configure.

15.7   Managing Portal Settings

After you have created users, user groups, organizations, roles, sites and teams your portal will be ready to host content and applications. You can configure Liferay's portal settings to fit your environment and your particular portal project. Many configurations can be performed through Liferay's portlet-driven user interface. This section covers how to configure portal settings such as password policies, authentication settings, mail host names, email notifications, display settings and monitoring.

Now that you have been navigating in the control panel, you should be pretty familiar with how it works. All the options appear in the left navigation, their interfaces appear in the middle and any sub-options appear on the right. We have focused so far on the maintenance of users and portal security. The remaining links in the *Portal* category focus on various portal settings which cover how the portal operates and integrates with other systems you may have. Let's begin our discussion of Liferay's portal settings by examining how to configure password policies.

Password Policies

Password policies can enhance the security of your portal. You can set requirements on password strength, frequency of password expiration and more. Additionally, you can apply different password policies to different sets of portal users.

If you are viewing a page other than the control panel, select *Control Panel* from the *Go to* menu of the Dockbar. Next, click on the *Password Policies* link on the left side of the screen under the *Portal* heading. You will see there is already a default password policy in the system. You can edit this in the same manner as you edit other resources in the portal: click *Actions* and then click *Edit*.

The Password Policy settings form contains the following fields. Enabling specific settings via the check boxes prompts setting-specific options to appear.

Name: requires you to enter a name for the password policy.

Description: lets you describe the password policy so other administrators will know what it's for.

Changeable: determines whether or not a user can change his or her password.

Change Required: determines whether or not a user must change his or her password after logging into the portal for the first time.

Minimum Age: lets you choose how long a password must remain in effect before it can be changed.

Reset Ticket Max Age: determines how long a password reset link remains valid.

Password Syntax Checking: allows you to set a minimum password length and to choose whether or not dictionary words can be in passwords. You can also specify detailed requirements such as minimum numbers of alpha numeric characters, lower case letters, upper case letters, numbers or symbols.

Password History: lets you keep a history (with a defined length) of passwords and prevents users from changing their passwords to one that was previously used.

Password Expiration: lets you choose how long passwords can remain active before they expire. You can select the age, the warning time and a grace limit.

Lockout: allows you to set a number of failed log-in attempts that triggers a user's account to lock. You can choose whether an administrator needs to unlock the account or if it becomes unlocked after a specific duration.

From the list of password policies, you can perform several other actions.

Edit: brings you to the form above and allows you to modify the password policy.

Permissions: allows you to define which users, user groups or roles have permission to edit the password policy.

Assign Members: takes you to a screen where you can search and select users in the portal to be assigned to this password policy. The password policy will be enforced for any users who are added here.

Delete: shows up for any password policies you add beyond the default policy. You cannot delete the default policy.

Next, let's examine Liferay's Portal Settings.

Portal Settings

Most global portal settings can be configured from the Portal Settings section of the control panel. The Configuration heading contains the following links:

General: lets you configure global settings, such as the company name, domain, the virtual host, a global portal logo and more.

Authentication: allows you to configure log in IDs, connection to LDAP and Single Sign-On.

Users: has three tabs, labeled Fields, Reserved Credentials and Default User Associations. The Fields tab enables or disables some user fields, such as birthday or terms of use. The Reserved Credentials tab lets you reserve screen names and email addresses so users cannot register using them. You might use this to prevent users from registering on the portal with user names that contain profanity or that sound official, such as *admin* or *president*. The Default User Associations tab lets you configure default membership to roles, user groups, sites for new users and provides a check box which allows you to retroactively apply these to existing users.

Mail Host Names: lets you add a list of other mail host names to be associated with your organization. For example, your main domain might be `mycompany.com` but you might use `mycompany-marketing.com` for your email newsletters. Any domain names associated with your organization can go here.

Email Notifications: allows you to configure Liferay to send email notifications for certain events, such as user registrations, password changes, etc. You can customize those messages here.

Let's discuss these settings next.

Figure 15.13: Portal Settings Pages

General

The General link takes you to a page with three headings: Main Configuration, Navigation and Additional Information. Under the Main Configuration heading, you can set the name of the company, organization or site which is running the portal. This name also defines the name of your portal's default site. Its default name is `liferay.com` so you will definitely want to set this to reflect your own company. You can also set the mail domain, virtual host and content delivery network address here. Under the Navigation heading, you can set a home page for your portal here as well as default landing and logout pages. Under the Additional Information heading, you can specify a Legal name, ID, company type, SIC code, ticker symbol, industry and industry type.

Authentication

The Authentication page has several tabs: General, LDAP, CAS, Facebook, NTLM, OpenID, Open SSO and SiteMinder. You can use any of these authentication methods to configure how users will authenticate to Liferay. Since Liferay supports quite a few authentication methods, there are different settings for each.

The settings on the General tab of the Authentication page affect only Liferay functionality and don't have anything to do with the integration options on the other tabs. The General tab allows you to customize Liferay's standard authentication behavior. Specifically, the General tab allows you to select from several global authentication settings:

- Authenticate via email address (default), screen name or user ID (a numerical ID auto-generated in the database not recommended).

- Enable/Disable automatic log in. If enabled, Liferay allows a user to check a box which will cause the site to "remember" the user's log in by placing a cookie on his or her browser. If disabled, users will always have to log in manually.

- Enable/Disable forgotten password functionality.

- Enable/Disable request password reset links.

- Enable/Disable account creation by strangers. If you are running an Internet site, you will probably want to leave this on so visitors can create accounts on your site.

- Enable/Disable account creation by those using an email address in the domain of the company running the site (which you just set on the General page of Portal Settings). This is handy if you are using Liferay to host both internal and external web sites. You can make sure all internal IDs have to be created by administrators but external users can register for IDs themselves.

- Enable / Disable email address verification. If you enable this, Liferay will send users a verification email with a link back to the portal to verify the email address they entered is a valid one they can access.

By default, all settings except for the last are enabled. User authentication by email address is an important default for the following reasons:

1. An email address is, by definition, unique to the user who owns it.

2. People can generally remember their email addresses. If you have users who haven't logged into the portal for a while, it is possible they will forget their screen names, especially if they weren't allowed to use their screen names of choice (because they were already taken).

3. If a user changes his or her email address, it is more likely the user will forget to update his or her email address in his or her profile, if the email address is not used to authenticate. If the user's email address is not updated, all notifications sent by the portal will fail to reach the user. So it is important to keep the email address at the forefront of a user's mind when he or she logs in to help the user keep it up to date.

We'll examine how to set up LDAP authentication next.

15.8   Integrating Liferay users into your enterprise

LDAP

You can use the LDAP tab of the Authentication page to connect Liferay to an LDAP directory. There are two places for you to configure the LDAP settings: here in the control panel or in the `portal-ext.properties` file (which is covered in chapter 20). We recommend you use the control panel since your configuration settings will be stored in the database. Note that if you use both, the settings in the database will be merged with the settings in `portal-ext.properties`. If there's a conflict or overlapping data, the LDAP servers set in the control panel take precedence over the servers set in `portal-ext.properties`. Configuring the LDAP settings from the control panel is easier and does not require a restart of Liferay. The only compelling reason to use the `portal-ext.properties` file is if you have many Liferay nodes which will be configured to run against the same LDAP directory. In that case, for your initial deployment, it may be easier to copy the `portal-ext.properties` file to all of the nodes so the first time they start up, the settings are correct. Regardless of which method you use, the available settings are the same.

You configure the global values from the LDAP tab of the Authentication page.

Enabled: Check this box to enable LDAP Authentication.

Required: Check this box if LDAP authentication is required. Liferay will then not allow a user to log in unless he or she can successfully bind to the LDAP directory first. Uncheck this box if you want to allow users with Liferay accounts but no LDA accounts to log in to the portal.

LDAP Servers: Liferay supports connections to multiple LDAP servers. You can you the Add button beneath this heading to add LDAP servers. We explain how to configure new LDAP servers below.

Import/Export: You can import and export user data from LDAP directories using the following options:

- *Import Enabled:* Check this box to cause Liferay to do a mass import from your LDAP directories. If you want Liferay to only synchronize users when they log in, leave this box unchecked. Definitely leave this unchecked if you are working in a clustered environment. Otherwise, all of your nodes would try to do a mass import when each of them starts up.

- *Import on Startup Enabled:* Check this box to have Liferay run the import when it starts up. Note: This box only appears if you check the *Import Enabled* box above.

- *Export Enabled:* Check this box to enable Liferay to export user accounts from the database to LDAP. Liferay uses a listener to track any changes made to the User object and will push these changes out to the LDAP server whenever the User object is updated. Note that by default on every login, fields such as LastLoginDate are updated. When export is enabled, this has the effect of causing a user export every time the user logs in. You can disable this by setting the following property in your portal-ext.properties file:

  users.update.last.login=false

Use LDAP Password Policy: Liferay uses its own password policy by default. This can be configured on the Password Policies page of the control panel. Check the *Use LDAP Password Policy* box if you want to use the password policies defined by your LDAP directory. Once this is enabled, the Password Policies tab will display a message stating you are not using a local password policy. You will now have to use your LDAP directory's mechanism for setting password policies. Liferay does this by parsing the messages in the LDAP controls returned by your LDAP server. By default, the messages in the LDAP controls that Liferay is looking for are the messages returned by the Fedora Directory Server. If you are using a different LDAP server, you will need to customize the messages in Liferay's portal-ext.properties file, as there is not yet a GUI for setting this. See below for instructions describing how to do this.

Once you've finished configuring LDAP, click the *Save* button. Next, let's look at how to add LDAP servers.

Adding LDAP Servers

The Add button beneath the LDAP servers heading allows you to add LDAP servers. If you have more than one, you can arrange the servers by order of preference using the up/down arrows. When you add an LDAP Server, you will need to provide several pieces of data so Liferay can bind to that LDAP server and search it for user records. Regardless of how many LDAP servers you add, each server has the same configuration options.

Server Name: Enter a name for your LDAP server.

Default Values: Several leading directory servers are listed here. If you are using one of these, select it and click the Reset Values button. The rest of the form will be populated with the proper default values for that directory.

Connection: These settings cover the basic connection to LDAP.

- *Base Provider URL:* This tells the portal where the LDAP server is located. Make sure the machine on which Liferay is installed can communicate with the LDAP server. If there is a firewall between the two systems, check to make sure the appropriate ports are opened.

- *Base DN:* This is the Base Distinguished Name for your LDAP directory. It is usually modeled after your organization. For a commercial organization, it may look similar to this: dc=companynamehere,dc=com.

- *Principal:* By default, the administrator ID is populated here. If you have removed the default LDAP administrator, you will need to use the fully qualified name of the administrative credential you use instead. You need an administrative credential because Liferay will be using this ID to synchronize user accounts to and from LDAP .

- *Credentials:* This is the password for the administrative user.

This is all you need to make a regular connection to an LDAP directory. The rest of the configuration is optional. Generally, the default attribute mappings provide enough data to synchronize back to the Liferay database when a user attempts to log in. To test the connection to your LDAP server, click the *Test LDAP Connection* button.

If you are running your LDAP directory in SSL mode to prevent credential information from passing through the network unencrypted, you will have to perform extra steps to share the encryption key and certificate between the two systems.

For example, assuming your LDAP directory happens to be Microsoft Active Directory on Windows Server 2003, you would take the following steps to share the certificate:

Click Start → Administrative Tools → Certificate Authority. Highlight the machine that is the certificate authority, right click on it, and click *Properties*.

From the General menu, click *View Certificate*. Select the Details view, and click *Copy To File*. Use the resulting wizard to save the certificate as a file. As with the CAS install (see the below section entitled Single Sign-On), you will need to import the certificate into the *cacerts keystore*. The import is handled by a command like the following:

```
keytool -import -trustcacerts -keystore /some/path/jdk1.5.0_11/jre/   \
    lib/security/cacerts -storepass changeit -noprompt -alias MyRootCA   \
    -file /some/path/MyRootCA.cer
```

The *keytool* utility ships as part of the Java SDK.

Once this is done, go back to the LDAP page in the control panel. Modify the LDAP URL in the Base DN field to the secure version by changing the protocol to **https** and the port to **636** like the following:

```
ldaps://myLdapServerHostname:636
```

Save the changes. Your Liferay Portal will now use LDAP in secure mode for authentication.

Users: This section contains settings for finding users in your LDAP directory.

- *Authentication Search Filter:* The search filter box can be used to determine the search criteria for user logins. By default, Liferay uses users' email addresses for their login names. If you have changed this setting, you will need to modify the search filter here, which has been configured to use the email address attribute from LDAP as a search criterion. For example, if you changed Liferay's authentication method to use screen names instead of the email addresses, you would modify the search filter so it can match the entered log in name:

    ```
    (cn=@screen\_name@)
    ```

- *Import Search Filter:* Depending on the **LDAP** server, there are different ways to identify the user. Generally, the default setting[1] is fine but if you want to search for only a subset of users or users that have different object classes, you can change this.

---

[1] objectClass=inetOrgPerson

- *User Mapping:* The next series of fields allows you to define mappings from LDAP attributes to Liferay fields. Though your LDAP user attributes may be different from LDAP server to LDAP server, there are five fields Liferay requires to be mapped for the user to be recognized. You must define a mapping to the corresponding attributes in LDAP for the following Liferay fields:

  - *Screen Name*
  - *Password*
  - *Email Address*
  - *Full Name*
  - *First Name*
  - *Middle Name*
  - *Last Name*
  - *Job Title*
  - *Group*

The control panel provides default mappings for commonly used LDAP attributes. You can also add your own mappings if you wish.

- *Test LDAP Users:* Once you have your attribute mappings set up (see above), click the *Test LDAP Users* button and Liferay will attempt to pull LDAP users and match them with their mappings as a preview.

Groups: This section contains settings for mapping LDAP groups to Liferay.

- *Import Search Filter:* This is the filter for finding LDAP groups you want to map to Liferay. Enter the LDAP group attributes you want retrieved for this mapping. The following attributes can be mapped:

  - Group Name
  - Description
  - User

- *Test LDAP Groups:* Click the **Test LDAP Groups** to display a list of the groups returned by your search filter.

Export: This section contains settings for exporting user data from LDAP.

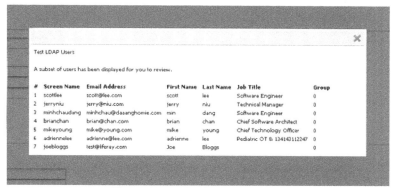

Figure 15.14: Testing LDAP Users

- *Users DN:* Enter the location in your LDAP tree where the users will be stored. When Liferay does an export, it will export the users to this location.

- *User Default Object Classes:* When a user is exported, the user is created with the listed default object classes. To find out what your default object classes are, use an LDAP browser tool such as JXplorer to locate a user and view the Object Class attributes stored in LDAP for that user.

- *Groups DN:* Enter the location in your LDAP tree where the groups will be stored. When Liferay does an export, it will export the groups to this location.

- *Group Default Object Classes:* When a group is exported, the group is created with the listed default object classes. To find out what your default object classes are, use an LDAP browser tool such as *Jxplorer* to locate a group and view the Object Class attributes stored in LDAP for that group.

Once you've set all your options and tested your connection, click *Save*. From here, you can add another LDAP server or set just a few more options that apply to all of your LDAP server connections.

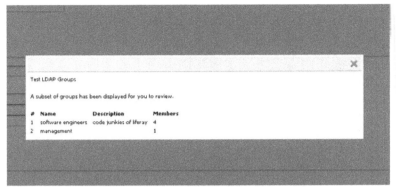

Test LDAP Groups

A subset of groups has been displayed for you to review.

#	Name	Description	Members
1	software engineers	code junkies of liferay	4
2	management		1

Figure 15.15: Mapping LDAP Groups

LDAP Options Not Available in the GUI

Although most of the LDAP configuration can be done from the control panel, there are several configuration parameters that are only available by editing `portal-ext.properties`. These options will be available in the GUI in future versions of Liferay Portal but for now they can only be configured by editing the properties file.

If you need to change any of these options, copy the LDAP section from the `portal.properties` file into your `portal-ext.properties` file. Note that since you have already configured LDAP from the GUI, any settings from the properties file that match settings already configured in the GUI will be ignored. The GUI, which stores the settings in the database, always takes precedence over the properties file.

```
ldap.auth.method=bind
#ldap.auth.method=password-compare
```

Set either bind or password-compare for the LDAP authentication method. Bind is preferred by most vendors so you don't have to worry about encryption strategies. Password compare does exactly what it sounds like: it reads the user's password out of LDAP, decrypts it and compares it with the user's password in Liferay, syncing the two.

```
ldap.auth.password.encryption.algorithm=
ldap.auth.password.encryption.algorithm.types=MD5,SHA
```

Set the password encryption to used to compare passwords if the property `ldap.auth.method` is set to `password-compare`.

```
ldap.import.method=[user,group]
```

If you set this to `user`, Liferay will import all users from the specified portion of the LDAP tree. If you set this to `group`, Liferay will search all the groups and import the users in each group. If you have users who do not belong to any groups, they will not be imported.

```
ldap.error.password.history=history
ldap.error.password.not.changeable=not allowed to change
ldap.error.password.syntax=syntax ldap.error.password.trivial=trivial
ldap.error.user.lockout=retry limit
ldap.error.password.age=age ldap.error.password.expired=expired
```

These properties are a list of phrases from error messages which can possibly be returned by the LDAP server. When a user binds to LDAP, the server can return *controls* with its response of success or failure. These controls contain a message describing the error or the information that is coming back with the response. Though the controls are the same across LDAP servers, the messages can be different. The properties described here contain snippets of words from those messages and will work with Red Hat's Fedora Directory Server. If you are not using that server, the word snippets may not work with your LDAP server. If they don't, you can replace the values of these properties with phrases from your server's error messages. This will enable Liferay to recognize them. Next, let's look at the Single Sign-On solutions Liferay supports.

SSO

Single Sign-On solutions allow you to provide a single login credential for multiple systems. This allows you to have people authenticate to the Single Sign-On product and they will be automatically logged in to Liferay and to other products as well.

Liferay supports several single sign-on solutions. Of course, if your product is not yet supported, you may choose to implement support for it yourself by use of the extension environment. Alternatively, your organization can choose to sponsor support for it. Please contact `sales@liferay.com` for more information about this.

Authentication: Central Authentication Service (CAS)

CAS is an authentication system originally created at Yale University. It is a widely-used open source single sign-on solution and was the first SSO product to be supported by Liferay.

Please follow the documentation for CAS to install it on your application server of choice.

Your first step will be to copy the CAS client .jar file to Liferay's library folder. On Tomcat, this is in `[Tomcat Home]/webapps/ROOT/WEB-INF/lib`. Once you've done this, the CAS client will be available to Liferay the next time you start it.

The CAS Server application requires a properly configured Secure Socket Layer certificate on your server to work. If you wish to generate one yourself, you will need to use the `keytool` utility that comes with the JDK. Your first step is to generate the key. Next, you export the key into a file. Finally, you import the key into your local Java key store. For public, Internet-based production environments, you will need to either purchase a signed key from a recognized certificate authority (such as Thawte or Verisign) or have your key signed by a recognized certificate authority. For Intranets, you should have your IT department pre-configure users' browsers to accept the certificate so they don't get warning messages about the certificate.

To generate a key, use the following command:

```
keytool -genkey -alias tomcat -keypass changeit -keyalg RSA
```

Instead of the password in the example (`changeit`), use a password you will remember. If you are not using Tomcat, you may want to use a different alias as well. For First and Last names, enter `localhost` or the host name of your server. It cannot be an IP address.

To export the key to a file, use the following command:

```
keytool -export -alias tomcat -keypass changeit -file server.cert
```

Finally, to import the key into your Java key store, use the following command:

```
keytool -import -alias tomcat -file %FILE_NAME% -keypass changeit -keystore   \
   \$JAVA\_HOME/jre/lib/security/cacerts
```

If you are on a Windows system, replace `$JAVA_HOME` above with `%JAVA_HOME%`. Of course, all of this needs to be done on the system on which CAS will be running.

Once your CAS server is up and running, you can configure Liferay to use it. This is a simple matter of navigating to the *Settings → Authentication → CAS* tab in the control panel. Enable CAS authentication and then modify the URL properties to point to your CAS server.

Enabled: Check this box to enable CAS single sign-on.

Import from LDAP: A user may be authenticated from CAS and not yet exist in the portal. Select this to automatically import users from LDAP if they do not exist in the portal.

The rest of the settings are various URLs, with defaults included. Change *localhost* in the default values to point to your CAS server. When you are finished, click *Save*. After this, when users click the *Sign In* link, they will be directed to the CAS server to sign in to Liferay.

Authentication: Facebook

Liferay Portal also enables users to log in using their Facebook accounts. To enable this feature, you simply need to select the *Enable* box and enter the Application ID and Application Secret which should have been provided to you by Facebook. Facebook SSO works by taking the primary Facebook email address and searching for the same email address in Liferay's `User_` table. If a match is found, the user is automatically signed on (provided the user clicked *allow* from the Facebook dialog). If there isn't a match, the user is prompted in Liferay to add a user from Facebook. Once selected, a new user is created by retrieving four fields from Facebook (first name, last name, email address and gender).

Authentication: NTLM

NTLM is a Microsoft protocol that can be used for authentication through Microsoft Internet Explorer. Though Microsoft has adopted Kerberos in modern versions of Windows server, NTLM is still used when authenticating to a workgroup. Liferay Portal now supports NTLM v2 authentication. NTLM v2 is more secure and has a stronger authentication process than NTLMv1.

Enabled: Check this box to enable NTLM authentication.

Domain Controller: Enter the IP address of your domain controller. This is the server that contains the user accounts you want to use with Liferay.

Domain: Enter the domain / workgroup name.

Service Account: You need to create a service account for NTLM. This account will be a computer account, not a user account.

Service Password: Enter the password for the service account.

Authentication: OpenID

OpenID is a new single sign-on standard which is implemented by multiple vendors. The idea is multiple vendors can implement the standard and then users can register for an ID with the vendor they trust. The credential issued by that vendor can be used by all the web sites that support OpenID. Some high profile OpenID vendors are

- AOL http://openid.aol.com/screenname

- LiveDoor http://profile.livedoor.com/username

- LiveJournal http://username.livejournal.com

Please see the OpenID site http://www.openid.net for a more complete list.

A main benefit of OpenID for the user is he or she no longer has to register for a new account on every site in which he or she wants to participate. Users can register on *one* site (the OpenID provider's site) and then use those credentials to authenticate to many web sites which support OpenID. Many web site owners often struggle to build communities because end users are reluctant to register for so many different accounts. Supporting OpenID makes it easier for site owners to build their communities because the barriers to participating (i.e., the effort it takes to register for and keep track of many accounts) are removed. All of the account information is kept with the OpenID provider, making it much easier to manage this information and keep it up to date.

Liferay Portal can act as an OpenID consumer, allowing users to automatically register and sign in with their OpenID accounts. Internally, the product uses OpenID4Java http://code.google.com/p/openid4java/ to implement the feature.

OpenID is enabled by default in Liferay but can be disabled here.

Atlassian Crowd

Atlassian Crowd is a web-based Single Sign-On product similar to CAS. Crowd can be used to manage authentication to many different web applications and directory servers.

Because Atlassian Crowd implements an OpenID producer, Liferay works and has been tested with it. Simply use the OpenID authentication feature in Liferay to log in using Crowd.

Authentication: OpenSSO

OpenSSO is an open source single sign-on solution that comes from the code base of Sun's System Access Manager product. Liferay integrates with OpenSSO, allowing you to use OpenSSO to integrate Liferay into an infrastructure that contains a multitude of different authentication schemes against different repositories of identities.

You can set up OpenSSO on the same server as Liferay or a different box. Follow the instructions at the OpenSSO site http://opensso.dev.java.net to install OpenSSO. Once you have it installed, create the Liferay administrative user in it. Users are mapped back and forth by screen names. By default, the Liferay administrative user has a screen name of *test*, so in OpenSSO, you would register the user with the ID of *test* and an email address of *test@liferay.com*. Once you have the user set up, log in to Open SSO using this user.

In the same browser window, go to the URL for your server running Liferay and log in as the same user, using the email address *test@liferay.com*. Go to the control panel and click *Settings* → *Authentication* → *OpenSSO*. Modify the three URL fields (Login URL, Logout URL and Service URL) so they point to your OpenSSO server (i.e., only modify the host name portion of the URLs), click the *Enabled* check box and then click *Save*. Liferay will then redirect users to OpenSSO when they click the *Sign In* link.

Authentication: SiteMinder

SiteMinder is a single sign-on implementation from Computer Associates. Liferay 5.2 introduced built-in integration with SiteMinder. SiteMinder uses a custom HTTP header to implement its single sign-on solution.

To enable SiteMinder authentication in Liferay, check the *Enabled* box on the *SiteMinder* tab. If you are also using LDAP with Liferay, you can check the *Import from LDAP* box. If this box is checked, users authenticated from SiteMinder who do not exist in the portal will be imported from LDAP.

The last field defines the header SiteMinder is using to keep track of the user. The default value is already populated. If you have customized the field for your installation, enter the custom value here.

When you are finished, click *Save*. Next, let's examine how to configure portal-wide user settings.

Users

The Users page of Portal Settings has three tabs: Fields, Reserved Credentials and Default User Associations.

The Fields tab allows you to enable/disable the following fields:

- Enable/disable requiring the Terms of Use

- Enable/disable user screen names autogeneration

- Enable/disable requiring the last names

- Enable/disable the birthday field

- Enable/disable the gender field

The next tab is Reserved Credentials. You can enter screen names and email addresses here that you don't want others to use. Liferay will then prevent users from registering with these screen names and email addresses. You might use this feature to prevent users from creating IDs that look like administrative IDs or that have reserved words in their names.

The Default User Associations tab has three fields allowing you to list (one per line) sites, roles and user groups you want new users to become members of automatically. By default, Liferay assigns new users to both the Users role and the Power Users role.

If you have defined other user groups, sites or roles you want newly created users to be members of by default, enter them here. For example, you may have defined site templates in certain user groups to pre-populate end users' private pages. If there is a particular configuration you want everyone to have, you may want to enter those user groups here.

15.9   Summary

In this chapter, we began to examine Liferay's control panel. Site memberships and teams aren't the only way for portal administrators to group and manage users: organizations can be used to arrange users into hierarchical structures and user groups are a flexible way to collect groups of users that transcend organizational hierarchies. You can create roles to define permissions and scope them for the entire portal or for a particular site or organization. User groups can be assigned to roles; in this case, each member of the user group is assigned to the role.

We also looked at how to configure password policies for users. Next, we looked at the different authentication options provided by Liferay. You can configure Liferay so that users can authenticate via LDAP, CAS, Facebook, NTLM, OpenID, OpenSSO, or SiteMinder. Finally, we examined some general configuration options for the portal users. We'll continue our coverage of Liferay's Control Panel in the next chapter.

CHAPTER 16

USING THE CONTROL PANEL

In this chapter, we continue our coverage of Liferay's control panel that we began in chapter 15. We'll cover the following topics:

- Portal settings including mail host names, email notifications, identification, and display settings

- Custom fields

- Monitoring

- Plugins configuration

- Server administration, including resources, log levels, properties, captcha data migration, file uploads, mail, external services, scripts, and shutdown settings

- Portal instances

Let's begin with mail host names.

Mail Host Names

Mail Host Names appears after Authentication and Users on the Portal Settings page of the control panel. You can enter other mail host names (one per line) besides the one you configured on the General tab. This lets the portal know which mail host names are owned by your organization.

Email Notifications

There are five tabs under the Email Notifications page of Portal Settings. The Sender tab allows you to set the portal's administrative name and email address. By default, these are `Joe Bloggs` and `test@liferay.com`. You can change them to whatever you want. This name and email address will appear in the From field in all email messages sent by the portal.

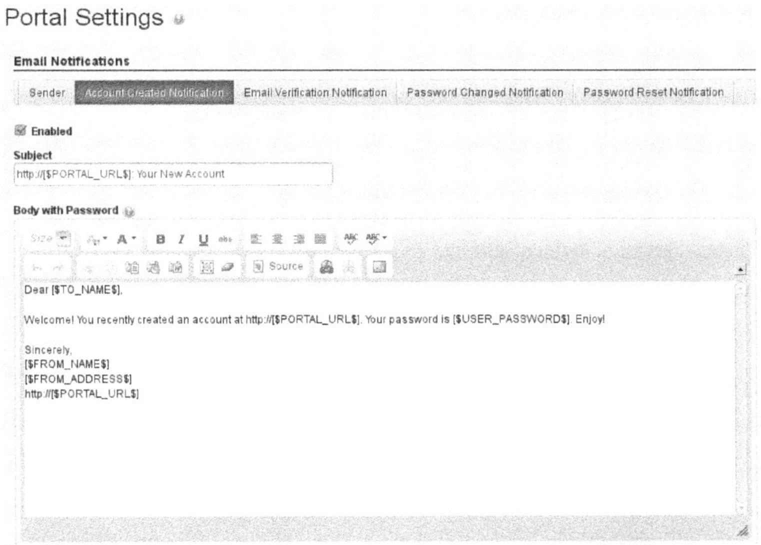

Figure 16.1: Automated Emails: Account Created Notification

The other four tabs are Account Created Notification, Email Verification Notification, Password Changed Notification and Password Reset Notification.

These tabs allow you to customize the email messages that are sent to users each
time any of those four events occur.

Definition of Terms

[$FROM_ADDRESS$]	test@liferay.com
[$FROM_NAME$]	Joe Bloggs
[$PORTAL_URL$]	localhost
[$TO_ADDRESS$]	The address of the email recipient
[TO_NAME]	The name of the email recipient
[$USER_ID$]	The user ID
[$USER_PASSWORD$]	The user password
[$USER_SCREENNAME$]	The user screen name

Figure 16.2: Definition of Terms for Automated Emails

A list of tokens, entitled "Definition of Terms," is provided so you can insert
certain values (such as the portal URL or the user ID) when you are setting up
the custom email messages.

Identification

The identification section has several links for addresses, phone numbers and
other information you can configure in your portal. This allows you to set up
contact information for the organization that owns the portal. Developers can
query for this information in their applications.

Miscellaneous: Display Settings

This section allows you to set the default portal language and the time zone.
You can also set up a portal-wide logo which appears in the top left corners of
portal pages.

Liferay's default theme is configured to display the portal logo. For custom
themes, you can choose whether or not to display the logo. Be careful to choose
an image file that fits the space. If you pick something too big, it might overlap
with the navigation. Next, let's look at how to customize different types of
portal assets using custom fields.

16.1   Custom Fields

Custom fields appear beneath Portal Settings in the Portal section of the control
panel. Custom fields are a way to add attributes to many types of assets in the
portal. For example, if you're using Liferay Portal to create a site for rating

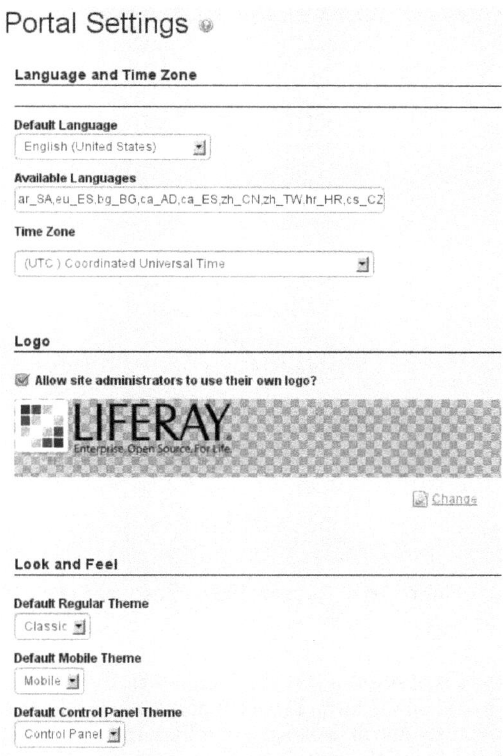

Figure 16.3: Server Configuration Miscellaneous Display Settings

books, you might assign the User object a custom field called Favorite Books. If you're using the wiki for book reviews, you might add fields for Book Title and Book Author.

To add a custom field, click on the *Custom Fields* link in the control panel Then choose a resource, click on the *Edit* link next to it and select *Add Custom Field*.

Figure 16.4: Custom Fields Resource List

From here you will need to add the custom field key. The key appears as the label for the field on the form. For some portal assets (like the User), custom fields are a separate section of the form. For others, as can be seen above, custom fields are integrated with the default fields on the form. Additionally, developers can access custom fields programatically through the `<liferay-ui:custom-attribute />` tag.

You can create fields of many different types: text fields (indexed or secret), integers, selection of multiple values and more. Once you've created a field, you cannot change its type.

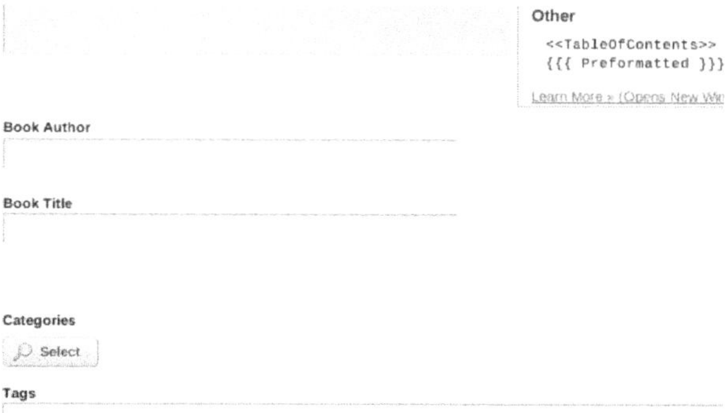

Figure 16.5: Custom Fields Integrated with the Rest of the Fields on the Wiki Form

16.2 Monitoring

The next link on the left side of the control panel is for monitoring. You can use the Monitoring page to view all of the live sessions in the portal. For performance reasons, this setting is usually turned off in production.

16.3 Plugins Configuration

The Plugins Configuration page contains tabs for three types of plugins: portlets, themes and layouts. You can use these tabs to view which roles can add plugins to pages or you can make the plugins active or inactive.

Note that this is for basic configuration: if you want to view the existing permission configuration for a given portlet and/or modify that configuration for existing roles, this is where you can do that. If you need to add permissions to new roles for a given portlet, use the Roles section of the control panel and the *Actions → Define Permissions* button. Next, let's look at how to apply server configurations.

16.4   Server Administration

The Server Administration page of the control panel lets you perform various tasks related to the portal server itself, as opposed to the resources in the portal. Clicking the link makes this clear: you're immediately presented with a graph showing the resources available in the JVM.

Resources

The first tab is called *Resources* . This tab contains the aforementioned graph plus several server wide actions that an administrator can execute. These are:

Garbage collection: You can send in a request to the JVM to begin the garbage collection task.

Clearing VM caches: You can send in a request to the JVM to clear a single VM cache.

Clearing caches across the cluster: You can send in a request to the JVM to clear content cached across the entire cluster.

Clearing database caches: You can send in a request to the JVM to clear the database cache.

Reindex all search indexes: You can send in a request to regenerate all search indexes. If you are not using a Solr search server this will impact portal performance so try to do this at non-peak times.

Reset Document Library preview and thumbnail files: You can send in a request to reset the preview and thumbnail files for each item in your portal's Documents and Media libraries.

Generate Thread Dump: If you are performance testing, you can generate a thread dump which can be examined later to determine if there are any deadlocks and where they might be.

Verify database tables of all plugins: Checks all tables against their indexes for accuracy of data retrieval.

Clean up Permissions: This process removes the assignment of some permissions on the Guest, User and Power User roles to simplify the management of "User Customizable Pages". Notably, "Add To Page" permissions is removed from the Guest and User roles for all portlets. Likewise the same permission is reduced in scope for Power Users from portal wide to scoped to "User Personal Site."

Log Levels

The Log Levels tab of the Server Administration page allows you to dynamically modify the log levels for any class hierarchy in the portal. If you have custom code you have deployed which isn't in the list, you can use the *Add Category* tab to add it. If you change the log level near the top of the class hierarchy (such as at com.liferay), all the classes under that hierarchy will have their log levels changed. If you are testing something specific, it is much better to be as specific as you can when you change log levels. Modifying them too high in the hierarchy generates a lot more log messages than you need.

Properties

Liferay and the JVM contain many settings which are defined as properties. There are two subtabs of the properties tab of the Server Administration page: one showing system properties and one showing portal properties.

The system properties tab shows an exhaustive list of system properties for the JVM, as well as many Liferay system properties. This information can be used for debugging purposes or to check the configuration of the currently running portal.

The portal properties tab tab shows an exhaustive list of the portal properties. These properties can be customized; you can peruse the full list of customizable properties in chapter 20. If you need to check the current value of a particular property, it can be viewed from this screen without having to shut down the portal or open any properties files.

Captcha

By default, Liferay ships with its own simple captcha service which is designed to thwart bots from registering for accounts on sites powered by Liferay. If you want to instead use Google's reCaptcha service, you can enable this setting from the Captcha tab of the Server Administration page.

Simply check the *Enable ReCaptcha* box and enter your public and private keys into the provided fields, then click *Save*. Liferay Portal will then use reCaptcha instead of simple captcha.

Data Migration

If you are upgrading from a previous release of Liferay Portal or if you need to migrate your data from one system to another, the Data Migration tab helps you to do that without your developers having to write custom scripts.

The first section lets you copy your entire Liferay database from the current database under which it is running to the database you specify in this set of fields. You'll need to enter the driver class name (and the driver will need to be on Liferay's classpath), the JDBC URL of the database to which you'll be copying your data and the credentials of a user with access to that database. Once you have all of this information entered, click *Execute* to copy the data.

The next section helps you migrate your documents. If you want to move off of the Jackrabbit JSR-170 repository to the file system, or to the Jackrabbit repository from the file system, or to any of the other repositories supported by the documents and media library, you can do so very easily. Make sure you have already set up your `portal-ext.properties` file so the hook is properly configured before running this migration. Select the Document Library hook that represents where you want your documents migrated and click *Execute*. Your documents will be migrated to the new repository. You can then shut down Liferay, make the new repository the default in the `portal-ext.properties` file and then restart.

Similarly, you can migrate images from the Image Gallery in the same manner.

File Uploads

Since Liferay allows users to upload files in various places, you may want to lock down the type of files and the size of files users are allowed to upload. The File Uploads tab of the Server Configuration tab lets you set the overall maximum file size and then override that size for specific applications within Liferay. You can limit the allowed file extensions generally or by application. You have a lot of flexibility as to how you want files to be managed within your portal.

Mail

Rather than using the `portal-ext.properties` file as we did in the installation chapter, you can configure a mail server from the Mail tab of the Server Configuration tab. If the portal is to receive mail (see our coverage of the Message Boards portlet in chapter 7), you can connect a POP mail server. If the portal is to send mail, which it needs to do to send notifications to users, you can connect to an SMTP server here as well and this is highly recommended.

Note that if you add your mail server settings here, they will override anything in your `portal-ext.properties` file.

External Services

Liferay Portal enables users to upload and share content via the Documents and Media library, a customizable and permissionable online repository. Users can upload files of any type to the Documents and Media library. Liferay ships with PDFBox and uses it to generate automatic previews for certain types of documents, by default. You can also install three additional tools that offer higher quality previews and document conversion functionality: OpenOffice or Libre-Office, ImageMagick and Xuggler. With Liferay configured to use these tools, you can generate automatic previews for many types of files incuding text files, office suite files, PDFs, images, audio files and videos. Users will also be able to use the conversion functionality to download documents in a variety of formats. Please see chapter 4 on Documents and Media for more information.

LibreOffice is available here: LibreOffice, ImageMagick is available here: ImageMagick and Xuggler is available here: Xuggler. Make sure to choose the correct versions of these applications for your operating system. You can build Xuggler 3.4.1012, which works with Liferay 6.1, from source or you can install it from the binaries:

- Source
- Linux (32-bit)
- Linux (64-bit)
- Mac OS X
- Windows

Once you've installed these tools, you can use the External Services tab of the control panel to configure Liferay to use them.

OpenOffice/LibreOffice configuration

OpenOffice and LibreOffice are open source office suites which are usually run in graphical mode to create documents but they can also be run in "server" mode. When run in server mode, OpenOffice and LibreOffice can be used to convert documents to and from all of the file types it supports. Once configured, Liferay makes use of this feature to automatically convert content on the fly. You can install OpenOffice or LibreOffice on the same machine upon which Liferay is running or you can connect to a separate host.

If you've installed OpenOffice or LibreOffice on the same machine that's running Liferay, you can start it in server mode with the following command:

```
soffice --headless --accept="socket,host=127.0.0.1,port=8100;urp;"
--nofirststartwizard
```

Once OpenOffice or LibreOffice has been installed and is running in server mode, you can configure Liferay to use it either in your `portal-ext.properties` file or from the control panel. To enable OpenOffice/LibreOffice in your `portal-ext.properties` file, add the following line:

```
openoffice.server.enabled=true
```

If OpenOffice or LibreOffice is running on another server or on a non-default port, you must also specify these values. The default values are as follows:

```
openoffice.server.host=127.0.0.1
openoffice.server.port=8100
```

By default, when Liferay uses OpenOffice or LibreOffice to perform conversions, it uses a cache. The first time a document is converted, a copy is saved in the Liferay temp folder `/liferay/document_conversion/`. When Liferay receives a conversion request, it checks this folder to see if the converted document already exists. If the converted document is found, Liferay returns it to the user. Otherwise, it performs a fresh conversion and saves a copy in the temp folder. If the cache is turned off, Liferay will always regenerate the file regardless of whether a previously existing conversion already exists in the temp folder. You can turn the cache off by setting the following property:

```
openoffice.cache.enabled=false
```

To configure Liferay to use OpenOffice/LibreOffice from the control panel, navigate to the *Server Administration → External Services* page and check the *Enabled* box for OpenOffice. If OpenOffice/LibreOffice is running on a non-default port, you must also specify the port number. By default, OpenOffice runs on port 8100, which is the default port in the control panel. If you have something else running on this port, find an open port and specify it both in the command to start OpenOffice/LibreOffice in server mode and on the control panel's External Services configuration page. When you are finished, click *Save*. Now Liferay can perform many types of document conversions.

ImageMagick configuration

Once you've installed the correct version of *ImageMagick* for your operating system, which should include the installation of Ghostscript, you need to configure Liferay to use ImageMagick. You can do this either in your `portal-ext.properties` file or from the control panel. To enable ImageMagick in your `portal-ext.properties` file, add the following lines and make sure the search path points to the directories for the ImageMagick and Ghostscript executables. You may also need to configure the path for fonts used by Ghostscript when in Mac or Unix environments.

```
imagemagick.enabled=true
imagemagick.global.search.path[apple]=/opt/local/bin:/opt/local/share     \
    /ghostscript/fonts:/opt/local/share/fonts/urw-fonts
imagemagick.global.search.path[unix]=/usr/local/bin:/usr/local/share/ghostscript/fonts:    \
    /usr/local/share/fonts/urw-fonts
imagemagick.global.search.path[windows]=C:\\Program Files\\ImageMagick
```

To enable ImageMagick from the control panel, navigate to the *Server Administration → External Services* page, check the *Enabled* checkbox for ImageMagick and verify the paths to the ImageMagick and Ghostscript executables are correct.

Note that some older versions of ImageMagick are unable to properly run with Liferay. If this is the case, update to the latest version (ImageMagick 6.7.9-6 2012-09-25 Q16 or later). To check for the latest ImageMagick versions, visit their web site.[1] See Liferay's issues ticketing system[2] for information on efforts to identify incompatible application versions with Liferay.

Xuggler configuration

Once you've installed the correct version of *Xuggler* for your operating system, you need to configure your environment variables. Depending on where you installed Xuggler, a configuration similar to the following should work on Unix-like systems:

```
export XUGGLE_HOME=/usr/local/xuggler
export LD_LIBRARY_PATH=$XUGGLE_HOME/lib:$LD_LIBRARY_PATH
export PATH=$XUGGLE_HOME/bin:$PATH
```

Once your environment variables are set up correctly, you can configure Liferay to use Xuggler either in your `portal-properties` file or from the control

---

[1] http://www.imagemagick.org/script/binary-releases.php
[2] http://issues.liferay.com/browse/LPS-30291

panel. If you'd like to use your portal-ext.properties file, just add the following line:

```
xuggler.enabled=true
```

To configure Liferay to use Xuggler in the control panel, navigate to the *Server Administration → External Services* page and check *Enabled.* That's it! You've successfully configured the Documents and Media library to use Xuggler for audio and video files.

Script

Liferay includes a scripting console which lets administrators execute migration or management code instantly. Several scripting languages are supported, including JavaScript, Groovy, Python, Ruby and Beanshell. For further information about Liferay's APIs, see the JavaDoc or *Liferay in Action.*

Shutdown

If you ever need to shut down your Liferay Portal server while users are logged in, you can use the Shutdown tab to inform your logged-in users of the impending shutdown. You can define the number of minutes until the shutdown and a custom message that will be displayed.

Users will see your message at the top of their portal pages for the duration of time you specified. When the time expires, all portal pages will display a message saying the portal has been shut down. At this point, the server will need to be restarted to restore access. Next, let's examine how to manage multiple portal instances.

16.5   Portal Instances

Liferay Portal allows you to run more than one portal instance on a single server. The Portal Instances page of the control panel lets you manage these instances. Data for each portal instance are kept separate from every other portal instance. All portal data, however, is kept in the same database.

Each portal instance requires its own domain name. Liferay will direct users to the proper portal instance based on this domain name. So before you configure an instance, configure its domain name in your network first. When you're ready to add an instance, click the *Add* button here.

You'll be prompted for four fields and a check box:

Web ID: A general convention is to use the domain name for this. It's a user-generated ID for the instance.

Virtual Host: Put the domain name you configured in your network here. When **users** are directed to your Liferay server via this domain name, Liferay will then be able to send them to the proper portal instance.

Mail Domain: Enter the domain name for the mail host for this instance. Liferay will use this to send email notifications from the portal.

Max Users: Enter the maximum numbers of user accounts you would like your portal instance to support.

Active: Use this check box to choose whether to create an active or an inactive portal instance.

When you are finished filling out the form, click *Save*. Now navigate to the portal using your new domain name. You will see you are brought to what looks like a clean install of Liferay. This is your new portal instance which can now be configured any way you like.

16.6   Plugins Installation

The *Plugins Installation* page of the control panel shows all of the plugins currently installed. These are divided into tabs for portlets, themes, layout templates, hook plugins and web plugins. If you want to install a new plugin, click the *Install More Portlets* button. You will then be brought to the Plugin Installer, where you can browse Liferay's repository of portlets or install your own plugins. We covered the plugins installer and explained how to install plugins manually in chapter 13.

16.7   Summary

In this chapter, we finished our overview of Liferay's control panel that we began in chapter 15. We saw how to configure mail host names, email notifications, identification, and portal display settings. We showed how you add custom fields to various portal entities such as users, pages, documents, wiki articles, message board posts, and more.

Next, we saw how to view and configure overall server settings. We saw how to view the memory currently being used by the server, as well as how to initiate garbage collection, a thread dump, search engine re-indexing and the clearing of various caches. We learned how to debug parts of the portal by changing log levels and by viewing the various properties defined in the portal.

Finally, we learned how to properly notify users that the portal is about to shut down and how to set up exernal services like OpenOffice integration. We looked at how to create multiple portal instances on a single installation of Liferay and we showed how to view currently installed plugins.

We hope this information helps you become an effective Liferay Portal Administrator.

CHAPTER 17

ADVANCED PORTAL OPERATION

In this chapter we discuss several advanced features of Liferay Portal, including audit trails and portal maintainence, backup, and logging. Audit trails allow portal administrators to track the activities of portal users–this can be very useful for troubleshooting or figuring out who's resposible for certain actions that have taken place on your portal. It's generally not much more complicated to maintain a running Liferay instance than it is to maintain the application server upon which it's running. However, Liferay provides tools for logging, patching, and upgrading Liferay that you should know how to use. It's also important to follow secure backup procedures to protect your Liferay instance's source code, database, and properties files.

We'll discuss the following topics in this section:

- Audit trails

- Liferay Monitoring using Google Analytics

- Backing Up a Liferay Installation

- Changing Logging Levels

- Patching Liferay

- Upgrading Liferay

Let's get started with audit trails.

17.1 Audit Trails

EE Only Feature

You've just finished lunch and are ready to get back to work. You have a site in Liferay you use to manage your project, and before you left, you were about to create a folder in your Documents and Media library for sharing some requirements documentation. Sitting down at your desk, you navigate to the repository and attempt to create the folder.

You do not have permission to perform this action, Liferay helpfully tells you.

"*What?*" you blurt accidentally in surprise. "This is *my* project!"

"Ah, you too?" asks a co-worker helpfully from over the cube wall. "I lost access to a wiki I was updating just a few minutes ago. I was about to enter a support ticket for it."

"Forget the ticket. Let's go see the portal admin now," you say.

And off you go, two floors down, to the far end of the building where, as you approach, you can already hear stress in the portal admin's voice as he tries to reassure someone on the phone.

"Yes, Mr. Jones. Yes, I'll fix it." (*Jones? The president of the company?* goes through your mind.) "I'll get on it right away, Mr. Jones. It was just a mistake; I'll fix it. Thank you, Mr. Jones," and he hangs up the phone.

"Problems?" you ask the portal admin, whose name is Harry. He does look rather harried.

"Yeah, Tom," he says. "Somebody changed a bunch of permissions in the portal–it wasn't me. I'm assuming you and Dick are here because of the same problem?"

"Yup," you say. "I lost access to a document repository folder."

"And I lost access to a wiki," Dick says helpfully.

"It was probably due to some site membership change. Let's take a look at the audit portlet in the control panel and see what happened."

When in the course of human events it becomes necessary to see what users are doing on your portal, you'll find Liferay makes this easy. If you're a Liferay Enterprise Edition customer, you have access to two plugins–a hook and a portlet–that, in combination with some settings in `portal-ext.properties`, enable you to see all the activity that occurs in your portal. Using this, you can quickly find out what changes were made and by whom. If you've delegated permission granting to any group of people, this is an essential feature you're likely to use.

We'll come back to Tom, Dick and Harry's story later in the chapter. For now, let's look at how to install Liferay's audit plugins so you can do the same thing Harry's about to do.

Installing and configuring the audit plugins

Liferay's audit functionality is composed of two parts: a back-end piece that hooks into Liferay events and a front-end piece that gives you an interface to see what's happening. Both of these are available as EE-only plugins in the Customer Portal or Liferay Marketplace, and you'll need to install both to get audit functionality working (plugins installation is covered in chapter 13).

Once installed, there are two properties in your `portal-ext.properties` file which you can use to tweak the settings.

com.liferay.portal.servlet.filters.audit.AuditFilter: By default, this is set to `false`, because the audit plugins aren't installed by default. When you set it to `true`, the audit hook is able to capture more information about events, such as the client host and the client's IP address.

audit.message.com.liferay.portal.model.Layout.VIEW: In the code, pages are *layouts*. Setting this to `true`, therefore, records audit events for page views. It's turned off by default because this may be too fine-grained for most installations.

Once you've decided if you're going to use one or both of the two settings above, place them in your `portal-ext.properties` file and restart your Liferay server. Once it comes up, audit events are captured by Liferay, and you'll be able to use them to see what's happening in your portal.

Using audit events

Now that you're capturing audit events, it's easy to use them to view activities in your portal. Navigate to the control panel and you'll find a new entry in the *Portal* section labeled *Audit Reports* (see figure 17.1).

Figure 17.1: Once the Audit Reports plugins are installed, an entry appears in the control panel.

Clicking the entry shows you a list of the events Liferay has already captured (see figure 17.2), along with an interface for searching for events. You can browse the list if you want, but it's likely you'll need to use the search to find what you're looking for.

Figure 17.2 shows Stephen Professor logged in and did some things on the site. To see the detail of any of these events, all you need to do is click one to see more information. You'll then see something like figure 17.3.

As you can see, depending on how many users you have in your portal, this list can get populated very quickly. For this reason, it's a good idea to keep the `audit.message.com.liferay.portal.model.Layout.VIEW` property set to `false`. This way, you don't clutter up your audit events with multiple page view events, which will definitely be the most often triggered event in your portal.

Now that you know how to browse and view audit events, let's look at searching for specific events.

Viewing audit reports

Finding what you want in a big list of events is, to use the expression, like searching for a needle in a haystack. This is why the audit portlet gives you a robust searching mechanism. By default, it looks pretty simple: there's only a single field for searching. Clicking the *advanced* link, however, reveals a search dialog broken out by various fields you can use in your search.

Figure 17.2: Liferay captures and stores events as soon as the audit plugins are installed.

Let's look at the options we have for search.

Match: You can match all fields you've specified or any single field.

User ID: Specify the user ID you'd like to search for. This would be the user who performed some action in the portal you'd like to audit.

User Name: Specify the user name you'd like to search for. This is often easier than searching for a user ID, especially if you don't have access to the Liferay database to find the user ID.

Resource ID: Specify the ID of the resource that was modified or viewed in this audit record.

Resource Name: Specify the name of the resource that was modified or viewed in this audit record. For example, you could search for User resources to see if someone modified a user's account.

Resource Action: Specify an action that was performed on the resource. This could be any one of the following: add, `assign`, `delete`, `impersonate`, `login`, `login_failure`, `logout`, `unassign`, or `update`.

Session ID: Specify the session ID to search for. You'd use this if you were correlating a session ID from your web server logs with activity in Liferay.

Event ID	10517
Create Date	9/9/11 8:01 PM

User ID	10433
User Name	Stephen Professor

Resource ID	10433
Resource Name	User (com.liferay.portal.model.User)
Resource Action	Update (UPDATE)

Client Host	127.0.0.1
Client IP	127.0.0.1
Server Name	localhost
Session ID	73E770750392641CD7811182E120A885
Additional Information	{"attributes":[{"newValue":"true","name":"agreedToTermsOfUse","oldValue":"false"}]}

Figure 17.3: Clicking an event in the list shows the details of that event.
This event shows it must've been Stephen Professor's first time logging
into the site, because he's accepting the terms of use.

Client IP: Specify the IP address of the client that performed the activity you
wish to audit.

Client Host: Specify the host name of the client that performed the activity
you wish to audit.

Server Name: Specify the server name upon which the activity occurred. If
you're using a cluster, each member of the cluster can be individually queried.

Server Port: Specify the server port upon which the activity occurred. You'd
need this if you run a "vertical" cluster of multiple VMs on the same machine.

Start Date: Specify the low end of the date range you wish to search.

End Date: Specify the high end of the date range you wish to search.

Using this form, if you wanted to check to see if someone in the portal unas-
signed a user from a particular role, you might search for a resource name of
user and a resource action of *unassign*. The results of such a search might look
something like figure 17.4.

Once you have the results of your search, you can click on any of the records
returned to see the detail page for that record. Figure 17.5 shows, in this particular case, the default administrative user removed Stephen Professor from the

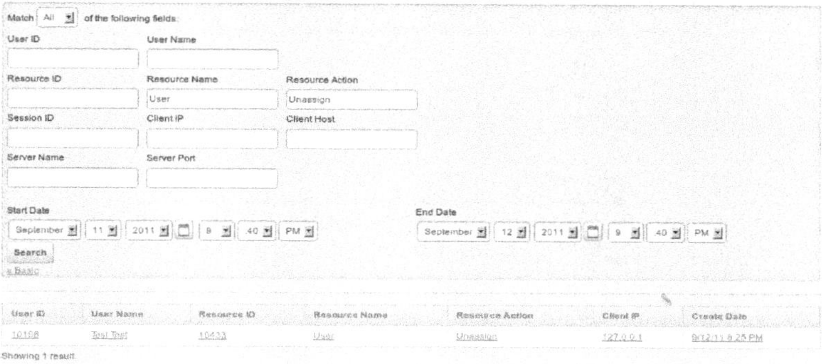

Figure 17.4: Searching audit events is easy with the search form provided by the audit portlet. You can quickly drill down to find the types of events you're looking for.

role of Power User.

As you can see, Liferay's audit portlets give you a lot of power to see what's happening in your portal. You can use this information to troubleshoot problems, determine ownership of particular actions, or, as Harry is about to do, find out who made permission changes they weren't supposed to make.

Conclusion of the Story

"Okay," says Harry, "let's fire up Liferay's audit system and see if we can figure out what happened."

You and Dick stand behind Harry's chair and watch as he enters a query into a form on the audit portlet. Clicking *search*, the screen fills up with audit events.

"Wow, that's a lot of unassign events." Harry says. "And look who the culprit is," he adds sarcastically.

"Who's Melvin Dooitrong?" Dick asks.

"That's my new intern," Harry says. "I'm gonna kill him." Harry pushes out his chair and walks down the row of cubes to the end, where a kid no more than 20 years old with disheveled hair sits, earbuds in his ears.

"Hey Melvin," Harry says as Melvin turns around to face him. "Didn't I ask you to move that set of users from site membership to organization member-

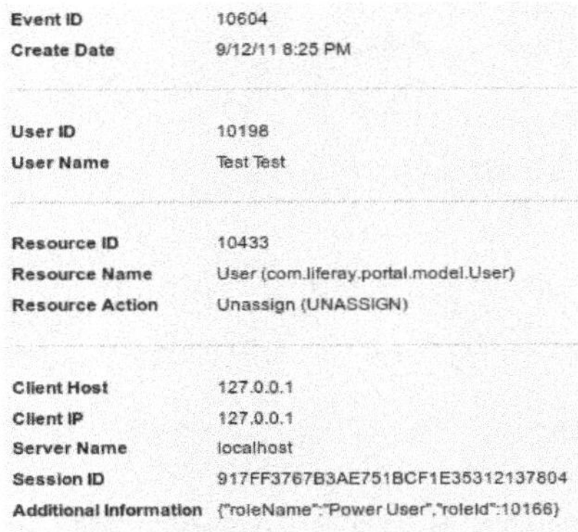

Event ID	10604
Create Date	9/12/11 8:25 PM
User ID	10198
User Name	Test Test
Resource ID	10433
Resource Name	User (com.liferay.portal.model.User)
Resource Action	Unassign (UNASSIGN)
Client Host	127.0.0.1
Client IP	127.0.0.1
Server Name	localhost
Session ID	917FF3767B3AE751BCF1E35312137804
Additional Information	{"roleName":"Power User","roleId":10166}

Figure 17.5: If you've delegated portal administration to multiple users, you can use the audit plugins to determine who made what change. And, of course, you'll never leave the default administrative user enabled in a production system, right?

ship?"

"Yeah," Melvin says, "I did that already."

"How'd you do it?"

"It was going to take a while to do it manually, so I wrote a script and executed it in the scripting host," Melvin replies, matter-of-factly.

"You did, did you? Well, guess what? Your script removed *everybody* from *all* sites."

"*What?*"

"Yeah, and now you're going to start adding them back, one by one, manually, starting with Mr. Jones...."

Tom and Dick back away slowly from Melvin's cube as Harry and Melvin continue to have their—let's call it a discussion. One thing is clear: they're having a better day than Melvin is.

Now that we've seen how you can use audit trails, let's look at some tools and best practices for maintaining your Liferay installation.

17.2 Liferay monitoring using Google Analytics

Liferay includes built-in support for Google Analytics, allowing administrators to make use of Google's tool set for analyzing site traffic data. When you sign up for Google Analytics, a snippet of code is provided which needs to be added to your web pages to allow Google's system to register the page hit. It can be a tedious process to add this code to every page on a site, especially if it's a large site and there is a lot of user-generated content.

This problem can be solved in Liferay by putting Google's code into a custom theme written specifically for the web site on which the portal is running. Doing this, however, requires a theme developer to make specific changes to the theme and it prevents users from using the many themes that are freely available for Liferay "out of the box."

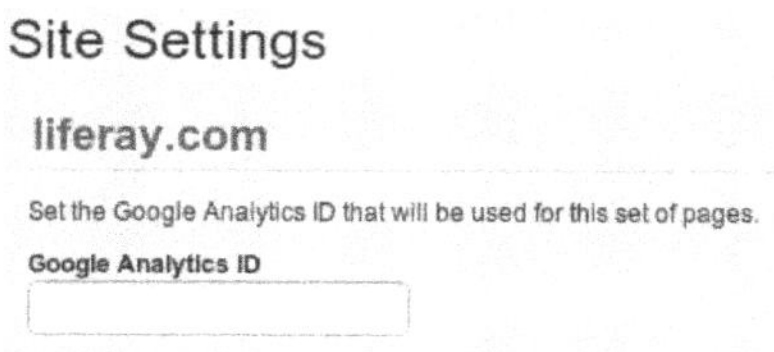

Site Settings

liferay.com

Set the Google Analytics ID that will be used for this set of pages.

Google Analytics ID

Figure 17.6: Setting up Google Analytics for your site is very easy: sign up for the ID and then enter it into this field.

Because of this, support for Google Analytics has been built into Liferay, and can be turned on through a simple user interface. This allows Liferay administrators to make use of Google Analytics on a community by community basis and turn it on and off when needed.

To enable Google Analytics support, go to *Site Settings* in the control panel, and then select *Analytics* on the right. You'll see a very simple form, pictured below.

Put your Google Analytics ID (which should have been provided to you when you signed up for the service) in the field and click *Save*. All the pages in the community you selected will now have the Google Analytics code in them and will be tracked.

This is a fairly simple procedure, and it gives you the ability to take advantage of some great tools to help you visualize who's coming to your site and from where. Next, we discuss some topics germane to maintaining your Liferay installation as it's used. Let's start with backup.

17.3 Backing up a Liferay installation

Once you have an installation of Liferay Portal running, you'll want to have proper backup procedures in place in case of a catastrophic hardware failure of some kind. Liferay isn't very different from any other application that may be running on your application server. Nevertheless, there are some specific components you should include in your backup plan.

Backing up source code

If you have extended Liferay or have written any plugins, they should be stored in a source code repository such as Git, Subversion, or CVS, unless you're Linus Torvalds, and then tarballs are okay too (that's a joke). Your source code repository should be backed up on a regular basis to preserve your ongoing work. This probably goes without saying in your organization, as nobody wants to lose source code that's taken months to produce, but we thought we should mention it anyway.

If you're extending Liferay with an Ext plugin, you'll want to make sure you also store the version of the Liferay source on which your extension environment is based. This allows your developers convenient access to all the tools they need to build your extension and deploy it to a server.

Let's look at the items that need to be backed up in your Liferay installation.

Backing up Liferay's file system

Liferay's configuration file, `portal-ext.properties`, gets stored in the *Liferay Home* folder, which is generally one folder up from where your application server is installed (see chapter 14 for specific details for your application server). At a minimum, this file should be backed up, but it is generally best to back up your whole application server.

If you've followed the non-plugin procedure (see chapter 19) to modify your Ehcache configuration, you'll have cache configuration files in the deploy location of Liferay. You'll need to back up this location. If you're using the plugin procedure (i.e., the recommended procedure), your cache configuration settings are stored in your source code repository, which is backed up separately.

Liferay stores configuration files, search indexes, and cache information in a folder called `data` in Liferay Home. If you're using the File System store or the Advanced File System store, the media repository is stored here (by default) too. You should always back up the contents of your Liferay Home folder.

If you've modified the location where the Document Library stores files, you should also back up this location.

That about covers the file system locations Liferay uses. Next, let's discuss how to back up Liferay's database.

Backing up Liferay's database

Liferay's database is the central repository for all of the Portal's information and is the most important component that needs to be backed up. You can do this by backing up the database live (if your database allows this) or by exporting the database and then backing up the exported file. For example, MySQL ships with a `mysqldump` utility which allows you to export the entire database and data into a large SQL file. This file can then be backed up. In case of a database failure, this file can be used to recreate the state of the database at the time the dump was created.

If you're using Liferay's Documents and Media Library with the Jackrabbit JSR-170 repository to store documents in a database, the Jackrabbit database should be backed up also. If you've placed your search index into a database (not recommended; see chapter 19 for information on using Cluster Link or Solr), that database should be backed up as well.

Search indexes can be backed up as well, if you wish to avoid reindexing your entire portal after you do your restore. This is easiest to do if you have a separate Solr environment upon which your index is stored. If you're in a clustered configuration and you're replicating indexes, you'll need to back up each index replica.

Restoring your application server, your Liferay Home folder, the locations of any file system-based media repositories, and your database from a backup system should give you a functioning portal. Restoring search indexes should avoid the need to reindex when you bring your site back up after a catastrophic failure. Good, consistent backup procedures are key to successfully recovering from a hardware failure.

But what about maintenance while your server is running? Liferay lets you view a lot of what is going on through its logging system.

17.4   Liferay's Logging System

Liferay uses Log4j extensively to implement logging for nearly every class in the portal. If you need to debug something specific while the system is running, you can use the control panel to set logging levels by class dynamically.

To view the log levels, go to the control panel, click *Server Administration* in the Server section, and then click the *Log Levels* tab.

A paginated list of logging categories appears. These categories correspond to Liferay classes that have log messages in them. By default, all categories are set to display messages only if there is an error that occurs in the class. This is why you see ERROR displayed in all of the drop-down list boxes on the right side of the portlet.

Each category is filtered by its place in the class hierarchy. For example, if you wanted to see logging for a specific class that is registered in Liferay, you would browse to that specific class and change its log level to something that is more descriptive, such as DEBUG. Once you click the *Save* button at the bottom of the list, you'll start seeing DEBUG messages from that class in your application server's log file.

If you're not sure which class you want to see log messages for, you can find a place higher up in the hierarchy and select the package name instead of an individual class name. If you do this, messages for every class lower in the hierarchy will be displayed in your application server's log file.

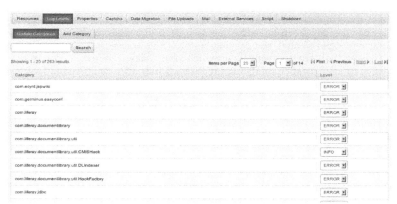

Figure 17.7: Log levels can be dynamically changed at runtime, whenever you need to debug an issue.

Be careful when you do this. If you set the log level to DEBUG somewhere near the top of the hierarchy (such as `com.liferay`, for example), you may wind up with a lot of messages in your log file. This could make it difficult to find the one you were looking for, and causes the server to do more work writing messages to the log.

If you want to set the log level for one of your own classes in a deployed plugin, you can register that class with Liferay to can control the log levels more easily, so long as your class uses Log4J to do its logging.

You will first need to implement Log4J logging in your class, with a statement such as the following (taken from Liferay's `JCRStore` class):

```
private static Log _log = LogFactory.getLog(JCRStore.class);
```

You would then use this `_log` variable to create log messages in your code for the various logging levels:

```
_log.error("Reindexing " + node.getName(), e1);
```

To enable your logging messages to appear in your server's log file via the control panel, click the *Add Category* tab on the same *Log Levels* page.

Figure 17.8: Adding your own logging classes is as simple as specifying it in this field.

You'll see you can add a logging category. Put in the fully qualified name of your class or of the package that contains the classes whose log messages you want to view, choose a log level, then click the *Save* button. You will now start to see log messages from your own class or classes in the server's log file.

Logs are great for figuring out issues in production. But what if Liferay contacts you via its support channel with a bug fix or a security enhancement? Read on to learn how to patch Liferay.

17.5   Patching Liferay

While we strive for perfection with every release of Liferay Portal, the reality of the human condition dictates that releases of the product may not be as perfect as originally intended. But we've planned for that. Included with every Liferay

EE Only Feature

bundle is a patching tool that can handle the installation of two types of patches: hot fixes and fix packs.

A hot fix is provided to a customer when a customer contacts Liferay about an issue, and Liferay's support team–working with the customer–determines that the problem is indeed an issue with the product that needs to be fixed. Support fixes the bug and provides a hot fix to the customer immediately. This is a short-term fix that solves the issue for the customer as quickly as possible

On a regular schedule, these hot fixes are bundled together into fix packs. Fix packs are provided to all of Liferay's customers and are component-based. This means any issues with the content management system will be bundled together separately from issues with another component, such as the message boards. This lets you determine which patches are critical and which are not, based on your usage. Of course, if Liferay issues a security advisory, that's something you're always going to want to patch.

Now that you know what patching is all about, let's check out the tool.

Installing the patching tool

If you're using a Liferay bundle, congratulations! The patching tool is already installed. Your job isn't done yet, however, because Liferay *might* have updated the patching tool. Always check the Customer Portal to see if the patching tool has been updated first. But even if you forget to check, the patching tool will tell you if it needs to be updated when you run it. A lot of planning and forethought has gone into the patching system to make it run as smoothly as possible.

You follow the same procedure whether you're installing or upgrading the patching tool. Once you've obtained it from the customer portal, unzip it to the Liferay Home folder. This is the folder where you've placed your `por-tal-ext.properties` file and where by default the `data` folder resides. This is generally one folder up from where your application server is installed, but some application servers are different. If you don't know where Liferay Home is on your system, check chapter 14 to see where this folder is for your specific application server.

If you're upgrading the patching tool, all you need to do is unzip the new version on top of the old version. Note that if you're doing this on LUM (Linux, Unix, Mac) machines, you'll need to make the `patching-tool.sh` script executable.

After the patching tool is installed, you need to let it auto-discover your Liferay installation. Then it will determine what your release level is and what your application server environment is. This is a simple command to run on LUM:

```
./patching-tool.sh auto-discovery
```

or on Windows:

```
patching-tool auto-discovery
```

From here on, for brevity we'll use the LUM version of the command. Why? Because Liferay is open source; there's no open source variant of Windows (ReactOS is still in alpha, so it doesn't count); and therefore my (RS) unscientific impression is that more people will run Liferay on open source technology than not. If I'm wrong, I'm wrong, but there are still many other examples of documentation that defaults to Windows, so we still get to be different.

If you've installed the patching tool in a non-standard location, you'll have to give this command another parameter to point it to your Liferay installation. For example, if you've installed a Liferay/Tomcat bundle in **/opt/Liferay**, you'd issue this command:

```
./patching-tool.sh auto-discovery /opt/Liferay/tomcat-7.0.21
```

In all, this is pretty simple. Now let's see how to use the patching tool to get your patches installed.

Installing patches

The absolute first thing you must do when installing one or more patches is to shut down your server. On Windows operating systems, files that are in use are locked by the OS, and won't be patched. On LUM systems, you can generally replace files that are running, but of course that still leaves the old ones loaded in memory. So your best bet is to shut down the application server that's running Liferay before you install a patch.

Liferay distributes patches as `.zip` files, whether they are hot fixes or fix packs. When you receive one, either via a LESA ticket (hot fix) or through downloading a fix pack from the customer portal, you'll need to place it in the `patches` folder, which is inside the patching tool's home folder. Once you've done that, it's a simple matter to install it. First, execute

```
./patching-tool.sh info
```

This shows you a list of patches you've already installed, along with a list of patches that *can* be installed, from what's in the `patches` folder. To install the available patches, issue the following command:

```
./patching-tool.sh install
```

Your patches are now installed. You can verify this by using the `./patching-tool.sh info` command, which now shows your patch in the list of installed patches. Let's look now at how you'd manage your patches.

Handling hot fixes and patches

As stated above, hot fixes are short term fixes provided as quickly as possible and fix packs are larger bundles of hot fixes provided to all customers at regular intervals. If you already have a hot fix installed, and the fix pack which contains that hot fix is released, you can rest assured the patching tool will manage this for you. Fix packs always supercede hot fixes, so when you install your fix pack, the hot fix that it already contains is uninstalled, and the fix pack version is installed in its place.

Sometimes there can be a fix to a fix pack. This is also handled automatically. If a new version of a fix pack is released, you can use the patching tool to install it. The patching tool uninstalls the old fix pack and installs the new version in its place.

Fix pack dependencies

Some fix packs require other fix packs to be installed first. If you attempt to install a fix pack that depends on another fix pack, the patching tool will notify you of this so you can go to the customer portal and obtain the fix pack dependency. Once all the necessary fix packs are available in the `patches` folder, the patching tool will install them.

The patching tool can also remove patches.

Removing or reverting patches

Have you noticed that the patching tool only seems to have an `install` command? This is because patches are managed not by the command, but by what appears in the `patches` folder. You manage the patches you have installed by adding or removing patches from this folder. If you currently have a patch installed and you don't want it installed, remove it from the `patches` folder. Then run the `./patching-tool.sh install` command, and the patch is removed.

If you want to remove all patches you've installed, use the

```
./patching-tool.sh revert
```

command. This removes all patches from your installation.

What we've described so far is the simplest way to use the patching tool, but you can also use the patching tool in the most complex, multi-VM, clustered environments. This is done by using profiles.

Using profiles with the patching tool

When you ran the auto-discovery task after installing the patching tool, it created a default profile that points to the application server it discovered. This is the easiest way to use the patching tool, and is great for smaller, single server installations. But we realize many Liferay installations are sized accordingly to serve millions of pages per day, and the patching tool has been designed for this as well. So if you're running a small, medium, or large cluster of Liferay machines, you can use the patching tool to manage all of them using profiles.

The auto-discovery task creates a properties file called `default.properties`. This file contains the detected configuration for your application server. But you're not limited to only one server which the tool can detect. You can have it auto-discover other runtimes, or you can manually create new profiles yourself.

To have the patching tool auto-discover other runtimes, you'll need to use a few more command line parameters:

```
./patching-tool.sh [name of profile] auto-discovery [path/to/runtime]
```

This will run the same discovery process, but on a path you choose, and the profile information will go into a `[your profile name].properties` file.

Alternatively, you can manually create your profiles. Using a text editor, create a `[profile name].properties` file in the same folder as the patching tool script. You can place the following properties in the file:

patching.mode: This can be `binary` (the default) or `source`, if you're patching the source tree you're working with. Liferay patches contain both binary and source patches. If your development team is extending Liferay, you'll want to provide the patches you install to your development team so they can patch their source tree.

jdk.version: Patches are compiled for both JDK 5 and JDK 6. Specify the one (either `jdk5` or `jdk6`) your application server is running against.

patches.folder: Specify the location where you'll copy your patches. By default, this is `./patches`.

war.path: No, no one's angry. This is a property for which you specify the location of the Liferay installation inside your application server. Alternatively, you can specify a .war file here, and you'll be able to patch a Liferay .war for installation to your application server.

global.lib.path: Specify the location where .jar files on the global classpath are stored. If you're not sure, search for your `portal-service.jar` file; it's on the global classpath. This property is only valid if your `patching.mode` is `binary`.

source.path: Specify the location of your Liferay source tree. This property is only valid if your `patching.mode` is `source`.

You can have as many profiles as you want, and use the same patching tool to patch all of them. This helps to keep all your installations in sync.

Now that you know how to patch an existing installation of Liferay, let's turn to how you'd upgrade Liferay from an older release to the current release.

17.6   Upgrading Liferay

Liferay upgrades are fairly straightforward. A consistent set of steps is all you need to follow to upgrade a standard Liferay installation. Things do get more complicated if your organization has used Ext plugins to customize Liferay. It's possible that API changes in the new version will break your existing code. This, however, is usually pretty easy for your developers to fix. Portlet plugins which use Liferay APIs should be reviewed and their services rebuilt against the new release. Theme plugins may require some modifications to take advantage of new features, and if they're using Liferay APIs, they should be reviewed. Much effort has been made to make upgrades as painless as possible; however, this is not a guarantee everything will work without modification. Ext plugins are the most complicating factor in an upgrade, so it is important to test as much as possible.

As a general rule, you can upgrade from one major release to the next major release. For example, you can upgrade directly from Liferay 5.2.x to 6.0.x, but not from 5.2.x to 6.1.x. If you need to upgrade over several major releases, you'll need to run the upgrade procedure for each major release until you reach the release you want. This doesn't mean you need to run the procedure for every point release or service pack; you only need to run the procedure for the major releases. A good practice is to use the latest version of each major release to upgrade your system.

Now that we've gotten the general philosophy of upgrading out of the way, let's outline the procedure you'll undergo for upgrading a Liferay 6.0 installation to a 6.1 installation. If you're running a previous version of Liferay and need to upgrade to 6.0 first, please see the instructions in the previous version of this document.

Preparing to Upgrade Liferay Portal 6.0 to Liferay Portal 6.1

There are a few things you should prepare before you actually perform the upgrade. Specifically, you need to make sure you've migrated to permission algorithm 6, reviewed your image gallery usage, reviewed new Liferay 6.1 defaults, and cataloged all the plugins you have installed. After you've performed these three tasks, you're ready to upgrade. Let's look at them one by one.

Migrate to Algorithm 6

If your Liferay installation has existed for a while, you may be on a different permission algorithm than the one that's available in Liferay Portal 6.1. Permission algorithms 1-5 were deprecated in Liferay Portal 6.0, and they've now been removed in 6.1, which means you must migrate *before* you upgrade.

If you're on Liferay 5.2 or below, you need to upgrade to the latest available release of Liferay 6.0 first. Please follow the instructions in the *Liferay Portal Administrator's Guide* to do this. We will assume for the rest of this section that you have 6.0 running, and that it's configured to use an older algorithm than algorithm 6.

The first thing you need to do, if this is not done already, is to upgrade your installation to algorithm 5. If you've already done that, great! You can skip the rest of this paragraph. If not, shut down your server, edit your **portal-ext.properties** file, and modify/add the following property so that it reads like this:

```
permissions.user.check.algorithm=5
```

Restart your server. As Liferay starts, it upgrades your permissions algorithm to algorithm 5. Review your system to make sure that your permissions configuration is working properly (it should be).

Next, log in as an Administrator and navigate to the Control Panel. Go to *Server Administration* and select *Data Migration* from the menu along the top of the screen. A section entitled *Legacy Permissions Migration* appears at the bottom of the page.

Figure 17.9: Update your permissions algorithm by clicking the *Execute* button.

Algorithms 5 and 6 do not support adding permissions at the user level. If you have permissions set for individual users, the converter can simulate this for you. To do this, it auto-generates roles for each individual permission, and then assigns those roles to the users who have individualized permissions. If you have a lot of these, you'll likely want to go through and clean them up after the conversion process. To generate these roles, check the *Generate Custom Roles* box. If you do not generate the roles, all custom permissions set for individual users are discarded.

Click *Execute* to convert all existing users and roles to algorithm 6. When the process completes, shut down your server. Edit your `portal-ext.properties` file and modify the algorithm property to show that you're now using algorithm 6:

```
permissions.user.check.algorithm=6
```

Restart your server. Congratulations! You've successfully migrated your installation to use the latest, highest performing permissions algorithm. Next, you'll need to explicitly set your Image Gallery storage option.

Migrate Your Image Gallery Images

Liferay 6.1 introduces a major change to how Liferay handles files. No longer do we have a separate Document Library and Image Gallery; instead, these have been combined into Documents and Media. If you were using Liferay's Image

Gallery to store images, these can be migrated over during an upgrade, but you'll have to take some extra steps first.

In Liferay 6.0, you had three ways you could store images in the Image Gallery. You could use the `DatabaseHook` and store them as BLOBs in the database; you could use the `DLHook` to store them in the Document Library, or you could use the `FileSystemHook` to store them in a folder on your server's file system. Before you upgrade, you'll need to set whichever property you were using in your 6.0 `portal-ext.properties` file, because by default, none of them are enabled in 6.1. Setting one of the properties triggers the migration during the upgrade process. Below are the three properties; you'll need to set only *one* of them (the one you were using).

```
image.hook.impl=com.liferay.portal.image.DatabaseHook
image.hook.impl=com.liferay.portal.image.DLHook
image.hook.impl=com.liferay.portal.image.FileSystemHook
```

By default, Liferay 6.0 used the `FileSystemHook`. If you never customized this property for your installation, you'd use the `FileSystemHook` property above. If you customized the property, you should know which one you used, and it is likely already in your `portal-ext.properties` file.

The third thing you need to do to prepare for your upgrade is to review the new property defaults.

Review the New 6.1 Properties Defaults

The next thing you'll need to look at are the defaults that have changed from 6.0 to 6.1. These are preserved in `portal-legacy-6.0.properties` in the source. The 6.0 values are:

```
users.last.name.required=true
layout.types=portlet,panel,embedded,article,url,link_to_layout
editor.wysiwyg.portal-web.docroot.html.portlet.message_boards.edit_message.bb_code.jsp=   \
    bbcode
setup.wizard.enabled=false discussion.subscribe.by.default=false
message.boards.subscribe.by.default=false
```

The 6.1 values have changed to:

```
users.last.name.required=false
layout.types=portlet,panel,embedded,url,link_to_layout
editor.wysiwyg.portal-web.docroot.html.portlet.message_boards.edit_message.bb_code.jsp=   \
    ckeditor_bbcode
setup.wizard.enabled=true discussion.subscribe.by.default=true
message.boards.subscribe.by.default=true
```

If you don't like the defaults, you can change them back in one shot by adding a system property to your JVM's startup. This differs by application servers. In Tomcat, you'd modify `setenv.sh/setenv.bat` and append the option `-Dexternal-properties=portal-legacy-6.0.properties` to the environment variable JAVA_OPTS. The scripts `setenv.sh` or `setenv.bat` are not delivered with default Tomcat, but do exist in the bundles. If they're there, Tomcat uses them in the startup process, so it's a nice way to separate your own settings from Tomcat's default shell scripts. Alternatively, of course, you can override some or all of them in your `portal-ext.properties` along with your other overrides.

If you're not using Tomcat, check your application server's documentation to see how to modify runtime properties. Your final task is to catalog all the plugins you have installed, so you can install the new versions in your upgraded system.

Catalog all the plugins you have installed

Finally, you need to take note of any plugins you have installed. Liferay's plugins are usually version-specific, so you'll need to obtain new versions of them for the new release of Liferay. If you have custom plugins created by your development team, they'll need to build, test, and optionally modify them to work with the new release of Liferay. Don't attempt an upgrade without collecting all the plugins you'll need first.

Once you've upgraded your permissions algorithm, reviewed your properties, and collected all the plugins you'll need, you're ready to follow the upgrade procedure. Remember to back up your system before you begin.

There are two different procedures to upgrade Liferay. The first one, upgrading a Liferay bundle, is the most common. The second procedure is for upgrading a Liferay installation on an application server. We'll go over both.

In both cases, Liferay auto-detects whether the database requires an upgrade the first time the new version is started. When Liferay does this, it upgrades the database to the format required by the new version. To perform this task, Liferay *must* be accessing the database with an ID that can create, drop and modify tables. Make sure you have granted these permissions to the ID before you attempt to upgrade Liferay. And, of course, we'll run the risk of overly repeating ourselves: back up your database.

Let's look at upgrading a bundle, which is the easiest upgrade path.

Upgrading a bundle

If you're running a Liferay bundle, the best way to do the upgrade is to follow the steps below. The new Liferay is installed in a newer version of your bundle runtime. For example, the Liferay/Tomcat bundle for 6.0 used Tomcat 6 by default; the 6.1 bundle uses Tomcat 7. Though there is a Tomcat 6 bundle of Liferay 6.1, that bundle also uses a newer release of Tomcat than the one from 6.0. This is the case for all runtimes Liferay supports. We generally recommend you use the latest version of your runtime bundle, as it will be supported the longest.

1. Obtain the new bundle. Unzip the bundle to an appropriate location on your system.

2. Copy your `portal-ext.properties` file and your `data` folder to the new bundle.

3. Review your `portal-ext.properties` file as described above. Make sure you're using permissions algorithm 6. If you were using the Image Gallery, make the necessary modifications so your files are migrated to Documents and Media. Review the new defaults and decide whether you want to use them. Review any other modifications you've made.

4. Start your application server. Watch the console as Liferay starts: it upgrades the database automatically.

5. When the upgrade completes, install any plugins you were using in your old version of Liferay. Make sure you use the versions of those plugins that are designed for Liferay 6.1. If you have your own plugins, your development team will need to migrate the code in these ahead of time and provide .war files for you.

6. Browse around in your new installation and verify everything is working. Have your QA team test everything. If all looks good, you can delete the old application server with the old release of Liferay in it from the bundle directory. You have a backup of it anyway, right?

   As you can see, upgrading a bundle is generally pretty simple. But not everybody can use bundles: sometimes, specific application servers or application server versions are mandated by the environment you're in or by management. For this reason, Liferay also ships as an installable .war file that can be used on any supported application server.

Upgrading using a .war file

Running a manual upgrade is almost as easy as upgrading a bundle:

1. Verify your application server is supported by Liferay. You can do this by viewing the appropriate document on the Customer Portal (EE), in chapter 14 (because there are installation instructions for it), or on liferay.com (CE). If your application server isn't supported by Liferay 6.1, *do not continue!* You'll need to upgrade or switch to a supported application server first.

2. Obtain the Liferay Portal .war file and the dependency .jars archive.

3. Copy your customized `portal-ext.properties` file to a safe place and review it as described above, making all the appropriate changes.

4. Undeploy the old version of Liferay and shut down your application server.

5. Copy the new versions of Liferay's dependency .jars to a location on your server's class path, overwriting the ones you already have for the old version of Liferay. This location is documented for your application server in chapter 14.

6. Deploy the new Liferay .war file to your application server. Follow the deployment instructions in chapter 14.

7. Start (or, if your app server has a console from which you've installed the .war, restart) your application server. Watch the console as Liferay starts: it should upgrade the database automatically. Verify your portal is operating normally, and then install any plugins you were using in your old version of Liferay. Make sure you use the versions of theose plugins designed for Liferay 6.1. If you have your own plugins, your development team will need to migrate the code in these ahead of time and provide .war files to you.

8. Browse around in your new installation and verify everything is working. Have your QA team test everything. If all looks good, you're finished.

That's all there is to it. Most everything is handled by Liferay's upgrade procedure. Note as stated above, if you have to upgrade over several Liferay versions, you will need to repeat these steps for each major release.

17.7 Summary

Liferay Portal is an easy environment to maintain. Backup procedures are simple and straightforward. Administrators have all the options they need to view and diagnose a running Liferay Portal server through its tunable logs.

Patching Liferay is easy to do with Liferay's patching tool. It handles for you all the management of available patches, and makes it easy to install and uninstall them.

Upgrading Liferay is also a snap, because Liferay does most of the work automatically. With easy migration tools and automated database upgrade scripts, you'll have your new version of Liferay Portal up and running in no time.

CHAPTER 18

USING SCRIPTING FOR ADVANCED FLEXIBILITY

Liferay provides a robust script engine that can be used to interpret scripts in Beanshell, Javascript, Groovy, Python and Ruby. The script engine came out of Liferay's involvement with the Romulus project (http://www.ict-romulus.eu). It was originally developed to support non Java-based portlets, but has now been extended to handle a lot more. For example, when Liferay's workflow framework was introduced, the script engine was leveraged to support the execution of scripts from within a workflow module. A script console is now included in the Server Administration portlet in the control panel. It allows system administrators an easy way to execute scripts to perform repetitive user maintenance operations, bulk manipulations using the Liferay API to ensure consistency, or even system level operations.

This chapter helps you to understand Liferay's script engine and covers the following topics:

- Accessing Liferay's service layer from a script

- Running scripts from the script console

- Using the script engine with workflow

- Leveraging custom Java tools in the script engine

The most common thing you'll want to do is access Liferay's services. If you have any familiarity with Liferay's developer tools and API, this will be a snap for you.

18.1 Accessing Liferay Services

In many cases, you'll want to interact with one of Liferay's many services. This is possible from all of the scripting languages supported, but the syntax is a little different for each language.

To illustrate the correct syntax for interacting with Liferay services, let's look at a simple example that uses the `UserLocalService` to retrieve a list of users and then prints their names to the log file. We'll initially implement the example in Java pseudo-code.

```
import com.liferay.portal.model.User;
import com.liferay.portal.service.UserLocalServiceUtil;
import java.util.List;
          .
          .
          .

int userCount = UserLocalServiceUtil.getUsersCount();
List<User> users = UserLocalServiceUtil.getUsers(0, userCount);
\index{User}

for (User user:users) {
    System.out.println("User Name: " + user.getFullName());
}


          .
          .
          .
```

Let's see first how this would work in Beanshell, which is very similar to Java.

Beanshell

Beanshell is a Java scripting language that's designed to run Java code with little or no changes. In this example, we only have one small change to make because Beanshell doesn't support the use of Java Generics.

```
import com.liferay.portal.model.User;
import com.liferay.portal.service.UserLocalServiceUtil;
import java.util.List;

int userCount = UserLocalServiceUtil.getUsersCount();
List users = UserLocalServiceUtil.getUsers(0, userCount);
\index{User}

for (User user:users) {
    System.out.println("User Name: " + user.getFullName());
}
```

Next, we'll show the same thing in Groovy, another scripting language designed to be similar to Java.

Groovy

Groovy is also based on Java and is perhaps a little easier than Beanshell because literally any code written in Java also runs in Groovy. This means we can execute the exact same code from our Java example without any changes.

```
import com.liferay.portal.model.User;
import com.liferay.portal.service.UserLocalServiceUtil;
import java.util.List;

int userCount = UserLocalServiceUtil.getUsersCount();
List<User> users = UserLocalServiceUtil.getUsers(0, userCount);
\index{User}

for (User user:users) {
    System.out.println("User Name: " + user.getFullName());
}
```

Of course, we could make this somewhat Groovier by simplyfing the program as follows:

```
import com.liferay.portal.service.UserLocalServiceUtil

userCount = UserLocalServiceUtil.getUsersCount()
users = UserLocalServiceUtil.getUsers(0, userCount)
for ( user in users){
    System.out.println("User Name: " + user.getFullName())
}
```

The script engine supports more than just Java-like languages. Despite the name, you should be aware that Javascript bears little resemblance to Java, but you can still use it in Liferay's script engine.

Javascript

Liferay uses the Rhino Javascript Engine to provide Javascript support in the
script engine. The following code provides a Javascript version of our original
Java program.

```
userCount = Packages.com.liferay.portal.service.UserLocalServiceUtil.getUsersCount();
users = new Packages.java.util.ArrayList;
users = Packages.com.liferay.portal.service.UserLocalServiceUtil.getUsers(0, userCount);
user = Packages.com.liferay.portal.service.UserLocalServiceUtil.createUser(0);

for (i=0;i<users.size();i++) {
    Packages.java.lang.System.out.println(users.get(i).getFullName());
}
```

You can see the Javascript example is compact. Ruby is even more compact.

Ruby

Ruby is supported throgh the use of JRuby and our previous example could be
implemented in Ruby as follows:

```
userCount = com.liferay.portal.service.UserLocalServiceUtil.getUsersCount();
users = com.liferay.portal.service.UserLocalServiceUtil.getUsers(0, userCount);
users.each{ |user| print user.getFullName() + "\n"}
```

Python users aren't left out either.

Python

Lastly, Liferay provides Python support based on Jython and the previous example could be implemented with the following code.

```
from com.liferay.portal.service import UserLocalServiceUtil
from com.liferay.portal.model import User

userCount = UserLocalServiceUtil().getUsersCount()
users = UserLocalServiceUtil().getUsers(0,userCount)
\index{User}

for user in users:
    print user.getFullName()
```

As you can see, Liferay's services can be accessed from any of these languages. Let's look at some practical examples of how you'd use this.

18.2   Running scripts from the control panel

To see a very simple example of the script console in action, log into the portal as an administrator and navigate to the control panel → Server Administration → Script. Change the script type to Groovy and modify the current code to look like the following:

```
number = com.liferay.portal.service.UserLocalServiceUtil.getUsersCount();
out.println(number);
```

Click the execute button and check the console or the log for your output.

Let's implement a more realistic example. We'll retrieve some user information from the database, make some changes and then update the database with our changes. Our company has updated the terms of use and requires that everyone be presented with the updated terms of use on the next log in. When users agree to the terms of use, a boolean attribute called **agreedToTermsOf-Use** is set in their user records. As long as the boolean is **true**, Liferay will not present the user with the terms of use. However, if we set this flag to **false** for everyone, all users will have to agree to it again to use the site.

We'll again use Groovy, so ensure the script type is set to Groovy and execute the following code to check the status of the **agreedToTermsOfUse** attribute:

```
import com.liferay.portal.service.UserLocalServiceUtil

userCount = UserLocalServiceUtil.getUsersCount()
users = UserLocalServiceUtil.getUsers(0, userCount)
\index{User}

for (user in users) {
    println("User Name: " + user.getFullName() + " -- " + user.getAgreedToTermsOfUse())
}
```

Now we'll actually update each user in the system to set his or her **agreed-ToTermsOfUse** attribute to false. We'll be sure to skip the default user as the default user is not required to agree to the Terms of Use. We'll also skip the admin user that's currently logged in and running the script. If you're logged in as somoene other than test@liferay.com, be sure to update the following script before running it.

```
import com.liferay.portal.service.UserLocalServiceUtil

userCount = UserLocalServiceUtil.getUsersCount()
users = UserLocalServiceUtil.getUsers(0, userCount)
\index{User}

for (user in users){
```

```
if(!user.isDefaultUser() &&
    !user.getEmailAddress().equalsIgnoreCase("test@liferay.com")) {

        user.setAgreedToTermsOfUse(false)
        UserLocalServiceUtil.updateUser(user)
\index{User}

    }

}
```

To verify the script has updated the records, run the first script again and you should see all users (except the default user and your ID) have been updated.

That's all that's needed to run scripts and to access the Liferay service layer. There are, however, some things to keep in mind when working with the script console:

- There is no undo

- There is no preview

- When using Local Services, no permissions checking is enforced

- Scripts are executed synchronously, so be careful with scripts that might take a long time to execute.

For these reasons, you want to use the script console with care, and test run your scripts on non-production systems before you run them on production.

Of course, the script engine has uses beyond the script console. One of the main uses of it is in designing workflows.

18.3 Leveraging the Script Engine in Workflow

Liferay's Kaleo workflow engine provides a robust system for reviewing and approving content in an enterprise environment. Just with the standard feature set, it is a powerful and robust workflow solution. Adding scripting features brings it to the next level.

The default workflow definition included with Kaleo gives you a quick look into how the feature works. The final step in the workflow runs a script that makes content available for use. As you can see in the snippet below, it uses Javascript to access the Java class associated with the workflow to set the status of the content to *approved*.

```
<script>
<![CDATA[
    Packages.com.liferay.portal.kernel.workflow.WorkflowStatusManagerUtil.updateStatus
      (Packages.com.liferay.portal.kernel.workflow.WorkflowConstants.toStatus("approved"),
        workflowContext);]]>
</script>
<script-language>javascript</script-language>
```

At virtually any point in a workflow, you can use Liferay's scripting engine
to access workflow APIs or other APIs outside of workflow. There are a lot
of different ways you could use this, but some practical ones might be getting
a list of users with a specific workflow-related role; sending an email to the
designated content approver with a list of people to contact if he is unable to
review the content; or creating an alert to be displayed in the Alerts portlet for
any user assigned to approve content.

Of course, before you try any of this, you might want to know what the
appropriate syntax is for inserting a script into the workflow. In an XML workflow definition, a script can be used in any XML type that can contain an tag
- those types being `<state>`, `<task>`, `<fork>` and `<join>`. Inside of one of
those types, format your script like so:

```
<actions>
    <action>
        <script>
            <![CDATA[*the contents of your script*]]>
        </script>
        <script-language>*your scripting language of choice*</script-language>
    </action>
    ...
</actions>
```

Here's an example of a workflow script created in Groovy. This one is designed to be used with a `Condition` statement in Kaleo. It accesses Liferay's
Asset Framework to determine the category of an asset in the workflow so the
correct approval process can be automatically determined.

```
<script>
        <![CDATA[
            import com.liferay.portal.kernel.util.GetterUtil;
            import com.liferay.portal.kernel.workflow.WorkflowConstants;
            import com.liferay.portal.kernel.workflow.WorkflowHandler;
            import com.liferay.portal.kernel.workflow.WorkflowHandlerRegistryUtil;
            import com.liferay.portlet.asset.model.AssetCategory;
            import com.liferay.portlet.asset.model.AssetEntry;
            import com.liferay.portlet.asset.model.AssetRenderer;
            import com.liferay.portlet.asset.model.AssetRendererFactory;
            import com.liferay.portlet.asset.service.AssetEntryLocalServiceUtil;

            import java.util.List;
```

```
String className = (String)workflowContext.get(
    WorkflowConstants.CONTEXT_ENTRY_CLASS_NAME);

WorkflowHandler workflowHandler =
    WorkflowHandlerRegistryUtil.getWorkflowHandler(className);

AssetRendererFactory assetRendererFactory =
    workflowHandler.getAssetRendererFactory();

long classPK =
    GetterUtil.getLong((String)workflowContext.get
        (WorkflowConstants.CONTEXT_ENTRY_CLASS_PK));

AssetRenderer assetRenderer =
    workflowHandler.getAssetRenderer(classPK);

AssetEntry assetEntry = assetRendererFactory.getAssetEntry(
    assetRendererFactory.getClassName(), assetRenderer.getClassPK());

List<AssetCategory> assetCategories = assetEntry.getCategories();

returnValue = "Content Review";

for (AssetCategory assetCategory : assetCategories) {
    String categoryName = assetCategory.getName();

    if (categoryName.equals("legal")) {
        returnValue = "Legal Review";

        return;
    }
}
        ]]>
    </script>
    <script-language>groovy</script-language>
```

Within a workflow, the next task or state is chosen based on the what the
method returns.

The combination of Liferay's scripting and workflow engines is incredibly
powerful, but as it provides users with the ability to execute code, it can also be
very dangerous. When configuring your permissions, be aware of the potential consequences of poorly, or maliciously, written scripts inside of a workflow
definition. For more information on creating definitions with Kaleo Workflow
see *Chapter 6: Workflow with Kaleo.*

18.4   Custom Java Tools in the Script Engine

There are several challenges when working with the Script Engine, including
debugging and logging. One approach to overcome these challenges is to de-

velop custom Java utilities that can be called from your scripts. These utilities can write to a custom log file or the Liferay log file. You can also place breakpoints in your utility code and step through it using your favorite debugger.

Liferay's use of Spring and `PortletBeanLocatorUtil` makes calling these Java utilities from your script easy, regardless of the scripting language you're using.

Let's begin by creating a Liferay Hook project. If you're using Liferay IDE or Liferay Developer Studio, select *File* → *New* → *Liferay Project*. Name the project *script-utils* and accept the display name generated by the wizard. Be sure to select *Hook* for the Plugin Type and then select *Finish*.

You're using a Liferay Hook Plugin to deploy your utility, but you're not using any of the typical hook features. You just need a way to make your code available to the portal and the Hook Plugin is the least obtrusive way to do this. This means you don't need to add anything to the `liferay-hook.xml` file. Instead, you'll begin by adding your utility code.

You'll be following the Dependency Injection design pattern so begin by creating the interface. Right click on the `docroot/WEB-INF/src` folder and select *New* → *Interface*. You'll create your interface in the `com.liferay.sample` package. Name it `ScriptUtil`.

Next, add two methods to the interface.

```
package com.liferay.samples;

public interface ScriptUtil {

    public String operationOne();

    public String operationTwo(String name);

}
```

Next, create the implementation class. Right click on the `docroot/WEB-INF/src` folder and select *New* → *Class*. Create the interface in the `com.liferay.sample` package and name it `ScriptUtilImpl`. Be sure to select `com.-liferay.sample.ScriptUtil` as the Interface.

Next, add implementations for the two methods.

```
package com.liferay.samples;

import com.liferay.portal.kernel.log.Log;
import com.liferay.portal.kernel.log.LogFactoryUtil;

public class ScriptUtilImpl implements ScriptUtil {
```

Figure 18.1: Creating a new utilities project is easy if you use Liferay IDE
or Liferay Developer Studio.

```
@Override
public String operationOne() {

    return "Hello out there!";
}

@Override
public String operationTwo(String name) {

    _log.debug("Inside of Operation Two");

    return "Hello " + name + "!";
}
```

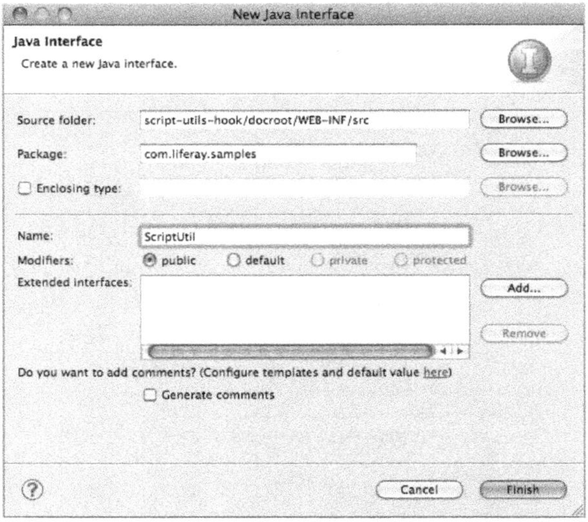

Figure 18.2: Create a new Java Interface which you'll later implement.

```
private static Log _log = LogFactoryUtil.getLog(ScriptUtilImpl.class);
```

```
}
```

Liferay makes extensive use of the Spring Framework and you'll be using it here to inject your implementation class into the application. Spring needs a bean definition which you'll declare in an XML file named `applicationContext.xml`. Create this file in the `docroot/WEB-INF/` directory and add the following code:

```
<?xml version="1.0" encoding="UTF-8"?>
<!DOCTYPE beans PUBLIC "-//SPRING//DTD BEAN//EN"
   "http://www.springframework.org/dtd/spring-beans.dtd">

<beans>
    <bean id="com.liferay.sample.ScriptUtil" class="com.liferay.sample.ScriptUtilImpl" />
</beans>
```

Upon deployment, you'll need the portal to create a `BeanLocator` for your plugin. The `BeanLocator` reads the bean definitions you provided.

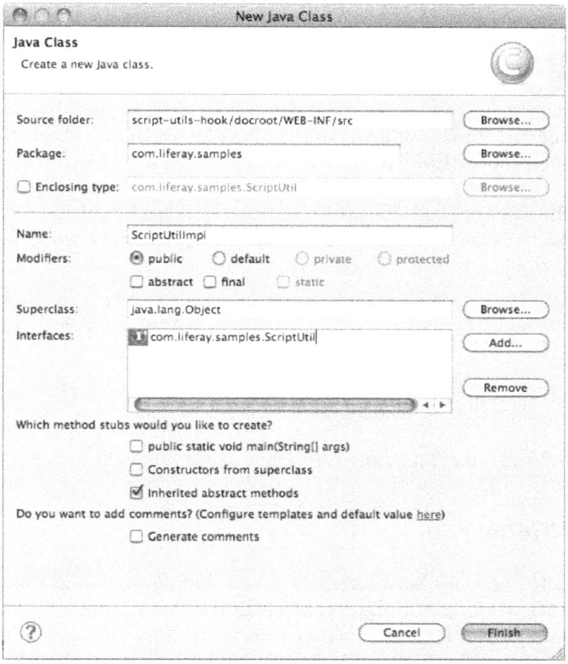

Figure 18.3: Create a new Java Class that implements the interface you created earlier.

If you're adding your utility to a Service Builder enabled plugin, then you'll already have a `BeanLocator` and you can skip this step. Since this Hook plugin is not already using Service Builder, you'll need to define a context loader listener in our Hook to provide a `BeanLocator`. Open the `docroot/WEB-INF/-web.xml` file and replace its contents with the following code:

```
<?xml version="1.0"?>
<!DOCTYPE web-app PUBLIC "-//Sun Microsystems, Inc.//DTD Web Application 2.3//EN"
    "http://java.sun.com/dtd/web-app_2_3.dtd">

<web-app>
    <listener>
```

```
        <listener-class>
            com.liferay.portal.kernel.spring.context.PortletContextLoaderListener
        </listener-class>
    </listener>
</web-app>
```

Save all of the changes you've made and deploy the hook. Once the hook has been deployed successfully, the `ScriptUtil` can be used in your script engine code.

To see the `ScriptUtil` code in action, navigate back to the *control panel* → *Server Administration* → *Script*. Change the script type to Groovy and enter the following script:

```
myUtil =
    com.liferay.portal.kernel.bean.PortletBeanLocatorUtil.locate("script-utils-hook",
    "com.liferay.samples.ScriptUtil")

println(myUtil.operationOne())

println(myUtil.operationTwo("Joe Bloggs"))
```

You should see the results of your script displayed right under the script.

18.5   Summary

In this chapter we saw how Liferay's script engine opens up many exciting posibilities for working with Liferay regardless of your language of choice. We learned how you can leverage Liferay's Services Oriented Architecture (SOA) from any of the popular scripting languages Liferay supports. We then saw how those scripts could be used to simplify administrative tasks by leveraging the Administrator Script Console. Next, we discovered how you could enhance workflow by using the power of scripts. Lastly, we saw how you could overcome some of the limitations of running scripts in Liferay by creating custom Java utilities that could be executed from within your scripts.

As you can see, Liferay's script engine opens up many exciting possibilities for working with Liferay regardless of your language of choice.

CHAPTER 19

CONFIGURING LIFERAY FOR HIGH AVAILABILITY

Liferay Portal is a robust, enterprise-ready portal solution. As such, it is fully ready to support mission-critical, enterprise applications in an environment configured for multiple redundancies and 24/7 uptimes. The product, however, like other products of its kind, doesn't come configured this way out of the box, so there are some steps that need to be taken to tune it for your needs.

This chapter covers these topics in detail. Liferay runs on so many different Java EE application servers that we can't cover all the differences between them. For this reason, we'll discuss Liferay configurations only. For example, we'll look at how to configure Liferay to work in a clustered environment, but not how to create the cluster in your application server. The documentation for your particular application server is always a much better place to learn those kinds of things.

This chapter explains how to configure Liferay for a number of advanced scenarios, such as

- Clustering

- Distributed Caching

- Deploying Customized versions of Liferay

- Performance Testing and Tuning

During this discussion, we'll mention a number of other open source products upon which Liferay relies for much of this functionality. These products all have their own documentation which should be consulted for a fuller view of what these products can do. For example, Liferay uses Ehcache for its caching mechanism. We'll cover how to configure Ehcache to enable caches in Liferay, but will refer you to that product's documentation for further information about that product.

Sometimes Liferay supports multiple products which perform the same function. There are, for example, several single sign-on implementations you can use with Liferay. We'll leave it up to you to select which product best fits the needs of your project without recommending one product over another.

With all of that said, let's get started configuring Liferay for the enterprise.

19.1   Liferay Clustering

Liferay Portal is designed to serve everything from the smallest to the largest web sites. Out of the box, it's configured optimally for a single server environment. If one server isn't sufficient to serve the high traffic needs of your site, Liferay scales to the size you need.

Liferay works well in clusters of multiple machines (horizontal cluster) or in clusters of multiple VMs on a single machine (vertical cluster), or any mixture of the two. Once you have Liferay installed in more than one application server node, there are several optimizations that need to be made. At a minimum, Liferay should be configured in the following way for a clustered environment:

- All nodes should be pointing to the same Liferay database or database cluster.

- Documents and Media repositories should be accessible to all nodes of the cluster.

- Search should be configured for replication or should use a separate search server.

- The cache should be replicating across all nodes of the cluster.

- Hot deploy folders should be configured for each node if you're not using server farms.

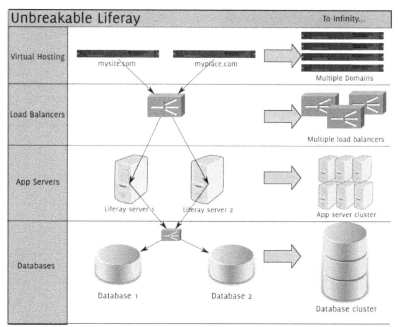

Figure 19.1: Liferay is designed to scale to as large an installation as you
need.

If you haven't configured your application server to use farms for deployment, the hot deploy folder should be a separate folder for all the nodes, and
plugins will have to be deployed to all of the nodes individually. This can be
done via a script. If you do have farms configured, you can deploy normally
to any node's deploy folder, and your farm configuration should take care of
syncing the deployment to all nodes.

Many of these configuration changes can be made by adding or modifying properties in your `portal-ext.properties` file. Remember that this file
overrides the defaults in the `portal.properties` file. The original version of
this file can be found in the Liferay source code or can be extracted from the
`portal-impl.jar` file in your Liferay installation. It is a best practice to copy

the relevant section you want to modify from `portal.properties` into your `portal-ext.properties` file, and then modify the values there.

Note: This chapter documents a Liferay-specific cluster configuration, without getting into specific implementations of third party software, such as Java EE application servers, HTTP servers, and load balancers. Please consult your documentation for those components of your cluster for specific details of those components. Before configuring Liferay in a cluster configuration, make sure your OS is not defining the hostname of your box to the local network at 127.0.0.1.

We'll take each of the points above one by one to present a clear picture of how to cluster Liferay.

All nodes should be pointing to the same Liferay database

This is pretty self-explanatory. Each node should be configured with a data source that points to one Liferay database (or a database cluster) that all the nodes will share. This ensures all the nodes operate from the same basic data set. This means, of course, Liferay cannot (and should not) use the embedded HSQL database that is shipped with the bundles (but you already knew that, right?). And, of course, it goes without saying the database server is a separate physical box from the server which is running Liferay.

Beyond a database cluster, there are two more advanced options you can use to optimize your database configuration: a read-writer database configuration, and sharding.

Read-Writer database configuration

Liferay allows you to use two different data sources for reading and writing. This enables you to split your database infrastructure into two sets: one that is optimized for reading and one that is optimized for writing. Since all major databases support replication in one form or another, you can then use your database vendor's replication mechanism to keep the databases in sync in a much faster manner than if you had a single data source which handled everything.

Enabling a read-writer database is simple. In your `portal-ext.properties` file, configure two different data sources for Liferay to use, one for reading, and one for writing:

```
jdbc.read.driverClassName=com.mysql.jdbc.Driver
jdbc.read.url=jdbc:mysql://dbread.com/lportal?useUnicode=true&characterEncoding=UTF-8   \
    &useFastDateParsing=false
jdbc.read.username=**your user name**
jdbc.read.password=**your password**
jdbc.write.driverClassName=com.mysql.jdbc.Driver
jdbc.write.url=jdbc:mysql://dbwrite.com/lportal?useUnicode=true&characterEncoding=UTF-8  \
    &useFastDateParsing=false
jdbc.write.username=**your user name**
jdbc.write.password=**your password**
```

Of course, specify the user name and password to your database in the above configuration.

After this, enable the read-writer database configuration by uncommenting the Spring configuration file which enables it in your **spring.configs** property (line to uncomment is in bold):

```
spring.configs=\
META-INF/base-spring.xml,\
META-INF/hibernate-spring.xml,\
META-INF/infrastructure-spring.xml,\
META-INF/management-spring.xml,\
META-INF/util-spring.xml,\
META-INF/editor-spring.xml,\
META-INF/jcr-spring.xml,\
META-INF/messaging-spring.xml,\
META-INF/scheduler-spring.xml,\
META-INF/search-spring.xml,\
META-INF/counter-spring.xml,\
META-INF/document-library-spring.xml,\
META-INF/lock-spring.xml,\
META-INF/mail-spring.xml,\
META-INF/portal-spring.xml,\
META-INF/portlet-container-spring.xml,\
META-INF/wsrp-spring.xml,\
META-INF/mirage-spring.xml,\
**META-INF/dynamic-data-source-spring.xml,\**
#META-INF/shard-data-source-spring.xml,\
META-INF/ext-spring.xml
```

The next time you restart Liferay, it will now use the two data sources you have defined. Be sure you have correctly set up your two databases for replication before starting Liferay.

Next, we'll look at database sharding.

Database Sharding

Liferay starting with version 5.2.3 supports database sharding for different portal instances. Sharding is a term used to describe an extremely high scalability configuration for systems with massive amounts of users. In diagrams, a database is normally pictured as a cylinder. Instead, picture it as a glass bottle full of data. Now take that bottle and smash it onto a concrete sidewalk. There will be shards of glass everywhere. If that bottle were a database, each shard now is a database, with a subset of the data in each shard.

This allows you to split up your database by various types of data that might be in it. For example, some implementations of sharding a database split up the users: those with last names beginning with A to D go in one database; E to I go in another; etc. When users log in, they are directed to the instance of the application that is connected to the database that corresponds to their last names. In this manner, processing is split up evenly, and the amount of data the application needs to sort through is reduced.

By default, Liferay allows you to support sharding through different portal instances, using the *round robin shard selector*. This is a class which serves as the default algorithm for sharding in Liferay. Using this algorithm, Liferay selects from several different portal instances and evenly distributes the data across them. Alternatively, you can use the manual shard selector. In this case, you'd need to use the UI provided in the control panel to configure your shards.

Of course, if you wish to have your developers implement your own sharding algorithm, you can do that. This is a great use of the Ext plugin. You can select which algorithm is active via the `portal-ext.properties` file:

```
shard.selector=com.liferay.portal.dao.shard.RoundRobinShardSelector
#shard.selector=com.liferay.portal.dao.shard.ManualShardSelector
#shard.selector=[your implementation here]
```

Enabling sharding is easy. You'll need to make sure you are using Liferay's data source implementation instead of your application server's. Set your various database shards in your `portal-ext.properties` file this way:

```
jdbc.default.driverClassName=com.mysql.jdbc.Driver
jdbc.default.url=jdbc:mysql://localhost/lportal?useUnicode=true&characterEncoding=UTF-8  \
    &useFastDateParsing=false
jdbc.default.username=
jdbc.default.password=
jdbc.one.driverClassName=com.mysql.jdbc.Driver
jdbc.one.url=jdbc:mysql://localhost/lportal1?useUnicode=true&characterEncoding=UTF-8
    &useFastDateParsing=false
jdbc.one.username=
jdbc.one.password=
jdbc.two.driverClassName=com.mysql.jdbc.Driver
jdbc.two.url=jdbc:mysql://localhost/lportal2?useUnicode=true&characterEncoding=UTF-8    \
    &useFastDateParsing=false
jdbc.two.username=
jdbc.two.password=
shard.available.names=default,one,two
```

Once you do this, you can set up your DNS so several domain names point to your Liferay installation (e.g., abc1.com, abc2.com, abc3.com). Next, go to the control panel and click *Portal Instances* in the Server category. Create two to three instances bound to the DNS names you have configured.

If you're using the `RoundRobinShardSelector` class, Liferay automatically enters data into each instance one by one. If you're using the `ManualShard-Selector` class, you'll have to specify a shard for each instance using the UI.

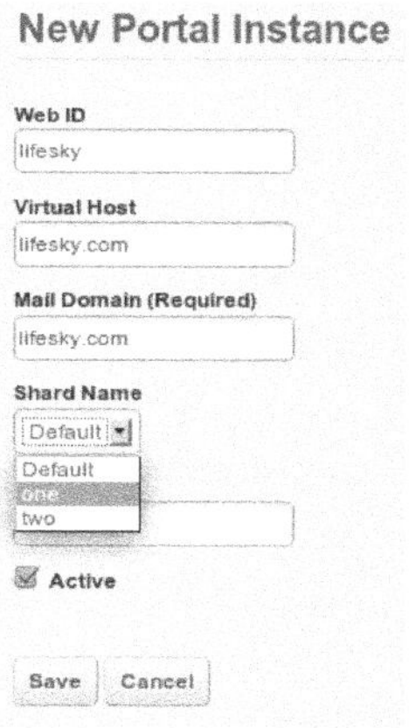

New Portal Instance

Web ID

> lifesky

Virtual Host

> lifesky.com

Mail Domain (Required)

> lifesky.com

Shard Name

> Default
> Default
> one
> two

☑ Active

Save   Cancel

Figure 19.2: When creating a shard using the manual shard selector, specify the shard you want to use for that instance.

The last thing you need to do is modify the `spring.configs` section of your `portal-ext.properties` file to enable the sharding configuration, which by default is commented out. To do this, your `spring.configs` should look like this (modified section is in bold):

```
spring.configs=\
    META-INF/base-spring.xml,\
    \
    META-INF/hibernate-spring.xml,\
    META-INF/infrastructure-spring.xml,\
    META-INF/management-spring.xml,\
    \
    META-INF/util-spring.xml,\
    \
    META-INF/jpa-spring.xml,\
```

```
    \
    META-INF/executor-spring.xml,\
    \
    META-INF/audit-spring.xml,\
    META-INF/cluster-spring.xml,\
    META-INF/editor-spring.xml,\
    META-INF/jcr-spring.xml,\
    META-INF/ldap-spring.xml,\
    META-INF/messaging-core-spring.xml,\
    META-INF/messaging-misc-spring.xml,\
    META-INF/mobile-device-spring.xml,\
    META-INF/notifications-spring.xml,\
    META-INF/poller-spring.xml,\
    META-INF/rules-spring.xml,\
    META-INF/scheduler-spring.xml,\
    META-INF/scripting-spring.xml,\
    META-INF/search-spring.xml,\
    META-INF/workflow-spring.xml,\
    \
    META-INF/counter-spring.xml,\
    META-INF/mail-spring.xml,\
    META-INF/portal-spring.xml,\
    META-INF/portlet-container-spring.xml,\
    META-INF/staging-spring.xml,\
    META-INF/virtual-layouts-spring.xml,\
    \
    #META-INF/dynamic-data-source-spring.xml,\
    *META-INF/shard-data-source-spring.xml,\*
    #META-INF/memcached-spring.xml,\
    #META-INF/monitoring-spring.xml,\
    \
    classpath*:META-INF/ext-spring.xml
```

That's all there is to it. Your system is now set up for sharding. Now that you've got your database set up and optimized for a large installation, let's turn to clustering the Documents and Media Library.

Documents and Media Library clustering

Liferay 6.1 introduces a new Documents and Media Library which is capable of mounting several repositories at a time and presenting a unified interface to the user. By default, users can make use of the Liferay repository, which is already mounted. This repository is built into Liferay Portal and can use as its back-end one of several different store implementations. In addition to this, many different kinds of third party repositories can be mounted. If you have a separate repository you've mounted, all nodes of the cluster will point to this repository. Your avenue for improving performance at that point is to cluster your third party repository, using the documentation for the repository you have chosen. If you don't have a third party repository, there are ways you can configure the Liferay repository to perform well in a clustered configuration.

The main thing to keep in mind is you need to make sure every node of the cluster has the same access to the file store as every other node. For this reason, you'll need to take a look at your store configuration.

There are several options available for configuring how Liferay's Documents and Media library stores files. Each option is a *store* which can be configured through the `portal-ext.properties` file by setting the `dl.store.impl=` property. Let's consider the ramifications of the various store options.

Using the File System store

This is the default store. It's a simple file storage implementation that uses a local folder to store files. You can use the file system for your clustered configuration, but you'd have to make sure the folder to which you point the store can handle things like concurrent requests and file locking. For this reason, you need to use a Storage Area Network or a clustered file system.

The file system store was the first store created for Liferay and is heavily bound to the Liferay database. By default, documents are stored in a `docu-ment_library` subfolder of the `data` folder in a Liferay bundle. Of course, you can change this path to anything you want by using the `dl.store.file.sys-tem.root.dir=` property.

Figure 19.3: Liferay's file system store creates a folder structure based on primary keys in Liferay's database.

This store creates a folder structure based on primary keys in the Liferay database. If, for example, you upload a presentation with the file name `work-flow.odp` into a folder called *stuff*, the file system store creates a folder structure which looks like figure 19.3.

The first folder is the company ID to which the site belongs. The second folder is the group ID of the site where the document resides. The third is the ID of the document itself, and finally the file name of the document is renamed to a version number for storing multiple versions of the document.

As you can see, this binds your documents very closely to Liferay, and may not be exactly what you want. But if you've been using the default settings for a while and need to migrate your documents, Liferay provides a migration utility in the control panel in

Server Administration → Data Migration. Using this utility, you can move your documents very easily from one store implementation to another.

Speaking of other store implementations, let's look at some others Liferay provides.

Using the Advanced File System store

Liferay's advanced file system store is similar to the default file system store. Like that store, it saves files to the local file system—which, of course, could be a remote file system mount. It uses a slightly different folder structure to store files, which is pictured below.

So what makes the advanced file system store *advanced*? Several operating systems have limitations on the number of files which can be stored in a particular folder. The advanced file system store overcomes this limitation by programmatically creating a structure that can expand to millions of files, by alphabetically nesting the files in folders. This not only allows for more files to be stored, but also improves performance as there are less files stored per folder.

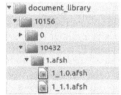

The same rules apply to the advanced file system store as apply to the default file system store. To cluster this, you'll need to point the store to a network mounted file system that all the nodes can access, and that networked file system needs to support concurrent requests and file locking. Otherwise, you may experience data corruption issues if two users attempt from two different nodes to write to the same file at the same time.

Figure 19.4: The advanced file system store creates a more nested folder structure than the file system store.

You may decide the advanced file system store for whatever reason doesn't serve your needs. If this is the case, you can of course mount other file systems into the documents and media library. In addition to this, you can also redefine the Liferay store to use one of three other supported protocols. We'll look at these next.

Using the CMIS store

Though you can mount as many different CMIS (Content Management Interoperability Services) repositories as you like in the documents and media library, you may wish also to redefine the Liferay repository to point to a CMIS repository as well. Why? Because, as you know, users are users, and it's possible they may find a way to create a folder or upload content to the Liferay repository. It would be nice if that Liferay repository was connected to a clustered CMIS repository by the administrator without having to mount it through the UI. The CMIS store allows you to do just that.

If you wish to use the CMIS store, all you need to do is set the following four directives in your `portal-ext.properties` file:

```
dl.store.cmis.credentials.username=yourusername
dl.store.cmis.credentials.password=yourpassword
dl.store.cmis.repository.url=http://localhost:8080/url/to/your/cmis/repository
dl.store.cmis.system.root.dir=Liferay Home
```

Now the Liferay repository is connected to CMIS via the CMIS store. As long as all nodes are pointing to your CMIS repository, everything in your Liferay cluster should be fine, as the CMIS protocol prevents multiple simultaneous file access from causing data corruption.

From here, we'll move on to the JCR store.

Using the JCR store

Liferay Portal supports as a store the Java Content Repository standard. Under the hood, Liferay uses Jackrabbit—which is a project from Apache—as its JSR-170 compliant document repository. By default, Jackrabbit is configured to store the documents on the local file system upon which Liferay is installed, in the `[Liferay Home]/liferay/jackrabbit` folder. Inside this folder is Jackrabbit's configuration file, called `repository.xml`.

Using the default settings, the JCR store is not very different from the file system stores, except you can use any JCR client to access the files. You can, however, modify Jackrabbit's configuration so it stores files in a database that can be accessed by all nodes, and so that it operates as a cluster within Liferay's cluster.

To move the default repository location to a shared folder, you do not need to edit Jackrabbit's configuration file. Instead, find the section in `portal.properties` labeled JCR and copy/paste that section into your `portal-ext.properties` file. One of the properties, by default, is the following:

```
jcr.jackrabbit.repository.root=${liferay.home}/data/jackrabbit
```

Change this property to point to a shared folder that all the nodes can see. A new Jackrabbit configuration file is then generated in that location, and you'll have to edit that file to modify Jackrabbit's configuration.

Note that because of file locking issues, this isn't the best way to share Jackrabbit resources, unless you're using a networked file system that can handle concurrency and file locking. If you have two people logged in at the same time uploading content, you could encounter data corruption using this method, and because of this, we don't recommend it for a production system. Instead, if you want to use the Java Content Repository in a cluster, you should redirect Jackrabbit into your database of choice. You can use the Liferay database or another database for this purpose. This requires editing Jackrabbit's configuration file.

The default Jackrabbit configuration file has sections commented out for moving the Jackrabbit configuration into the database. This has been done to make it as easy as possible to enable this configuration. To move the Jackrabbit configuration into the database, simply comment out the sections relating to the file system and comment in the sections relating to the database. These by default are configured for a MySQL database. If you are using another database, you will likely need to modify the configuration, as there are changes to the configuration file that are necessary for specific databases. For example, the default configuration uses Jackrabbit's `DbFileSystem` class to mimic a file system in the database. While this works well in MySQL, it doesn't work for all databases. For example, if you're using an Oracle database, you'll need to modify this to use `OracleFileSystem`.

Modify the JDBC database URLs so they point to your database. This, of course, must be done on all nodes of the cluster. Don't forget to create the database first, and grant the user ID you are specifying in the configuration file access to create, modify, and drop tables. After this, be sure to uncomment the `<Cluster/>` section at the bottom of the file. For further information, it's best to check out the Jackrabbit documentation. Please see the Jackrabbit documentation at `http://jackrabbit.apache.org` for further information.

Once you've configured Jackrabbit to store its repository in a database, the next time you bring up Liferay, the necessary database tables are created automatically. Jackrabbit, however, does not create indexes on these tables, and so over time this can be a performance penalty. To fix this, you'll need to manually go into your database and index the primary key columns for all the Jackrabbit tables.

Note that this configuration doesn't perform as well as the advanced file system store, because you're storing documents in a database instead of in the file system. But it does have the benefit of clustering well. Next, we'll look at Amazon's S3 store.

Using Amazon Simple Storage Service   Amazon's simple storage service (S3)
is a cloud-based storage solution which you can use with Liferay. All you need
is an account, and you can store your documents to the cloud from all nodes,
seamlessly.

This is easy to set up. When you sign up for the service, Amazon assigns you
some unique keys which link you to your account. In Amazon's interface, you
can create "buckets" of data optimized by region. Once you've created these to
your specifications, all you need to do is declare them in `portal-ext.proper-`
`ties`:

```
dl.store.s3.access.key=
dl.store.s3.secret.key=
dl.store.s3.bucket.name=
```

Once you have these configured, set your store implementation to the `S3-`
`Store`:

```
dl.store.impl=com.liferay.portlet.documentlibrary.store.S3Store
```

Consult the Amazon Simple Storage documentation for additional details on
using Amazon's service.

We have one more store to go over: the Documentum store.

 EE Only Feature

Using the Documentum store   If you have a Liferay Portal EE license, you
have access to the Documentum hook which adds support for Documentum to
Liferay's Documents and Media library. Install this hook by using the Liferay
Marketplace.

This hook doesn't add an option to make the Liferay repository into a Documentum repository, as the other store implementations do. Instead, it gives you
the ability to mount Documentum repositories via the Documents and Media
library UI.

There's not really a lot to this; it's incredibly easy. Click *Add* → *Repository*,
and in the form that appears, choose *Documentum* as the repository type. After
that, give it a name and specify the Documentum repository and cabinet, and

Liferay mounts the repository for you. That's really all there is to it. If all your nodes are pointing to a Documentum repository, you can cluster Documentum to achieve higher performance.

Now that we've covered the available ways you can configure documents and media for clustering, we can move on to configuring search.

Clustering search

You can configure search for clustering in one of two ways: use pluggable enterprise search (recommended), or configure Lucene so indexes replicate across the individual file systems of the nodes in the cluster. We'll look at both ways to do this.

Using Pluggable Enterprise Search

As an alternative to using Lucene, Liferay supports pluggable search engines. The first implementation of this uses the open source search engine *Solr*, but in the future there will be many such plugins for your search engine of choice. This allows you to use a completely separate product for search, and this product can be installed on another application server or cluster of servers. Your search engine then operates completely independently of your Liferay Portal nodes in a clustered environment, acting as a search service for all the nodes simultaneously.

This makes it much easier to deal with search indexes. You no longer have to maintain indexes on every node in your cluster, and you get to offload indexing activity to a separate server, so your nodes can concentrate their CPU power on serving pages. Each Liferay node sends requests to the search engine to update the search index when needed, and these updates are then queued and handled automatically by the search engine, independently. It's kind of like having an army of robots ready and willing to do your bidding.

First, you'll need to configure your Solr server, and then you need to install Liferay's Solr plugin to redirect searches over to it.

Configuring the Solr Search Server   Since Solr is a standalone search engine, you'll need to download it and install it first according to the instructions on the Solr web site (`http://lucene.apache.org/solr`). Of course, it's best to use a server that is separate from your Liferay installation, as your Solr server becomes responsible for all indexing and searching for your entire cluster. You definitely don't want both Solr and Liferay on the same box. Solr is distributed

as a .war file with several .jar files which need to be available on your application server's classpath. Once you have Solr up and running, integrating it
with Liferay is easy, but it requires a restart of your application server.

The first thing you need to define on the Solr box is the location of your
search index. Assuming you're running a Linux server and you've mounted a
file system for the index at /solr, create an environment variable that points
to this folder. This environment variable needs to be called $SOLR_HOME. So for
our example, we would define:

```
$SOLR_HOME=/solr
```

This environment variable can be defined anywhere you need: in your operating system's start up sequence, in the environment for the user who is logged
in, or in the start up script for your application server. If you're using Tomcat to
host Solr, modify setenv.sh or setenv.bat and add the environment variable
there.

Once you've created the environment variable, you then can use it in your
application server's start up configuration as a parameter to your JVM. This is
configured differently per application server, but again, if you're using Tomcat,
edit catalina.sh or catalina.bat and append the following to the $JAVA-
_OPTS variable:

```
-Dsolr.solr.home=$SOLR_HOME
```

This takes care of telling Solr where to store its search index. Go ahead
and install Solr to this box according to the instructions on the Solr web site
(http://lucene.apache.org/solr). Once it's installed, shut it down, as
there is some more configuration to do.

Installing the Solr Liferay Plugin   Next, you have a choice. If you have installed Solr on the same system upon which Liferay is running (not recommended), you can simply go to the Liferay Marketplace and install the *solr-web*
plugin. This, however, defeats much of the purpose of using Solr, because the
goal is to offload search indexing to another box to free up processing for your
installation of Liferay. For this reason, you really shouldn't run Liferay and your
search engine on the same box. Unfortunately, the configuration in the plugin
is set exactly that way, presumably to allow you to experiment with different
search configurations. To run them separately–as you would in a production
environment–, you'll have to make a change to a configuration file in the plugin before you install it so you can tell Liferay where to send indexing requests.

In this case, go to the Liferay Marketplace and download the plugin to your system.

Open or extract the plugin. Inside the plugin, you'll find a file called `sol-r-spring.xml` in the `WEB-INF/classes/META-INF` folder. Open this file in a text editor and you will see the entry which defines where the Solr server can be found by Liferay:

```
<bean class="com.liferay.portal.spring.context.PortletBeanFactoryPostProcessor" />

<!-- Solr search engine -->
\index{Solr}

<bean id="com.liferay.portal.search.solr.server.BasicAuthSolrServer"
    class="com.liferay.portal.search.solr.server.BasicAuthSolrServer">
    <constructor-arg type="java.lang.String" value="http://localhost:8080/solr" />
</bean>
```

Modify this value so it points to the server where Solr is running. Then save the file and put it back into the plugin archive in the same place it was before.

Next, extract the file `schema.xml` from the plugin. It should be in the `doc-root/WEB-INF/conf` folder. This file tells Solr how to index the data coming from Liferay, and can be customized for your installation. Copy this file to `$SOLR_HOME/conf` on your Solr box (you may have to create the `conf` directory).

Before you start Solr, you should provide Solr with a list of **synonyms** and **stop words**. Synonyms are words that should be equivalent in search. For example, if a user searches for *important information*, you may want to show results for *required information* or *critical information*. You can define these in `synonyms.txt`. Stop words are defined in `stopwords.txt` and are words that should not be indexed: articles, pronouns, and other words that have little value in a search. Place these files in your `$SOLR_HOME/conf` folder. Examples for both of these files are found in the Solr archive in the `solr-4.1.0/examp-le/solr/collection1/conf` folder. Additional Solr configuration options, most importantly `solrconfig.xml` and `elevate.xml`, are in the `$SOLR_HOME-/conf` folder. Now you can start Solr. After Solr has started, hot deploy the `solr-web` plugin to all your nodes. See the next section for instructions on hot deploying to a cluster.

Once the plugin is hot deployed, your Liferay server's search is automatically upgraded to use Solr. It's likely, however, that initial searches will come up with nothing: this is because you need to reindex everything using Solr.

Go to the control panel. In the *Server* section, click *Server Administration*. Click the *Execute* button next to *Reindex all search indexes* at the bottom of the page. Liferay will begin sending indexing requests to Solr for execution. Once

Solr has indexed all your data, you'll have a search server running independently of all your Liferay nodes.

Installing the plugin to your nodes has the effect of overriding any calls to Lucene for searching. All Liferay's search boxes will now use Solr as the search index. This is ideal for a clustered environment, as it allows all your nodes to share one search server and one search index, and this search server operates independently of all your nodes. If, however, you don't have the server hardware upon which to install a separate search server, you can sync the search indexes between all your nodes, as is described next.

Clustering Lucene indexes on all nodes

Lucene, the search indexer which Liferay uses, can be configured to sync indexes across each cluster node. This is the easiest configuration to implement, though of course, it's not as "clean" a configuration as using pluggable enterprise search. Sometimes, however, you just don't have another server to use for search indexing, so you need a way to keep all your nodes in sync. Liferay provides a method called Cluster Link which can send indexing requests to all nodes in the cluster to keep them in sync. This configuration doesn't require any additional hardware, and it performs very well. It may increase network traffic when an individual server reboots, since a full reindex will be needed. But this should rarely happen, making it a good tradeoff if you don't have the extra hardware to implement a Solr search server.

You can enable Cluster Link by setting the following property in your `portal-ext.properties` file:

```
cluster.link.enabled=true
```

To cluster your search indexes, you also need to set the following property:

```
lucene.replicate.write=true
```

If you have `cluster.link.enabled=true` but `lucene.replicate.write=false`, you'll enable cache replication but not index replication.

Of course, `cluster.link.enabled=true` and `lucene.replicate.write=true` need to be set on all your nodes. That's all you need to do to sync your indexes. Pretty easy, right? Of course, if you have existing indexes, you'll want to do a reindex as described in the previous section once you have Cluster Link enabled on all your nodes.

Next, we'll show how to share indexes in a database. This is actually not a recommended configuration, as it's slow (databases are always slower than file systems), but for completeness, we'll go ahead and tell you how to do it anyway. But you've been forewarned: it's far better to use one of the other methods of clustering your search index.

Sharing a search index (not recommended unless you have a file locking-aware SAN)

If you wish to have a shared index (and we really hope you don't), you'll need to either share the index on the file system or in the database. This requires changing your Lucene configuration.

The Lucene configuration can be changed by modifying values in your `portal-ext.properties` file. Open your `portal.properties` file and search for the text *Lucene*. Copy that section and then paste it into your `portal-ext.properties` file.

If you wish to store the Lucene search index on a file system that is shared by all of the Liferay nodes (not recommended: you've been warned), you can modify the location of the search index by changing the `lucene.dir` property. By default, this property points to the `lucene` folder inside the Liferay home folder:

```
lucene.dir=${liferay.home}/data/lucene/
```

Change this to the folder of your choice. You'll need to restart Liferay for the changes to take effect. You can point all of the nodes to this folder and they will use the same index.

Like Jackrabbit, however, this is not the best way to share the search index, as it could result in file corruption if different nodes try reindexing at the same time. We do not recommend this for a production system. A better way (though still not great) is to share the index via a database, where the database can enforce data integrity on the index. This is very easy to do; it is a simple change to your `portal-ext.properties` file. Of course, we also don't recommend this for a production system, as accessing the index from a database will be slower than from a file system. If, however, you have no other option and want to do this anyway, keep reading.

There is a single property called `lucene.store.type`. By default this is set to go to the file system. You can change this so that the index is stored in the database by making it the following:

```
lucene.store.type=jdbc
```

The next time Liferay is started, new tables are created in the Liferay database, and the index is stored there. If all the Liferay nodes point to the same database tables, they will be able to share the index. Again, performance on this is not very good. Your DBAs may be able to tweak the database indexes a bit to improve performance. For better performance, you should consider using a separate search server or syncing the indexes on the nodes' file systems.

Note: MySQL users need to modify their JDBC connection string for this to work. Add the following parameter to your connection string:

```
emulateLocators=true
```

Alternatively, you can leave the configuration alone, and each node will have its own index. This ensures against collisions when multiple nodes update the index. However, the indices will quickly get out of sync since they don't replicate. For this reason, this is not a recommended configuration either. Again, for a better configuration, replicate the indexes with Cluster Link or use a separate search server (see the section on Solr above).

Distributed Caching

Liferay uses **Ehcache**, which has robust distributed caching support. This means that the cache can be distributed across multiple Liferay nodes running concurrently. Enabling this cache can increase performance dramatically. For example, say that two users are browsing the message boards. The first user clicks a thread to read it. Liferay must look up that thread from the database and format it for display in the browser. With a distributed Ehcache running, this thread is stored in a cache for quick retrieval, and that cache is then replicated to the other nodes in the cluster. Say then that the second user who is being served by another node in the cluster wants to read the same forum thread and clicks on it. This time, the data is retrieved more quickly. Because the thread is in the cache, no trip to the database is necessary.

This is much more powerful than having a cache running separately on each node. The power of *distributed* caching allows for common portal destinations to be cached for multiple users. The first user can post a message to the thread he or she was reading, and the cache is updated across all the nodes, making the new post available immediately from the local cache. Without that, the second user would need to wait until the cache was invalidated on the node he or she connected to before he or she could see the updated forum post.

There are two ways to enable distributed caching. If you use the default settings, it's very easy. If you need to tweak the cache for your site, there are a few more steps, but it's still pretty easy.

Enabling distributed caching

You must have Cluster Link enabled in order to activate distributed caching. Since you already did this, you have only one more property to add to your `portal-ext.properties` file:

```
ehcache.cluster.link.replication=true
```

What this does is enable some RMI (Remote Method Invocation) cache listeners that are designed to replicate the cache across a cluster.

Once you enable distributed caching, of course, you should do some due diligence and test your system under a load that best simulates the kind of traffic your system needs to handle. If you'll be serving up a lot of message board messages, your script should reflect that. If web content is the core of your site, your script should reflect that too.

As a result of a load test, you may find that the default distributed cache settings aren't optimized for your site. In this case, you'll need to tweak the settings yourself. You can modify the Liferay installation directly or you can use a plugin to do it. Either way, the settings you change are the same. Let's see how to do this with a plugin first.

Modifying the cache settings with a plugin

A benefit of working with plugins is that you can quickly install a plugin on each node of your cluster without taking down the cluster. We'll cover this first. If you're not a developer, don't worry–even though you'll create a plugin, you won't have to write any code.

Since we're assuming you're an administrator and not a developer, we'll take the easiest route, and use Liferay's graphical development tools, rather than the command line Plugins SDK by itself. If you're a Liferay EE customer, download Liferay Developer Studio from the Customer Portal. Set it up with all the defaults from the first start wizard, and you're good to go (skip the next paragraph).

If you're not a Liferay EE customer, download Eclipse and install Liferay IDE from the Eclipse Marketplace. Download the Plugins SDK for your edition of Liferay from either the Customer Portal (EE) or the Downloads page on liferay.com. Connect Liferay IDE to your Plugins SDK using the instructions found in the *Liferay Developer's Guide.*

Next, create a hook plugin by selecting *File → New → Liferay Project.* Select *Hook* as the project type and give your project a name. Click *Finish* and your project is created.

In your project, create a text file called `portlet.properties` in the `docroot/WEB-INF/src` folder. This file can override properties in your portal just like `portal-ext.properties`. Into this file place the following three properties:

```
net.sf.ehcache.configurationResourceName=
ehcache.single.vm.config.location=
ehcache.multi.vm.config.location=
```

Liferay's configuration files are, of course, used by default. If you're overriding these properties, it's because you want to customize the configuration for your own site. A good way to start with this is to extract Liferay's configuration files and then customize them. If you're running an application server (such as Tomcat) that allows you to browse to the running instance of Liferay, you can extract Liferay's configuration files from Liferay itself. If you're not, you can extract them from Liferay's .war file or Liferay's source code. In either place, you'll find the files in the `portal-impl.jar` file, which is in Liferay's `WEB-INF/lib` folder. The files you want are `hibernate-clustered.xml`, `liferay-single-vm.xml`, and `liferay-multi-vm-clustered.xml`, and they'll be in the `/ehcache` folder in this .jar. Once you have these, make a subfolder of the `docroot` folder in your project. Place the files you extracted into this folder and then specify this folder in the properties above.

For example, if you created a folder called `custom_cache` in your project's `docroot` folder, you'd copy the three XML configuration files (`hibernate-clustered.xml`, `liferay-single-vm.xml`, and `liferay-multi-vm-clustered.xml`) there. Then you'd edit your `portlet.properties` and specify your configuration files in the three properties above:

```
net.sf.ehcache.configurationResourceName=/custom_cache/hibernate-clustered.xml
ehcache.single.vm.config.location=/custom_cache/liferay-single-vm.xml
ehcache.multi.vm.config.location=/custom_cache/liferay-multi-vm-clustered.xml
```

Save the file and deploy the plugin (deploying plugins is covered in the *Liferay Developer's Guide*), and the settings you've placed in those files will override the default Liferay settings. In this way, you can tweak your cache settings so that your cache performs optimally for the type of traffic generated by your site. The strength of doing it this way is that you don't have restart your server to change the cache settings. This is a great benefit, but beware: since Ehcache doesn't allow for changes to cache settings while the cache is alive, reconfiguring a cache while the server is running will flush the cache.

There is, of course, another way to do this if you don't want to create a plugin. It requires you to restart the server to enable the new cache settings, but you don't have to work with any developer tools to do it.

Modifying the Ehcache settings directly

This method is pretty similar to the plugin method, except that you have to modify the Liferay installation directly. You'll still need to extract Liferay's configuration files as described in the previous section. Next, shut down your server and find the location in the server where Liferay is installed (this may not be possible on all application servers, and if this is the case, you'll need to use the plugin method described above). For example, say you're running Liferay on Tomcat. Tomcat stores the deployed version of Liferay in [Tomcat Home]/webapps/ROOT. Inside this folder is the folder structure WEB-INF/classes. You can create a new folder in here called custom_cache to store the custom versions of the cache configuration files. Copy the files you extracted from Liferay into this folder.

You then need to modify the properties in portal-ext.properties that point to these files. Copy/paste the **Hibernate** section of portal.properties into your portal-ext.properties file and then modify the net.sf.ehcache.configurationResourceName property to point to the clustered version of the configuration file that is now in your custom folder:

```
net.sf.ehcache.configurationResourceName=/custom_cache/hibernate-clustered.xml
```

Now that Liferay is pointing to your custom file, you can modify the settings in this file to change the cache configuration for Hibernate.

Next, copy/paste the *Ehcache* section from the portal.properties file into your portal-ext.properties file. Modify the properties so they point to the files in your custom folder. For example:

```
ehcache.multi.vm.config.location=/custom_cache/liferay-multi-vm-clustered.xml
```

You can now take a look at the settings in these files and tune them to fit your environment and application. Let's examine how to do that next.

Customizing Hibernate cache settings

By default, Hibernate (Liferay's database persistence layer) is configured to use Ehcache as its cache provider. This is the recommended setting. If you're using the default settings using Cluster Link, you already have this enabled. If, however, you need to customize the settings, you'll have to customize it in one of the ways described above: either in a plugin or in the deployed instance of Liferay. The first thing, of course, is to start off with the clustered version of the file. Copy the `hibernate-clustered.xml` configuration file to your plugin or to a place in Liferay's classpath (as described above) where you can refer to it. Then change the following property to point to the file:

```
net.sf.ehcache.configurationResourceName=/path/to/hibernate-clustered.xml
```

Next, open this file in a text editor. You'll notice that the configuration is already set up to perform distributed caching through a multi-cast connection. The configuration, however, might not be set up optimally for your particular application. Notice that by default, the only object cached in the Hibernate cache is the User object (`com.liferay.``portal``.model.impl.UserImpl`). This means that when a user logs in, his or her User object will go in the cache so that any portal operation that requires access to it (such as permission checking) can retrieve that object very quickly from the cache.

You may wish to add other objects to the cache. For example, a large part of your application may be document management using the Documents and Media portlet. In this case, you may want to cache media objects, such as `DLFileEntryImpl` to improve performance as users access documents. To do that, add another block to the configuration file with the class you want to cache:

```
<cache
    eternal="false"
    maxElementsInMemory="10000"
    name="com.liferay.portlet.documentlibrary.model.impl.DLFileEntryImpl"
    overflowToDisk="false"
    timeToIdleSeconds="600"
>
    <cacheEventListenerFactory
        class="com.liferay.portal.cache.ehcache.LiferayCacheEventListenerFactory"
        properties="replicatePuts=false,replicateUpdatesViaCopy=false"
        propertySeparator=","
    />
    <bootstrapCacheLoaderFactory class=
    "com.liferay.portal.cache.ehcache.LiferayBootstrapCacheLoaderFactory" />
</cache>
```

Your site may use the message boards portlet, and those message boards may get a lot of traffic. To cache the threads on the message boards, configure a block with the `MBMessageImpl` class:

```
<cache
    eternal="false"
    maxElementsInMemory="10000"
    name="com.liferay.portlet.messageboards.model.impl.MBMessageImpl"
    overflowToDisk="false"
    timeToIdleSeconds="600"
>
    <cacheEventListenerFactory
        class="com.liferay.portal.cache.ehcache.LiferayCacheEventListenerFactory"
        properties="replicatePuts=false,replicateUpdatesViaCopy=false"
        propertySeparator=","
    />
    <bootstrapCacheLoaderFactory class=
      "com.liferay.portal.cache.ehcache.LiferayBootstrapCacheLoaderFactory" />
</cache>
```

Note that if your developers have overridden any of these classes in an Ext plugin, you'll have to specify the overridden versions rather than the stock ones that come with Liferay Portal. You can customize the other ehcache configuration files in exactly the same way. Refer to Ehcache's documentation for information on how to do this.

As you can see, it's easy to add specific data to be cached. Be careful, however, as too much caching can actually reduce performance if the JVM runs out of memory and starts garbage collecting too frequently. You'll likely need to experiment with the memory settings on your JVM as well as the cache settings above. You can find the specifics about these settings in the documentation for Ehcache.

The last thing we'll cover about caching is a special EE-only optimization that can be made to the cache.

Enhanced distributed cache algorithm

 EE Only Feature

By default, Liferay's distributed cache uses the RMI replication mechanism, which uses a point to point communication topology. As you can guess, this kind of structure doesn't scale well for a large cluster with many nodes. Because each node has to send the same event to other nodes N − 1 times, network traffic becomes a bottleneck when N is too large. Ehcache also has a performance issue of its own, in that it creates a replication thread for each cache entity. In a large system like Liferay Portal, it's very common to have more than 100 cached entities. This translates to 100+ cache replication threads. Threads are expensive, because they take resources (memory and CPU power). Most of the time, these threads are sleeping, because they only need to work when a cached entity has to talk to remote peers.

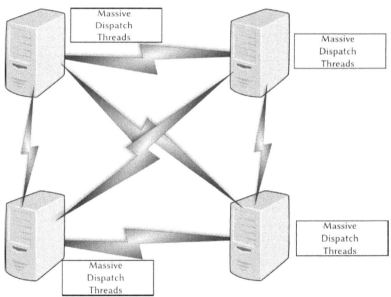

Figure 19.5: The default algorithm requires each node to create massive amounts of dispatch threads to update the cache for each node in the cluster.

Putting heap memory aside (because the amount of memory on the heap depends on the application(s) running), consider the stack memory footprint of those 100+ threads. By default on most platforms, the thread stack size is 2

MB; for 100 threads, that's more than 200 MB. If you include the heap memory size, this number can become as high as 500 MB for just one node. And that massive amount of threads can also cause frequent context switch overhead, which translates to increased CPU cycles.

For large installations containing many nodes, Liferay has developed an alternative algorithm for handling cache replication that can can fix both the 1 to N − 1 network communication bottleneck, as well as the massive threads bottleneck. The default implementation uses JGroups' UDP multicast to communicate.

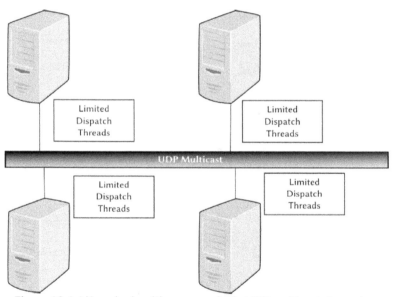

Figure 19.6: Liferay's algorithm uses a single UDP multicast channel, so that nodes don't have to create a thread for each other node in the cluster.

To reduce the number of replication threads, we provide a small pool of dispatching threads. These deliver cache cluster events to remote peers. Since all cache entities' cluster events must go through our pool of dispatching threads to communicate, this gives us a chance to coalesce events: if two modifications to the same cache object happen at almost the same time, we can combine the changes into one, and then we only need to notify remote peers once. This reduces traffic on the network. We should also note that newer versions of Ehcache support the JGroups replicator and can also fix the 1 to N − 1 network communication; however, they cannot fix the massive threads issue and they cannot coalesce cache events.

For EE customers who are interested in this feature, all you have to do to enable the alternate algorithm is to install a plugin from the Liferay Marketplace. Search for the *Ehcache Cluster EE* plugin, which is free to all EE customers, and install it on all your nodes. The new algorithm is immediately activated and you can reap the benefits right away.

Now we can look at the last consideration when clustering Liferay: hot deploy.

Hot Deploy

Plugins which are hot deployed will need to be deployed separately to all the Liferay nodes. The best way to do this is to configure your application server to support *farms*. This is a feature that enables you to deploy an application on one node and then it replicates automatically to each of the other nodes. This, of course, is configured differently for each application server, so you'll need to consult your application server's documentation to learn how to do this. It's by far the best way to handle hot deploy, and is the recommended configuration. If you have this working, great! You can skip the rest of this section completely.

If for some reason your application server doesn't support this feature or you can't use it, you'll need to come up with a way to deploy applications across your cluster. Each node needs to have its own hot deploy folder. This folder needs to be writable by the user under which Liferay is running, because plugins are moved from this folder to a temporary folder when they are deployed. This is to prevent the system from entering an endless loop, because the presence of a plugin in the folder is what triggers the hot deploy process.

When you want to deploy a plugin to the entire cluster, copy that plugin to the hot deploy folders of all of the Liferay nodes. Depending on the number of nodes, it may be best to create a script to do this. Once the plugin has been deployed to all of the nodes, you can then make use of it (by adding the portlet to a page or choosing the theme as the look and feel for a page or page hierarchy).

All of the above will get basic Liferay clustering working; however, the configuration can be further optimized. We will see how to do this next.

19.2   Performance Tuning

Once you have your portal up and running, you may find a need to tune it for performance, especially if your site winds up generating more traffic than you'd anticipated. There are some definite steps you can take with regard to improving Liferay's performance.

Memory

Memory is one of the first things to look at when you want to optimize performance. If you have any disk swapping, you want to avoid it at all costs: it has a serious impact on performance. Make sure your server has an optimal amount of memory and your JVM is tuned to use it.

There are three basic JVM command switches that control the amount of memory in the Java heap.

```
-Xms
-Xmx
-XX:MaxPermSize
```

These three settings control the amount of memory available to the JVM initially, the maximum amount of memory into which the JVM can grow, and the separate area of the heap called Permanent Generation space.

The first two settings should be set to the same value. This prevents the JVM from having to reallocate memory if the application needs more. Setting them to the same value causes the JVM to be created up front with the maximum amount of memory you want to give it.

```
-Xms1024m -Xmx1024m -XX:MaxPermSize=256m
```

This is perfectly reasonable for a moderately sized machine or a developer machine. These settings give the JVM 1024MB for its regular heap size and have a PermGen space of 256MB. If you're having performance problems, and your profiler is showing that there's a lot of garbage collection going on, the first thing you might want to look at is increasing the memory available to the JVM. You'll be able to tell if memory is a problem by running a profiler (such as Jprobe, YourKit, or the NetBeans profiler) on the server. If you see Garbage Collection (GC) running frequently, you definitely want to increase the amount of memory available to the JVM.

Note that there is a law of diminishing returns on memory, especially with 64 bit systems. These systems allow you to create very large JVMs, but the larger the JVM, the more time it takes for garbage collection to take place. For this reason, you probably won't want to create JVMs of more than 2 GB in size. To take advantage of higher amounts of memory on a single system, run multiple JVMs of Liferay instead.

Issues with PermGen space can also affect performance. PermGen space contains long-lived classes, anonymous classes and interned Strings (immutable String objects that are kept around for a long time to increase String processing performance). Hibernate–which Liferay uses extensively–has been known to make use of PermGen space. If you increase the amount of memory available to the JVM, you may want to increase the amount of PermGen space accordingly.

Garbage Collection

As the system runs, various Java objects are created. Some of these objects are long-lived, and some are not. The ones that are not become *de-referenced*, which means that the JVM no longer has a link to them because they have ceased to be useful. These may be variables that were used for methods which have already returned their values, objects retrieved from the database for a user that is no longer logged on, or a host of other things. These objects sit in memory and fill up the heap space until the JVM decides it's time to clean them up.

Normally, when garbage collection (GC) runs, it stops all processing in the JVM while it goes through the heap looking for dead objects. Once it finds them, it frees the memory they were taking up, and then processing can continue. If this happens in a server environment, it can slow down the processing of requests, as all processing comes to a halt while GC is happening.

There are some JVM switches that you can enable which can reduce the amount of time processing is halted while garbage collecting happens. These can improve the performance of your Liferay installation if applied properly. As always, you will need to use a profiler to monitor garbage collection during a load test to tune the numbers properly for your server hardware, operating system, and application server.

The Java heap is divided into sections for the young generation, the old generation, and the permanent generation. The young generation is further divided into three sections: Eden, which is where new objects are created, and two "survivor spaces, which we can call the *From* and *To* spaces. Garbage collection occurs in stages. Generally, it's more frequently done in the young generation, less frequently done in the old generation, and even less frequently done in the permanent generation, where long-lived objects reside. When garbage collection runs in the young generation, Eden is swept for objects which are no longer referenced. Those that are still around are moved to the *To* survivor space, and

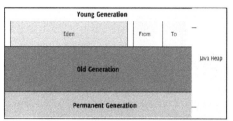

Figure 19.7: Java Memory

the *From* space is then swept. Any other objects in that space which still have references to them are moved to the *To* space, and the *From* space is then cleared out altogether. After this, the *From* and the *To* spaces swap roles, and processing is freed up again until the next time the JVM determines that garbage collection needs to run.

After a predetermined number of *generations* of garbage collection, surviving objects may be moved to the old generation. Similarly, after a predetermined number of *generations* of garbage collection in the old generation, surviving objects may be moved to the permanent generation.

By default, the JDK uses a serial garbage collector to achieve this. This works very well for a short-lived desktop Java application, but is not necessarily the best performer for a long-lived, server-based application like Liferay. For this reason, you may wish to switch to the Concurrent Mark-Sweep (CMS) collector.

In CMS garbage collection, rather than halting application processing altogether, this garbage collector makes one short pause in application execution to mark objects directly reachable from the application code. Then it allows the application to run while it marks all objects which are reachable from the set it marked. Finally, it adds another phase called the *remark* phase which finalizes marking by revisiting any objects modified while the application was running. It then sweeps through and garbage collects. Though it sounds more complicated, this has the effect of greatly reducing the amount of time that execution needs to be halted to clean out dead objects.

Just about every aspect of the way memory management works in Java can be tuned. In your profiling, you may want to experiment with some of the following settings to see if any of them can increase your performance.

NewSize, MaxNewSize: The initial size and the maximum size of the New or Young Generation.

+UseParNewGC: Causes garbage collection to happen in parallel, using multiple CPUs. This decreases garbage collection overhead and increases application throughput.

+UseConcMarkSweepGC: Use the Concurrent Mark-Sweep Garbage Collector. This uses shorter garbage collection pauses, and is good for applications that have a relatively large set of long-lived data, and that run on machines with two or more processors, such as web servers.

+CMSParallelRemarkEnabled: For the CMS GC, enables the garbage collector to use multiple threads during the CMS remark phase. This decreases the pauses during this phase.

SurvivorRatio: Controls the size of the two survivor spaces. It's a ratio between the survivor space size and Eden. The default is 25. There's not much bang for the buck here, but it may need to be adjusted.

ParallelGCThreads: The number of threads to use for parallel garbage collection. Should be equal to the number of CPU cores in your server.

A sample configuration using the above parameters might look something like this:

```
JAVA_OPTS="$JAVA_OPTS -XX:NewSize=700m -XX:MaxNewSize=700m -Xms2048m
-Xmx2048m -XX:MaxPermSize=128m -XX:+UseParNewGC -XX:+UseConcMarkSweepGC
-XX:+CMSParallelRemarkEnabled -XX:SurvivorRatio=20
-XX:ParallelGCThreads=8"
```

Again, you should always follow the procedure of adjusting the settings, then testing under load, then adjusting again. Every system is different and these are general guidelines to follow. Next, we'll see some modifications we can make to Liferay's properties to help increase performance.

Properties File Changes

There are also some changes you can make to your `portal-ext.properties` file once you are in a production environment.

Set the following to false to disable checking the last modified date on server side CSS and JavaScript.

```
last.modified.check=false
```

Set this property to true to load the theme's merged CSS files for faster loading for production. By default it is set to false for easier debugging for development. You can also disable fast loading by setting the URL parameter `css_fast_load` to 0.

```
theme.css.fast.load=true
```

Set this property to true to load the combined JavaScript files from the property `javascript.files` into one compacted file for faster loading for production.

```
javascript.fast.load=true
```

These are various things the Liferay engineering team has done to increase performance generally. If your developers make use of Liferay's tools and platform, their JavaScript and themes can also take advantage of these properties.

Let's look at one final, general way of increasing Liferay's performance: disabling unused servlet filters.

Disabling unused servlet filters

Liferay comes by default with a number of servlet filters enabled and running. It is likely that for your installation, you don't need them all. Since servlet filters intercept the HTTP request and do some processing on it before Liferay even has a chance to start building the page, you can increase performance by disabling the ones you're not using.

You can disable servlet filters you're not using by using your `portal-ext.properties` file. Copy the *Servlet Filters* section from the original `portal.properties` file into your customized file, and then go through the list and see if there are any you can disable, by setting them to `false`.

For example, if you are not using CAS for single sign-on, disable the CAS Filter. If you are not using NTLM for single sign-ons, disable the NTLM Filter. The fewer servlet filters you are running, the less processing power is needed for each request.

As you can see, there are many things you can do to increase Liferay's performance generally. But don't forget to load test your own applications! It may be that a performance issue comes from a custom-built application that's doing something it shouldn't do. Always load test your system before putting it into production: that's the best way of finding out potential performance problems, and that way, you'll find them during performance testing, and not when your system is in production.

19.3   Summary

We've seen how good a fit Liferay Portal is for the enterprise. It can be scaled linearly to grow to whatever size you need to serve your users. Clustering is a snap, and Liferay harmonizes very well with whatever environment you may have.

Liferay Portal is also built for performance. You can take advantage of read-writer database configurations, as well as database sharding. You can tune it to support over 3300 concurrent users on a single server with mean login times under half a second and maximum throughput of more than 79 logins per second. We've seen some tips for tuning Liferay Portal, and we have to keep in mind the adage about tuning: load test and profile, tune, repeat.

In all, Liferay Portal gives you all the options you need to build a high-performance, robust environment that supports your enterprise.

INDEX

www.ingramcontent.com/pod-product-compliance
Lightning Source LLC
Chambersburg PA
CBHW051218050326
40689CB00007B/730